CODE OF FEDERAL REGULATIONS

Title 46
Shipping

Parts 41 to 69

Revised as of October 1, 2013

Containing a codification of documents
of general applicability and future effect

As of October 1, 2013

With Ancillaries

Published by the Office of the Federal Register
National Archives and Records Administration
as a Special Edition of the Federal Register

U.S. GOVERNMENT OFFICIAL EDITION NOTICE

Legal Status and Use of Seals and Logos

The seal of the National Archives and Records Administration (NARA) authenticates the Code of Federal Regulations (CFR) as the official codification of Federal regulations established under the Federal Register Act. Under the provisions of 44 U.S.C. 1507, the contents of the CFR, a special edition of the Federal Register, shall be judicially noticed. The CFR is prima facie evidence of the original documents published in the Federal Register (44 U.S.C. 1510).

It is prohibited to use NARA's official seal and the stylized Code of Federal Regulations logo on any republication of this material without the express, written permission of the Archivist of the United States or the Archivist's designee. Any person using NARA's official seals and logos in a manner inconsistent with the provisions of 36 CFR part 1200 is subject to the penalties specified in 18 U.S.C. 506, 701, and 1017.

Use of ISBN Prefix

This is the Official U.S. Government edition of this publication and is herein identified to certify its authenticity. Use of the 0–16 ISBN prefix is for U.S. Government Printing Office Official Editions only. The Superintendent of Documents of the U.S. Government Printing Office requests that any reprinted edition clearly be labeled as a copy of the authentic work with a new ISBN.

 U.S. GOVERNMENT PRINTING OFFICE

U.S. Superintendent of Documents • Washington, DC 20402–0001

http://bookstore.gpo.gov

Phone: toll-free (866) 512-1800; DC area (202) 512-1800

Table of Contents

	Page
Explanation	v

Title 46:

    Chapter I—Coast Guard, Department of Homeland Security (Continued) 3

Finding Aids:

    Table of CFR Titles and Chapters 425

    Alphabetical List of Agencies Appearing in the CFR 445

    List of CFR Sections Affected 455

Cite this Code: CFR

To cite the regulations in this volume use title, part and section number. Thus, 46 CFR 42.01–1 *refers to title 46, part 42, section 01–1.*

Explanation

The Code of Federal Regulations is a codification of the general and permanent rules published in the Federal Register by the Executive departments and agencies of the Federal Government. The Code is divided into 50 titles which represent broad areas subject to Federal regulation. Each title is divided into chapters which usually bear the name of the issuing agency. Each chapter is further subdivided into parts covering specific regulatory areas.

Each volume of the Code is revised at least once each calendar year and issued on a quarterly basis approximately as follows:

Title 1 through Title 16..as of January 1
Title 17 through Title 27 ....as of April 1
Title 28 through Title 41 ....as of July 1
Title 42 through Title 50 ....as of October 1

The appropriate revision date is printed on the cover of each volume.

LEGAL STATUS

The contents of the Federal Register are required to be judicially noticed (44 U.S.C. 1507). The Code of Federal Regulations is prima facie evidence of the text of the original documents (44 U.S.C. 1510).

HOW TO USE THE CODE OF FEDERAL REGULATIONS

The Code of Federal Regulations is kept up to date by the individual issues of the Federal Register. These two publications must be used together to determine the latest version of any given rule.

To determine whether a Code volume has been amended since its revision date (in this case, October 1, 2013), consult the "List of CFR Sections Affected (LSA)," which is issued monthly, and the "Cumulative List of Parts Affected," which appears in the Reader Aids section of the daily Federal Register. These two lists will identify the Federal Register page number of the latest amendment of any given rule.

EFFECTIVE AND EXPIRATION DATES

Each volume of the Code contains amendments published in the Federal Register since the last revision of that volume of the Code. Source citations for the regulations are referred to by volume number and page number of the Federal Register and date of publication. Publication dates and effective dates are usually not the same and care must be exercised by the user in determining the actual effective date. In instances where the effective date is beyond the cut-off date for the Code a note has been inserted to reflect the future effective date. In those instances where a regulation published in the Federal Register states a date certain for expiration, an appropriate note will be inserted following the text.

OMB CONTROL NUMBERS

The Paperwork Reduction Act of 1980 (Pub. L. 96–511) requires Federal agencies to display an OMB control number with their information collection request.

Many agencies have begun publishing numerous OMB control numbers as amendments to existing regulations in the CFR. These OMB numbers are placed as close as possible to the applicable recordkeeping or reporting requirements.

PAST PROVISIONS OF THE CODE

Provisions of the Code that are no longer in force and effect as of the revision date stated on the cover of each volume are not carried. Code users may find the text of provisions in effect on any given date in the past by using the appropriate List of CFR Sections Affected (LSA). For the convenience of the reader, a "List of CFR Sections Affected" is published at the end of each CFR volume. For changes to the Code prior to the LSA listings at the end of the volume, consult previous annual editions of the LSA. For changes to the Code prior to 2001, consult the List of CFR Sections Affected compilations, published for 1949-1963, 1964-1972, 1973-1985, and 1986-2000.

"[RESERVED]" TERMINOLOGY

The term "[Reserved]" is used as a place holder within the Code of Federal Regulations. An agency may add regulatory information at a "[Reserved]" location at any time. Occasionally "[Reserved]" is used editorially to indicate that a portion of the CFR was left vacant and not accidentally dropped due to a printing or computer error.

INCORPORATION BY REFERENCE

What is incorporation by reference? Incorporation by reference was established by statute and allows Federal agencies to meet the requirement to publish regulations in the Federal Register by referring to materials already published elsewhere. For an incorporation to be valid, the Director of the Federal Register must approve it. The legal effect of incorporation by reference is that the material is treated as if it were published in full in the Federal Register (5 U.S.C. 552(a)). This material, like any other properly issued regulation, has the force of law.

What is a proper incorporation by reference? The Director of the Federal Register will approve an incorporation by reference only when the requirements of 1 CFR part 51 are met. Some of the elements on which approval is based are:

(a) The incorporation will substantially reduce the volume of material published in the Federal Register.

(b) The matter incorporated is in fact available to the extent necessary to afford fairness and uniformity in the administrative process.

(c) The incorporating document is drafted and submitted for publication in accordance with 1 CFR part 51.

What if the material incorporated by reference cannot be found? If you have any problem locating or obtaining a copy of material listed as an approved incorporation by reference, please contact the agency that issued the regulation containing that incorporation. If, after contacting the agency, you find the material is not available, please notify the Director of the Federal Register, National Archives and Records Administration, 8601 Adelphi Road, College Park, MD 20740-6001, or call 202-741-6010.

CFR INDEXES AND TABULAR GUIDES

A subject index to the Code of Federal Regulations is contained in a separate volume, revised annually as of January 1, entitled CFR INDEX AND FINDING AIDS. This volume contains the Parallel Table of Authorities and Rules. A list of CFR titles, chapters, subchapters, and parts and an alphabetical list of agencies publishing in the CFR are also included in this volume.

An index to the text of "Title 3—The President" is carried within that volume.

The Federal Register Index is issued monthly in cumulative form. This index is based on a consolidation of the "Contents" entries in the daily Federal Register.

A List of CFR Sections Affected (LSA) is published monthly, keyed to the revision dates of the 50 CFR titles.

REPUBLICATION OF MATERIAL

There are no restrictions on the republication of material appearing in the Code of Federal Regulations.

INQUIRIES

For a legal interpretation or explanation of any regulation in this volume, contact the issuing agency. The issuing agency's name appears at the top of odd-numbered pages.

For inquiries concerning CFR reference assistance, call 202-741-6000 or write to the Director, Office of the Federal Register, National Archives and Records Administration, 8601 Adelphi Road, College Park, MD 20740-6001 or e-mail *fedreg.info@nara.gov*.

SALES

The Government Printing Office (GPO) processes all sales and distribution of the CFR. For payment by credit card, call toll-free, 866-512-1800, or DC area, 202-512-1800, M-F 8 a.m. to 4 p.m. e.s.t. or fax your order to 202-512-2104, 24 hours a day. For payment by check, write to: US Government Printing Office – New Orders, P.O. Box 979050, St. Louis, MO 63197-9000.

ELECTRONIC SERVICES

The full text of the Code of Federal Regulations, the LSA (List of CFR Sections Affected), The United States Government Manual, the Federal Register, Public Laws, Public Papers of the Presidents of the United States, Compilation of Presidential Documents and the Privacy Act Compilation are available in electronic format via *www.ofr.gov*. For more information, contact the GPO Customer Contact Center, U.S. Government Printing Office. Phone 202-512-1800, or 866-512-1800 (toll-free). E-mail, *ContactCenter@gpo.gov*.

The Office of the Federal Register also offers a free service on the National Archives and Records Administration's (NARA) World Wide Web site for public law numbers, Federal Register finding aids, and related information. Connect to NARA's web site at *www.archives.gov/federal-register*.

The e-CFR is a regularly updated, unofficial editorial compilation of CFR material and Federal Register amendments, produced by the Office of the Federal Register and the Government Printing Office. It is available at *www.ecfr.gov*.

CHARLES A. BARTH,
Director,
Office of the Federal Register.
October 1, 2013.

THIS TITLE

Title 46—SHIPPING is composed of nine volumes. The parts in these volumes are arranged in the following order: Parts 1–40, 41–69, 70–89, 90–139, 140–155, 156–165, 166–199, 200–499, and 500 to end. The first seven volumes containing parts 1–199 comprise chapter I—Coast Guard, DHS. The eighth volume, containing parts 200—499, includes chapter II—Maritime Administration, DOT and chapter III—Coast Guard (Great Lakes Pilotage), DHS. The ninth volume, containing part 500 to end, includes chapter IV—Federal Maritime Commission. The contents of these volumes represent all current regulations codified under this title of the CFR as of October 1, 2013.

For this volume, Susannah Hurley was Chief Editor. The Code of Federal Regulations publication program is under the direction of Michael L. White, assisted by Ann Worley.

Title 46—Shipping

(This book contains parts 41 to 69)

	Part
CHAPTER I—Coast Guard, Department of Homeland Security (Continued)	42

CHAPTER I—COAST GUARD, DEPARTMENT OF HOMELAND SECURITY (CONTINUED)

EDITORIAL NOTE: Nomenclature changes to chapter I appear at 69 FR 18803, Apr. 9, 2004.

SUBCHAPTER E—LOAD LINES

Part		Page
41	[Reserved]	
42	Domestic and foreign voyages by sea	5
43	[Reserved]	
44	Special service limited domestic voyages	65
45	Great Lakes load lines	72
46	Subdivision load lines for passenger vessels	92
47	Combination load lines	98

SUBCHAPTER F—MARINE ENGINEERING

50	General provisions	100
51	[Reserved]	
52	Power boilers	109
53	Heating boilers	127
54	Pressure vessels	131
56	Piping systems and appurtenances	166
57	Welding and brazing	242
58	Main and auxiliary machinery and related systems	256
59	Repairs to boilers, pressure vessels and appurtenances	284
60	[Reserved]	
61	Periodic tests and inspections	290
62	Vital system automation	300
63	Automatic auxiliary boilers	315
64	Marine portable tanks and cargo handling systems	321

SUBCHAPTER G—DOCUMENTATION AND MEASUREMENT OF VESSELS

66	[Reserved]	
67	Documentation of vessels	330
68	Documentation of vessels: Exceptions to coastwise qualification	367
69	Measurement of vessels	385

SUBCHAPTER E—LOAD LINES

PART 41 [RESERVED]

PART 42—DOMESTIC AND FOREIGN VOYAGES BY SEA

Subpart 42.01—Authority and Purpose

Sec.
42.01-1 Authority for regulations.
42.01-5 OMB control numbers assigned pursuant to the Paperwork Reduction Act.
42.01-10 Purpose of regulations.

Subpart 42.03—Application

42.03-5 U.S.-flag vessels subject to the requirements of this subchapter.
42.03-10 Foreign vessels subject to this subchapter.
42.03-15 The Great Lakes of North America.
42.03-17 Special load line marks for vessels carrying timber deck cargo.
42.03-20 Equivalents.
42.03-25 Experimental installations.
42.03-30 Exemptions for vessels.
42.03-35 U.S.-flag vessels and Canadian vessels navigating on sheltered waters of Puget Sound and contiguous west coast waters of United States and Canada.

Subpart 42.05—Definition of Terms Used in This Subchapter

42.05-1 Approved.
42.05-10 Assigning authority.
42.05-20 Commandant.
42.05-25 Coast Guard District Commander or District Commander.
42.05-27 Credential.
42.05-30 Existing vessel.
42.05-40 Great Lakes.
42.05-45 International voyage.
42.05-47 Marine inspector or inspector.
42.05-50 New vessel.
42.05-55 Officer in Charge, Marine Inspection.
42.05-60 Recognized classification society.
42.05-63 Ship(s) and vessel(s).
42.05-65 Surveyor.

Subpart 42.07—Control, Enforcement, and Rights of Appeal

42.07-1 Load lines required.
42.07-5 Marks placed on vessel to indicate load lines.
42.07-10 Submergence of load line marks.
42.07-15 Zones and seasonal areas.
42.07-20 Logbook entries.
42.07-25 Approval of the Commandant.
42.07-30 Approval of the assigning authority.
42.07-35 American Bureau of Shipping as an assigning authority.
42.07-40 Recognized classification society as an assigning authority.
42.07-43 Change in assigning authority.
42.07-45 Load line certificates.
42.07-50 Penalties for violations.
42.07-55 Cancellation of load line certificates or exemption certificates.
42.07-60 Control.
42.07-75 Right of appeal.

Subpart 42.09—Load Line Assignments and Surveys—General Requirements

42.09-1 Assignment of load lines.
42.09-5 All vessels—division into types.
42.09-10 Stability, subdivision, and strength.
42.09-15 Surveys by the American Bureau of Shipping or assigning authority.
42.09-20 Surveys of foreign vessels.
42.09-25 Initial or periodic survey requirements for all vessels.
42.09-30 Additional survey requirements for steel-hull vessels.
42.09-35 Additional survey requirements for wood-hull vessels.
42.09-40 Annual surveys.
42.09-45 Correction of deficiencies.
42.09-50 Repairs or alterations to vessel after it has been surveyed.

Subpart 42.11—Applications for Load Line Assignments, Surveys, and Certificates

42.11-1 General.
42.11-5 Applications for load line assignments, surveys, and certificates for U.S.-flag vessels.
42.11-10 Applications for load line assignments and certificates for vessels other than U.S.-flag vessels.
42.11-15 Application for timber load lines.
42.11-20 Application for annual survey.

Subpart 42.13—General Rules for Determining Load Lines

42.13-1 Assumptions.
42.13-5 Strength of vessel.
42.13-10 Freeboards assigned vessels.
42.13-15 Definitions of terms.
42.13-20 Deck line.
42.13-25 Load line mark.
42.13-30 Lines to be used with the load line mark.
42.13-35 Mark of assigning authority.
42.13-40 Details of marking.
42.13-45 Verification of marks.

§ 42.01-1

Subpart 42.15—Conditions of Assignment of Freeboard

42.15-1   Information to be supplied to the master.
42.15-5   Superstructure end bulkheads.
42.15-10 Doors.
42.15-15 Positions of hatchways, doorways and ventilators.
42.15-20 Cargo and other hatchways.
42.15-25 Hatchways closed by portable covers and secured weathertight by tarpaulins and battening devices.
42.15-30 Hatchways closed by weathertight covers of steel or other equivalent material fitted with gaskets and clamping devices.
42.15-35 Machinery space openings.
42.15-40 Miscellaneous openings in freeboard and superstructure decks.
42.15-45 Ventilators.
42.15-50 Air pipes.
42.15-55 Cargo ports and other similar openings.
42.15-60 Scuppers, inlets, and discharges.
42.15-65 Side scuttles.
42.15-70 Freeing ports.
42.15-75 Protection of the crew.
42.15-80 Special conditions of assignment for Type "A" vessels.

Subpart 42.20—Freeboards

42.20-3   Freeboard assignment: Type "A" vessels.
42.20-5   Freeboard assignment: Type "B" vessels.
42.20-6   Flooding standard: Type "A" vessels.
42.20-7   Flooding standard: Type "B" vessel, 60 percent reduction.
42.20-8   Flooding standard: Type "B" vessel, 100 percent reduction.
42.20-9   Initial conditions of loading.
42.20-10 Free surface.
42.20-11 Extent of damage.
42.20-12 Conditions of equilibrium.
42.20-13 Vessels without means of propulsion.
42.20-15 Freeboard tables.
42.20-20 Correction to the freeboard for vessels under 328 feet in length.
42.20-25 Correction for block coefficient.
42.20-30 Correction for depth.
42.20-35 Correction for position of deck line.
42.20-40 Standard height of superstructure.
42.20-45 Length of superstructure.
42.20-50 Effective length of superstructure.
42.20-55 Trunks.
42.20-60 Deduction for superstructures and trunks.
42.20-65 Sheer.
42.20-70 Minimum bow height.
42.20-75 Minimum freeboards.

Subpart 42.25—Special Requirements for Vessels Assigned Timber Freeboards

42.25-1   Application of this subpart.
42.25-5   Definitions of terms used in this subpart.
42.25-10 Construction of vessel.
42.25-15 Stowage.
42.25-20 Computation for freeboard.

Subpart 42.30—Zones, Areas, and Seasonal Periods

42.30-1   Basis.
42.30-5   Northern Winter Seasonal Zones and area.
42.30-10 Southern Winter Seasonal Zone.
42.30-15 Tropical Zone.
42.30-20 Seasonal Tropical Areas.
42.30-25 Summer Zones.
42.30-30 Enclosed seas.
42.30-35 The Winter North Atlantic Load Line.

Subpart 42.50—Load Line Certificates—Model Forms

42.50-1   General.
42.50-5   International load line certificates.
42.50-10 Load line certificates for non-adherent foreign flag vessels.
42.50-15 Coastwise load line certificates for U.S.-flag vessels.

AUTHORITY: 46 U.S.C. 5101–5116; Department of Homeland Security Delegation No. 0170.1; section 42.01–5 also issued under the authority of 44 U.S.C. 3507.

Subpart 42.01—Authority and Purpose

§ 42.01-1   Authority for regulations.

The statutory authority to prescribe rules and regulations requiring certain vessels to have and display load line marks indicating the maximum amidship draft to which such vessels may be safely loaded and certification thereof by the assigning authority is in 46 U.S.C. 5101–5116.

[CGD 80–120, 47 FR 5721, Feb. 8, 1982, as amended by CGD 97–057, 62 FR 51043, Sept. 30, 1997]

§ 42.01-5   OMB control numbers assigned pursuant to the Paperwork Reduction Act.

(a) *Purpose.* This section collects and displays the control numbers assigned to information collection and recordkeeping requirements in this subchapter by the Office of Management

Coast Guard, DHS

§ 42.03-5

and Budget (OMB) pursuant to the Paperwork Reduction Act of 1980 (44 U.S.C. 3501 *et seq.*). The Coast Guard intends that this section comply with the requirements of 44 U.S.C. 3507(f) which requires that agencies display a current control number assigned by the Director of the OMB for each approved agency information collection requirement.

(b) *Display.*

46 CFR part or section where identified or described	Current OMB control No.
Part 42	1625-0013
Part 44	1625-0013
Part 45	1625-0013
Part 46	1625-0013

[49 FR 38120, Sept. 27, 1984, as amended by USCG-2004-18884, 69 FR 58345, Sept. 30, 2004]

§ 42.01-10 **Purpose of regulations.**

(a) The load line marks when placed on a vessel shall indicate the maximum amidships draft to which such vessel can be lawfully submerged, in the various circumstances and seasons applicable to such vessel.

(b) This subchapter sets forth the uniform minimum requirements for load line marks on various categories of vessels. It also sets forth requirements for surveys relating to the assignment of load lines, the issuing of load line certificates by authorized issuing authorities, and the carriage of load line certificates aboard vessels.

(c) The rules and regulations in this subchapter also provide for the enforcement of load line requirements and control over vessels when it is believed such vessels may be in violation of applicable load line requirements.

[CGFR 68-60, 33 FR 10049, July 12, 1968, as amended by CGD 80-120, 47 FR 5721, Feb. 8, 1982]

Subpart 42.03—Application

§ 42.03-5 **U.S.-flag vessels subject to the requirements of this subchapter.**

(a) *Vessels engaged in foreign voyages or international voyages other than solely Great Lakes voyages.* (1) All U.S. flag vessels which engage in foreign voyages or international voyages by sea (other than solely in Great Lakes voyages) are subject to this part; except the following:

(i) Ships of war;

(ii) New vessels of less than 79 feet in length;

(iii) Existing vessels of less than 150 gross tons;

(iv) Pleasure yachts not engaged in trade; and

(v) Fishing vessels.

(2) As provided in Article 4(4) of the 1966 Convention, in order for existing vessels to take advantage of any reduction in freeboards from those previously assigned, the regulations in subparts 42.13 to 42.25, inclusive, of this part shall be fully complied with. Except for due cause, such vessels shall not be required to increase their freeboards under the provisions of the 1966 Convention.

(3) All U.S.-flag vessels authorized to engage in foreign or international voyages may also engage in domestic voyages by sea and, as permitted by § 45.9 of this part and part 47 of this subchapter, in Great Lakes voyages without additional load line marks and/or certificates. Where additional load line marks and certificates are provided to specifically cover "Special Service, Coastwise" or "Great Lakes" operation, such vessels are subject to the applicable provisions of parts 44 and 45 of this subchapter.

(b) *Vessels engaged in domestic voyages by sea.* (1) All U.S.-flag vessels which engage in domestic voyages by sea (coastwise and intercoastal voyages) shall be subject to the applicable provisions of this part except the following:

(i) Merchant vessels of less than 150 gross tons.

(ii) Vessels which are mechanically propelled and numbered by a State or the Coast Guard under the Federal Boat Safety Act of 1971 (46 U.S.C. 1451 *et seq.*) and not required by other laws to be inspected or certified by the U.S. Coast Guard. (This exception includes all mechanically propelled vessels of less than 150 gross tons, and uninspected motor propelled oceanographic vessels of less than 300 gross tons while operating pursuant to 46 U.S.C. 2113.

(iii) Pleasure craft not used or engaged in trade or commerce.

(iv) Barges of less than 150 gross tons.

(v) Vessels engaged exclusively in voyages on waters within the United States or its possessions and which are determined not to be "coastwise" or "Great Lakes" voyages.

(vi) Ships of war.

(vii) U.S. public vessels other than those vessels of 150 gross tons or over and engaged in commercial activities.

(2) In order for existing vessels to take advantage of any reduction in freeboards from those previously assigned, paragraph (a)(2) of this section applies.

(c) *Vessels engaged solely on Great Lakes voyages.* A U.S. flag vessel 79 feet and more and 150 gross tons or over that engages solely on Great Lakes voyages is subject to the applicable provisions of this part and part 45 of this subchapter and must comply with the regulations in force on the date the keel is laid or a similar progress in construction is made.

(d) *Special service coastwise voyage.* A U.S. flag vessel 150 gross tons or over that engages in a "special service coastwise voyage" is subject to the applicable provisions of this part and part 44 of this subchapter.

(e) *Hopper dredges engaged in limited service domestic voyages.* Self-propelled hopper dredges over 79 feet (24 meters) in length with working freeboards, on limited service domestic voyages within 20 nautical miles (37 kilometers) from the mouth of a harbor of safe refuge, are subject to the provisions of this subchapter that apply to a Type "B" vessel and to the provisions of subpart E of part 44 of this chapter.

[CGFR 68–60, 33 FR 10049, July 12, 1968, as amended by CGFR 68–126, 34 FR 9011, June 5, 1969; CGD 73–49R, 38 FR 12289, May 10, 1973; CGD 80–120, 47 FR 5721, Feb. 8, 1982; CGD 86–016, 51 FR 9962, Mar. 24, 1986; CDG 76–080, 54 FR 36976, Sept. 6, 1989; CGD 97–057, 62 FR 51043, Sept. 30, 1997]

§ 42.03–10 **Foreign vessels subject to this subchapter.**

(a) *General.* All existing foreign merchant vessels of 150 gross tons or over, and new foreign vessels of 79 feet in length or more, loading at or proceeding from any port or place within the jurisdiction of the United States or its possessions for a foreign voyage by sea, or arriving within the jurisdiction of the United States or its possessions from a foreign voyage by sea, in both cases the Great Lakes excepted, are subject to 46 U.S.C. 5101–5116, and the regulations in this part applicable to such service. All foreign merchant vessels of 150 gross tons or over, loading at or proceeding from any port or place within the United States on the Great Lakes of North America, or arriving within the jurisdiction of the United States on the Great Lakes, are subject to 46 U.S.C. 5101–5116 and the regulations in part 45 of this subchapter applicable to such service.

(b) *Canadian vessels.* All vessels of Canadian registry and holding valid certificates issued pursuant to Canadian laws and regulations are assumed to be in compliance with the applicable provisions of 46 U.S.C. 5101–5116, the International Convention on Load Lines, 1966, and the regulations in this subchapter.

(c) *Vessels of countries signatory to or adhering to the 1966 Convention.* The enforcement and control of load line requirements regarding vessels of countries signatory to or adhering to The International Convention on Load Lines, 1966, (the 1966 Convention) are as described in § 42.07–60 in this part, which is in accord with provisions of Article 21 of the 1966 Convention. Such vessels when holding currently valid certificates issued pursuant to the 1966 Convention, or recognized under such Convention, are assumed to be in compliance with the applicable provisions of such Convention. Such vessels are deemed to be in compliance with the load line requirements found to be equally effective as those established in this part and therefore in compliance with the applicable load line provisions of 46 U.S.C. 5101–5116, as amended, and the regulations in this part as authorized by such laws. Vessels engaged in navigation on the Great Lakes are subject to application of seasonal international marks as specified in part 45 of this subchapter.

(d) *Vessels of countries not signatory to or adhering to the 1966 Convention.* (1) Vessels of countries not signatory to or adhering to the 1966 Convention, when within the jurisdiction of the United States, shall be subject to 46 U.S.C.

5101–5116, and the regulations in this subchapter as authorized by such laws.

(2) Vessels of countries signatory to or adhering only to International Load Line Convention, London, 1930 (the 1930 Convention), and holding valid certificates issued under that Convention, are subject to the applicable law described in paragraph (a) of this section and the regulations prescribed thereunder in this subchapter.

[CGD 80–120, 47 FR 5722, Feb. 8, 1982, as amended by CGD 97–057, 62 FR 51043, Sept. 30, 1997; USCG–1998–4442, 63 FR 52190, Sept. 30, 1998]

§ 42.03–15 The Great Lakes of North America.

(a) The term "Great Lakes of North America" means those waters of North America which are defined in § 42.05–40, and in the exception in Article 5(2)(a) of the 1966 Convention.

(b) The expressions in the regulations in this part, such as "voyages by sea," "proceed to sea," "arrive from the high seas," etc., shall be construed as having no application to voyages on the Great Lakes or portions thereof unless specifically provided otherwise in part 45 of this subchapter.

[CGFR 68–60, 33 FR 10050, July 12, 1968]

§ 42.03–17 Special load line marks for vessels carrying timber deck cargo.

(a) Certain vessels having load line marks not related to carriage of timber deck cargo may be assigned timber load lines if they are in compliance with the applicable requirements governing timber deck cargoes in this subchapter. The timber load lines apply and may be used only when the vessel is carrying timber deck cargo.

(b) A new or existing vessel having timber load lines assigned to it, when carrying timber deck cargo, may be loaded to the vessel's timber load line applicable to the voyage and season.

[CGFR 68–60, 33 FR 10050, July 12, 1968, as amended by CGD 80–120, 47 FR 5722, Feb. 8, 1982]

§ 42.03–20 Equivalents.

(a) Where in this subchapter it is provided that a particular fitting, material, appliance, apparatus, or equipment, or type thereof, shall be fitted or carried in a vessel, or that a particular provision shall be made or arrangement shall be adopted, the assigning authority, with the prior approval of the Commandant, may accept in substitution therefor any other fitting, material, apparatus, or equipment or type thereof, or any other provision or arrangement: *Provided,* That it can be demonstrated by trial thereof or otherwise that the substitution is at least as effective as that required by the regulations in this subchapter.

(b) In any case where it is shown to the satisfaction of the assigning authority and the Commandant that the use of any particular equipment, apparatus, or arrangement not specifically required by law is unreasonable or impracticable, appropriate alternatives may be permitted under such conditions as are consistent with the minimum standards set forth in this subchapter.

[CGFR 68–60, 33 FR 10050, July 12, 1968]

§ 42.03–25 Experimental installations.

(a) Complete information (including plans, necessary instructions and limitations, if any) on proposed experimental installations affecting any fitting, material, appliance, apparatus, arrangement, or otherwise shall be submitted to the assigning authority for evaluation. After acceptance by the assigning authority, the complete information of such installation shall be forwarded to the Commandant for specific approval prior to installation. Complete information shall also be furnished for any associated installation(s) deemed necessary to prevent endangering the vessel during the trial period of proposed experimental installations.

(b) The use of approved experimental installations shall be permitted only when in accordance with instructions and limitations as specifically prescribed for such installations by the Commandant.

[CGFR 68–60, 33 FR 10050, July 12, 1968]

§ 42.03–30 Exemptions for vessels.

(a) For an individual vessel or category of vessels, upon the specific recommendation of the assigning authority, the Commandant may authorize an

§ 42.03–30

exemption from one or more load line requirements. Such recommendation and authorization will depend upon provision of any additional features as deemed necessary by the authorities to ensure the vessel's safety in the services and under the conditions specified in paragraph (b) of this section.

(b) Exemptions from specific load line requirements for vessels meeting requirements of paragraph (a) of this section are authorized, subject to certain conditions, including type of voyage engaged in, as follows:

(1) For vessels engaged on international voyages between the United States and near neighboring ports of its possessions or of foreign countries. The exemptions may be permitted because the requirements are deemed to be unreasonable or impracticable due to the sheltered nature of the waters on which the voyages occur or other conditions. These exemptions shall be valid only so long as such a vessel shall remain engaged on specific designated voyages. If the voyage involves a foreign country or countries, the United States will require an exemption agreement with such country or countries prior to the issuance of the appropriate load line certificate.

(2) For vessels engaged on international voyages which embody features of a novel kind, and where nonexemption may seriously impede research, development, and incorporation of novel features into vessels. If the voyage or voyages intended involve a foreign country or countries, then the United States will require an exemption agreement with such country or countries prior to the issuance of a Load Line Exemption Certificate. If the Commandant grants an exemption pursuant to this paragraph (b)(2) to a U.S. flag vessel that operates on the Great Lakes of North America, he may notify the Chairman of the Board of Steamship Inspection of Canada of the nature of the exemption, but no special exemption certificate is issued.

(3) For a vessel not normally engaged on international voyages but which is required to undertake a single international voyage under exceptional circumstances.

(4) For self-propelled hopper dredges engaged on international voyages or on limited service domestic voyages by sea. These vessels may be exempt from applicable hatch cover requirements of § 42.15–25 of this part by showing they meet the requirements in § 174.310 of this chapter. When a Load Line Exemption Certificate is issued for this exemption, it must have an endorsement that only seawater is allowed in the vessel's hoppers.

(c) A vessel given one or more exemptions from load line requirements under the provisions of paragraph (b)(1) of this section will be issued the appropriate load line certificate, using Form A1, A2, or A3. In each case the exemptions shall be specified on the load line certificate together with the Convention authority which authorizes such exemptions.

(d) A vessel given one or more exemptions under the provisions of paragraph (b)(2) or (b)(3) of this section will be issued a Load Line Exemption Certificate, using Form E1. This certificate shall be in lieu of a regular load line certificate, and the vessel shall be considered as in compliance with applicable load line requirements.

(e) The Commandant may exempt from any of the requirements of this part a vessel that engages on a domestic voyage by sea or a voyage solely on the Great Lakes and embodies features of a novel kind, if the novel features and any additional safety measures required are described on the face of the issued certificate.

(f) A vessel that is not usually engaged on domestic voyages by sea or on voyages on the Great Lakes but that, in exceptional circumstances, is required to undertake a single such voyage between two specific ports is—

(1) Subject to 46 U.S.C. 5101–5116 and the applicable regulations of this subchapter; and

(2) Issued a single voyage load line authorization by the Commandant that states the conditions under which the voyage may be made and any additional safety measures required for a single voyage.

[CGFR 68–126, 34 FR 9011, June 5, 1969, as amended by CGD 73–49R, 38 FR 12289, May 10, 1973; CGD 76–080, 54 FR 36976, Sept. 6, 1989; USCG–1998–4442, 63 FR 52190, Sept. 30, 1998]

§ 42.03-35 U.S.-flag vessels and Canadian vessels navigating on sheltered waters of Puget Sound and contiguous west coast waters of United States and Canada.

(a) In a Treaty between the United States and Canada proclaimed on August 11, 1934, the respective Governments were satisfied of the sheltered nature of certain waters of the west coast of North America. It was agreed to exempt vessels of the United States and Canadian vessels from load line requirements when such vessels engage on international voyages originating on, wholly confined to, and terminating on such waters. In Article I of this Treaty these waters are described as follows: "* * * the waters of Puget Sound, the waters lying between Vancouver Island and the mainland, and east of a line from a point 1 nautical mile west of the city limits of Port Angeles in the State of Washington to Race Rocks on Vancouver Island, and of a line from Hope Island, British Columbia, to Cape Calvert, Calvert Island, British Columbia, the waters east of a line from Cape Calvert to Duke Point on Duke Island, and the waters north of Duke Island and east of Prince of Wales Island, Baranof Island, and Chicagof Island, the waters of Peril, Neva, and Olga Straits to Sitka, and the waters east of a line from Port Althorp of Chicagof Island to Cape Spencer, Alaska, are sheltered waters * * *."

(b) U.S.-flag vessels and Canadian vessels navigating on the treaty waters on a voyage as described in paragraph (a) of this section are by virtue of this Treaty of August 11, 1934, not subject to load line requirements in 46 U.S.C. 5101–5116, the 1966 Convention, and the regulations in this subchapter. Vessels navigating these sheltered waters and passing outside their boundary on any voyage cannot claim the benefits of this Treaty and shall be in compliance with the applicable load line requirements in 46 U.S.C. 5101–5116, the 1966 Convention, and the regulations in this subchapter.

(c) Since subdivision requirements apply to all passenger vessels subject to the 1960 International Convention on Safety of Life at Sea, those passenger vessels navigating on the waters described in paragraph (a) of this section shall be in compliance with such 1960 Convention requirements and the regulations in part 46 of this subchapter. The Coast Guard issues to such a vessel a stability letter. The assigning authority is authorized to issue to such a passenger vessel an appropriate load line certificate, modified to meet the conditions governing her service assignment, and marking.

[CGFR 68–60, 33 FR 10051, July 12, 1968, as amended by CGFR 68–126, 34 FR 9011, June 5, 1969; USCG–1998–4442, 63 FR 52190, Sept. 30, 1998]

Subpart 42.05—Definition of Terms Used in This Subchapter

§ 42.05-1 Approved.

This term means approved by the Commandant, U.S. Coast Guard, unless otherwise stated.

[CGFR 68–60, 33 FR 10051, July 12, 1968]

§ 42.05-10 Assigning authority.

This term means the "American Bureau of Shipping" or such other recognized classification society which the Commandant may approve as the load line assigning and issuing authority for a vessel, as provided in sections 3 of the load line acts.

[CGFR 68–60, 33 FR 10051, July 12, 1968]

§ 42.05-20 Commandant.

This term means the Commandant (CG–ENG), Attn: Office of Design and Engineering Systems, U.S. Coast Guard Stop 7509, 2703 Martin Luther King Jr. Avenue SE., Washington, DC 20593–7509.

[CGFR 68–60, 33 FR 10051, July 12, 1968, as amended by CGD 88–070, 53 FR 34534, Sept. 7, 1988; USCG 2013–0671, 78 FR 60147, Sept. 30, 2013]

§ 42.05-25 Coast Guard District Commander or District Commander.

These terms mean an officer of the Coast Guard designated as such by the Commandant to command all Coast Guard activities within his district. This includes enforcement of load line requirements as described in this subchapter.

[CGFR 68–60, 33 FR 10051, July 12, 1968]

§ 42.05-27 Credential.

As used in this subchapter, *credential* means any or all of the following:
(a) Merchant mariner's document.
(b) Merchant mariner's license.
(c) STCW endorsement.
(d) Certificate of registry.
(e) Merchant mariner credential.

[USCG 2006-24371, 74 FR 11265, Mar. 16, 2009]

§ 42.05-30 Existing vessel.

(a) As used in this part 42, for a vessel engaged on international voyages or on domestic voyages by sea, the term *existing vessel* means a vessel which is not a new vessel. With few exceptions an *existing vessel* is a vessel the keel of which was laid, or which was at a similar stage of construction, prior to July 21, 1968. (See § 42.05-50 for the definition of a new vessel.)

(b)–(c) [Reserved]

(d) As used in part 44 of this subchapter, for a vessel marked with load lines for special service on a coastwise or interisland voyage, the term *existing vessel* means one whose keel was laid prior to September 28, 1937. (See § 44.01-20 of this subchapter.)

(e) As used in part 45 of this subchapter, *existing vessel* in all regulations pertaining to a vessel engaged solely on Great Lakes voyages before April 14, 1973, means a vessel whose keel was laid before August 27, 1936. The regulations pertaining to these vessels that are in effect after April 14, 1973, do not use the term *existing vessel*.

(f) As used in part 46 of this subchapter, for a passenger vessel marked with subdivision load lines, the term *existing vessel* means a vessel whose keel was laid or was converted to such service prior to May 26, 1965. (See § 46.05-30 of this subchapter.)

[CGFR 68-60, 33 FR 10051, July 12, 1968, as amended by CGD 73-49R, 38 FR 12290, May 10, 1973; CGD 80-120, 47 FR 5722, Feb. 8, 1982]

§ 42.05-40 Great Lakes.

(a) This term means the Great Lakes of North America.

(b) As used in this part, the term *solely navigating the Great Lakes* includes any special service coastwise navigation performed by the vessel.

(c) In concurrence with related Canadian regulations, the waters of the St. Lawrence River west of a rhumb line drawn from Cap de Rosiers to West Point, Anticosti Island, and west of a line along 63° W. longitude from Anticosti Island to the north shore of the St. Lawrence River shall be considered as a part of the Great Lakes. In addition, the Victoria Bridge, Montreal, Canada, is the dividing line between fresh water and salt water in the St. Lawrence River.

[CGFR 68-60, 33 FR 10051, July 12, 1968, as amended by CGD 73-49R, 38 FR 12290, May 10, 1973]

§ 42.05-45 International voyage.

(a) The term *international voyage* as used in this part shall have the same meaning as the term *international voyage* in Article 2(4) of the 1966 Convention. Except for vessels operating solely on the waters indicated in Article 5(2) of the 1966 Convention, an *international voyage* means a sea voyage from any country to a port outside such country, or conversely. For this purpose, every territory for the international relations of which any specific Contracting Government is responsible or for which the United Nations are the administering authority is regarded as a separate country.

(b) The 1966 Convention does not apply to vessels solely navigating the Great Lakes. Accordingly, such vessels shall not be considered as being on an *international voyage* for the purpose of this subchapter.

(c) For the purpose of administration of load line requirements in this subchapter, the Commonwealth of Puerto Rico, the Territory of Guam, the Virgin Islands, and all possessions and lands held by the United States under a protectorate or mandate shall each be considered to be a *territory* of the United States.

[CGFR 68-60, 33 FR 10051, July 12, 1968]

§ 42.05-47 Marine inspector or inspector.

These terms mean any person from the civilian or military branch of the Coast Guard assigned under the superintendence and direction of an Officer in Charge, Marine Inspection, or any other person as may be designated for the performance of duties with respect to the inspection, enforcement, and administration of title 52, Revised Statutes, and acts amendatory thereof or supplemental thereto, and rules and regulations thereunder.

[CGFR 68–60, 33 FR 10051, July 12, 1968]

§ 42.05–50 New vessel.

(a) As used in this part 42, for a vessel engaged on international voyages or on domestic voyages by sea, the term *new vessel* means a vessel, the keel of which is laid, or which is at a similar stage of construction, on or after July 21, 1968. (See § 42.05–30 for definition of an existing vessel.)

(1) This definition applies to all vessels of countries signatory to or acceding to the 1966 Convention prior to April 21, 1968, and to vessels of countries not adhering to an applicable Convention as indicated in Article 16(4) of the 1966 Convention.

(2) For countries which accede to the 1966 Convention after April 21, 1968, a *new vessel* (foreign) shall be one whose keel is constructively laid 3 months or more after such date.

(b)–(c) [Reserved]

(d) As used in part 44 of this subchapter, for a vessel marked with load lines for special service on a coastwise or interisland voyage, the term *new vessel* means one whose keel is laid on or after September 28, 1937. (See § 44.01–20 of this subchapter.)

(e) As used in part 45 of this subchapter, for a vessel engaged solely on Great Lakes voyages, the term *new vessel* means one whose keel is laid on or after August 27, 1936. (See § 45.01–10 of this subchapter.)

(f) As used in part 46 of this subchapter, for a passenger vessel marked with subdivision load lines, the term *new vessel* means a vessel whose keel is laid or is converted to such service on or after May 26, 1965. (See § 46.05–25 of this subchapter.)

[CGFR 68–60, 33 FR 10051, July 12, 1968 as amended by CGD 80–120, 47 FR 5722, Feb. 8, 1982]

§ 42.05–55 Officer in Charge, Marine Inspection.

This term means any person from the civilian or military branch of the Coast Guard designated as such by the Commandant and who, under the superintendence and direction of the Coast Guard District Commander, is in charge of a marine inspection zone, and may supervise or perform the duties of a marine inspector.

[CGFR 68–60, 33 FR 10052, July 12, 1968]

§ 42.05–60 Recognized classification society.

The term *recognized classification society* means the American Bureau of Shipping or other classification society recognized by the Commandant, as provided in 46 U.S.C. 5107, and who also may be approved as a load line assigning and issuing authority.

[CGFR 68–60, 33 FR 10052, July 12, 1968, as amended by USCG–1998–4442, 63 FR 52190, Sept. 30, 1998]

§ 42.05–63 Ship(s) and vessel(s).

The terms *ship(s)* and *vessel(s)* are interchangeable or synonymous words, and include every description of watercraft, other than a seaplane on the water, used or capable of being used as a means of transportation on water.

[CGFR 68–126, 34 FR 9011, June 5, 1969]

§ 42.05–65 Surveyor.

The term *surveyor* means any person designated by the American Bureau of Shipping or other classification society recognized by the Commandant as the person who actually examines the vessel and/or materials associated with such examination, and who ascertains such vessel complies with applicable load line requirements.

[CGFR 68–60, 33 FR 10052, July 12, 1968]

Subpart 42.07—Control, Enforcement, and Rights of Appeal

§ 42.07–1 Load lines required.

(a) The vessels listed in §§ 42.03–5 and 42.03–10 as subject to the applicable requirements in this subchapter shall have load lines accurately marked amidships, port and starboard, as provided in this part 42 or the 1966 Convention, unless otherwise stated. Those vessels issued load line exemption certificates may not be required to have load line marks (see § 42.03–30).

§ 42.07-5

(b) For vessels marked with international load lines and navigating the Great Lakes, such vessels are also subject to requirements in part 45 of this subchapter while on the Great Lakes. See § 45.9 of this subchapter for load line marks used by such vessels.

(c) For Great Lakes vessels operating solely on Great Lakes voyages, the requirements for the applicable load line marks are in part 45 of this subchapter. Great Lakes vessels when making other international or unlimited coastwise voyages shall comply with the applicable requirements in parts 42, 44, and 45 of this subchapter.

(d) For coastwise steam colliers, barges, and self-propelled barges in special services, the requirements for the applicable load line marks are in part 44 of this subchapter. These requirements also include certain regulations governing such vessels when they additionally engage in Great Lakes voyages, international voyages or unlimited coastwise voyages. Load line requirements in this part 42 also apply to such vessels when engaged on international or unlimited coastwise voyages.

(e) Existing U.S.-flag vessels, as defined in § 42.05-30(a) of this chapter, engaged in international or coastwise voyages, may retain the load line assigned under previous regulations, provided:

(1) The vessel has not been assigned a reduced freeboard under the regulations in this part 42, and

(2) The form of the load line certificate issued to and carried on board the vessel conforms to the requirements of subpart 42.50 of this part or § 44.05-35 or § 46.10-30 of this chapter.

(f) This part applies to foreign vessels of countries—

(1) Signatory to or adhering to the 1966 Convention;

(2) Adhering to the 1930 Convention and not acceding to the 1966 Convention, or;

(3) Not adhering to either the 1930 Convention or the 1966 Convention but subject to the load line acts.

[CGFR 68–60, 33 FR 10052, July 12, 1968, as amended by CGFR 68–126, 34 FR 9011, June 5, 1969; CGD 73–49R, 38 FR 12290, May 10, 1973; CGD 80–120, 47 FR 5722, Feb. 8, 1982]

§ 42.07-5 Marks placed on vessel to indicate load lines.

(a) Load line marks to indicate the maximum amidship's draft to which a vessel can be lawfully submerged, in the various circumstances and seasons, shall be permanently marked on each side of the vessel in the form, manner, and location as required by this subchapter.

(b) The load line marks placed on a vessel shall be attested to by a valid load line certificate as required by § 42.07–45(b). The issuing authority shall not deliver any required load line certificate to the vessel until after its surveyor has ascertained that the vessel meets the applicable survey requirements and the correct placement of the marks on the vessel's sides has been confirmed.

(c) The requirements for load line marks apply to all new and existing vessels as specified in §§ 42.03–5 and 42.03–10, except when a vessel has been issued a load line exemption certificate in lieu of a load line certificate.

[CGFR 68–60, 33 FR 10052, July 12, 1968, as amended by CGFR 68–126, 34 FR 9012, June 5, 1969]

§ 42.07-10 Submergence of load line marks.

(a) Except as provided otherwise in this section, vessels of the types described in paragraphs (a)(1) through (a)(3) of this section shall not be so loaded as to submerge at any time when departing for a voyage by sea, or on the Great Lakes, or during the voyage, or on arrival, the applicable load lines marked on the sides of the vessel for the season of the year and the zone or area in which the vessel may be operating.

(1) Merchant vessels of 150 gross tons or over, as described in § 42.03–5 or § 42.03–10, and on voyages subject to 46 U.S.C. 5101–5116.

(2) All new vessels of 79 feet or over in length on voyages subject to the 1966 Convention.

(3) All vessels of 150 gross tons or over, other than merchant vessels covered by paragraph (a)(1) of this section, on voyages subject to the 1966 Convention.

(b) When loading a vessel in a favorable zone for a voyage on which the vessel will enter a less favorable zone, such allowances must be made that the vessel when crossing into the less favorable zone, will conform to the regulations and freeboard for the less favorable zone.

(c) When a vessel is in fresh water of unit density, the appropriate load line may be submerged by the amount of the fresh water allowance shown on the applicable load line certificate. Where the density is other than unity, an allowance shall be made proportional to the difference between 1.025 and the actual density. This paragraph does not apply to vessels when navigating the Great Lakes.

(d) When a vessel departs from a port situated on a river or inland waters, deeper loading shall be permitted corresponding to the weight of fuel and all other materials required for consumption between the port of departure and the sea. This paragraph does not apply to vessels when navigating the Great Lakes.

[CGFR 68–60, 33 FR 10052, July 12, 1968, as amended by CGFR 68–126, 34 FR 9012, June 5, 1969; USCG–1998–4442, 63 FR 52190, Sept. 30, 1998]

§ 42.07-15 Zones and seasonal areas.

(a) A vessel subject to 46 U.S.C. 5101–5116 or the 1966 Convention shall comply, as applicable, with the requirements regarding the zones and seasonal areas described in subpart 42.30.

(b) A port located on the boundary line between two zones or areas shall be regarded as within the zone or seasonal area from or into which the vessel arrives or departs.

[CGFR 68–60, 33 FR 10053, July 12, 1968, as amended by USCG–1998–4442, 63 FR 52190, Sept. 30, 1998]

§ 42.07-20 Logbook entries.

(a) As described in § 3.13–35 of Subchapter A (Procedures Applicable to the Public) of this chapter, official logbooks (Form CG–706–C), are furnished free to certain vessels, and after they have served their purpose they are filed with the applicable Officer in Charge, Marine Inspection.

(b) The master shall be responsible for having entered in the vessel's "official logbook" if carried, otherwise in his own log considered as its official logbook, the data required by section 6 of the load line acts. These logbooks entries shall be made before a vessel departs from her loading port or place and consist of:

(1) A statement of the load line marks applicable to the voyage; and,

(2) A statement of the position of the load line marks, port and starboard, at the time of departing from a port or place; i.e., the distance in inches of the water surface above or below the applicable load line; and,

(3) The actual drafts of the vessel, forward and aft, as nearly as the same can be ascertained, at the time of departing from a port or place.

(c) Where the master uses his own log, it shall be kept by the master or owner for 1 year after the actions noted therein have been completed and upon request shall be furnished to any load line enforcement officer.

[CGFR 68–60, 33 FR 10053, July 12, 1968]

§ 42.07-25 Approval of the Commandant.

(a) Where the requirements in this subchapter state that the approval of the Commandant is necessary, the owner or his agent shall furnish all information necessary, including background material, and/or final plans, calculations, and conclusions reached, as will enable the Commandant to obtain a comprehensive understanding of and reach a decision relative to the question or problem at issue prior to proceeding with the work. All information, plans and calculations submitted will remain with the Commandant as a part of the record on the vessel.

(b) If the owner or his agent desires to have information, plans, and calculations returned with Commandant's actions noted thereon, or if distribution of such information is necessary or required by regulations in this subchapter to owners, masters of vessels, etc., then the owner or his agent shall furnish multiple copies of the information as required.

[CGFR 68–60, 33 FR 10053, July 12, 1968]

§ 42.07-30 Approval of the assigning authority.

(a) Where the requirements in this subchapter state the approval of an assigning authority is required, the owner or his agent shall furnish the required information, including plans, etc., as required by and which will enable the assigning authority to obtain a comprehensive understanding of the matter and to reach pertinent decisions prior to proceeding with the work. When requested the assigning authority shall furnish the Coast Guard all information, etc., on any question at issue and decisions reached.

(b) All information required under this subchapter by an assigning authority with respect to a specific vessel shall be retained until 5 years after termination of certification by such authority.

[CGFR 68-60, 33 FR 10053, July 12, 1968]

§ 42.07-35 American Bureau of Shipping as an assigning authority.

(a) The American Bureau of Shipping, with its home office at ABS Plaza, 16855 Northchase Drive, Houston, TX 77060, is hereby appointed as the prime assigning and issuing authority under the provisions of Articles 13 and 16(3) of the 1966 Convention and as directed by 46 U.S.C. 5107. In this capacity the American Bureau of Shipping is empowered to assign load lines, to perform surveys required for load line assignments, and to determine that the position of and the manner of marking vessels has been done in accordance with applicable requirements.

(b) On behalf of the United States of America, the American Bureau of Shipping is authorized to issue or reissue, under its own seal and signature of its officials, the appropriate load line certificates or International Load Line Exemption Certificate as described in subpart 42.50 of this part or in parts 44 to 46, inclusive, of this subchapter. Except for the International Load Line Exemption Certificate, the required load line certificate issued to a specific vessel shall certify to the correctness of the load line marks assigned and marked on the vessel and compliance with authorized conditions, restrictions, and/or exemptions, if any. The International Load Line Exemption Certificate when issued to a vessel shall certify as to the compliance with the information applicable to the vessel.

(c) The designation and delegation to the American Bureau of Shipping as an assigning and issuing authority shall be in effect indefinitely unless for due cause it shall be terminated by proper authority and notice of cancellation is published in the FEDERAL REGISTER.

(d) The American Bureau of Shipping is authorized to revalidate from time to time by endorsement a load line certificate or an International Load Line Exemption Certificate.

(e) Before revalidating any certificate by endorsement, the American Bureau of Shipping shall verify that the required load line marks assigned are marked on the vessel and the vessel is in compliance with authorized conditions, restrictions, and/or exemptions, if any.

(f) The American Bureau of Shipping shall issue all load line certificates in duplicate; one copy shall be delivered to the owner or master of the vessel, and one copy (together with a summary of data used to determine the assigned load lines) shall be forwarded to the Commandant.

(g) The American Bureau of Shipping shall prepare a load line survey report on each new vessel or existing vessel when brought into complete compliance with this part prior to issuing the required load line certificate described in subpart 42.50 of this part. At the time the certificate is delivered, one copy of this report shall be delivered to the master of the vessel, and one copy shall be forwarded to the Commandant. When a load line survey report is superseded or revised, one copy shall be delivered to the master of the vessel, and one copy shall be forwarded to the Commandant.

(h) The load line survey report or stability information furnished to a specific vessel shall include a statement of the locations of all watertight subdivision bulkheads, including steps or recesses therein, which may be involved in the vessel's load line assignment.

[CGFR 68–60, 33 FR 10053, July 12, 1968, as amended by CGFR 68–126, 34 FR 9012, June 5, 1969; CGD 80–143, 47 FR 25149, June 10, 1982; CGD 96–041, 61 FR 50727, Sept. 27, 1996; USCG–1998–4442, 63 FR 52190, Sept. 30, 1998; USCG–2000–7790, 65 FR 58459, Sept. 29, 2000]

§ 42.07–40 Recognized classification society as an assigning authority.

(a) On behalf of the United States of America, under the provisions of Articles 13 and 16(3) and as provided in 46 U.S.C. 5107, the Commandant, at the request of a shipowner, may appoint any other recognized classification society, which he may approve, as the assigning and issuing authority who shall perform the same functions and duties as indicated in § 42.07–35 for the American Bureau of Shipping.

(b) The appointment of a recognized classification society as the assigning and issuing authority will be limited to vessels specifically designated by the Commandant.

[CGFR 68–60, 33 FR 10053, July 12, 1968, as amended by USCG–1998–4442, 63 FR 52190, Sept. 30, 1998]

§ 42.07–43 Change in assigning authority.

(a) If the owner desires a change in assigning and issuing authority for a vessel, a special request shall be made in writing to the Commandant at least 90 days prior to the expiration date of the present certificate or the annual endorsement thereon.

(b) A change in the assigning authority does not presume any change in assigned load lines.

[CGFR 68–60, 33 FR 10053, July 12, 1968]

§ 42.07–45 Load line certificates.

(a) The load line certificates for which the Government of the United States of America assumes full responsibility may be issued by the Commandant, the American Bureau of Shipping, or a recognized classification society when appointed as an authorized assigning and issuing authority for specifically designated vessels.

(b) The load line certificate shall certify to the correctness of the load line marks assigned to the vessel and that the vessel is in compliance with applicable requirements. A certificate issued under this subchapter also shall describe the applicable load line marks, conditions, restrictions, and/or exemptions, if any, the vessel shall observe, according to the season of the year and the zone or area in which the vessel may operate. The load line exemption certificate issued under § 42.03–30 shall certify the special conditions the vessel shall observe.

(c) A load line assignment and certificate issued to any vessel under the authority of the regulations in this subchapter (or under the authority of any Government adhering to the 1966 Convention, under the provisions of Article 19(5) of the 1966 Convention) shall cease to be valid upon the transfer of such vessel to the flag of another Government.

(d) Each loadline certificate is issued for the following length of time:

(1) An international and coastwise certificate is issued for 5 years and may be extended by the Commandant up to 150 days from the date of the—

(i) Survey that is endorsed on the certificate by the surveyor authorized by the Coast Guard; or

(ii) Last day of the 5-year period.

(2) A Great Lakes certificate is issued for 5 years and may be extended by the Commander, Ninth Coast Guard District, up to 365 days from date of the—

(i) Survey that is endorsed on the certificate by the surveyor authorized by the Coast Guard; or

(ii) Last day of the 5-year period.

(e) The form of certificate certifying to the correctness of the load line marks, assigned under the regulations in this part, may be in the form of temporary or provisional certificate, signed by the authorized surveyor pending early issuance of appropriate certificate as shown in subpart 42.50 of this part as follows:

(1) International Load Line Certificate, 1966, issued to U.S. vessels engaged in foreign voyages, or engaged in coastwise or intercoastal voyages (provided such vessels qualify to engage in foreign voyages without restriction), as follows:

(i) Form *A1*, For general use.

(ii) Form *A2*, For sailing vessels.

(iii) Form *A3*, For general use, combined with timber deck cargo.

(2) Certificate issued to foreign vessels belonging to countries that have not ratified or acceded to the 1966 Convention as follows:

(i) Form *B*, For general use.

(3) Coastwise load line certificate (other than for special service as provided for by part 44 of this subchapter) issued to U.S. vessels engaged solely in coastwise and/or intercoastal voyages (which may be subject to restrictions as to manning, routes, seasons, waters of operations, etc., as shown on the face of the certificate), as follows:

(i) Form *C1*, For general use.
(ii) Form *C2*, For sailing ships.
(iii) Form *C3*, For general use, combined with timber deck cargo.

(f) The form of certificate certifying to the correctness of exemptions granted under the regulations in this part shall be as shown in subpart 42.50 of this part as follows:

(1) International load line exemption certificate issued under special conditions to U.S.-flag vessels engaged in foreign voyages, as follows:

(i) Form *E1*, For general international use.

(ii) Where this certificate is intended to expire after a single voyage, this information shall be noted on the face of the certificate.

(2) International load line certificate Form A1, A2, or A3 issued under special conditions to U.S.-flag vessels on international voyages between the United States and near neighboring ports of its possessions or of foreign countries. Exemptions, if any, shall be specified on the certificate.

(g) The issuing authority shall provide the printed forms it may use under the regulations in this subchapter. These forms shall be approved by the Commandant before final printing. The international load line certificate and exemption certificate forms shall exactly reproduce the arrangement of the printed part of the model Forms *A1*, *A2*, *A3*, and *E1* indicated in subpart 42.50 of this part for all official copies and any certified copies issued.

(h) Where a vessel qualifies for and is issued a Form E1 International Load Line Exemption Certificate for foreign voyages but is also or solely engaged in coastwise or intercoastal voyages by sea, this certificate shall be considered equivalent to a valid coastwise load line certificate. In such case the vessel shall be deemed in full compliance with 46 U.S.C. 5101–5116 and the regulations in this part promulgated thereunder.

[CGFR 68–60, 33 FR 10054, July 12, 1968, as amended by CGFR 68–126, 34 FR 9012, June 5, 1969; CGD 73–49R, 38 FR 12290, May 10, 1973; CGD–74; 153, 39 FR 25324, July 10, 1974; CGD 80–120, 47 FR 5722, Feb. 8, 1982; CGD 96–006, 61 FR 35964, July 9, 1996; USCG–1998–4442, 63 FR 52190, Sept. 30, 1998]

§ 42.07–50 Penalties for violations.

(a) The penalties for violation of various provisions of the load line acts or the regulations established thereunder are set forth in 46 U.S.C. 5116. The Secretary of Transportation by 49 CFR 1.46(b) has transferred to the Commandant authority to assess, collect, remit or litigate any monetary penalty imposed under these laws.

(b) The master and/or owner of a vessel that is operated, navigated, or used in violation of the provisions of the load line acts, or the regulations in this subchapter will be subject to the penalties as set forth in law, and the vessel shall also be liable therefor. Depending upon the gravity of the violations, the Coast Guard may do any one or more of the following:

(1) Detain a vessel if deemed to be overloaded in violation of title 46 U.S.C. 5112, in accordance with 46 U.S.C. 5113 and have the vessel surveyed by three disinterested surveyors.

(2) Assess and collect applicable monetary penalties for certain violations as provided in 46 U.S.C. 5112 and 5116.

(3) Initiate a criminal prosecution for certain violations when required by 46 U.S.C. 5112 or 5116.

(4) Initiate an action of libel against the vessel involved if there is a failure to pay monetary penalties assessed.

(5) Initiate a suspension or revocation proceeding, in addition to the foregoing actions described in this paragraph against any officer or seaman holding a valid Coast Guard credential and who may violate any provision of the load line acts, the 1966 Convention, or the regulations in this subchapter,

under the provisions of 46 U.S.C. chapter 77, and the regulations in 46 CFR part 5.

(c) In determining offenses, 46 U.S.C. 5116 provides that 'Each day of a continuing violation is a separate violation' and

(d) The procedures governing the assessment, collection, remission and litigation of any monetary penalty proposed under 46 U.S.C. 5116 for a violation of either load line law or the applicable regulations in this subchapter, as well as the appeal procedures to be allowed, are in 33 CFR subpart 1.07.

[CGFR 68–60, 33 FR 10054, July 12, 1968, as amended by CGFR 68–126, 34 FR 9012, June 5, 1969; CGD 80–120, 47 FR 5722, Feb. 8, 1982; CGD 97–057, 62 FR 51043, Sept. 30, 1997; USCG 2006–24371, 74 FR 11265, Mar. 16, 2009]

§ 42.07–55 Cancellation of load line certificates or exemption certificates.

(a) Since vessels described in § 42.03–5 or § 42.03–10 when found qualified are issued appropriate load line certificates or load line exemption certificates, under U.S. responsibility as indicated in § 42.07–45 such certificates may be canceled by proper U.S. authority for due cause, including one or more of the causes listed in paragraph (b) of this section. Such action may occur prior to the expiration date on the certificate and normal certificate surrender. The cancellation of such certificate means that the correctness of load line marks and compliance with conditions of assignment for the named vessel no longer are recognized by the United States and that the existing assigned load line marks are voided.

(b) Certain causes for automatic cancellation of certificates are:

(1) The conditions of assignment have not been maintained as required by this subchapter.

(2) Material alterations have taken place in the hull or superstructure of the vessel, which will necessitate the assignment of an increased freeboard.

(3) The fittings and appliances have not been maintained in an effective condition for the protection of openings, guardrails, freeing ports, and means of access to crew's quarters.

(4) The structural strength of the vessel is lowered to such an extent that the vessel is unsafe.

(5) The load line certificate or International Load Line Exemption Certificate is not endorsed to show the vessel has been surveyed annually or periodically by the issuing authority as required by this part or the 1966 Convention.

(6) Issuance of a new load line certificate for the same vessel.

(7) Surrender of a certificate for cancellation when required.

(8) The owner, master, or agent of the vessel has furnished false or fraudulent information in or with the application for a certificate.

[CGFR 68–60, 33 FR 10054, July 12, 1968, as amended by CGFR 68–126, 34 FR 9012, June 5, 1969]

§ 42.07–60 Control.

(a) The Director, Field Operations (DFO) or the Coast Guard District Commander may detain a vessel for survey if there is reason to believe that the vessel is proceeding on her journey in excess of the draft allowed by the regulations in this subchapter as indicated by the vessel's load line certificate, or otherwise. The Coast Guard District Commander may detain a vessel if it is so loaded as to be manifestly unsafe to proceed to sea.

(b) If the Director, Field Operations (DFO) orders a vessel detained, he shall immediately inform the Coast Guard District Commander thereof, who shall thereupon advise the Director, Field Operations (DFO) whether or not he deems that the vessel may proceed to sea with safety. If the Coast Guard District Commander orders a vessel detained, such officer will furnish the Director, Field Operations (DFO) immediate notification of such detention. The clearance shall be refused to any vessel which shall have been ordered detained, which shall be in effect until it is shown that the vessel is not in violation of the applicable law and the regulations in this subchapter.

(1) Where a vessel is detained for noncompliance with "material alteration" and "effective maintenance" requirements of paragraph (f)(1) of this section, the detention shall only be exercised insofar as may be necessary to

ensure that the vessel can proceed to sea without danger to passengers or crew.

(c) The detention of a vessel will be by written order of either the Coast Guard District Commander or the Director, Field Operations (DFO), depending on who orders the detention. The Coast Guard District Commander will immediately arrange for a survey in the manner prescribed by 46 U.S.C. 5113. Unless the owner or agent waives in writing and stipulates to accept the Coast Guard's survey, the Coast Guard District Commander shall appoint three disinterested surveyors and, where practicable, one of them shall be from the Surveying Staff of the American Bureau of Shipping. Such surveyors shall conduct a survey to ascertain whether or not the vessel is loaded in violation of the applicable provisions in the load line acts, and the regulations in this subchapter. If the survey confirms the allegation that the vessel is in violation of either law or the applicable regulations in this subchapter, "the owner and agent shall bear the costs of the survey in addition to any penalty or fine imposed", as provided in these laws.

(d) Whenever a vessel is detained, the master or owner may, within 5 days, appeal to the Commandant who may, if he desires, order a further survey, and may affirm, set aside, or modify the order of the detaining officer.

(e) Where a foreign vessel is detained or intervention action of any other kind is taken against a foreign vessel, the officer carrying out the action shall immediately inform in writing the Consul or the diplomatic representative of the State whose flag the vessel is flying, of the decision involved together with all pertinent circumstances under which intervention was deemed necessary.

(f) Under 46 U.S.C. 5109 a vessel of a foreign country which has ratified the 1966 Convention, or which holds a recognized and valid 1930 Convention certificate, or which holds a valid Great Lakes Certificate, shall be exempt from the provisions of the regulations in this subchapter insofar as the marking of the load lines and the certificating thereof are concerned, so long as such country similarly recognizes the load lines established by this subchapter for the purpose of a voyage by sea subject to the proviso in paragraph (f)(1) of this section or the alternative proviso in paragraph (f)(2) of this section.

(1) If the foreign vessel is marked with load lines and has on board a valid International or Great Lakes Load Line Certificate certifying to the correctness of the marks, the control provisions in this part which are in accord with Article 21 of the 1966 Convention shall be observed. In this connection, the vessel shall not be loaded beyond the limits allowed by the certificate. The position of the load lines on the vessel shall correspond with the certificate. The vessel shall not have been so materially altered as to make the vessel manifestly unfit to proceed to sea without danger to human life, in regard to:

(i) The hull or superstructure (if necessitating assignment of an increased freeboard); and/or,

(ii) The appliances and fittings for protection of openings, guardrails, freeing ports, and means of access to crew's quarters (if necessitating replacement or other effective maintenance).

(2) (Alternatively provided) If the foreign vessel has on board an International Load Line Exemption Certificate in lieu of an International Load Line Certificate, 1966, in such case, verify that it is valid and any conditions stipulated therein are met.

(g) A foreign vessel of a nation for which the 1966 Convention has not come into force does not qualify for an International Load Line Certificate, 1966. In lieu thereof, such a vessel shall be required to have on board a valid Form *B* load line certificate or a recognized 1930 Convention certificate.

[CGFR 68–60, 33 FR 10055, July 12, 1968, as amended by CGFR 68–126, 34 FR 9012, June 5, 1969; USCG–1998–4442, 63 FR 52190, Sept. 30, 1998; USCG–2012–0832, 77 FR 59777, Oct. 1, 2012]

§ 42.07–75 Right of appeal.

Any person directly affected by a decision or action taken under this subchapter, by or on behalf of the Coast

Guard, may appeal therefrom in accordance with subpart 1.03 of this chapter.

[CGD 88–033, 54 FR 50380, Dec. 6, 1989]

Subpart 42.09—Load Line Assignments and Surveys—General Requirements

§ 42.09-1 Assignment of load lines.

(a) The assignment of load lines is conditioned upon the structural efficiency and satisfactory stability of the vessel, and upon the provisions provided on the vessel for her effective protection and that of the crew. Certain vessels, such as vessels carrying all their cargo as deck cargo, or vessels where design or service require special conditions to be applicable, shall have certain stability limitations imposed on them, as may be necessary. When stability limitations for a vessel are prescribed, the assigning authority shall furnish the master the vessel's maximum draft permitted and other conditions, including reference to Commandant approved operating stability features, which may be applicable.

(1) No load line assignment shall be made under this part to a vessel proceeding on a foreign voyage, or where the load line assignment is related to the flooded stability provisions and the vessel is proceeding on a domestic voyage, until the applicable light ship characteristics are established and incorporated into the vessel's stability data approved by the Commandant and furnished to the master of the vessel.

(2) If load line assignments are made to vessels for coastwise voyages before the results of the required stability characteristics are determined and incorporated into the vessel's stability data approved by the Commandant, then such load line assignments shall be regarded as conditional and shall be subject to verification or modification for removal of the conditional status. Any vessel with a conditional load line assignment shall not be loaded beyond a conservative safe draft. Where the Commandant deems it unnecessary, the requirement for furnishing stability information to the masters of coastwise vessels assigned load lines not related to flooded stability may be omitted and the assigning authority and others concerned will be so notified.

(b) Each vessel subject to load line requirements shall carry on board a valid certificate attesting to compliance with such requirements. (See §§ 42.07–35 and 42.07–40 for additional data furnished to the vessel.)

(c) The master of the vessel for which a load line certificate has been issued shall be responsible for the maintenance of such certificate on board such vessel and for compliance with its terms and conditions. Additionally, the master shall be responsible for having the current load line survey report on board the vessel. This report shall be made available to surveyors when carrying out subsequent load line surveys.

[CGFR 68–60, 33 FR 10055, July 12, 1968, as amended by CGFR 68–126, 34 FR 9012, June 5, 1969]

§ 42.09-5 All vessels—division into types.

(a) For the purposes of this part, each vessel to which this part applies is either a Type "A" or a Type "B" vessel.

(b) A Type "A" vessel is a vessel that—

(1) Is designed to carry only liquid cargoes in bulk;

(2) Has a high degree of watertight and structural integrity of the deck exposed to the weather, with only small openings to cargo compartments that are closed by watertight gasketed covers of steel or other material considered equivalent by the Commandant; and

(3) Has a low permeability of loaded cargo compartments.

(c) A Type "B" vessel is any vessel that is not a Type "A" vessel.

(d) Requirements governing the assignment of freeboards for Types "A" and "B" vessels are in subparts 42.20 and 42.25 of this part.

[CGD 79–153, 48 FR 38647, Aug. 25, 1983]

§ 42.09-10 Stability, subdivision, and strength.

(a) *All vessels.* Where regulations in this part, or in part 46 of this subchapter, require or permit load line assignment on the basis of the vessel's ability to meet specified flooding, including damage stability requirements,

§ 42.09–15

the owner shall furnish the necessary plans and calculations demonstrating that the vessel is in compliance with the applicable requirements. This material shall be furnished to the assigning authority for approval review at the earliest practicable date except where specifically required by part 46 of this subchapter for passenger vessels to be submitted to the Commandant for approval.

(1) When stability information is required, the plans shall include the location and extent of all watertight subdivision bulkheads, etc., involved.

(2) Additional stability, subdivision, and strength requirements are in §§ 42.09–1, 42.13–1, 42.13–5, and 42.15–1. The applicable flooded stability requirements are in §§ 42.20–3 through 42.20–13.

(b) *Passenger vessels.* In passenger vessels where the positions of the maximum load lines is subject to determination by the application of subdivision and stability requirements in this subchapter, the provisions of both parts 42 and 46 shall be accounted for and developed as necessary. See subchapter H (Passenger Vessels) of this chapter for related data required to be submitted to the Commandant.

(c) *Light ship data.* All plans, etc., necessary for obtaining the Commandant's approval of test results (light ship data) and stability information shall be furnished by the owner. In the absence of existing acceptable light ship stability information, such data shall be obtained from a stability test performed under the supervision of the Commandant. Results of such tests, if satisfactory, will be approved by the Commandant.

[CGFR 68–60, 33 FR 10056, July 12, 1968, as amended by CGFR 68–126, 34 FR 9012, June 5, 1969; CGD 79–153, 48 FR 38647, Aug. 25, 1983]

§ 42.09–15 Surveys by the American Bureau of Shipping or assigning authority.

(a) *General.* Before issuing a certificate or placement of load line marks on a vessel, the assigning and issuing authority shall make an initial or periodic survey of the vessel as required by this subchapter. A load line survey report shall be made, reflecting information and facts based on initial surveys, including required and special elements as may be deemed necessary by the assigning authority or the Commandant.

(b) *Initial survey.* An initial survey shall be made before the vessel is put in service or the first time the assigning authority is requested to survey a vessel. The survey shall include a complete examination of its structure and equipment insofar as required by the applicable requirements in this subchapter. This survey shall be such as to ensure that the arrangements, materials, scantlings, and subsequent placement of load line marks fully comply with applicable requirements.

(c) *Periodical survey.* A periodical survey shall be made at intervals not exceeding five (5) years from an initial or previous periodic survey. The survey shall be similar to the initial survey insofar as extent and purpose are concerned.

(1) If the load line marks are found to be correct for the condition the vessel is then in, the assigning and issuing authority shall issue a new load line certificate, valid for such time as the condition of the vessel then warrants but in no case for a period of longer than 5 years. If, after a survey has been passed, a loadline certificate can not be issued before the current certificate expires, the current certificate may be extended by an endorsement in accordance with the requirements contained in § 42.07–45(d). This endorsement of the assigning authority shall be placed on the back of the certificate, as shown on the forms in subpart 42.50. However, if there have been alterations which affect the vessel's freeboards, such extension shall not be granted. This prohibition is the same as in Article 19(2) of the 1966 Convention.

(2) The periodical survey, including certificate extension or reissue, for a vessel holding an international load line exemption certificate for more than one voyage, shall be the same as for any other vessel covered by this section except for load line marks. However, other conditions specified in the exemption certificate shall be verified.

(d) *Annual surveys for endorsements.* Vessels subject to initial and periodic surveys shall have annual surveys, within 3 months either way of the certificate's anniversary date. The annual surveys shall be made by and prove satisfactory to the assigning and issuing authority prior to executing the required annual endorsements on load line certificates or exemption certificates. The scope shall be as defined in § 42.09–40 and such as to ensure that the applicable load line marks are found to be correct for the condition the vessel is then in.

[CGFR 68–60, 33 FR 10056, July 12, 1968, as amended by CGFR 68–126, 34 FR 9012, June 5, 1969; CGD 73–49R, 38 FR 12290, May 10, 1973]

§ 42.09–20 **Surveys of foreign vessels.**

(a) *General.* Foreign vessels of countries which have not ratified or acceded to the 1966 Convention, or which do not have valid certificates issued under other international convention or treaty and recognized by the United States of America, if desiring to depart from a port or place in the United States, the Commonwealth of Puerto Rico, the Territory of Guam, or other U.S. possessions, shall be subjected to survey, marking, and certification by a load line assigning and issuing authority as authorized under § 42.07–35 or § 42.07–40, unless:

(1) The vessel is exempted by the provision of 46 U.S.C. 5102; or

(2) The vessel is under tow and carrying neither passengers nor cargo.

(b) *Scope of survey.* A periodical survey described in § 42.09–15(c) shall be conducted by and prove satisfactory to the assigning and issuing authority. It shall be made prior to issue or reissue of the applicable certificate.

(c) *Certification of load lines.* The assigning and issuing authority after determining the vessel meets the applicable requirements in this part may issue a load line certificate subject to requirements in § 42.07–45 and on the applicable form described in subpart 42.50 of this part: *Provided,* That the load line certificate issued shall be valid for a period of 1 year. The certificate may be revalidated by endorsement for additional 1 year periods if the condition of the vessel so warrants, but in any event the certificate shall become void five (5) years from date of issue, or at the expiration of the fourth (4th) yearly validation, whichever occurs first. Whenever the condition of the vessel warrants special limitations, such information and facts shall be attested to on the front or back of the certificate as necessary, by the assigning and issuing authority.

[CGFR 68–60, 33 FR 10056, July 12, 1968, as amended by CGFR 68–126, 34 FR 9013, June 5, 1969; CGD 80–120, 47 FR 5723, Feb. 8, 1982; USCG–1998–4442, 63 FR 52190, Sept. 30, 1998]

§ 42.09–25 **Initial or periodic survey requirements for all vessels.**

(a) Before a survey may be completed, the vessel shall be placed in a drydock or hauled out. The surveyor shall be given complete access to all parts of the vessel to ensure that the vessel complies with all applicable requirements.

(b) The surveyor shall examine on all vessels the items, etc., listed in this paragraph to determine if in satisfactory condition and meeting applicable requirements in this subchapter.

(1) Cargo hatch coamings, covers, beams and supports, gaskets, clamps, locking bars, tarpaulins, battens, cleats and wedges of hatches on exposed freeboard, quarter and superstructure decks, and elsewhere as may be necessary.

(2) Structure of the vessel, coamings, closures, and all means of protection provided for openings, such as for ventilators, companionways, machinery casings, fiddleys, funnels, enclosed superstructures on the freeboard deck (and their end bulkheads) or equivalent protective deck houses, openings in the freeboard and superstructure decks, and significant openings at higher levels in the vessel.

(3) Transverse watertight subdivision bulkheads, as fitted, including any openings therein and closures for such openings. They shall be examined throughout their vertical and transverse extent.

(4) All air-pipe outlets, their closures, all scuppers, and all sanitary discharges in the vessel's sides, including nonreturn valves installed.

(5) The main and auxiliary sea inlets and discharges in the machinery space, and elsewhere if existent, and the valves and controls for these items.

(6) All gangways, cargo ports, and airports, including dead covers or other

§ 42.09-30

similar openings in the vessel's sides and their closures.

(7) All guardrails, bulwarks, gangways, and freeing port shutters, including securing devices, and bars.

(8) All eye plates or similar fittings for timber (or other) deck-cargo lashings, including the lashings, sockets for uprights and protective devices as may be necessary for ventilators and steering arrangements.

[CGFR 68-60, 33 FR 10056, July 12, 1968, as amended by CGFR 68-126, 34 FR 9013, June 5, 1969]

§ 42.09-30 Additional survey requirements for steel-hull vessels.

(a) In addition to the requirements in § 42.09-25, the surveyor of the assigning authority shall examine the items, etc., listed in this section, to determine if in satisfactory condition and meeting applicable requirements in this subchapter.

(b) When the vessel is in drydock, the hull plating, etc., shall be examined.

(c) The holds, 'tween decks, peaks, bilges, machinery spaces, and bunkers shall be examined to determine the condition of the framing, etc.

(d) The deep tanks and other tanks which form part of the vessel shall be examined internally.

(e) If a double bottom is fitted, the tanks normally shall be examined internally. Where double bottom and other tanks are used for fuel-oil bunkers, such tanks need not be cleaned out, if the surveyor is able to determine by an external examination that their general condition is satisfactory.

(f) The deck shall be examined.

(g) Where, owing to the age and condition of the vessel or otherwise, the surveyor deems it necessary, the shell and deck plating may be required to be drilled or other acceptable means used, in order to ascertain the then thickness of such plating.

[CGFR 68-60, 33 FR 10057, July 12, 1968]

§ 42.09-35 Additional survey requirements for wood-hull vessels.

(a) In addition to the requirements in § 42.09-25, the surveyor of the assigning authority shall examine the items, etc., listed in this section, to determine if in satisfactory condition and meeting the applicable requirements in this subchapter.

(b) When the vessel is in drydock or hauled out, the keel, stem, stern frame or sternpost, outside planking, and caulking shall be examined.

(c) The fasteners shall be examined. Bolts, screws, or equivalent fastenings, as deemed necessary by the surveyor, must be backed out, or otherwise dealt with, to ensure soundness.

(d) The holds, 'tween decks, peaks, bilges, machinery spaces, and bunkers shall be examined.

(e) The entire structure, including decks, shall be examined. If considered necessary by the surveyor, borings shall be made, or other means may be used, to ascertain the condition of the materials. Should these measures disclose sufficient cause, further examination to satisfy the surveyor as to the true condition shall be made and check locations listed. This list shall be submitted to the assigning and issuing authority for record purposes, and for use in subsequent surveys.

[CGFR 68-60, 33 FR 10057, July 12, 1968]

§ 42.09-40 Annual surveys.

(a) Relative to §§ 42.09-15(d) and 42.09-20(c), the assigning and issuing authority shall make an annual survey of each vessel holding an appropriate certificate issued under this subchapter.

(b) The annual survey shall be of such scope and extent so as to ensure:

(1) The maintenance in an effective condition of the fittings and appliances for the:

(i) Protection of openings;

(ii) Guardrails;

(iii) Freeing ports; and,

(iv) Means of access to crew's quarters.

(2) That there have not been alterations made to the hull or superstructure which would affect the calculations determining the position of the load line marks.

(c) The assigning and issuing authority shall report on the annual survey made to the owner of the vessel.

[CGFR 68-60, 33 FR 10057, July 12, 1968 as amended by CGD 80-143, 47 FR 25149, June 10, 1982]

§ 42.09-45 Correction of deficiencies.

(a) During and after any survey made by the assigning and issuing authority, those items, fittings, etc., which are found to be in an unsatisfactory condition by the surveyor shall be repaired or renewed in order to place the vessel in a satisfactory condition.

(b) No load line certificate shall be issued, endorsed, extended, or reissued or delivered to a vessel subject to this subchapter until after unsatisfactory conditions have been corrected as required by paragraph (a) of this section.

[CGFR 68–60, 33 FR 10057, July 12, 1968, as amended by CGFR 68–126, 34 FR 9013, June 5, 1969]

§ 42.09-50 Repairs or alterations to vessel after it has been surveyed.

(a) After any survey of the vessel made under §§ 42.09–25 to 42.09–40, inclusive, as applicable, has been completed and deficiencies corrected as provided in § 42.09–45, no change shall be made in the vessel's structure, equipment, arrangement, material, or scantlings as covered by such survey, without the prior specific approval of the assigning and issuing authority.

(b) To avoid a freeboard or other penalty, any vessel which undergoes repairs, alterations, or modifications, including outfitting related thereto, shall continue to comply with the applicable requirements consistent with the load line certificate held.

(c) An existing vessel, which had a load line assigned under previous regulations which undergoes repairs, alterations, or modifications of a major character, shall meet the requirements for a new vessel in this part insofar as the assigning and issuing authority and the Commandant deem reasonable and practicable.

[CGFR 68–60, 33 FR 10057, July 12, 1968, as amended by CGD 80–120, 47 FR 5723, Feb. 8, 1982]

Subpart 42.11—Applications for Load Line Assignments, Surveys, and Certificates

§ 42.11-1 General.

(a) As described in this subchapter under §§ 42.07–35, 42.07–40, 42.09–15, and 42.09–20, the American Bureau of Shipping or other recognized classification societies approved as load line assigning and issuing authorities perform the duties connected with making load line assignments to vessels.

(b) The Commandant is responsible for the administration of the load line acts, the 1966 Convention, other treaties regarding load lines, and the implementing regulations in this subchapter which include prescribed form and content of applicable load line certificates.

(c) Except in special instances for Coast Guard vessels, the Commandant does not perform the duties of a load line assigning authority.

[CGFR 68–60, 33 FR 10057, July 12, 1968, as amended by CGFR 68–126, 34 FR 9013, June 5, 1969; CGD 80–120, 47 FR 5723, Feb. 8, 1982]

§ 42.11-5 Applications for load line assignments, surveys, and certificates for U.S.-flag vessels.

(a) Normally, the owner, master, or agent of a vessel shall apply in writing, on a timely basis, to the American Bureau of Shipping for the assignment, survey, and certification of load lines. When nonconcurrent, a separate application shall be made for each function desired and submitted on a timely basis. The mailing address of the home office of American Bureau of Shipping is ABS Plaza, 16855 Northchase Drive, Houston, TX 77060.

(b) After the Commandant has approved a recognized classification society as a load line assigning and issuing authority for a vessel, as described in a written request of the shipowner, the owner shall apply in writing, on a timely basis, direct to the approved assigning and issuing authority for the assignment, survey, and certification of load lines. When nonconcurrent, a separate application shall be made to such authority for each function desired, and submitted on a timely basis.

[CGFR 68–60, 33 FR 10057, July 12, 1968, as amended by CGFR 68–126, 34 FR 9013, June 5, 1969; CGD 96–041, 61 FR 50727, Sept. 27, 1996; USCG–2000–7790, 65 FR 58459, Sept. 29, 2000]

§ 42.11-10 Applications for load line assignments and certificates for vessels other than U.S.-flag vessels.

(a) The application for the assignment of load lines and certificate for a

§ 42.11-15

foreign vessel belonging to (or which will belong to) either a country ratifying or acceding to the International Convention on Load Lines, 1966, or to a country with which the United States of America has a reciprocal load line agreement in effect shall be made by the Government whose flag the vessel flies, or will fly. The application may be made direct to the American Bureau of Shipping, or after receiving the Commandant's approval, to a recognized classification society which that country has requested as an assigning and issuing authority. When the load line assignment and certificate are authorized pursuant to the requirements in this part, the certificate must contain a statement that it has been issued at the request of a specific Government, which shall be named therein.

(1) When the load line assignment is performed under the applicable regulations in this subchapter, the assigning and issuing authority shall transmit to the requesting Government at the earliest practicable date, one copy of each certificate issued, the load line survey report used for computing the freeboard, and the freeboard computations. For information, the assigning and issuing authority shall also notify the Commandant of the names of the vessel and the Government involved and the date and place where the work was done.

(b) For a foreign vessel of a country not included in paragraph (a) of this section, the owner, master, or agent normally shall apply in writing to the American Bureau of Shipping, or to any other recognized assigning and issuing authority after it has been approved by the Commandant, for the assignment, survey, and certification of load lines, or for reissue of a load line certificate, as may be necessary for the vessel to clear ports of the United States, the Commonwealth of Puerto Rico, the Territory of Guam, or other U.S. possessions. Normally the same requirements, conditions, procedures, distribution of applicable certificates, etc., shall be applied to such foreign vessels which are applied to similar U.S.-flag vessels of 150 gross tons or over.

[CGFR 68-60, 33 FR 10058, July 12, 1968, as amended by CGFR 68-126, 34 FR 9013, June 5, 1969]

§ 42.11-15 Application for timber load lines.

(a) The owner, master, or agent of a vessel having load lines assigned under this subchapter may apply to the assigning and issuing authority for timber load lines when making his application for a load line certificate. After the vessel has been found in compliance with the applicable requirements in this subchapter, it may be marked with timber load lines, which will also be certified to in the load line certificate.

[CGFR 68-60, 33 FR 10058, July 12, 1968, as amended by CGFR 68-126, 34 FR 9013, June 5, 1969]

§ 42.11-20 Application for annual survey.

(a) The owner, master, or agent of a vessel holding a load line certificate shall apply to the assigning and issuing authority who issued the certificate for the annual survey required by § 42.09-40 or the International Convention on Load Lines, 1966.

[CGFR 68-60, 33 FR 10058, July 12, 1968]

Subpart 42.13—General Rules for Determining Load Lines

§ 42.13-1 Assumptions.

(a) The regulations in this part are based on the assumption that the nature and stowage of the cargo, ballast, etc., are such as will secure sufficient stability of the vessel and avoid excessive structural stress.

(b) The regulations in this part are also based on the assumption that, where there are other international requirements relating to stability or subdivision applicable to vessels, these requirements have been met.

[CGFR 68-60, 33 FR 10058, July 12, 1968]

§ 42.13-5 Strength of vessel.

(a) The assigning and issuing authority shall satisfy itself that the general structural strength of the vessel is sufficient for the draft corresponding to the freeboard assigned, and when requested shall furnish pertinent strength information to the Commandant.

(b) Vessels built and maintained in conformity with the requirements of a classification society recognized by the Commandant are considered to possess adequate strength for the purpose of the applicable requirements in this subchapter unless deemed otherwise by the Commandant.

[CGFR 68–60, 33 FR 10058, July 12, 1968, as amended by CGFR 68–126, 34 FR 9013, June 5, 1969]

§ 42.13–10 **Freeboards assigned vessels.**

(a) Vessels with mechanical means of propulsion, or lighters, barges, or other vessels without independent means of propulsion, shall be assigned freeboards in accordance with the provisions of §§ 42.13–1 to 42.20–75, inclusive.

(b) Vessels carrying timber deck cargoes may be assigned, in addition to the freeboards required by paragraph (a) of this section, timber freeboards in accordance with the provisions of §§ 42.25–1 to 42.25–20, inclusive.

(c) Vessels designed to carry sail, whether as the sole means of propulsion or as a supplementary means, and tugs, shall be assigned freeboards in accordance with the provisions of §§ 42.13–1 to 42.20–75, inclusive, and such additional freeboards as determined necessary by the Commandant under the procedure of paragraph (f) of this section.

(d) Vessels of wood or of composite construction, or of other materials the use of which the Commandant has approved, or vessels whose constructional features are such as to render the application of the provisions of §§ 42.13–1 to 42.25–20 unreasonable or impracticable, shall be assigned freeboards as determined necessary by the Commandant under the procedure of paragraph (f) of this section.

(e) The requirements in §§ 42.15–1 to 42.15–80, inclusive, shall apply to every vessel to which a minimum freeboard is assigned. Relaxations from these requirements may be granted to a vessel to which a greater than minimum freeboard is assigned provided the safety conditions of the vessel are determined to be satisfactory under paragraph (f) of this section.

(f) In each case specified by paragraphs (c) to (e) inclusive of this section, the assigning authority shall report to the Commandant the specific matters in which the vessel is deficient or requires special freeboard consideration due to design, arrangement, construction materials, propulsive method, or relaxation of requirements in this part. The report shall also furnish background data and recommendations of the assigning authority (including freeboard additions), as will enable the Commandant to reach a decision.

[CGFR 68–60, 33 FR 10058, July 12, 1968, as amended by CGFR 68–126, 34 FR 9013, June 5, 1969]

§ 42.13–15 **Definitions of terms.**

(a) *Length.* The length (L) shall be taken as 96 percent of the total length on a waterline at 85 percent of the least molded depth measured from the top of the keel, or as the length from the foreside of the stem to the axis of the rudder stock on that waterline, if that be greater. In vessels designed with a rake of keel the waterline on which this length is measured shall be parallel to the designed waterline.

(b) *Perpendiculars.* The forward and after perpendiculars shall be taken at the forward and after ends of the length (L). The forward perpendicular shall coincide with the foreside of the stem on the waterline on which the length is measured.

(c) *Amidships.* Amidships is at the middle of the length (L).

(d) *Breadth.* Unless expressly provided otherwise, the breadth (B) is the maximum breadth of the vessel, measured amidships to the molded line of the frame in a vessel with a metal shell and to the outer surface of the hull in a vessel with a shell of any other material.

(e) *Molded depth.* (1) The molded depth is the vertical distance measured from the top of the keel to the top of the freeboard deck beam at side. In wood and composite vessels the distance is measured from the lower edge of the keel rabbet. Where the form at the lower part of the midship section is of a hollow character, or where thick

§ 42.13-15

garboards are fitted, the distance is measured from the point where the line of the flat of the bottom continued inwards cuts the side of the keel.

(2) In vessels having rounded gunwales, the molded depth shall be measured to the point of intersection of the molded lines of the deck and sides, the lines extending as though the gunwale were of angular design.

(3) Where the freeboard deck is stepped and the raised part of the deck extends over the point at which the molded depth is to be determined, the molded depth shall be measured to a line of reference extending from the lower part of the deck along a line parallel with the raised part.

(f) *Depth for freeboard* (D). (1) The depth for freeboard (D) is the molded depth amidships, plus the thickness of the freeboard deck stringer plate, where fitted, plus

$$T(L-S)/L$$

if the exposed freeboard deck is sheathed;

where:

T is the mean thickness of the exposed sheathing clear of deck openings; and

S is the total length of superstructures as defined in paragraph (j)(4) of this section.

(2) The depth for freeboard (D) in a vessel having a rounded gunwale with a radius greater than 4 percent of the breadth (B) or having topsides of unusual form is the depth for freeboard of a vessel having a midship section with vertical topsides and with the same round of beam and area of topside section equal to that provided by the actual midship section.

(g) *Block coefficient.* The block coefficient (C_b) is given by

$$C_b = \Delta/L.B.d_1$$

where Δ is the volume of the molded displacement of the vessel, excluding bossing, in a vessel with a metal shell, and is the volume of displacement to the outer surface of the hull in a vessel with a shell of any other material, both taken at a molded draft of d_1; and, d_1 is 85 percent of the least molded depth.

(h) *Freeboard.* The freeboard assigned is the distance measured vertically downward amidships from the upper edge of the deck line to the upper edge of the related load line.

(i) *Freeboard deck.* (1) The freeboard deck is normally the uppermost complete deck exposed to weather and sea, which has permanent means of closing all openings in the weather part thereof, and below which all openings in the sides of the vessel are fitted with permanent means of watertight closing. In a vessel having a discontinuance freeboard deck, the lowest line of the exposed deck and the continuation of that line parallel to the upper part of the deck is taken as the freeboard deck. At the option of the owner and subject to the approval of the assigning authority a lower deck may be designated as the freeboard deck, provided it is a complete and permanent deck continuous in a fore and aft direction at least between the machinery space and peak bulkheads and continuous athwartships. When this lower deck is stepped the lowest line of the deck and the continuation of that line parallel to the upper part of the deck is taken as the freeboard deck.

(2) When a lower deck is designated as the freeboard deck, that part of the hull which extends above the freeboard deck is treated as a superstructure so far as concerns the application of the conditions of assignment and the calculation of freeboard. It is from this deck that the freeboard is calculated.

(j) *Superstructure.* (1) A superstructure is a decked structure on the freeboard deck, extending from side to side of the vessel or with the side plating not being inboard of the shell plating more than 4 percent to the breadth (B). A raised quarter deck is regarded as a superstructure.

(2) An enclosed superstructure is a superstructure with:

(i) Enclosing bulkheads of efficient construction;

(ii) Access openings, if any in these bulkheads fitted with doors complying with the requirements of § 42.15-10; and,

(iii) All other openings in sides or ends of the superstructure fitted with efficient weathertight means of closing.

NOTE: A bridge or poop shall not be regarded as enclosed unless access is provided for the crew to reach machinery and other working spaces inside the superstructures by alternative means, which are available at all times when bulkhead openings are closed.

Coast Guard, DHS § 42.13-30

(3) The height of a superstructure is the least vertical height measured at side from the top of the superstructure deck beams to the top of the freeboard deck beams.

(4) The length of a superstructure (S) is the mean length of the part of the superstructure which lies within the length (L).

(k) *Flush deck vessel.* A flush deck vessel is one which has no superstructure on the freeboard deck.

(l) *Weathertight.* Weathertight means that in any sea conditions water will not penetrate into the vessel.

[CGFR 68-60, 33 FR 10058, July 12, 1968, as amended by CGFR 68-126, 34 FR 9013, June 5, 1969; 43 FR 31928, July 24, 1978]

§ 42.13-20 Deck line.

(a) The deck line is a horizontal line 12 inches in length and 1 inch in breadth. It shall be marked amidships on each side of the vessel, and its upper edge shall normally pass through the point where the continuation outwards of the upper surface of the freeboard deck intersects the outer surface of the shell (as illustrated in Figure 42.13-20(a)), provided that the deck line may be placed with reference to another fixed point on the vessel on condition that the freeboard is correspondingly corrected. The location of the reference point and the identification of the freeboard deck shall in all cases be indicated on the International Load Line Certificate (1966), and, as applicable, on all other load line certificates issued pursuant to this part 42.

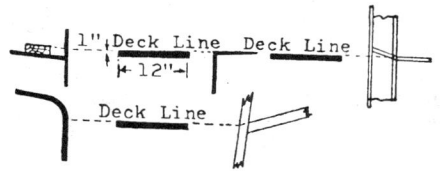

FIGURE 42.13-20(A)—DECK LINE

[CGFR 68-60, 33 FR 10059, July 12, 1968, as amended by CGFR 68-126, 34 FR 9014, June 5, 1969]

§ 42.13-25 Load line mark.

(a) The load line mark shall consist of a ring 12 inches in outside diameter and 1 inch wide which is intersected by a horizontal line 18 inches in length and 1 inch in breadth, the upper edge of which passes through the center of the ring. The center of the ring shall be placed amidships and at a distance equal to the assigned summer freeboard measured vertically below the upper edge of the deck line (as illustrated in Figure 42.13-25(a)).

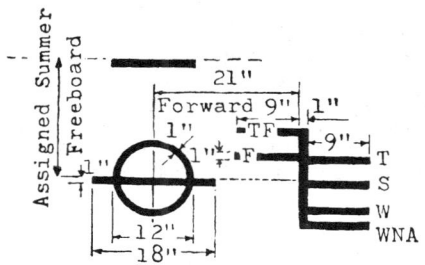

FIGURE 42.13-25(A)—LOAD LINE MARK AND LINES TO BE USED WITH THIS MARK

[CGFR 68-60, 33 FR 10059, July 12, 1968]

§ 42.13-30 Lines to be used with the load line mark.

(a) The lines which indicate the load line assigned in accordance with the regulations in this part shall be horizontal lines 9 inches in length and 1 inch in breadth which extend forward of, unless expressly provided otherwise, and at right angles to, a vertical line 1 inch in breadth marked at a distance 21 inches forward of the center of the ring (as illustrated in Figure 42.13-25(a)).

(b) The following load lines shall be used:

(1) The summer load line indicated by the upper edge of the line which passes through the center of the ring and also by a line marked *S*.

(2) The winter load line indicated by the upper edge of a line marked *W*.

(3) The winter North Atlantic load line indicated by the upper edge of a line marked *WNA*.

(4) The tropical load line indicated by the upper edge of a line marked *T*.

(5) The fresh water load line in summer indicated by the upper edge of a line marked *F*. The fresh water load line in summer is marked abaft the vertical line. The difference between the fresh water load line in summer

§ 42.13-35

and the summer load line is the allowance to be made for loading in fresh water at the other load lines.

(6) The tropical fresh water load line indicated by the upper edge of a line marked *TF*, and marked abaft the vertical line.

(c) If timber freeboards are assigned, the timber load lines shall be marked in addition to ordinary load lines. These lines shall be horizontal lines 9 inches in length and 1 inch in breadth which extend abaft unless expressly provided otherwise, and are at right angles to, a vertical line 1 inch in breadth marked at a distance 21 inches abaft the center of the ring (as illustrated in Figure 42.13-30(c)).

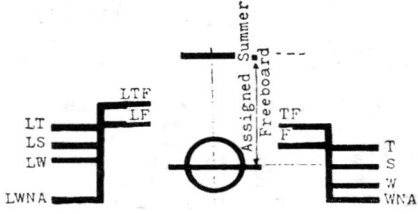

FIGURE 42.13-30(C)—TIMBER LOAD LINE MARK AND LINES TO BE USED WITH THIS MARK

(d) The following timber load lines shall be used:

(1) The summer timber load line indicated by the upper edge of a line marked *LS*.

(2) The winter timber load line indicated by the upper edge of a line marked *LW*.

(3) The winter North Atlantic timber load line indicated by the upper edge of a line marked *LWNA*.

(4) The tropical timber load line indicated by the upper edge of a line marked *LT*.

(5) The fresh water timber load line in summer indicated by the upper edge of a line marked *LF* and marked forward of the vertical line.

NOTE: The difference between the fresh water timber load line in summer and the summer timber load line is the allowance to be made for loading in fresh water at the other timber load lines.

(6) The tropical fresh water timber load line indicated by the upper edge of a line marked *LTF* and marked forward of the vertical line.

(e) Where the characteristics of a vessel, or the nature of the vessel's service or navigational limits make any of the seasonal lines inapplicable, these lines may be omitted.

(f) Where a vessel is assigned a greater than minimum freeboard so that the load line is marked at a position corresponding to, or lower than, the lowest seasonal load line assigned at minimum freeboard in accordance with the present Convention, only the fresh water load line need be marked.

(g) On sailing vessels only the fresh water load line and the winter North Atlantic load line need be marked (as illustrated in Figure 42.13-30(g)).

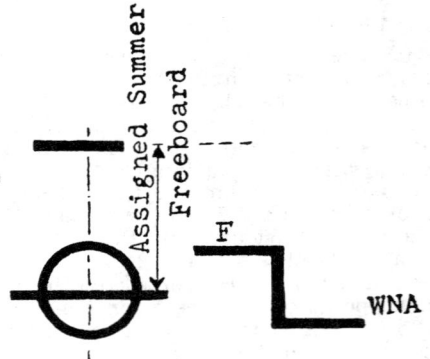

FIGURE 42.13-30(G)—LOAD LINE MARK ON SAILING VESSEL AND LINES TO BE USED WITH THIS MARK

(h) Where a winter North Atlantic load line is identical with the winter load line corresponding to the same vertical line, this load line shall be marked *W*.

(i) Additional load lines required by other international conventions in force may be marked at right angles to and abaft the vertical line specified in paragraph (a) of this section.

[CGFR 68-60, 33 FR 10059, July 12, 1968, as amended by CGFR 68-126, 34 FR 9014, June 5, 1969]

§ 42.13-35 Mark of assigning authority.

(a) The mark of the assigning authority by whom the load lines are assigned may be indicated alongside the load line ring above the horizontal line which passes through the center of the ring, or above and below it. This mark shall consist of not more than four initials to identify the assigning authority's name, each measuring approximately 4½ inches in height and 3 inches in width.

[CGFR 68–60, 33 FR 10060, July 12, 1968]

§ 42.13–40 Details of marking.

(a) The ring, lines and letters shall be painted in white or yellow on a dark ground or in black on a light ground. They shall also be permanently marked on the sides of the vessels to the satisfaction of the assigning authority. The marks shall be plainly visible and, if necessary, special arrangements shall be made for this purpose.

[CGFR 68–60, 33 FR 10060, July 12, 1968, as amended by CGFR 68–126, 34 FR 9014, June 5, 1969]

§ 42.13–45 Verification of marks.

(a) The International Load Line Certificate (1966) shall not be delivered to the vessel until § 42.07–5 has been fully complied with under the authority and provisions of subparts 42.07 and 42.09 of this part.

[CGFR 68–60, 33 FR 10060, July 12, 1968, as amended by CGFR 68–126, 34 FR 9014, June 5, 1969]

Subpart 42.15—Conditions of Assignment of Freeboard

§ 42.15–1 Information to be supplied to the master.

(a) The master of every new vessel shall be supplied with sufficient information in a form approved by the assigning and issuing authority, to enable him to arrange for the loading and ballasting of his vessel in such a way as to avoid the creation of any unacceptable stresses in the vessel's structure: *Provided*, That this requirement need not apply to any particular length, design or class of vessel where the Commandant considers it to be unnecessary and so notifies the assigning and issuing authority.

(b) The master of every new vessel, which is not already provided with stability information under an international convention for the safety of life at sea in force, shall be supplied with sufficient information in a form approved by the Commandant, to give him guidance as to the stability of the vessel under varying conditions of service, and a copy shall be furnished to the Commandant.

[CGFR 68–60, 33 FR 10060, July 12, 1968, as amended by CGFR 68–126, 34 FR 9014, June 5, 1969]

§ 42.15–5 Superstructure end bulkheads.

(a) Bulkheads at exposed ends of enclosed superstructures shall be of efficient construction and shall be to the satisfaction of the assigning authority.

[CGFR 68–60, 33 FR 10060, July 12, 1968, as amended by CGFR 68–126, 34 FR 9014, June 5, 1969]

§ 42.15–10 Doors.

(a) All access openings in bulkheads at ends of enclosed superstructures shall be fitted with doors of steel or other equivalent material, permanently and strongly attached to the bulkhead, and framed, stiffened and fitted so that the whole structure is of equivalent strength to the unpierced bulkhead and weathertight when closed. The means for securing these doors weathertight shall consist of gaskets and clamping devices or other equivalent means and shall be permanently attached to the bulkhead or to the doors themselves, and the doors shall be so arranged that they can be operated from both sides of the bulkhead.

(b) Except as otherwise provided in these regulations, the height of the sills of access openings in bulkheads at ends of enclosed superstructures shall be at least 15 inches above the deck.

[CGFR 68–60, 33 FR 10060, July 12, 1968]

§ 42.15–15 Positions of hatchways, doorways and ventilators.

(a) For the purpose of this part two positions of hatchways, doorways and ventilators are defined as follows:

(1) Position 1: Upon exposed freeboard and raised quarter decks, and upon exposed superstructure decks situated forward of a point located a quarter of the vessel's length from the forward perpendicular.

(2) Position 2: Upon exposed superstructure decks situated abaft a quarter of the vessel's length from the forward perpendicular.

[CGFR 68–60, 33 FR 10060, July 12, 1968, as amended by CGFR 68–126, 34 FR 9014, June 5, 1969]

§ 42.15–20 Cargo and other hatchways.

(a) The construction and the means for securing the weathertightness of cargo and other hatchways in positions 1 and 2 shall be at least equivalent to the requirements of §§ 42.15–25 and 42.15–30.

(b) Coamings and hatchway covers to exposed hatchways on decks above the superstructure deck shall comply with the requirements of the assigning authority.

[CGFR 68–60, 33 FR 10060, July 12, 1968, as amended by CGFR 68–126, 34 FR 9014, June 5, 1969]

§ 42.15–25 Hatchways closed by portable covers and secured weathertight by tarpaulins and battening devices.

(a) *Hatchway coamings.* (1) The coamings of hatchways closed by portable covers secured weathertight by tarpaulins and battening devices shall be of substantial construction, and their height above the deck shall be at least as follows:

(i) 23½ inches if in position 1.
(ii) 17½ inches if in position 2.

(b) *Hatchway covers.* (1) The width of each bearing surface for hatchway covers shall be at least 2½ inches.

(2) Where covers are made of wood, the finished thickness shall be at least 2⅜ inches in association with a span of not more than 4.9 feet.

(3) Where covers are made of mild steel, the strength shall be calculated with assumed loads not less than 358 pounds per square foot on hatchways in position 1, and not less than 266 pounds per square foot on hatchways in position 2, and the product of the maximum stress thus calculated and the factor 4.25 shall not exceed the minimum ultimate strength of the material. They shall be so designed as to limit the deflection to not more than 0.0028 times the span under these loads.

(4) The assumed loads on hatchways in position 1 may be reduced to 205 pounds per square foot for vessels of 79 feet in length and shall be not less than 358 pounds per square foot for vessels of 328 feet in length. The corresponding loads on hatchways in position 2 may be reduced to 154 pounds per square foot and 266 pounds per square foot respectively. In all cases values at intermediate lengths shall be obtained by linear interpolation.

(c) *Portable beams.* (1) Where portable beams for supporting hatchway covers are made of mild steel the strength shall be calculated with assumed loads not less than 358 pounds per square foot on hatchways in position 1 and not less than 266 pounds per square foot on hatchways in position 2 and the product of the maximum stress thus calculated and the factor 5 shall not exceed the minimum ultimate strength of the material. They shall be so designed as to limit the deflection to not more than 0.0022 times the span under these loads. For vessels of not more than 328 feet in length the requirements of paragraph (b)(4) of this section are applicable.

(d) *Pontoon covers.* (1) Where pontoon covers used in place of portable beams and covers are made of mild steel the strength shall be calculated with the assumed loads given in paragraph (b)(3) of this section, and the product of the maximum stress thus calculated and the factor 5 shall not exceed the minimum ultimate strength of the material. They shall be so designed as to limit the deflection to not more than 0.0022 times the span. Mild steel plating forming the tops of covers shall be not less in thickness than 1 percent of the spacing of stiffeners or 0.24 inches if that be greater. For vessels of not more than 328 feet in length the requirements of paragraph (b)(4) of this section are applicable.

(2) The strength and stiffness of covers made of materials other than mild steel shall be equivalent to those of mild steel to the satisfaction of the assigning authority.

(e) *Carriers or sockets.* (1) Carriers or sockets for portable beams shall be of substantial construction, and shall provide means for the efficient fitting and securing of the beams. Where rolling types of beams are use, the arrangements shall ensure that the beams remain properly in position when the hatchway is closed.

(f) *Cleats.* (1) Cleats shall be set to fit the taper of the wedges. They shall be at least 2½ inches wide and spaced not more than 23½ inches center to center; the cleats along each side or end shall be not more than 6 inches from the hatch corners.

(g) *Battens and wedges.* (1) Battens and wedges shall be efficient and in good condition. Wedges shall be of tough wood or other equivalent material. They shall have a taper of not more than 1 in 6 and shall be not less than ½-inch thick at the toes.

(h) *Tarpaulins.* (1) At least two layers of tarpaulin in good condition shall be provided for each hatchway in positions 1 and 2.

(2) The tarpaulins shall be waterproof and of ample strength. They shall be of a material of at least a standard weight and quality as approved by the assigning and issuing authority.

(i) *Security of hatchway covers.* (1) For all hatchways in position 1 or 2, steel bars or other equivalent means shall be provided in order efficiently and independently to secure each section of hatchway covers after the tarpaulins are battened down. Hatchway covers of more than 4.9 feet in length shall be secured by at least two such securing appliances.

[CGFR 68–60, 33 FR 10060, July 12, 1968, as amended by CGFR 68–126, 34 FR 9014, June 5, 1969]

§ 42.15–30 Hatchways closed by weathertight covers of steel or other equivalent material fitted with gaskets and clamping devices.

(a) *Hatchway coamings.* At positions 1 and 2 the height above the deck of hatchway coamings fitted with weathertight hatch covers of steel or other equivalent material fitted with gaskets and clamping devices shall be as specified in § 42.15–25(a)(1). The height of these coamings may be reduced, or the coamings omitted entirely, on condition that the assigning authority is satisfied that the safety of the vessel is not thereby impaired in any sea conditions. Where coamings are provided they shall be of substantial construction.

(b) *Weathertight covers.* (1) Where weathertight covers are of mild steel the strength shall be calculated with assumed loads not less than 358 pounds per square foot on hatchways in position 1, and not less than 255 pounds per square foot on hatchways in position 2, and the product of the maximum stress thus calculated and the factor of 4.25 shall not exceed the minimum ultimate strength of the material. They shall be so designed as to limit the deflection to not more than 0.0028 times the span under these loads. Mild steel plating forming the tops of covers shall be not less in thickness than one percent of the spacing of stiffeners or 0.24 inches if that be greater. The provisions of § 42.15–25(b)(4) are applicable for vessels of not more than 328 feet in length.

(2) The strength and stiffness of covers made of materials other than mild steel shall be equivalent to those of mild steel to the satisfaction of the assigning authority.

(c) *Means for securing weathertightness.* (1) The means for securing and maintaining weathertightness shall be to the satisfaction of the assigning authority.

(2) The arrangements shall ensure that the tightness can be maintained in any sea conditions. For this purpose tests for tightness shall be required at the initial surveys, and may be required at periodical surveys and at annual surveys or at more frequent intervals.

[CGFR 68–60, 33 FR 10061, July 12, 1968, as amended by CGFR 68–126, 34 FR 9014, June 5, 1969]

§ 42.15–35 Machinery space openings.

(a) Machinery space openings in position 1 or 2 shall be properly framed and efficiently enclosed by steel casings of ample strength, and where the casings are not protected by other structures their strength shall be specifically considered. Access openings in such casings shall be fitted with doors complying with the requirements of § 42.15–10(a), the sills of which shall be at least 23½ inches above the deck if in position 1, and at least 15 inches above the deck if in position 2. Other openings in such casings shall be fitted with equivalent covers, permanently attached in their proper positions.

(b) Coamings of any fiddley, funnel, or machinery space ventilators in an exposed position on the freeboard or superstructure deck shall be as high above the deck as is reasonable and practicable. Fiddley openings shall be fitted with strong covers of steel or other equivalent material permanently attached in their proper positions and capable of being secured weathertight.

[CGFR 68–60, 33 FR 10061, July 12, 1968]

§ 42.15–40 Miscellaneous openings in freeboard and superstructure decks.

(a) Manholes and flush scuttles in position 1 or 2 or within superstructures other than enclosed superstructures shall be closed by substantial covers capable of being made watertight. Unless secured by closely spaced bolts, the covers shall be permanently attached.

(b) Openings in freeboard decks other than hatchways, machinery space openings, manholes, and flush scuttles shall be protected by an enclosed superstructure, or by a deckhouse or companionway of equivalent strength and weathertightness. Any such opening in an exposed superstructure deck or in the top of a deckhouse on the freeboard deck which gives access to a space below the freeboard deck or a space within an enclosed superstructure shall be protected by an efficient deckhouse or companionway. Doorways in such deckhouses or companionways shall be fitted with doors complying with the requirements of § 42.15–10(a).

(c) In position 1 the height above the deck of sills to the doorways in companionways shall be at least 23½ inches. In position 2 they shall be at least 15 inches.

[CGFR 68–60, 33 FR 10061, July 12, 1968, as amended by CGFR 68–126, 34 FR 9014, June 5, 1969]

§ 42.15–45 Ventilators.

(a) Ventilators in position 1 or 2 to spaces below the freeboard decks or decks of enclosed superstructures shall have coamings of steel or other equivalent material, substantially constructed and efficiently connected to the deck. Where the coaming of any ventilator exceeds 35½ inches in height it shall be specially supported.

(b) Ventilators passing through superstructures other than enclosed superstructures shall have substantially constructed coamings of steel or other equivalent material at the freeboard deck.

(c) Ventilators in position 1 the coamings of which extend to more than 14.8 feet above the deck, and in position 2 the coamings of which extend to more than 7.5 feet above the deck, need not be fitted with closing arrangements unless specifically required by the assigning authority.

(d) Except as provided in paragraph (c) of this section ventilator openings shall be provided with efficient weathertight closing appliances. In vessels of not more than 328 feet in length the closing appliances shall be permanently attached; where not so provided in other vessels, they shall be conveniently stowed near the ventilators to which they are to be fitted. Ventilators in position 1 shall have coamings of a height of at least 35½ inches above the deck; in position 2 the coamings shall be of a height at least 30 inches above the deck.

(e) In exposed positions, the height of coamings may be required to be increased to the satisfaction of the assigning authority.

[CGFR 68–60, 33 FR 10061, July 12, 1968, as amended by CGFR 68–126, 34 FR 9014, June 5, 1969]

§ 42.15–50 Air pipes.

(a) Where air pipes to ballast and other tanks extend above the freeboard or superstructure decks, the exposed parts of the pipes shall be of substantial construction; the height from the deck to the point where water may have access below shall be at least 30 inches on the freeboard deck and 17½ inches on the superstructure deck. Where these heights may interfere with the working of the vessel, a lower height may be approved, provided the assigning authority is satisfied that the closing arrangements and other circumstances justify a lower height.

Satisfactory means permanently attached, shall be provided for closing the openings of the air pipes.

[CGFR 68–60, 33 FR 10062, July 12, 1968, as amended by CGFR 68–126, 34 FR 9014, June 5, 1969]

§ 42.15–55 Cargo ports and other similar openings.

(a) Cargo ports and other similar openings in the sides of vessels below the freeboard deck shall be fitted with doors so designed as to ensure watertightness and structural integrity commensurate with the surrounding shell plating, to the satisfaction of the assigning authority. The arrangements shall be subject to tightness tests at the initial survey and at such subsequent surveys or more frequent intervals as deemed necessary. The number of such openings shall be the minimum compatible with the design and proper working of the vessel.

(b) Unless permitted by the Commandant the lower edge of such openings shall not be below a line drawn parallel to the freeboard deck at side, which has at its lowest point the upper edge of the uppermost load line.

[CGFR 68–60, 33 FR 10062, July 12, 1968, as amended by CGFR 68–126, 34 FR 9014, June 5, 1969]

§ 42.15–60 Scuppers, inlets, and discharges.

(a) Discharges led through the shell either from spaces below the freeboard deck or from within superstructures and deckhouses on the freeboard deck fitted with doors complying with the requirements of § 42.15–10 shall be fitted with efficient and accessible means for preventing water from passing inboard. Normally, each separate discharge shall have one automatic nonreturn valve with a positive means of closing it from a position above the freeboard deck. Where, however, the vertical distance from the summer load waterline to the inboard end of the discharge pipe exceeds $0.01L$, the discharge may have two automatic nonreturn valves without positive means of closing: *Provided*, That the inboard valve is always accessible for examination under service conditions; where that vertical distance exceeds $0.02L$ a single automatic nonreturn valve without positive means of closing may be accepted subject to the approval of the assigning authority. The means for operating the positive action valve shall be readily accessible and provided with an indicator showing whether the valve is open or closed.

(b) In manned machinery spaces main and auxiliary sea inlets and discharges in connection with the operation of machinery may be controlled locally. The controls shall be readily accessible and shall be provided with indicators showing whether the valves are open or closed.

(c) Scuppers and discharge pipes originating at any level and penetrating the shell either more than 17½ inches below the freeboard deck or less than 23½ inches above the summer load waterline shall be provided with a nonreturn valve at the shell. This valve, unless required by paragraph (a) of this section, may be omitted if the piping is of thickness as specified in part 56 in subchapter F (Marine Engineering) of this chapter.

(d) Scuppers leading from superstructures or deckhouses not fitted with doors complying with the requirements of § 42.15–10 shall be led overboard.

(e) All valves and shell fittings required by this section shall be of steel, bronze, or other approved ductile material. Valves of ordinary cast iron or similar material are not acceptable. All pipes to which this section refers shall be of steel or other equivalent material to the satisfaction of the assigning authority.

[CGFR 68–60, 33 FR 10062, July 12, 1968, as amended by CGFR 68–126, 34 FR 9014, June 5, 1969]

§ 42.15–65 Side scuttles.

(a) Side scuttles to spaces below the freeboard deck or to spaces within enclosed superstructures shall be fitted with efficient hinged inside deadlights arranged so that they can be effectively closed and secured watertight.

(b) No side scuttle shall be fitted in a position so that its sill is below a line drawn parallel to the freeboard deck at side and having its lowest point 2.5 percent of the breadth (B) above the load waterline, or 19½ inches, which ever is the greater distance.

§ 42.15-70

(c) The side scuttles, together with their glasses, if fitted, and deadlights, shall be of substantial and approved construction.

[CGFR 68-60, 33 FR 10062, July 12, 1968]

§ 42.15-70 Freeing ports.

(a) Where bulwarks on the weather portions of freeboard or superstructure decks form wells, ample provision shall be made for rapidly freeing the deck of water and for draining them. Except as provided in paragraphs (b) and (c) of this section, the minimum freeing port area (A) on each side of the vessel for each well on the freeboard deck shall be that given by the following formulae in cases where the sheer in way of the well is standard or greater than standard. The minimum area for each well on superstructure decks shall be one-half of the area given by the formulae.

(1) Where the length of bulwark (l) in the well is 66 feet or less $A = 7.6 + 0.115l$ (square feet)

(2) Where l exceeds 66 feet $A = 0.23l$ (square feet)

(3) l need in no case be taken as greater than $0.7L$.

(4) If the bulwark is more than 3.9 feet in average height the required area shall be increased by 0.04 square feet per foot of length of well for each foot difference in height. If the bulwark is less than 3 feet in average height, the required area may be decreased by 0.04 square feet per foot of length of well for each foot difference in height.

(b) In vessels with no sheer the area calculated according to paragraph (a) of this section shall be increased by 50 percent. Where the sheer is less than the standard the percentage shall be obtained by linear interpolation.

(c) Where a vessel is fitted with a trunk which does not comply with the requirements of § 42.20-55(a)(5) or where continuous or substantially continuous hatchway side coamings are fitted between detached superstructures the minimum area of the freeing port openings shall be calculated from table 42.15-70(c):

TABLE 42.15-70(c)

Breadth of hatchway or trunk in relation to the breadth of vessel	Area of freeing ports in relation to the total area of the bulwarks
40 percent or less	20 percent.
75 percent or more	10 percent.

NOTE: The area of freeing ports at intermediate breadths shall be obtained by linear interpolation.

(d) In vessels having superstructures which are open at either or both ends, adequate provision for freeing the space within such superstructures shall be provided to the satisfaction of the assigning authority.

(e) The lower edges of the freeing ports shall be as near the deck as practicable. Two-thirds of the freeing port area required shall be provided in the half of the well nearest the lowest point of the sheer curve.

(f) All such openings in the bulwarks shall be protected by rails or bars spaced approximately 9 inches apart. If shutters are fitted to freeing ports, ample clearance shall be provided to prevent jamming. Hinges shall have pins or bearings of noncorrodible material. If shutters are fitted with securing appliances, these appliances shall be of approved construction.

[CGFR 68-60, 33 FR 10062, July 12, 1968, as amended by CGFR 68-126, 34 FR 9014, June 5, 1969]

§ 42.15-75 Protection of the crew.

(a) The strength of the deckhouses used for the accommodation of the crew shall be to the satisfaction of the assigning authority.

(b) Efficient guard rails or bulwarks must be fitted on all exposed parts of the freeboard and superstructure decks as follows:

(1) The height of the bulwarks or guard rails must be at least 39½ inches from the deck, provided that where this height would interfere with the normal operation of the vessel, a lesser height may be approved if the Commandant and the assigning authority are satisfied that adequate protection is provided.

(2) On each vessel that is initially surveyed for load line assignment after January 1, 1976, and that is exclusively

engaged in towing operations, the minimum bulwark or rail height on the freeboard deck may be reduced to 30 inches provided the assigning authority is satisfied that adequate grabrails are provided around the periphery of the deckhouse.

(3) Portable rails may be used when operating conditions warrant their use.

(c) The opening below the lowest course of the guard rails shall not exceed 9 inches. The other courses shall be not more than 15 inches apart. In the case of vessels with rounded gunwales the guard rail supports shall be placed on the flat of the deck.

(d) Satisfactory means (in the form of guard rails, life lines, gangways or underdeck passages, etc.) shall be provided for the protection of the crew in getting to and from their quarters, the machinery space and all other parts used in the necessary work of the vessel.

(e) Deck cargo carried on any vessel shall be so stowed that any opening which is in way of the cargo and which gives access to and from the crew's quarters, the machinery space and all other parts used in the necessary work of the vessel, can be properly closed and secured against the admission of water. Effective protection for the crew in the form of guard rails or life lines shall be provided above the deck cargo if there is no convenient passage on or below the deck of the vessel.

[CGFR 68–60, 33 FR 10062, July 12, 1968, as amended by CGFR 68–126, 34 FR 9014, June 5, 1969; CGD 74–164, 41 FR 1470, Jan. 8, 1976]

§ 42.15–80 Special conditions of assignment for Type "A" vessels.

(a) *Machinery casings.* Machinery casings on Type "A" vessels as defined in § 42.09–5(b) must be protected by an enclosed poop or bridge of at least standard height, or by a deckhouse of equal height and equivalent strength, except that machinery casings may be exposed if there are no openings giving direct access from the freeboard deck to the machinery space. A door complying with the requirements of § 42.15–10 is permitted in the machinery casing if it leads to a space or passageway which is as strongly constructed as the casing and is separated from the stairway to the engine room by a second weathertight door of steel or equivalent material.

(b) *Gangway and access.* (1) An efficiently constructed fore and aft permanent gangway of sufficient strength shall be fitted on Type "A" vessels at the level of the superstructure deck between the poop and the midship bridge or deckhouse where fitted, or equivalent means of access shall be provided to carry out the purpose of the gangway, such as passages below deck. Elsewhere, and on Type "A" vessels without a midship bridge, arrangements to the satisfaction of the assigning authority shall be provided to safeguard the crew in reaching all parts used in the necessary work of the ship.

(2) Safe and satisfactory access from the gangway level shall be available between separates crew accommodations and also between crew accommodations and the machinery space.

(c) *Hatchways.* Exposed hatchways on the freeboard and forecastle decks or on the tops of expansion trunks on Type "A" vessels shall be provided with efficient watertight covers of steel or other equivalent material.

(d) *Freeing arrangements.* (1) Type "A" vessels with bulwarks shall have open rails fitted for at least half the length of the exposed parts of the weather deck or other effective freeing arrangements. The upper edge of the sheer strake shall be kept as low as practicable.

(2) Where superstructures are connected by trunks, open rails shall be fitted for the whole length of the exposed parts of the freeboard deck.

[CGFR 68–60, 33 FR 10063, July 12, 1968, as amended by CGFR 68–126, 34 FR 9014, June 5, 1969; CGD 79–153, 48 FR 38647, Aug. 25, 1983]

Subpart 42.20—Freeboards

§ 42.20–3 Freeboard assignment: Type "A" vessels.

(a) A Type "A" vessel is assigned a freeboard not less than that based on table 42.20–15(a)(1) provided that the vessel meets the flooding standard in § 42.20–6.

(b) A vessel that meets the requirements of subpart D, F, or G of part 172 of this chapter is considered by the Coast Guard as meeting the flooding

§ 42.20-5

standard referenced in paragraph (a) of this section.

[CGD 79-153, 48 FR 38647, Aug. 25, 1983 as amended by CGD 79-023, 49 FR 26593, June 28, 1984]

§ 42.20-5 Freeboard assignment: Type "B" vessels.

(a) Each Type "B" vessel is assigned a freeboard from table 42.20-15(b)(1) that is increased or decreased by the provisions of this section.

(b) Each Type "B" vessel that has a hatchway in position 1, must have the freeboard assigned in accordance with paragraph (a) of this section increased by the amount given in table 42.20-5(b) unless the hatch cover complies with:
  (1) Section 42.15-25(d); or
  (2) Section 42.15-30.

TABLE 42.20-5(b)—FREEBOARD INCREASE OVER TABULAR FREEBOARD FOR TYPE "B" VESSELS WITH HATCH COVERS NOT COMPLYING WITH § 42.15-25(d) OR § 42.15-30.

[Metric]

Length of ship (meters)	Freeboard increase [1] (millimeters)
[2]108	50
109	52
110	55
111	57
112	59
113	62
114	64
115	68
116	70
117	73
118	76
119	80
120	84
121	87
122	91
123	95
124	99
125	103
126	108
127	112
128	116
129	121
130	126
131	131
132	136
133	142
134	147
135	153
136	159
137	164
138	170
139	175
140	181
141	186
142	191
143	196
144	201
145	206
146	210

TABLE 42.20-5(b)—FREEBOARD INCREASE OVER TABULAR FREEBOARD FOR TYPE "B" VESSELS WITH HATCH COVERS NOT COMPLYING WITH § 42.15-25(d) OR § 42.15-30.—Continued

[Metric]

Length of ship (meters)	Freeboard increase [1] (millimeters)
147	215
148	219
149	224
150	228
151	232
152	236
153	240
154	244
155	247
156	251
157	254
158	258
159	261
160	264
161	267
162	270
163	273
164	275
165	278
166	280
167	283
168	285
169	287
170	290
171	292
172	294
173	297
174	299
175	301
176	304
177	306
178	308
179	311
180	313
181	315
182	318
183	320
184	322
185	325
186	327
187	329
188	332
189	334
190	336
191	339
192	341
193	343
194	346
195	348
196	350
197	353
198	355
199	357
[3]200	358

[1] Freeboards at intermediate lengths of ship shall be obtained by linear interpolation.
[2] 108 and below.
[3] Ships above 200 meters in length are subject to individual determination by the Commandant.

[English]

Length of ship (feet)	Freeboard increase [1] (inches)
[2]350	2.0
360	2.3

[English]

Length of ship (feet)	Freeboard increase [1] (inches)
370	2.6
380	2.9
390	3.3
400	3.7
410	4.2
420	4.7
430	5.2
440	5.8
450	6.4
460	7.0
470	7.6
480	8.2
490	8.7
500	9.2
510	9.6
520	10.0
530	10.4
540	10.7
550	11.0
560	11.4
570	11.8
580	12.1
590	12.5
600	12.8
610	13.1
620	13.4
630	13.6
640	13.9
650	14.1
[3]660	14.3

[1] Freeboards at intermediate lengths of ship be obtained by linear interpolation.
[2] 350 and below.
[3] Ships above 660 feet in length are subject to individual determination by the Commandant.

(c) Any Type "B" vessel that is greater than 100 meters (328 feet) in length and any hopper dredge meeting the requirements in subpart C of part 44 of this chapter may have a reduced freeboard from that assigned under table 42.20-15(b)(1) in accordance with paragraph (d) or paragraph (e) of this section if—

(1) The measures provided for the protection of the crew are adequate;
(2) The freeing arrangements are adequate; and
(3) The hatchway covers in positions 1 and 2 comply with the provisions of § 42.15-30 and have adequate strength, special care being given to their sealing and securing arrangements.

(d) The freeboards for a Type "B" vessel which comply with paragraph (c) of this section may be reduced up to 60 percent of the total difference between the freeboards in table 42.20-15(b)(1) and table 42.20-15(a)(1) provided that the vessel meets the flooding standard in § 42.20-7.

(e) The freeboards for a Type "B" vessel which complies with paragraph (c) of this section may be reduced up to the total difference between the freeboard tables referenced in paragraph (d) of this section provided that the vessel meets the flooding standard in § 42.20-8 and the provisions of § 42.15-80 (a), (b) and (d) as if it were a Type "A" vessel.

[CGD 79–153, 48 FR 38647, Aug. 25, 1983, as amended by CGD 76–080, 54 FR 36976, Sept. 6, 1989]

§ 42.20–6 Flooding standard: Type "A" vessels.

(a) Design calculations must be submitted that demonstrate that the vessel will remain afloat in the conditions of equilibrium specified in § 42.20–12 assuming the damage specified in § 42.20–11 as applied to the following flooding standards:

(1) If the vessel is over 150 meters (492 feet) in length it must be able to withstand the flooding of any one compartment, except the machinery space.
(2) If the vessel is over 225 meters (738 feet) in length, it must be able to withstand the flooding of any one compartment, treating the machinery space as a floodable compartment.

(b) When doing the calculations required in paragraph (a) of this section, the following permeabilities must be assumed:

(1) 0.95 in all locations except the machinery space.
(2) 0.85 in the machinery space.

[CGD 79–153, 48 FR 38648, Aug. 25, 1983]

§ 42.20–7 Flooding standard: Type "B" vessel, 60 percent reduction.

(a) Design calculations must be submitted that demonstrate that the vessel will remain afloat in the conditions of equilibrium specified in § 42.20–12 assuming the damage specified in § 42.20–11 as applied to the following flooding standards:

(1) If the vessel is 225 meters (738 feet) or less in length, it must be able to withstand the flooding of any one compartment, except the machinery space.
(2) If the vessel is over 225 meters (738 feet) in length, it must be able to withstand the flooding of any one compartment, treating the machinery space as a floodable compartment.

(b) When doing the calculations required in paragraph (a) of this section,

§ 42.20-8

the following permeabilities must be assumed:

(1) 0.95 in all locations except the machinery space.

(2) 0.85 in the machinery space.

[CGD 79-153, 48 FR 38648, Aug. 25, 1983]

§ 42.20-8 Flooding standard: Type "B" vessel, 100 percent reduction.

(a) Design calculations must be submitted that demonstrate that the vessel will remain afloat in the conditions of equilibrium specified in § 42.20-12 assuming the damage specified in § 42.20-11 as applied to the following flooding standards:

(1) If the vessel is 225 meters (738 feet) or less in length, it must be able to withstand the flooding of any two adjacent fore and after compartments excluding the machinery space;

(2) If the vessel is over 225 meters (738 feet) in length, the flooding standard of paragraph (a)(1) of this section must be applied, treating the machinery space, taken alone, as a floodable compartment.

(b) When doing the calculations required in paragraph (a) of this section, the following permeabilities must be assumed:

(1) 0.95 in all locations except the machinery space.

(2) 0.85 in the machinery space.

[CGD 79-153, 48 FR 38648, Aug. 25, 1983]

§ 42.20-9 Initial conditions of loading.

When doing the calculations required in §§ 42.20-6(a), 42.20-7(a) and 42.20-8(a), the initial condition of loading before flooding must be assumed to be as specified in this section:

(a) The vessel is assumed to be loaded to its summer load waterline with no trim.

(b) When calculating the vertical center of gravity, the following assumptions apply:

(1) The cargo is assumed to be homogeneous.

(2) Except as specified in paragraph (b)(3) of this section, all cargo compartments are assumed to be fully loaded. This includes compartments intended to be only partially filled. In the case of liquid cargoes, fully loaded means 98 percent full.

(3) If the vessel is intended to operate at its summer load waterline with empty compartments, these empty compartments are assumed to be empty rather than fully loaded if the resulting height of the vertical center of gravity is not less than the height determined in accordance with paragraph (b)(2) of this section.

(4) Fifty percent of the total capacity of all tanks and spaces fitted to contain consumable liquids or stores must be assumed to be distributed to accomplish the following:

(i) Each tank and space fitted to contain consumable liquids or stores must be assumed either completely empty or completely filled.

(ii) The consumables must be distributed so as to produce the greatest possible height above the keel for the center of gravity.

(5) Weights are calculated using the following values for specific gravities:

Salt water—1.025
Fresh water—1.000
Oil fuel—0.950
Diesel oil—0.900
Lube oil—0.900

[CGD 79-153, 48 FR 38648, Aug. 25, 1983]

§ 42.20-10 Free surface.

When doing the calculations required in §§ 42.20-6(a), 42.20-7(a) and 42.20-8(a), the effect of free surface of the following liquids must be included:

(a) For each type of consumable liquid, the maximum free surface of at least one transverse pair of tanks or a single centerline tank must be included. The tank or combination of tanks must be that resulting in the greatest free surface effect.

(b) For cargo liquids, unless the compartment is assumed to be empty as required by § 42.20-9(b)(3), the free surface of those compartments containing liquids is calculated at an angle of heel of not more than 5 degrees.

[CGD 79-153, 48 FR 38649, Aug. 25, 1983]

§ 42.20-11 Extent of damage.

When doing the calculations required by §§ 42.20-6(a), 42.20-7(a) and 42.20-8(a), the following must be assumed:

(a) The vertical extent of damage in all cases must be assumed to be from the baseline upward without limit.

(b) The transverse extent of damage is assumed to be equal to B/5 or 11.5 meters (37.7 feet), whichever is less. The transverse extent is measured inboard from the side of the ship perpendicularly to the center line at the level of the summer load waterline.

(c) If damage of a lesser extent than that specified in paragraph (a) or (b) of this section results in a more severe condition, the lesser extent must be assumed.

(d) The following assumptions apply to the transverse damage specified in paragraph (b) of this section for a stepped or recessed bulkhead:

(1) A transverse watertight bulkhead that has a step or recess located within the transverse extent of assumed damage may be considered intact if the step or recess is not more than 3.05 meters (10 feet) in length.

(2) If a transverse watertight bulkhead has a step or recess of more than 3.05 meters (10 feet) in length, within the transverse extent of assumed damage, the two compartments adjacent to this bulkhead must be considered as flooded.

(3) If within the transverse extent of damage, a transverse bulkhead has a step or recess more than 3.05 meters (10 feet) in length that coincides with the double bottom tank top or the inner boundary of a wing tank, respectively, all adjacent compartments within the transverse extent of assumed damage must be considered to be flooded simultaneously.

(e) If a wing tank has openings into adjacent compartments, the wing tank and adjacent compartments must be considered as one compartment. This provision applies even where these openings are fitted with closing appliances except:

(1) Valves fitted in bulkheads between tanks which are controlled from above the bulkhead deck.

(2) Secured manhole covers fitted with closely spaced bolts.

(f) Only transverse watertight bulkheads that are spaced apart at least $\frac{1}{3}(L)^{2/3}$ or 14.5 meters ($0.495(L)^{2/3}$ or 47.6 feet), whichever is less, may be considered effective. If transverse bulkheads are closer together, then one or more of these bulkheads must be assumed to be non-existent in order to achieve the minimum spacing between bulkheads.

[CGD 79–153, 48 FR 38649, Aug. 25, 1983]

§ 42.20–12 Conditions of equilibrium.

The following conditions of equilibrium are regarded as satisfactory:

(a) *Downflooding.* The final waterline after flooding, taking into account sinkage, heel, and trim, is below the lower edge of any opening through which progressive flooding can take place. Such openings include air pipes, ventilators, and openings which are closed by means of weathertight doors (even if they comply with § 42.15–10) or covers (even if they comply with § 42.15–30 or § 42.15–45(d)) but may exclude those openings closed by means of:

(1) Manhole covers and flush scuttles which comply with § 42.15–40;

(2) Cargo hatch covers which comply with § 42.09–5(b);

(3) Hinged watertight doors in an approved position which are secured closed while at sea and so logged; and

(4) Remotely operated sliding watertight doors, and side scuttles of the non-opening type which comply with § 42.15–65.

(b) *Progressive flooding.* If pipes, ducts, or tunnels are situated within the assumed extent of damage penetration as defined in § 42.20–11 (a) and (b), progressive flooding cannot extend to compartments other than those assumed to be floodable in the calculation for each case of damage.

(c) *Final angle of heel.* The angle of heel due to unsymmetrical flooding does not exceed 15 degrees. If no part of the deck is immersed, an angle of heel of up to 17 degrees may be accepted.

(d) *Metacentric height.* The metacentric height of the damaged vessel, in the upright condition, is positive.

(e) *Residual stability.* Through an angle of 20 degrees beyond its position of equilibrium, the vessel must meet the following conditions:

(1) The righting arm must be positive.

(2) The maximum righting arm must be at least 0.1 meter (4 inches).

(3) The area under the righting arm curve within the 20 degree range must

§ 42.20–13

not be less than 0.0175 meter-radians (0.689 inch-radians).

(4) Each submerged opening must be weathertight (e.g. a vent fitted with a ball check valve).

(f) *Intermediate stages of flooding.* The Commandant is satisfied that the stability is sufficient during intermediate stages of flooding.

[CGD 79–153, 48 FR 38649, Aug. 25, 1983]

§ 42.20–13 Vessels without means of propulsion.

(a) A lighter, barge, or other vessel without independent means of propulsion is assigned a freeboard in accordance with the provisions of this subpart as modified by paragraphs (b), (c), and (d) of this section.

(b) A barge that meets the requirements of § 42.09–5(b) may be assigned Type "A" freeboard if the barge does not carry deck cargo.

(c) An unmanned barge is not required to comply with § 42.15–75, § 42.15–80(b), or § 42.20–70.

(d) An unmanned barge that has only small access openings closed by watertight gasketed covers of steel or equivalent material on the freeboard deck, may be assigned a freeboard 25 percent less than that calculated in accordance with this subpart.

[CGD 79–153, 48 FR 38649, Aug. 25, 1983]

§ 42.20–15 Freeboard tables.

(a) *Type "A" vessel.* (1) The tabular freeboard for Type "A" vessel shall be determined from table 42.20–15(a)(1):

TABLE 42.20–15(a)(1)—FREEBOARD TABLE FOR TYPE "A" VESSELS

Length of vessel (feet)	Freeboard [1] (inches)
80	8.0
90	8.9
100	9.8
110	10.8
120	11.9
130	13.0
140	14.2
150	15.5
160	16.9
170	18.3
180	19.8
190	21.3
200	22.9
210	24.5
220	26.2
230	27.8
240	29.5
250	31.1

TABLE 42.20–15(a)(1)—FREEBOARD TABLE FOR TYPE "A" VESSELS—Continued

Length of vessel (feet)	Freeboard [1] (inches)
260	32.8
270	34.6
280	36.3
290	38.0
300	39.7
310	41.4
320	43.2
330	45.0
340	46.9
350	48.8
360	50.7
370	52.7
380	54.7
390	56.8
400	58.8
410	60.9
420	62.9
430	65.0
440	67.0
450	69.1
460	71.1
470	73.1
480	75.1
490	77.1
500	79.0
510	80.9
520	82.7
530	84.5
540	86.3
550	88.0
560	89.6
570	91.1
580	92.6
590	94.1
600	95.5
610	96.9
620	98.3
630	99.6
640	100.9
650	102.1
660	103.3
670	104.4
680	105.5
690	106.6
700	107.7
710	108.7
720	109.7
730	110.7
740	111.7
750	112.6
760	113.5
770	114.4
780	115.3
790	116.1
800	117.0
810	117.8
820	118.6
830	119.3
840	120.1
850	120.7
860	121.4
870	122.1
880	122.7
890	123.4
900	124.0
910	124.6
920	125.2
930	125.7
940	126.2
950	126.7

Coast Guard, DHS § 42.20-15

TABLE 42.20-15(a)(1)—FREEBOARD TABLE FOR TYPE "A" VESSELS—Continued

Length of vessel (feet)	Freeboard [1] (inches)
960	127.2
970	127.7
980	128.1
990	128.6
1,000	129.0
1,010	129.4
1,020	129.9
1,030	130.3
1,040	130.7
1,050	131.0
1,060	131.4
1,070	131.7
1,080	132.0
1,090	132.3
1,100	132.6
1,110	132.9
1,120	133.2
1,130	133.5
1,140	133.8
1,150	134.0
1,160	134.3
1,170	134.5
1,180	134.7
1,190	135.0
1,200	135.2
1,200 [2]	

[1] Freeboards at intermediate lengths of vessels shall be obtained by linear interpolation.
[2] Vessels above 1,200 feet in length shall be dealt with by the Commandant.

(b) *Type "B" vessels.* (1) The tabular freeboard for Type "B" vessels shall be determined from table 42.20-15(b)(1):

TABLE 42.20-15(b)(1)—FREEBOARD TABLE FOR TYPE "B" VESSELS

Length of vessel (feet)	Freeboard [1] (inches)
80	8.0
90	8.9
100	9.8
110	10.8
120	11.9
130	13.0
140	14.2
150	15.5
160	16.9
170	18.3
180	19.8
190	21.3
200	22.9
210	24.7
220	26.6
230	28.5
240	30.4
250	32.4
260	34.4
270	36.5
280	38.7
290	41.0
300	43.3
310	45.7
320	48.2
330	50.7
340	53.2
350	55.7

TABLE 42.20-15(b)(1)—FREEBOARD TABLE FOR TYPE "B" VESSELS—Continued

Length of vessel (feet)	Freeboard [1] (inches)
360	58.2
370	60.7
380	63.2
390	65.7
400	68.2
410	70.7
420	73.2
430	75.7
440	78.2
450	80.7
460	83.1
470	85.6
480	88.1
490	90.6
500	93.1
510	95.6
520	98.1
530	100.6
540	103.0
550	105.4
560	107.7
570	110.0
580	112.3
590	114.6
600	116.8
610	119.0
620	121.1
630	123.2
640	125.3
650	127.3
660	129.3
670	131.3
680	133.3
690	135.3
700	137.1
710	139.0
720	140.9
730	142.7
740	144.5
750	146.3
760	148.1
770	149.8
780	151.5
790	153.2
800	154.8
810	156.4
820	158.0
830	159.6
840	161.2
850	162.8
860	164.3
870	165.9
880	167.4
890	168.9
900	170.4
910	171.8
920	173.3
930	174.7
940	176.1
950	177.5
960	178.9
970	180.3
980	181.7
990	183.1
1,000	184.4
1,010	185.8
1,020	187.2
1,030	188.5
1,040	189.8
1,050	191.0

§ 42.20-20

TABLE 42.20–15(b)(1)—FREEBOARD TABLE FOR TYPE "B" VESSELS—Continued

Length of vessel (feet)	Freeboard [1] (inches)
1,060	192.3
1,070	193.5
1,080	194.8
1,090	196.1
1,100	197.3
1,110	198.6
1,120	199.9
1,130	201.2
1,140	202.3
1,150	203.5
1,160	204.6
1,170	205.8
1,180	206.9
1,190	208.1
1,200	209.3
1,200 [2]	

[1] Freeboards at intermediate lengths of vessel shall be obtained by linear interpolation.
[2] Vessels above 1,200 feet in length shall be dealt with by the Commandant.

[CGFR 68–60, 33 FR 10064, July 12, 1968, as amended by CGFR 68–126, 34 FR 9015, June 5, 1969]

§ 42.20–20 Correction to the freeboard for vessels under 328 feet in length.

(a) The tabular freeboard for a Type "B" vessel of between 79 feet and 328 feet in length having enclosed superstructures with an effective length of up to 35 percent of the length of the vessel shall be increased by:

$0.09 (328 - L) [0.35 - (E/L)]$ inches

where:

L=length of vessel in feet.
E=effective length of superstructure in feet as defined in § 42.20-50.

[CGFR 68–60, 33 FR 10064, July 12, 1968]

§ 42.20–25 Correction for block coefficient.

If the block coefficient (C_b) exceeds 0.68, the tabular freeboard specified in § 42.20–5 (b) and (d), and 42.20–20(a) must be multiplied by the factor (C_b+0.68)/1.36.

[CGD 79–153, 48 FR 38650, Aug. 25, 1983]

§ 42.20–30 Correction for depth.

(a) Where D exceeds $L^1/_{15}$ the freeboard shall be increased by $[D - (L/15)]$ R inches, where R is $L/131.2$ at lengths less than 393.6 feet and 3 at 393.6 feet length and above.

(b) Where D is less than $L/15$ no reduction shall be made except in a vessel with an enclosed superstructure covering at least $0.6L$ amidships, with a complete trunk, or combination of detached enclosed superstructures and trunks which extend all fore and aft, where the freeboard shall be reduced at the rate prescribed in paragraph (a) of this section.

(c) Where the height of superstructure or trunk is less than the standard height, the reduction shall be in the ratio of the actual to the standard height as defined in § 42.20-40.

[CGFR 68–60, 33 FR 10064, July 12, 1968]

§ 42.20–35 Correction for position of deck line.

(a) Where the actual depth to the upper edge of the deck line is greater or less than D, the difference between the depths shall be added to or deducted from the freeboard.

[CGFR 68–60, 33 FR 10065, July 12, 1968]

§ 42.20–40 Standard height of superstructure.

(a) The standard height of a superstructure shall be as given in table 42.20–40(a):

TABLE 42.20–40(a) STANDARD HEIGHTS (IN FEET) [1]

Length (L) (in feet)	Raised quarter deck	All other super structures
98.5 or less	3.0	5.9
246	3.9	5.9
410 or more	5.9	7.5

[1] The standard heights at intermediate lengths of the vessel shall be obtained by linear interpolation.

[CGFR 68–60, 33 FR 10065, July 12, 1968, as amended by CGFR 68–126, 34 FR 9015, June 5, 1969]

§ 42.20–45 Length of superstructure.

(a) Except as provided in paragraph (b) of this section, the length of a superstructure (S) shall be the mean length of the parts of the superstructure which lie within the length (L).

(b) Where the end bulkhead of an enclosed superstructure extends in a fair convex curve beyond its intersection with the superstructure sides, the length of the superstructure may be increased on the basis of an equivalent plane bulkhead. This increase shall be two-thirds of the fore and aft extent of curvature. The maximum curvature which may be taken into account in determining this increase is one-half the breadth of the superstructure at the point of intersection of the curved end of the superstructure with its side.

[CGFR 68–60, 33 FR 10065, July 12, 1968, as amended by CGFR 68–126, 34 FR 9015, June 5, 1969]

§ 42.20–50 Effective length of superstructure.

(a) Except as provided for in paragraph (b) of this section the effective length (E) of an enclosed superstructure of standard height shall be its length.

(b) In all cases where an enclosed superstructure of standard height is set in from the sides of the vessel as permitted in § 42.13–15(j), the effective length shall be the length modified by the ratio of b/Bs,

where:

"b" is the breadth of the superstructure at the middle of its length;
"Bs" is the breadth of the vessel at the middle of the length of the superstructure.

(1) Where a superstructure is set in for a part of its length, this modification shall be applied only to the set in part.

(c) Where the height of an enclosed superstructure is less than the standard height, the effective length shall be its length reduced in the ratio of the actual height to the standard height. Where the height exceeds the standard, no increase shall be made to the effective length of the superstructure.

(d) The effective length of a raised quarter deck if fitted with an intact front bulkhead, shall be its length up to a maximum of 0.6L. Where the bulkhead is not intact, the raised quarter deck shall be treated as a poop of less than standard height.

(e) Superstructures which are not enclosed shall have no effective length.

[CGFR 68–60, 33 FR 10065, July 12, 1968]

§ 42.20–55 Trunks.

(a) A trunk or similar structure which does not extend to the sides of the vessel shall be regarded as efficient on the following conditions:

(1) The trunk is at least as strong as a superstructure;

(2) The hatchways are in the trunk deck, and the hatchway coamings and covers comply with the requirements of §§ 42.15–15 to 42.15–30, inclusive, and the width of the trunk deck stringer provides a satisfactory gangway and sufficient lateral stiffness; however, small access openings with watertight covers may be permitted in the freeboard deck;

(3) A permanent working platform fore and aft fitted with guard rails is provided by the trunk deck, or by detached trunks connected to superstructures by efficient permanent gangways;

(4) Ventilators are protected by the trunk by watertight covers or by other equivalent means;

(5) Open rails are fitted on the weather parts of the freeboard deck in way of the trunk for at least half their length;

(6) The machinery casings are protected by the trunk, by a superstructure of at least standard height, or by a deckhouse of the same height and of equivalent strength;

(7) The breadth of the trunk is at least 60 percent of the breadth of the vessel; and,

(8) Where there is no superstructure, the length of the trunk is at least 0.6L.

(b) The full length of an efficient trunk reduced in the ratio of its mean breadth to B shall be its effective length.

(c) The standard height of a trunk is the standard height of a superstructure other than a raised quarter deck.

(d) Where the height of a trunk is less than the standard height, its effective length shall be reduced in the ratio of the actual to the standard height. Where the height of hatchway coamings on the trunk deck is less than that required under § 42.15–25(a), a reduction from the actual height of trunk shall be made which corresponds to the difference between the actual and required height of coaming.

[CGFR 68–60, 33 FR 10065, July 12, 1968, as amended by CGFR 68–126, 34 FR 9015, June 5, 1969]

§ 42.20-60 Deduction for superstructures and trunks.

(a) Where the effective length of superstructures and trunks is 1.0L, the deduction from the freeboard shall be 14 inches at 79 feet length of vessel, 34 inches at 279 feet length, and 42 inches at 400 feet length and above; deductions at intermediate lengths shall be obtained by linear interpolation.

(b) Where the total effective length of superstructures and trunks is less than 1.0L the deduction shall be a percentage obtained from table 42.20-60(b)(1) or table 42.20-60(b)(2):

TABLE 42.20-60(b)(1)—PERCENTAGE OF DEDUCTION FOR TYPE "A" VESSELS

	Total effective length of superstructures and trunks										
	0	0.1L	0.2L	0.3L	0.4L	0.5L	0.6L	0.7L	0.8L	0.9L	1.0L
Percentage of deduction for all types of superstructures [1]	0	7	14	21	31	41	52	63	75.3	87.7	100

[1] Percentages at intermediate lengths of superstructures and trunks shall be obtained by linear interpolation.

TABLE 42.20-60(b)(2)—PERCENTAGE OF DEDUCTION FOR TYPE "B" VESSELS
[Percentage of deduction [1]]

		Total effective length of superstructures and trunks										
	Line	0	0.1L	0.2L	0.3L	0.4L	0.5L	0.6L	0.7L	0.8L	0.9L	1.0L
Vessels with forecastle and without detached bridge	I	0	5	10	15	23.5	32	46	63	75.3	87.7	100
Vessels with forecasle and detached bridge	II	0	6.3	12.7	19	27.5	36	46	63	75.3	87.7	100

[1] Percentages at intermediate lengths of superstructures and trunks shall be obtained by linear interpolation.

(c) For vessels of Type "B":

(1) Where the effective length of a bridge is less than 0.2L, the percentages shall be obtained by linear interpolation between lines I and II;

(2) Where the effective length of a forecastle is more than 0.4L, the percentages shall be obtained from line II; and,

(3) Where the effective length of a forecastle is less than 0.07L, the percentages in table 42.20-60(b)(2) of this paragraph shall be reduced by:

$$5(0.07L - f)/0.07L$$

L is the length of vessel as defined in § 42.13-15(a),
f is the effective length of the forecastle.

[CGFR 68-60, 33 FR 10065, July 12, 1968, as amended by CGFR 68-126, 34 FR 9015, June 5, 1969]

§ 42.20-65 Sheer.

(a) *General.* (1) The sheer shall be measured from the deck at side to a line of reference drawn parallel to the keel through the sheer line amidships.

(2) In vessels designed with a rake of keel, the sheer shall be measured in relation to a reference line drawn parallel to the design load waterline.

(3) In flush deck vessels and in vessels with detached superstructures the sheer shall be measured at the freeboard deck.

(4) In vessels with topsides of unusual form in which there is a step or break in the topsides, the sheer shall be considered in relation to the equivalent depth amidships.

(5) In vessels with a superstructure of standard height which extends over the whole length of the freeboard deck, the sheer shall be measured at the superstructure deck. Where the height exceeds the standard the least difference (Z) between the actual and standard heights shall be added to each end ordinate. Similarly, the intermediate ordinates at distances of $\frac{1}{6}L$ and $\frac{1}{3}L$ from each perpendicular shall be increased by 0.444Z and 0.111Z respectively.

(6) Where the deck of an enclosed superstructure has at least the same sheer as the exposed freeboard deck, the sheer of the enclosed portion of the freeboard deck shall not be taken into account.

(7) Where an enclosed poop or forecastle is of standard height with greater sheer than that of the freeboard deck, or is of more than standard height, an addition to the sheer of the freeboard deck shall be made as provided in paragraph (c)(4) of this section.

(b) *Standard sheer profile.* (1) The ordinates of the standard sheer profile are given in table 42.20–65(b)(1):

TABLE 42.20–65(b)(1)—STANDARD SHEER PROFILE

[Where L is in feet]

	Station	Ordinate (in inches)	Ordinate (in inches)	Factor
After half	After Perpendicular.	0.1	L+10	1
	⅙ L from A.P	0.0444 ...	L+4.44 ...	3
	⅓ L from A.P	0.0111 ...	L+1.11 ...	3
	Amidships		0	1
Forward half.	Amidships		0	1
	⅓ L from F.P	0.0222 ...	L+2.22 ...	3
	⅙ L from F.P	0.0888 ...	L+8.88 ...	3
	Forward Perpendicular.	0.2	L+20	1

(c) *Measurement of variation from standard sheer profile.* (1) Where the sheer profile differs from the standard, the four ordinates of each profile in the forward or after half shall be multiplied by the appropriate factors given in the table of ordinates. The difference between the sums of the respective products and those of the standard divided by 8 measures the deficiency or excess of sheer in the forward or after half. The arithmetical mean of the excess or deficiency in the forward and after halves measures the excess or deficiency of sheer.

(2) Where the after half of the sheer has an excess and the forward half of the sheer has a deficiency, no credit shall be allowed for the part in excess and deficiency only shall be measured.

(3) Where the forward half of the sheer profile exceeds the standard, and the after portion of the sheer profile is not less than 75 percent of the standard, credit shall be allowed for the part in excess; where the after part is less than 50 percent of the standard, no credit shall be given for the excess sheer forward. Where the after sheer is between 50 percent and 75 percent of the standard, intermediate allowances may be granted for excess sheer forward.

(4) Where sheer credit is given for a poop or forecastle, the following formula shall be used:

$s = (y/3)(L'/L)$

where:

s = sheer credit, to be deducted from the deficiency or added to the excess of sheer.

y = difference between actual and standard height of superstructure at the end ordinate.

L' = mean enclosed length of poop or forecastle up to a maximum length of $0.5L$.

L = length of vessel as defined in §42.13–15(a).

(i) The formula in this paragraph (c)(4) of this section provides a curve in the form of a parabola tangent to the actual sheer curve at the freeboard deck and intersecting the end ordinate at a point below the superstructure deck a distance equal to the standard height of a superstructure. The superstructure deck shall not be less than standard height above this curve at any point. This curve shall be used in determining the sheer profile for forward and after halves of the vessel.

(d) *Correction for variations from standard sheer profile.* (1) The correction for sheer shall be the deficiency or excess of sheer (see paragraphs (c) (1) to (4) inclusive of this section) multiplied by:

$0.75 - (S/2L)$

where:

S is the total length of enclosed superstructures.

(e) *Addition for deficiency in sheer.* (1) Where the sheer is less than the standard, the correction for deficiency in sheer (see paragraph (d)(1) of this section) shall be added to the freeboard.

(f) *Deduction for excess sheer.* (1) In vessels where an enclosed superstructure covers $0.1L$ before and $0.1L$ abaft amidships, the correction for excess of sheer as calculated under the provisions of paragraph (d)(1) of this section shall be deducted from the freeboard; in vessels where no enclosed superstructure covers amidships, no deduction shall be made from the freeboard; where an enclosed superstructure covers less than $0.1L$ before and $0.1L$ abaft amidships, the deduction

§ 42.20-70 Minimum bow height.

shall be obtained by linear interpolation. The maximum deduction for excess sheer shall be at the rate of 1½ inches per 100 feet of length.

[CGFR 68-60, 33 FR 10066, July 12, 1968, as amended by CGFR 68-126, 34 FR 9016, June 5, 1969]

§ 42.20-70 Minimum bow height.

(a) The bow height defined as the vertical distance at the forward perpendicular between the waterline corresponding to the assigned summer freeboard and the designed trim and the top of the exposed deck at side shall be not less than:

(1) For vessels below 820 feet in length,

$0.672L[1-(L/1640)][1.36/(C_b+0.68)]$ inches;

where:

L is the length of the vessel in feet.
C_b is the block coefficient which is to be taken as not less than 0.68.

(2) For vessels of 820 feet and above in length,

$275.6[1.36/(C_b+0.68)]$ inches;

where:

C_b is the block coefficient which is to be taken as not less than 0.68.

(b) Where the bow height required in paragraph (a) of this section is obtained by sheer, the sheer shall extend for at least 15 percent of the length of the vessel measured from the forward perpendicular. Where it is obtained by fitting a superstructure, such superstructure shall extend from the stem to a point at least $0.07L$ abaft the forward perpendicular, and it shall comply with the following requirements:

(1) For vessels not over 328 feet in length it shall be enclosed as defined in §42.13-15(j); and,

(2) For vessels over 328 feet in length it need not comply with §42.13-15(j) but shall be fitted with closing appliances to the satisfaction of the assigning authority.

(c) Vessels which, to suit exceptional operational requirements, cannot meet the requirements of paragraphs (a) and (b) of this section may be given special consideration by the assigning authority.

[CGFR 68-60, 33 FR 10066, July 12, 1968, as amended by CGFR 68-126, 34 FR 9016, June 5, 1969]

§ 42.20-75 Minimum freeboards.

(a) *Summer freeboard.* (1) The minimum freeboard in summer must be the freeboard derived from the tables in §42.20-15 as modified by the corrections in §§42.20-3 and 42.20-5, as applicable, and §§42.20-20, 42.20-25, 42.20-30, 42.20-35, 42.20-60, 42.20-65 and, if applicable, §42.20-70.

(2) The freeboard in salt water, as calculated in accordance with paragraph (a)(1) of this section, but without the correction for deck line, as provided by §42.20-35, shall not be less than 2 inches. For vessels having in position 1 hatchways with covers which do not comply with the requirements of §§42.15-25(d)(1), 42.15-30, or 42.15-80, the freeboard shall be not less than 6 inches.

(b) *Tropical freeboard.* (1) The minimum tropical freeboard shall be the freeboard obtained by a deduction from the summer freeboard of one forty-eighth of the summer draft measured from the top of the keel to the center of the ring of the load line mark.

(2) The freeboard in salt water, as calculated in accordance with paragraph (b)(1) of this section, but without the correction for deck line, as provided by §42.20-35, shall not be less than 2 inches. For vessels having in position 1 hatchways with covers which do not comply with the requirements of §42.15-25(d)(1), §42.15-30, or §42.15-80, the freeboard shall be not less than 6 inches.

(c) *Winter freeboard.* (1) The minimum winter freeboard shall be the freeboard obtained by an addition to the summer freeboard of one forty-eighth of summer draft, measured from the top of the keel to the center of the ring of the load line mark.

(d) *Winter North Atlantic freeboard.* (1) The minimum freeboard for vessels of not more than 328 feet in length which enter any part of the North Atlantic defined in §42.30-35 during the winter seasonal period shall be the winter freeboard plus 2 inches. For other vessels the winter North Atlantic freeboard shall be the winter freeboard.

(e) *Fresh water freeboard.* (1) The minimum freeboard in fresh water of unit density shall be obtained by deducting from the minimum freeboard in salt water:

($\Delta/40\ T$) inches

where:

Δ=displacement in salt water in tons at the summer load waterline; and,
T=tons per inch immersion in salt water at the summer load waterline.

(2) Where the displacement at the summer load waterline cannot be certified, the deduction shall be one forty-eighth of summer draft, measured from the top of the keel to the center of the ring of the load line mark.

[CGFR 68–60, 33 FR 10066, July 12, 1968, as amended by CGFR 68–126, 34 FR 9016, June 5, 1969; CGD 79–153, 48 FR 38650, Aug. 25, 1983]

Subpart 42.25—Special Requirements for Vessels Assigned Timber Freeboards

§ 42.25-1 Application of this subpart.

(a) The provisions of this subpart 42.25 apply only to vessels to which timber load lines are assigned.

[CGFR 68–60, 33 FR 10067, July 12, 1968]

§ 42.25-5 Definitions of terms used in this subpart.

(a) *Timber deck cargo.* The term "timber deck cargo" means a cargo of timber carried on an uncovered part of a freeboard or superstructure deck. The term does not include wood pulp or similar cargo.

(b) *Timber load line.* A timber deck cargo may be regarded as giving a vessel a certain additional buoyancy and a greater degree of protection against the sea. For that reason, vessels carrying a timber deck cargo may be granted a reduction of freeboard calculated according to the provisions of § 42.25-20 and marked on the vessel's side in accordance with the provisions of § 42.13-30(c) and (d). However, in order that such special freeboard may be granted and used, the timber deck cargo shall comply with certain conditions which are laid down in § 42.25-15, and the vessel itself shall also comply with certain conditions relating to its construction which are set out in § 42.25-10.

[CGFR 68–60, 33 FR 10067, July 12, 1968, as amended by CGFR 68–126, 34 FR 9016, June 5, 1969]

§ 42.25-10 Construction of vessel.

(a) *Superstructure.* (1) Vessels, shall have a forecastle of at least standard height and a length of at least $0.07L$. In addition, if the vessel is less than 328 feet in length, a poop of at least standard height, or a raised quarter deck with either a deckhouse or a strong steel hood of at least the same total height shall be fitted aft.

(b) *Double bottom tanks.* (1) Double bottom tanks where fitted within the midship half length of the vessel shall have adequate watertight longitudinal subdivision.

(c) *Bulwarks.* (1) The vessel shall be fitted either with permanent bulwarks at least 39½ inches in height, specially stiffened on the upper edge and supported by strong bulwark stays attached to the deck and provided with necessary freeing ports, or with efficient rails of the same height and of specially strong construction.

[CGFR 68–60, 33 FR 10067, July 12, 1968, as amended by CGFR 68–126, 34 FR 9016, June 5, 1969]

§ 42.25-15 Stowage.

(a) *General.* (1) Openings in the weather deck over which cargo is stowed shall be securely closed and battened down. The ventilators shall be efficiently protected.

(2) Timber deck cargo shall extend over at least the entire available length which is the total length of the well or wells between superstructures. Where there is no limiting superstructure at the after end, the timber shall extend at least to the after end of the aftermost hatchway. The timber shall be stowed as solidly as possible, to at least the standard height of a superstructure other than a raised quarter deck.

(3) On a vessel within a seasonal winter zone in winter, the height of the deck cargo above the weather deck shall not exceed one-third of the extreme breadth of the vessel.

(4) The timber deck cargo shall be compactly stowed, lashed, and secured. It shall not interfere in any way with the navigation and necessary work of the vessel.

(b) *Upright.* (1) Uprights, when required by the nature of the timber, shall be of adequate strength considering the breadth of the vessel; the spacing shall be suitable for the length and character of timber carried, but shall not exceed 9.8 feet. Strong angles or metal sockets or equally efficient means shall be provided for securing the uprights.

(c) *Lashings.* (1) Timber deck cargo shall be efficiently secured throughout its length by independent overall lashings spaced not more than 9.8 feet apart. Eye plates for these lashings shall be efficiently attached to the sheer strake or to the deck stringer plate at intervals of not more than 9.8 feet. The distance from an end bulkhead of a superstructure to the first eye plate shall be not more than 6.6 feet. Eye plates and lashings shall be provided 23½ inches and 4.9 feet from the ends of timber deck cargoes where there is no bulkhead.

(2) Lashings shall be not less than ¾-inch close link chain or flexible wire rope of equivalent strength, fitted with sliphooks and turnbuckles, which shall be accessible at all times. Wire rope lashings shall have a short length of long link chain to permit the length of lashings to be regulated.

(3) When timber is in lengths less than 11.8 feet the spacing of the lashings shall be reduced or other suitable provisions made to suit the length of timber.

(4) All fittings required for securing the lashings shall be of strength corresponding to the length of the lashings.

(d) *Stability.* (1) Provision shall be made for a safe margin of stability at all stages of the voyage, regard being given to additions of weight, such as those due to absorption of water and icing and to losses of weight such as those due to consumption of fuel and stores.

(e) *Protection of crew, access to machinery spaces, etc.* (1) In addition to the requirements of § 42.15–75(e) guardrails or life lines spaced not more than 13 inches apart vertically shall be provided on each side of the deck cargo to a height of at least 39½ inches above the cargo.

(f) *Steering arrangements.* (1) Steering arrangements shall be effectively protected from damage by cargo and, as far as practicable, shall be accessible. Efficient provision shall be made for steering in the event of a breakdown in the main steering arrangements.

[CGFR 68–60, 33 FR 10067, July 12, 1968, as amended by CGFR 68–126, 34 FR 9016, June 5, 1969]

§ 42.25–20 Computation for freeboard.

(a) The minimum summer freeboards must be computed in accordance with §§ 42.20–5 (a) and (b), 42.20–13, 42.20–15, 42.20–20, 42.20–25, 42.20–30, 42.20–35, 42.20–60, and 42.20–65, except that § 42.20–60 is modified by substituting the percentages in table 42.25–20(a) for those given in § 42.20–60:

TABLE 42.25–20(a)—PERCENTAGE OF DEDUCTION FOR SUPERSTRUCTURE
[Total Effective Length of Superstructure]

	0	0.1L	0.2L	0.3L	0.4L	0.5L	0.6L	0.7L	0.8L	0.9L	1.0L
Percentage of deduction for all types of superstructure [1]	20	31	42	53	64	70	76	82	88	94	100

[1] Percentages at intermediate lengths of superstructures shall be obtained by linear interpolation.

(b) The winter timber freeboard shall be obtained by adding to the summer timber freeboard one thirty-sixth of the molded summer timber draft.

(c) The winter North Atlantic timber freeboard shall be the same as the winter North Atlantic freeboard prescribed in § 42.20–75(d)(1).

(d) The tropical timber freeboard shall be obtained by deducting from the summer timber freeboard one forty-eighth of the molded summer timber draft.

Coast Guard, DHS §42.30-10

(e) The fresh water timber freeboard shall be computed in accordance with §42.20-75(e) (1) or (2) based on the summer timber load waterline.

[CGFR 68-60, 33 FR 10067, July 12, 1968, as amended by CGFR 68-126, 34 FR 9016, June 5, 1969; CGD 79-153, 48 FR 38650, Aug. 25, 1983]

Subpart 42.30—Zones, Areas, and Seasonal Periods

§42.30-1 Basis.

(a) The zones and areas in this subpart are, in general, based on the following criteria:

(1) Summer: not more than 10 percent winds of force 8 Beaufort (34 knots) or more.

(2) Tropical: not more than 1 percent winds of force 8 Beaufort (34 knots) or more. Not more than one tropical storm in 10 years in an area of 5° square in any 1 separate calendar month.

(b) In certain special areas, for practical reasons, some degree of relaxation has been found acceptable.

(c) A chart is attached to the International Convention on Load Lines, 1966, which illustrates the zones and areas defined in this Convention and in this subpart.

[CGFR 68-60, 33 FR 10068, July 12, 1968, as amended by CGFR 68-126, 34 FR 9016, June 5, 1969]

§42.30-5 Northern Winter Seasonal Zones and area.

(a) *North Atlantic Winter Seasonal Zones I and II.* (1) The North Atlantic Winter Seasonal Zone I lies within the meridian of longitude 50° W. from the coast of Greenland to latitude 45° N.; thence the parallel of latitude 45° N. to longitude 15° W.; thence the meridian of longitude 15° W. to latitude 60° N.; thence the parallel of latitude 60° N. to the Greenwich Meridian, thence this meridian northwards.

(i) Seasonal periods:

Winter: October 16 to April 15.
Summer: April 16 to October 15.

(2) The North Atlantic Winter Seasonal Zone II lies within the meridian of longitude 68°30′ W. from the coast of the United States to latitude 40° N.; thence the rhumb line to the point latitude 36° N., longitude 73° W.; thence the parallel of latitude 36° N. to longitude 25° W.; and thence the rhumb line to Cape Torinana. Excluded from this zone are the North Atlantic Winter Seasonal Zone I and the Baltic Sea bounded by the parallel of the latitude of The Skaw in the Skagerrak.

(i) Seasonal periods:

Winter: November 1 to March 31.
Summer: April 1 to October 31.

(b) *North Atlantic Winter Seasonal Area.* (1) The boundary of the North Atlantic Winter Seasonal Area is the meridian of longitude 68°30′ W. from the coast of the United States to latitude 40° N.; thence the rhumb line to the southernmost intersection of the meridian of longitude 61° W. with the coast of Canada; and thence the east coasts of Canada and the United States.

(i) Seasonal periods:

(*a*) For vessels over 328 feet in length:

Winter: December 16 to February 15.
Summer: February 16 to December 15.

(*b*) For vessels of 328 feet and under in length:

Winter: November 1 to March 31.
Summer: April 1 to October 31.

(c) *North Pacific Winter Seasonal Zone.* The southern boundary of the North Pacific Winter Seasonal Zone is the parallel of latitude 50° N. from the east coast of the Union of Soviet Socialist Republics, to the west coast of Sakhalin; thence the west coast of Sakhalin to the southern extremity of Cape Kril'on: thence the rhumb line to Wakkanai, Hokkaido, Japan; thence the east and south coasts of Hokkaido to longitude 145° E., thence the meridian of longitude 145° E. to latitude 35° N., thence the parallel of latitude 35° N. to longitude 150° W. and thence the rhumb line to the southern extremity of Dall Island, Alaska.

(1) Seasonal periods:

Winter: October 16 to April 15.
Summer: April 16 to October 15.

[CGFR 68-60, 33 FR 10068, July 12, 1968, as amended by CGFR 68-126, 34 FR 9016, June 5, 1969]

§42.30-10 Southern Winter Seasonal Zone.

(a) The northern boundary of the Southern Winter Seasonal Zone is the rhumb line from the east coast of the American continent at Cape Tres Puntas to the point latitude 34° S., longitude 50° W.; thence the parallel of latitude 34° S. to longitude 17° E.; thence the rhumb line to the point latitude 35°10′ S., longitude 20° E.; thence the rhumb line to the point latitude 34° S. longitude 28° E.; thence along the rhumb line to the point latitude 35°30′ S., longitude 118° E.; thence the rhumb line to Cape Grim on the northwest coast of Tasmania; thence along the north and east coasts of Tasmania to the southernmost point of Bruny Island; thence the rhumb line to Black Rock Point on Stewart Island; thence the rhumb line to the point latitude 47° S., longitude 170° E.; thence along the rhumb line to the point latitude 33° S., longitude 170° W.; and thence the parallel of latitude 33° S. to the west coast of the American continent.

(1) Valparaiso is to be considered as being on the boundary line of the Summer and the Winter Seasonal Zones.

(2) Seasonal periods:

Winter: April 16 to October 15.
Summer: October 16 to April 15.

[CGFR 68–60, 33 FR 10068, July 12, 1968]

§ 42.30–15 **Tropical Zone.**

(a) *Northern boundary of the Tropical Zone.* The northern boundary of the Tropical Zone is the parallel of latitude 13° N. from the east coast of the American continent to longitude 60° W.; thence the rhumb line to a point in latitude 10° N., longitude 58° W.; thence the parallel of latitude 10° N. to longitude 20° W.; thence the meridian of longitude 20° W. to latitude 30° N.; thence the parallel of latitude 30° N. to the west coast of Africa; from the east coast of Africa the parallel of latitude 8° N. to longitude 70° E.; thence the meridian of longitude 70° E. to latitude 13° N.; thence the parallel of latitude 13° N. to the west coast of India; thence around the south coast of India to latitude 10°30′ N. on the east coast of India; thence the rhumb line to a point in latitude 9° N., longitude 82° E.; thence the meridian of longitude 82° E. to latitude 8° N.; thence the parallel of latitude 8° N. to the west coast of Malaysia; thence the coast of Southeast Asia to the east coast of Vietnam at latitude 10° N.; thence the parallel of latitude 10° N. to longitude 145° E.; thence the meridian of longitude 145° E. to latitude 13° N.; and thence the parallel of latitude 13° N. to the west coast of the American continent.

(1) Saigon is to be considered as being on the boundary line of the Tropical Zone and the Seasonal Tropical Area.

(b) *Southern boundary of the Tropical Zone.* The southern boundary of the Tropical Zone is the rhumb line from the Port of Santos, Brazil, to the point where the meridian of longitude 40° W. intersects the Tropic of Capricorn; thence the Tropic of Capricorn to the west coast of Africa; from the east coast of Africa the parallel of latitude 20° S. to the west coast of Madagascar; thence the west and north coasts of Madagascar to longitude 50° E.; thence the meridian of longitude 50° E. to latitude 10° S.; thence the parallel of latitude 10° S. to longitude 98° E.; thence the rhumb line to Port Darwin, Australia; thence the coasts of Australia and Wessel Island eastwards to Cape Wessel; thence the parallel of latitude 11° S. to the west side of Cape York; from the east side of Cape York the parallel of latitude 11° S. to longitude 150° W.; thence the rhumb line to the point latitude 26° S., longitude 75° W.; and thence the rhumb line to the west coast of the American continent at latitude 30° S.

(1) Coquimbo and Santos are to be considered as being on the boundary line of the Tropical and Summer Zones.

(c) *Areas to be included in the Tropical Zone.* The following areas are to be treated as included in the Tropical Zone:

(1) The Suez Canal, the Red Sea, and the Gulf of Aden, from Port Said to the meridian of longitude 45° E.

(i) Aden and Berbera are to be considered as being on the boundary line of the Tropical Zone and the Seasonal Tropical Area.

(2) The Persian Gulf of the meridian of longitude 59° E.

(3) The area bounded by the parallel of latitude 22° S. from the east coast of Australia to the Great Barrier Reef, thence the Great Barrier Reef to latitude 11° S. The northern boundary of

Coast Guard, DHS § 42.30-20

the area is the southern boundary of the Tropical Zone.

[CGFR 68-60, 33 FR 10068, July 12, 1968]

§ 42.30-20 Seasonal Tropical Areas.

The following are Seasonal Tropical Areas:

(a) *In the North Atlantic.* It is an area bounded on the north by the rhumb line from Cape Catoche, Yucatan, to Cape San Antonio, Cuba, the north coast of Cuba to latitude 20° N., thence the parallel of latitude 20° N. to longitude 20° W.; on the west by the coast of the American continent; on the south and east by the northern boundary of the Tropical Zone.

(1) Seasonal periods:

Tropical: November 1 to July 15.
Summer: July 16 to October 31.

(b) *In the Arabian Sea.* An area bounded on the west by the coast of Africa, the meridian of longitude 45° E. in the Gulf of Aden, the coast of South Arabia and the meridian of longitude 59° E. in the Gulf of Oman; on the north and east by the coasts of Pakistan and India; on the south by the northern boundary of the Tropical Zone.

(1) Seasonal periods:

Tropical: September 1 to May 31.
Summer: June 1 to August 31.

(c) *In the Bay of Bengal.* The Bay of Bengal north of the northern boundary of the Tropical Zone.

(1) Seasonal periods:

Tropical: December 1 to April 30.
Summer: May 1 to November 30.

(d) *In the South Indian Ocean.* (1) An area bounded on the north and west by the southern boundary of the Tropical Zone and the east coast of Madagascar; on the south by the parallel of latitude 20° S.; on the east by the rhumb line from a point in latitude 20° S., longitude 50° E., to a point in latitude 15° S., longitude 51°30′ E., and thence by the meridian of longitude 51°30′ E. to latitude 10° S.

(i) Seasonal periods:

Tropical: April 1 to November 30.
Summer: December 1 to March 31.

(2) An area bounded on the north by the southern boundary of the Tropical Zone; on the east by the coast of Australia; on the south by the parallel of latitude 15° S. from longitude 51°30′ E., to longitude 120° E. and thence the meridian of longitude 120° E. to the coast of Australia; on the west by the meridian of longitude 51°30′ E.

(i) Seasonal periods:

Tropical: May 1 to November 30.
Summer: December 1 to April 30.

(e) *In the China Sea.* An area bounded on the west and north by the coasts of Vietnam and China from latitude 10° N. to Hong Kong; on the east by the rhumb line from Hong Kong to the Port of Sual (Luzon Island), and the west coasts of the Islands of Luzon, Samar, and Leyte to latitude 10° N.; on the south by the parallel of latitude 10° N.

(1) Hong Kong and Sual are to be considered as being on the boundary of the Seasonal Tropical Area and Summer Zone.

(2) Seasonal periods:

Tropical: January 21 to April 30.
Summer: May 1 to January 20.

(f) *In the North Pacific.* (1) An area bounded on the north by the parallel of latitude 25° N.; on the west by the meridian of longitude 160° E.; on the south by the parallel of latitude 13° N.; on the east by the meridian of longitude 130° W.

(i) Seasonal periods:

Tropical: April 1 to October 31.
Summer: November 1 to March 31.

(2) An area bounded on the north and east by the west coast of the American continent; on the west by the meridian of longitude 123° W. from the coast of the American continent to latitude 33° N., longitude 123° W.; to the point latitude 13° N., longitude 105° W.; on the south by the parallel of latitude 13° N.

(i) Seasonal periods:

Tropical: March 1 to June 30, and November 1 to November 30.
Summer: July 1 to October 31, and December 1 to February 28/29.

(g) *In the South Pacific.* (1) The Gulf of Carpentaria south of latitude 11° S.

(i) Seasonal periods:

Tropical: April 1 to November 30.
Summer: December 1 to March 31.

(2) An area bounded on the north and east by the southern boundary of the Tropical Zone; on the south by the

53

§ 42.30-25

Tropic of Capricorn from the east coast of Australia to longitude 150° W.; thence by the meridian of longitude 150° W. to latitude 20° S. and thence by the parallel of latitude 20° S. to the point where it intersects the southern boundary of the Tropical Zone; on the west by the boundaries of the area within the Great Barrier Reef included in the Tropical Zone, and by the east coast of Australia.

(i) Seasonal periods:

Tropical: April 1 to November 30.
Summer: December 1 to March 31.

[CGFR 68-60, 33 FR 10068, July 12, 1968, as amended by CGFR 68-126, 34 FR 9016, June 5, 1969]

§ 42.30-25 Summer Zones.

(a) The remaining areas constitute the Summer Zones.

(1) However, for vessels of 328 feet and under in length, the area bounded on the north and west by the east coast of the United States; on the east by the meridian of longitude 68°30′ W. from the coast of the United States to latitude 40° N. and thence by the rhumb line to the point latitude 36° N., longitude 73° W.; on the south by the parallel of latitude 36° N.; is a Winter Seasonal Area.

(i) Seasonal periods:

Winter: November 1 to March 31.
Summer: April 1 to October 31.

[CGFR 68-60, 33 FR 10069, July 12, 1968, as amended by CGFR 68-126, 34 FR 9016, June 5, 1969]

§ 42.30-30 Enclosed seas.

(a) *Baltic Sea.* This sea bounded by the parallel of latitude of The Skaw in the Skagerrak is included in the Summer Zones.

(1) However, for vessels of 328 feet and under in length, it is a Winter Seasonal Area.

(i) Seasonal periods:

Winter: November 1 to March 31.
Summer: April 1 to October 31.

(b) *Black Sea.* This sea is included in the Summer Zones.

(1) However, for vessels of 328 feet and under in length, the area north of latitude 44° N. is a Winter Seasonal Area.

(i) Seasonal periods:

Winter: December 1 to February 28/29.
Summer: March 1 to November 30.

(c) *Mediterranean.* This sea is included in the Summer Zones.

(1) However, for vessels of 328 feet and under in length, the area bounded on the north and west by the coasts of France and Spain and the meridian of longitude 3° E. from the coast of Spain to latitude 40° N.; on the south by the parallel of latitude 40° N. from longitude 3° E. to the west coast of Sardinia; on the east by the west and north coasts of Sardinia from latitude 40° N. to longitude 9° E., thence by the meridian of longitude 9° E. to the south coast of Corsica, thence by the west and north coasts of Corsica to longitude 9° E. and thence by the rhumb line to Cape Sicie; is a Winter Seasonal Area.

(i) Seasonal periods:

Winter: December 16 to March 15.
Summer: March 16 to December 15.

(d) *Sea of Japan.* This sea south of the parallel of latitude 50° N. is included in the Summer Zones.

(1) However, for vessels of 382 feet and under in length, the area between the parallel of latitude 50° N. and the rhumb line from the east coast of Korea at latitude 38° N. to the west coast of Hokkaido, Japan, at latitude 43°12′ N., is a Winter Seasonal Area.

(i) Seasonal periods:

Winter: December 1 to February 28/29.
Summer: March 1 to November 30.

[CGFR 68-60, 33 FR 10069, July 12, 1968, as amended by CGFR 68-126, 34 FR 9016, June 5, 1969]

§ 42.30-35 The Winter North Atlantic Load Line.

(a) The part of the North Atlantic referred to in § 42.20-75(d)(1) comprises:

(1) That part of the North Atlantic Winter Seasonal Zone II which lies between the meridians of 15° W. and 50° W.; and

(2) The whole of the North Atlantic Winter Seasonal Zone I, the Shetland Islands to be considered as being on the boundary.

[CGFR 68-60, 33 FR 10069, July 12, 1968]

Subpart 42.50—Load Line Certificates—Model Forms

§ 42.50-1 General.

(a) The provisions of this subpart set forth the requirements for the text of the various load line certificates issued to vessels complying with the applicable requirements in this part. See §§ 42.07-35 and 42.07-40 for requirements regarding load line assigning and issuing authorities. See § 42.07-45 for requirements regarding load line certificates, their text and arrangement.

(b) The 1966 international load line certificate and exemption certificate shall be the same as set forth in this subpart in the model Forms A1, A2, A3, and E1, except for the following authorized variations which shall also apply to model Forms B, C1, C2, and C3:

(1) As indicated in § 42.13-30, the freeboards and load line marks which are not applicable to a specific vessel need not be entered on the certificate issued.

(2) The provisions of Note 3 on the front of the certificate forms (other than Model E1) may be changed to correctly describe the situation applicable to the vessel concerning information and instructions furnished the master about loading and ballasting the vessel to provide a guide as to stability under various conditions and as to avoid unacceptable stresses in the vessel's structure.

(c) In the load line certificate the assigning and issuing authority shall set forth its full official designation; i.e., its legal name, address of home office, and reference to the authorization from the Commandant where an assigning and issuing authority other than the American Bureau of Shipping is designated.

[CGFR 68-126, 34 FR 9017, June 5, 1969]

§ 42.50-5 International load line certificates.

(a) The various forms of certificates certifying to the correctness of the load line marks assigned under the regulations in this subchapter and/or certain exemptions therefrom for U.S.-flag vessels engaged in foreign voyages, or engaged in coastwise or intercoastal voyages (provided such vessels qualify to engage in foreign voyages without restriction), are A1, A2, A3, and E1. The detailed application of these forms is as specified in § 42.07-45 (e), (f), and (h).

(b) The text and arrangement of the printed portions of Form *A1* (printed front and back) are as follows:

INTERNATIONAL LOAD LINE CERTIFICATE (1966)

[Form *A1*]

(Official seal of issuing authority.)
(Certificate No. _____)

Issued under the provisions of the International Convention on Load Lines, 1966, under the authority of the Government of the United States of America, and the Commandant, U.S. Coast Guard:
By

(Insert full official designation of issuing authority)

and duly authorized for assigning purposes under the provisions of the Convention.

Name of ship	Official number or distinctive letters	Port of registry	Length (*L*) as defined in Article 2(8) i.e., 46 CFR 42.13-15
Freeboard assigned as:[1]	A new ship .... An existing ship	Type of ship:[1]	Type "A". Type "B". Type "B" with reduced freeboard. Type "B" with increased freeboard.

FREEBOARD FROM DECK LINE			LOAD LINE
Tropical	___ (inches)	(T)	___ (inches) above (S).
Summer	___ (inches)	(S)	Upper edge of line at level of center of ring.
Winter	___ (inches)	(W)	___ (inches) below (S).

§ 42.50-5   46 CFR Ch. I (10-1-13 Edition)

| Name of ship | Official number or distinctive letters | Port of registry | Length (*L*) as defined in Article 2(8) i.e., 46 CFR 42.13–15 |

Winter (North Atlantic) ____ (inches) .... (WNA) .... ____ (inches) below (S).
Allowance for fresh water for all freeboards .... ____ (inches).

(All measurements are to upper edge of the respective horizontal lines)

The upper edge of the deck line from which these freeboards are measured is ____ inches above or below the top of the ____ deck at side; i.e., freeboard[1] deck.

Date of initial or periodical survey _____
This is to certify that this ship has been surveyed and that the freeboards have been assigned and load lines shown above have been marked in accordance with the International Convention on Load Lines, 1966.
This certificate is valid until _____,[2] subject to annual surveys in accordance with Article 14(1)(c) of the Convention, and endorsement thereof on the reverse side of the certificate.
Issued at _____ (Place of issue of certificate), _____, 19____ (Date of issue)

_____
(Signature of official issuing the certificate)

[Seal of issuing authority]

The undersigned declares that he is duly authorized by the said Government to issue this certificate.

(Signature)

NOTES

1. When a ship departs from a port situated on a river or inland waters, deeper loading shall be permitted corresponding to the weight of fuel and all other materials required for consumption between the point of departure and the sea.
2. When a ship is in fresh water of unit density, the appropriate load line may be submerged by the amount of the fresh water allowance shown above. Where the density is other than unity, an allowance shall be made proportional to the difference between 1.025 and the actual density.
3. It is the owner's responsibility to furnish the master with information and instructions for loading and ballasting this vessel to provide guidance as to stability of the vessel under varying conditions of service and to avoid unacceptable stresses in the vessel's structure.

[1] The issuing authority is authorized to delete or change words whenever it is inapplicable to a specific vessel and to arrange wording so appropriate word insertions may be made, which accurately describe the facts.
[2] At the expiration of this certificate, applicable reissuance should be obtained in accordance with the Load Line Regulations.

(REVERSE SIDE OF CERTIFICATE)

ANNUAL SURVEYS

This is to certify that at an annual survey required by Article 14(1)(c) of the Convention, this ship was found to comply with the relevant provisions of the Convention.
Place .... Date ....

(Signature and seal of issuing authority)
Place .... Date ....

Coast Guard, DHS § 42.50–5

Place .... (Signature and seal of issuing authority) .... Date ....

Place .... (Signature and seal of issuing authority) .... Date ....

(Signature and seal of issuing authority)

EXTENSION OF LOAD LINE CERTIFICATE

The provisions of the Convention being fully complied with by this ship, the validity of this certificate is, in accordance with Article 19(2) of the Convention, extended until.

Place .... Date ....

(Signature and seal of issuing authority)

NOTES

4. The Winter North Atlantic Load Line applies only to vessels of 328 feet in length or less, which enter any part of the North Atlantic Ocean during the winter months as defined by the Load Line Regulations in 46 CFR 42.30–5 and 42.30–35. The periods during which the other seasonal load lines apply in different parts of the world are as stated in the Load Line Regulations in 46 CFR 42.30–5 to 42.30–30, inclusive.

5. The Load Line Certificate will be canceled by the Commandant, U.S. Coast Guard, if:

(a) The annual surveys have not been carried out within 3 months either way of each anniversary of the certificate date.

(b) The certificate is not endorsed to show that the ship has been surveyed as indicated in (a).

(c) Material alterations have been made to the hull or superstructure of the vessel, such as would necessitate the assignment of an increased freeboard.

(d) The fittings and appliances for the protection of the openings, guardrails, freeing ports, or the means of access to the crew's quarters have not been maintained in as effective a condition as they were when the certificate was issued.

(e) The structural strength of the ship is lowered to such an extent that the ship is unsafe.

6. When this certificate has expired or has been canceled, it must be delivered to the issuing authority.

(c) The text and arrangement of the printed portion of Form *A2* shall be identical with the information on the face and reverse sides of Form *A1* certificate in paragraph (b) of this section except for the identification of model form, description of the "Freeboard from deck line," the "Load Line," and the illustration of load line marks, which shall be as follows:

INTERNATIONAL LOAD LINE CERTIFICATE (1966)

[Form *A2*]

*   *   *   *   *   *   *

FREEBOARD FROM DECK LINE			LOAD LINE
Tropical			
Summer .... ___ (inches)			Upper edge of line at level of center of ring.
Winter			
Winter—North Atlantic .. ___ (inches) .... (WNA)			Upper edge of line ___ (inches) below upper edge at level of center of ring.
Allowance for fresh water for all freeboards			___ (inches).

(All measurements are to upper edge of the respective horizontal lines)

The upper edge of the deck line from which these freeboards are measured is ___ inches above or below the top of the ___ deck at side; i.e., freeboard[1] deck.

§ 42.50-5

* * * * * * *

[1] The issuing authority is authorized to delete or change words whenever it is inapplicable to a specific vessel and to arrange wording so appropriate word insertions may be made, which accurately describe the facts.

(d) The text and arrangement of the printed portion of Form *A3* shall be identical with the information on the face and reverse sides of Form *A1* certificate in paragraph (b) of this section except for the identification of model form, description of the "Freeboard from deck line," the "Load Line," and the illustration of load line marks, which shall be as follows:

INTERNATIONAL LOAD LINE CERTIFICATE (1966)

[Form *A3*]

* * * * * * *

The timber freeboards given in this certificate are applicable only when this ship carries a timber deck cargo and complies with special requirements of the Load Line Regulations regarding timber deck cargoes.

	FREEBOARD FROM DECK LINE			LOAD LINE
Tropical	___ (inches)	(T)	___	(inches) above (S).
Summer	___ (inches)	(S)		Upper edge of line at level of center of ring.
Winter	___ (inches)	(W)	___	(inches) below (S).
Winter—North Atlantic	___ (inches)	(WNA)	___	(inches) below (S)
Timber—tropical	___ (inches)	(LT)	___	(inches) above (LS).
Timber—summer	___ (inches)	(LS)	___	(inches) above (S).
Timber—winter	___ (inches)	(LW)	___	(inches) below (LS).
Timber—winter—North Atlantic.	___ (inches)	(LWNA)	___	(inches) below (LS).
Allowance for fresh water for all freeboards other than timber			___	(inches).
Allowance for fresh water for all timber freeboards			___	(inches).

(All measurements are to upper edge of the respective horizontal lines)

The upper edge of the deck line from which these freeboards are measured is ___ inches above or below the top of the _____ deck at side; i.e., freeboard[1] deck.

Coast Guard, DHS § 42.50–5

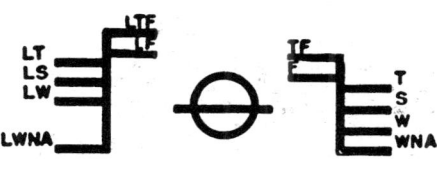

* * * * * * *

[1] The issuing authority is authorized to delete or change words whenever it is inapplicable to a specific vessel and to arrange wording so appropriate word insertions may be made, which accurately describe the facts.

(e) The text and arrangement of the printed portions of Form E1 are as follows:

INTERNATIONAL LOAD LINE EXEMPTION CERTIFICATE

[Form *E1*]

(Official seal of issuing authority.)
(Certificate No. ____)
Issued under the provisions of the International Convention on Load Lines, 1966, under the authority of the Government of the United States of America, and the Commandant U.S. Coast Guard:
By _____

(Insert full official designation of issuing authority)

and duly authorized for assigning and exemption purposes under the provisions of the Convention.

Name of ship   Official numbers of distinctive letters   Port of registry

This is to certify that the above-mentioned ship is exempted from the provisions of the 1966 Convention, under the authority conferred by Article 6(2),[1] Article 6(4),[1] of the Convention referred to above and that this ship has been surveyed accordingly.
The provisions of the Convention from which the ship is exempted under Article 6(2) are:

The voyage for which exemption is granted under Article 6(4) is:
From: _____
To: _____
Conditions, if any, on which the exemption is granted under either Article 6(2) or Article 6(4):

This certificate is valid until _____,[2] subject, where appropriate, to annual surveys in accordance with Article 14(1)(c) of the Convention, and endorsement thereof on the reverse side of the certificate.

§ 42.50-10

Issued at

(Place of issue of certificate)

(Date of issue)

(Signature of official issuing the certificate)

[Seal of issuing authority]

The undersigned declares that he is duly authorized by the said Government to issue this certificate.

(Signature)

¹ The issuing authority is authorized to delete whichever reference is inapplicable.
² At the expiration of this certificate, applicable reissuance should be obtained in accordance with the Load Line Regulations, if permitted.

(Reverse side of exemption certificate)

ANNUAL SURVEYS

This is to certify that this ship continues to comply with the conditions under which this exemption was granted.

Place .... Date ....

(Signature and seal of issuing authority)

Place .... Date ....

(Signature and seal of issuing authority)

Place .... Date ....

(Signature and seal of issuing authority)

Place .... Date ....

(Signature and seal of issuing authority)

EXTENSION OF LOAD LINE CERTIFICATE

This ship continues to comply with the conditions under which this exemption was granted and the validity of this certificate is, in accordance with Article 19(4)(a) of the Convention, extended until.

Place .... Date ....

(Signature and seal of issuing authority)

[CGFR 68-60, 33 FR 10070, July 12, 1968, as amended by CGFR 68-126, 34 FR 9017, June 5, 1969]

§ 42.50-10 **Load line certificates for nonadherent foreign flag vessels.**

(a) The form of load line certificate certifying to the correctness of the load line marks assigned under the regulations in this subchapter to nonadherent foreign flag vessels as specified in § 42.07-45(e)(2) is:

(1) Form B for general use. The period of validity shall be as expressed in § 42.09-20(c).

(b) The text and arrangement of the printed portion of Form B shall be identical with the information on the face and reverse sides of Form A1 certificate in § 42.50-5(b) except for title of certificate, model form, the first paragraph, and the wording of the certificate for issuance and revalidation, which shall be as follows:

Coast Guard, DHS § 42.50–10

LOAD LINE CERTIFICATE

(Form *B*)

(Official seal of issuing authority.)
(Certificate No. ____)
Issued under the authority of the Commandant, U.S. Coast Guard, United States of America, under the provisions of the Load Line Act of March 2, 1929, as amended (46 U.S.C. 85–85g), and the Load Line Regulations in 46 CFR part 42:
By _____

(Insert full official designation of issuing authority)

and duly authorized for assigning purposes under the provisions of the Load Line Act of March 2, 1929, as amended.

* * * * * * *

This is to certify that this ship has been surveyed and the freeboards have been assigned and load lines shown above have been marked upon the vessel in manner and location as required by the Load Line Regulations of the Commandant, U.S. Coast Guard, in 46 CFR part 42.

This certificate remains in force until _____,[2] subject to annual revalidation in accordance with the Load Line Regulations, and endorsement thereof on the reverse side of this certificate.

Issued at _____ (Place of issue of certificate), _____, 19___
(Date of issue)

(Signature of official issuing the certificate)

[Seal of issuing authority]

* * * * * * *

[2] Expiration date is not to exceed 5 years from original date of issue of this certificate. At expiration applicable reissuance of this certificate should be obtained in accordance with the Load Line Regulations.

* * * * * * *

(Reverse Side of Certificate)

ANNUAL REVALIDATION OF CERTIFICATE

This is to certify that the provisions of the Load Line Regulations of the Commandant, U.S. Coast Guard, are fully complied with by the condition of this ship on the dates indicated, and in each case this certificate is revalidated for a 1 year interval as follows:

(1) Until.
Place .... Date.
(Signature and seal of issuing authority).

(1) Until.
Place .... Date.
(Signature and seal of issuing authority)

(1) Until.
Place .... Date.
(Signature and seal of issuing authority)

(1) Until.
Place .... Date.
(Signature and seal of issuing authority)

[CGFR 68–126, 34 FR 9017, June 5, 1969]

§ 42.50-15 Coastwise load line certificates for U.S.-flag vessels.

(a) The forms of the coastwise load line certificate, other than for special service which are provided for in part 44 of this subchapter, certifying to the correctness of the load line marks assigned under the regulations in this part are C1, C2 and C3. The detailed application of these forms is as specified in § 42.07-45(e).

(b) Space shall be provided on the face of each of the coastwise load line certificates so that there may be entered thereon a record of the restrictions applicable to the vessel, if any.

(c) The text and arrangement of the printed portions of Form *C1* are as follows:

COASTWISE LOAD LINE CERTIFICATE

[Form *C1*]

(Official seal of issuing authority.)
(Certificate No. ____)
Issued under the authority of the Commandant, U.S. Coast Guard, under the provisions of the Coastwise Load Line Act, 1935, as amended (46 U.S.C. 88–88g), and the Load Line Regulations in 46 CFR part 42:
By _____

(Insert full official designation of issuing authority)

and duly authorized for assigning purposes under the provisions of this law for vessels engaging in coastwise and/or intercoastal voyages.

Name of ship	Official number or distinctive letters	Port or registry	Length (L) as defined in 46 CFR 42.13-15

Freeboard assigned as:[1] .. A new ship. .... Type of ship:[1] .... Type "A".
                      An existing ship. ....   Type "B".
                                                                                                         Type "B" with reduced freeboard.
                                                                                                         Type "B" with increased freeboard.

		FREEBOARD FROM DECK LINE		LOAD LINE
Tropical	___ (inches)	(T)	___	(inches) above (S).
Summer	___ (inches)	(S)		Upper edge of line at level of center of ring.
Winter	___ (inches)	(W)	___	(inches) below (S).
Allowance for fresh water for all freeboards			___	(inches)

(All measurements are to upper edge of the respective horizontal lines)

The upper edge of the deck line from which these freeboards are measured is ____ inches above or below the top of the _____ deck at side; i.e., freeboard[1] deck.

* * * * * * *

Date of initial or periodical survey _____
The following is a record of the restrictions applicable to the above named ship:

62

Coast Guard, DHS § 42.50–15

(List restrictions. If none, insert "None.")

This is to certify that this ship has been surveyed and that the freeboards have been assigned and load lines shown above have been marked in accordance with the Commandant, U.S. Coast Guard, Coastwise Load Line Regulations in 46 CFR parts 42 to 46, inclusive as applicable.

This certificate remains in force until _____,[2] subject to annual surveys in accordance with applicable Load Line Regulations, and endorsement thereof on the reverse side of the certificate.

Issued at _____

(Place of issue of certificate)   (Date of issue)

By

(Signature of official issuing the certificate)

[Seal of issuing authority]

NOTES

1. When a ship departs from a port situated on a river or inland waters, deeper loading shall be permitted corresponding to the weight of fuel and all other materials required for consumption between the point of departure and the sea.

2. When a ship is in fresh water of unit density the appropriate load line may be submerged by the amount of the fresh water allowance shown above. Where the density is other than unity, an allowance shall be made proportional to the difference between 1.025 and the actual density.

3. It is the owner's responsibility to furnish the master with information and instructions for loading and ballasting this vessel to provide guidance as to stability of the vessel under varying conditions of service and to avoid unacceptable stresses in the vessel's structure.

[1] The issuing authority is authorized to delete or change words inapplicable to a specific vessel and to arrange wording so appropriate word insertions may be made, which accurately describe the facts.

[2] At the expiration of this certificate, applicable reissuance should be obtained in accordance with the Load Line Regulations.

(Reverse side of Coastwise Load Line Certificate)

ANNUAL SURVEYS

This is to certify that this ship has been surveyed on the dates indicated to determine in each case whether this certificate should remain in force for an additional 1 year and the survey has been completed to my satisfaction.

(1).
     Signature of Surveyor   Place   Date

(2).
     Signature of Surveyor   Place   Date

(3).
     Signature of Surveyor   Place   Date

(4).
     Signature of Surveyor   Place   Date

EXTENSION OF LOAD LINE CERTIFICATE

The provisions of the Coastwise Load Line Regulations of the Commandant, U.S. Coast Guard, being fully complied with by this ship, this certificate is extended under the authority of 46 CFR 42.07–45 and 42.09–15 until.

Place .... Date ....

....

(Name of issuing authority and signature of Surveyor)

§ 42.50-15

NOTES

4. The periods and areas during which the seasonal load lines apply are as stated in the Load Line Regulations in 46 CFR subpart 42.30, as appropriate.

5. This Coastwise Load Line Certificate will be canceled by the Commandant, U.S. Coast Guard, if:

(a) The annual surveys have not been carried out within three months either way of each anniversary of the certificate date.

(b) The certificate is not endorsed to show that the ship has been surveyed as indicated in (a).

(c) Material alterations have been made to the hull or superstructure of the vessel, such as would necessitate the assignment of an increased freeboard.

(d) The fittings and appliances for the protection of the openings, guardrails, freeing ports, or the means of access to the crew's quarters have not been maintained in as effective a condition as they were when the certificate was issued.

(e) The structural strength of the ship is lowered to such an extent that the ship is unsafe.

6. When this certificate has expired or has been canceled, it must be delivered to the issuing authority.

* * * * * *

(d) The text and arrangement of the printed portion of Form *C2* shall be identical with the information on the face and revese sides of Form *C1* certificate in paragraph (c) of this section except for the identification of model form, description of the "Freeboard from deck line", the "Load Line", and the illustration of load line marks, which shall be as follows:

COASTWISE LOAD LINE CERTIFICATE

[Form *C2*]

* * * * * *

	FREEBOARD FROM DECK LINE		LOAD LINE
Tropical	___ (inches)		Upper edge of line at level center of ring.
Summer	......do		
Winter	......do		Do.
Allowance for fresh water for all freeboards			___ (inches).

(All measurements are to upper edge of the respective horizontal lines)

The upper edge of the deck line from which these freeboards are measured is ___ inches above or below the top of the _____ deck at side; i.e., freeboard[1] deck.

* * * * * *

(e) The text and arrangement of the printed portion of Form *C3* shall be identical with the information on the face and reverse sides of Form *C1* certificate in paragraph (c) of this section except for the identification of model form, description of the "Freeboard from deck line," the "Load Line," and the illustration of load line marks, which shall be as follows:

Coast Guard, DHS   **Pt. 44**

COASTWISE LOAD LINE CERTIFICATE

[Form *C3*]

*   *   *   *   *   *   *

The timber freeboards given in this certificate are applicable only when this ship carries a timber deck cargo and complies with the special requirements of the Load Line Regulations regarding timber deck cargoes.

FREEBOARD FROM DECK LINE LOAD LINE   LOAD LINE

Tropical .... ___ (inches) .... (T) .... ___ (inches) above (S).
Summer .... ___ (inches) .... (S) .... Upper edge of line at level of center of ring.
Winter .... ___ (inches) .... (W) .... ___ (inches) below (S).
Timber—tropical .... ___ (inches) .... (LT) .... ___ (inches) above (LS).
Timber—summer .... ___ (inches) .... (LS) .... ___ (inches) above (S).
Timber—winter .... ___ (inches) .... (LW) .... ___ (inches) below (LS).
    Allowance for fresh water for all freeboards other than timber .... ___ (inches).
    Allowance for fresh water for all timber freeboards .... ___ (inches).

(All measurements are to upper edge of the respective horizontal lines)

The upper edge of the deck line from which these freeboards are measured is ___ inches above or below the top of the _____ deck at side; i.e., freeboard[1] deck.

*   *   *   *   *   *   *

[1] The issuing authority is authorized to delete or change words inapplicable to a specific vessel and to arrange wording so appropriate word insertions may be made, which accurately describe the facts.

[CGFR 68-60, 33 FR 10073, July 12, 1968, as amended by CGFR 68-126, 34 FR 9018, June 5, 1969]

PART 43 [RESERVED]

PART 44—SPECIAL SERVICE LIMITED DOMESTIC VOYAGES

Subpart A—Administration

Sec.
44.01-1 Establishment of load lines for special services.
44.01-5 Administration; special service.
44.01-10 Approval by Commandant, U.S. Coast Guard, of special service.
44.01-11 Assignment and marking load lines; special service.
44.01-12 Voyage limits; special service.
44.01-13 Heavy weather plan.
44.01-15 Special service certificate.
44.01-20 New and existing vessels; special service.

Subpart B—Rules for Assigning Special Service Load Lines

44.05-1 General.
44.05-5 Definitions.
44.05-10 Load line markings.
44.05-15 Existing vessels.
44.05-20 Conditions of assignment.
44.05-25 Freeboards.
44.05-30 Load line certificate.
44.05-35 Form of load line certificate.

Subpart C—Rules for Assigning Working Freeboards to Hopper Dredges

44.300 Applicability.
44.310 Definitions.
44.320 Submission of plans and calculations.
44.330 Obtaining working freeboards for hopper dredges.
44.340 Operating restrictions.

§ 44.01-1

AUTHORITY: 46 U.S.C. 5101–5116; Department of Homeland Security Delegation No. 0170.1.

SOURCE: CGFR 65–50, 30 FR 16755, Dec. 30, 1965, unless otherwise noted.

Subpart A—Administration

§ 44.01-1 Establishment of load lines for special services.

(a) Load lines are established for steam colliers, tugs, barges, and self-propelled barges engaged in special services in conformity with regulations in this part.

(b) Load lines for steam colliers, barges, and self-propelled barges engaged on specially limited coastwise voyages as described in § 44.01–12 shall be established pursuant to the regulations in this part.

(c) Variance for tugs is not permitted.

[CGFR 65–50, 30 FR 16755, Dec. 30, 1965, as amended by USCG–1998–4442, 63 FR 52190, Sept. 30, 1998]

§ 44.01-5 Administration; special service.

(a) The administrative provisions of §§ 42.01–1 to 42.11–20 inclusive of this subchapter, relating to vessels engaged in foreign and coastwise voyages, where applicable, shall apply to vessels subject to this part except as modified in paragraph (b) of this section.

(b) Application for the assignment of load lines under this part for the types of vessels described in § 44.01–1 shall be made in writing to the American Bureau of Shipping unless another society has been specifically approved by the Commandant as a load line assigning authority. In the latter case application shall be made to the society so approved. Applications shall state the following information:

(1) Name of vessel and official number.

(2) Type of vessel (steam collier, barge, or self-propelled barge).

(3) Date keel was laid.

(4) Normal sea speed of vessel.

(5) Limits of voyage for which approval is requested.

(6) Normal maximum distance offshore in course of voyage.

(7) Length of voyage in days and nautical miles.

(8) Statement of weather conditions to be expected.

(9) Cargo to be carried.

(10) Whether vessel is to be operated manned or unmanned.

[CGFR 65–50, 30 FR 16755, Dec. 30, 1965, as amended by CGFR 68–60, 33 FR 10076, July 12, 1968]

§ 44.01-10 Approval by Commandant, U.S. Coast Guard, of special service.

(a) Subject to the conditions contained in this part, the Commandant, U.S. Coast Guard, has determined that load lines at variance from the position fixed by the International Convention on Load Lines, 1966, but not above the actual line of safety, may be assigned steam colliers, barges, or self-propelled barges (separately by class) for certain specifically limited coastwise voyages between ports of the continental United States or between islands of a group over which the United States has jurisdiction.

[CGFR 65–50, 30 FR 16755, Dec. 30, 1965, as amended by CGFR 68–60, 33 FR 10076, July 12, 1968]

§ 44.01-11 Assignment and marking load lines; special service.

(a) The assignment and marking of special service load lines and certifications thereof shall be in accordance with this part to the satisfaction of the American Bureau of Shipping. The load line certificate shall define the voyage limits and seasonal restrictions governing the validity of the load lines.

§ 44.01-12 Voyage limits; special service.

(a) Special service load lines may be assigned for operation not more than a specified limited distance offshore which shall not exceed 20 nautical miles. The offshore distance shall be measured from the coastline except where a line of inland waters has been otherwise established.

(b) For continental United States ports, special service load lines may be issued for operation between but not to exceed the extreme port limits specified below, or for operation between intermediate ports within the extreme limits specified:

(1) Central and Northern Atlantic Coast—From Norfolk, Virginia, to Eastport, Maine.

(2) Southeast Atlantic Coast—from Key West, Florida, to Jacksonville, Florida, except that the special service load line is not valid for manned vessels during the hurricane season, i.e., July 1st to November 15th, both dates inclusive, unless the vessel is operated in accordance with a Coast Guard approved heavy weather plan.

(3) Gulf of Mexico Coast—from the mouth of the Rio Grande River, Texas, to Key West, Florida, except that the special service load line is not valid for manned vessels during the hurricane season, i.e., July 1st to November 15th, both dates inclusive, unless the vessel is operated in accordance with a Coast Guard approved heavy weather plan.

(4) Pacific Coast—From San Francisco, California, to San Diego, California.

(c) Assignment of special service load lines for voyage limits between the islands of a group over which the United States has jurisdiction shall be made only upon authorization by the Commandant, U.S. Coast Guard, after submittal to him of the information called for by § 44.01–5(b).

[CGFR 65–50, 30 FR 16755, Dec. 30, 1965, as amended by CGD 79–142, 45 FR 57402, Aug. 28, 1980]

§ 44.01–13 Heavy weather plan.

(a) Each heavy weather plan under § 44.01–12(b) must be prepared by the vessel owner or operator and approved by the cognizant Officer in Charge, Marine Inspection. Approval of a heavy weather plan is limited to the current hurricane season.

(b) The cognizant Officer in Charge, Marine Inspection, is—

(1) The Officer in Charge, Marine Inspection, within whose area the work site is located for a vessel that will be operating in a limited geographical area; or

(2) The Officer in Charge, Marine Inspection, within whose area the point of departure is located for a transiting vessel.

(c) The required content of the heavy weather plan is determined on a case-by-case basis by the cognizant Officer in Charge, Marine Inspection, based on knowledge of the local conditions. The heavy weather plan may contain weather radio frequencies and time schedules for seeking a harbor of safe refuge. A single heavy weather plan may be accepted for more than one vessel operating at a single work site or on a single route.

(d) The vessel owner or operator must place a copy of the heavy weather plan on each vessel to which it applies and ensure that it remains there throughout the hurricane season.

[CGD 79–142, 45 FR 57402, Aug. 28, 1980]

§ 44.01–15 Special service certificate.

(a) The use of the special service load line certificate issued under this part is limited to voyages only as described in the certificate. If the vessel engages on any voyage not contemplated by the certificate where a load line is required, the load line prescribed by part 42 of this subchapter shall govern.

(b) Vessels engaged on special services in the coastwise trade and the interisland trade will be certificated on the form shown in § 44.05–35.

[CGFR 65–50, 30 FR 16755, Dec. 30, 1965, as amended by CGFR 68–60, 33 FR 10076, July 12, 1968]

§ 44.01–20 New and existing vessels; special service.

(a) A new vessel marked with load lines for special service on a coastwise or inter-island voyage is a vessel whose keel was laid on or after September 28, 1937. An existing vessel is one whose keel was laid before that date.

Subpart B—Rules for Assigning Special Service Load Lines

§ 44.05–1 General.

(a) The load line regulations in this part are complementary to those in part 42 or part 45 (Great Lakes load line regulations) of this subchapter, as reference is made thereto.

[CGFR 65–50, 30 FR 16755, Dec. 30, 1965, as amended by CGFR 68–60, 33 FR 10076, July 12, 1968]

§ 44.05–5 Definitions.

(a) A steam collier is a vessel mechanically propelled, and specially designed for the carriage of coal in bulk.

§ 44.05-10

(b) A towed barge is a vessel without sufficient means of self-propulsion and which requires to be towed.

(c) A self-propelled barge is a vessel mechanically propelled of the type specially designed for use in limited coastwise and Great Lakes service and capable of transiting interconnecting canals.

§ 44.05-10 Load line markings.

(a) The load line marks on the vessel's sides must be in accordance with § 42.13-25(a) of this subchapter, except seasonal markings such as "Winter North Atlantic" which are not applicable to the voyage are omitted.

(b) In the case of vessels which engage in special services on coastwise voyages and voyages on the Great Lakes, the marks on the vessel's sides are to be in accordance with Figure 44.05-10(b), except that the lines marked "SW" and "MS" shall be used only where applicable.

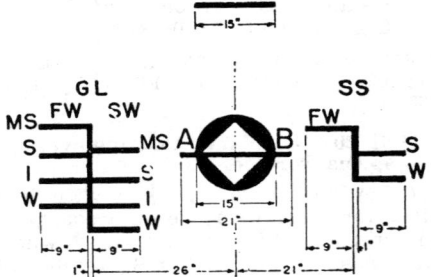

FIGURE 44.05-10(B)

(c) The load lines aft of the combined disk and diamond will be applicable for voyages on the Great Lakes and those on the forward side will be applicable to limited coastwise voyages. The summer line on the ocean will correspond to the summer line on the Lakes and the winter line on the ocean will correspond to the intermediate line on the Lakes.

(d) In the case of vessels which operate both on special service coastwise voyages and on unlimited coastwise voyages, the marks on the ship's sides are to be in accordance with figure 44.05-10 (d). The load lines aft of the disk will be applicable to voyages in special service coastwise or inter-island voyages and those on the forward side will be applicable to unlimited coastwise voyages. (A vessel marked for both special service and unlimited coastwise voyages and furnished with a load line certificate on the international form shall, when entering the foreign trade, arrange that the load line markings are in accord with the vessel's international load line certificate by the elimination of the marks aft of the disk.)

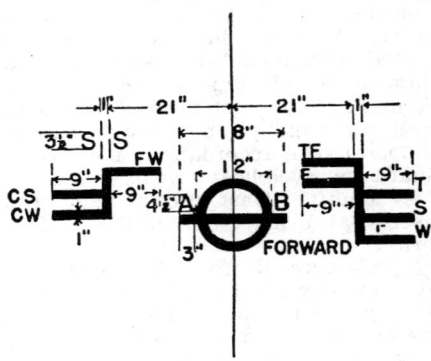

FIGURE 45.05-10(D)

[CGFR 65-50, 30 FR 16755, Dec. 30, 1965, as amended by CGD 80-120, 47 FR 5723, Feb. 8, 1982; USCG-2004-18884, 69 FR 58345, Sept. 30, 2004]

§ 44.05-15 Existing vessels.

(a) In assigning load lines to an existing vessel the provisions of the regulations in this part shall be complied with in principle and detail insofar as is reasonable and practicable, having regard to the proven efficacy of existing arrangements for a special service voyage, and having particular regard to the provision of sufficient means for the protection and safety of the crew.

(b) Where it is neither reasonable nor practicable to comply with this part in its entirety, the assigning authority will, in each case, report to the Commandant, U.S. Coast Guard, the specific matters in which the vessel is deficient with such recommendations as may seem desirable. Upon the receipt of this report the Commandant, U.S. Coast Guard, shall determine such addition to the freeboard as will, in the judgment of the Commandant, U.S.

Coast Guard, make the vessel as safe as if it had fully complied with this part.

§ 44.05-20 Conditions of assignment.

(a) *Steam colliers.* The conditions of assignment for steam colliers shall be in accordance with the requirements of part 42 of this subchapter, except that in the case of steam colliers constructed with bulwarks, the freeing port may be of a practically continuous slot type, located as low as possible, the clear area of the slot to be not less than 20 percent of the superficial area of the unpierced bulwarks. If, due to sheer, or other conditions, the assigning authority considers that extra local provision should be made for freeing decks of water, the slots are to be located so as to have maximum efficacy.

(b) *Towed barges.* The conditions of assignment for towed cargo barges where the cargo is carried under deck shall be in accordance with §§ 45.10-5 to 45.10-100 of this subchapter. In the case of tank barges and cargo barges carrying cargo only on deck, compliance will also be required with the supplementary conditions of §§ 45.20-1 to 45.20-70 of this subchapter. In the case of cargo barges of the open type, assignment will be limited to barges in unmanned operation and the construction of the vessel must be such as to satisfy the assigning authority that no unusual hazards will be experienced.

(c) *Self-propelled barges.* The conditions of assignment for self-propelled cargo barges carrying cargo under decks shall be in accordance with the provisions of §§ 45.10-5 to 45.10-100 of this subchapter. In the case of self-propelled tank barges and self-propelled cargo barges carrying cargo only on deck, compliance will also be required with the supplementary conditions of §§ 45.20-1 to 45.20-70 of this subchapter.

[CGFR 65-50, 30 FR 16755, Dec. 30, 1965, as amended by CGFR 68-60, 33 FR 10076, July 12, 1968]

§ 44.05-25 Freeboards.

(a) *General.* (1) When the assigning authority is satisfied that the requirements of this part as applicable to the type of vessel under consideration are complied with the freeboards will be computed as described in this section.

(2) The requirements in §§ 42.09-1 and 42.09-10 that relate to the assignment of freeboards and to stability are applicable to each vessel subject to the requirements in this part.

(3) The assigning authority that assigns a vessel subject to the requirements in this part a freeboard under part 45 of this chapter shall do so in accordance with the requirements in effect as of October 1, 1972.

(b) *Steam colliers.* Steam colliers that have constructional features similar to those of a tanker which afford extra invulnerability against the sea may be assigned a reduction of freeboard from that determined under part 42 of this subchapter. The amount of such reduction shall be determined by the assigning authority, in relation to the freeboard assigned to tankers, having regard to the degree of compliance with the supplementary conditions of assignment laid down for these ships, but without regard to the degree of subdivision provided. The freeboard assigned to such a vessel shall in no case be less than would be assigned the vessel as a tanker, as determined under part 42 of this subchapter.

(c) *Towed cargo barges with cargo under deck.* The freeboard is to be computed under §§ 45.15-1 to 45.15-97 of this subchapter. The fresh water and seasonal markings where applicable are to be determined under part 42 of this subchapter.

(d) *Towed cargo barges with cargo only on deck.* The freeboard for barges of this type is to be computed in accordance with the requirements of §§ 45.20-1 to 45.20-70 of this subchapter. The fresh water and seasonal markings where applicable are to be the same as determined under part 42 of this subchapter.

(e) *Towed cargo barges of the open type.* The load line shall be placed where, in the judgment of the assigning authority, the draft will be such that no unusual hazard will be experienced. In general, drafts assigned will be such that the barge will remain afloat with a reasonable freeboard after flooding of the net available open space.

(f) *Towed tank barges.* The freeboard is to be computed in accordance with §§ 45.20-1 to 45.20-70 of this subchapter. The fresh water and seasonal markings

§ 44.05-30

where applicable are to be determined under part 42 of this subchapter.

(g) *Self-propelled cargo barges.* The freeboard is to be computed under §§ 45.15-1 to 45.20-15 of this subchapter. The fresh water and seasonal markings where applicable are to be determined under part 42 of this subchapter.

(h) *Self-propelled tank barges.* The freeboard is to be computed in accordance with §§ 45.20-1 to 45.20-70 of this subchapter. The fresh water and seasonal markings where applicable are to be determined under part 42 of this subchapter.

[CGFR 65-50, 30 FR 17655, Dec. 30, 1965, as amended by CGFR 68-60, 33 FR 10077, July 12, 1968; CGD 73-49R, 38 FR 12290, May 10, 1973]

§ 44.05-30 Load line certificate.

(a) The load line certificates for a special service coastwise or special inter-island voyage shall be issued in addition to any other applicable load line certificates and shall be on the form shown in § 44.05-35.

§ 44.05-35 Form of load line certificate.

(a) Where no other Load Line certificate is issued:

LOAD LINE CERTIFICATE FOR A SPECIAL SERVICE COASTWISE OR INTER-ISLAND VOYAGE

Issued under the authority of the Commandant, U.S. Coast Guard, United States of America, under the provisions of the Coastwise Load Line Act of August 27, 1935, as amended.

[SEAL]

Issued by _____
Certificate No. _____

This certificate is valid only for coastwise or inter-island voyages that are between the limits of _____ and _____ provided the vessel is engaged solely in the trade stated herein.

Ship _____
Official No. _____
Port of registry _____
Trade of vessel _____
Gross tonnage _____

Freeboard from deck line	Load line
Tropical (T)	Above (S).
Summer (S)	Upper edge of line through center of disk.
Winter (W)	Below (S).

*Allowance for fresh water for all freeboards (except on the Great Lakes) _____
The upper edge of the deck line from which these freeboards are measured is _____ inches above the top of the ____ deck at side.

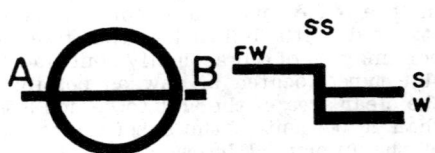

This is to certify that this ship has been surveyed and the freeboards and load lines shown above have been found to be correctly marked upon the vessel in manner and location as provided by the Load Line Regulations of the Commandant, U.S. Coast Guard, applicable to vessels engaged on this special service voyage.

**This certificate remains in force until _____. Issued at _____ on the _____ day of _____, 19___.

(Here follows the signature or seal and description of the assigning authority)

NOTES: (1) In accordance with the Load Line Regulations, the disk or diamond and the lines must be permanently marked by center punch marks or cutting.

(2) The load line assignment given by this certificate necessarily assumes that the nature and stowage of cargo, balast, etc., are such as to secure sufficient stability for the vessel. Accordingly, it is the owner's responsibility to furnish the Master of the vessel with stability information and instructions when this is necessary to maintenance of sufficient stability.

(On the reverse side of the load line certificate, the provision for annual inspection endorsement and for renewal of the certificate is to be the same as for vessels engaged in the foreign trade.)

(b) Where the Special Service Load Line Certificate is issued in addition to

*Where seagoing steamers navigate a river or inland water, deeper loading is permitted corresponding to the weight of fuel, etc., required for consumption between the point of departure and the open sea.

**Upon the expiration of the certificate renewal must be obtained as provided by the Load Line Regulations and the certificate so endorsed. Endorsement should also be made in the spaces provided on the occasion of each annual inspection required by the Load Line Regulations.

a Great Lakes Load Line Certificate, the wording of the Special Service Load Line Certificate is to be identical to that given in paragraph (a) of this section, but the markings indicated in the form shall be replaced by the following markings:

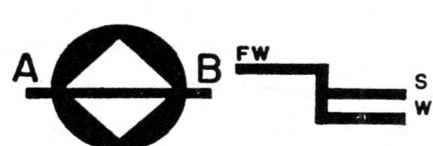

(c) Where the Special Service Load Line Certificate is issued in addition to an Unlimited Coastwise or International Load Line Certificate, the wording of the Special Service Load Line Certificate is to be identical to that given in paragraph (a) of this section, but the markings indicated in the form shall be replaced by the following markings:

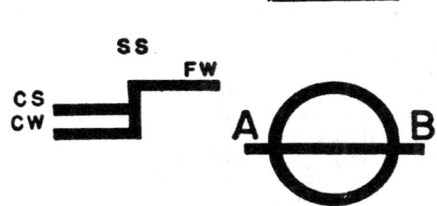

Subpart C—Rules for Assigning Working Freeboards to Hopper Dredges

SOURCE: CGD 76–080, 54 FR 36977, Sept. 6, 1989, unless otherwise noted.

§ 44.300 Applicability.

This subpart applies to each self-propelled hopper dredge—

(a) For which a working freeboard assignment is desired after January 1, 1990; and

(b) That operates with a working freeboard assigned under this subpart.

§ 44.310 Definitions.

Hopper dredge means a self-propelled dredge with an open hold or hopper in the hull of the dredge that receives dredged material.

Working freeboard means one-half the distance between the mark of the load line assigned under this subchapter and the freeboard deck.

§ 44.320 Submission of plans and calculations.

To request a working freeboard, calculations, plans, and stability information necessary to demonstrate compliance with this subpart must be submitted to the:

(a) Commanding Officer, Marine Safety Center, U.S. Coast Guard, 4200 Wilson Boulevard Suite 400, Arlington, VA 22203 for visitors. Send all mail to Commanding Officer (MSC), Attn: Marine Safety Center, U.S. Coast Guard Stop 7410, 4200 Wilson Boulevard Suite 400, Arlington, VA 20598–7410; or

(b) American Bureau of Shipping, ABS Plaza, 16855 Northchase Drive, Houston, TX 77060.

[CGD 76–080, 54 FR 36977, Sept. 6, 1989, as amended by USCG–1998–4442, 63 FR 52190, Sept. 30, 1998; USCG–2000–7790, 65 FR 58459, Sept. 29, 2000; USCG–2007–29018, 72 FR 53965, Sept. 21, 2007; USCG–2009–0702, 74 FR 49228, Sept. 25, 2009; USCG 2013–0671, 78 FR 60147, Sept. 30, 2013]

§ 44.330 Obtaining working freeboards for hopper dredges.

A hopper dredge may be issued a working freeboard on a limited service domestic voyage load line certificate or a Great Lakes load line certificate if the following are met:

(a) The hopper dredge structure must have adequate strength for any draft up to the working freeboard draft. Dredges built and maintained in conformity with the requirements of a classification society recognized by the Commandant usually meet this requirement.

(b) The hopper dredge must—

(1) Meet subpart I of part 174 of this chapter; and

(2) Have on its bridge remote draft indicators that:

(i) Show the fore, aft, and mean draft of the dredge at all times while the dredge is operating; and

§ 44.340 Operating restrictions.

(ii) Have each indicator marked with the assigned freeboard and the working freeboard.

§ 44.340 Operating restrictions.

(a) Each hopper dredge assigned a working freeboard may be operated at drafts from the normal freeboard to the working freeboard if the—

(1) Seas are not more than 10 feet;
(2) Winds are not more than 35 knots;
(3) Area of operation is not more than 20 nautical miles (37 kilometers) from the mouth of a harbor of safe refuge; and
(4) Specific gravity of the spoil carried is not more than the highest specific gravity of spoil used in the stability calculations required by subchapter S of this chapter.

(b) The Assigning Authority designates on the face of the dredge's load line certificate—

(1) Each restriction contained in paragraph (a)(1) through (a)(3) of this section; and
(2) The maximum specific gravity of the spoils allowed to be carried.

PART 45—GREAT LAKES LOAD LINES

Subpart A—General

Sec.
45.1 Purpose.
45.3 Definitions.
45.5 Seasonal application of load lines.
45.9 Seasonal application of load lines for vessels not marked under this part.
45.11 Issue of load line certificate.
45.13 Form of certificate.
45.15 Exemptions.

Subpart B—Load Line Marks

45.31 Deck line.
45.33 Diamond.
45.35 Seasonal load lines.
45.37 Salt water load lines.
45.39 Marking.

Subpart C—Freeboards

45.51 Types of ships.
45.53 Summer freeboard.
45.55 Freeboard coefficient.
45.57 Correction: Position of deckline.
45.58 Correction: Short superstructure.
45.59 Definitions for superstructure corrections.
45.61 Correction for superstructures and trunks.
45.63 Correction for sheer.
45.65 Excess sheer limitations.
45.67 Sheer measurement.
45.69 Correction for bow height.
45.71 Midsummer freeboard.
45.73 Winter freeboard.
45.75 Intermediate freeboard.
45.77 Salt water freeboard.

Subpart D—Conditions of Assignment

45.101 Purpose.
45.103 Structural stress and stability.
45.105 Information supplied to the master.
45.107 Strength of hull.
45.109 Strength of superstructures and deckhouses.
45.111 Strength of bulkheads at ends of superstructures.
45.113 Access openings in bulkheads at ends of enclosed superstructures.
45.115 Bulwarks and guardrails.
45.117 Freeing port area: General.
45.119 Freeing port area: Changes from standard sheer.
45.121 Freeing port area: Changes for trunks and side coamings.
45.123 Freeing port area: Changes for bulwark height.
45.125 Crew passageways.
45.127 Position of structures, openings, and fittings.
45.129 Hull fittings: General.
45.131 Ventilators.
45.133 Air pipes.
45.135 Hull openings at or below freeboard deck.
45.137 Cargo ports.
45.139 Side scuttles.
45.141 Manholes and flush scuttles.
45.143 Hull openings above freeboard deck.
45.145 Hatchway covers.
45.147 Hatchway coamings.
45.149 Machinery space openings.
45.151 Other openings.
45.153 Through-hull piping: General.
45.155 Inlets and discharge piping: Valves.
45.157 Scuppers and gravity drains.
45.159 Special conditions of assignment for type A vessels.

Subpart E—Unmanned River Barges on Lake Michigan Routes

45.171 Purpose.
45.173 Eligible barges.
45.175 Applicable routes.
45.177 Freeboard requirements.
45.179 Cargo limitations.
45.181 Load line exemption requirements for the Burns Harbor and Milwaukee routes.
45.183 Load line requirements for the St. Joseph and Muskegon routes.
45.185 Tow limitations.
45.187 Weather limitations.
45.191 Pre-departure requirements.
45.193 Towboat power requirements.

Coast Guard, DHS

§ 45.195 Additional equipment requirements for the Muskegon route.

§ 45.197 Operational plan requirements for the Muskegon route.

APPENDIX A TO PART 45—LOAD LINE CERTIFICATE FORM

AUTHORITY: 46 U.S.C. 5104, 5108; Department of Homeland Security Delegation No. 0170.1.

SOURCE: CGD 73–49R, 38 FR 12290, May 10, 1973, unless otherwise noted.

Subpart A—General

§ 45.1 Purpose.

This part prescribes requirements for assignment of freeboards, issuance of loadline certificates, and marking of loadlines for service on the Great Lakes of North America.

[CGD 73–49R, 38 FR 12290, May 10, 1973, as amended by USCG–1998–4442, 63 FR 52190, Sept. 30, 1998]

§ 45.3 Definitions.

As used in this part:

(a) *Length* (L) means 96 percent of the total length on a waterline at 85 percent of the least moulded depth measured from the top of the keel or the length from the foreside of the stem to the axis of the rudder stock on that waterline, if that is greater. In ships designed with a rake of keel the waterline on which this length is measured must be parallel to the designed waterline.

(b) *Perpendiculars* means the forward and after perpendiculars at the forward and after ends of the length (L). The forward perpendicular coincides with the foreside of the stem on the waterline on which the length is measured.

(c) *Amidships* means the middle of the length (L).

(d) *Breadth* unless expressly provided otherwise, means the maximum breadth of the ship, measured amidships to the moulded line of the frame in a ship with a metal shell and to the outer surface of the hull in a ship with a shell of any other material.

(e) *Moulded Depth* means the vertical distance measured amidships from the top of the keel to the top of the freeboard deck beam at side except that—

(1) In vessels of other than metal construction, the distance is measured from the lower edge of the keel rabbet;

(2) Where the form at the lower part of the midship section is of a hollow character, or where thick garboards are fitted, the distance is measured from the point where the line of the flat of the bottom continued inwards cuts the side of the keel;

(3) In ships having rounded gunwales, this distance is measured to the point of intersection of the moulded lines of the deck and side, the lines extending as though the gunwale were of angular design; and

(4) Where the freeboard deck is stepped and the raised part of the deck extends over the point at which the moulded depth is to be determined, the distance is measured to a line of reference extending from the lower part of the deck along a line parallel with the raised part.

(f) *Depth for Freeboard* (D) means—

(1) Moulded depth amidships plus the thickness of the stringer plate with no allowance for sheathing; and

(2) In a vessel having a rounded gunwale with a radius greater than 4 percent of the breadth (B) or having topsides of unusual form, the depth for freeboard (D) of a vessel having a midship section with vertical topsides and with the same round of beam and area of topside section equal to that provided by the actual midship section.

(g) *Freeboard* means the distance measured vertically downwards amidships from the upper edge of the deck line to the upper edge of the related load line.

(h) *Freeboard Deck* means, normally, the uppermost complete deck exposed to weather and sea that has permanent means of closing all openings in the weather part thereof and below which all openings in the sides of the ship are fitted with permanent means of watertight closings except that—

(1) In a ship having a discontinuous freeboard deck, the lowest line of the exposed deck and the continuation of that line parallel to the upper part of the deck is the freeboard deck.

(2) At the option of the owner and subject to the approval of the Commandant a lower deck may be designated as the freeboard deck, if it is a

complete and permanent deck continuous in a fore and aft direction at least between the machinery space and peak bulkheads and continuous athwartships;

(3) When this lower deck is stepped the lowest line of the deck and the continuation of that line parallel to the upper part of the deck is taken as the freeboard deck.

(i) *Superstructure* means a deck structure on the freeboard deck, extending from side to side of the ship or with the side plating not being inboard of the shell plating more than 4 percent of the breadth (B). A raised quarterdeck is a superstructure.

(j) *Enclosed superstructure* means a superstructure with enclosing bulkheads.

(k) *Height* of a superstructure means the least vertical height measured at side from the top of the superstructure deck beams to the top of the freeboard deck beams.

(l) *Length of a superstructure* (S) means the mean length of the part of the superstructure which extends to the sides of the vessel and lies within the length (L).

(m) *Flush deck ship* means a ship that has no superstructure on the freeboard deck.

(n) *Weathertight* means that in any sea conditions water will not penetrate into the ship.

(o) *Watertight* means designed to withstand a static head of water.

(p) *Exposed positions* means exposed to weather and sea.

(q) *Intact bulkhead* with respect to superstructure means a bulkhead with no openings.

(r) *Steel* means steel and materials with which structures can be made equivalent to steel with respect to such parameters as yield strength, total deflection, flexural life, or resistance to galvanic or stress corrosion.

§ 45.5 Seasonal application of load lines.

For the purposes of the law and regulations prohibiting submergence of load lines (46 U.S.C. 88c; 46 CFR 42.07–10), the fresh water and salt water load lines marked under this part apply during the following seasons:

(a) Summer load lines apply April 16 through April 30 and September 16 through September 30.

(b) Except for hopper dredges operating at working freeboards in accordance with subpart C of part 44 of this chapter, the Assigning Authority may not allow for lesser freeboards.

(c) Intermediate load lines apply October 1 through October 31 and April 1 through April 15.

(d) Winter load lines apply November 1 through March 31.

§ 45.9 Seasonal application of load lines for vessels not marked under this part.

(a) For the purposes of the law and regulations prohibiting submergence of load lines (46 U.S.C. 88c; 46 CFR 42.07–10) the marks assigned to vessels holding international load line certificates apply during the following seasons:

(1) Vessels assigned freeboards as new vessels under the International Load Line Convention, 1966—

(i) Winter—November 1 through March 31.

(ii) Summer—April 1 through April 30 and October 1 through October 31.

(iii) Tropical—May 1 through September 30;

(2) Vessels assigned freeboards as existing vessels under the International Load Line Convention, 1966—

(i) Winter—November 1 through March 31;

(ii) Summer—April 1 through April 30 and October 1 through October 31;

(iii) Tropical—September 16 through September 30;

(iv) Tropical Fresh—May 1 through September 15.

(b) Except for hopper dredges operating at working freeboards in accordance with subpart C of part 44 of this chapter, the Assigning Authority may not allow for lesser freeboards.

[CGD 73–49R, 38 FR 12290, May 10, 1973, as amended by CGD 76–080, 54 FR 36977, Sept. 6, 1989]

§ 45.11 Issue of load line certificate.

(a) A vessel 79 feet in length and more, and 150 gross tons or over, the keel of which is laid or which has reached a similar stage of construction after April 14, 1973, must meet the requirements of this part.

(b) Except as prescribed in paragraph (a) of this section, any vessel that meets the requirements in subparts C and D of this part and the survey requirements in §§ 42.09–15 through 42.09–50 of this subchapter is entitled to assignment of freeboards and issue of a load line certificate under this part by the Commandant or his authorized representative.

(c) A vessel, the keel of which was laid or was at a similar stage of construction before April 14, 1973, that meets the requirements of this part that were in effect before April 14, 1973, and the survey requirements in §§ 42.09–15 through 42.09–50 of this subchapter is entitled to the assignment of freeboards calculated under the provisions of this part in effect before April 14, 1973, and to a load line certificate issued under this part by the Commandant or his authorized representative.

§ 45.13 Form of certificate.

The form of a load line certificate issued under this part is specified in appendix A to this part.

§ 45.15 Exemptions.

(a) The Commandant may exempt a ship from any of the requirements in this part if the chairman of the board of Steamship Inspections, Department of Transport, Canada, and the Commandant agree that the sheltered nature or the condition of that voyage make it unreasonable or impracticable to apply requirements of this part.

(b) The Commandant may exempt a vessel that embodies features of a novel kind from any of the requirements of this part if those requirements might seriously impede research into the development of such features and their incorporation in ships. Any such vessel must comply with the safety requirements that, in the opinion of the Commandant, are adequate for the service for which the vessel is intended and will insure the overall safety of the vessel. If the Commandant grants an exemption pursuant to this paragraph he communicates the details of the exemption and the reasons therefor to the chairman of the board of Steamship Inspections.

(c) A vessel that is not normally engaged on voyages to which this part applies but that, in exceptional circumstances, is required to undertake a single such voyage between two specific ports may be exempted by the Commandant from any of the requirements of this part, if the ship complies with safety requirements that, in the opinion of the Commandant are adequate for the voyage that is to be undertaken by the vessel.

(d) Unmanned dry cargo river barges carrying non-hazardous cargoes on certain routes on Lake Michigan may be exempted from load line requirements in accordance with the conditions specified in subpart E of this part.

[CGD 73–49R, 38 FR 12290, May 10, 1973, as amended by CGD 84–058, 50 FR 19533, May 9, 1985; USCG–1998–4623, 67 FR 19690, Apr. 23, 2002]

Subpart B—Load Line Marks

§ 45.31 Deck line.

(a) Each vessel must be marked with a deck line on the outer surface of the shell on each side of the vessel with the upper edge of the line passing through the point where the upper surface of the freeboard deck intersects the outer surface of the shell or if the summer freeboard is correspondingly adjusted under § 45.57, the deck line may be placed above or below the freeboard deck. Figure 1 illustrates the deck line markings.

(b) Each deck line must be at least 12-inches long and 1-inch wide.

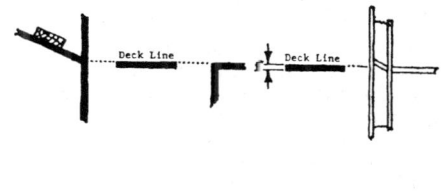

§ 45.33 Diamond.

(a) Each vessel must be marked with the diamond mark described in figure 2 of § 45.35 amidships below the upper edge of the deck line on each side with the center of the loadline mark at a distance below the deck line equal to the summer freeboard assigned under this part.

(b) The width of each line in the loadline mark must be 1 inch.

§ 45.35 Seasonal load lines.

Each vessel must have the summer (S), midsummer (MS), intermediate (I), and winter (W) loadlines for fresh water freeboards calculated under §§ 45.71 through 45.75 marked in accordance with § 45.39.

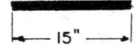
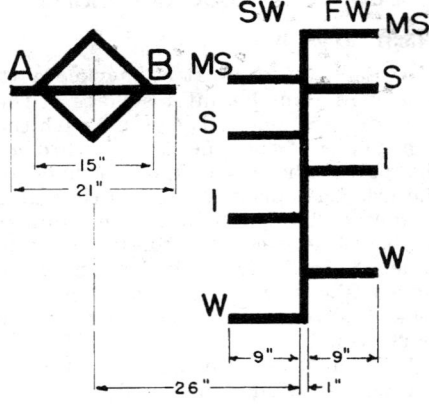

§ 45.37 Salt water load lines.

Each vessel that operates in the salt water of the St. Lawrence River must—

(a) Be marked with the summer (S), midsummer (MS), intermediate (I) and winter (W) load line marks under § 45.77 for salt water; and

(b) Be marked with the letters "FW" above the fresh water marks and the letters "SW" above the salt water marks as described in figure 2.

§ 45.39 Marking.

(a) The diamond, lines, and letters must be painted in white or yellow on a dark ground or in black on a light ground and permanently marked on the sides of the vessel.

(b) The upper edge of the line that passes through the center of the diamond must indicate summer freeboard assigned under § 45.53.

(c) Unless otherwise authorized the seasonal load lines must be horizontal lines extending forward of, and at right angles to, a vertical line marked at a distance 26 inches forward of the vertical centerline of the diamond as described in figure 2.

(d) The salt water load lines must be horizontal lines extending abaft the vertical line required by paragraph (b) of this section as described in figure 2.

(e) The upper edge of each seasonal and salt water load line mark must indicate the minimum freeboard for that mark.

(f) When two freeboards assigned under this part differ by 2 inches or less, the line for the lesser freeboard must be omitted and the line for the greater freeboard must be identified with the seasonal letters for both freeboards.

(g) Seasonal freeboards that are limited by a summer freeboard assigned under § 45.53(c) must not be marked but the identifying letter must be marked adjacent to the summer mark.

(h) The identity of the authority that assigns the freeboard must be indicated alongside the load line diamond above the horizontal line that passes through the center of the diamond with two initials approximately 4½ inches high and 3 inches wide.

Subpart C—Freeboards

§ 45.51 Types of ships.

(a) For the purpose of this subpart, a type A vessel has—

(1) No cargo ports or similar sideshell openings below the freeboard deck;

(2) Only small freeboard deck openings fitted with watertight gasketed hatch covers of steel;

(3) No dimension of a freeboard deck cargo opening greater than 6 feet and the total area not exceeding 18 ft^2; and

(4) No more than two freeboard deck cargo openings to a single cargo space.

(b) For the purposes of this subpart a type B vessel is a vessel that does not meet the requirements in paragraph (a) of this section.

§ 45.53 Summer freeboard.

(a) Except as required in paragraph (c) of this section, the minimum freeboard in summer for a type A vessel is F in the following formula modified by the corrections in this subpart:

F (inches)=$10.2 \times P_1 \times D$

where P_1 is defined in § 45.55 and D is the depth for freeboard in feet.

(b) Except as required in paragraph (c) of this section, the minimum freeboard in summer for a type B vessel is F in the formula modified by the corrections in this subpart:

F (inches)=$12 \times P_1 \times D$

where P_1 is defined by § 45.55 and D is the depth for freeboard in feet.

(c) Seasonal freeboards assigned under §§ 45.71 through 45.75 must be calculated on the basis of the summer freeboard calculated under paragraph (a) or (b) of this section.

(d) If a minimum freeboard is required for a vessel under this part which is greater than that required by paragraph (a) or (b) of this section because of scantling or subdivision requirements, the summer freeboard and the seasonal freeboards assigned under this subpart must be no less than that minimum freeboard, except the midsummer seasonal freeboard may be calculated on the basis of the summer freeboard assigned under this paragraph.

(e) If a greater than the calculated minimum freeboard is requested by the applicant for the load line certificate, that greater freeboard may be assigned as the summer freeboard and—

(1) The intermediate and winter seasonal freeboards assigned must be calculated under paragraph (a) or (b) of this section; and

(2) The midsummer seasonal freeboard must be calculated on the basis of the summer freeboard assigned under this paragraph.

§ 45.55 Freeboard coefficient.

(a) For ships less than 350 feet in length (L), the freeboard coefficient is P_1 in the formula:

$P_1 = P + A[(L/D) - (L/D_s)]$

where P is a factor, which is a function of the length from table 1 and "A" is a coefficient, which is a function of length (L), from table 2; L/D is the ratio of the length (L) to the depth for freeboard (D); L/D_s is the ratio of the length (L) to a standard depth (D_s) from table 3.

D is not to be used as less than that which will give a ration of L to D that is:

(a) More than 15 when L=400 feet or less, or

(b) More than 21 when L=700 feet or more, with the ratio for intermediate lengths being calculated proportionately.

(b) For ships 350 feet or more in length (L), the coefficient "A" is zero and the formula is:

$P_1 = P$

where P is a factor, which is a function of length from table (1).

§ 45.57 Correction: Position of deckline.

(a) Where the depth to the upper edge of the deckline is greater or less than D, the difference between the depths must be added to or deducted from the freeboard.

(b) When the Commandant or the approved assigning authority approves a location for the deckline that is above or below the freeboard deck, the minimum summer freeboard must be corrected by—

(1) Adding the difference between the depth and D if the depth is greater than D; and

(2) Subtracting the difference between the depth and D, if the depth is less than D.

(c) Except for the adjustment allowed in paragraph (b) of this section, no freeboard of less than 2 in. may be assigned.

§ 45.58 Correction: Short superstructure.

The minimum freeboard in summer for a type B vessel that is 79 ft. or more but less than 500 ft. in length and has enclosed superstructures with an effective length of 25 percent or less of the length of the vessel must be increased by—

0.03 (500—L) (0.25—E/L) inches

where:

(L)=length of vessel in feet;

§ 45.59

(E)=effective length of superstructure in feet as defined in § 45.59.

§ 45.59 Definitions for superstructure corrections.

For the purpose of §§ 45.58 through 45.61—

(a) The standard height of a superstructure (H^s) other than a raised quarter deck and the standard height of a trunk (H^s) is determined by the formula:

$H^s=[6.0+(L/300)]$ ft

(b) The length of superstructure (S) is the length of those parts of the superstructure which extends to the sides of the vessel and that lie within the length (L).

(c) The effective length (E) of a trunk is its length in the ratio of its mean breadth to B.

(d) The effective length (E) of an enclosed superstructure of standard height or greater is its length "S".

(e) Where the height of an enclosed superstructure or trunk is less than the standard height (H_s), the effective length (E) is its length reduced in the ratio of its height to H_s.

(f) The effective length (E) of a raised quarter deck of ⅔ H_s or greater that has no openings in the front bulkhead is its length up to a maximum of 0.6L.

(g) The effective length (E) of a raised quarter deck of less than ⅔ H_s or that does not have an intact front bulkhead is its length reduced by the ratio of its height to H_s.

TABLE 12(1)
TABLES OF P VALUES

Length of Ship (feet)	Value of P
80	0.1100
90	0.1136
100	0.1172
110	0.1208
120	0.1244
130	0.1281
140	0.1318
150	0.1355
160	0.1393
170	0.1430
180	0.1468
190	0.1506
200	0.1545
210	0.1583
220	0.1622
230	0.1661
240	0.1700
250	0.1740
260	0.1780

TABLE 12(1)—Continued
TABLES OF P VALUES

Length of Ship (feet)	Value of P
270	0.1820
280	0.1860
290	0.1900
300	0.1941
310	0.1982
320	0.2023
330	0.2065
340	0.2106
350	0.2148
360	0.2190
370	0.2233
380	0.2275
390	0.2318
400	0.2361
410	0.2400
420	0.2437
430	0.2472
440	0.2506
450	0.2537
460	0.2567
470	0.2595
480	0.2621
490	0.2645
500	0.2667
510	0.2688
520	0.2706
530	0.2723
540	0.2738
550	0.2751
560	0.2762
570	0.2772
580	0.2779
590	0.2785
600	0.2788
610	0.2790
620	0.2790
630	0.2789
640	0.2785
650	0.2779
660	0.2772
670	0.2768
680	0.2760
690	0.2751
700	0.2740
710	0.2728
720	0.2715
730	0.2700
740	0.2684
750	0.2667
760	0.2648
770	0.2628
780	0.2607
790	0.2584
800	0.2560
810	0.2532
820	0.2504
830	0.2476
840	0.2448
850	0.2420
860	0.2392
870	0.2364
880	0.2336
890	0.2308
900	0.2280
910	0.2252
920	0.2224
930	0.2196
940	0.2168
950	0.2140
960	0.2112

Table 12(1)—Continued
TABLES OF P VALUES

Length of Ship (feet)	Value of P
970	0.2084
980	0.2056
990	0.2028
1000	0.2000

Table 12(2)
VALUES OF "A" FOR USE IN THE EXPRESSION $P_1 = P + "A" (L/D - L/D_s)$

Length of Ship (feet)	Value of "A"
80	0.00864
90	0.00806
100	0.00750
110	0.00696
120	0.00644
130	0.00594
140	0.00546
150	0.00500
160	0.00456
170	0.00414
180	0.00374
190	0.00336
200	0.00300
210	0.00266
220	0.00234
230	0.00204
240	0.00176
250	0.00150
260	0.00126
270	0.00104
280	0.00084
290	0.00066
300	0.00050
310	0.00036
320	0.00024
330	0.00014
340	0.00006
350	0.00000

Table 12(3)
VALUES OF L/DS

Length of Ship (feet)	Value of L/D_s
80	6.50000
90	6.76563
100	7.03125
110	7.29688
120	7.56250
130	7.82813
140	8.09375
150	8.35938
160	8.62500
170	8.89063
180	9.19625
190	9.42188
200	9.68750
210	9.95313
220	10.21875
230	10.48438
240	10.75000
250	11.01563
260	11.28125
270	11.54688
280	11.81250
290	12.07813
300	12.34375

Table 12(3)—Continued
VALUES OF L/DS

Length of Ship (feet)	Value of L/D_s
310	12.60938
320	12.87500
330	13.14063
340	13.40625
350	13.67188
360	13.93750
370	14.20313
380	14.46875
390	14.73438
400	15.00000

(h) Superstructures which are not enclosed have no effective length.

(i) When a lower deck is designated as the freeboard deck, that part of the hull which extends above the freeboard deck is treated as a superstructure so far as concerns the application of the conditions of assignment and the calculation of freeboard.

(j) A bridge or poop is enclosed only when access is provided whereby the crew may reach accommodations, machinery, or other working spaces inside the superstructure by alternative means that are available at all times when bulkhead openings are closed.

§ 45.61 Correction for superstructures and trunks.

(a) Where the effective length E of superstructures and trunks that meet the requirements of subpart D of this part is $1.0L$, the minimum summer freeboard may be corrected by subtracting $\frac{1}{2}H_s$.

(b) Where the effective length of superstructures and trunks is less than $1.0L$ the minimum summer freeboard may be corrected by subtracting a percentage of one-half of the standard superstructure height (H_s) determined by the formula:

Percentage = $(E/2L)(1 + E/L) \times 100$

(c) To be eligible for the correction a trunk must—

(1) Be at least as strong and as stiff as a superstructure;

(2) Have no opening in the freeboard deck in way of the trunk, except small access openings;

(3) Have hatchway coamings and covers that meet §§ 45.143 through 45.147;

(4) Provide a permanent working platform fore and aft with guardrails;

§ 45.63

(5) Provide fore and aft access between detached trunks and superstructures by permanent gangways;
(6) Be at least 60 percent of the breadth of the ship in way of the trunk; and
(7) Be at least 0.6 L in length, if no superstructure, is provided.

§ 45.63 Correction for sheer.

(a) The minimum summer freeboard must be increased by the deficiency, or may be decreased by the excess as limited by § 45.65, of sheer calculated from table 4, multiplied by:

$$0.75 - (S/2L)$$

where S is the total length of enclosed superstructures. Trunks are not included.

§ 45.65 Excess sheer limitations.

The decrease in freeboard allowed in § 45.63 is limited as follows:

SHEER CALCULATION—TABLE 4

Station	Actual ordinate	S. M.	Product
After Half:			
AP		1	
L/6-AP		3	
L/3-AP		3	
Midship		1	
Sum of Aft Products			
After Standard Sheer .2665L+26.65[1]			
Difference: Sum-STD			+Excess/−Deficiency
AFT Sheer: Diff÷8			Excess/Deficiency
Fwd. Half:			
FP		1	
L/6-FP		3	
L/3-FP		3	
Midships		1	
Sum of Fwd Products			
Fwd Standard Sheer .5330L+53.30[1]			
Difference: Sum-STD			+Excess/−Deficiency
FWD Sheer: Diff÷8			Excess/Deficiency

[1] L in Standard Sheer=L or 500 whichever is less.

Sheer Summation

Aft Sheer±	
Fwd Sheer±	
Net Sheer±	
Mean: Net÷2	Excess/Deficiency

(a) In vessels having no enclosed superstructure from 0.1 L abaft amidships to 0.1 L forward of amidships, no decrease is allowed.

(b) In vessels having enclosed superstructures amidships less than 0.1 L before and abaft amidships, the decrease must be reduced by linear interpolation.

(c) If excess sheer exists in the forward half, and the after half is at least 75 percent of standard sheer, the full decrease is allowed. If the after sheer is between 50 percent and 75 percent of standard sheer an intermediate decrease, determined by linear interpolation, is allowed for the excess sheer forward. If the after sheer is 50 percent of standard or less, no decrease is allowed for the excess sheer forward.

(d) Where an enclosed poop or forecastle is of standard height with greater sheer than that of the freeboard deck, or is greater than standard height, an addition to the sheer of the freeboard deck may be made using the following formula:

$$S = vL'/3L$$

Where

s=sheer credit, to be deducted from the deficiency or added to the excess of sheer.

v=difference between actual and standard height of superstructure at the end ordinate.

L'=mean enclosed length of poop or forecastle up to a maximum length of 0.5 L.

Coast Guard, DHS § 45.77

The superstructure deck must not be less than standard height above this curve at any point. This curve must be used in determining the sheer profile for forward and after halves of the vessel.

(e) The maximum decreased for excess sheer must be no more than 1½ inches per 100 feet of length.

(f) Where the deck of an enclosed superstructure has at least the same sheer as the exposed freeboard deck, the sheer of the enclosed portion of the freeboard deck cannot be taken into account.

§ 45.67 Sheer measurement.

(a) The sheer is measured from the freeboard deck at side to a line of reference drawn parallel to the keel through the sheer line at amidships;

(b) In ships designed with a rake of keel or designed to trim by the stern, the sheer must be measured in reference to a line drawn through the sheer line at amidships parallel to the design load waterline.

(c) In flush deck ships and in ships with detached superstructures, the sheer must be measured at the freeboard deck.

(d) In ships with a step or break in the topsides, the sheer must be measured from the equivalent depth amidships.

(e) In vessels with a superstructure of standard height that extends over the whole length of the freeboard deck, the sheer must be measured on the superstructure deck. Where the height of superstructure exceeds the standard, the least difference (Z) between the actual and standard heights must be added to each end ordinate. Similarly, the intermediate ordinates at distance of ⅙ L and ⅓ L from each perpendicular must be increased by 0.444 Z and 0.111 Z respectively.

§ 45.69 Correction for bow height.

(a) The minimum summer freeboard of all manned vessels must be increased by the same amount in inches as any deficiency which may be shown by the following formulas:

(1) For vessels having a length of not less than 79 feet and not greater than 550 feet,

0.593 L (1.0−L/1640) inches—actual bow height

(2) For vessels having a length greater than 550 feet,

(341.6−0.227 L) inches—actual bow height

(b) Where the bow height is obtained by sheer, the sheer must extend for at least 15 percent of the length of the vessel measured from the forward perpendicular.

(c) Where the bow height is obtained by a superstructure, the superstructure must be enclosed and extend from the stem to a point at least 0.06 L abaft the forward perpendicular.

(d) Vessels which, to suit exceptional operational requirements, cannot meet the requirements of paragraph (c) of this section may be given special consideration by the Commandant.

(e) The bow height is defined as the vertical distance at the forward perpendicular between the waterline corresponding to the assigned summer freeboard at the designed trim and the top of the exposed deck at side.

§ 45.71 Midsummer freeboard.

The minimum midsummer freeboard (fms) in inches is obtained by the formula:

$fms = f(s) - 0.3 Ts$

where:

$f(s)$=summer freeboard in inches
Ts=distance in feet between top of keel and the summer load line.

§ 45.73 Winter freeboard.

The minimum winter freeboard (fw) in inches is obtained by the formula:

$fw = f(s) + T s (200)/L$

where:

L=length L in feet but not less than 400 feet.

§ 45.75 Intermediate freeboard.

The minimum intermediate freeboard (f_I) in inches is obtained by the formula:

$f_I = f(s) + T s(100)/L$

where:

L=length L in feet but not less than 400 feet.

§ 45.77 Salt water freeboard.

(a) The salt water addition in inches to freeboard applicable to each fresh water mark is obtained by the formula:

Addition=$\Delta/41T$

§ 45.101

where:

Δ=displacement in fresh water, in tons of 2,240 pounds, at the summer load waterline.

T=tons per inch immersion, of 2,240 pounds, in fresh water at the summer load waterline.

(b) When the displacement at the summer load waterline cannot be certified, the addition in inches to the minimum freeboard in fresh water may be obtained by multiplying 0.25 by the summer draught in feet measured from the top of the keel to the center of the load line diamond.

Subpart D—Conditions of Assignment

§ 45.101 Purpose.

This subpart prescribes conditions that a vessel must meet to be eligible for assignment of a loadline under this part.

§ 45.103 Structural stress and stability.

(a) The nature and stowage of the cargo, ballast, and other variable weights must be such as to make the vessel stable and avoid unacceptable structural stress.

(b) The vessel must meet all applicable stability and subdivision requirements of this chapter.

§ 45.105 Information supplied to the master.

Unless otherwise authorized by the Commandant, the vessel must have onboard, in a form approved by the Commandant, sufficient information.

(a) To enable the master to load and ballast the vessel in a manner that avoids unacceptable stresses in the vessel's structure; and

(b) To guide the master as to the stability of the ship under varying conditions of service.

§ 45.107 Strength of hull.

The general structural strength of the hull must be sufficient for the draught corresponding to the freeboard assigned and must be approved by the Commandant. Ships built and maintained in conformity with the requirements of a classification society may be recognized by the Commandant as possessing adequate strength.

§ 45.109 Strength of superstructures and deckhouses.

Each superstructure or deckhouse used for accommodations of the crew must be approved by the Commandant or the approved assigning authority with regard to general strength and weathertightness. The Commandant may use the requirements of the assigning authority as a guide.

§ 45.111 Strength of bulkheads at ends of superstructures.

Bulkheads at ends of enclosed superstructures must have sufficient strength to withstand impact of boarding seas.

§ 45.113 Access openings in bulkheads at ends of enclosed superstructures.

(a) Access openings in bulkheads at ends of enclosed superstructures must have doors of steel or material as strong as steel that are permanently attached to the bulkhead and framed, stiffened, and fitted so that the bulkhead and door are as strong as the bulkhead and weather tight when closed.

(b) The means for securing the doors weathertight must be permanently attached to the doors or bulkheads and arranged so that the doors can be secured weathertight from both sides of the bulkhead.

(c) Access openings in bulkheads at ends of enclosed superstructures must have sills that are at least 12 inches above the deck.

§ 45.115 Bulwarks and guardrails.

(a) The exposed parts of freeboard and superstructures decks and deckhouses on the freeboard deck must have guardrails or bulwarks that are at least 36 inches high above the deck.

(b) Guardrails must have at least three courses with no more than a 9-inch opening below the lowest course and no more than 15 inches between other courses. If the sheer strake projection is at least 8 inches above the deck, a guardrail may have two courses with no more than 15 inches between courses.

(c) In way of trunks at least half the protection required by paragraph (a) of this section must be in the form of open rails.

§ 45.117 Freeing port area: General.

(a) Where bulwarks on the weather portins of freeboard or superstructure decks form wells, the bulwarks must have the area prescribed in this section and §§ 45.119 and 45.121 for rapidly freeing and draining the decks of water.

(b) Except as required in §§ 45.119 and 45.121 the minimum freeing port area in square feet on each side of the ship for each well on the freeboard deck and on the raised quarterdeck must be at least as great as A in the following formulas:

(1) Where the length of bulwark (l) in the well is 66 feet or less, $A = 7.6 + 0.115\,(l)$

(2) Where (l) exceeds 66 feet, $A = 0.23\,(l)$ but (l) need in no case be taken as greater than 0.7L.

(c) In ships having erections on deck that are open at either or both ends, provision for freeing the space within such erections must be approved by the Commandant or the assigning authority.

(d) The lower edges of the freeing ports must be as near the deck as practicable. Two-thirds of the freeing port area required must be provided in the half of the well nearest the lowest point of the sheer curve.

(e) All freeing port openings in the bulwarks must be protected by rails or bars spaced approximately 9 inches. If shutters are fitted to freeing ports, ample clearance must be provided to prevent jamming. Hinges must have pins or bearings of noncorrodible material. If shutters are fitted with securing appliances, these appliances must be of approved construction.

(f) The minimum freeing port area for each well on superstructure decks must be one-half of the area required by paragraph (b) of this section.

§ 45.119 Freeing port area: Changes from standard sheer.

The freeing port area required by § 45.117(b) must be multiplied by the factor in the following table 5 if the sheer differs from the standard sheer defined in § 45.63. table 4.

TABLE 5
Freeing port area: Sheer correction.

Ratio of sums of actual sheer ord./std. sheer ord. Greater than:	Multiplier for area required by § 45.117(b)
1.0	1.0
1.0	1.00
0.9	1.05
0.8	1.10
0.7	1.15
0.6	1.20
0.5	1.25
0.4	1.30
0.3	1.35
0.2	1.40
0.1	1.45
No sheer	1.50

§ 45.121 Freeing port area: Changes for trunks and side coamings.

If a vessel has a trunk and does not meet the requirements of § 45.61 or has continuous or substantially continuous hatchway side coamings between detached superstructures, the minimum area of the freeing port openings must be obtained from the following table:

Breadth of hatchway or trunk in relation to the breadth of ship	Area of freeing ports in relation to the total area of the bulwarks (percent)
40 percent or less	20
75 percent or more	10

The area of freeing ports at intermediate breadths must be obtained by linear interpolation.

§ 45.123 Freeing port area: Changes for bulwark height.

(a) For the purposes of freeing port area only, bulwark height is considered standard at 24 in for ships 240 ft in length and less; and 48 in for ships 480 ft in length or greater. The standard bulwark height for ships of intermediate length is obtained by direct interpolation.

(b) If the bulwark is more than standard height, the area required by § 45.117 must be increased by 0.04 square feet per foot (ft^2/ft) of length of well for each foot difference in height.

(c) For ships greater than 480 ft in length that have an average bulwark height less than 3 ft, the area required by § 45.117 may be decreased by 0.04 $ft^2/$

§ 45.125

ft of length for each foot difference in height.

§ 45.125 Crew passageways.

The vessel must have means for protection of the crew from boarding seas such as life lines, gangways, and underdeck passages to facilitate passing between their quarters and machinery spaces and other spaces essential to the operation of the ship.

§ 45.127 Position of structures, openings, and fittings.

For the purposes of this part—
(a) *Position 1* means in an exposed position on—
(1) The freeboard deck or a raised quarter deck;
(2) A superstructure deck or a trunk deck and forward of a point ¼ L from the forward perpendicular; or
(3) A trunk deck whose height is less than H_s.
(b) *Position 2* means—
(1) On a superstructure deck aft of a point ¼ L abaft the forward perpendicular; or
(2) On a superstructure and trunk combination, that is H_s or more n height, aft or a point ¼ L abaft the forward perpendicular.

§ 45.129 Hull fittings: General.

Hull fittings must be securely mounted in the hull so as to avoid increases in hull stresses and must be protected from local damage caused by movement of equipment or cargo.

§ 45.131 Ventilators.

(a) Ventilators passing through superstructures other than enclosed superstructures must have coamings of steel or equivalent material at the freeboard deck.
(b) Ventilators in position 1 must have coamings at least 30 in. above the deck and ventilators in position 2 must have coamings at least 24 in. above the deck. The Commandant or the assigning authority may also require coamings in other exposed positions.
(c) Ventilators in position 1 or 2 to spaces below freeboard decks or decks of enclosed superstructures or trunks must have coamings of steel permanently connected to the deck and any ventilator coaming that is more than 36 in. high must be specially supported.
(d) Except as provided in paragraph (e) of this section ventilator openings must have weathertight closing appliances that are permanently attached or, where approved by the Commandant or the assigning authority conveniently stowed near the ventilators to which they are to be fitted.
(e) Ventilators in position 1, the coamings of which extend to more than 12.5 ft above the deck, and in position 2, the coamings of which extend to more than 6 ft above the deck, need not have closing appliances unless specifically required by the Commandant.

§ 45.133 Air pipes.

(a) Where an air pipe to any tank extends above the freeboard or superstructure deck—
(1) The exposed part of the air pipe must be made of steel and of sufficient thickness to avoid breaking from impact of boarding seas.
(2) The air pipe must have a permanently attached means of closing its opening; and
(3) The height from the deck to any point where water may obtain access below deck must be at least 30 in above the freeboard deck, 24 in above raised quarter decks, and 12 in above other superstructure decks.
(b) If the height required in paragraph (a) of this section interferes with working the ship, the Commandant may approve a lower height after considering the closing arrangements.

§ 45.135 Hull openings at or below freeboard deck.

Closures for hull openings at or below the freeboard deck must be as strong as the structure to which they are attached and must be watertight.

§ 45.137 Cargo ports.

(a) Unless otherwise authorized by the Commandant, the lower edge of any opening for cargo, personnel, machinery access, or similar opening in the side of a ship must be above a line that is drawn parallel to the freeboard deck at side and has as its lowest point the upper edge of the uppermost loadline.

(b) The number of cargo ports in the sides of a ship must be—
(1) No more than the minimum necessary for working the ship; and
(2) Approved by the Commandant.

§ 45.139 Side scuttles.

(a) The sill of each side scuttle must be above a line that is drawn parallel to the freeboard deck at side having its lowest point 2.5 percent of the breadth or 20 in above the summer load waterline, whichever is higher.

(b) Except as provided for in paragraph (c) of this section, each side scuttle to a space below the freeboard deck, or to a space within an enclosed superstructure, must have a hinged inside deadlight which is designed so that it can be secured watertight over the side scuttle.

(c) A side scuttle of a superstructure end bulkhead door, companionway door, or deckhouse door may have a portable inside deadlight which is designed so that it can be:
(1) Secured watertight over the side scuttle; and
(2) Stowed inside the superstructure, companionway, or deckhouse when not in use, in a readily accessible location on or adjacent to the door.

[CGD 73–49R, 38 FR 12290, May 10, 1973, as amended by CCGD 80–116, 46 FR 56788, Nov. 19, 1981]

§ 45.141 Manholes and flush scuttles.

Manholes and flush scuttles in position 1 or 2 or within any superstructure other than an enclosed superstructure must have permanently attached covers, unless the cover is secured by closely spaced bolts around its entire perimeter.

§ 45.143 Hull openings above freeboard deck.

Closures for openings above the freeboard deck must be as strong as the structure to which they are attached and must be weathertight.

§ 45.145 Hatchway covers.

(a) Hatchways in position 1 and 2 must have weathertight hatch covers with gaskets and clamping devices.
(b) The maximum ultimate strength of the hatchway cover material must be at least 4.25 times the maximum stress in the structure calculated with the following assumed loads:
(1) For ships 350 ft or more in length, at least 250 lb/ft^2 in position 1 and 200 lb/ft^2 in position 2.
(2) For ships less than 350 ft in length, at least AL in the following formula:
(i) Position 1:

$AL=200+C$

where $C=50(L-79)/271$

(ii) Position 2:

$Al=150+C$

(c) Hatchway covers must be so designed as to limit the deflection to not more than 0.0028 times the span under the loads described in paragraph (b) of this section and the thickness of mild steel plating forming the tops of covers must be at least 1 percent of the spacing of stiffeners or 0.24 in, whichever is greater.

§ 45.147 Hatchway coamings.

(a) Except where the Commandant determines that the safety of the vessel will not be impaired in any sea condition, each hatchway must have a coaming that is at least—
(1) 18 inches in position 1; and
(2) 12 inches in position 2.
(b) Each hatchway coaming required by this section must be made of steel or equivalent material.
(c) The height of these coamings may be reduced or omitted if the Commandant is satisfied that safety of the ship is not thereby impaired in any sea conditions.

§ 45.149 Machinery space openings.

(a) Machinery space openings in position 1 or 2 must be framed and enclosed by steel casings, and where the casings are not protected by other structures that meet the requirements of § 45.109, their strength must be approved by the Commandant or the assigning authority.

(b) Access openings in casings required by paragraph (a) of this section must have doors complying with the requirements of § 45.113. Other openings in such casings shall be fitted with equivalent covers, permanently attached.

§ 45.151

(c) Except as provided in paragraph (d) of this section, coamings of any funnel or machinery space ventilator that must be kept open for the essential operations of the ship must—

(1) In position 1, extend at least 12.5 ft above the deck; and

(2) In position 2, extend at least 6 ft above the deck.

(d) The Commandant may approve a lesser height for protected coamings.

(e) Coamings of any fiddley or skylight over a machinery space opening in the freeboard or superstructure deck or the top of a deckhouse on the freeboard deck, must have covers of steel permanently attached and capable of being secured weathertight.

§ 45.151 Other openings.

Each opening other than hatchways, machinery space openings, manholes, or flush scuttles—

(a) In freeboard decks, must be protected by an enclosed superstructure or by a deckhouse or companionway that is equal in strength and weathertightness to an enclosed superstructure; or

(b) In exposed superstructure decks or in the top of a deckhouse on freeboard decks that gives access to a space below the freeboard deck or a space within an enclosed superstructure, must be protected by a deckhouse or companionway.

§ 45.153 Through-hull piping: General.

(a) All through-hull pipes required by this subpart must be made of steel or material equivalent to the hull in strength and fatigue resistance.

(b) All valves used as shell fittings and all shell fittings on which such valves are mounted must be made of steel, or bronze or other ductile material approved by the Commandant.

§ 45.155 Inlets and discharge piping: Valves.

(a) Except as provided in paragraphs (d) and (e) of this section each pipe that discharges overboard through the hull of the ship must have—

(1) An automatic nonreturn valve with a positive means for closing; or

(2) Two automatic nonreturn valves with the inboard valve accessible for examination in service.

(b) The means for operating a valve described by paragraph (a)(1) of this section must be readily accessible and have indicators that show when the valve is not closed.

(c) If the pipe discharges from a space that is not manned or does not have continuous bilge water monitoring, a valve described in paragraph (a)(1) of this section must be operable above the freeboard deck.

(d) Each pipe that discharges from a space within an enclosed superstructure or deckhouse may have at least one accessible automatic nonreturn valve if the space is regularly visited by the crew.

(e) Through-hull piping systems in machinery spaces may have valves with positive means for closing at the shell if the controls are readily accessible and have indicators showing when the valves are not closed (nonreturn valves are not required).

§ 45.157 Scuppers and gravity drains.

Scuppers and gravity deck drains from spaces above the freeboard deck that penetrate the shell below a line 24″ or .05B above the summer loadline, whichever is greater, must have an automatic nonreturn valve. This valve may be omitted if the piping is of thickness not less than extra heavy pipe.

§ 45.159 Special conditions of assignment for type A vessels.

The lower freeboards allowed for type A vessels allow water on deck for greater percentages of time. Therefore the following additional requirements must be met to qualify for type A freeboards:

(a) Machinery casings must be protected by an enclosed superstructure or deckhouse unless intact bulkheads are used on all sides on the freeboard deck.

(b) Exposed machinery casings may be fitted with weathertight doors providing they lead to a space or passageway as strong as an enclosed superstructure from which a second interior weathertight door is provided for access to the engine room.

(c) Hatchways on the exposed freeboard or forecastle decks must be provided with watertight covers of steel.

(d) Unless a separate fore and aft access is provided below the freeboard deck, a permanent fore and aft gangway must be fitted at the superstructure deck level between poop and all other deckhouses used in the essential operation of the vessel.

(e) Type "A" vessels must be fitted with open rails for at least half the length of the exposed parts of the weather deck. Where superstructures are connected by trunks, open rails must be fitted for the whole length of the exposed parts of the freeboard deck.

Subpart E—Unmanned River Barges on Lake Michigan Routes

SOURCE: USCG–1998–4623, 67 FR 19690, Apr. 23, 2002, unless otherwise noted.

§ 45.171 Purpose.

(a) This subpart establishes a special load line regime under which certain unmanned, river-service, dry-cargo barges may be exempted from the normal Great Lakes load line requirements while operating on certain Lake Michigan routes. Depending upon the route, the barge may only need a limited service domestic voyage load line, or may be conditionally exempted from load line assignment.

(b) Except as provided in this subpart, barges operating on Lake Michigan must have either an international load line assignment issued in accordance with the International Convention on Load Lines, 1966, as amended, or a Great Lakes load line assignment issued in accordance with the requirements of this part.

(c) The requirements of this subpart are summarized in table 45.171:

Table 45.171:
Load Line Requirements for Dry Cargo River Barges Operating on Lake Michigan

	Voyages between Calumet Harbor, IL and:			
	Burns Harbor, IN	Milwaukee, WI	St. Joseph, MI	Muskegon, MI
1) Load line requirement	Conditionally exempted from load line assignment (must meet requirements below)		"Limited service domestic voyage" load line	
2) Where to register/apply	Exempted barges must be registered with the USCG Marine Safety Unit 555A Plainfield Road, Willowbrook, IL 60527 Fax: (630) 986-2120		Apply for load line to ABS Americas 16855 Northchase Dr. Houston, TX 77060	
3) Eligible barges	Dry cargo river barges Built and maintained in accordance with ABS River Rules Length-to-depth ratio less than 22 All weathertight and watertight closures are in proper working condition			
	No age limitation	Not more than 10 years old	No age limitation	
4) Freeboard requirement	All barges: freeboard must be at least 24 inches (610 mm) Open hopper barges: coaming height + freeboard must be at least 54 inches (1,372 mm)			
5) Tow limitations	Barges must be unmanned Not more than 5 nautical miles from shore			
	No limit on number of barges		Not more than 3 barges per tow	
6) Cargo limitations	Dry cargoes only. Liquid cargoes, even in drums or tank containers, are prohibited No hazardous materials. HazMats are defined in 46 CFR part 148 and 49 CFR chapter 1, subchapter C			
7) Weather limitations Voyage may not begin; or if these conditions arise during transit, voyage must be discontinued and tow must proceed to shelter.	"Fair weather" only		Ice conditions: adverse conditions that imperil tow or access to shelter	
			Waves: 4 feet (1.2 m)	
			Sustained winds: 16 kts from NE, E, SE 21 kts from N, NW, W, SW, S	Sustained winds: 16 kts from N, NW, W, SW 21 kts from NE, E, SE, S
8) Pre-departure preps:	Required -- as specified in § 45.191			
9) Towboat requirements			Sufficient to handle tow, but at least--	
(a) Power:	Sufficient to handle tow		1,000 HP	1,500 HP
(b) Communication system:	Recommended -- § 45.195(a)	Recommended -- § 45.195(a)	Recommended -- § 45.195(a)	Required -- § 45.195(a)
(c) Cutting gear:	Recommended -- § 45.195(b)	Recommended -- § 45.195(b)	Recommended -- § 45.195(b)	Required -- § 45.195(b)
(d) Operational plan:	Recommended -- § 45.197	Recommended -- § 45.197	Recommended -- § 45.197	Required -- § 45.197

[USCG–1998–4623, 67 FR 19690, Apr. 23, 2002, as amended at 75 FR 70601, Nov. 18, 2010; 75 FR 78928, Dec. 17, 2010; 76 FR 32326, June 6, 2011]

§ 45.173 Eligible barges.

Only barges meeting the following requirements are eligible for the special load line regime under this subpart:

(a) Unmanned, river service, dry-cargo barges;

(b) Barges that have been designed and built to at least the minimum scantlings of the American Bureau of Shipping River Rules which were in effect at the time of construction;

(c) Barges with a length-to-depth ratio less than 22;

(d) Barges on the Milwaukee route must not be more than 10 years old; and

(e) All weathertight and watertight closures (dogs, gaskets, covers, etc.) must be in proper working condition.

[USCG–1998–4623, 67 FR 19690, Apr. 23, 2002, as amended at 75 FR 70603, Nov. 18, 2010]

§ 45.175 Applicable routes.

This subpart applies to the following routes, including intermediate ports, on Lake Michigan, between Calumet Harbor, IL, and—

(a) Milwaukee, WI (the "Milwaukee route");

(b) Burns Harbor, IN (the "Burns Harbor route");

(c) St. Joseph, MI (the "St. Joseph route"); and

(d) Muskegon, MI (the "Muskegon route").

[USCG–1998–4623, 75 FR 70604, Nov. 18, 2010]

§ 45.177 Freeboard requirements.

(a) All barges must have a minimum freeboard of 24 inches (610 mm).

(b) Additionally, open hopper barges must have a combined freeboard plus cargo box coaming height of at least 54 inches (1,372 mm).

§ 45.179 Cargo limitations.

(a) Only dry cargoes may be carried. Liquid cargoes, even in drums or tank containers, may not be carried.

(b) Hazardous materials, as defined in part 148 of this chapter and 49 CFR chapter 1, subchapter C, may not be carried.

§ 45.181 Load line exemption requirements for the Burns Harbor and Milwaukee routes.

Barges operating on the Burns Harbor and Milwaukee routes may be conditionally exempted from load line assignment provided that the following requirements are met:

(a) *Registration.* Before the barge's first voyage onto Lake Michigan, the owner or operator must register the barge in writing with the Commanding Officer, Marine Safety Unit Chicago, 555A Plainfield Road, Willowbrook, IL, 60527. The registration may be faxed to MSU Chicago in advance at (630) 986–2120, with the original following by mail. The registration may be in any form, but must be signed by the owner or operator. No load line exemption certificate will be returned. However, the registration will be kept on file.

(b) The registration must include the following information:

(1) Barge name and official documentation number;

(2) Owner and operator (points-of-contact, company addresses and telephone numbers);

(3) Service route (Milwaukee and/or Burns Harbor);

(4) Design type (covered/uncovered hopper, deck, etc.);

(5) External dimensions;

(6) Types of cargo; and

(7) Place built and original delivery date.

(c) The registration must include a statement certifying that:

(1) The barge has been designed and built to at least the minimum scantlings of the ABS River Rules which were in effect at the time of construction; and

(2) The owner or operator agrees to maintain the barge in serviceable condition and comply with the applicable provisions of 46 CFR part 45, subpart E.

(d) *Expiration.* Registration is valid only until the earliest of the following events:

(1) The tenth anniversary of the delivery date (for barges on the Milwaukee route),

(2) The barge no longer is fit for this service (due to damage), or

(3) The barge changes ownership or operators (registration is not transferable to new owners or operators; the barge must be re-registered if it is to continue in Lake Michigan service).

(e) *Notification.* The owner or operator of an exempted barge must notify the OCMI of the transfer of ownership or change of operator, withdrawal from Lake Michigan service (due to damage, age, or other circumstances), or other disposition of the barge.

[USCG–1998–4623, 67 FR 19690, Apr. 23, 2002, as amended by USCG–2006–25556, 72 FR 36330, July 2, 2007; 75 FR 70604, Nov. 18, 2010]

§ 45.183 Load line requirements for the St. Joseph and Muskegon routes.

(a) *Load line certificate.* (1) The load line issued under this subpart must be a limited-service, domestic-voyage load line.

(2) Except as provided under paragraph (b)(2)(vi) of this section, the term of the certificate is 5 years.

(3) The load line certificate is valid for the St. Joseph and Muskegon routes, and intermediate ports. However, operators must comply with the route-specific requirements on the certificate.

(4) The freeboard assignment, operational limitations, and towboat requirements of this subpart must appear on the certificate.

(b) *Conditions of assignment.* (1) An initial load line survey under § 42.09–25 of this chapter and subsequent annual surveys under § 42.09–40 of this chapter are required.

(2) At the request of the barge owner, the initial load line survey may be conducted with the barge afloat if the following conditions are met:

(i) The barge is less than 10 years old;

§ 45.185

(ii) The draft during the survey does not exceed 15 inches (380 millimeters);

(iii) The barge is empty and thoroughly cleaned of all debris, excessive rust, scale, mud, and water. All internal structure must be accessible for inspection;

(iv) Gaugings are taken to the extent necessary to verify that the scantlings are in accordance with approved drawings;

(v) The hull plating (bottom and sides) and stiffeners below the light waterline are closely examined internally. If the surveyor determines that sufficient cause exists, the surveyor may require that the barge be drydocked or hauled out and further external examination conducted; and

(vi) The initial load line certificate is to be issued for a term of 5 years or until the barge reaches 10 years of age, whichever occurs first. Once this certificate expires, the barge must be drydocked or hauled out and fully examined internally and externally.

[USCG-1998-4623, 67 FR 19690, Apr. 23, 2002, as amended at 75 FR 70604, Nov. 18, 2010]

§ 45.185 Tow limitations.

(a) Barges must not be manned.

(b) No more than a total of three barges per tow may operate on the Milwaukee, St. Joseph, and Muskegon routes. A mixed tow of load-lined and exempted barges is still limited to three barges on those routes.

(c) Tows must not be more than 5 nautical miles from shore.

[USCG-1998-4623, 67 FR 19690, Apr. 23, 2002, as amended at 75 FR 70604, Nov. 18, 2010]

§ 45.187 Weather limitations.

(a) Tows on the Burns Harbor route must operate during fair weather conditions only.

(b) The weather limits (ice conditions, wave height, and sustained winds) for the Milwaukee, St. Joseph, and Muskegon routes are specified in § 45.171, table 45.171.

(c) If weather conditions are expected to exceed these limits at any time during the voyage, the tow must not leave harbor or, if already underway, must proceed to the nearest appropriate harbor of safe refuge.

[USCG-1998-4623, 76 FR 32327, June 6, 2011]

§ 45.191 Pre-departure requirements.

Before beginning each voyage, the towing vessel master must conduct the following:

(a) *Weather forecast.* Determine the marine weather forecast along the planned route, and contact the dock operator at the destination port to get an update on local weather conditions.

(b) *Inspection.* Inspect each barge of the tow to ensure that they meet the following requirements:

(1) A valid load line certificate, if required, is on board;

(2) The barge is not loaded deeper than permitted;

(3) The deck and side shell plating are free of visible holes, fractures, or serious indentations, as well as damage that would be considered in excess of normal wear;

(4) The cargo box side and end coamings are watertight;

(5) All hatch and manhole dogs are in working condition, and all covers are closed and secured watertight;

(6) All voids are free of excess water; and

(7) Precautions have been taken to prevent shifting of cargo.

(c) *Verifications.* On voyages north of St. Joseph, the towing vessel master must contact a mooring/docking facility in St. Joseph, Holland, Grand Haven, and Muskegon to verify that sufficient space is available to accommodate the tow. The tow cannot venture onto Lake Michigan without confirmed space available.

(d) *Log entries.* Before getting underway, the towing vessel master must note in the logbook that the pre-departure barge inspections, verification of mooring/docking space availability, and weather forecast checks were performed, and record the freeboards of each barge.

[USCG-1998-4623, 67 FR 19690, Apr. 23, 2002, as amended at 75 FR 70604, Nov. 18, 2010; 75 FR 78928, Dec. 17, 2010; 76 FR 32327, June 6, 2011]

§ 45.193 Towboat power requirements.

The towing vessel must meet the following requirements:

(a) *General.* The towing vessel must have adequate horsepower (HP) to handle the tow, but not less than the amount specified for the routes below.

(b) *Milwaukee and St. Joseph routes:* a minimum of 1,000 HP.
(c) *Muskegon route:* a minimum of 1,500 HP.

[USCG–1998–4623, 67 FR 19690, Apr. 23, 2002, as amended at 75 FR 70604, Nov. 18, 2010]

§ 45.195 Additional equipment requirements for the Muskegon route.

Towboats on the Muskegon route must meet these additional equipment requirements:
(a) *Communication equipment.* Two independent voice communication systems in operable condition, such as Very High Frequency (VHF) radio, radiotelephone, or cellular phone. At least two persons aboard the vessel must be capable of using the communication systems.
(b) *Cutting gear.* Equipment that can quickly cut the towline at the towing vessel. The cutting gear must be in operable condition and appropriate for the type of towline being used, such as wire, polypropylene, or nylon. At least two persons aboard the vessel must be capable of using the cutting gear.

§ 45.197 Operational plan requirements for the Muskegon route.

Towing vessels on the Muskegon route must have on board an operational plan that is available for ready reference by the master. The plan must include the following:
(a) The cargo limitations, the general operational requirements, and the special operational requirements of this subpart.
(b) A list of mooring and docking facilities (with phone numbers) in St. Joseph, Holland, Grand Haven, and Muskegon, that can accommodate the tow.
(c) A list of towing firms (with phone numbers) that have the capability to render assistance to the tow, if required.
(d) Guidelines for possible emergency situations, such as barge handling under adverse weather conditions, and other emergency procedures.

[USCG–1998–4623, 67 FR 19690, Apr. 23, 2002, as amended at 75 FR 70604, Nov. 18, 2010]

APPENDIX A TO PART 45—LOAD LINE CERTIFICATE FORM

GREAT LAKES LOAD LINE CERTIFICATE

No. ____

Issued under the authority of the Commandant, U.S. Coast Guard, United States of America, under the provisions of the Act of August 27, 1935, as amended to establish load lines on the Great Lakes of North America and the Load Line regulations in force on _____, 19___, By _____, duly authorized by the Commandant to issue said load line certificate.

Ship _____
Certificate No. _____
Official No _____
Length (LBP) _____
Gross tonnage _____
Port of registry _____

Type of Ship:

TYPE "A"
TYPE "B"
TYPE "B" with increased freeboard

FREEBOARD FROM DECK LINE

Midsummer	MS
Summer	S
Intermediate	I
Winter	W

LOAD LINE

.... above S
Upper edge of line through center of diamond
 below S
 below S

Increase for salt water for all freeboards ____ inches.

The upper edge of the deck line from which these freeboards are measured is ____ inches above or below the top of the _____ deck at side.

This is to certify that this ship has been surveyed and the freeboards and load lines shown above have been found to be correctly marked upon the vessel in manner and location as provided by the load line regulations of the Commandant, U.S. Coast Guard, applicable to the Great Lakes.

This certificate[1] remains in force until _____. Issued at _____ on the _____ day of _____, 19___.

(Here follows the signature, seal, if any, and the name of the authority issuing the certificate.)

NOTES

(1) In accordance with the Great Lakes Load Line Regulations the diamond and

---

[1] Upon the expiration of the certificate, renewal must be obtained as provided by the Great Lakes Load Line Regulations and the certificate so endorsed.

lines must be permanently marked. The "MS" loadline shall be assigned only to those particular vessels that qualify under the regulations.

(2) The "SW" marks need only be assigned to Great Lakes vessels loading in salt water of the St. Lawrence River west of a straight line from Cap de Rosiers to West Point Anticosti Island, and west of a line along longitude 63 degrees west from Anticosti Island to the north shore of the St. Lawrence River. In such cases these limits shall be indicated on the certificate.

(3) The load line assignment given by this certificate necessarily assumes that the nature and stowage of cargo, ballast, etc., are such as to secure sufficient stability for the vessel. Accordingly, it is the owner's responsibility to furnish the Master of the vessel with stability information and instructions when this is necessary to maintenance of sufficient stability.

(On the reverse side of the load line certificate, or on a separate sheet, attached and forming part of the certificate, provision is to be made for annual inspection and renewal endorsements.)

PART 46—SUBDIVISION LOAD LINES FOR PASSENGER VESSELS

Subpart 46.01—Purpose

Sec.
46.01-1 Purpose.
46.01-15 Application of regulations.
46.01-20 Penalties for violations.

Subpart 46.05—Definitions Used in This Part

46.05-1 Passenger vessel.
46.05-10 Foreign voyage.
46.05-15 Coastwise voyages.
46.05-20 Great Lakes voyage.
46.05-25 New passenger vessel.
46.05-30 Existing passenger vessel.

Subpart 46.10—Administration

46.10-1 Relaxation from regulations.
46.10-5 Load line requirements for subdivision.
46.10-10 Marks to indicate subdivision load lines.
46.10-15 Survey for the establishment and renewal of subdivision load line marks.
46.10-20 Application for the assignment and renewal of subdivision load lines.
46.10-25 Equivalents.
46.10-30 Subdivision load line certificates.
46.10-35 Validity of subdivision load line certificates.
46.10-40 Nonsubmergence subdivision load line (Great Lakes).
46.10-45 Nonsubmergence subdivision load lines in salt water.
46.10-50 Drills and inspections.
46.10-55 Logbook entries.
46.10-60 Control.
46.10-65 Construction.
46.10-70 Plans and inspections of new and converted vessels.

Subpart 46.15—Subdivision Load Lines for Passenger Vessels Engaged in Foreign, Coastwise, and Great Lakes Voyages

46.15-1 Procedure for determination of subdivision load line.
46.15-5 Engineering requirements.
46.15-10 Subdivision load lines.

AUTHORITY: 46 U.S.C. 3306; 46 U.S.C. 5101–5116; E.O. 12234, 3 CFR, 1980 Comp., p. 277; Department of Homeland Security Delegation No. 0170.1.

SOURCE: CGFR 65–50, 30 FR 16769, Dec. 30, 1965, unless otherwise noted.

Subpart 46.01—Purpose

§ 46.01-1 Purpose.

(a) The purpose of the regulations in this part is to set forth uniform minimum requirements applicable to passenger vessels required to have subdivision load lines. These requirements deal with the following:

(1) Load line requirements applicable before a passenger vessel will be marked with and certificated as to subdivision load lines.

(2) Assigning, marking, and recording of subdivision load lines.

(3) Administration of subdivision load lines.

(4) Application of requirements to passenger vessels.

§ 46.01-15 Application of regulations.

(a) The regulations in this part establish subdivision load lines required on passenger vessels engaged in foreign voyages, as well as on passenger vessels of 150 gross tons or over engaged in coastwise or Great Lakes voyages.

(b) When engaged in voyages subject to this part, no passenger vessel required to be marked with subdivision load lines shall depart from or arrive at any port or place under the jurisdiction of the United States, nor shall such United States vessel operate on the high seas nor the Great Lakes, unless such vessel has been marked with subdivision load lines in accordance with the regulations in this part, has on board a valid certificate certifying to the correctness of the location of such subdivision load line marks, and is otherwise in compliance with the applicable requirements of law and regulations in this part.

(c) No passenger vessel of the United States of 150 gross tons or over and subject to 46 U.S.C. 5101–5116, shall engage in coastwise voyages or voyages on the Great Lakes unless such vessel has been marked with subdivision load lines in accordance with the regulations in this part and has on board a valid certificate certifying to the correctness of the location of such subdivision load line marks.

(d) No foreign passenger vessel belonging to a country that has ratified or acceded to the applicable International Convention for Safety of Life at Sea shall arrive or depart from any port or place under the jurisdiction of the United States, and no foreign passenger vessel subject to 46 U.S.C. 5101–5116, shall arrive or depart from any port or place under the jurisdiction of the United States, including ports on the Great Lakes, unless that vessel has been marked with subdivision load lines in accordance with the regulations in this part and has on board a valid certificate certifying to the correctness of the location of such subdivision load line marks.

(e) Subdivision load lines shall be marked on both sides of passenger vessels where determined and in a manner described in subpart 46.15 as applicable to the vessel's service. The subdivision load line certificates shall be in accordance with §§ 46.10–30 and 46.10–35.

[CGFR 65–50, 30 FR 16769, Dec. 30, 1965 as amended by CGD 80–120, 47 FR 5723, Feb. 8, 1982; CGD 97–057, 62 FR 51044, Sept. 30, 1997; USCG–1998–4442, 63 FR 52190, Sept. 30, 1998]

§ 46.01–20 Penalties for violations.

(a) Penalties for violations of the regulations in this part by passenger vessels of the United States engaged in foreign voyages shall be in accordance with those laws which require the inspection and certification of the vessel. In addition, for passenger vessels subject to 46 U.S.C. 5101–5116, which engage in voyages described in § 42.03–5, § 42.03–10, or § 45.01–1, the penalties for violations of the regulations in this part shall be those set forth in the load line act applicable to the vessel.

(b) For a further description of the actions which may be taken see § 42.07–50, of this subchapter. The procedures governing the assessment, collection, remission and mitigation of any monetary penalty imposed for a violation of a law or the regulations prescribed thereunder in this part, as well as the appeal procedures followed, are in subpart 2.50 of part 2 of subchapter A (Procedures Applicable to the Public) of this chapter.

[CGFR 65–50, 30 FR 16769, Dec. 30, 1965, as amended by CGFR 68–60, 33 FR 10077, July 12, 1968; CGD 80–120, 47 FR 5723, Feb. 8, 1982; CGD 97–057, 62 FR 51044, Sept. 30, 1997]

Subpart 46.05—Definitions Used in This Part

§ 46.05–1 Passenger vessel.

(a) For the purpose of the regulations in this part, a vessel is a passenger vessel if:

(1) Engaged on an international voyage by sea, it carries or is authorized to carry more than 12 passengers; or,

(2) Engaged on a coastwise voyage by sea or a voyage on the Great Lakes, it carries or is authorized to carry more than 16 persons in addition to the crew.

§ 46.05–10 Foreign voyage.

(a) A foreign voyage for the purpose of marking passenger vessels with subdivision load lines is a voyage by sea between a port under the jurisdiction of the United States and a port of a foreign country, its colonies, territories, or protectorates, or conversely (a voyage exclusively on the Great Lakes excepted).

§ 46.05–15 Coastwise voyages.

(a) A coastwise voyage by sea, for the purpose of marking passenger vessels with subdivision load lines, is a voyage in which a vessel in the usual course of her employment proceeds from one port or place in the United States to another port or place in the United States or from a port or place in a possession to another port or place in the same possession, and passes outside the line dividing inland waters from the high seas (a voyage exclusively on the

Great Lakes excepted), as well as a voyage in which a vessel proceeds from a port or place in the United States or her possessions and passes outside the line dividing inland waters from the high seas and navigates on the high seas, and then returns to the same port or place.

§ 46.05-20 Great Lakes voyage.

A Great Lakes voyage is any voyage from a United States port or place on the Great Lakes to another United States port or place on the Great Lakes or to a Canadian port or place on the Great Lakes, or conversely.

§ 46.05-25 New passenger vessel.

A new passenger vessel is a vessel whose keel was laid or was a vessel converted into a passenger vessel on or after May 26, 1965.

[CGFR 65–50, 30 FR 16769, Dec. 30, 1965, as amended by CGFR 68–60, 33 FR 10077, July 12, 1968]

§ 46.05-30 Existing passenger vessel.

An existing passenger vessel in respect to its voyage is any passenger vessel that is not a new passenger vessel as defined in § 46.05–25.

Subpart 46.10—Administration

§ 46.10-1 Relaxation from regulations.

(a) New passenger vessels making foreign voyages by sea shall comply with the requirements in this part. An existing passenger vessel engaged in foreign voyages by sea may be permitted relaxation from the requirements of this part if, in the opinion of the Commandant, U.S. Coast Guard, such requirements are unreasonable or impracticable.

(b) A new passenger vessel making coastwise voyages by sea or making Great Lakes voyages shall comply with the requirements in this part. An existing passenger vessel making coastwise voyages by sea or Great Lakes voyages may be permitted relaxation from the requirements of this part if, in the opinion of the Commandant, U.S. Coast Guard, such requirements are unreasonable or impracticable.

§ 46.10-5 Load line requirements for subdivision.

(a) The load line requirements of parts 42, 44, 45 of this subchapter as applicable to the passenger vessel and her service, shall be complied with before a passenger vessel will be marked with and certificated as to subdivision load lines.

[CGFR 65–50, 30 FR 16769, Dec. 30, 1965, as amended by CGFR 68–60, 33 FR 10077, July 12, 1968]

§ 46.10-10 Marks to indicate subdivision load lines.

(a) Marks to indicate the maximum mean draft to which a passenger vessel may be lawfully submerged shall be permanently marked on each side of the passenger vessel in the form, manner, and location provided in this part.

(b) The Commandant, U.S. Coast Guard, will determine the position of the subdivision load lines by the application of the requirements contained in this part and parts 170 and 171 of this chapter. The correct marking of subdivision load lines will be certified by the American Bureau of Shipping or a classification society approved by the Commandant for that purpose.

(c) Certificates certifying to the correctness of subdivision load line marks shall not be furnished until it is determined that the marks have been correctly placed upon the passenger vessel.

(d) In the case of passenger vessels that are required by the International Convention for Safety of Life at Sea to have on board a safety certificate, the certification of subdivision, load line marks shall be made by letter to the cognizant Officer in Charge, Marine Inspection, U.S. Coast Guard.

[CGFR 65–50, 30 FR 16769, Dec. 30, 1965, as amended by CGFR 68–60, 33 FR 10077, July 12, 1968; CGD 79–023, 48 FR 51007, Nov. 4, 1983; CGD 88–070, 53 FR 34534, Sept. 7, 1988; USCG–2009–0702, 74 FR 49228, Sept. 25, 2009]

§ 46.10-15 Survey for the establishment and renewal of subdivision load line marks.

(a) Every passenger vessel to be marked with and certificated for subdivision load lines must comply with the requirements as set forth in subchapter H (Passenger Vessels) of this chapter for ocean, coastwise, and Great Lakes service as applicable to the particular vessel and the service in which she is to be employed.

(b) Every passenger vessel marked with a subdivision load line shall be subjected to the surveys specified in this paragraph. The details of the surveys or inspections indicated in paragraphs (b)(1) through (3) of this section shall be as set forth in the applicable sections of part 71 of subchapter H (Passenger Vessels) of this chapter.

(1) A survey before the vessel is put in service.

(2) A periodical survey once every 12 months.

(3) Additional surveys as occasion arises.

(4) Surveys required by part 42, part 44, or part 45 of this subchapter.

[CGFR 65–50, 30 FR 16769, Dec. 30, 1965, as amended by CGFR 68–60, 33 FR 10077, July 12, 1968]

§ 46.10–20 Application for the assignment and renewal of subdivision load lines.

(a) Application for assignment and renewal of subdivision load lines and certification thereof shall be made in writing to the Commandant (CG–ENG), Attn: Office of Design and Engineering Systems, U.S. Coast Guard Stop 7509, 2703 Martin Luther King Jr. Avenue SE., Washington, DC 20593–7509.

[CGFR 65–50, 30 FR 16769, Dec. 30, 1965, as amended by CGFR 68–60, 33 FR 10077, July 12, 1968; CGD 88–070, 53 FR 34534, Sept. 7, 1988; USCG 2013–0671, 78 FR 60147, Sept. 30, 2013]

§ 46.10–25 Equivalents.

(a) Where in the regulations in this part it is provided that a particular fitting, appliance, apparatus, or type thereof, shall be fitted or carried in a vessel engaged on foreign voyages by sea or that any particular arrangement shall be adopted, there may be substituted any other fitting or appliance or type thereof or any other arrangement provided that the Commandant, U.S. Coast Guard, shall have been satisfied by suitable trials that the fitting, appliance, or apparatus, or type thereof, or that the arrangement substituted is at least as effective as that specified in this part.

(b) Where, in the application of the regulations in this part to passenger vessels engaged in coastwise voyages by sea and on Great Lakes voyages, it is desired to substitute other construction, arrangement, fitting, or appliance, or type thereof, such substitution may be made if approved by the Commandant, U.S. Coast Guard, provided the degree of safety provided by this part is obtained.

§ 46.10–30 Subdivision load line certificates.

(a) Passenger vessels engaged in foreign voyages by sea shall have their subdivision load lines certified on the safety certificate required by the International Convention for Safety of Life at Sea, 1960. Safety certificates shall be issued by the Commandant, U.S. Coast Guard, for a period not to exceed one year. These vessels will also be provided with the load line certificate required by part 42 of this subchapter, the minimum freeboard shown thereon to be not less than the minimum freeboard corresponding to the principal passenger condition. The fact that they are subdivision load lines is to be noted on the load line certificate.

(b) Passenger vessels engaged on coastwise voyages by sea or Great Lakes voyages shall have the position of their subdivision load lines recorded on a load line certificate in the form required by part 42 or part 45 of this subchapter. The fact that they are subdivision load lines is to be noted on the load line certificate.

(c) A note shall be added to the load line certificate below the signature of the assigning—authority in the following form:

The bulkhead deck used for determining the position of the subdivision load lines certified above is _____ (here described bulkhead deck).

(d) Annual inspections of passenger vessels shall be as required by §§ 42.09–40 and 46.10–15 of this subchapter and renewal of passenger vessels' load line certificates shall be as required by §§ 42.09–15 and 42.09–20.

(e) Each new passenger vessel which receives its first load line certificate shall also be provided with a copy of the load line survey report as required by § 42.09–1(c) or § 45.01–30 of this subchapter.

[CGFR 65–50, 30 FR 16769, Dec. 30, 1965, as amended by CGFR 68–60, 33 FR 10077, July 12, 1968; CGFR 68–126, 34 FR 9019, June 5, 1969; CGD 80–120, 47 FR 5723, Feb. 8, 1982; CGD 88–070, 53 FR 34534, Sept. 7, 1988]

§ 46.10–35 Validity of subdivision load line certificates.

(a) Subdivision load line certificates issued to passenger vessels shall only be valid during the time for which the certificates are issued.

(b) If, due to any cause, the conditions as required by this part are changed, or the regulations in this part are not carried out, the load line certificate may be cancelled and the load lines considered nonexistent: *Provided*, That if the conditions causing the cancellation of the certificate are satisfactorily corrected, the load line certificate shall be reinstated for the remainder of its term.

(c) A valid subdivision load line certificate for foreign voyages by sea shall be valid for coastwise voyages by sea and Great Lakes voyages. A valid subdivision load line certificate for coastwise voyages by sea shall be valid for Great Lakes voyages but not for foreign voyages by sea. A valid subdivision load line certificate for Great Lakes voyages shall not be valid for foreign or coastwise voyages by sea.

§ 46.10–40 Nonsubmergence subdivision load line (Great Lakes).

(a) Passenger vessels on the Great Lakes of 150 gross tons or over shall not submerge the subdivision load line applicable to the voyage.

§ 46.10–45 Nonsubmergence subdivision load lines in salt water.

(a) Passenger vessels required to be marked with subdivision load lines, engaged on foreign and coastwise voyages other than the Great Lakes voyages, shall not submerge in salt water the subdivision load line applicable to the voyage. Passenger vessels engaged on ocean, foreign or coastwise voyages may be marked with fresh water load lines. A passenger vessel on foreign or coastwise voyages (except Great Lakes voyages) may have an allowance made for the degree of brackishness of the water in which the vessel is floating but not for the weight of fuel, water, etc., required for consumption between the point of departure and the open sea, and no allowance is to be made for bilge or ballast water that may be in the passenger vessel at the time of departure.

§ 46.10–50 Drills and inspections.

(a) For the required drills and inspections to be conducted on passenger vessels, see subpart 78.17 of subchapter H (Passenger Vessels) of this chapter.

§ 46.10–55 Logbook entries.

(a) For required logbook entries to be made on passenger vessels, see subpart 78.17 of subchapter H (Passenger Vessels) of this chapter.

§ 46.10–60 Control.

The Director, Field Operations (DFO) or the Coast Guard District Commander may detain a passenger vessel for a survey if there is reason to believe that such a vessel is proceeding on her journey in excess of the draft allowed by the regulations in this part as indicated by the vessel's load lines certified on the safety certificate, load line certificate, or otherwise. The Coast Guard District Commander may detain a passenger vessel if it is so loaded as to be manifestly unsafe to proceed to sea. Except as otherwise required by this section, § 42.07–60 of this subchapter applies to all passenger vessels assigned load lines under the load line acts and the regulations of this subchapter.

[USCG–2012–0832, 77 FR 59777, Oct. 1, 2012]

§ 46.10–65 Construction.

(a) The watertight subdivision of every passenger vessel must be as efficient as possible, having regard to its intended service. This principle is given effect by applying the requirements in part 171 of this chapter.

(b) Passenger vessels engaged in foreign voyages by sea or coastwise voyages by sea or voyages on the Great Lakes, to be marked with subdivision load lines shall comply with the requirements in this part.

[CGFR 65–50, 30 FR 16769, Dec. 30, 1965, as amended by CGD 79–023, 48 FR 51007, Nov. 4, 1983]

§ 46.10–70 Plans and inspections of new and converted vessels.

(a) Plans for a new passenger vessel or a vessel to be converted to a passenger vessel shall be submitted to the Commandant as required by subpart 71.65 of subchapter H (Passenger Vessels) of this chapter.

(b) Inspections shall be made during the construction or conversion of the vessel as required by subpart 71.20 of subchapter H (Passenger Vessels) of this chapter.

(c) Upon completion of construction or conversion of a passenger vessel, a stability test must be performed and stability information must be supplied to the operator as required by part 170 of this chapter.

[CGFR 65–50, 30 FR 16769, Dec. 30, 1965, as amended by CGD 79–023, 48 FR 51007, Nov. 4, 1983]

Subpart 46.15—Subdivision Load Lines for Passenger Vessels Engaged in Foreign, Coastwise, and Great Lakes Voyages

§ 46.15–1 Procedure for determination of subdivision load line.

The procedure for determining the subdivision load line as well as special construction features of the vessel must be as set forth in subpart 72.01 and parts 170 and 171 of this chapter.

[CGD 79–023, 48 FR 51007, Nov. 4, 1983]

§ 46.15–5 Engineering requirements.

(a) Bilge and ballast systems, piping, inlets and discharges, ash chutes, astern power, and auxiliary steering shall be in accordance with the provisions of subchapter F (Marine Engineering) of this chapter.

§ 46.15–10 Subdivision load lines.

(a) Subdivision load lines shall be located by measuring vertically down from the deck line required by part 42 of this subchapter.

(b) The length, width, and manner of marking the lines shall be as provided in subpart 42.13 of this subchapter.

(c) No subdivision load line is to be placed so that the freeboard is reduced from that determined by the highest seasonal mark permitted by part 42.

(d) When the highest subdivision load line is located on a vessel used as a passenger vessel in a position between the highest and lowest seasonal load line marks, the seasonal load line marks above the subdivision load line will be omitted and those below will be marked.

(e) When the freeboard from the highest subdivision load line on a vessel used as a passenger vessel is greater than the freeboard from the lowest load line permitted by part 42 of this subchapter, the load lines required by part 42 of this subchapter shall be omitted and the disk with its horizontal line located in line with the highest subdivision load line.

(f) One fresh water line shall be marked. When a subdivision and a normal load line are combined, the normal fresh water line only shall be used unless the position of the subdivision load line is such that confusion will result, in which case a subdivision fresh water line may be used, marked FC_1 and the normal fresh water line omitted.

(g) Subdivision load lines shall be aft of the vertical line. The vertical line shall be extended as necessary to connect the lowest and highest load lines marked on the vessel.

(h) When a vessel has spaces used for cargo and passengers alternatively so that the position of the subdivision load line varies with the service, subdivision load lines for the principal passenger condition shall be marked and denoted by C_1 and the alternative conditions marked and denoted by C_2, C_3, etc. The position of each load line and the conditions under which a particular load line is applicable shall be noted in the certificate.

(i) The principal passenger condition for a vessel having spaces used for passengers and cargo alternatively is the condition where only those spaces appropriated exclusively to passengers are taken into consideration for determination of the subdivision load line.

(j) For Great Lakes vessels, references to part 42 shall read part 45 and a "diamond" shall be substituted for the "disk". No "fresh water" line will be marked.

[CGFR 65–50, 30 FR 16769, Dec. 30, 1965, as amended by CGFR 68–60, 33 FR 10077, July 12, 1968]

PART 47—COMBINATION LOAD LINES

Subpart A—General

Sec.
47.100 Purpose.
47.110 Definitions used in this part.

Subparts B–E [Reserved]

Subpart F—International and Great Lakes Service; Stability Limited Deck Cargo Barges

47.600 Description of service.
47.610 Conditions of assignment.
47.620 Load line marks.
47.630 Restrictions.
47.640 Form of certificate.

Subpart G [Reserved]

AUTHORITY: 46 U.S.C. 5115; Department of Homeland Security Delegation No. 0170.1.

SOURCE: CGD 86–016, 51 FR 9962, Mar. 24, 1986, unless otherwise noted.

Subpart A—General

§ 47.100 Purpose.

(a) The purpose of the regulations in this part is to set forth simplified alternative marking schemes for those vessels operating in more than one service. Operating requirements for a given vessel could vary depending on the service, the season of the year, stability requirements, manning requirements and tonnage requirements. The conditions of assignment, restrictions applicable, form of the certificate and the load line marks are described.

§ 47.110 Definitions used in this part.

(a) *International service* means:
(1) A voyage by sea between a port under the jurisdiction of the United States and a port of a foreign country, its colonies, territories, or protectorates, or conversely (a voyage exclusively on the Great Lakes is excepted); or
(2) A voyage that proceeds beyond 20 nautical miles from the territorial sea baseline.

(b) *Great Lakes service* means a voyage from a United States port or place on the Great Lakes to another United States port or place on the Great Lakes or to a Canadian port or place on the Great Lakes, or conversely. In concurrence with related Canadian regulations, the waters of the St. Lawrence River west of a rhumb line drawn from Cap de Rosiers to West Point, Anticosti Island, and west of a line along 63° W. Longitude from Anticosti Island to the north shore of the St. Lawrence River shall be considered as part of the Great Lakes. In addition, the Victoria Bridge, Montreal, Canada, is the dividing line between fresh water and salt water in the St. Lawrence River.

Subparts B–E [Reserved]

Subpart F—International and Great Lakes Service; Stability Limited Deck Cargo Barges

§ 47.600 Description of service.

This subpart applies to deck cargo barges operating in International and Great Lakes service and meeting the conditions of assignment in § 47.610 of this subpart.

§ 47.610 Conditions of assignment.

Owners or operators of deck cargo barges which are draft limited by the intact stability requirements of 46 CFR 174.015 (a)(1) and (a)(2) may elect to be assigned load lines under this subpart in order to load to a draft corresponding to the intact stability requirement of 10 foot-degrees (46 CFR 174.015(a)(2)) while engaging in Great Lakes service during the summer season.

§ 47.620 Load line marks.

(a) A plimsoll mark (disc and line through center) applicable to International service must be placed at the draft corresponding to 15-degrees of righting energy as calculated in fulfilling the requirements of 46 CFR 174.015(a)(1).

(b) The seasonal ladder representing summer, winter, and winter North Atlantic seasons must be as shown in Figure 1 below.

(c) An equivalent Great Lakes summer seasonal line must be placed on the seasonal ladder at the draft corresponding to 10 foot-degrees of righting energy as calculated in fulfilling the requirements of 46 CFR 174.015(a)(2) and be marked with a (T).

(d) The fresh water mark may be omitted by request of the owner or operator.

§ 47.630 Restrictions.

(a) The mark (T) applies only to Great Lakes service from May 1 through September 30.

(b) Notations are to be placed on the face of the load line certificate to the effect that:

(1) The barge must be operated in compliance with the draft vs. cargo vertical center of gravity tables in the U.S. Coast Guard approved stability letter, and

(2) The mark (T) is applicable only for Great Lakes service from May 1 through September 30 as per 46 CFR 45.9.

§ 47.640 Form of certificate.

The form of the certificate is as specified in § 42.50–5(b) of this subchapter with the exception that the illustrated load line marks are as shown in Figure 1 below.

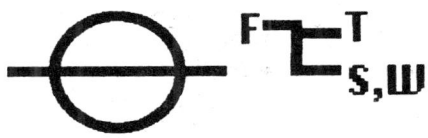

Figure 1. Load Line Marks

Subpart G [Reserved]

SUBCHAPTER F—MARINE ENGINEERING

PART 50—GENERAL PROVISIONS

Subpart 50.01—Basis and Purpose of Regulations

Sec.
50.01–10 Purpose of regulations.
50.01–15 Scope of regulations.
50.01–20 OMB control numbers assigned pursuant to the Paperwork Reduction Act.

Subpart 50.05—Application

50.05–1 General.
50.05–5 Existing boilers, pressure vessels or piping systems.
50.05–10 Alterations or repairs.
50.05–15 Vessels subject to regulations in this subchapter.
50.05–20 Steam-propelled motorboats.

Subpart 50.10—Definition of Terms Used in This Subchapter

50.10–1 Commandant.
50.10–5 Coast Guard District Commander or District Commander.
50.10–10 Officer in Charge, Marine Inspection, (OCMI).
50.10–15 Marine inspector or inspector.
50.10–20 Headquarters.
50.10–23 Marine Safety Center.
50.10–25 Coast Guard Symbol.
50.10–30 Coast Guard number.
50.10–35 Constructed.

Subpart 50.20—Plan Submittal and Approval

50.20–1 General.
50.20–5 Procedures for submittal of plans.
50.20–10 Number of copies of plans required.
50.20–15 Previously approved plans.
50.20–25 Calculations.
50.20–30 Alternative materials or methods of construction.
50.20–33 [Reserved]
50.20–35 Marine inspector's decisions.
50.20–40 Right of appeal.

Subpart 50.25—Acceptance of Material and Piping Components

50.25–1 General.
50.25–3 Manufacturer or mill certification.
50.25–5 Products requiring manufacturer or mill certification.
50.25–7 Testing of products required to be certified in presence of marine inspector.
50.25–10 Acceptance of piping components by specific letter or approved plan.

Subpart 50.30—Fabrication Inspection

50.30–1 Scope.
50.30–10 Class I, I-L and II-L pressure vessels.
50.30–15 Class II pressure vessels.
50.30–20 Class III pressure vessels.

AUTHORITY: 43 U.S.C. 1333; 46 U.S.C. 3306, 3703; E.O. 12234, 45 FR 58801, 3 CFR, 1980 Comp., p. 277; Department of Homeland Security Delegation No. 0170.1; Section 50.01–20 also issued under the authority of 44 U.S.C. 3507.

SOURCE: CGFR 68–82, 33 FR 18808, Dec. 18, 1968, unless otherwise noted.

Subpart 50.01—Basis and Purpose of Regulations

§ 50.01–10 Purpose of regulations.

(a) The purpose of the regulations in this subchapter is to set forth minimum requirements for marine engineering details for various types of vessels in accordance with the intent of title 52 of the Revised Statutes and acts amendatory thereof or supplemental thereto as well as to implement various international conventions for safety of life at sea and other treaties, which contain requirements affecting marine engineering. The regulations in this subchapter have the force of law.

(b) All marine engineering details, such as boilers, pressure vessels, main and auxiliary machinery, piping, valves, and fittings, shall be designed, constructed, and installed in accordance with the provisions of this subchapter, except when specifically modified by the regulations in another subchapter in this chapter for a particular type of vessel or where a specific installation may be required or permitted.

[CGFR 68–82, 33 FR 18808, Dec. 18, 1968, CGD 95–012, 60 FR 48049, Sept. 18, 1995]

§ 50.01–15 Scope of regulations.

(a) This subchapter provides the specifications, standards and requirements for strength and adequacy of design, construction, installation, inspection, and choice of materials for machinery, boilers, pressure vessels, safety valves, and piping systems upon which safety of life is dependent.

(b) Since this subchapter contains the marine engineering details, it implements the requirements for inspection and certification of vessels as set forth in other subchapters for specific types of vessels.

§ 50.01–20 OMB control numbers assigned pursuant to the Paperwork Reduction Act.

(a) *Purpose.* This section collects and displays the control numbers assigned to information collection and recordkeeping requirements in this subchapter by the Office of Management and Budget (OMB) pursuant to the Paperwork Reduction Act of 1980 (44 U.S.C. 3501 *et seq.*). The Coast Guard intends that this section comply with the requirements of 44 U.S.C. 3507(f) which requires that agencies display a current control number assigned by the Director of the OMB for each approved agency information collection requirement.

(b) *Display.*

46 CFR Part or Section where Identified or Described	Current OMB Control No.
Parts 50 through 64	1625–0097

[49 FR 38120, Sept. 27, 1984, as amended by CGD 88–072, 53 FR 34297, Sept. 6, 1988; USCG–2004–18884, 69 FR 58345, Sept. 30, 2004]

Subpart 50.05—Application

§ 50.05–1 General.

(a) The regulations in this subchapter shall apply to the marine engineering details of installations on vessels required to be inspected and certificated under other subchapters in this chapter as described in § 50.01–10.

(b) The regulations in this subchapter are not retroactive in effect, except as provided in § 50.05–5 or § 50.05–10, or if specifically so provided for at the time specific regulations are amended or added.

(c) The requirements in this subchapter revised or added subsequent to July 1, 1969, shall be applicable to the installations contracted for after the effective dates of such requirements. Normally, materials, items of equipment, or installations in vessels which have been accepted and passed as satisfactory and meeting the applicable requirements in this subchapter then in effect and which are maintained in good and serviceable condition to the satisfaction of the Officer in Charge, Marine Inspection, may be continued in use until replacement is deemed necessary by such officer or as specified in the regulations.

(d) Items of equipment, which are in use on vessels, previously approved by the Commandant but not complying with the latest specification requirements may be continued in use so long as they are maintained in good and serviceable condition to the satisfaction of the Officer in Charge, Marine Inspection, until replacement is deemed necessary by such officer or as specified in the regulations.

(e) Industrial systems and components on mobile offshore drilling units must meet subpart 58.60 of this chapter.

[CGFR 68–82, 33 FR 18808, Dec. 18, 1968, as amended by CGD 73–251, 43 FR 56799, Dec. 4, 1978; CGD 77–147, 47 FR 21809, May 20, 1982; USCG–2000–7790, 65 FR 58459, Sept. 29, 2000]

§ 50.05–5 Existing boilers, pressure vessels or piping systems.

(a) Whenever doubt exists as to the safety of an existing boiler, pressure vessel, or piping system, the marine inspector may require that it be gaged or checked to determine the extent of deterioration, and if necessary for safety may require the recalculation and reduction of the maximum allowable working pressure.

(b) For the purpose of recalculating the maximum allowable working pressure of boilers, pressure vessels, or piping which have deteriorated in service, the applicable design formulas in effect at the time it was contracted for or built or the currently effective design formulas in this subchapter shall be used: *Provided,* That such recalculation based on currently effective design formulas in this subchapter does not permit a higher pressure than that originally allowed by the regulations in effect at the time such work was contracted for or built.

(c) When existing vessels are reboilered, the mountings and attachments shall be renewed in accordance with the regulations in this subchapter in effect at the time such reboilering work is contracted for. The existing steam piping shall be examined. Those portions which are in good condition and comply with minimum thickness requirements in effect at the time such reboilering work is contracted for may be continued in service. The steam piping replaced shall be in accordance with the regulations in this subchapter in effect for new construction.

(d) For the purpose of this section, existing equipment includes only items which have previously met all Coast Guard requirements for installation aboard a vessel certificated by the Coast Guard, including requirements for design, fabrication, testing, and inspection at the time the equipment was new.

[CGFR 68–82, 33 FR 18808, Dec. 18, 1968, as amended by CGD 81–79, 50 FR 9430, Mar. 8, 1985]

§ 50.05-10 Alterations or repairs.

(a) When alteration or repair of boilers, pressure vessels, machinery, safety valves or piping systems becomes necessary, the work shall be done under the cognizance of the Officer in Charge Marine Inspection. It shall be done in accordance with the regulations in effect at the time such vessel or installation was contracted for or built (whichever is latest), or in accordance with the regulations in effect for new construction.

(b) When alterations or repairs are made to a U.S. flag vessel in a port or place not in the United States, a notice containing details of the proposed alterations or repairs must be submitted to the appropriate Officer in Charge, Marine Inspection.

[CGFR 68–82, 33 FR 18808, Dec. 18, 1968, as amended by CGD 73–251, 43 FR 56799, Dec. 4, 1978]

§ 50.05-15 Vessels subject to regulations in this subchapter.

(a) Passenger vessels, tank vessels, cargo and miscellaneous vessels, nautical schoolships, mobile offshore drilling units, and oceanographic vessels are subject to the regulations in this subchapter to the extent prescribed by various laws and regulations as described in § 50.01-1. The applicable provisions in this subchapter shall apply to all such U.S. flag vessels, and to all such foreign vessels which carry passengers from any port in the United States except as follows:

(1) Any vessel of a foreign nation signatory to the International Convention for Safety of Life at Sea, 1974, and which has on board a current, valid Convention certificate attesting to the sufficiency of the marine engineering details as prescribed by applicable regulations in this chapter.

(2) Any vessel of a foreign nation having inspection laws approximating those of the United States together with reciprocal inspection arrangements with the United States, and which has on board a current, valid certificate of inspection issued by its government under such arrangements.

(3) Any vessel operating exclusively on inland waters which are not navigable waters of the United States.

(4) Any vessel laid up and dismantled and out of commission.

(5) With the exception of vessels of the U.S. Maritime Administration, any vessel with the title vested in the United States and which is used for public purposes.

(b) Notwithstanding the exceptions previously noted in paragraphs (a) (1) and (2) of this section, foreign vessels of novel design or construction or whose operation involves potential unusual risks shall be subject to inspection to the extent necessary to safeguard life and property in U.S. ports, as further provided by § 2.01-13 in subchapter A (Procedures Applicable to the Public) of this chapter.

[CGFR 68–82, 33 FR 18808, Dec. 18, 1968, as amended by CGD 73–251, 43 FR 56799, Dec. 4, 1978; CGD 80–161, 48 FR 15472, Apr. 11, 1983; CGD 90–008, 55 FR 30660, July 26, 1990; CGD 95–012, 60 FR 48049, Sept. 18, 1995]

§ 50.05-20 Steam-propelled motorboats.

(a) The requirements covering design of the propelling engine, boiler, and the auxiliary machinery, and the inspection thereof on all motor boats which are more than 40 feet in length and which are propelled by machinery driven by steam shall be in accordance with the applicable provisions of this subchapter.

(b) If the engines, boilers, and auxiliary machinery are found to be in safe operating condition at the initial or subsequent periodical inspection, the Officer in Charge, Marine Inspection, shall issue a letter to that effect. Such letter shall be posted on the vessel under glass. The letter will be valid for a specified period of time, as determined by the Officer in Charge, Marine Inspection. The owner, within 30 days prior to its expiration, shall make application to the nearest Officer in Charge, Marine Inspection for a renewal thereof.

Subpart 50.10—Definition of Terms Used in This Subchapter

§ 50.10-1 Commandant.

The term *Commandant* means the Commandant U.S. Coast Guard.

§ 50.10-5 Coast Guard District Commander or District Commander.

The term *Coast Guard District Commander* or *District Commander* means an officer of the Coast Guard designated as such by the Commandant to command all Coast Guard activities within his district, which include the inspections, enforcement, and administration of Subtitle II, Title 46, U.S. Code, Title 46 and Title 33 U.S. Code, and regulations under these statutes.

[CGFR 68-82, 33 FR 18808, Dec. 18, 1968, as amended by CGD 95-028, 62 FR 51200, Sept. 30, 1997]

§ 50.10-10 Officer in Charge, Marine Inspection, (OCMI).

The term *Officer in Charge, Marine Inspection*, (OCMI) means any person from the civilian or military branch of the Coast Guard designated as such by the Commandant and who, under the superintendence and direction of the Coast Guard District Commander, is in charge of an inspection zone for the performance of duties with respect to the inspections, enforcement, and administration of Subtitle II, Title 46, U.S. Code, Title 46 and Title 33 U.S. Code, and regulations under these statutes.

[CGFR 68-82, 33 FR 18808, Dec. 18, 1968, as amended by CGD 95-028, 62 FR 51200, Sept. 30, 1997]

§ 50.10-15 Marine inspector or inspector.

The term *marine inspector* or *inspector* means any person from the civilian or military branch of the Coast Guard assigned under the superintendence and direction of an Officer in Charge, Marine Inspection, or any other person as may be designated for the performance of duties with respect to the inspections, enforcement and the administration of Subtitle II, Title, 46, U.S. Code, Title 46 and Title 33, U.S. Code, and regulations under these statutes.

[CGFR 68-82, 33 FR 18808, Dec. 18, 1968, as amended by CGD 95-028, 62 FR 51200, Sept. 30, 1997]

§ 50.10-20 Headquarters.

The term *Headquarters* means the Commandant (CG-00), Attn: Commandant, U.S. Coast Guard Stop 7000, 2703 Martin Luther King Jr. Avenue SE., Washington, DC 20593-7000.

[CGFR 68-82, 33 FR 18808, Dec. 18, 1968, as amended by CGD 88-070, 53 FR 34534, Sept. 7, 1988; USCG 2013-0671, 78 FR 60147, Sept. 30, 2013]

§ 50.10-23 Marine Safety Center.

The term *Marine Safety Center* refers to the Commanding Officer, Marine Safety Center, U.S. Coast Guard, 4200 Wilson Boulevard, Suite 400, Arlington, VA 22203 for visitors. Send all mail to Commanding Officer (MSC), Attn: Marine Safety Center, U.S. Coast Guard Stop 7410, 4200 Wilson Boulevard, Suite 400, Arlington, VA 20598-7410, in a written or electronic format. Information for submitting the VSP electronically can be found at *http://www.uscg.mil/HQ/MSC*.

[USCG-2007-29018, 72 FR 53965, Sept. 21, 2007; USCG-2009-0702, 74 FR 49228, Sept. 25, 2009; USCG 2013-0671, 78 FR 60147, Sept. 30, 2013]

§ 50.10-25 Coast Guard Symbol.

(a) The term *Coast Guard Symbol* means that impression stamped on the nameplates of boilers, pressure vessels, and safety valves by a marine inspector upon the satisfactory completion of the tests and inspection of the product. It may also be used by a marine inspector to identify workmanship test plates and welding samples.

§ 50.10-30

(b) The impression of the Coast Guard Symbol for stamping nameplates and specimens is shown in Figure 50.10–25(b).

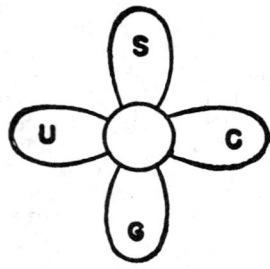

FIGURE 50.10–25(B)—COAST GUARD SYMBOL

§ 50.10-30 Coast Guard number.

(a) The Coast Guard number means that number assigned to boilers and pressure vessels by the Officer in Charge, Marine Inspection, who makes the final tests and inspections.

(b) The Coast Guard number shall be stamped on the nameplates of boilers and pressure vessels.

(c) The Coast Guard number is comprised of the following:

(1) Three capital letters which identify the office of the issuing Officer in Charge, Marine Inspection (see table 50.10–30); followed by,

(2) An OCMI serial number, by which the particular boiler or pressure vessel can be identified; the first two digits of which will identify the calendar year the number was assigned.

TABLE 50.10–30—PREVIOUS SECTOR OFFICE IDENTIFICATION LETTERS IN COAST GUARD NUMBERS FOR BOILERS AND PRESSURE VESSELS

Identification	Sector Office
ALB	Albany.
ANC	Anchorage.
BAL	Baltimore.
BOS	Boston.
BUF	Buffalo.
CHA	Charleston.
CHI	Chicago.
CIN	Cincinnati.
CLE	Cleveland.
COR	Corpus Christi.
DET	Detroit.
DUL	Duluth.
GAL	Galveston.
GUA	Guam.
HON	Honolulu.
HOU	Houston.
HRV	Hampton Roads, VA.
HUN	Huntington.
JAC	Jacksonville.
JUN	Juneau.
LIS	Long Island.
LOS	Los Angeles.
LOU	Louisville.
MEM	Memphis.
MIA	Miami.
MIL	Milwaukee.
MIN	Minneapolis.
MOB	Mobile.
MOR	Morgan City.
NAS	Nashville.
NEW	New Orleans.
NYC	New York.
PAD	Paducah.
PAT	Port Arthur.
PHI	Philadelphia.
PIT	Pittsburgh.
POM	Portland, ME.
POR	Portland, OR.
PRO	Providence.
ROT	Rotterdam.
SAV	Savannah.
SDC	San Diego.
SEA	Seattle.
SFC	San Francisco.
SIM	Saint Ignace.
SJP	San Juan.
SLM	St. Louis.
STB	Sturgeon Bay.
TAM	Tampa.
TOL	Toledo.
VAL	Valdez.
WNC	Wilmington, NC.

[CGFR 68–82, 33 FR 18808, Dec. 18, 1968, as amended by CGFR 69–127, 35 FR 9975, June 17, 1970; CGD 74–219, 39 FR 40158, Nov. 14, 1974; CGD 78–161, 44 FR 13492, Mar. 12, 1979; USCG–2000–7790, 65 FR 58459, Sept. 29, 2000; USCG–2006–25556, 72 FR 36330, July 2, 2007]

§ 50.10-35 Constructed.

The term *constructed* means the keel has been laid or, for vessels with no keel, assembly of at least 50 tons or 1% of the estimated mass of all structural material, whichever is less, has been completed.

[CGD 83–043, 60 FR 24772, May 10, 1995]

Coast Guard, Dept. of Homeland Security § 50.20-25

Subpart 50.20—Plan Submittal and Approval

§ 50.20-1 General.

(a) The required vessel, equipment, or installation plans, as listed in this subchapter, are general in character, but include all plans which normally show the intended construction and safety features coming under the cognizance of the Coast Guard. In a particular case, however, not all of the plans enumerated may be applicable, and in such cases the Coast Guard will so notify the submitter.

(b) Manufacturers of pressure vessels and other components, which require specific fabrication inspection in accordance with the requirements of this subchapter, shall submit and obtain approval of the applicable construction plans prior to the commencement of such fabrication. Manufacturers of automatically controlled boilers shall submit and obtain approval of the applicable control system plans prior to installation of the boiler. Manufacturers of boilers which must meet the requirements of part 52 of this subchapter shall submit the applicable construction plans for review prior to installation.

[CGFR 68–82, 33 FR 18808, Dec. 18, 1968, as amended by CGD 81–79, 50 FR 9431, Mar. 8, 1985]

§ 50.20-5 Procedures for submittal of plans.

(a) As the relative locations of shipyards, design offices, and Coast Guard offices vary throughout the country, no specific routing will be required in the submittal of plans. In general, one of the procedures outlined in this section apply, but if a more expeditious procedure can be used, there will normally be no objection to it.

(b) The plans may be submitted in duplicate to the Officer in Charge, Marine Inspection, at or nearest the place where the vessel is to be built. Alternatively, the plans may be submitted in triplicate to the Marine Safety Center.

(c) In the case of classed vessels, upon specific request by the submitter, the American Bureau of Shipping will arrange to forward the necessary plans to the Coast Guard indicating its action thereon. In this case, the plans will be returned directly to the submitter as noted in paragraph (c) of this section.

[CGFR 68–82, 33 FR 18808, Dec. 18, 1968, as amended by CGD 88–070, 53 FR 34534, Sept. 7, 1988; CGD 77–140, 54 FR 40598, Oct. 2, 1989; CGD 95–012, 60 FR 48049, Sept. 18, 1995; CGD 95–072, 60 FR 50462, Sept. 29, 1995]

§ 50.20-10 Number of copies of plans required.

(a) Three copies of each plan are normally required so that one copy can be returned to the submitter. If the submitter desires additional copies of approved plans, a suitable number should be submitted to permit the required distribution.

§ 50.20-15 Previously approved plans.

(a) A manufacturer wishing to fabricate equipment in accordance with a plan previously approved (including work accomplished under a different contract) shall not be required to resubmit such plans provided:

(1) Certification is submitted that the proposed equipment conforms in every respect to the plan previously approved, and such certification contains the drawing number, title, date, and last revision or change date, and date of previous approval;

(2) The current regulations, including adopted specifications, standards or codes, pertaining to the proposed equipment are the same as those current when the original plan was approved; and

(3) A copy of the approved plan is available for review by the approving office.

[CGFR 68–82, 33 FR 18808, Dec. 18, 1968, as amended by CGD 77–140, 54 FR 40598, Oct. 2, 1989]

§ 50.20-25 Calculations.

(a) Calculations shall be forwarded with plans submitted for approval and shall clearly substantiate compliance with the regulations in this subchapter. Care shall be taken to identify sources of equations, factors and other information upon which the calculations are based.

(b) The results of the calculations, such as the maximum allowable working pressure (MAWP), test pressure, and safety device settings, shall be clearly identified.

§ 50.20-30 Alternative materials or methods of construction.

(a) When new or alternative procedures, designs, or methods of construction are submitted for approval and for which no regulations have been provided, the Commandant will act regarding the approval or disapproval thereof.

(b) If, in the development of industrial arts, improved materials or methods of construction are developed, their use in lieu of those specified will be given consideration upon formal application to the Commandant, with full information as to their characteristics, together with such scientific data and evidence as may be necessary to establish the suitability of such materials or methods of construction for the purpose intended.

§ 50.20-33 [Reserved]

§ 50.20-35 Marine inspector's decisions.

(a) When it becomes necessary for a marine inspector to make decisions on matters covered by the regulations in this subchapter or by requirements in referenced specifications, standards or codes, the inspector shall inform the owner or his representative of the requirement, which will be identified by source, section and paragraph number, on which the decisions are based. Whenever it is necessary to make decisions in matters not specifically covered by the regulations in this subchapter or by referenced requirements, the marine inspector shall clearly state the reasons which caused him to arrive at such decisions.

(b) If the owner or his representative disagrees with a decision made by the marine inspector, he shall take up the matter with the local Officer in Charge, Marine Inspection. The owner or his representative may appeal the decision of the Officer in Charge, Marine Inspection, in accordance with § 50.20-40.

§ 50.20-40 Right of appeal.

Any person directly affected by a decision or action taken under this subchapter, by or on behalf of the Coast Guard, may appeal therefrom in accordance with subpart 1.03 of this chapter.

[CGD 88-033, 54 FR 50380, Dec. 6, 1989]

Subpart 50.25—Acceptance of Material and Piping Components

§ 50.25-1 General.

(a) Materials and piping components used in the construction of boilers, pressure vessels, pressure piping systems, and related components are accepted by review of manufacturer or mill certificates under § 50.25-3 of this part, product marking in accordance with an adopted industry standard, or technical information indicating their compliance with the requirements of this subchapter.

(b) Plate, bar stock, pipe, tube, pipe joining fittings (tees, elbows, reducers, etc.), bolting, castings, forgings, and flanges, are accepted by review of manufacturer or mill certificates under §§ 50.25-3, 50.25-5, and 50.25-7 of this part.

(c) Valves, fluid conditioner fittings, and special purpose fittings complying with an adopted industry standard and marked in accordance with the standard are accepted through review of the marking indicating compliance with the adopted industry standard.

(d) Valves, fluid conditioner fittings, special purpose fittings, and pipe joining fittings not complying with an adopted industry standard are accepted for use on a case-by-case basis. Acceptance is granted by the Marine Safety Center or the Officer in Charge, Marine Inspection, having cognizance over the installation of the product. To obtain acceptance of a product, the manufacturer must submit, via the vessel owner or representative, the information described in § 50.25-10 of this part to the Marine Safety Center or the cognizant Officer in Charge, Marine Inspection.

(e) Components designed for hydraulic service which require shock testing under § 58.30-15(f) of this chapter and nonmetallic flexible hose assemblies must be accepted by the Commandant

(CG–ENG). Manufacturers desiring acceptance of these products must submit information necessary to show compliance with §§ 56.60–25(c) or 58.30–15 of this chapter, as applicable. Acceptance of specific installations of acceptable nonmetallic flexible hose assemblies and shock tested hydraulic components is granted by the Marine Safety Center or the cognizant Officer in Charge, Marine Inspection, as described in paragraph (d) of this section.

(f) The vessel owner or representative shall make available to the Officer in Charge, Marine Inspection, the manufacturer or mill certificates, specific letters of acceptance, or approved plans necessary to verify that piping components comply with the requirements of this subchapter.

[CGD 77–140, 54 FR 40598, Oct. 2, 1989, as amended by CGD 95–072, 60 FR 50462, Sept. 29, 1995; CGD 96–041, 61 FR 50727, Sept. 27, 1996; USCG–2004–18884, 69 FR 58345, Sept. 30, 2004; USCG–2003–16630, 73 FR 65160, Oct. 31, 2008; USCG–2012–0832, 77 FR 59777, Oct. 1, 2012]

§ 50.25–3 Manufacturer or mill certification.

(a) A manufacturer or mill producing materials used in certain products for installation on inspected vessels, shall issue a certificate or mill test report which shall report the results of chemical analysis and mechanical properties required by the ASTM specification.

(b) This certificate shall be made available to the marine inspector and Officer in Charge, Marine Inspection, upon request to the fabricator. (For exception refer to § 50.25–5(d).)

[CGFR 68–82, 33 FR 18808, Dec. 18, 1968, as amended by CGD 77–140, 54 FR 40598, Oct. 2, 1989]

§ 50.25–5 Products requiring manufacturer or mill certification.

(a) Products required to be certified by a manufacturer or by mill certificate shall be fabricated and tested in accordance with the applicable specifications. Such products will not normally be subject to mill inspection by the Coast Guard except as required by § 50.25–7.

(b) The Officer in Charge, Marine Inspection, having cognizance over the installation of the products required to be certified shall ensure that adequate control has been exercised to identify the product with its manufacturer or mill certificate.

(c) In the event that the Officer in Charge, Marine Inspection, determines that handling of a product has been such that proper identification is not possible, he may:

(1) Require testing in his presence based on the applicable material or fabrication specification; or

(2) Reject the product on the basis that it cannot be properly identified.

(d) A product conforming to an acceptable material specification may, at the discretion of the Officer in Charge, Marine Inspection, be accepted without referring to its manufacturer or mill certification, if:

(1) The product is marked in accordance with the identification marking requirements of the specification;

(2) The marking alone is sufficient to identify that specification; and

(3) In the opinion of the Officer in Charge, Marine Inspection, the application of the product does not require knowledge of the exact chemical analysis or mechanical properties enumerated on the manufacturer or mill certificate.

[CGFR 68–82, 33 FR 18808, Dec. 18, 1968, as amended by CGD 77–140, 54 FR 40598, Oct. 2, 1989]

§ 50.25–7 Testing of products required to be certified in presence of marine inspector.

(a) Certified products are not normally tested in the presence of a marine inspector. The Commandant may, however, assign a marine inspector to witness tests required by the applicable specifications to satisfy himself that the requirements are met.

(b) Marine inspectors shall have free entry at all times to those parts of the plant where material subject to the regulations in this subchapter is being manufactured. The manufacturer shall provide marine inspectors all reasonable facilities to satisfy them that the material is being manufactured in accordance with the requirements of the Commandant.

(c) Unless otherwise authorized, required tests and inspections described in applicable specifications shall be made at the place of manufacture prior

§ 50.25-10

to shipment. Unless otherwise specified, tests shall be performed at room temperature. These tests when performed in the presence of a marine inspector will be so conducted as not to interfere unnecessarily with the operation of the plant.

(d) Marine inspectors shall assure themselves that test specimens are marked for positive identification with the materials which they represent.

[CGFR 68–82, 33 FR 18808, Dec. 18, 1968, as amended by CGD 77–140, 54 FR 40599, Oct. 2, 1989]

§ 50.25-10 Acceptance of piping components by specific letter or approved plan.

(a) A manufacturer of a piping component which does not comply with an adopted industry standard and requires acceptance by specific letter or approved plan must do the following:

(1) Submit an engineering type catalog or representative drawings of the component which includes the pressure and temperature ratings of the component and identify the service for which it is intended.

(2) Identify materials used to fabricate the component. Materials must meet the requirements of subpart 56.60 of this chapter. If the component is not manufactured to accepted material specifications, the manufacturer must prove equivalency to accepted material specifications by comparing details of the materials' chemical composition, mechanical properties, method of manufacture, and complete chemical and mechanical test results with an accepted material specification.

(3) Identify the industry standard, if any, to which the component is manufactured.

(4) Submit a description of non-destructive testing performed on the component.

(5) Submit a description of the marking applied to the component.

(6) Submit information showing compliance with the requirements of part 56, subparts 56.15, 56.20, 56.25, 56.30, or 56.35 of this chapter, as applicable.

(7) Submit any additional information necessary to evaluate the component's acceptability for its intended application.

(b) If the component is found to comply with the requirements of this subchapter, the component is designated as acceptable for its intended installation. This acceptance is in the form of a specific letter relating directly to the particular component or in the form of an approved piping system plan in which the component is identified as an integral part.

[CGD 77–140, 54 FR 40599, Oct. 2, 1989]

Subpart 50.30—Fabrication Inspection

§ 50.30-1 Scope.

(a) The manufacturer shall notify the Officer in Charge, Marine Inspection, of the intended fabrication of pressure vessels that will require Coast Guard inspection.

(b) For exemption of certain pressure vessels from shop inspection see § 54.01-15 of this subchapter.

(c) For a classification delineation of boilers and pressure vessels refer to tables 54.01-5(a) and 54.01-5(b) of this subchapter.

[CGFR 68–82, 33 FR 18808, Dec. 18, 1968, as amended by CGD 81–79, 50 FR 9431, Mar. 8, 1985]

§ 50.30-10 Class I, I-L and II-L pressure vessels.

(a) Classes I, I-L and II-L pressure vessels shall be subject to shop inspection at the plant where they are being fabricated, or when determined necessary by the Officer in Charge, Marine Inspection.

(b) The manufacturer shall submit Class I, I-L and II-L pressure vessels, as defined in parts 54 and 56 of this subchapter for shop inspection at such stages of fabrication as may be requested by the Officer in Charge, Marine Inspection.

[CGD 95–012, 60 FR 48049, Sept. 18, 1995]

§ 50.30-15 Class II pressure vessels.

(a) Class II pressure vessels shall be subject to shop inspections at the plant where they are being fabricated, as or when determined necessary by the Officer in Charge, Marine Inspection. The inspections described in this section

Coast Guard, Dept. of Homeland Security

are required, unless specifically exempted by other regulations in this subchapter.

(b) The first inspection of Class II welded pressure vessels shall be performed during the welding of the longitudinal joint. At this time the marine inspector shall check the material and fit-up of the work, and ascertain that only welders who have passed the required tests are employed.

(c) A second inspection of Class II welded pressure vessels shall be made during the welding of the circumferential joints. At this time the marine inspector shall check any new material being used which may not have been examined at the time of the first inspection, also the fit-up of the vessel at this stage of fabrication, and in addition, observe the welding and ascertain that only welders who have passed the required tests are employed.

§ 50.30–20 Class III pressure vessels.

(a) Class III pressure vessels shall be subject to shop inspection at the plant where they are being fabricated, as or when determined necessary by the Officer in Charge, Marine Inspection. The inspection described in this section is required, unless specifically exempted by other regulations in this subchapter.

(b) For Class III welded pressure vessels, one inspection shall be made during the welding of the longitudinal joint. If there is no longitudinal joint, the inspection shall be made during the welding of a circumferential joint. At this time the marine inspector shall check the material and fit-up of the work and see that only welders who have passed the required tests are employed.

PART 51 [RESERVED]

PART 52—POWER BOILERS

Subpart 52.01—General Requirements

Sec.
52.01–1 Incorporation by reference.
52.01–2 Adoption of section I of the ASME Boiler and Pressure Vessel Code.
52.01–3 Definitions of terms used in this part.
52.01–5 Plans.
52.01–10 Automatic controls.
52.01–35 Auxiliary, donkey, fired thermal fluid heater, and heating boilers.
52.01–40 Materials and workmanship.
52.01–50 Fusible plugs (modifies A–19 through A–21).
52.01–55 Increase in maximum allowable working pressure.
52.01–90 Materials (modifies PG–5 through PG–13).
52.01–95 Design (modifies PG–16 through PG–31 and PG–100).
52.01–100 Openings and compensation (modifies PG–32 through PG–39, PG–42 through PG–55).
52.01–105 Piping, valves and fittings (modifies PG–58 and PG–59).
52.01–110 Water-level indicators, water columns, gauge-glass connections, gauge cocks, and pressure gauges (modifies PG–60).
52.01–115 Feedwater supply (modifies PG–61).
52.01–120 Safety valves and safety relief valves (modifies PG–67 through PG–73).
52.01–130 Installation.
52.01–135 Inspection and tests (modifies PG–90 through PG–100).
52.01–140 Certification by stamping (modifies PG–104 through PG–113).
52.01–145 Manufacturers' data report forms (modifies PG–112 and PG–113).

Subpart 52.05—Requirements for Boilers Fabricated by Welding

52.05–1 General (modifies PW–1 through PW–54).
52.05–15 Heat treatment (modifies PW–10).
52.05–20 Radiographic and ultrasonic examination (modifies PW–11 and PW–41.1).
52.05–30 Minimum requirements for attachment welds (modifies PW–16).
52.05–45 Circumferential joints in pipes, tubes and headers (modifies PW–41).

Subpart 52.15—Requirements for Watertube Boilers

52.15–1 General (modifies PWT–1 through PWT–15).
52.15–5 Tube connections (modifies PWT–9 and PWT–11).

Subpart 52.20—Requirements for Firetube Boilers

52.20–1 General (modifies PFT–1 through PFT–49).
52.20–17 Opening between boiler and safety valve (modifies PFT–44).
52.20–25 Setting (modifies PFT–46).

Subpart 52.25—Other Boiler Types

52.25–1 General.
52.25–3 Feedwater heaters (modifies PFH–1).
52.25–5 Miniature boiler (modifies PMB–1 through PMB–21).

§ 52.01–1

52.25–7 Electric boilers (modifies PEB–1 through PEB–19).
52.25–10 Organic fluid vaporizer generators (modifies PVG–1 through PVG–12).
52.25–15 Fired thermal fluid heaters.
52.25–20 Exhaust gas boilers.

AUTHORITY: 46 U.S.C. 3306, 3307, 3703; E.O. 12234, 45 FR 58801, 3 CFR, 1980 Comp., p. 277; Department of Homeland Security Delegation No. 0170.1.

SOURCE: CGFR 68–82, 33 FR 18815, Dec. 18, 1968, unless otherwise noted.

Subpart 52.01—General Requirements

§ 52.01–1 Incorporation by reference.

(a) Certain material is incorporated by reference into this part with the approval of the Director of the Federal Register under 5 U.S.C. 552(a) and 1 CFR part 51. To enforce any edition other than that specified in this section, the Coast Guard must publish notice of change in the FEDERAL REGISTER and the material must be available to the public. All approved material is available for inspection at the National Archives and Records Administration (NARA). For information on the availability of this material at NARA, call 202–741–6030 or go to *http://www.archives.gov/federal_register/code_of_federal_regulations/ibr_locations.html*. The material is also available for inspection at the Coast Guard Headquarters. Contact Commandant (CG–ENG), Attn: Office of Design and Engineering Systems, U.S. Coast Guard Stop 7509, 2703 Martin Luther King Jr. Avenue SE., Washington, DC 20593–7509. The material is also available from the sources listed in paragraph (b) of this section.

(b) *American Society of Mechanical Engineers (ASME) International*, Three Park Avenue, New York, NY 10016–5990:

(1) 2001 ASME Boiler and Pressure Vessel Code, Section I, Rules for Construction of Power Boilers (July 1, 2001) ("Section I of the ASME Boiler and Pressure Vessel Code"), 52.01–2; 52.01–5; 52.01–50; 52.01–90; 52.01–95; 52.01–100; 52.01–105; 52.01–110; 52.01–115; 52.01–120; 52.01–135; 52.01–140; 52.01–145; 52.05–1; 52.05–15; 52.05–20; 52.05–30; 52.05–45; 52.15–1; 52.15–5; 52.20–1; 52.20–25; 52.25–3; 52.25–5; 52.25–7; and 52.25–10.

(2) 1998 ASME Boiler and Pressure Vessel Code, Section II, Part A—Ferrous Material Specifications and Part B—Nonferrous Material Specifications (1998) ("Section II of the ASME Boiler and Pressure Vessel Code"), 52.01–90.

(3) [Reserved]

[USCG–2003–16630, 73 FR 65160, Oct. 31, 2008, as amended by USCG–2009–0702, 74 FR 49228, Sept. 25, 2009; USCG–2012–0832, 77 FR 59777, Oct. 1, 2012; USCG 2013–0671, 78 FR 60147, Sept. 30, 2013]

§ 52.01–2 Adoption of section I of the ASME Boiler and Pressure Vessel Code.

(a) Main power boilers and auxiliary boilers shall be designed, constructed, inspected, tested, and stamped in accordance with section I of the ASME Boiler and Pressure Vessel Code (incorporated by reference; see 46 CFR 52.01–1), as limited, modified, or replaced by specific requirements in this part. The provisions in the appendix to section I of the ASME Boiler and Pressure Vessel Code are adopted and shall be followed when the requirements in section I make them mandatory. For general information, table 52.01–1(a) lists the various paragraphs in section I of the ASME Boiler and Pressure Vessel Code that are limited, modified, or replaced by regulations in this part.

TABLE 52.01–1(a)—LIMITATIONS AND MODIFICATIONS IN THE ADOPTION OF SECTION I OF THE ASME CODE

Paragraphs in section I, ASME Code[1] and disposition	Unit of this part
PG–1 replaced by	54.01–5(a)
PG–5 through PG–13 modified by	52.01–90
PG–16 through PG–31 modified by	52.01–95
PG–32 through PG–39 modified by	52.01–100
PG–42 through PG–55 modified by	52.01–100
PG–58 and PG–59 modified by	52.01–105
PG–60 modified by	52.01–110
PG–61 modified by	52.01–115 (56.50–30)
PG–67 through PG–73 modified by	52.01–120
PG–90 through PG–100 modified by	52.01–135 (52.01–95)
PG–91 modified by	52.01–135(b)
PG–99 modified by	52.01–135(c)
PG–100 modified by	52.01–95(e)
PG–104 through PG–113 modified by	52.01–140(a)
PG–112 and PG–113 modified by	52.01–145
PW–1 through PW–54 modified by	52.05–1
PW–10 modified by	52.05–15
PW–11.1 modified by	52.05–20
PW–16 modified by	52.05–30
PW–41 modified by	52.05–20, 52.05–45
PWT–1 through PWT–15 modified by	52.15–1

Coast Guard, Dept. of Homeland Security § 52.01-3

TABLE 52.01–1(a)—LIMITATIONS AND MODIFICATIONS IN THE ADOPTION OF SECTION I OF THE ASME CODE—Continued

Paragraphs in section I, ASME Code[1] and disposition	Unit of this part
PWT–9 modified by	52.15–5
PWT–9.2 replaced by	52.15–5(b)
PWT–11 modified by	52.15–5
PWT–11.3 replaced by	52.15–5(b)
PFT–1 through PFT–49 modified by	52.20–1
PFT–44 modified by	52.20–17
PFT–46. modified by	52.20–25
PFH–1 modified by	52.25–3
PMB–1 through PMB–21 modified by	52.25–5
PEB–1 through PEB–19 modified by	52.25–7
PVG–1 through PVG–12 modified by	52.25–10
A–19 through A–21 modified by	52.01–50

[1] The references to specific provisions in the ASME Code are coded. The first letter "P" refers to section I, while the letter "A" refers to the appendix to section I. The letter or letters following "P" refer to a specific subsection of section I. The number following the letter or letters refers to the paragraph so numbered in the text.

(b) References to the ASME Code, such as paragraph PG–1, indicate:

P=Section I, Power Boilers ASME Code.
G=Subsection—General.
1=Paragraph 1.

(c) When a section or paragraph of the regulations in this part relates to material in section I of the ASME Code, the relationship with the code will be shown immediately following the heading of the section or at the beginning of the paragraph as follows:

(1) (Modifies P____.) This indicates that the material in P____ is generally applicable but is being altered, amplified or augmented.

(2) (Replaces P____.) This indicates that P____ does not apply.

(3) (Reproduces P____.) This indicates that P____ is being identically reproduced for convenience, not for emphasis.

[CGFR 68–82, 33 FR 18815, Dec. 18, 1968, as amended by CGFR 69–127, 35 FR 9975, June 17, 1970; CGD 81–79, 50 FR 9431, Mar. 8, 1985. Redesignated and amended by CGD 88–032, 56 FR 35821, July 29, 1991; USCG –2003–16630, 73 FR 65160, Oct. 31, 2008]

§ 52.01–3 Definitions of terms used in this part.

(a) *Types of boilers*—(1) *Main power boiler.* A main power boiler is a steam boiler used for generating steam for main propulsion.

(2) *Auxiliary or donkey boiler.* An auxiliary or donkey boiler is a steam boiler used for all purposes, including emergency propulsion, for which steam may be required other than main propulsion.

(3) *Watertube boiler.* A watertube boiler is a steam boiler in which the boiler tubes contain water and steam. The heat is applied to the outside surface of the tubes.

(4) *Internally fired firetube boiler (scotch boiler).* An internally fired firetube boiler is a steam boiler containing furnaces, one or more combustion chambers and tubes or flues, which are surrounded by water and through which the products of combustion pass from the furnace to the uptake. In such boilers no part of the shell is in contact with the fire or products of combustion.

(5) *Externally fired firetube or flue boiler (horizontal return tubular).* An externally fired firetube or flue boiler is a steam boiler, part of the outer shell of which is exposed to fire or to the products of combustion, and containing flues through which such products pass from the furnace to the uptake.

(6) *High temperature water boiler.* A high temperature water boiler is a boiler containing water at a temperature exceeding 250 °F.

(7) *Packaged boiler.* A packaged boiler is a steam boiler equipped, and shipped complete with fuel burning equipment, mechanical draft equipment, feed water apparatus and all necessary controls for manual or automatic operation, all completely mounted on a common base and requiring only to be connected to fuel, water and electric supplies to be ready for use.

(8) *Fired steam boiler.* A pressure vessel in which steam is generated by the application of heat resulting from the combustion of fuel is classed as a fired steam boiler.

(9) *Unfired steam boiler.* A pressure vessel in which steam is generated by means other than fuel combustion is classed as an unfired steam boiler. (See § 54.01–10 of this subchapter.)

(10) *Hybrid boiler.* A hybrid boiler is a steam boiler whose design employs features from both watertube and firetube boilers.

(b) *Parts of boilers*—(1) *Shell.* The shell is the structure forming the outer envelope of a boiler drum, or pressure vessel consisting of one or more plates

§ 52.01-3

properly joined (or of seamless construction) as specified in this part. This does not include tube sheets or heads.

(2) *Heads.* The heads are the ends of a boiler or pressure vessel. They may be flat or dished, stayed or unstayed.

(i) *Dished heads.* Dished heads are heads formed to a segment of a sphere or to a hemispherical or elliptical section and may be attached to the shell so that the pressure will be either on the concave or on the convex side.

(ii) *Stayed heads.* Stayed heads are heads supported in whole or in part by stays, furnaces, flues, tubes, etc.

(3) *Water wall.* A water wall is a series of tubes or elements spaced along or integral with a wall of a furnace to protect the wall and provide additional heating surface.

(4) *Header.* A header is a hollow forging, pipe, or welded plate of cylindrical, square, or rectangular cross section, serving as a manifold to which tubes are connected.

(5) *Superheater.* A superheater is an appliance for the purpose of increasing the temperature of steam.

(6) *Economizer.* An economizer is a feed-water heater usually located in the uptake or casing of a boiler to absorb heat from the waste gases.

(7) *Domes.* Domes are superstructures of shells, attached by riveting, bolting, or welding. They generally consist of a cylindrical shell with one end flanged for attachment to the main shell and the other end closed by a head which may be integral with, riveted, or welded to the shell.

(8) *Steam chimneys.* Steam chimneys are superstructures of steam boilers which are fitted with a lining inside of which the products of combustion pass to the smokestack. They may be constructed in the form of a dome integral with the boiler or as independent steam vessels connected by piping to the boiler.

(9) *Furnace.* A furnace is a firebox or a large flue in which the fuel is burned.

(i) *Corrugated furnace.* A corrugated furnace is a cylindrical shell wherein corrugations are formed circumferentially for additional strength and to provide for expansion.

(ii) *Plain furnace.* A plain furnace is a cylindrical shell usually made in sections joined by means of riveting or welding.

(10) *Combustion chamber.* A combustion chamber is that part of an internally fired boiler in which combustible gases may be burned after leaving the furnace.

(i) *Separate combustion chamber.* A separate combustion chamber is a combustion chamber which is connected to one furnace only.

(ii) *Common combustion chamber.* A common combustion chamber is a combustion chamber connected to two or more furnaces in a boiler.

(iii) *Crown or top plate.* A crown or top plate is the top of a combustion chamber and is usually supported by girder stays or by sling stays or braces.

(iv) *Curved bottom plate.* A curved bottom plate is the bottom of a separate combustion chamber formed to an arc of a circle and usually designed to be self-supporting.

(v) *Combustion chamber tube sheet.* A combustion chamber tube sheet is the plate forming the end of a combustion chamber in which the tubes are secured.

(vi) *Combustion chamber back sheet.* A combustion chamber back sheet is the plate opposite the tube sheet forming the back of the combustion chamber. It is usually stayed to the back head of the boiler by means of screw staybolts, or, in the case of double-ended boilers, to the back of the combustion chamber of the other end of the boiler.

(11) *Flues.* Flues are cylindrical shells made of seamless or welded tubing, or with a riveted longitudinal joint, the ends being attached by riveting or welding. Their purpose is to provide additional heating surface and to form a path for the products of combustion.

(12) *Tubes.* Tubes are cylindrical shells of comparatively small diameter constituting the main part of the heating surface of a boiler or superheater.

(i) *Seamless tube.* A seamless tube is a tube without any longitudinal joint.

(ii) *Electric-resistance-welded tube.* An electric-resistance-welded tube is a tube the longitudinal joint of which is made by the electric-resistance butt welding process.

(iii) *Stay tube.* A stay tube is a thickwalled tube, the end of which is

Coast Guard, Dept. of Homeland Security §52.01-3

usually thickened by upsetting to compensate for threading. Such tubes are used for staying tube sheets into which they are screwed and expanded.

(13) *Tube sheet.* A tube sheet is a portion of a boiler drum, or header perforated for the insertion of tubes.

(14) *Ligament.* The ligament is the section of metal between the holes in a tube sheet.

(i) *Longitudinal ligament.* A longitudinal ligament is the minimum section of metal between two tube holes on a line parallel with the axis of the drum.

(ii) *Circumferential ligament.* A circumferential ligament is the minimum section of metal between two tube holes on a line around the circumference of the drum.

(iii) *Diagonal ligament.* A diagonal ligament is the minimum section of metal between two tube holes in adjacent rows, measured diagonally from one row to the other.

(c) *Stays and supports*—(1) *Surfaces to be stayed.* Surfaces to be stayed or reinforced include flat plates, heads, or areas thereof, such as segments of heads, wrapper sheets, furnace plates, side sheets, combustion chamber tops, etc., which are not self-supporting; and curved plates, constituting the whole or parts of a cylinder subject to external pressure, which are not entirely self-supporting.

(2) *Through stay.* A through stay is a solid bar extending through both heads of a boiler and threaded at the ends for attachment by means of nuts. With this type of stay the ends are usually upset to compensate for the threading. (See Figure 52.01–3(a).)

(3) *Solid screw staybolt.* A solid screw staybolt is a threaded bar screwed through the plates, the ends being riveted over or fitted with nuts or welded collars. (See Figure 52.01–3(b).)

(4) *Welded collar.* A welded collar is a beveled ring formed around the end of a screw stay by means of arc- or gas-welding. It is used in lieu of a nut. (See Figure 52.01–3(1).)

(5) *Hollow screw staybolt.* A hollow screw staybolt is a hollow threaded bar screwed through the plate, the ends being riveted over or fitted with nuts or welded collars. (See Figure 52.01–3(c).)

(6) *Flexible staybolt.* A flexible staybolt is a bar made with ball-and-socket joint on one end, the cup of the socket being screwed into the outside sheet and covered with a removable cap, the plain end of the staybolt being threaded, screwed through the inside sheet and riveted over. (See Figure 52.01–3(d).)

(7) *Sling stay.* A sling stay is a flexible stay consisting of a solid bar having one or both ends forged for a pin connection to a crowfoot or other structural fitting secured to the stayed plate. (See Figure 52.01–3(e).)

(8) *Crowfoot.* A crowfoot is a forged fitting with palms or lugs secured to the head to form a proper connection with a sling stay. (See Figure 52.01–3(f).)

(9) *Crowfoot stay.* A crowfoot stay is a solid bar stay terminating in a forged fork with palms or lugs for attachment to the plate. (See Figure 52.01–3(g).)

(10) *Diagonal stay.* A diagonal stay is a bar or formed plate forged with palms or lugs for staying the head of the boiler to the shell diagonally. (See Figure 52.01–3(h).)

(11) *Gusset stay.* A gusset stay is a triangular plate used for the same purpose as a diagonal stay and attached to the head and the shell by angles, flanges, or other suitable means of attachment. (See Figure 52.01–3(i).)

(12) *Dog stay.* A dog stay is a staybolt, one end of which extends through a girder, dog, or bridge, and is secured by a nut, the other end being screwed through the plate which it is supporting and riveted over or fitted with a nut or welded collar. (See Figure 52.01–3(j).)

(13) *Girder.* A girder is a bridge, built up of plates of structural shapes separated by distance pieces, a forging, or a formed plate, which spans an area requiring support, abutting thereon and supporting the girder stays or staybolts. (See Figure 52.01–3(k).)

(14) *Structural stiffeners.* Structural stiffeners are rolled shapes or flanged plates which are used to stiffen a surface which is not entirely self-supporting.

(15) *Reinforcement.* A reinforcement is a doubling plate, washer, structural shape, or other form for stiffening or strengthening a plate.

§ 52.01-3

(d) *Pressure relief devices.* For boilers, pressure vessels, and pressure piping, a pressure relief device is designed to open to prevent a rise of internal fluid pressure in excess of a specified value due to exposure to emergency or abnormal conditions. It may also be designed to prevent excessive internal vacuum. It may be a pressure relief valve, a nonreclosing pressure relief device or a vacuum relief valve.

(1) *Pressure relief valve.* A pressure relief valve is a pressure relief device which is designed to reclose and prevent the further flow of fluid after normal conditions have been restored.

(i) *Safety valve.* A safety valve is a pressure relief valve actuated by inlet static pressure and characterized by rapid opening or pop action. Examples of types used on boilers include:

(A) *Spring-loaded safety valve.* A spring-loaded safety valve is a safety valve fitted with a spring which normally holds the valve disk in a closed position against the seat and allows it to open or close at predetermined pressures. Spring-loaded safety valves are characterized by pop action.

(B) *Pressure loaded pilot actuated safety valve.* A pressure loaded pilot actuated safety valve is one which is held in a closed position by steam pressure and controlled in operation by a pilot actuator valve.

(C) *Spring loaded pilot actuated safety valve.* A spring loaded, pilot actuated safety valve is one in which a spring is used in the conventional way to hold the disk against the seat, but which has a piston attached to the spindle and enclosed within a cylinder, which when subjected to a limiting or set pressure, unbalances the spring load thereby opening the valve.

(D) *Spring loaded pilot valve.* A spring loaded pilot valve is a conventional safety valve designed to actuate another spring loaded safety valve through a pressure transmitting line led from the body of the pilot valve.

(ii) *Relief valve.* A relief valve is a pressure relief valve actuated by inlet static pressure which opens in proportion to the increase in pressure over the opening pressure.

(iii) *Safety relief valve.* A safety relief valve is a pressure relief valve characterized by rapid opening or pop action, or by opening in proportion to the increase in pressure over the opening pressure, depending on application.

(A) *Conventional safety relief valve.* A conventional safety relief valve has its spring housing vented to the discharge side of the valve. The performance characteristics (opening pressure, closing pressure, lift and relieving capacity) are directly affected by changes of the back pressure on the valve.

(B) *Balanced safety relief valve.* A balanced safety relief valve incorporates means of minimizing the effect of back pressure on the operational characteristics (opening pressure, closing pressure, lift and relieving capacity).

(C) *Internal spring safety relief valve.* An internal spring safety relief valve incorporates the spring and all or part of the operating mechanism within the pressure vessel.

(iv) *Pilot operated pressure relief valve.* A pilot operated pressure relief valve is a pressure relief valve in which the major relieving device is combined with and is controlled by a self-actuated auxiliary pressure relief valve.

(v) *Power actuated relief valve.* A power actuated pressure relief valve is a pressure relief valve in which the major relieving device is combined with and controlled by a device requiring an external source of energy.

(vi) *Temperature actuated pressure relief valve.* A temperature actuated pressure relief valve is a pressure relief valve. A spring loaded, pilot actuated internal temperature.

(2) *Nonreclosing pressure relief device.* A nonreclosing pressure relief device is a pressure relief device not designed to reclose after operation.

(i) *Rupture disk device.* A rupture disk device is a device actuated by inlet static pressure and designed to function by the bursting of a pressure retaining disk.

(ii) *Explosion rupture disk device.* An explosion rupture disk device is a rupture disk device designed for use at high rates of pressure rise.

(iii) *Breaking pin device.* A breaking pin device is a device actuated by inlet static pressure and designed to function by the breakage of a load carrying section of a pin which supports a pressure retaining member.

Coast Guard, Dept. of Homeland Security § 52.01-3

(iv) *Shear pin device.* A shear pin device is a device actuated by inlet static pressure and designed to function by the shearing of a load carrying pin which supports the pressure retaining member.

(v) *Fusible plug device.* A fusible plug device is a device designed to function by the yielding or melting of a plug of suitable melting temperature.

(vi) *Frangible disk device.* A frangible disk device is the same as a rupture disk device.

(vii) *Bursting disk device.* A bursting disk device is the same as a rupture disk device.

(3) *Vacuum relief valve.* A vacuum relief valve is a valve designed to admit fluid to prevent an excessive internal vacuum.

(e) *Other boiler attachments*—(1) *Mountings.* Mountings are nozzle connections, distance pieces, valves, or fittings attached directly to the boiler.

(2) *Main steam stop valve.* A main steam stop valve is a valve usually connected directly to the boiler for the purpose of shutting off the steam from the main steam line.

(3) *Auxiliary steam stop valve.* An auxiliary steam stop valve is a valve usually connected directly to the boiler for the purpose of shutting off the steam from the auxiliary lines (including the whistle lines).

(4) *Manifold.* A manifold is a fitting with two or more branches having valves either attached by bolting or integral with the fitting.

(5) *Feed valve.* A feed valve is a valve in the feed-water line which controls the boiler feed.

(6) *Blowoff valve.* A blowoff valve is a valve connected directly to the boiler for the purpose of blowing out water, scum or sediment.

(7) *Dry pipe.* A dry pipe is a perforated or slotted pipe placed in the highest part of the steam space of a boiler to prevent priming.

(8) *Water column.* A water column is a fitting or tube equipped with a water glass attached to a boiler for the purpose of indicating the water level.

(9) *Test cocks.* Test cocks are small cocks on a boiler for indicating the water level.

(10) *Salinometer cocks.* Salinometer cocks are cocks attached to a boiler for the purpose of drawing off a sample of water for salinity tests.

(11) *Fusible plugs.* Fusible plugs are plugs made with a bronze casing and a tin filling which melts at a temperature of 445° to 450 °F. They are intended to melt in the event of low water and thus warn the engineer on watch.

(f) *Boiler fabrication*—(1) *Repair.* Repair is the restoration of any damaged or impaired part to an effective and safe condition.

(2) *Alteration.* Alteration is a structural modification to or departure from an approved design or existing construction.

(3) *Expanding.* Expanding is the process of enlarging the end of a tube to make it fit tightly in the tube sheet.

(4) *Beading.* Beading is the process of turning over the protruding end of a tube after expanding to form a supporting collar for the tube sheet.

(5) *Bell-mouthing.* Bell-mouthing is the process of flaring the end of a tube beyond where it is expanded in the tube sheet.

(6) *Telltale hole.* A telltale hole is a small hole having a diameter not less than three-sixteenths inch drilled in the center of a solid stay, and extending to at least one-half inch beyond the inside surface of the sheet.

(7) *Access or inspection openings.* Access or inspection openings are holes cut in the shells or heads of boilers or boiler pressure part for the purpose of inspection and cleaning.

(8) *Openings.* Openings are holes cut in shells or heads of boilers or boiler pressure parts for the purpose of connecting nozzles, domes, steam chimneys, or mountings.

(g) *Pressure.* The term pressure is an abbreviation of the more explicit expression "difference in pressure intensity." It is measured in terms such as pounds per square inch (p.s.i.).

(1) *Gage (or gauge) pressure.* Gage pressure is the difference between the pressure at the point being measured and the ambient pressure for the gage. It is measured in units such as pounds per square inch gage (p.s.i.g.).

(2) *Absolute pressure.* Absolute pressure is the difference between the pressure at the point being measured and

§ 52.01-5

that of a perfect vacuum. It is measured in units such as pounds per square inch absolute (p.s.i.a.).

(3) *Internal pressure.* Internal pressure refers to a situation where the pressure inside exceeds that outside the volume being described.

(4) *External pressure.* External pressure refers to a situation where the pressure outside exceeds that inside the volume being described.

(5) *Maximum allowable working pressure.* For a definition of maximum allowable working pressure, see § 54.10-5 of this subchapter.

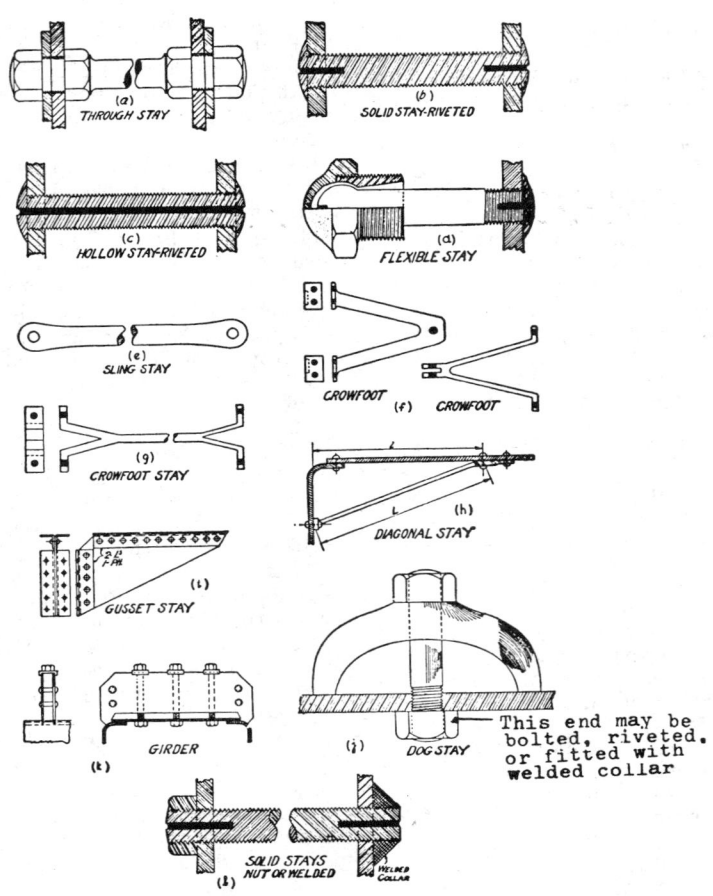

FIGURE 52.01-3—ACCEPTABLE TYPES OF BOILER STAYS

[CGFR 68-82, 33 FR 18815, Dec. 18, 1968, as amended by CGFR 69-127, 35 FR 9976, June 17, 1970; CGD 81-79, 50 FR 9431, Mar. 8, 1985; CGD 83-043, 60 FR 24772, May 10, 1995]

§ 52.01-5 Plans.

(a) Manufacturers intending to fabricate boilers to be installed on vessels shall submit detailed plans as required by subpart 50.20 of this subchapter. The plans, including design calculations, must be certified by a registered professional engineer as meeting the design requirements in this part and in section I of the ASME Boiler and Pressure Vessel Code (incorporated by reference; see 46 CFR 52.01–1).

(b) The following information must be included:

(1) Calculations for all pressure containment components including the maximum allowable working pressure and temperature, the hydrostatic or pneumatic test pressure, the maximum steam generating capacity and the intended safety valve settings.

(2) Joint design and methods of attachment of all pressure containment components.

(3) A bill of material meeting the requirements of section I of the ASME Code, as modified by this subpart.

(4) A diagrammatic arrangement drawing of the assembled unit indicating the location of internal and external components including any interconnecting piping.

(Approved by the Office of Management and Budget under control number 1625–0097)

[CGD 81–79, 50 FR 9432, Mar. 8, 1985, as amended by USCG–2006–25697, 71 FR 55746, Sept. 25, 2006; USCG–2003–16630, 73 FR 65160, Oct. 31, 2008]

§ 52.01–10 Automatic controls.

(a) Each main boiler must meet the special requirements for automatic safety controls in § 62.35–20(a)(1) of this chapter.

(b) Each automatically controlled auxiliary boiler having a heat input rating of less than 12,500,000 Btu/hr. (3.66 megawatts) must meet the requirements of part 63 of this chapter.

(c) Each automatically controlled auxiliary boiler with a heat input rating of 12,500,000 Btu/hr. (3.66 megawatts) or above, must meet the requirements for automatic safety controls in part 62 of this chapter.

[CGFR 68–82, 33 FR 18815, Dec. 18, 1968, as amended by CGD 81–030, 53 FR 17837, May 18, 1988; CGD 88–057, 55 FR 24236, June 15, 1990]

§ 52.01–35 Auxiliary, donkey, fired thermal fluid heater, and heating boilers.

(a) To determine the appropriate part of the regulations where requirements for miscellaneous boiler types, such as donkey, fired thermal fluid heater, heating boiler, etc., may be found, refer to table 54.01–5(a) of this subchapter.

(b) Fired vessels in which steam is generated at pressures exceeding 103 kPa gage (15 psig) shall meet the requirements of this part.

[CGFR 68–82, 33 FR 18815, Dec. 18, 1968, as amended by CGD 81–79, 50 FR 9432, Mar. 8, 1985]

§ 52.01–40 Materials and workmanship.

All materials to be used in any of the work specified in the various sections of this part shall be free from injurious defects and shall have a workmanlike finish. The construction work shall be executed in a workmanlike manner with proper tools or equipment and shall be free from defects which would impair strength or durability.

§ 52.01–50 Fusible plugs (modifies A–19 through A–21).

(a) All boilers, except watertube boilers, with a maximum allowable working pressure in excess of 206 kPa gauge (30 psig), if fired with solid fuel not in suspension, or if not equipped for unattended waterbed operation, must be fitted with fusible plugs. Fusible plugs must comply with only the requirements of A19 and A20 of section I of the ASME Boiler and Pressure Vessel Code (incorporated by reference; see 46 CFR 52.01–1) and be stamped on the casing with the name of the manufacturer, and on the water end of the fusible metal "ASME Std." Fusible plugs are not permitted where the maximum steam temperature to which they are exposed exceeds 218 °C (425 °F).

(b) Vertical boilers shall be fitted with one fusible plug located in a tube not more than 2 inches below the lowest gage cock.

(c) Externally fired cylindrical boilers with flues shall have one plug fitted to the shell immediately below the fire line not less than 4 feet from the front end.

(d) Firebox, Scotch, and other types of shell boilers not specifically provided for, having a combustion chamber common to all furnaces, shall have one plug fitted at or near the center of the crown sheet of the combustion chamber.

§ 52.01-55

(e) Double-ended boilers, having individual combustion chambers for each end, in which combustion chambers are common to all the furnaces in one end of the boiler, shall have one plug fitted at or near the center of the crown sheet of each combustion chamber.

(f) Boilers constructed with a separate combustion chamber for each individual furnace shall be fitted with a fusible plug in the center of the crown sheet of each combustion chamber.

(g) Boilers of types not provided for in this section shall be fitted with at least one fusible plug of such dimensions and located in a part of the boiler as will best meet the purposes for which it is intended.

(h) Fusible plugs shall be so fitted that the smaller end of the filling is in direct contact with the radiant heat of the fire, and shall be at least 1 inch higher on the water side than the plate or flue in which they are fitted, and in no case more than 1 inch below the lowest permissible water level.

(i) The lowest permissible water level shall be determined as follows:

(1) Vertical firetube boilers, one-half of the length of the tubes above the lower tube sheets.

(2) Vertical submerged tube boilers 1 inch above the upper tube sheet.

(3) Internally fired firetube boilers with combustion chambers integral with the boiler, 2 inches above the highest part of the combustion chamber.

(4) Horizontal-return tubular and dry back Scotch boilers, 2 inches above the top row of tubes.

(j) [Reserved]

(k)(1) Fusible plugs shall be cleaned and will be examined by the marine inspector at each inspection for certification, periodic inspection, and oftener if necessary. If in the marine inspector's opinion the condition of any plug is satisfactory, it may be continued in use.

(2) When fusible plugs are renewed at other than the inspection for certification and no marine inspector is in attendance, the Chief Engineer shall submit a written report to the Officer in Charge, Marine Inspection, who issued the certificate of inspection informing him of the renewal. This letter report shall contain the following information:

(i) Name and official number of vessel.

(ii) Date of renewal of fusible plugs.

(iii) Number and location of fusible plugs renewed in each boiler.

(iv) Manufacturer and heat number of each plug.

(v) Reason for renewal.

[CGFR 68–82, 33 FR 18815, Dec. 18, 1968, as amended by CGD 81–79, 50 FR 9432, Mar. 8, 1985; USCG–1999–4976, 65 FR 6500, Feb. 9, 2000; USCG–2003–16630, 73 FR 65160, Oct. 31, 2008]

§ 52.01-55 Increase in maximum allowable working pressure.

(a) When the maximum allowable working pressure of a boiler has been established, an increase in the pressure settings of its safety valves shall not be granted unless the boiler design meets the requirements of this subchapter in effect at the time the boiler was contracted for or built; but in no case will a pressure increase be authorized for boilers constructed prior to the effective date of the regulations dated November 19, 1952, if the minimum thickness found by measurement shows that the boiler will have a factor of safety of less than 4½. The piping system, machinery, and appurtenances shall meet the present requirements of this subchapter for the maximum allowable working pressure requested. An increase in pressure shall be granted only by the Commandant upon presentation of data or plans proving that the requested increase in pressure is justified.

(b) When an existing boiler is replaced by a new boiler designed to operate at pressures in excess of the pressure indicated on the certificate of inspection for the previous boiler, an analysis of the complete system shall be made, including machinery and piping, to insure its compatibility with the increased steam pressure. The maximum allowable working pressure on the certificate of inspection shall be based on the results of this analysis.

§ 52.01-90 Materials (modifies PG-5 through PG-13).

(a) Material subject to stress due to pressure must conform to specifications as indicated in paragraphs PG–5 through PG–13 of section I of the ASME Boiler and Pressure Vessel Code (incorporated by reference; see 46 CFR 52.01–1) except as noted otherwise in this section.

(b) Material not fully identified with an ASME Boiler and Pressure Vessel Code-approved specification may be accepted as meeting Coast Guard requirements providing it satisfies the conditions indicated in paragraph PG–10 of section I of the ASME Boiler and Pressure Vessel Code.

(c) (*Modifies PG–5.*) When the maximum allowable working pressure (See PG–21) exceeds 15 pounds per square inch, cross pipes connecting the steam and water drums of water tube boilers, headers, cross boxes, and all pressure parts of the boiler proper, shall be made of a wrought or cast steel listed in tables 1A and 1B of section II of the ASME Boiler and Pressure Vessel Code (incorporated by reference; see 46 CFR 52.01–1).

(d) (*Modifies PG–8.2.*) The use of cast iron is prohibited for mountings, fittings, valves, or cocks attached directly to boilers operating at pressures exceeding 15 pounds per square inch.

[USCG–2003–16630, 73 FR 65161, Oct. 31, 2008]

§ 52.01–95 Design (modifies PG–16 through PG–31 and PG–100).

(a) *Requirements.* Boilers required to be designed to this part shall meet the requirements of PG–16 through PG–31 of section I of the ASME Boiler and Pressure Vessel Code (incorporated by reference; see 46 CFR 52.01–1) except as noted otherwise in this section.

(b) *Superheater.* (1) The design pressure of a superheater integral with the boiler shall not be less than the lowest setting of the drum safety valve.

(2) Controls shall be provided to insure that the maximum temperature at the superheater outlets does not exceed the allowable temperature limit of the material used in the superheater outlet, in the steam piping, and in the associated machinery under all operating conditions including boiler overload. Controls need not be provided if the operating superheater characteristic is demonstrated to be such that the temperature limits of the material will not be exceeded. Visible and audible alarms indicating excessive superheat shall be provided in any installation in which the superheater outlet temperature exceeds 454 °C (850 °F). The setting of the excessive superheat alarms must not exceed the maximum allowable temperature of the superheater outlet, which may be limited by the boiler design, the main steam piping design, or the temperature limits of other equipment subjected to the temperature of the steam.

(3) Arrangement shall be made for venting and draining the superheater in order to permit steam circulation through the superheater when starting the boiler.

(c) *Economizer.* The design pressure of an economizer integral with the boiler and connected to the boiler drum without intervening stop valves shall be at least equal to 110 percent of the highest setting of the safety valves on the drum.

(d) *Brazed boiler steam air heaters.* Boiler steam air heaters utilizing brazed construction are permitted at temperature not exceeding 525 °F. Refer to § 56.30–30(b)(1) of this subchapter for applicable requirements.

(e) *Stresses.* (*Modifies PG–22.*) The stresses due to hydrostatic head shall be taken into account in determining the minimum thickness of the shell or head of any boiler pressure part unless noted otherwise. Additional stresses, imposed by effects other than internal pressure or static head, which increase the average stress over substantial sections of the shell or head by more than 10 percent of the allowable stress shall be taken into account. These effects include the weight of the vessel and its contents, method of support, impact loads, superimposed loads, localized stresses due to the reactions of supports, stresses due to temperature gradients and dynamic effects.

(f) *Cylindrical components under internal pressure.* (*Modifies PG–27.*) The minimum required thickness and maximum allowable working pressure of boiler piping, tubes, drums and headers shall be as required by the formula in PG–27 of section I of the ASME Boiler and Pressure Vessel Code except that

§ 52.01-100

threaded boiler tubes are not permitted.

[CGFR 68–82, 33 FR 18815, Dec. 18, 1968, as amended by CGD 81–79, 50 FR 9432, Mar. 8, 1985; USCG–2003–16630, 73 FR 65161, Oct. 31, 2008]

§ 52.01-100 Openings and compensation (modifies PG–32 through PG–39, PG–42 through PG–55).

(a) The rules for openings and compensation shall be as indicated in PG–32 through PG–55 of section I of the ASME Boiler and Pressure Vessel Code (incorporated by reference; see 46 CFR 52.01–1) except as noted otherwise in this section.

(b) (*Modifies PG–39.*) Pipe and nozzle necks shall be attached to vessel walls as indicated in PG–39 of section I of the ASME Boiler and Pressure Vessel Code except that threaded connections shall not be used under any of the following conditions:

(1) Pressures greater than 4,137 kPa (600 psig);

(2) Nominal diameters greater than 51 mm (2 in.); or

(3) Nominal diameters greater than 19 mm (0.75 in.) and pressures above 1,034 kPa (150 psig).

(c) (*Modifies PG–42.*) Butt welding flanges and fittings must be used when full radiography is required by § 56.95–10.

[CGD 81–79, 50 FR 9432, Mar. 8, 1985, as amended by USCG–2003–16630, 73 FR 65161, Oct. 31, 2008]

§ 52.01-105 Piping, valves and fittings (modifies PG–58 and PG–59).

(a) Boiler external piping within the jurisdiction of the ASME Boiler and Pressure Vessel Code must be as indicated in PG–58 and PG–59 of section I of the ASME Boiler and Pressure Vessel Code (incorporated by reference; see 46 CFR 52.01–1) except as noted otherwise in this section. Piping outside the jurisdiction of the ASME Boiler and Pressure Vessel Code must meet the appropriate requirements of part 56 of this subchapter.

(b) In addition to the requirements in PG–58 and PG–59 of section I of the ASME Boiler and Pressure Vessel Code, boiler external piping must:

(1) Meet the design conditions and criteria in § 56.07–10 of this subchapter, except § 56.07–10(b);

(2) Be included in the pipe stress calculations required by § 56.35–1 of this subchapter;

(3) Meet the nondestructive examination requirements in § 56.95–10 of this subchapter;

(4) Have butt welding flanges and fittings when full radiography is required; and

(5) Meet the requirements for threaded joints in § 56.30–20 of this subchapter.

(c) Steam stop valves, in sizes exceeding 152mm (6 inch) NPS, must be fitted with bypasses for heating the line and equalizing the pressure before the valve is opened.

(d) *Feed connections.* (1) Feed water shall not be discharged into a boiler against surfaces exposed to hot gases or radiant heat of the fire.

(2) Feed water nozzles of boilers designed for pressures of 2758 kPa (400 psi), or over, shall be fitted with sleeves or other suitable means employed to reduce the effects of metal temperature differentials.

(e) *Blowoff connections.* (1) Firetube and drum type boilers shall be fitted with a surface and a bottom blowoff valve or cock attached directly to the boiler or to a short distance piece. The surface blowoff valve shall be located within the permissible range of the water level, or fitted with a scum pan or pipe at this level. The bottom blowoff valve shall be attached to the lowest part of the boiler or fitted with an internal pipe leading to the lowest point inside the boiler. Watertube boilers designed for pressures of 2413 kPa (350 psig) or over are not required to be fitted with a surface blowoff valve. Boilers equipped with a continuous blowdown valve on the steam drum are not required to be fitted with an additional surface blowoff connection.

(2) Where blowoff pipes are exposed to radiant heat of the fire, they must be protected by fire brick or other suitable heat-resisting material.

(f) *Dry pipes.* Internal dry pipes may be fitted to the steam drum outlet provided the dry pipes have a diameter equal to the steam drum outlet and a wall thickness at least equal to standard commercial pipe of the same diameter. Openings in dry pipes must be as near as practicable to the drum outlet and must be slotted or drilled. The width of the slots must not be less than 6mm (0.25 in.). The diameter of the holes must not be less than 10mm (0.375 in.). Where dry pipes are used, they must be provided with drains at each end to prevent an accumulation of water.

[CGD 81–79, 50 FR 9432, Mar. 8, 1985, as amended by USCG–2003–16630, 73 FR 65161, Oct. 31, 2008]

§ 52.01–110 **Water-level indicators, water columns, gauge-glass connections, gauge cocks, and pressure gauges (modifies PG–60).**

(a) *Boiler water level devices.* Boiler water level devices shall be as indicated in PG–60 of section I of the ASME Boiler and Pressure Vessel Code (incorporated by reference; see 46 CFR 52.01–1) except as noted otherwise in this section.

(b) *Water level indicators. (Modifies PG–60.1.)* (1) Each boiler, except those of the forced circulation type with no fixed water line and steam line, shall have two independent means of indicating the water level in the boiler connected directly to the head or shell. One shall be a gage lighted by the emergency electrical system (See subpart 112.15 of subchapter J (Electrical Engineering) of this chapter) which will insure illumination of the gages under all normal and emergency conditions. The secondary indicator may consist of a gage glass, or other acceptable device. Where the allowance pressure exceeds 1724 kPa (250 psi), the gage glasses shall be of the flat type instead of the common tubular type.

(2) Gage glasses shall be in continuous operation while the boiler is steaming.

(3) Double-ended firetube boilers shall be equipped as specified in this paragraph and paragraph (e) of this section except that the required water level indicators shall be installed on each end of the boiler.

(4) Externally fired flue boilers, such as are used on central western river vessels, shall be equipped as specified in paragraphs (b) (1) through (3) of this section except that float gages may be substituted for gage glasses.

(c) *Water columns. (Modifies PG–60.2.)* The use of water columns is generally limited to firetube boilers. Water column installations shall be close hauled to minimize the effect of ship motion on water level indication. When water columns are provided they shall be fitted directly to the heads or shells of boilers or drums by 1 inch minimum size pipes with shutoff valves attached directly to the boiler or drums, or if necessary, connected thereto by a distance piece both at the top and bottom of the water columns. Shutoff valves used in the pipe connections between the boiler and water column or between the boiler and the shutoff valves, required by PG–60.6 of section I of the ASME Boiler and Pressure Vessel Code for gauge glasses, shall be locked or sealed open. Water column piping shall not be fitted inside the uptake, the smoke box, or the casing. Water columns shall be fitted with suitable drains. Cast iron fittings are not permitted.

(d) *Gage glass connections. (Modifies PG–60.3.)* Gage glasses and gage cocks shall be connected directly to the head or shell of a boiler as indicated in paragraph (b)(1) of this section. When water columns are authorized, connections to the columns may be made provided a close hauled arrangement is utilized so that the effect of ship roll on the water level indication is minimized.

(e) *Gage cocks. (Modifies PG–60.4.)* (1) When the steam pressure does not exceed 250 pounds per square inch, three test cocks attached directly to the head or shell of a boiler may serve as the secondary water level indicator.

(2) See paragraph (d) of this section for restrictions on cock connections.

(f) *Pressure gages. (Modifies PG–60.6.)* Each double-ended boiler shall be fitted with two steam gages, one on either end on the boiler.

(g) *Salinometer cocks.* In vessels operating in salt water, each boiler shall be equipped with a salinometer cock or valve which shall be fitted directly to the boiler in a convenient position. They shall not be attached to the water gage or water column.

(h) *High-water-level alarm.* Each watertube boiler for propulsion must

§ 52.01-115

have an audible and a visible high-water-level alarm. The alarm indicators must be located where the boiler is controlled.

[CG FR 68-82, 33 FR 18815, Dec. 18, 1968, as amended by CGD 81-79, 50 FR 9433, Mar. 8, 1985; CGD 83-043, 60 FR 24772, May 10, 1995; USCG-2003-16630, 73 FR 65161, Oct. 31, 2008]

§ 52.01-115 Feedwater supply (modifies PG-61).

Boiler feedwater supply must meet the requirements of PG-61 of section I of the ASME Boiler and Pressure Vessel Code (incorporated by reference; see 46 CFR 52.01-1) and § 56.50-30 of this subchapter.

[USCG-2003-16630, 73 FR 65161, Oct. 31, 2008]

§ 52.01-120 Safety valves and safety relief valves (modifies PG-67 through PG-73).

(a)(1) Boiler safety valves and safety relief valves must be as indicated in PG-67 through PG-73 of section I of the ASME Boiler and Pressure Vessel Code (incorporated by reference; see 46 CFR 52.01-1) except as noted otherwise in this section.

(2) A safety valve must:

(i) Be stamped in accordance with PG-110 of section I of the ASME Boiler and Pressure Vessel Code;

(ii) Have its capacity certified by the National Board of Boiler and Pressure Vessel Inspectors;

(iii) Have a drain opening tapped for not less than 6mm (¼ in.) NPS; and

(iv) Not have threaded inlets for valves larger than 51mm (2 in.) NPS.

(3) On river steam vessels whose boilers are connected in batteries without means of isolating one boiler from another, each battery of boilers shall be treated as a single boiler and equipped with not less than two safety valves of equal size.

(4) (*Modifies PG-70.*) The total rated relieving capacity of drum and superheater safety valves as certified by the valve manufacturer shall not be less than the maximum generating capacity of the boiler which shall be determined and certified by the boiler manufacturer. This capacity shall be in compliance with PG-70 of section I of the ASME Boiler and Pressure Vessel Code.

(5) In the event the maximum steam generating capacity of the boiler is increased by any means, the relieving capacity of the safety valves shall be checked by an inspector, and, if determined to be necessary, valves of increased relieving capacity shall be installed.

(6) (*Modifies PG-67.*) Drum safety valves shall be set to relieve at a pressure not in excess of that allowed by the Certificate of Inspection. Where for any reason this is lower than the pressure for which the boiler was originally designed and the revised safety valve capacity cannot be recomputed and certified by the valve manufacturer, one of the tests described in PG-70(3) of section I of the ASME Boiler and Pressure Vessel Code shall be conducted in the presence of the Inspector to insure that the relieving capacity is sufficient at the lower pressure.

(7) On new installations the safety valve nominal size for propulsion boilers and superheaters must not be less than 38mm (1½ in.) nor more than 102mm (4 in.). Safety valves 38mm (1½ in.) to 114mm (4½ in.) may be used for replacements on existing boilers. The safety valve size for auxiliary boilers must be between 19mm (¾ in.) and 102mm (4 in.) NPS. The nominal size of a safety valve is the nominal diameter (as defined in 56.07-5(b)) of the inlet opening.

(8) Lever or weighted safety valves now installed may be continued in use and may be repaired, but when renewals are necessary, lever or weighted safety valves shall not be used. All such replacements shall conform to the requirements of this section.

(9) Gags or clamps for holding the safety valve disk on its seat shall be carried on board the vessel at all times.

(10) (*Modifies PG-73.2.*) Cast iron may be used only for caps and lifting bars. When used for these parts, the elongation must be at least 5 percent in 51mm (2 inch) gage length. Nonmetallic material may be used only for gaskets and packing.

(b)(1) (*Modifies PG-68.*) Superheater safety valves shall be as indicated in PG-68 of section I of the ASME Boiler and Pressure Vessel Code except as noted otherwise in this paragraph.

Coast Guard, Dept. of Homeland Security § 52.01-130

(2) The setting of the superheater safety valve shall not exceed the design pressure of the superheater outlet flange or the main steam piping beyond the superheater. To prevent damage to the superheater, the drum safety valve shall be set at a pressure not less than that of the superheater safety valve setting plus 5 pounds minimum plus approximately the normal load pressure drop through the superheater and associated piping, including the controlled desuperheater if fitted. See also § 52.01–95(b) (1).

(3) Drum pilot actuated superheater safety valves are permitted provided the setting of the pilot valve and superheater safety valve is such that the superheater safety valve will open before the drum safety valve.

(c)(1) (*Modifies PG–71.*) Safety valves shall be installed as indicated in PG–71 of section I of the ASME Boiler and Pressure Vessel Code except as noted otherwise in this paragraph.

(2) The final setting of boiler safety valves shall be checked and adjusted under steam pressure and, if possible, while the boiler is on the line and the steam is at operating temperatures, in the presence of and to the satisfaction of a marine inspector who, upon acceptance, shall seal the valves. This regulation applies to both drum and superheater safety valves of all boilers.

(3) The safety valve body drains required by PG–71 of section I of the ASME Boiler and Pressure Vessel Code shall be run as directly as possible from the body of each boiler safety valve, or the drain from each boiler safety valve may be led to an independent header common only to boiler safety valve drains. No valves of any type shall be installed in the leakoff from drains or drain headers and they shall be led to suitable locations to avoid hazard to personnel.

(d)(1) (*Modifies PG–72.*) The operation of safety valves shall be as indicated in PG–72 of section I of the ASME Boiler and Pressure Vessel Code except as noted in paragraph (d)(2) of this section.

(2) (*Modifies PG–73.*) The lifting device required by PG–73.1.3 of section I of the ASME Boiler and Pressure Vessel Code shall be fitted with suitable relieving gear so arranged that the controls may be operated from the fireroom or engineroom floor.

[CGFR 68–82, 33 FR 18815, Dec. 18, 1968, as amended by CGD 81–79, 50 FR 9433, Mar. 8, 1985; USCG–2003–16630, 73 FR 65161, Oct. 31, 2008]

§ 52.01-130 Installation.

(a) *Foundations.* (1) Plans showing details of proposed foundations and support for boilers and the proposed means of bracing boilers in the vessel shall be submitted for approval to the Officer in Charge, Marine Inspection, in the district where the installation is being made.

(2) Provision shall be made in foundations for expansion of the boilers when heated.

(3) Boilers shall be provided with chocks to prevent movement in the event of collision unless a bolted or riveted construction satisfactorily provides for this contingency.

(b) *Protection of adjacent structure.* (1) Boilers shall be so placed that all parts are readily accessible for inspection and repair.

(2) In vessels having a double bottom or other extensive surfaces directly below the boiler, the distance between such surface and a boiler shall in no case be less than 18 inches at the lowest part.

(3) In certain types of vessels where the boiler foundation forms the ashpit, such foundations shall be efficiently ventilated, except in cases where the ashpit is partially filled with water at all times.

(4) The pans of oil-burning, watertube boilers shall be arranged to prevent oil from leaking into the bilges and shall be lined with firebrick or other heat resisting material.

(5) The distance between a boiler and a compartment containing fuel oil shall not be less than 24 inches at the back end of a boiler and 18 inches elsewhere, except that for a cylindrical part of a boiler or a knuckle in the casing of a water-tube boiler, these distances may be reduced to 18 inches, provided all parts are readily accessible for inspection and repair.

(6) All oil-burning boilers shall be provided with oiltight drip pans under the burners and elsewhere as necessary to prevent oil draining into the bilges.

§52.01-135

(c) *Boiler uptakes.* (1) Where dampers are installed in the uptakes or funnels, the arrangement shall be such that it will not be possible to shut off the gas passages from the operating boilers.

(2) Each main power boiler and auxiliary boiler shall be fitted with a separate gas passage.

§52.01-135 Inspection and tests (modifies PG-90 through PG-100).

(a) *Requirements.* Inspection and test of boilers and boiler pressure parts shall be as indicated in PG-90 through PG-100 of section I of the ASME Boiler and Pressure Vessel Code (incorporated by reference; see 46 CFR 52.01-1) except as noted otherwise in this section.

(b) The inspections required by PG-90 through PG-100 of the ASME Code shall be performed by the "Authorized Inspector" as defined in PG-91 of section I of the ASME Boiler and Pressure Vessel Code (incorporated by reference; see 46 CFR 52.01-1). The Authorized Inspector shall hold a valid commission issued by the National Board of Boiler and Pressure Vessel Inspectors. After installation, boilers will be inspected for compliance with this part by the "Marine Inspector" as defined in §50.10-15 of this subchapter.

(c) *Hydrostatic test (Modifies PG-99).* Each new boiler shall be hydrostatically tested after installation to 1½ times the maximum allowable working pressure as indicated in PG-99 of section I of the ASME Boiler and Pressure Vessel Code (incorporated by reference; see 46 CFR 52.01-1). Before the boilers are insulated, accessible parts of the boiler shall be emptied, opened up and all interior surfaces shall be examined by the marine inspector to ascertain that no defects have occurred due to the hydrostatic test.

(d) *Operating tests.* In addition to hydrostatic tests prescribed in paragraph (c) of this section, automatically controlled auxiliary boilers must be subjected to operating tests as specified in §§ 61.30-20, 61.35-1, 61.35-3, 62.30-10, 63.15-9, 63.25-3, and 63.25-5 of this chapter, as appropriate, or as directed by the Officer in Charge, Marine Inspection, for propulsion boilers. These tests are to be performed after final installation.

[CGFR 68-82, 33 FR 18815, Dec. 18, 1968, as amended by CGFR 69-127, 35 FR 9976, June 17, 1970; CGD 81-79, 50 FR 9433, Mar. 8, 1985; CGD 88-057, 55 FR 24236, June 15, 1990; USCG-2003-16630, 73 FR 65162, Oct. 31, 2008]

§52.01-140 Certification by stamping (modifies PG-104 through PG-113).

(a) All boilers built in accordance with this part must be stamped with the appropriate ASME Code symbol as required by PG-104 through PG-113 of section I of the ASME Boiler and Pressure Vessel Code (incorporated by reference; see 46 CFR 52.01-1).

(b)(1) Upon satisfactory completion of the tests and Coast Guard inspections, boilers must be stamped with the following:

(i) Manufacturer's name and serial number;

(ii) ASME Code Symbol;

(iii) Coast Guard symbol, which is affixed only by marine inspector (see §50.10-15 of this subchapter);

(iv) Maximum allowable working pressure _____ at _____ °C (°F): and

(v) Boiler rated steaming capacity in kilograms (pounds) per hour (rated joules (B.T.U.) per hour output for high temperature water boilers).

(2) The information required in paragraph (b)(1) of this section must be located on:

(i) The front head or shell near the normal waterline and within 610 mm (24 inches) of the front of firetube boilers; and

(ii) The drum head of water tube boilers.

(3) Those heating boilers which are built to section I of section I of the ASME Boiler and Pressure Vessel Code (incorporated by reference; see 46 CFR 52.01-1), as permitted by §53.01-10(e) of this subchapter, do not require Coast Guard stamping and must receive full ASME stamping including the appropriate code symbol.

(c) The data shall be legibly stamped and shall not be obliterated during the life of the boiler. In the event that the portion of the boiler upon which the data is stamped is to be insulated or otherwise covered, a metal nameplate as described in PG-106.6 of section I of the ASME Boiler and Pressure Vessel

Code (incorporated by reference; see 46 CFR 52.01–1) shall be furnished and mounted. The nameplate is to be maintained in a legible condition so that the data may be easily read.

(d) Safety valves shall be stamped as indicated in PG–110 of the ASME Boiler and Pressure Vessel Code.

[CGD 81–79, 50 FR 9433, Mar. 8, 1985, as amended by USCG–2003–16630, 73 FR 65162, Oct. 31, 2008]

§ 52.01–145 Manufacturers' data report forms (modifies PG–112 and PG–113).

The manufacturers' data report forms required by PG–112 and PG–113 of section I of the ASME Boiler and Pressure Vessel Code (incorporated by reference; see 46 CFR 52.01–1) must be made available to the marine inspector for review. The Authorized Inspector's National Board commission number must be included on the manufacturers' data report forms.

[CGD 81–79, 50 FR 9434, Mar. 8, 1985, as amended by USCG–2003–16630, 73 FR 65161, Oct. 31, 2008]

Subpart 52.05—Requirements for Boilers Fabricated by Welding

§ 52.05–1 General (modifies PW–1 through PW–54).

(a) Boilers and component parts, including piping, that are fabricated by welding shall be as indicated in PW–1 through PW–54 of section I of the ASME Boiler and Pressure Vessel Code (incorporated by reference; see 46 CFR 52.01–1) except as noted otherwise in this subpart.

[CGFR 68–82, 33 FR 18815, Dec. 18, 1968, as amended by USCG–2003–16630, 73 FR 65162, Oct. 31, 2008]

§ 52.05–15 Heat treatment (modifies PW–10).

(a) Vessels and vessel parts shall be preheated and postweld heat treated in accordance with PW–38 and PW–39 of section I of the ASME Boiler and Pressure Vessel Code (incorporated by reference; see 46 CFR 52.01–1) (reproduces PW–10). This includes boiler parts made of pipe material even though they may be nondestructively examined under § 52.05–20.

[CGFR 68–82, 33 FR 18815, Dec. 18, 1968, as amended by USCG–2003–16630, 73 FR 65162, Oct. 31, 2008]

§ 52.05–20 Radiographic and ultrasonic examination (modifies PW–11 and PW–41.1).

Radiographic and ultrasonic examination of welded joints must be as described in PW–11 of section I of the ASME Boiler and Pressure Vessel Code (incorporated by reference; see 46 CFR 52.01–1), except that parts of boilers fabricated of pipe material such as drums, shells, downcomers, risers, cross pipes, headers, and tubes containing only circumferentially welded butt joints, must be nondestructively examined as required by § 56.95–10 of this subchapter even though they may be exempted by the limits on size specified in table PW–11 and PW–41.1 of section I of the ASME Boiler and Pressure Vessel Code.

[USCG–2003–16630, 73 FR 65162, Oct. 31, 2008]

§ 52.05–30 Minimum requirements for attachment welds (modifies PW–16).

(a) The location and minimum size of attachment welds for nozzles and other connections shall be as required by PW–16 of section I of the ASME Boiler and Pressure Vessel Code (incorporated by reference; see 46 CFR 52.01–1) except as noted otherwise in this section.

(b) When nozzles or couplings are attached to boilers, as shown in Figure PW–16 (a) and (c) of section I of the ASME Boiler and Pressure Vessel Code and are welded from one side only, backing strips shall be used unless it can be determined visually or by acceptable nondestructive test methods that complete penetration has been obtained.

(c) When attachments as shown in Figure PW–16 (y) and (z) of section I of the ASME Boiler and Pressure Vessel Code are employed they shall be limited to 2-inch pipe size for pressure exceeding 150 pounds per square inch.

[CGFR 68–82, 33 FR 18815, Dec. 18, 1968, as amended by USCG–2003–16630, 73 FR 65161, Oct. 31, 2008]

§ 52.05–45 Circumferential joints in pipes, tubes and headers (modifies PW–41).

(a) Circumferential welded joints of pipes, tubes and headers shall be as required by PW–41 of section I of the ASME Boiler and Pressure Vessel Code (incorporated by reference; see 46 CFR 52.01–1) except as noted otherwise in this section.

(b) (*Modifies PW–41.1*) Circumferential welded joints in pipes, tubes, and headers of pipe material must be nondestructively examined as required by § 56.95–10 of this subchapter and PW–41 of section I of the ASME Boiler and Pressure Vessel Code.

(c) (*Modifies PW–41.5*) Butt welded connections shall be provided whenever radiography is required by § 56.95–10 of this subchapter for the piping system in which the connection is to be made. When radiography is not required, welded socket or sleeve type joints meeting the requirements of PW–41.5 of section I of the ASME Boiler and Pressure Vessel Code may be provided.

[CGFR 68–82, 33 FR 18815, Dec. 18, 1968, as amended by CGD 81–79, 50 FR 9434, Mar. 8, 1985; USCG–2003–16630, 73 FR 65161, Oct. 31, 2008]

Subpart 52.15—Requirements for Watertube Boilers

§ 52.15–1 General (modifies PWT–1 through PWT–15).

Watertube boilers and parts thereof shall be as indicated in PWT–1 through PWT–15 of section I of the ASME Boiler and Pressure Vessel Code (incorporated by reference; see 46 CFR 52.01–1) except as noted otherwise in this subpart.

[CGD 81–79, 50 FR 9434, Mar. 8, 1985; USCG–2003–16630, 73 FR 65161, Oct. 31, 2008]

§ 52.15–5 Tube connections (modifies PWT–9 and PWT–11).

(a) Tubes, pipe and nipples shall be attached to sheets, heads, headers, and fittings as indicated in PWT–11 of section I of the ASME Boiler and Pressure Vessel Code (incorporated by reference; see 46 CFR 52.01–1) except as noted otherwise in this section.

(b) (*Replaces PWT–9.2 and PWT–11.3.*) Threaded boiler tubes shall not be permitted as described by PWT–9.2 and PWT–11.3 of section I of the ASME Boiler and Pressure Vessel Code.

(c) In welded wall construction employing stub and welded wall panels which are field welded, approximately 10 percent of the field welds shall be checked using any acceptable nondestructive test method.

(d) Nondestructive testing of the butt welded joints shall meet the requirements of § 56.95–10 of this subchapter.

[CGFR 68–82, 33 FR 18815, Dec. 18, 1968, as amended by CGFR 69–127, 35 FR 9976, June 17, 1970; CGD 81–79, 50 FR 9434, Mar. 8, 1985; USCG–2003–16630, 73 FR 65161, Oct. 31, 2008]

Subpart 52.20—Requirements for Firetube Boilers

§ 52.20–1 General (modifies PFT–1 through PFT–49).

Firetube boilers and parts thereof shall be as indicated in PFT–1 through PFT–49 of section I of the ASME Boiler and Pressure Vessel Code (incorporated by reference; see 46 CFR 52.01–1) except as noted otherwise in this subpart.

[USCG–2003–16630, 73 FR 65161, Oct. 31, 2008]

§ 52.20–17 Opening between boiler and safety valve (modifies PFT–44).

When a discharge pipe is used, it must be installed in accordance with the requirements of § 52.01–105.

[CGD 81–79, 50 FR 9434, Mar. 8, 1985]

§ 52.20–25 Setting (modifies PFT–46).

(a) The method of supporting firetube boilers shall be as indicated in PFT–46 of section I of the ASME Boiler and Pressure Vessel Code (incorporated by reference; see 46 CFR 52.01–1) except as noted otherwise in this section.

(b) The foundations shall meet the requirements of § 52.01–130.

[CGFR 68–82, 33 FR 18815, Dec. 18, 1968, as amended by USCG–2003–16630, 73 FR 65161, Oct. 31, 2008]

Subpart 52.25—Other Boiler Types

SOURCE: CGD 81–79, 50 FR 9434, Mar. 8, 1985, unless otherwise noted.

Coast Guard, Dept. of Homeland Security

§ 52.25-1 General.

Requirements for fired boilers of various sizes and uses are referenced in table 54.01–5(a) of this subchapter.

§ 52.25-3 Feedwater heaters (modifies PFH-1).

In addition to the requirements in PFH–1 of section I of the ASME Boiler and Pressure Vessel Code (incorporated by reference; see 46 CFR 52.01–1), feedwater heaters must meet the requirements in this part or the requirements in part 54.

[CGFR 68–82, 33 FR 18815, Dec. 18, 1968, as amended by USCG–2003–16630, 73 FR 65161, Oct. 31, 2008]

§ 52.25-5 Miniature boilers (modifies PMB-1 through PMB-21).

Miniature boilers must meet the applicable provisions in this part for the boiler type involved and the mandatory requirements in PMB–1 through PMB–21 of of section I of the ASME Boiler and Pressure Vessel Code (incorporated by reference; see 46 CFR 52.01–1)

[CGFR 68–82, 33 FR 18815, Dec. 18, 1968, as amended by USCG–2003–16630, 73 FR 65161, Oct. 31, 2008]

§ 52.25-7 Electric boilers (modifies PEB-1 through PEB-19).

Electric boilers required to comply with this part must meet the applicable provisions in this part and the mandatory requirements in PEB–1 through PEB–19 except PEB–3 of section I of the ASME Boiler and Pressure Vessel Code (incorporated by reference; see 46 CFR 52.01–1).

[CGFR 68–82, 33 FR 18815, Dec. 18, 1968, as amended by USCG–2003–16630, 73 FR 65161, Oct. 31, 2008]

§ 52.25-10 Organic fluid vaporizer generators (modifies PVG-1 through PVG-12).

(a) Organic fluid vaporizer generators and parts thereof shall meet the requirements of PVG–1 through PVG–12 of section I of the ASME Boiler and Pressure Vessel Code (incorporated by reference; see 46 CFR 52.01–1) except as noted otherwise in this section.

(b) The application and end use of organic fluid vaporizer generators shall be approved by the Commandant.

[CGFR 68–82, 33 FR 18815, Dec. 18, 1968, as amended by USCG–2003–16630, 73 FR 65161, Oct. 31, 2008]

§ 52.25-15 Fired thermal fluid heaters.

(a) Fired thermal fluid heaters shall be designed, constructed, inspected, tested, and stamped in accordance with the applicable provisions in this part.

(b) Each fired thermal fluid heater must be fitted with a control which prevents the heat transfer fluid from being heated above its flash point.

(c) The heat transfer fluid must be chemically compatible with any cargo carried in the cargo tanks serviced by the heat transfer system.

(d) Each fired thermal fluid heater must be tested and inspected in accordance with the requirements of subpart 61.30 of this chapter.

[CGFR 68–82, 33 FR 18815, Dec. 18, 1968, as amended by CGD 88–057, 55 FR 24236, June 15, 1990]

§ 52.25-20 Exhaust gas boilers.

Exhaust gas boilers with a maximum allowable working pressure greater than 103 kPa gage (15 psig) or an operating temperature greater than 454 °C. (850 °F.) must be designed, constructed, inspected, tested and stamped in accordance with the applicable provisions in this part. The design temperature of parts exposed to the exhaust gas must be the maximum temperature that could normally be produced by the source of the exhaust gas. This temperature must be verified by testing or by the manufacturer of the engine or other equipment producing the exhaust. Automatic exhaust gas boiler control systems must be designed, constructed, tested, and inspected in accordance with § 63.25–7 of this chapter.

[CGD 88–057, 55 FR 24236, June 15, 1990]

PART 53—HEATING BOILERS

Subpart 53.01—General Requirements

Sec.
53.01–1 Incorporation by reference.
53.01–3 Adoption of section IV of the ASME Boiler and Pressure Vessel Code.
53.01–5 Scope (modifies HG–100).

§ 53.01-1

53.01-10 Service restrictions and exceptions (replaces HG–101).

Subpart 53.05—Pressure Relieving Devices (Article 4)

53.05-1 Safety valve requirements for steam boilers (modifies HG–400 and HG–401).
53.05-2 Relief valve requirements for hot water boilers (modifies HG–400.2).
53.05-3 Materials (modifies HG–401.2).
53.05-5 Discharge capacities and valve markings.

Subpart 53.10—Tests, Inspection, Stamping, and Reporting (Article 5)

53.10-1 General.
53.10-3 Inspection and tests (modifies HG–500 through HG–540).
53.10-10 Certification by stamping.
53.10-15 Manufacturers' data report forms.

Subpart 53.12—Instruments, Fittings, and Controls (Article 6)

53.12-1 General (modifies HG–600 through HG–640).

AUTHORITY: 46 U.S.C. 3306, 3703; E.O. 12234, 45 FR 58801, 3 CFR, 1980 Comp., p. 277; Department of Homeland Security Delegation No. 0170.1.

SOURCE: CGFR 68–82, 33 FR 18826, Dec. 18, 1968, unless otherwise noted.

Subpart 53.01—General Requirements

§ 53.01-1 Incorporation by reference.

(a) Certain material is incorporated by reference into this part with the approval of the Director of the Federal Register under 5 U.S.C. 552(a) and 1 CFR part 51. To enforce any edition other than that specified in this section, the Coast Guard must publish notice of change in the FEDERAL REGISTER and the material must be available to the public. All approved material is available for inspection at the National Archives and Records Administration (NARA). For information on the availability of this material at NARA, call 202–741–6030 or go to *http://www.archives.gov/federal_register/code_of_federal_regulations/ibr_locations.html*. The material is also available for inspection at the Coast Guard Headquarters. Contact Commandant (CG–ENG), Attn: Office of Design and Engineering Systems, U.S. Coast Guard Stop 7509, 2703 Martin Luther King Jr. Avenue SE., Washington, DC 20593–7509. You may also inspect this material at the sources listed below.

(b) *American Society of Mechanical Engineers (ASME) International,* Three Park Avenue, New York, NY 10016–5990:

(1) 2001 ASME Boiler and Pressure Vessel Code, Section I, Rules for Construction of Power Boilers (July 1, 2001) ("Section I of the ASME Boiler and Pressure Vessel Code"), 53.01–10.

(2) 2004 ASME Boiler and Pressure Vessel Code, Section IV, Rules for Construction of Heating Boilers (July 1, 2004) ("Section IV of the ASME Boiler and Pressure Vessel Code"), 53.01–3; 53.01–5; 53.01–10; 53.05–1; 53.05–2; 53.05–3; 53.05–5; 53.10–1; 53.10–3; 53.10–10; 53.10–15; and 53.12–1.

(c) *Underwriters Laboratories Inc.,* 333 Pfingston Road, Northbrook, IL 60062–2096:

(1) UL 174, Standard for Household Electric Storage Tank Water Heaters, Tenth Edition, Feb. 28, 1996 (Revisions through and including Nov. 10, 1997) ("UL 174"), 53.01–10.

(2) UL 1453, Standard for Electric Booster and Commercial Storage Tank Water Heaters, Fourth Edition, Sep. 1, 1995 ("UL 1453"), 53.01–10.

[USCG–2003–16630, 73 FR 65163, Oct. 31, 2008, as amended by USCG–2009–0702, 74 FR 49228, Sept. 25, 2009; USCG–2012–0832, 77 FR 59777, Oct. 1, 2012; USCG 2013–0671, 78 FR 60147, Sept. 30, 2013]

§ 53.01-3 Adoption of section IV of the ASME Boiler and Pressure Vessel Code.

(a) Heating boilers shall be designed, constructed, inspected, tested, and stamped in accordance with section IV of the ASME Boiler and Pressure Vessel Code (incorporated by reference; see 46 CFR 53.01–1) as limited, modified, or replaced by specific requirements in this part. The provisions in the appendices to section IV of the ASME Boiler and Pressure Vessel Code are adopted and shall be followed when the requirements in section IV make them mandatory. For general information, table 53.01–3(a) lists the various paragraphs in section IV of the ASME Boiler and Pressure Vessel Code that are limited, modified, or replaced by regulations in this part.

TABLE 53.01–3(a)—LIMITATIONS AND MODIFICATIONS IN THE ADOPTION OF SECTION IV OF THE ASME BOILER AND PRESSURE VESSEL CODE

Paragraphs in Section IV of the ASME Boiler and Pressure Vessel Code [1] and disposition	Unit of this part
HG–100 modified by	53.01–5(b)
HG–101 replaced by	53.01–10
HG–400 modified by	53.05–1
HG–400.2 modified by	53.05–2
HG–401 modified by	53.05–1
HG–401.2 modified by	53.05–3
HG–500 through HG–540 modified by	53.10–3
HG–600 through HG–640 modified by	53.12–1

[1] The references to specific provisions in the ASME Boiler and Pressure Vessel Code are coded. The first letter, such as "H," refers to section IV. The second letter, such as "G," refers to a part or subpart in section IV. The number following the letters refers to the paragraph so numbered in the text of the part or subpart in section IV.

(b) References to the ASME Boiler and Pressure Vessel Code, such as paragraph HG–307, indicate:

H = Section IV of the ASME Boiler and Pressure Vessel Code.

G = Part containing general requirements.

3 = Article in part.

307 = Paragraph within Article 3.

(c) When a paragraph or a section of the regulations in this part relates to material in section IV of the ASME Boiler and Pressure Vessel Code, the relationship with the code will be shown immediately following the heading of the section or at the beginning of the paragraph, as follows:

(1) (Modifies H_____.) This indicates that the material in H_____ is generally applicable but is being altered, amplified or augmented.

(2) (Replaces H_____.) This indicates that H_____ does not apply.

(3) (Reproduces H_____.) This indicates that H_____ is being identically reproduced for convenience, not for emphasis.

[CGFR 68–82, 33 FR 18826, Dec. 18, 1968, as amended by CGFR 69–127, 35 FR 9976, June 17, 1970; CGD 81–79, 50 FR 9435, Mar. 8, 1985. Redesignated and amended by CGD 88–032, 56 FR 35821, July 29, 1991; USCG–2003–16630, 73 FR 65163, Oct. 31, 2008]

§ 53.01–5 Scope (modifies HG–100).

(a) The regulations in this part apply to steam heating boilers, hot water boilers (which include hot water heating boilers and hot water supply boilers), and to appurtenances thereto. The requirements in this part shall be used in conjunction with section IV of the ASME Boiler and Pressure Vessel Code (incorporated by reference; see 46 CFR 53.01–1). table 54.01–5(a) of this subchapter gives a breakdown by parts in this subchapter of the regulations governing various types of pressure vessels and boilers.

(b) *Modifies HG–100.* The requirements of part HG of section IV of the ASME Boiler and Pressure Vessel Code shall be used except as noted otherwise in this part.

[USCG–2003–16630, 73 FR 65163, Oct. 31, 2008]

§ 53.01–10 Service restrictions and exceptions (replaces HG–101).

(a) *General.* The service restrictions and exceptions shall be as indicated in this section in lieu of the requirements in HG–101 of section IV of the ASME Boiler and Pressure Vessel Code (incorporated by reference; see 46 CFR 53.01–1).

(b) *Service restrictions.* (1) Boilers of wrought materials shall be restricted to a maximum of 103 kPa gage (15 psig) for steam and a maximum of 689 kPa (100 psig) or 121 °C (250 °F) for hot water. If operating conditions exceed these limits, design and fabrications shall be in accordance with part 52 of this subchapter.

(2) Boilers of cast iron materials shall be restricted to a maximum of 103 kPa gage (15 psig) for steam and to a maximum of 206 kPa gage (30 psig) or 121 °C (250 °F) for hot water.

(c) *Hot water supply boilers.* (1) Electrically fired hot water supply boilers that have a capacity not greater than 454 liters (120 gallons), a heat input not greater than 58.6 kilowatts (200,000 BTU per hour), and are listed as approved under Underwriters' Laboratories UL 174 or UL 1453 (both incorporated by reference; see 46 CFR 53.01–1) are exempted from the requirements of this part provided they are protected by a pressure relief device. This relief device need not comply with § 53.05–2.

(2) Oil fired hot water supply boilers shall not be exempted from the requirements of this part on the basis of size or heat input.

(d) *Exhaust gas type boilers* shall be restricted to a working pressure equal to or less than 103 kPa gage (15 psig) and an operating temperature equal to or less than 454 °C (850 °F). The design temperature of parts exposed to the exhaust gas must be the maximum temperature that could normally be produced by the source of exhaust gas. This temperature shall be verified by testing or by the manufacturer of the engine or other equipment producing the exhaust.

(e) Heating boilers whose operating conditions are within the service restrictions of § 53.01–10(b)(1) may be constructed in accordance with section I of the ASME Boiler and Pressure Vessel Code (incorporated by reference; see 46 CFR 53.01–1). In addition, these heating boilers must:

(1) Be stamped with the appropriate ASME Code symbol in accordance with PG–104 through PG–113 of section IV of the ASME Boiler and Pressure Vessel Code;

(2) Meet the service restrictions of § 53.01–10(b)(2) if made of cast iron;

(3) Have safety valves which meet the requirements of § 52.01–120 of this subchapter;

(4) If a hot water supply boiler, have a temperature relief valve or a pressure-temperature relief valve in accordance with § 53.05–2(c);

(5) If automatically controlled, meet the applicable requirements in part 63 of this subchapter; and

(6) Meet the inspection and test requirements of § 53.10–3.

(f) *Controls and miscellaneous accessories.* Refer to part 63 of this subchapter for the requirements governing controls and miscellaneous accessories.

[CGFR 68–82, 33 FR 18826, Dec. 18, 1968, as amended by CGD 81–79, 50 FR 9435, Mar. 8, 1985; USCG–2003–16630, 73 FR 65163, Oct. 31, 2008]

Subpart 53.05—Pressure Relieving Devices (Article 4)

SOURCE: CGD 81–79, 50 FR 9435, Mar. 8, 1985, unless otherwise noted.

§ 53.05–1 Safety valve requirements for steam boilers (modifies HG–400 and HG–401).

(a) The pressure relief valve requirements and the safety valve requirements for steam boilers must be as indicated in HG–400 and HG–401 of section IV of the ASME Boiler and Pressure Vessel Code (incorporated by reference; see 46 CFR 53.01–1) except as noted otherwise in this section.

(b) Each steam boiler must have at least one safety valve.

[CGD 81–79, 50 FR 9435, Mar. 8, 1985, as amended by USCG–2003–16630, 73 FR 65163, Oct. 31, 2008]

§ 53.05–2 Relief valve requirements for hot water boilers (modifies HG–400.2).

(a) The relief valve requirements for hot water boilers must be as indicated in article 4 of section IV of the ASME Boiler and Pressure Vessel Code (incorporated by reference; see 46 CFR 53.01–1) except as noted otherwise in this section.

(b) *Hot water heating boilers.* Each hot water heating boiler must have at least one safety relief valve.

(c) *Hot water supply boilers.* Each hot water supply boiler must have at least one safety relief valve and a temperature relief valve or a pressure-temperature relief valve. The valve temperature setting must not be more than 99 °C (210 °F).

[CGD 81–79, 50 FR 9435, Mar. 8, 1985, as amended by USCG–2003–16630, 73 FR 65163, Oct. 31, 2008]

§ 53.05–3 Materials (modifies HG–401.2).

Materials for valves must be in accordance with HG–401.2 of section IV of the ASME Boiler and Pressure Vessel Code (incorporated by reference; see 46 CFR 53.01–1) except that nonmetallic materials may be used only for gaskets and packing.

[USCG–2003–16630, 73 FR 65164, Oct. 31, 2008]

§ 53.05–5 Discharge capacities and valve markings.

The discharge capacities and valve markings must be as indicated in HG–402 of section IV of the ASME Boiler and Pressure Vessel Code (incorporated by reference; see 46 CFR 53.01–1). The discharge capacities must be certified by the National Board of Boiler and Pressure Vessel Inspectors.

[USCG–2003–16630, 73 FR 65164, Oct. 31, 2008]

Subpart 53.10—Tests, Inspection, Stamping, and Reporting (Article 5)

§ 53.10-1 General.

The tests, inspection, stamping, and reporting of heating boilers shall be as indicated in article 5, part HG of section IV of the ASME Boiler and Pressure Vessel Code (incorporated by reference; see 46 CFR 53.01–1) except as noted otherwise in this subpart.

[USCG–2003–16630, 73 FR 65164, Oct. 31, 2008]

§ 53.10-3 Inspection and tests (modifies HG-500 through HG-540).

(a) The inspections required by HG–500 through HG–540 must be performed by the "Authorized Inspector" as defined in HG–515 of section IV of the ASME Boiler and Pressure Vessel Code (incorporated by reference; see 46 CFR 53.01–1). The Authorized Inspector shall hold a valid commission issued by the National Board of Boiler and Pressure Vessel Inspectors. After installation, heating boilers must be inspected for compliance with this part by a marine inspector.

(b) Automatically controlled boilers must be subjected to the operating tests prescribed in part 63 of this subchapter.

(c) All heating boilers must have the operation of their pressure relieving devices checked after the final installation.

[CGD 81–79, 50 FR 9436, Mar. 8, 1985, as amended by USCG–2003–16630, 73 FR 65164, Oct. 31, 2008]

§ 53.10-10 Certification by stamping.

Stamping of heating boilers shall be as indicated in HG–530 of section IV of the ASME Boiler and Pressure Vessel Code (incorporated by reference; see 46 CFR 53.01–1).

[USCG–2003–16630, 73 FR 65164, Oct. 31, 2008]

§ 53.10-15 Manufacturers' data report forms.

The manufacturers' data report forms required by HG–520 of section IV of the ASME Boiler and Pressure Vessel Code (incorporated by reference; see 46 CFR 53.01–1) must be made available to the marine inspector for review. The Authorized Inspector's National Board commission number must be included on the manufacturers' data report forms.

[USCG–2003–16630, 73 FR 65164, Oct. 31, 2008]

Subpart 53.12—Instruments, Fittings, and Controls (Article 6)

§ 53.12-1 General (modifies HG–600 through HG–640).

(a) The instruments, fittings and controls for heating boilers shall be as indicated in HG–600 through HG–640 of section IV of the ASME Boiler and Pressure Vessel Code (incorporated by reference; see 46 CFR 53.01–1) except as noted otherwise in this section.

(b) For control systems for automatic auxiliary heating equipment, the requirements in part 63 of this subchapter govern and shall be followed.

[CGFR 68–82, 33 FR 18826, Dec. 18, 1968, as amended by USCG–2003–16630, 73 FR 65164, Oct. 31, 2008]

PART 54—PRESSURE VESSELS

Subpart 54.01—General Requirements

Sec.
54.01–1 Incorporation by reference
54.01–2 Adoption of division 1 of section VIII of the ASME Boiler and Pressure Vessel Code.
54.01–5 Scope (modifies U–1 and U–2).
54.01–10 Steam-generating pressure vessels (modifies U–1(g)).
54.01–15 Exemptions from shop inspection and plan approval (modifiesU–1(c)(2)).
54.01–17 Pressure vessel for human occupancy (PVHO).
54.01–18 Plan approval.
54.01–25 Miscellaneous pressure components (modifies UG–11).
54.01–30 Loadings (modifies UG–22).
54.01–35 Corrosion (modifies UG–25).
54.01–40 External pressure (modifies UG– 28).

Subpart 54.03—Low Temperature Operation

54.03–1 Scope.
54.03–5 General.

Subpart 54.05—Toughness Tests

54.05–1 Scope (replaces UG–84).
54.05–3 Tests required.
54.05–5 Toughness test specimens.
54.05–6 Toughness test temperatures.
54.05–10 Certification of material toughness tests.

§ 54.01-1

54.05–15 Weldment toughness tests—procedure qualifications.
54.05–16 Production toughness testing.
54.05–17 Weld toughness test acceptance criteria.
54.05–20 Impact test properties for service of 0 °F. and below.
54.05–25 [Reserved]
54.05–30 Allowable stress values at low temperatures.

Subpart 54.10—Inspection, Reports, and Stamping

54.10–1 Scope (modifies UG–90 through UG–103 and UG–115 through UG–120).
54.10–3 Marine inspectors (replaces UG–90 and UG–91, and modifies UG–92 through UG–103).
54.10–5 Maximum allowable working pressure (reproduces UG–98).
54.10–10 Standard hydrostatic test (modifies UG–99).
54.10–15 Pneumatic test (modifies UG–100).
54.10–20 Marking and stamping.
54.10–25 Manufacturers' data report forms (modifies UG–120).

Subpart 54.15—Pressure-Relief Devices

54.15–1 General (modifies UG–125 through UG–137).
54.15–3 Definitions (modifies appendix 3).
54.15–5 Protective devices (modifies UG–125).
54.15–10 Safety and relief valves (modifies UG–126).
54.15–13 Rupture disks (modifies UG–127).
54.15–15 Relief devices for unfired steam boilers, evaporators, and heat exchangers (modifies UG–126).
54.15–25 Minimum relief capacities for cargo tanks containing compressed or liquefied gas.

Subpart 54.20—Fabrication by Welding

54.20–1 Scope (modifies UW–1 through UW–65).
54.20–2 Fabrication for hazardous materials (replaces UW–2(a)).
54.20–3 Design (modifies UW–9, UW–11(a), UW–13, and UW–16).
54.20–5 Welding qualification tests and production testing (modifies UW–26, UW–28, UW–29, UW–47, and UW–48).

Subpart 54.23—Fabrication by Brazing

54.23–1 Scope (modifies UB–1).

Subpart 54.25—Construction With Carbon, Alloy, and Heat Treated Steels

54.25–1 Scope.
54.25–3 Steel plates (modifies UCS–6).
54.25–5 Corrosion allowance (replaces UCS–25).
54.25–7 Requirements for postweld heat treatment (modifies UCS–56).
54.25–8 Radiography (modifies UW–11(a), UCS–57, UNF–57, UHA–33, and UHT–57).
54.25–10 Low temperature operation—ferritic steels (replaces UCS–65 through UCS–67).
54.25–15 Low temperature operation—high alloy steels (modifies UHA–23(b) and UHA–51).
54.25–20 Low temperature operation—ferritic steels with properties enhanced by heat treatment (modifies UHT–5(c), UHT–6, UHT–23, and UHT–82).
54.25–25 Welding of quenched and tempered steels (modifies UHT–82).

Subpart 54.30—Mechanical Stress Relief

54.30–1 Scope.
54.30–3 Introduction.
54.30–5 Limitations and requirements.
54.30–10 Method of performing mechanical stress relief.
54.30–15 Requirement for analysis and computation.

AUTHORITY: 33 U.S.C. 1509; 43 U.S.C. 1333; 46 U.S.C. 3306, 3703; E.O. 12234, 45 FR 58801, 3 CFR, 1980 Comp., p. 277; Department of Homeland Security Delegation No. 0170.1.

SOURCE: CGFR 68–82, 33 FR 18828, Dec. 18, 1968, unless otherwise noted.

Subpart 54.01—General Requirements

§ 54.01-1 Incorporation by reference.

(a) Certain material is incorporated by reference into this part with the approval of the Director of the Federal Register under 5 U.S.C. 552(a) and 1 CFR part 51. To enforce any edition other than that specified in this section, the Coast Guard must publish notice of change in the FEDERAL REGISTER and the material must be available to the public. All approved material is available for inspection at the National Archives and Records Administration (NARA). For information on the availability of this material at NARA, call 202–741–6030 or go to *http://www.archives.gov/federal_register/code_of_federal_regulations/ibr_locations.html*. The material is also available for inspection at the Coast Guard Headquarters. Contact Commandant (CG-ENG), Attn: Office of Design and Engineering Systems, U.S. Coast Guard Stop 7509, 2703 Martin Luther King Jr. Avenue SE., Washington,

DC 20593–7509. The material is also available from the sources listed below.

(b) *American Society of Mechanical Engineers (ASME) International,* Three Park Avenue, New York, NY 10016–5990:

(1) ASME Boiler and Pressure Vessel Code, Section VIII, Division 1, Rules for Construction of Pressure Vessels (1998 with 1999 and 2000 addenda) ("Section VIII of the ASME Boiler and Pressure Vessel Code"), 54.01–2; 54.01–5; 54.01–15; 54.01–18; 54.01–25; 54.01–30; 54.01–35; 54.03–1; 54.05–1; 54.10–1; 54.10–3; 54.10–5; 54.10–10; 54.10–15; 54.15–1; 54.15–5; 54.15–10; 54.15–13; 54.20–1; 54.20–3; 54.25–1; 54.25–3; 54.25–8; 54.25–10; 54.25–15; 54.25–20; 54.30–3; 54.30–5; 54.30–10; and

(2) [Reserved]

(c) *ASTM International,* 100 Barr Harbor Drive, P.O. Box C700, West Conshohocken, PA 19428–2959, 877–909–2786, *http://www.astm.org:*

(1) ASTM A 20/A 20M–97a, Standard Specification for General Requirements for Steel Plates for Pressure Vessels ("ASTM A 20"), 54.05–10; 54.25–10;

(2) ASTM A 203/A 203M–97 (Reapproved 2007)ε[1], Standard Specification for Pressure Vessel Plates, Alloy Steel, Nickel ("ASTM A 203"), (approved November 1, 2007), incorporation by reference approved for § 54.05–20;

(3) ASTM A 370–97a, Standard Test Methods and Definitions for Mechanical Testing of Steel Products ("ASTM A 370"), 54.25–20;

(4) ASTM E 23–96, Standard Test Methods for Notched Bar Impact Testing of Metallic Materials ("ASTM Specification E 23"), 54.05–5; and

(5) ASTM E 208–95a, Standard Test Method for Conducting Drop-Weight Test to Determine Nil-Ductility Transition Temperature of Ferritic Steels ("ASTM Specification E 208"), 54.05–5.

(d) *Compressed Gas Association (CGA),* 500 Fifth Avenue, New York, NY 10036:

(1) S–1.2, Pressure Relief Device Standards—Part 2—Cargo and Portable Tanks for Compressed Gases, 1979 ("CGA S–1.2"), 54.15–10; and

(2) [Reserved]

(e) *Manufacturers Standardization Society of the Valve and Fittings Industry, Inc. (MSS),* 127 Park Street NE, Vienna, VA 22180:

(1) SP–25–1998 Standard Marking System for Valves, Fittings, Flanges and Unions (1998) ("MSS SP–25"), 54.01–25; and

(2) [Reserved]

[USCG–2003–16630, 73 FR 65164, Oct. 31, 2008, as amended by USCG–2009–0702, 74 FR 49228, Sept. 25, 2009; USCG–2012–0832, 77 FR 59777, Oct. 1, 2012; USCG–2012–0866, 78 FR 13249, Feb. 27, 2013; USCG 2013–0671, 78 FR 60148, Sept. 30, 2013]

§ 54.01–2 Adoption of division 1 of section VIII of the ASME Boiler and Pressure Vessel Code.

(a) Pressure vessels shall be designed, constructed, and inspected in accordance with section VIII of the ASME Boiler and Pressure Vessel Code (incorporated by reference, see 46 CFR 54.01–1), as limited, modified, or replaced by specific requirements in this part. The provisions in the appendices to section VIII of the ASME Boiler and Pressure Vessel Code are adopted and shall be followed when the requirements in section VIII make them mandatory. For general information, table 54.01–2(a) lists the various paragraphs in section VIII of the ASME Boiler and Pressure Vessel Code that are limited, modified, or replaced by regulations in this part.

TABLE 54.01–2(a)—LIMITATIONS AND MODIFICATIONS IN THE ADOPTION OF SECTION VIII OF THE ASME BOILER AND PRESSURE VESSEL CODE

Paragraphs in section VIII of the ASME Boiler and Pressure Vessel Code[1] and disposition	Unit of this part
U–1 and U–2 modified by	54.01–5 through 54.01–15.
U–1(c) replaced by	54.01–5.
U–1(d) replaced by	54.01–5(a) and 54.01–15.
U–1(g) modified by	54.01–10.
U–1(c)(2) modified by	54.01–15.
UG–11 modified by	54.01–25.
UG–22 modified by	54.01–30.
UG–25 modified by	54.01–35.
UG–28 modified by	54.01–40.
UG–84 replaced by	54.05–1.
UG–90 and UG–91 replaced by	54.10–3.

§ 54.01-5

TABLE 54.01-2(a)—LIMITATIONS AND MODIFICATIONS IN THE ADOPTION OF SECTION VIII OF THE ASME BOILER AND PRESSURE VESSEL CODE—Continued

Paragraphs in section VIII of the ASME Boiler and Pressure Vessel Code[1] and disposition	Unit of this part
UG–92 through UG–103 modified by	54.10–1 through 54.10–15.
UG–98 reproduced by	54.10–5.
UG–115 through UG–120 modified by	54.10–1.
UG–116, except (k), replaced by	54.10–20(a).
UG–116(k) replaced by	54.10–20(b).
UG–117 replaced by	54.10–20(c).
UG–118 replaced by	54.10–20(a).
UG–119 modified by	54.10–20(d).
UG–120 modified by	54.10–25.
UG–125 through UG–137 modified by	54.15–1 through 54.15–15.
UW–1 through UW–65 modified by	54.20–1.
UW–2(a) replaced by	54.01–5(b) and 54.20–2.
UW–2(b) replaced by	54.01–5(b) and 54.20–2.
UW–9, UW–11(a), UW–13, and UW–16 modified by	54.20–3.
UW–11(a) modified by	54.25–8.
UW–26, UW–27, UW–28, UW–29, UW–47, and UW–48 modified by	54.20–5.
UB–1 modified by	54.23–1
UB–2 modified by	52.01–95(d) and 56.30–30(b)(1).
UCS–6 modified by	54.25–3.
UCS–56 modified by	54.25–7.
UCS–57, UNF–57, UHA–33, and UHT–57 modified by	54.25–8.
UCS–65 through UCS–67 replaced by	54.25–10.
UHA–23(b) and UHA–51 modified by	54.25–15.
UHT–5(c), UHT–6, and UHT–23 modified by	54.25–20.
UHT–82 modified by	54.25–20 and 54.25–25.
Appendix 3 modified by	54.15–3.

[1] The references to specific provisions in section VIII of the ASME Boiler and Pressure Vessel Code are coded. The first letter, such as "U," refers to division 1 of section VIII. The second letter, such as "G," refers to a subsection within section VIII. The number refers to the paragraph within the subsection.

(b) References to the ASME Boiler and Pressure Vessel Code, such as paragraph UG–125, indicate:

U = Division 1 of section VIII of the ASME Boiler and Pressure Vessel Code.

G = Part containing general requirements.

125 = Paragraph within part.

(c) When a paragraph or a section of the regulations in this part relates to material in section VIII of the ASME Boiler and Pressure Vessel Code, the relationship with the code will be shown immediately following the heading of the section or at the beginning of the paragraph, as follows:

(1) (Modifies U____.) This indicates that the material in U____ is generally applicable but is being altered, amplified or augmented.

(2) (Replaces U____.) This indicates that U____ does not apply.

(3) (Reproduces U____.) This indicates that U____ is being identically reproduced for convenience, not for emphasis.

[CGFR 68–82, 33 FR 18828, Dec. 18, 1968, as amended by CGFR 69–127, 35 FR 9976, June 17, 1970; CGFR 72–59R, 37 FR 6188, Mar. 25, 1972; CGD 72–206R, 38 FR 17226, June 29, 1973; CGD 73–254, 40 FR 40163, Sept. 2, 1975; CGD 77–147, 47 FR 21809, May 20, 1982; CGD 85–061, 54 FR 50963, Dec. 11, 1989. Redesignated by CGD 88–032, 56 FR 35822, July 29, 1991; USCG–2003–16630, 73 FR 65164, Oct. 31, 2008]

§ 54.01–5 Scope (modifies U–1 and U–2).

(a) This part contains requirements for pressure vessels. table 54.01–5(a) gives a breakdown by parts in this subchapter of the regulations governing various types of pressure vessels, boilers, and thermal units.

(b) Pressure vessels are divided into Classes I, I-L (low temperature), II, II-L (low temperature), and III. table 54.01–5(b) describes these classes and sets out additional requirements for welded pressure vessels.

(c) The requirements for pressure vessels by class are as follows:

(1) Class I-L and II-L pressure vessels must meet the applicable requirements in this part.

Coast Guard, Dept. of Homeland Security §54.01–5

(2) Pressure vessels containing hazardous materials as defined in §150.115 of this chapter must meet the requirements of this part or, as applicable, the requirements in 49 CFR parts 171–177 or part 64 of this chapter.

(3) Except as provided in paragraph (c)(4) of this section, Classes I, II, and III pressure vessels not containing hazardous materials must be designed and constructed in accordance with the requirements in Section VIII, division 1, of the ASME Boiler and Pressure Vessel Code (incorporated by reference; see 46 CFR 54.01–1) and must be stamped with the ASME "U" symbol. These pressure vessels must also comply with the requirements that are listed or prescribed in paragraphs (d) through (g) of this section. Compliance with other provisions in this part is not required.

(4) Classes II and III pressure vessels that have a net internal volume of less than 0.14 cubic meters (5 cubic feet) and do not contain hazardous materials must be stamped with either the ASME "U" or "UM" symbol. Compliance with other provisions in this part is not required.

(d) Pressure vessels described in paragraph (c)(3) of this section must—

(1) Have detailed plans that include the information required by §54.01–18 (approved by the Office of Management and Budget under OMB control number 2130–0181);

(2) Meet §54.01–35, §54.20–3(c), and §54.25–3 of this part;

(3) Have pressure relief devices required by subpart 54.15;

(4) Meet the applicable requirements in §§54.10–3, 54.10–20, and 54.10–25 for inspection, reports, and stamping;

(5) If welded, meet the post weld heat treatment and minimum joint and radiography requirement in table 54.01–5(b); and

(6) If a steam generating pressure vessel, meet §54.01–10.

(e) The plans required by paragraph (d)(1) of this section must be certified by a registered professional engineer to meet the design requirements in paragraph (d) of this section and in section VIII, division 1, of the ASME Boiler and Pressure Vessel Code. The certification must appear on all drawings and analyses. The plans must be made available to the Coast Guard prior to the inspection required by §54.10–3(c).

(f) If a pressure vessel has more than one independent chamber and the chambers have different classifications, each chamber must, as a minimum, meet the requirements for its classification. If a single classification for the entire pressure vessel is preferred, the classification selected must be one that is required to meet all of the regulations applicable to the classification that is not selected. For example, if one chamber is Class I and one chamber is Class II-L, the only single classification that can be selected is Class I-L.

(g) The design pressure for each interface between two chambers in a multichambered pressure vessel must be—

(1) The maximum allowable working pressure (gauge) in the chamber with the higher pressure; or

(2) If one chamber is a vacuum chamber, the maximum allowable working pressure (absolute) in the other chamber minus the least operating pressure (absolute) in the vacuum chamber.

TABLE 54.01–5(a)—REGULATION REFERENCE FOR BOILERS, PRESSURE VESSELS, AND THERMAL UNITS

Service and pressure temperature boundaries	Part of subchapter regulating mechanical design	Part of subchapter regulating automatic control
Main (power) boiler: All	52	62
Pressure vessel: All	54	NA
Fired auxiliary boiler [1] (combustion products or electricity):		
(a) Steam:		
More than 103 kPa (15 psig)	52	[2] 62 or 63
Equal to or less than 103 kPa (15 psig)	53	63
(b) Hot water heating:		
More than 689 kPa (100 psig) or 121 °C (250 °F)	52	63
Equal to or less than 689 kPa (100 psig) and 121 °C (250 °F)	53	63
(c) Hot water supply:		
More than 689 kPa (100 psig) or 121 °C (250 °F)	52	63
Equal to or less than 689 kPa (100 psig) and 121 °C (250 °F)	53	63
Other:		
(a) Fired thermal fluid heaters: All	52	63

§ 54.01–5

TABLE 54.01–5(a)—REGULATION REFERENCE FOR BOILERS, PRESSURE VESSELS, AND THERMAL UNITS—Continued

Service and pressure temperature boundaries	Part of subchapter regulating mechanical design	Part of subchapter regulating automatic control
(b) Unfired steam boiler: More than 206 kPa (30 psig) or 454 °C (850 °F)[3]	52	NA
Equal to or less than 206 kPa (30 psig) and 454 °C (850 °F)	54	NA
(c) Evaporators and heat exchangers: More than 103 kPa (15 psig)[4]	54	NA
(d) Unfired hot water supply or heating boiler: More than 103 kPa (15 psig)[4]	54	NA

[1] Including exhaust gas types.
[2] Boilers with heat input ratings >=12,500,000 Btu/hr. must have controls that meet part 62. Boilers with heat input ratings <12,500,000 Btu/hr. must have controls that meet part 63.
[3] Temperature of working fluid.
[4] Relief device is required even if designed for less than 103 kPa (15 psig).

TABLE 54.01–5(b)—PRESSURE VESSEL CLASSIFICATION

[Note to table 54.01–5(b): All classes of pressure vessels are subject to shop inspection and plan approval.[4]]

Class	Service contents	Class limits on pressure and temperature	Joint requirements [1 6 7]	Radiography requirements, section VIII of the ASME Boiler and Pressure Vessel Code (incorporated by reference, see 46 CFR 54.01–1) [3 7]	Post-weld heat treatment requirements [5 7]
I	(a) Vapor or gas (b) Liquid (c) Hazardous Materials[2].	Vapor or gas: Over 600 p.s.i. or 700 °F. Liquid: Over 600 p.s.i. or 400 °F.	(1) For category A; (1) or (2) for category B. All categories C and D must have full penetration welds extending through the entire thickness of the vessel wall or nozzle wall.	Full on all butt joints regardless of thickness. Exceptions listed in table UCS–57 of section VIII of the ASME Boiler and Pressure Vessel Code do not apply.	For carbon- or low-alloy steel, in accordance with table UCS–56 of section VIII of the ASME Boiler and Pressure Vessel Code, regardless of thickness. For other materials, in accordance with section VIII.
I–L Low Temperature.	(a) Vapor or gas, or liquid. (b) Hazardous Materials[2].	Over 250 p.s.i. and service temp. below 0 °F.	(1) For categories A and B. All categories C and D must have full penetration welds extending through the entire thickness of the vessel wall or nozzle wall. No backing rings or strips left in place.	Full on all butt joints regardless of thickness. Exceptions listed in table UCS–57 of section VIII of the ASME Boiler and Pressure Vessel Code do not apply.	For carbon- or low-alloy steel, in accordance with table UCS–56 of section VIII of the ASME Boiler and Pressure Vessel Code, regardless of thickness. For other materials, in accordance with section VIII.
II	(a) Vapor or gas (b) Liquid (c) Hazardous Materials[2 3 6].	Vapor or gas: 30 through 600 p.s.i. or 275 through 700 °F. Liquid: 200 through 600 p.s.i. or 250 through 400 °F.	(1) Or (2) for category A. (1), (2), or (3) for category B. Categories C and D in accordance with UW–16 of section VIII of the ASME Boiler and Pressure Vessel Code.	Spot, unless exempted by UW–11(c) of section VIII of the ASME Boiler and Pressure Vessel Code.	In accordance with section VIII of the ASME Boiler and Pressure Vessel Code.

Coast Guard, Dept. of Homeland Security § 54.01-15

TABLE 54.01–5(b)—PRESSURE VESSEL CLASSIFICATION—Continued

[Note to table 54.01–5(b): All classes of pressure vessels are subject to shop inspection and plan approval.[4]]

Class	Service contents	Class limits on pressure and temperature	Joint requirements [1][6][7]	Radiography requirements, section VIII of the ASME Boiler and Pressure Vessel Code (incorporated by reference, see 46 CFR 54.01–1)[3][7]	Post-weld heat treatment requirements [5][7]
II–L Low Temperature.	(a) Vapor or gas, or liquid. (b) Hazardous Materials[2].	0 through 250 p.s.i. and service temp. below 0 °F.	(1) For category A; (1) or (2) for category B. All categories C and D must have full-penetration welds extending through the entire thickness of the vessel wall or nozzle wall.	Spot. The exemption of UW–11(c) of section VIII of the ASME Boiler and Pressure Vessel Code does not apply.	Same as for I–L except that mechanical stress relief may be substituted if allowed under subpart 54.30 of this chapter.
III	(a) Vapor or gas ... (b) Liquid .... (c) Hazardous Materials [2][3][6].	Vapor or gas: Under 30 p.s.i. and 0 through 275 °F. Liquid: Under 200 p.s.i. and 0 through 250 °F.	In accordance with section VIII of the ASME Boiler and Pressure Vessel Code.	Spot, unless exempted by UW–11(c) of section VIII of the ASME Boiler and Pressure Vessel Code.	In accordance with section VIII of the ASME Boiler and Pressure Vessel Code.

[1] Welded joint categories are defined under UW–3 of section VIII of the ASME Boiler and Pressure Vessel Code. Joint types are described in table UW–12 of section VIII of the ASME Boiler and Pressure Vessel Code, and numbered (1), (2), etc.
[2] See 46 CFR 54.20–2.
[3] See 46 CFR 54.25–8(c) and 54.25–10(d).
[4] See 46 CFR 54.01–15 and 54.10–3 for exemptions.
[5] Specific requirements modifying table UCS–56 of section VIII of the ASME Boiler and Pressure Vessel Code appear in 46 CFR 54.25–7.
[6] See 46 CFR 54.20–3(c) and (f).
[7] Applies only to welded pressure vessels.

(Approved by the Office of Management and Budget under OMB control number 2130–0181)

[CGFR 68–82, 33 FR 18828, Dec. 18, 1968, as amended by CGFR 69–127, 35 FR 9976, June 17, 1970; CGD 77–147, 47 FR 21809, May 20, 1982; 55 FR 696, Jan. 8, 1990; CGD 88–057, 55 FR 24236, June 15, 1990; CGD 85–061, 55 FR 41917, Oct. 16, 1990; CGD 95–027, 61 FR 26000, May 23, 1996; USCG–2000–7790, 65 FR 58460, Sept. 29, 2000; USCG–2003–16630, 73 FR 65165, Oct. 31, 2008]

§ 54.01–10 Steam-generating pressure vessels (modifies U–1(g)).

(a) Pressure vessels in which steam is generated are classed as "Unfired Steam Boilers" except as required otherwise by paragraph (b) of this section. Unfired steam boilers must be fitted with an efficient water level indicator, a pressure gage, a blowdown valve, and an approved safety valve as required by § 54.15–15. Unfired steam boilers must be constructed in accordance with this part other than when the pressures are more than 206 kPa (30 psig) or the temperatures of the working fluid are more than 454 °C (850 °F) when such boilers must be constructed in accordance with part 52 of this subchapter.

(b) Vessels known as "Evaporators" or "Heat Exchangers" are not classified as unfired steam boilers. They shall be fitted with an approved safety device as required under § 54.15–15 and constructed in accordance with this part.

(c) An evaporator in which steam is generated shall be fitted with an efficient water level indicator, a pressure gage, and a blowdown valve.

[CGFR 68–82, 33 FR 18828, Dec. 18, 1968, as amended by CGD 81–79, 50 FR 9436, Mar. 8, 1985; CGD 95–012, 60 FR 48044, Sept. 18, 1995; USCG–2003–16630, 73 FR 65166, Oct. 31, 2008]

§ 54.01–15 Exemptions from shop inspection and plan approval (modifiesU–1(c)(2)).

(a) The following classifications are exempt from shop inspection and plan approval requirements of this part:

(1) Vessels containing water at a pressure not greater than 689 kPa (100

§ 54.01-17

pounds per square inch gauge or "psig"), and at a temperature not above 93 °C (200 °F) including those containing air, the compression of which serves only as a cushion. Air-charging lines may be permanently attached if the air pressure does not exceed 103 kPa (15 psig).

(2) Hot water supply storage tanks heated by steam or any other indirect means when none of the following limitations is exceeded:

(i) A heat input of 58 kW (200,000 B.t.u. per hour);

(ii) A water temperature of 93 °C (200 °F);

(iii) A nominal water-containing capacity of 454 liters (120 gallons); or

(iv) A pressure of 689 kPa (100 psig).

The exemption of any tank under this subparagraph requires that it shall be fitted with a safety relief valve of at least 1-inch diameter, set to relieve below the maximum allowable working pressure of the tank.

(3)(i) Vessels having an internal operating pressure not exceeding 103 kPa (15 psig) with no limitation on size. (See UG–28(f) of section VIII of the ASME Boiler and Pressure Vessel Code (incorporated by reference; see 46 CFR 54.01–1.)

(ii) Cargo tanks of pressure vessel configuration are not included in the exemption in paragraph (a)(3)(i) of this section.

(4) Class I, II, and III pressure vessels that meet the requirements of § 54.01–5(c)(3) and (c)(4).

(5) Condensers and heat exchangers, regardless of size, when the design is such that the liquid phase is not greater than 689 kPa (100 psig) and 200 °F (93 °C) and the vapor phase is not greater than 103 kPa (15 psig) provided that the Officer in Charge, Marine Inspection is satisfied that system overpressure conditions are addressed by the owner or operator.

(b) For fluid conditioner fittings see § 56.15–1 of this subchapter.

[CGFR 68–82, 33 FR 18828, Dec. 18, 1968, as amended by CGFR 69–127, 35 FR 9977, June 17, 1970; CGFR 70–143, 35 FR 19906, Dec. 30, 1970; CGD 77–147, 47 FR 21810, May 20, 1982; USCG–2003–16630, 73 FR 65166, Oct. 31, 2008; USCG–2010–0759, 75 FR 60002, Sept. 29, 2010]

§ 54.01-17 Pressure vessel for human occupancy (PVHO).

Pressure vessels for human occupancy (PVHO's) must meet the requirements of subpart B (Commercial Diving Operations) of part 197 of this chapter.

[CGD 76–009, 43 FR 53683, Nov. 16, 1978]

§ 54.01-18 Plan approval.

(a) Manufacturers intending to fabricate pressure vessels, heat exchangers, evaporators, and similar appurtenances, covered by the regulations in this part shall submit detailed plans in accordance with subpart 50.20 of this subchapter.

(b) The following information shall be submitted:

(1) Calculations for all pressure containment components including the maximum allowable working pressure, the hydrostatic or pneumatic test pressure, and the intended safety device setting.

(2) Joint design and methods of attachment of all pressure containment components.

(3) Foundations and supports (design and attachment).

(4) Pertinent calculations for pressure vessel foundations and/or supports.

(5) A bill of material meeting the requirements of section VIII of section VIII of the ASME Boiler and Pressure Vessel Code (incorporated by reference; see 46 CFR 54.01–1), as modified by this part.

(6) A diagrammatic arrangement drawing of the assembled unit indicating location of internal and external components.

[CGFR 68–82, 33 FR 18828, Dec. 18, 1968, as amended by USCG–2003–16630, 73 FR 65166, Oct. 31, 2008]

§ 54.01-25 Miscellaneous pressure components (modifies UG–11).

(a) Pressure components for pressure vessels shall be as required by UG–11 of section VIII of the ASME Boiler and Pressure Vessel Code (incorporated by reference; see 46 CFR 54.01–1) except as noted otherwise in this section.

(b) All pressure components conforming to an accepted ANSI (American National Standards Institute)

Coast Guard, Dept. of Homeland Security § 54.03-1

Standard referred to in an adopted code, specification or standard or in this subchapter shall also be marked in accordance with MSS SP-25 (incorporated by reference; see 46 CFR 54.01-1).

[CGFR 68-82, 33 FR 18828, Dec. 18, 1968, as amended by CGFR 69-127, 35 FR 9977, June 17, 1970; USCG-2003-16630, 73 FR 65167, Oct. 31, 2008]

§ 54.01-30 Loadings (modifies UG-22).

(a) The loadings for pressure vessels shall be as required by UG-22 of section VIII of the ASME Boiler and Pressure Vessel Code (incorporated by reference; see 46 CFR 54.01-1) except as noted otherwise in this section.

(b) In evaluating loadings for certain pressure vessel applications, the Commandant may require consideration of the following loads in addition to those listed in UG-22 of section VIII of the ASME Boiler and Pressure Vessel Code:

(1) Loading imposed by vessel's attitude in roll, list, pitch and trim.

(2) Dynamic forces due to ship motions.

[CGFR 68-82, 33 FR 18828, Dec. 18, 1968, as amended by USCG-2003-16630, 73 FR 65167, Oct. 31, 2008]

§ 54.01-35 Corrosion (modifies UG-25).

(a) Vessels or portions of vessels subject to corrosion shall be as required by UG-25 of section VIII of the ASME Boiler and Pressure Vessel Code (incorporated by reference; see 46 CFR 54.01-1) except as noted otherwise in this section.

(b) The pressure portions of pressure vessels shall:

(1) Normally have a corrosion allowance of one-sixth of the calculated thickness, or one-sixteenth inch, whichever is smaller, added to the calculated thickness as determined by the applicable design formula.

(2) Be specifically evaluated in cases where unusually corrosive cargoes will be involved, for the possible increase of this corrosion allowance.

(3) Have no additional thickness required when acceptable corrosion resistant materials are used.

(4) Not normally need additional thickness allowance when the effective stress (either S or SE depending on the design formula used) is 80 percent or less of the allowable stress listed in section VIII of the ASME Boiler and Pressure Vessel Code for calculating thickness.

(c) Telltale holes shall not be permitted in pressure vessels containing dangerous fluids, such as acid, poison, corrosives, etc.

(d) Exemption from these corrosion allowance requirements will be granted by the Commandant in those cases where:

(1) The contents of the pressure vessel is judged to be sufficiently noncorrosive; and,

(2) Where the external surface is also protected from corrosion. A suitable vapor barrier is adequate protection, while paint or other thin coatings exposed to weather or mechanical damage are not acceptable.

NOTE: No applied linings except as provided in part UCL of section VIII of the ASME Boiler and Pressure Vessel Code shall be acceptable.

[CGFR 68-82, 33 FR 18828, Dec. 18, 1968, as amended by CGFR 72-59R, 37 FR 6189, Mar. 25, 1972; USCG-2003-16630, 73 FR 65167, Oct. 31, 2008]

§ 54.01-40 External pressure (modifies UG-28).

(a) The exemption from external pressure consideration provided by the note under UG-28(f) does not apply.

(b) Vessels which may at times be subjected to partial vacuum due to nature of the contents, temperature, unloading operations, or other facet of employment shall either have vacuum breaker protection or be designed for not less than one-half atmosphere of external pressure.

[CGFR 70-143, 35 FR 19906, Dec. 30, 1970]

Subpart 54.03—Low Temperature Operation

§ 54.03-1 Scope.

The pressure vessels for low temperature operation shall be as required by section VIII of the ASME Boiler and Pressure Vessel Code (incorporated by reference; see 46 CFR 54.01-1) as modified by this subpart.

[CGFR 68-82, 33 FR 18828, Dec. 18, 1968, as amended by USCG-2003-16630, 73 FR 65167, Oct. 31, 2008]

§ 54.03-5 General.

(a) Requirements for ferritic steels, high alloy steels, and heat treated ferritic steels are contained in §§ 54.25-10, 54.25-15, and 54.25-20 respectively of this subchapter.

(b) Requirements for toughness testing of material product forms and weldments (including weld procedure qualification and production toughness tests) are contained in subpart 54.05.

(c) Materials suitable for a given minimum service temperature may be used in warmer service. Steels differing in chemical composition, mechanical properties, or heat treatments from those specified may be specially approved by the Commandant. Similarly, aluminum alloys and other nonferrous materials not intended to be covered by these sections may be specially considered by the Commandant for service at any low temperature.

[CGFR 68-82, 33 FR 18828, Dec. 18, 1968, as amended by CGFR 69-127, 35 FR 9977, June 17, 1970]

Subpart 54.05—Toughness Tests

§ 54.05-1 Scope (replaces UG-84).

The toughness tests of materials used in pressure vessels shall be as required by this subpart in lieu of requirements in UG-84 of section VIII of the ASME Boiler and Pressure Vessel Code (incorporated by reference; see 46 CFR 54.01-1)

[CGFR 68-82, 33 FR 18828, Dec. 18, 1968, as amended by USCG-2003-16630, 73 FR 65167, Oct. 31, 2008]

§ 54.05-3 Tests required.

(a) Where material or welding toughness tests are required by §§ 54.25-10, 54.25-15, 54.25-20, and subpart 57.03 or 57.06 of this subchapter, the following requirements shall apply:

(1) Additional requirements for ferritic steels with properties enhanced by heat treatment are in § 54.25-20.

(2) Certified reports of toughness tests by the material manufacturer will be acceptable evidence provided the specimens taken are representative of the material delivered and that the material is not subject to treatment during or following fabrication that will reduce its impact properties. If such treatment is subsequently applied to the material, test specimens shall be so taken and treated as to be representative of the material in the finished vessel.

(b) The requirements of this subpart are also applicable to nonpressure vessel type low temperature tanks and associated secondary barriers, as defined in § 38.05-4 of subchapter D (Tank Vessels) of this chapter.

[CGFR 68-82, 33 FR 18828, Dec. 18, 1968, as amended by CGFR 69-127, 35 FR 9977, June 17, 1970]

§ 54.05-5 Toughness test specimens.

(a) *Charpy V-notch impact tests.* Where required, Charpy V-notch tests shall be conducted in accordance with ASTM Specification E 23 (incorporated by reference, see § 54.01-1), "Notched Bar Impact Testing of Metallic Materials", using the Type A specimen shown in Figure 4 of the specification. Special attention is drawn to the fact that the Charpy Keyhole and U-notch specimens are not acceptable substitutes for the Charpy V-notch specimen and shall not be used to qualify materials within the scope of this subpart. Each set of Charpy impact tests shall consist of three specimens. For materials ½-inch thick or less, the largest possible Charpy specimens for that thickness shall be cut centered at the material's mid-thickness. For materials thicker than ½-inch, full size Charpy specimens shall be cut centered at a location as near as practicable to a point midway between the material's surface and half-thickness. Except where otherwise specified, transversely oriented specimens must be used. When longitudinal specimens are used, the required energy values may not be less than 1.5 times the values required for transversely oriented specimens. In all cases the notch shall be cut normal to the material's surface. Test specimens shall be taken at least one "t" from any heat treated edge (where "t" is the material's nominal thickness).

(b) *Drop weight tests.* Where required, drop weight tests shall be conducted for no-break performance in accordance with ASTM Specification E 208 (incorporated by reference, see § 54.01-1), "Conducting Drop-Weight Test to Determine Nil-Ductility Transition

Coast Guard, Dept. of Homeland Security §54.05-10

Temperature of Ferritic Steels". For material thicknesses between ½-inch and ⅝-inch, the ASTM E-208 specimen P-3, machined to ½-inch thickness, shall be used with a stop distance of 0.090-inch. In preparing weld specimens for dropweight testing, weld reinforcement shall be ground flush, the hard facing bead centered on and transverse to the weld, and the notch centered on and parallel to the weld axis.

(c) *Retest procedures.* (1) When Charpy V-notch impact specimens are used and the average value of the three initial specimens fails to meet the stated requirements by an amount not exceeding 15 percent, or the value for more than one specimen is below the required average value of when the value for one specimen is below the minimum value permitted for a single specimen by an amount not exceeding 15 percent, three additional specimens from the same material may be tested and the results combined with those previously obtained to form a new average. This new average of six specimens must exceed the specified minimum average. In the event the Charpy retests fail, the material may still be qualified by exhibiting a no-break performance when tested in accordance with the drop weight procedure, if applicable. Two drop weight specimens shall be tested for each Charpy V-notch set of three initial specimens which failed to qualify. Failure of either or both of these drop weight specimens will constitute rejection of the material or weldments represented, except as outlined in paragraph (c)(3) of this section.

(2) When drop weight specimens are used, retests shall be permitted only within the limits prescribed in ASTM Specification E 208 (incorporated by reference, see §54.01-1), except as outlined in paragraph (c)(3) of this section.

(3) If, for heat treated base material, the required toughness results are not obtained in the initial test or in the retest, the material may be reheat treated one time and tested again in accordance with the initial requirements for the material.

(d) *Alternate toughness tests.* The Charpy V-notch impact values of §§54.05-20(a) and 54.05-25(a) are representative of those which correlate with the nil-ductility transition temperature determined by the drop-weight tests for the steels specified in §54.25-10. For materials for which there are other data showing suitable correlation between Charpy V-notch and drop-weight tests, V-notch acceptance limits different from those tabulated herein may be specially approved by the Commandant, based upon the actual correlation. In the case of steels for which the tabulated Charpy V-notch values can be shown to be inapplicable or in the case of specially considered steels, or as an alternative to complying with the tabulated impact requirements, acceptance may be based upon the material exhibiting a no-break performance when tested in accordance with the drop-weight procedure. Whenever the drop-weight test is used as an alternative to the Charpy V-notch test, two drop-weight specimens shall be tested for each set of three Charpy V-notch specimens otherwise required. If the drop-weight test cannot be performed because of material thickness limitations (less than one-half inch) or product shape, or is otherwise inapplicable (because of heat treatment, chemistry, etc.), other tests and/or test criteria will be specified by the Commandant to assure the adequacy of the material for the intended application.

[CGFR 68–82, 33 FR 18828, Dec. 18, 1968, as amended by CGD 73–254, 40 FR 40163, Sept. 2, 1975; USCG–2000–7790, 65 FR 58460, Sept. 29, 2000]

§54.05-6 Toughness test temperatures.

Each toughness test must be conducted at temperatures not warmer than −20 °F or 10 °F below the minimum service temperature, whichever is lower, except that for service at or below −320 °F, the tests may be conducted at the service temperature in accordance with §54.25-10(a)(2).

[CGD 85–061, 54 FR 50964, Dec. 11, 1989]

§54.05-10 Certification of material toughness tests.

(a) *Plate material.* The manufacturer of plates may certify such material, provided it has been given an appropriate heat-treatment, by reporting the results of tests of one set of Charpy impact specimens or of two drop weight

§54.05–10

specimens, as applicable, taken from each plate as rolled. Impact specimens shall be taken as outlined in section 12 of ASTM A 20 (incorporated by reference, see §54.01–1). The long axis of the Charpy specimen must be perpendicular to the final direction of rolling. When the direction of maximum stress is unknown, the manufacturer may certify on the basis of specimens taken parallel to the final direction of rolling.

(b) *Pipe or tube material.* (1) The manufacturer of pipe, tube, or welded fittings formed from pipe or tube may certify such material by reporting the results of tests of one set of Charpy impact specimens, provided the requirement for production in this paragraph (b)(1) or paragraph (b)(2) of this section, as well as the requirement for sampling in paragraph (b)(3) of this section are met. The specimens shall have the major axis parallel to the length of pipe or tube. In the case of welding fittings, the specimens may be taken from the tubing prior to forming provided the fittings are normalized after forming. Such specimens shall be normalized before testing.

(2) One set of specimens may represent each five (5) short tons, or less, of the pipe, tubes, or welding fittings produced from one heat of steel poured from a single melting furnace charge and subsequently processed in the same manner, provided all are given a normalizing heat-treatment in a continuous treating furnace in which the temperature is automatically controlled and checked by recording pyrometer.

(3) One set of specimens may represent each five (5) short tons, or less, of the pipe, tubes, or welding fittings that have been given a normalizing heat-treatment as a single charge in a batch-treating furnace equipped with recording pyrometer provided all have been produced from a single melting furnace heat and are subsequently processed in the same manner. If more than one melting furnace heat is present in the batch heat-treating furnace, means of identification shall be provided and one set of specimens shall be taken from each heat.

(4) One set of impact specimens shall be taken from one pipe or tube picked at random from each heat or furnace batch or portion thereof to be certified.

(c) *Forgings and forged or rolled fittings.* (1) The manufacturer of forgings for any purpose may certify them by reporting the results of tests of one set of Charpy impact specimens or two drop-weight specimens, as applicable, taken from each 5 short tons of product from each melting heat provided the requirements in this paragraph for production and sampling are met.

(2) One or more test blocks shall be cut from billets or blooms selected at random from each heat of material. Each test block shall be forge-reduced in thickness to the thickness of the finished forgings to be certified, within the limitations set below. After forging to the reduced thickness, the test block shall be heat-treated in the same manner as the finished forgings represented, which heat-treatment of test blocks may be carried out in the furnace with the forgings, or separately. If carried out separately, both heat-treatments shall be done in automatically controlled furnaces equipped with calibrated recording pyrometers, the certified records of which shall be made available to the inspector.

(3) One set of Charpy impact specimens or two drop-weight specimens, as applicable, shall be cut from each such test block and these specimens shall represent all forgings (up to 5 short tons) that are from the same heat of material and given the same heat-treatment as the test block, and the thickness of which does not differ from that of the test block by more than plus or minus 50 percent of 1½ inches, whichever is less, except that forged flanges and tube sheets thicker than 5½ inches may be qualified from a 4-inch test block.

(4) As many test blocks shall be made as are required under the foregoing rule in paragraph (c)(3) of this section to cover the weight of product and range of thickness found in the forgings represented. The major axis of the test specimens shall be parallel to the length of the test block.

(d) *Bars and shapes, rolled or forged.* (1) The manufacturer of forged or rolled bars and shapes may certify such by reporting the results of one set of Charpy impact specimens, or two drop-weight specimens, as applicable, produced from each 5 short tons from a single melting furnace heat, processed in a similar manner and heat-treated as a single furnace batch, if heat-treated. The impact specimens shall be cut from the heaviest section, clear of fillets, of the shape being tested with the axis of the specimens parallel to the axis of the bar or shape.

(e) *Castings.* (1) The manufacturer of castings may certify them by reporting the results of one set of Charpy impact specimens or two drop-weight specimens, as applicable, taken from each 5 short tons of product from each melting furnace heat. These specimens shall be taken either directly from a production casting or from test coupons cast attached thereto provided the additional requirements in this paragraph are met.

(2) One set of Charpy impact or two drop-weight specimens may represent all castings (up to 5 short tons) that are from the same heat of material and that have a thickness that does not differ from the thickness of the section from which the specimens were taken by more than plus or minus 25 percent, or 1½ inches, whichever is less. A wider range of thicknesses from one heat may be covered by taking additional sets of specimens from thicker or thinner material as may be required.

(3) The test specimens shall be heat-treated in the same manner as the castings represented, which heat-treatment of specimens may be carried out in the furnace with the castings represented, or separately, but if carried out separately both heat-treatments shall be done in automatically controlled furnaces equipped with calibrated recording pyrometers, the certified records of which shall be made available to the marine inspector.

(f) *Small parts.* The manufacturer of small parts, either cast or forged, may certify a lot of not more than 20 duplicate parts or 5 short tons, whichever is less, by reporting the results of one set of Charpy impact specimens, or two drop-weight specimens, as applicable, taken from one such part selected at random, provided the same kind of material and the same process of production were used for all of the lot. When the part is too small to provide the specimens of at least minimum size, no impact test need be made. For such parts too small to impact test, toughness qualifications shall be determined by the Commandant based on material, chemical, and mechanical properties.

[CGFR 68–82, 33 FR 18828, Dec. 18, 1968, as amended by CFR 73–254, 40 FR 40164, Sept. 2, 1975; USCG–1999–5151, 64 FR 67178, Dec. 1, 1999]

§ 54.05–15 **Weldment toughness tests—procedure qualifications.**

(a) Plate for which Charpy V-notch impact testing is required in the parent material and for which V-notch minima are specified shall similarly have welding procedures qualified for toughness by Charpy V-notch testing. For these tests, the test plates shall be oriented with their final rolling direction parallel to the weld axis (i.e., so that transverse impact specimens result), and with the V-notch normal to the plate surface. The sample weld joint preparation shall be the same as that used in production. The number of test specimens and the location of their notches shall be as shown in Figure 54.05–15(a) and as described in paragraphs (a) (1) through (5) of this section.

(1) Three specimens with the notch centered in the weld metal.

(2) Three specimens with the notch centered on the fusion line between parent plate and weld. (The fusion line may be identified by etching the specimen with a mild reagent.)

(3) Three specimens with the notch centered in the heat affected zone, 1 mm from the fusion line.

(4) Same as paragraph (a)(3) of this section, but 3 mm from the fusion line.

(5) Same as paragraph (a)(3) of this section, but 5 mm from the fusion line.

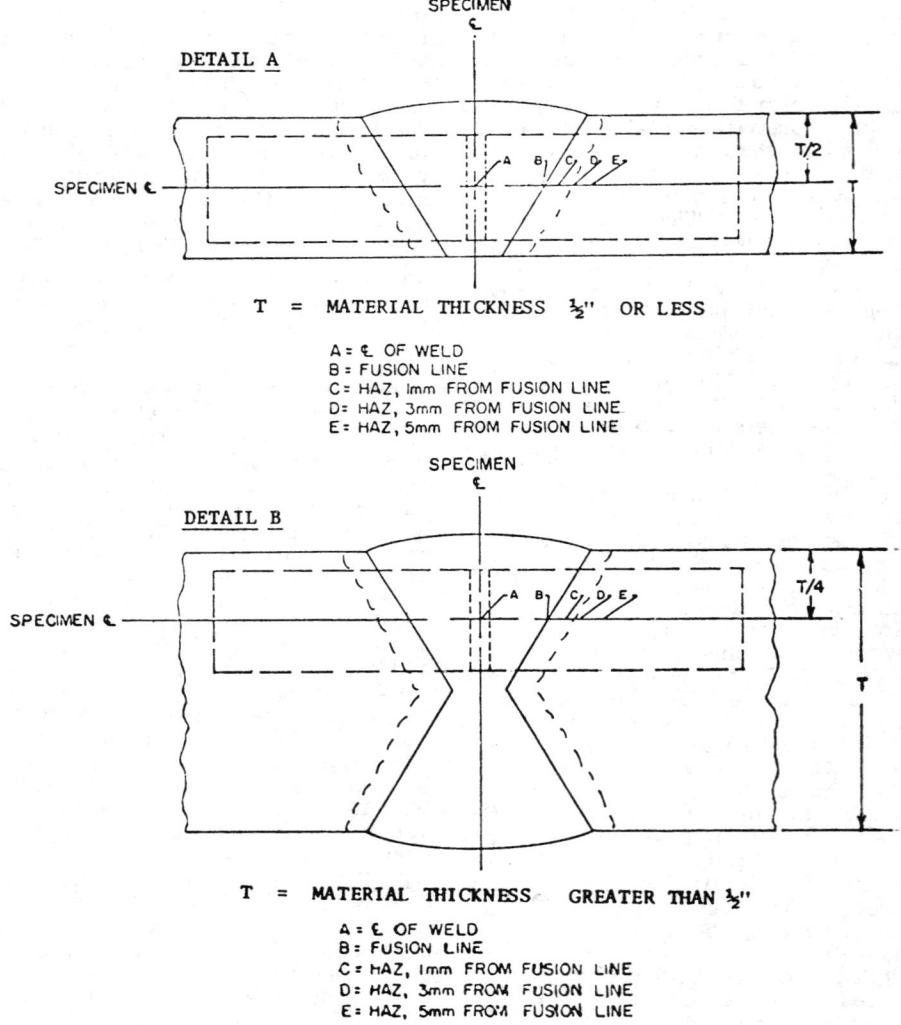

FIGURE 54.05-15(A)—CHARPY V-NOTCH SPECIMEN REMOVAL DETAILS

(b) Plate materials for which Charpy V-notch minimums are not specified, or for which a Charpy V-notch correlation with NDT is not known, and which are themselves tested for toughness by the drop-weight procedure, shall have welding procedures similarly qualified by the drop-weight test. For such qualifications, two drop-weight specimens are to be tested, with the notch positioned directly above and parallel to the centerline of the weld.

(c) Piping welding toughness tests shall be qualified, by making Charpy V-notch impact tests as prescribed in paragraph (a) of this section.

(d) Materials which are specially approved based on toughness criteria or tests, other than those discussed in paragraphs (a) and (b) of this section, shall have welding procedures tested and qualified for toughness as deemed appropriate and necessary by the Commandant.

(e) In the case of stainless steels, weld procedure toughness tests may be limited to weld metal only if this is all that is required by § 54.25–15.

§ 54.05-16 Production toughness testing.

(a) For vessels of welded construction, production toughness test plates shall be prepared for each 50 feet of longitudinal and circumferential butt weld in each Class I-L vessel, or for each 150 feet in each Class II-L vessel, except for material other than stainless steel that is exempted from impact test requirements by this subchapter. In the case of stainless steels, weld production toughness tests may be limited to weld metal only if this is all that is required be § 54.25–15. The test-plate thickness shall be the same as that of the vessel wall at the location of the production weld being sampled. The test plates shall be prepared, wherever possible, as run-off tabs attached at the ends of weld butts or seams. The rolling direction of the run-off tabs should be oriented parallel to the rolling direction of the adjacent production material. The test-plate material shall be taken from one of the heats of material used in the vessel, and both the electrodes and welding procedures shall be the same as used in the fabrication of the vessel. From each test plate, one set of three Charpy impact bars or two drop-weight specimens, as applicable according to the test used in procedure qualification, shall be taken transverse to the weld axis. For Charpy V-notch specimens, the notch shall be normal to the material surface and its location alternated (approximately) on successive tests between the weld metal and heat affected zone. Thus, approximately half of all weld production impact tests will be of weld metal and half of heat affected zone material. For the weld metal tests, the V-notch is to be centered between the fusion lines. For the heat affected zone tests, the notch is to be centered so as to sample, as nearly as practicable, the most critical location for toughness observed in the weld procedure qualification tests. Where the drop weight specimen is used in production weld testing, it shall be prepared in the same manner as specified for procedure qualification testing, § 54.05–15(b).

(b) For vessels not exceeding 5 cubic feet in volume, one set of impact specimens, or two drop-weight specimens, as applicable according to the test used in procedure qualification, may represent all vessels from the same heat of material not in excess of 100 vessels, or one heat-treatment furnace batch. In addition, when such vessels are welded, one weld test plate made from one of the heats of material used, and two sets of impact specimens or two drop-weight specimens, as applicable, cut therefrom, may represent the weld metal in the smallest of: One lot of 100 vessels or less; or each heat-treatment furnace batch; or each 50 feet of welding for Class I-L vessels; or each 150 feet of welding for Class II-L vessels.

(c) For several vessels or parts of vessels being welded in succession, the plate thickness of which does not vary by more than one-fourth inch, and which are made of the same grade of material, a test plate shall be furnished for each 50 feet of welding for Class I-L vessels or 150 feet of welding for Class II-L vessels. For each 50- or 150-foot increment of weld, as applicable, the test plates shall be prepared at the time of fabrication of the first vessel involving that increment.

(d) The test plates and any other test material from which toughness test specimens are cut shall be given the same heat-treatment as the production material they represent. Test specimens representing other material than the weld toughness test plates shall preferably be cut from a part of the vessel material but may be cut from like material that has been heat-treated within the temperature range specified by the producer in treating the actual vessel material.

(e) For nonpressure vessel type tanks and associated secondary barriers, as defined in § 38.05–4, subchapter D (Tank Vessels) of this chapter, production toughness test plates shall be prepared in accordance with paragraphs (a) and (d) of this section. One set of toughness

§ 54.05-17

test plates shall be prepared for each 165 feet (50 meters) of production butt type welds.

§ 54.05-17 **Weld toughness test acceptance criteria.**

(a) For Charpy V-notch impact tests the energy absorbed in both the weld metal and heat affected zone impact tests in weld qualification and production shall be:

(1) For weld metal specimens, not less than the transverse values required for the parent material.

(2) For heat affected zone specimens, when the specimens are transversely oriented, not less than the transverse values required for the parent material.

(3) For heat affected zone specimens, when the specimens are longitudinally oriented, not less than 1.5 times the transverse values required for the parent material.

(b) For drop-weight tests both specimens from each required set shall exhibit a no-break performance.

[CGFR 68-82, 33 FR 18828, Dec. 18, 1968, as amended by CGD 73-254, 40 FR 40164, Sept. 2, 1975]

§ 54.05-20 **Impact test properties for service of 0 °F and below.**

(a) *Test energy.* The impact energies of each set of transverse Charpy specimens may not be less than the values shown in table 54.05-20(a). Only one specimen in a set may be below the required average and the value of that specimen must be above the minimum impact value permitted on one specimen only. See § 54.05-5(c) for retest requirements.

TABLE 54.05-20(a)—CHARPY V-NOTCH IMPACT REQUIREMENTS

Size of specimen	Minimum impact value required for average of each set of 3 specimens foot-pounds [1]	Minimum impact value permitted on one specimen only of a set, foot-pounds
10 × 10 mm	20.0	13.5
10 × 7.5 mm	16.5	11.0
10 × 5 mm	13.5	9.0
10 × 2.5 mm	10.0	6.5

[1] Straight line interpolation for intermediate values is permitted.

(b) Transversely oriented Charpy V-notch impact specimens of ASTM A 203 (incorporated by reference, see § 54.01-1) nickel steels must exhibit energies not less than the values shown in § 54.05-20 (a). Requirements for 9 percent nickel steels are contained in § 54.25-20. Other nickel alloy steels, when specially approved by the Commandant, must exhibit a no-break performance when tested in accordance with the drop weight procedure. If, for such materials, there are data indicating suitable correlation with drop-weight tests, Charpy V-notch tests may be specially considered by the Commandant in lieu of drop-weight tests. If the drop-weight test cannot be performed because of material thickness limitations (less than one-half inch), or product shape, or is otherwise inapplicable (because of heat treatment, chemistry etc.) other tests or test criteria will be specified by the Commandant.

(c) Where sufficient data are available to warrant such waiver, the Commandant may waive the requirements for toughness testing austenitic stainless steel materials. Where required, austenitic stainless steels are to be tested using the drop-weight procedure and must exhibit a no-break performance. Where data are available indicating suitable correlation of Charpy V-notch results with drop-weight NDT or no-break performance, Charpy V-notch tests may be specially considered by the Commandant in lieu of dropweight tests. If the dropweight test cannot be performed because of material thickness limitations (less than one-half inch), or product shape, or is otherwise inapplicable (because of heat treatment, chemistry, etc.) other tests and/or test criteria will be specified by the Commandant.

[CGD 73-254, 40 FR 40164, Sept. 2, 1975, as amended by USCG-2000-7790, 65 FR 58460, Sept. 29, 2000]

§ 54.05-25 **[Reserved]**

§ 54.05-30 **Allowable stress values at low temperatures.**

(a) The Coast Guard will give consideration to the enhanced yield and tensile strength properties of ferrous and nonferrous materials at low temperature for the purpose of establishing allowable stress values for service temperature below 0 °F.

Coast Guard, Dept. of Homeland Security § 54.10–5

(b) The use of such allowable stress values must be specially approved by the Coast Guard for each application. Further information may be obtained by writing to the Commandant (CG–ENG), Attn: Office of Design and Engineering Systems, U.S. Coast Guard Stop 7509, 2703 Martin Luther King Jr. Avenue SE., Washington, DC 20593.

(c) Submittals must include information and calculations specified by the U.S. Coast Guard, Office of Design and Engineering Standards (CG–ENG) to demonstrate that the allowable stress for the material cannot be exceeded under any possible combination of vessel loads and metal temperature.

[CGD 73–133R, 39 FR 9179, Mar. 8, 1974, as amended by CGD 82–063b, 48 FR 4781, Feb. 3, 1983; CGD 95–072, 60 FR 50462, Sept. 29, 1995; CGD 96–041, 61 FR 50727, 50728, Sept. 27, 1996; USCG–2009–0702, 74 FR 49228, Sept. 25, 2009; USCG–2012–0832, 77 FR 59777, Oct. 1, 2012; USCG 2013–0671, 78 FR 60148, Sept. 30, 2013]

Subpart 54.10—Inspection, Reports, and Stamping

§ 54.10–1 Scope (modifies UG–90 through UG–103 and UG–115 through UG–120).

The inspection, tests, stamping, and reports for pressure vessels shall be as required by paragraphs UG–90 through UG–103 and UG–115 through UG–120 of section VIII of the ASME Boiler and Pressure Vessel Code (incorporated by reference; see 46 CFR 54.01–1) except as noted otherwise in this subpart.

[CGFR 68–82, 33 FR 18828, Dec. 18, 1968, as amended by USCG–2003–16630, 73 FR 65167, Oct. 31, 2008]

§ 54.10–3 Marine inspectors (replaces UG–90 and UG–91, and modifies UG–92 through UG–103).

(a) Only marine inspectors shall apply the Coast Guard Symbol. They will not apply any other code symbol to pressure vessels.

(b) All pressure vessels not exempted under provisions of § 54.01–15 shall be inspected by a marine inspector referring to procedures outlined in UG–92 through UG–103 of section VIII of the ASME Boiler and Pressure Vessel Code (incorporated by reference; see 46 CFR 54.01–1) and §§ 50.30–10, 50.30–15, and 50.30–20 of this subchapter. The marine inspector will then stamp the vessel with the Coast Guard Symbol.

(c) Pressure vessels described in § 54.01–5(c)(3), except pressure vessels in systems regulated under § 58.60 of this chapter, must be visually examined by a marine inspector prior to installation. The marine inspector also reviews the associated plans and manufacturers' data reports. If, upon inspection, the pressure vessel complies with the applicable requirements in § 54.01–5, the marine inspector stamps the pressure vessel with the Coast Guard Symbol.

[CGFR 68–82, 33 FR 18828, Dec. 18, 1968, as amended by CGD 77–147, 47 FR 21810, May 20, 1982; USCG–2003–16630, 73 FR 65167, Oct. 31, 2008]

§ 54.10–5 Maximum allowable working pressure (reproduces UG–98).

(a) The maximum allowable working pressure for a vessel is the maximum pressure permissible at the top of the vessel in its normal operating position at the designated coincident temperature specified for that pressure. It is the least of the values found for maximum allowable working pressure for any of the essential parts of the vessel by the principles given in paragraph (b) of this section and adjusted for any difference in static head that may exist between the part considered and the top of the vessel. (See appendix 3 of section VIII of the ASME Boiler and Pressure Vessel Code (incorporated by reference; see 46 CFR 54.01–1.)

(b) The maximum allowable working pressure for a vessel part is the maximum internal or external pressure, including the static head hereon, as determined by the rules and formulas in section VIII of the ASME Boiler and Pressure Vessel Code, together with the effect of any combination of loadings listed in UG–22 of section VIII of the ASME Boiler and Pressure Vessel Code (see 46 CFR 54.01–30) that are likely to occur, or the designated coincident operating temperature, excluding any metal thickness specified as corrosion allowance. (See UG–25 of section VIII of the ASME Boiler and Pressure Vessel Code.)

(c) Maximum allowable working pressure may be determined for more than one designated operating temperature,

§ 54.10-5

using for each temperature the applicable allowable stress value.

NOTE: Table 54.10–5 gives pictorially the interrelation among the various pressure levels pertinent to this part of the regulations. It includes reference to section VIII of the ASME Boiler and Pressure Vessel Code for definitions and explanations.

Table 54.10-5--Pictorial Inter-Relation Among Various Pressure Levels with References to Specific Requirements[1]

Pressure differential[2]	Test pressures	Relief Device pressure settings	Pressures upon which flow capacity of relief devices is based
↑ Increasing Pressure	Burst-proof test (UG-101(m) of section VIII of the ASME Boiler and Pressure Vessel Code		
	Yield-proof test (UG-101(j) of section VIII of the ASME Boiler and Pressure Vessel Code)		
	Standard hydrostatic test (UG-99 of section VIII of the ASME Boiler and Pressure Vessel Code)		
			Fire exposure, 120% MAWP
	Pneumatic test (UG-100 of section VIII of the ASME Boiler and Pressure Vessel Code)		
		Rupture disk burst (§ 54.15-13)	
			Normal, 110% MAWP

Coast Guard, Dept. of Homeland Security § 54.10-5

Increasing Pressure ↑	Maximum allowable working pressure (MAWP), UG-98 of section VIII of the ASME Boiler and Pressure Vessel Code	Maximum allowable working pressure (MAWP), UG-98 of section VIII of the ASME Boiler and Pressure Vessel Code	Maximum allowable working pressure (MAWP), UG-98 of section VIII of the ASME Boiler and Pressure Vessel Code
	Design pressure, UG-21 and Appendix 3 of section VIII of the ASME Boiler and Pressure Vessel Code	Design pressure, UG-21 and Appendix 3 of section VIII of the ASME Boiler and Pressure Vessel Code	Design pressure, UG-21 and Appendix 3 of section VIII of the ASME Boiler and Pressure Vessel Code
		Safety or relief valve setting (UG-133 of section VIII of the ASME Boiler and Pressure Vessel Code)	
	Operating Pressure (Appendix 3 of section VIII of the ASME Boiler and Pressure Vessel Code)	Operating Pressure (Appendix 3 of section VIII of the ASME Boiler and Pressure Vessel Code)	Operating Pressure (Appendix 3 of section VIII of the ASME Boiler and Pressure Vessel Code)

[1] For basic pressure definitions see 46 CFR 52.01-3(g) of this subchapter. Section VIII of the ASME Boiler and Pressure Vessel Code; see 46 CFR 54.01-1.

[2] For pressure differentials above 3,000 pounds per square inch (p.s.i.), special requirements may apply. Arrow of increasing pressure in left column signifies that, for example, the standard hydrostatic-test pressure is higher than the MAWP, which in turn is higher than the design pressure and the operating pressure, and so forth.

[USCG-2003-16630, 73 FR 65167, Oct. 31, 2008]

§ 54.10-10 Standard hydrostatic test (modifies UG-99).

(a) All pressure vessels shall satisfactorily pass the hydrostatic test prescribed by this section, except those pressure vessels noted under § 54.10-15(a).

(b) The hydrostatic-test pressure must be at least one and three-tenths (1.30) times the maximum allowable working pressure stamped on the pressure vessel, multiplied by the ratio of the stress value "S" at the test temperature to the stress value "S" at the design temperature for the materials of which the pressure vessel is constructed. The values for "S" shall be taken from tables UCS 23, UNF 23, UHA 23, or UHT 23 of section VIII of the ASME Boiler and Pressure Vessel Code (incorporated by reference, see 46 CFR 54.01-1). The value of "S" at test temperature shall be that taken for the material of the tabulated value of temperature closest to the test temperature. The value of "S" at design temperature shall be as interpolated from the appropriate table. No ratio less than one shall be used. The stress resulting from the hydrostatic test shall not exceed 90 percent of the yield stress of the material at the test temperature. External loadings which will exist in supporting structure during the hydrostatic test should be considered. The design shall consider the combined stress during hydrostatic testing due to pressure and the support reactions. This stress shall not exceed 90 percent of the yield stress of the material at the test temperature. In addition the adequacy of the supporting structure during hydrostatic testing should be considered in the design.

(c) The hydrostatic test pressure shall be applied for a sufficient period of time to permit a thorough examination of all joints and connections. The test shall not be conducted until the vessel and liquid are at approximately the same temperature.

(d) Defects detected during the hydrostatic test or subsequent examination shall be completely removed and then inspected. Provided the marine inspector gives his approval, they may then be repaired.

(e) Vessels requiring stress relieving shall be stress relieved after any welding repairs have been made. (See UW-40 of section VIII of the ASME Boiler and Pressure Vessel Code.)

(f) After repairs have been made the vessel shall again be tested in the regular way, and if it passes the test, the marine inspector may accept it. If it does not pass the test, the marine inspector can order supplementary repairs, or, if in his judgment the vessel is not suitable for service, he may permanently reject it.

[CGFR 68-82, 33 FR 18828, Dec. 18, 1968, as amended by USCG-2003-16630, 73 FR 65170, Oct. 31, 2008]

§ 54.10-15 Pneumatic test (modifies UG-100).

(a) Pneumatic testing of welded pressure vessels shall be permitted only for those units which are so designed and/or supported that they cannot be safely filled with water, or for those units which cannot be dried and are to be used in a service where traces of the testing medium cannot be tolerated.

(b) Proposals to pneumatically test shall be submitted to the cognizant Officer in Charge, Marine Inspection, for approval.

(c) Except for enameled vessels, for which the pneumatic test pressure shall be at least equal to, but need not exceed, the maximum allowable working pressure to be marked on the vessel, the pneumatic test pressure shall be at least equal to one and one-tenth (1.10) times the maximum allowable working pressure to be stamped on the vessel multiplied by the lowest ratio (for the materials of which the vessel is constructed) of the stress value "S" for the test temperature of the vessel to the stress value "S" for the design temperature (see UG-21 of section VIII of the ASME Boiler and Pressure Vessel Code (incorporated by reference; see 46 CFR 54.01-1)). In no case shall the pneumatic test pressure exceed one and one-tenth (1.10) times the basis for calculated test pressure as defined in UA-60(e) of section VIII of the ASME Boiler and Pressure Vessel Code.

(d) The pneumatic test of pressure vessels shall be accomplished as follows:

(1) The pressure on the vessel shall be gradually increased to not more than half the test pressure.

(2) The pressure will then be increased at steps of approximately one-tenth the test pressure until the test pressure has been reached.

(3) The pressure will then be reduced to the maximum allowable working pressure of the vessel to permit examination.

(e) Pressure vessels pneumatically tested shall also be leak tested. The test shall be capable of detecting leakage consistent with the design requirements of the pressure vessel. Details of the leak test shall be submitted to the Commandant for approval.

(f) After satisfactory completion of the pneumatic pressure test, the vessel may be stamped in accordance with §54.10–20. A marine inspector shall observe the pressure vessel in a loaded condition at the first opportunity following the pneumatic test. The tank supports and saddles, connecting piping, and insulation if provided shall be examined to determine if they are satisfactory and that no leaks are evident.

(g) The pneumatic test is inherently more hazardous than a hydrostatic test, and suitable precautions shall be taken to protect personnel and adjacent property.

[CGFR 68–82, 33 FR 18828, Dec. 18, 1968, as amended by USCG–2003–16530, 73 FR 65170, Oct. 31, 2008]

§54.10–20 Marking and stamping.

(a) *Pressure vessels (replaces UG–116, except paragraph (k), and UG–118).* Pressure vessels that are required by §54.10–3 to be stamped with the Coast Guard Symbol must also be stamped with the following information:

(1) Manufacturer's name and serial number.

(2) Coast Guard number, see §50.10–30 of this subchapter.

(3) Coast Guard Symbol, which is affixed only by the marine inspector.

(4) Maximum allowable working pressure ___ kPa (___ psig) at ___ °C (___ °F).

(5) Class.

(6) Minimum design metal temperature, if below −18 °C (0 °F).

(7) Water capacity in liters (U.S. gallons), if a cargo carrying pressure vessel.

(b) *Multichambered pressure vessels (replaces UG–116(k)).* In cases where more than one pressure vessel is involved in an integral construction, as with a heat exchanger, the manufacturer may elect to class the component pressure vessels differently. In such cases he shall stamp the combined structures as required in paragraph (a) of this section with information for each pressure vessel. Where an item for stamping is identical for both vessels, as with name and address of manufacturer, it need not be duplicated. However, where differences exist, each value and the vessel to which it applies shall be clearly indicated.

(c) *Stamping data (replaces UG–117).* Except as noted in paragraph (d) of this section, the data shall be stamped directly on the pressure vessel. The data shall be legibly stamped and shall not be obliterated during the service life of the pressure vessel. In the event that the portion of the pressure vessel upon which the data is stamped is to be insulated or otherwise covered, the data shall be reproduced on a metal nameplate. This plate shall be securely attached to the pressure vessel. The nameplate shall be maintained in a legible condition such that it may be easily read.

(1) Those parts of pressure vessels requiring Coast Guard shop inspection under this part which are furnished by other than the shop of the manufacturer responsible for the completed vessel shall be stamped with the Coast Guard Symbol, the Marine Inspection Office identification letters (see §50.10–30 of this subchapter) and the word "Part", the manufacturer's name and serial number, and the design pressure.

(d) *Thin walled vessels (Modifies UG–119).* In lieu of direct stamping on the pressure vessel, the information required by paragraph (a) of this section shall be stamped on a nameplate permanently attached to the pressure vessel when the pressure vessel is constructed of—

(1) Steel plate less than one-fourth inch thick; or

§ 54.10-25

(2) Nonferrous plate less than one-half inch thick.

[CGFR 68–82, 33 FR 18828, Dec. 18, 1968, as amended by CGFR 69–127, 35 FR 9977, June 17, 1970; CGD 72–206R, 38 FR 17226, June 29, 1973; CGD 77–147, 47 FR 21810, May 20, 1982; USCG–2003–16630, 73 FR 65170, Oct. 31, 2008]

§ 54.10–25 Manufacturers' data report forms (modifies UG–120).

(a) The Manufacturers' data report form, as provided by the Coast Guard, shall be completed in duplicate and certified by the manufacturer for each pressure vessel required to be shop inspected under these regulations. The original of this form shall be delivered to the Coast Guard inspector.

(b) Data forms for those parts of a pressure vessel requiring inspection, which are furnished by other than the shop of the manufacturer responsible for the completed unit, shall be executed in triplicate by the manufacturer of the parts. The original and one copy shall be delivered to the Coast Guard inspector who shall forward one copy of the report to the Officer in Charge, Marine Inspection, having cognizance over the final assembly. These partial data reports, together with the final inspection and tests, shall be the final Coast Guard inspector's authority to apply the Coast Guard symbol and number. A final data report shall be executed by the manufacturer or assembler who completes the final assembly and tests.

(c) If a pressure vessel is required to be inspected in accordance with § 54.10–3(c), the manufacturer's data reports required by UG–120 must be made available to the Coast Guard inspector for review prior to inspection of the pressure vessel.

(Approved by the Office of Management and Budget under control number 2130-0181)

[CGFR 69–127, 35 FR 9977, June 17, 1970 as amended by CGD 77–147, 47 FR 21810, May 20, 1982]

Subpart 54.15—Pressure-Relief Devices

§ 54.15–1 General (modifies UG–125 through UG–137).

(a) All pressure vessels built in accordance with applicable requirements in Division 1 of section VIII of the ASME Code must be provided with protective devices as indicated in UG–125 through UG–136 except as noted otherwise in this subpart.

(b) The markings shall be in accordance with this chapter for devices covered by § 54.15–10.

[CGFR 68–82, 33 FR 18828, Dec. 18, 1968, as amended by CGD 88–032, 56 FR 35822, July 29, 1991; USCG–2003–16630, 73 FR 65170, Oct. 31, 2008]

§ 54.15–3 Definitions (modifies appendix 3).

(a) Definitions applicable to this subpart are in § 52.01–3 of this subchapter.

[CGFR 68–82, 33 FR 18828, Dec. 18, 1968, as amended by USCG–2003–16630, 73 FR 65170, Oct. 31, 2008]

§ 54.15–5 Protective devices (modifies UG–125).

(a) All pressure vessels must be provided with protective devices. The protective devices must be in accordance with the requirements of UG–125 through UG–136 of section VIII of the ASME Boiler and Pressure Vessel Code (incorporated by reference; see 46 CFR 54.01–1) except as modified in this subpart.

(b) An unfired steam boiler evaporator or heat exchanger (see § 54.01–10) shall be equipped with protective devices as required by § 54.15–15.

(c) All pressure vessels other than unfired steam boilers shall be protected by pressure-relieving devices that will prevent the pressure from rising more than 10 percent above the maximum allowable working pressure, except when the excess pressure is caused by exposure to fire or other unexpected source of heat.

(d) Where an additional hazard can be created by exposure of a pressure vessel to fire or other unexpected sources of external heat (for example, vessels used to store liquefied flammable gases), supplemental pressure-relieving devices shall be installed to protect against excessive pressure. Such supplemental pressure-relieving devices shall be capable of preventing the pressure from rising more than 20 percent above the maximum allowable working pressure of the vessel. The minimum required relief capacities for compressed gas pressure vessels are given under §54.15-25. A single pressure-relieving device may be used to satisfy the requirements of this paragraph and paragraph (c) of this section, provided it meets the requirements of both paragraphs.

(e) Pressure-relieving devices should be selected on the basis of their intended service. They shall be constructed, located, and installed so that they are readily accessible for inspection and repair and so arranged that they cannot be readily rendered inoperative.

(f) Where pressure-indicating gages are used, they shall be chosen to be compatible with the pressure to be indicated. The size of the visual display, the fineness of graduations, and the orientation of the display will be considered. In no case shall the upper range of the gage be less than 1.2 times nor more than 2 times the pressure at which the relieving device is set to function.

(g) The Commandant may authorize or require the use of a rupture disk in lieu of a relief or safety valve under certain conditions of pressure vessel use and design. See §54.15-13.

(h) Vessels that are to operate completely filled with liquid shall be equipped with liquid relief valves unless otherwise protected against overpressure.

(i) The protective devices required under paragraph (a) of this section shall be installed directly on a pressure vessel except when the source of pressure is external to the vessel, and is under such positive control that the pressure in the vessel cannot exceed the maximum allowable working pressure at the operating temperature except as permitted in paragraphs (c) and (d) of this section.

(j) Pressure-relieving devices shall be constructed of materials suitable for the pressure, temperature, and other conditions of the service intended.

(k) The opening through all pipes and fittings between a pressure vessel and its pressure-relieving device shall have at least the area of the pressure-relieving device inlet, and in all cases shall have sufficient area so as not to unduly restrict the flow to the pressure-relieving device. The opening in the vessel shall be designed to provide direct and unobstructed flow between the vessel and its pressure-relieving device.

(1) Safety devices need not be provided by the pressure vessel manufacturer. However, overpressure protection shall be provided prior to placing the vessel in service.

[CGFR 68-82, 33 FR 18828, Dec. 18, 1968, as amended by CGD 88-032, 56 FR 35822, July 29, 1991; CGD 95-012, 60 FR 48049, Sept. 18, 1995; USCG-2003-16630, 73 FR 65170, Oct. 31, 2008]

§ 54.15-10 Safety and relief valves (modifies UG-126).

(a) All safety and relief valves for use on pressure vessels or piping systems shall be designed to meet the protection and service requirements for which they are intended and shall be set to relieve at a pressure which does not exceed the "maximum allowable working pressure" of the pressure vessel or piping system. Relief valves are not required to have huddling chambers for other than steam service. In addition, safety valves used on vessels in which steam is generated shall meet §52.01-120 of this subchapter except §52.01-120(a)(9). For steam service below 206 kPa (30 psig), bodies of safety valves may be made of cast iron. Safety relief valves used in liquefied compressed gas service shall meet subpart 162.017 or 162.018 in subchapter Q (Specifications) of this chapter as appropriate.

(b) Pilot-valve control or other indirect operation of safety valves is not permitted unless the design is such that the main unloading valve will open automatically at not over the set pressure and will discharge its full rated capacity if some essential part of the pilot or auxiliary device should fail. All other safety and relief valves shall be of the direct spring loaded type.

(c) Safety and relief valves for steam or air service shall be provided with a substantial lifting device so that the disk can be lifted from its seat when the pressure in the vessel is 75 percent of that at which the valve is set to blow.

(d) Safety and relief valves for service other than steam and air need not be provided with a lifting device although a lifting device is desirable if the vapors are such that their release will not create a hazard.

(e) If the design of a safety or relief valve is such that liquid can collect on the discharge side of the disk, the valve shall be equipped with a drain at the lowest point where liquid can collect (for installation, see UG–134 of section VIII of section VIII of the ASME Boiler and Pressure Vessel Code (incorporated by reference; see 46 CFR 54.01–1).

(f) Cast iron may be employed in the construction of relief valves for pressures not exceeding 125 pounds per square inch and temperatures not exceeding 450 °F. Seats or disks of cast iron are prohibited.

(g) The spring in a relief valve in service for pressures up to and including 250 pounds per square inch shall not be reset for any pressure more than 10 percent above or 10 percent below that for which the relief valve is marked. For higher pressures, the spring shall not be reset for any pressure more than 5 percent above or 5 percent below that for which the relief valve is marked.

(h) The rated relieving capacity of safety and relief valves for use on pressure vessels shall be based on actual flow test data and the capacity shall be certified by the manufacturer in accordance with one of the following:

(1) 120 percent of the valve set pressure for valves rated in accordance with CGA S–1.2 (incorporated by reference; see 46 CFR 54.01–1).

(2) 110 percent of the valve set pressure for valves rated in accordance with UG–131 of section VIII of section VIII of the ASME Boiler and Pressure Vessel Code.

(3) 103 percent of the valve set pressure for steam in accordance with PG–69 of section VIII of the ASME Boiler and Pressure Vessel Code.

[CGFR 68–82, 33 FR 18828, Dec. 18, 1968, as amended by CGD 81–79, 50 FR 9436, Mar. 8, 1985; USCG–2003–16630, 73 FR 65170, Oct. 31, 2008]

§ 54.15–13 Rupture disks (modifies UG–127).

(a) Paragraph UG–127 of section VIII of the ASME Boiler and Pressure Vessel Code (incorporated by reference; see 46 CFR 54.01–1) provides for the use of rupture disks in series with spring loaded safety or relief valves.

(b) For certain pressure vessels containing substances which may render a relief or safety valve inoperative, or where the installation of a valve is considered impractical, the Commandant may authorize or require the use of a rupture disk in parallel with or in lieu of a spring loaded safety or relief valve. These rupture disks shall:

(1) Comply with the general provisions of § 54.15–5 except as noted otherwise in this section;

(2) Have a capacity for discharge such that the volume of release is sufficient to prevent the internal pressure from exceeding 120 percent of the "maximum allowable working pressure" with the pressure vessel exposed to fire conditions (see § 54.15–25); and,

(3) Operate at a pressure level which does not produce fatigue failure of the disk. The normal maximum operating pressure multiplied by 1.3 shall not exceed the nominal disk burst pressure. (Notice that this restriction for protection of the rupture disk will usually require operation below the "maximum allowable working pressure" of the pressure vessel and therefore should be considered in design.)

(c) All disks shall be oriented so that if rupture occurs, the disk fragments and pressure vessel discharge will be directed away from operating personnel and vital machinery.

[CGFR 68–82, 33 FR 18828, Dec. 18, 1968, as amended by USCG–2003–16630, 73 FR 65170, Oct. 31, 2008]

§ 54.15–15 Relief devices for unfired steam boilers, evaporators, and heat exchangers (modifies UG–126).

(a) An approved safety valve set to relieve at a pressure not exceeding the "maximum allowable working pressure" of the shell shall be fitted to all unfired steam boilers and evaporators except for evaporators of the atmospheric type designed for vapor discharge direct to a distiller with no shutoff valve in the discharge line. The distiller connected to atmospheric evaporators shall be fitted with a vent to prevent a buildup in pressure. In no case shall the vent be less than 1½ inches in diameter. Evaporators operating between atmospheric pressure and 15 p.s.i.g., may use a rupture disc as an alternative to the safety valve.

(b) Safety valves for use on pressure vessels in which steam or pressure is generated shall comply with the requirements of § 54.15–10. Rupture discs used in lieu of these safety valves, as provided for in paragraph (a) of this section, shall comply with the requirements of § 54.15–13.

(c) The relieving capacity of evaporator safety valves required by paragraph (a) of this section shall be at least equal to the capacity of the orifice fitted in the steam supply to the evaporator. The orifice capacity shall be determined in accordance with the formula in paragraph (c) (1) or (2) of this section as appropriate:

(1) Where the set pressure of the evaporator shell safety valve is 58 percent or less than the setting of the safety valve in the steam supply:

$W = 51.45 A P$

(2) Where the set pressure of the evaporator shell safety valve exceeds 58 percent of the setting of the safety valve on the steam supply:

$W = 105.3 A \sqrt{P_1 (P - P_1)}$

where:

W=The required orifice capacity, in pounds per hour.
A=Cross-sectional area of rounded entrance orifice, in square inches. The orifice shall be installed near the steam inlet or the coils or tubes and where no orifice is employed the area used in the formula shall be that of the inlet connection or manifold.
P=Set pressure of steam supply safety valve, in pounds per square inch, absolute.
P_1=Set pressure of evaporator shell safety valve, in pounds per square inch, absolute.

(d) The relieving capacity of safety valves on unfired steam boilers shall not be less than the maximum generating capacity of the unfired steam boiler as certified by the manufacturer.

(e) On new installations and where the orifice size of an existing unfired steam boiler or evaporator is increased, an accumulation test shall be made by closing all steam outlet connections except the safety valves for a period of five minutes. When conducting the accumulation test, the water shall be at the normal operating level and the steam pressure shall be at the normal operating pressure, and while under this test the pressure shall not rise more than 6 percent above the safety valve setting.

(f) A heat exchanger with liquid in the shell and the heating medium in the tubes or coils, shall be fitted with a liquid relief valve meeting the requirement of § 54.15–5.

(g)(1) A heat exchanger with steam in the shell and liquid in the tubes or coils at a pressure exceeding that in the shell, shall have a liquid relief valve fitted to protect the shell against excess pressure.

(2) The discharge capacity of such relief valves shall be calculated on the basis of the discharge from one tube using the difference in pressures between that in the shell and that in the tubes and shall be not less than that determined by the following formula:

$Q = 29.81 K D 2 \sqrt{P_1 - P_2}$

where:

Q=Required relief valve discharge capacity, in gallons per minute, based on relief valve set pressure.
P_1=Pressure in the tube or coils, in pounds per square inch.
P_2=Set pressure of the shell relief valve, in pounds per square inch.
D=Internal diameter of the largest tube or coil, in inches.
K=Coefficient of discharge=0.62.

[CGFR 68–82, 33 FR 18828, Dec. 18, 1968, as amended by CGD 72–206R, 38 FR 17226, June 29, 1973]

§ 54.15–25 Minimum relief capacities for cargo tanks containing compressed or liquefied gas.

(a) Each tank shall be fitted with one or more safety relief valves designed, constructed, and flow tested in accordance with subpart 162.017 or 162.018 in subchapter Q (Specifications) of this chapter. Valves conforming to specification subpart 162.017 shall be limited to use on tanks whose maximum allowable working pressure is not in excess of 10 pounds per square inch. With specific approval of the Commandant, such valves may be connected to the vessel in lieu of being directly fitted to the tanks.

(b) The discharge pressure and the maximum overpressure permitted shall be in accordance with § 54.15–5.

(c) The rate of discharge for heat input of fire must meet the following formula:

§ 54.15-25

$Q = FGA^{0.82}$

where:

Q=minimum required rate of discharge in cubic meters (cubic feet) per minute of air at standard conditions 15 °C and 103 kPa (60 °F and 14.7 psia).

F=fire exposure factor for the following tank types:

F=1.0 for tanks without insulation located on the open deck.

F=0.5 for tanks on the open deck having insulation that has approved fire proofing, thermal conductance, and stability under fire exposure.

F=0.5 for uninsulated independent tasks installed in holds.

F=0.2 for insulated independent tanks in holds or for uninsulated independent tanks in insulated holds.

F=0.1 for insulated independent tanks in inerted holds or for uninsulated independent tanks in inerted, insulated holds.

F=0.1 for membrane and semi-membrane tanks.

G=gas factor of:

$$\text{"}G = [(177/LC)(\sqrt{ZT/M})] \qquad \text{SI units}$$

$$G = [(633,000/LC)(\sqrt{ZT/M})] \qquad \text{English units"}$$

where:

L=latent heat of the material being vaporized at the relieving conditions, in Kcal/kg (Btu per pound).

C=constant based on relation of specific heats (k), table §54.15-25(c) (if k is not known, C=.606(315)).

Z=compressibility factor of the gas at the relieving conditions (if not known, Z=1.0).

T=temperature in degrees K=(273 + degrees C) (R=(460 + degrees F)) at the relieving conditions (120% of the pressure at which the pressure relief valve is set).

M=molecular weight of the product.

A=external surface area of the tank in m² (sq. ft.) for the following tank types:

For a tank of a body of revolution shape:
A=external surface area.

For a tank other than a body of revolution shape:
A=external surface area less the projected bottom surface area.

For a grouping of pressure vessel tanks having insulation on the vessel's structure:
A=external surface area of the hold without the projected bottom area.

For a grouping of pressure tanks having insulation on the tank:
A=external surface area of the pressure tanks excluding insulation, and without the projected bottom area.[1]

---

[1] Figure 54.15–25(c) shows a method of determining the side external surface area of a grouping of vertical pressure tanks.

Coast Guard, Dept. of Homeland Security § 54.15-25

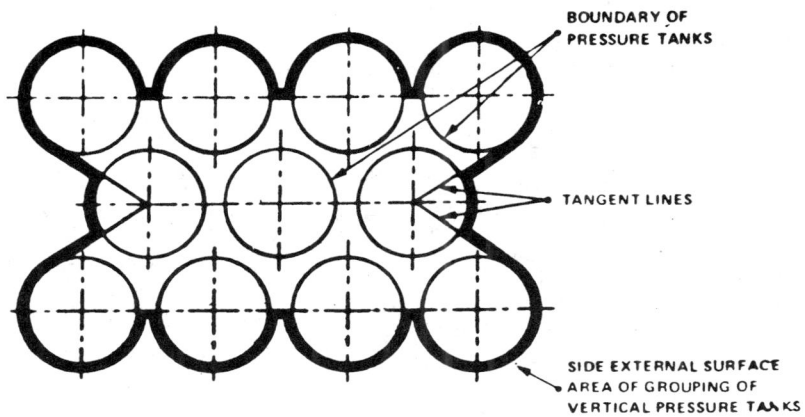

SIDE EXTERNAL SURFACE AREA OF GROUPING OF VERTICAL PRESSURE TANKS

Figure 54.15-25 (c)

TABLE 54.15–25(c)—CONSTANT C

k	C	
1.00	.606	(315)
1.02	.611	(318)
1.04	.615	(320)
1.06	.620	(322)
1.08	.624	(324)
1.10	.628	(327)
1.12	.633	(329)
1.14	.637	(331)
1.16	.641	(333)
1.18	.645	(335)
1.20	.649	(337)
1.22	.652	(339)
1.24	.658	(341)
1.26	.660	(343)
1.28	.664	(345)
1.30	.667	(347)
1.32	.671	(349)
1.34	.674	(351)
1.36	.677	(352)
1.38	.681	(354)
1.40	.685	(356)
1.42	.688	(358)
1.44	.691	(359)
1.46	.695	(361)
1.48	.698	(363)
1.50	.701	(364)
1.52	.704	(366)
1.54	.707	(368)
1.56	.710	(369)
1.58	.713	(371)
1.60	.716	(372)
1.62	.719	(374)
1.64	.722	(376)
1.66	.725	(377)
1.68	.728	(379)
1.70	.731	(380)
1.72	.734	(382)
1.74	.736	(383)
1.76	.739	(384)
1.78	.742	(386)
1.80	.745	(387)

TABLE 54.15–25(c)—CONSTANT C—Continued

k	C	
1.82	.747	(388)
1.84	.750	(390)
1.86	.752	(391)
1.88	.755	(392)
1.90	.758	(394)
1.92	.760	(395)
1.94	.763	(397)
1.96	.765	(398)
1.98	.767	(399)
2.00	.770	(400)
2.02	.772	(401)
2.20	.792	(412)

(c-1) For an independent tank that has a portion of the tank protruding above the open deck, the fire exposure factor must be calculated for the surface area above the deck and the surface area below the deck, and this calculation must be specially approved by the U.S. Coast Guard, Office of Design and Engineering Standards (CG-ENG)..

(d) In determining the total safety valve relieving capacity, the arrangement and location of the valves on the tank will be evaluated. The valves shall be placed so that a number of valves sufficient to provide the required relieving capacity shall always be in communication with the cargo vapor phase. The possible motions which the tank may see in its intended service and attendant changes in cargo liquid level will be considered. Shut off

§ 54.20-1

valves shall not be installed between the vessel and the safety relief valves. Manifolds for mounting multiple relief valves may be fitted with acceptable interlocking shut off valves so arranged that the required capacity of discharge will be "lined up" at all times.

(e)(1) Each safety relief valve shall be tested in the presence of a marine inspector before being placed in service except as noted otherwise in paragraph (e)(2) of this section. The test shall satisfactorily show that the valve will start to discharge at the required minimum pressure.

(2) Each safety relief valve fitted with a breaking pin and rupture disk need not be tested in the presence of a marine inspector before being placed in service. In lieu thereof, a certificate shall be furnished with the valve attested to by the manufacturer that the test requirements of paragraph (e)(1) of this section have been met.

[CGFR 68–82, 33 FR 18828, Dec. 18, 1968, as amended by CGD 74–289, 44 FR 26007, May 3, 1979; CGD 82–063b, 48 FR 4781, Feb. 3, 1983; CGD 95–072, 60 FR 50462, Sept. 29, 1995; CGD 96–041, 61 FR 50728, Sept. 27, 1996; USCG–2004–18884, 69 FR 58346, Sept. 30, 2004; USCG–2007–29018, 72 FR 53965, Sept. 21, 2007; USCG–2009–0702, 74 FR 49228, Sept. 25, 2009; USCG–2012–0832, 77 FR 59777, Oct. 1, 2012]

Subpart 54.20—Fabrication by Welding

§ 54.20-1 Scope (modifies UW-1 through UW-65).

(a) Pressure vessels and vessel parts that are fabricated by welding shall be as required by paragraphs UW-1 through UW-65 of section VIII of the ASME Boiler and Pressure Vessel Code (incorporated by reference; see 46 CFR 54.01-1) except as noted otherwise in this subchapter.

(b) [Reserved]

[CGFR 68–82, 33 FR 18828, Dec. 18, 1968, as amended by USCG–2003–16630, 73 FR 65170, Oct. 31, 2008]

§ 54.20-2 Fabrication for hazardous materials (replaces UW-2(a)).

(a) Pressure vessels containing hazardous materials as defined in § 150.115 of this chapter must be of the class and construction required by subchapter D,

I, O, or, when not specified, of a class determined by the Commandant.

(b) Class III pressure vessels must not be used for the storage or stowage of hazardous materials unless there is specific authorization in subchapters D, I, or O.

[CGD 77–147, 47 FR 21810, May 20, 1982]

§ 54.20-3 Design (modifies UW-9, UW-11(a), UW-13, and UW-16).

(a) Fabrication by welding shall be in accordance with the provisions of this part and with part 57 of this subchapter.

(b) Welding subject to UW-11(a) of section VIII of the ASME Boiler and Pressure Vessel Code (incorporated by reference; see 46 CFR 54.01-1) shall be modified as described in § 54.25-8 for radiographic examination.

(c) A butt welded joint with one plate edge offset, as shown in Figure UW-13.1(k) of section VIII of the ASME Boiler and Pressure Vessel Code, may only be used for circumferential joints of Class II and Class III pressure vessels.

(d) Attachment welds for nozzles and other connections shall be in accordance with UW-16 of section VIII of the ASME Boiler and Pressure Vessel Code. When nozzles or connections are made to pressure vessels, as shown in Figure UW-16.1 (a) and (c) of the ASME Code, and are welded from one side only, backing strips shall be used unless it can be determined visually that a full penetration weld has been achieved.

(e) When fabricating by welding the minimum joint requirements shall be as specified under the column headed "minimum joint requirements" in table 54.01-5(b) for various classes of pressure vessels.

(f) Joints in Class II or III pressure vessel cargo tanks must meet the following:

(1) Category A and B joints must be type (1) or (2).

(2) Category C and D joints must have full penetration welds extending through the entire thickness of the vessel wall or nozzle wall.

[CGFR 68–82, 33 FR 18828, Dec. 18, 1968, as amended by CGD 77–147, 47 FR 21810, May 20, 1982; CGD 85–061, 54 FR 50964, Dec. 11, 1989; USCG–2003–16630, 73 FR 65170, Oct. 31, 2008]

§ 54.20-5 Welding qualification tests and production testing (modifies UW-26, UW-28, UW-29, UW-47, and UW-48).

(a) *Performance and procedure qualification.* No production welding shall be done until welding procedures and welders have been qualified in accordance with part 57 of this subchapter.

(b) *Tests.* Production tests are required in accordance with § 57.06-1 of this subchapter.

[CGFR 68-82, 33 FR 18828, Dec. 18, 1968, as amended by CGFR 69-127, 35 FR 9977, June 17, 1970]

Subpart 54.23—Fabrication by Brazing

§ 54.23-1 Scope (modifies UB-1).

(a) Fabrication by brazing shall be in accordance with the provisions of this part and with part 57 of this subchapter.

[CGFR 69-127, 35 FR 9977, June 17, 1970]

Subpart 54.25—Construction With Carbon, Alloy, and Heat Treated Steels

§ 54.25-1 Scope.

The carbon, alloy, and heat treated steels used in construction of pressure vessels and parts shall be as indicated in section VIII of the ASME Boiler and Pressure Vessel Code (incorporated by reference; see 46 CFR 54.01-1) except as noted otherwise in this subpart.

[CGFR 68-82, 33 FR 18828, Dec. 18, 1968, as amended by USCG-2003-16630, 73 FR 65170, Oct. 31, 2008]

§ 54.25-3 Steel plates (modifies UCS-6).

The steels listed in UCS-6(b) of section VIII of the ASME Boiler and Pressure Vessel Code (incorporated by reference; see 46 CFR 54.01-1) will be allowed only in Class III pressure vessels (see table 54.01-5(b)).

[USCG-2003-16630, 73 FR 65170, Oct. 31, 2008]

§ 54.25-5 Corrosion allowance.

The corrosion allowance must be as required in 46 CFR 54.01-35.

[USCG-2003-16630, 73 FR 65170, Oct. 31, 2008]

§ 54.25-7 Requirement for postweld heat treatment (modifies UCS-56).

(a) Postweld heat treatment is required for all carbon and low alloy steel Class I, I-L, and II-L vessels regardless of thickness. (Refer to table 54.01-5(b) for applicable requirements.)

(b) Cargo tanks which are fabricated of carbon or low alloy steel as Class II pressure vessels, designed for pressures exceeding 100 pounds per square inch gage and used in the storage or transportation of liquefied compressed gases shall be postweld heat treated regardless of thickness.

[CGFR 69-127, 35 FR 9977, June 17, 1970]

§ 54.25-8 Radiography (modifies UW-11(a), UCS-57, UNF-57, UHA-33, and UHT-57).

(a) Full radiography is required for all Class I and Class I-L vessels regardless of thickness. (Refer to table 54.01-5(b) for applicable requirements.)

(b) Class II-L vessels shall be spot radiographed. The exemption provided in UW-11(c) of section VIII of the ASME Boiler and Pressure Vessel Code (incorporated by reference; see 46 CFR 54.01-1) does not apply. (Refer to table 54.01-5(b) for applicable requirements.)

(c) Each butt welded joint in a Class II or III pressure vessel cargo tank must be spot radiographed, in accordance with UW-52, regardless of diameter or thickness, and each weld intersection or crossing must be radiographed for a distance of at least 10 thicknesses from the intersection.

[CGFR 68-82, 33 FR 18828, Dec. 18, 1968, as amended by CGD 85-061, 54 FR 50964, Dec. 11, 1989; USCG-2003-16630, 73 FR 65170, Oct. 31, 2008]

§ 54.25-10 Low temperature operation—ferritic steels (replaces UCS-65 through UCS-67).

(a) *Scope.* (1) This section contains requirements for pressure vessels and nonpressure vessel type tanks and associated secondary barrier, as defined in § 38.05-4 and § 154.7 of this chapter, and their parts constructed of carbon and alloy steels which are stressed at operating or hydrostatic test temperatures below 0 °F.

(2) The service temperature is the minimum temperature of a product at which it may be contained, loaded and/

§ 54.25–10

or transported. However, the service temperature shall in no case be taken higher than given by the following formula:

$$t_s = t_w - 0.25(t_w - t_B)$$

where:
t_s = Service temperature.
t_w = Boiling temperature of gas at normal working pressure of container but not higher than +32 °F.
t_B = Boiling temperature of gas at atmospheric pressure.

Only temperatures due to refrigerated service usually need to be considered in determining the service temperature, except pressure vessel type cargo tanks operating at ambient temperatures must meet paragraph (d) of this section. "Refrigerated service", as used in this paragraph, means a service in which the temperature is controlled by the process and not by atmospheric conditions.

(b) *Specifications.* Materials used in the construction of vessels to operate below 0 °F. (but not below the designated minimum service temperature) shall conform to a specification given in table UCS-23 in section VIII of the ASME Boiler and Pressure Vessel Code (incorporated by reference; see 46 CFR 54.01–1) and the following additional requirements:

NOTE: For high alloy steels refer to § 54.25–15. For heat treated steels refer to § 54.25–20.

(1)(i) For minimum service temperatures not lower than −67 °F., ferritic steels shall be made with fine grain practice and shall have an austenitic grain size of 5 or finer, and shall be normalized. Consideration will be given to other heat treatments. Refer to § 57.03–1(d) of this subchapter. Plate for pressure vessel applications shall conform to the requirements of ASTM A 20 (incorporated by reference, see § 54.01–1). It may be produced by the open hearth, basic oxygen or electric furnace process and shall conform to the requirements of table 54.25–10(b)(1). (Other alloying elements may only be present in trace amounts.)

(ii) Mechanical properties shall be within the following limits:

Ultimate strength .... —58,000[1]–85,000[1] p.s.i.
Yield strength .... —Minimum 35,000 p.s.i.
                                    —Maximum 80 percent of ultimate.
Elongation minimum .... —20 percent in 8 inches, or
—24 percent in 2 inches, or
—22 percent in 5.65 √A, where "A" is the test specimen cross sectional area.

TABLE 54.25–10(b)(1)

Minimum service[1] temperature °F	Max. C[1] percent	Manganese range[1] percent
−30	0.20	0.70–1.35
−50	.16	1.15–1.50
−67	.12	1.30–1.60

[1] At service temperatures intermediate between those specified, intermediate amounts of carbon and manganese will be allowed (in proportion to the actual service temperature variation from that listed), provided all other chemical and mechanical properties specified for steels in this temperature range are satisfied.

	Range percent
Si	0.10–0.50

	Maximum
S	0.035
P	0.035
Ni	0.80
Cr	0.25
Mo	0.08
Cu	0.035
Nb	0.05
V	0.08

(2) For minimum service temperature below −67 °F., but not below the designated minimum service temperature, ferritic steels shall be normalized, low carbon, fully killed, fine grain, nickel alloy type, conforming to any one of the specifications in table 54.25–10(b)(2). Consideration will be given to other heat treatments. Refer to § 57.03–1(d) of this subchapter for quenched and tempered steels. The ultimate and yield strengths shall be as shown in the applicable specification and shall be suitable to the design stress levels adopted. The service temperature shall not be colder than the minimum specified in table 54.25–10(b)(2) for each steel.

TABLE 54.25–10(b)(2)

Steel	Minimum service temperature
A–203, 2¼ percent, Ni, normalized.	−80 °F. for Grade A. −75 °F. for Grade B.
A–203, 3½ percent, Ni, normalized.	−130 °F. for Grade D. −110 °F. for Grade E.
5 percent Ni, normalized	Dependent on chemical and physical properties.

(3) The materials permitted under paragraphs (b) (1) and (2) of this section shall be tested for toughness in accordance with and shall satisfy the applicable requirements of subpart 54.05.

(4) Welded pressure vessels or nonpressure vessel type tanks and associated secondary barriers, as defined in § 38.05–4 of subchapter D (Tank Vessels) of this chapter shall meet the toughness requirements of subparts 57.03 and 57.06 of this subchapter with regard to weld procedure qualifications and production testing.

(5) The material manufacturer's identification marking required by the material specification shall not be die-stamped on plate material less than one-fourth inch in thickness.

(c) *Design.* Pressure vessels must meet the requirements for Class I-L and II-L construction. (See table 54.01–5(b) for applicable requirements). Except as permitted by § 54.05–30, the allowable stress values used in the design of low temperature pressure vessels may not exceed those given in table UCS–23 of section VIII of the ASME Boiler and Pressure Vessel Code for temperatures of 0 °F. to 650 °F. For materials not listed in this table allowable stress values are determined in accordance with appendix P of section VIII of the ASME Boiler and Pressure Vessel Code.

(d) Weldments and all materials used in pressure vessel type cargo tanks operating at ambient temperatures and constructed of materials listed in table UCS–23 must pass Charpy impact tests in accordance with UG–84 at a temperature of −20 °F or colder, except as provided by paragraphs (d)(1), (d)(2), and (d)(3) of this section.

(1) Charpy impact tests are not required for any of the following ASTM materials if the thickness for each is ⅝ inch or less, unless otherwise indicated:

(i) A–182, normalized and tempered.
(ii) A–302, Grades C and D.
(iii) A–336, Grades F21 and F22 that are normalized and tempered.
(iv) A–387, Grades 21 and 22 that are normalized and tempered.
(v) A–516, Grades 55 and 60.
(vi) A–533, Grades B and C.
(vii) All other plates, structural shapes and bars, and other product forms, except for bolting, if produced to a fine grain practice and normalized.

(2) Charpy impact tests are not required for any of the following ASTM materials if the thickness for each is 1¼ inch or less:

(i) A–203.
(ii) A–508, Class 1.
(iii) A–516, normalized.
(iv) A–524.
(v) A–537.
(vi) A–612, normalized.
(vii) A–662, normalized.
(viii) A–724, normalized.

(3) Charpy impact tests are not required for any of the following bolt materials:

(i) A–193, Grades E5, B7, B7M, and B16.
(ii) A–307, Grade B
(iii) A–325, Type 1.
(iv) A–449.

[CGFR 68–82, 33 FR 18828, Dec. 18, 1968, as amended by CGFR 69–127, 35 FR 9977, June 17, 1970; CGD 73–133R, 39 FR 9178, Mar. 8, 1974; CGD 74–289, 44 FR 26007, May 3, 1979; CGD 77–069, 52 FR 31626, Aug. 21, 1987; CGD 85–061, 54 FR 50964, Dec. 11, 1989; USCG–1999–5151, 64 FR 67178, Dec. 1, 1999; USCG–2000–7790, 65 FR 58460, Sept. 29, 2000; USCG–2003–16630, 73 FR 65170, Oct. 31, 2008]

§ 54.25–15 Low temperature operation—high alloy steels (modifies UHA–23(b) and UHA–51).

(a) Toughness tests for the materials listed in UHA–51(a) in section VIII of the ASME Boiler and Pressure Vessel Code (incorporated by reference; see 46 CFR 54.01–1) for service temperatures below −425 °F., UHA–51(b)(1) through (5) for service temperatures below 0 °F., and UHA–51(c) for all service temperatures, shall be performed in accordance with the requirements of subpart 54.05. These requirements are also applicable to nonpressure vessel type, low temperature tanks and associated secondary barriers, as defined in § 38.05–4 in subchapter D (Tank Vessels) of this chapter. Such tests are required regardless of the vessel's design stress. Service temperature is defined in § 54.25–10(a)(2).

(b) Materials for pressure vessels with service temperatures below −320 °F. shall be of the stabilized or low carbon (less than 0.10 percent) austenitic stainless steel type, produced according to the applicable specifications of table UHA–23 of section VIII of the ASME Boiler and Pressure Vessel Code. These materials and their weldments shall be tested for toughness according

§ 54.25-20

to the requirements of subpart 54.05 except that the Charpy V-notch testing acceptance criteria will be in accordance with UHT–6(a)(4) and (5) of section VIII of the ASME Boiler and Pressure Vessel Code."

(c) Except as permitted by § 54.05–30, the allowable stress values used in the design of low temperature pressure vessels may not exceed those given in table UHA–23 of section VIII of the ASME Boiler and Pressure Vessel Code for temperatures of −20 °F. to 100 °F.

[CGFR 68–82, 33 FR 18828, Dec. 18, 1968, as amended by CGD 73–133R, 39 FR 9178, Mar. 8, 1974; CGD 73–254, 40 FR 40164, Sept. 2, 1975; USCG–2003–16630, 73 FR 65171, Oct. 31, 2008]

§ 54.25-20 Low temperature operation—ferritic steels with properties enhanced by heat treatment (modifies UHT–5(c), UHT–6, UHT–23, and UHT–82).

(a) For service temperatures below 0 °F. but not below the designated minimum service temperature, steel conforming to the specifications of table 54.25–20(a) may be used in the fabrication of pressure vessels and nonpressure vessel tanks and associated secondary barriers, as defined in § 38.05–4 of subchapter D (Tank Vessels) of this chapter. The ultimate and yield strengths shall be as shown in the applicable specification and shall be suitable for the design stress levels adopted. The service temperature shall not be colder than −320 °F. Service temperature is defined in § 54.25–10(a) (2).

TABLE 54.25–20(a)

Steel	Minimum service temperature, °F.
A–333, 9 percent Ni, grade 8	−320
A–334, 9 percent Ni, grade 8	−320
A–353, 9 percent Ni, double normalized and tempered	−320
A–522, 9 percent Ni, NNT, Q and T, forging	−320
A–553, 9 percent Ni, quenched and tempered	−320

(b) The materials permitted under paragraph (a) of this section shall be tested for toughness in accordance with the requirements of UHT–6 of section VIII of the ASME Boiler and Pressure Vessel Code (incorporated by reference; see 46 CFR 54.01–1) except that tests shall be conducted at the temperature specified in § 54.05–6 in lieu of that in UHT–5(c) of section VIII of the ASME Boiler and Pressure Vessel Code.

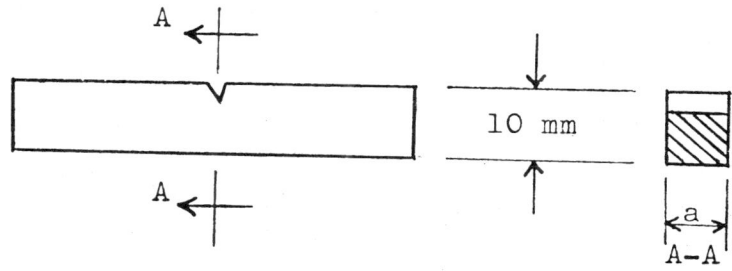

CHARPY V-NOTCH SPECIMEN

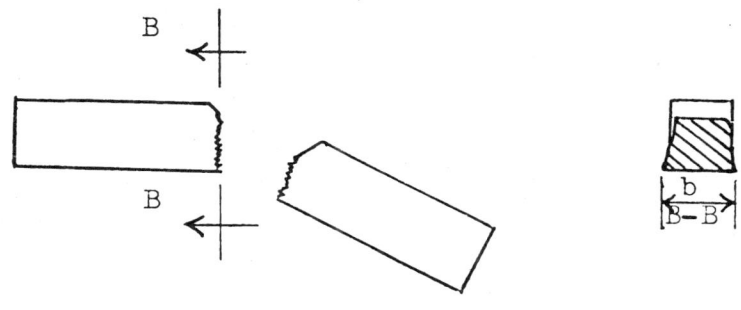

BROKEN SPECIMEN

LATERAL EXPANSION = (b-a)

(c) The qualification of welding procedures, welders and weld-production testing for the steels of table 54.25–20(a) must conform to the requirements of part 57 of this subchapter and to those of subpart 54.05 of this part except that the acceptance criteria for Charpy V-notch testing must be in accordance with UHT–6(a)(4) of section VIII of the ASME Boiler and Pressure Vessel Code.

(d) The values of absorbed energy in foot-pounds and of fracture appearance in percentage shear, which are recorded for information when complying with paragraphs (b) and (c) of this section shall also be reported to the marine inspector or the Commandant, as applicable.

(e) Except as permitted by §54.05–30, the allowable stress values may not exceed those given in table UHT–23 of section VIII of the ASME Boiler Pressure and Vessel Code for temperatures of 150 °F and below.

[CGFR 68–82, 33 FR 18828, Dec. 18, 1968, as amended by CGD 73–133R, 39 FR 9179, Mar. 8, 1974; USCG–2000–7790, 65 FR 58460, Sept. 29, 2000; USCG–2003–16630, 73 FR 65171, Oct. 31, 2008]

§ 54.25–25 Welding of quenched and tempered steels (modifies UHT–82).

(a) The qualification of welding procedures, welders, and weld-production testing must conform to the requirements of part 57 of this subchapter. The requirements of 46 CFR 57.03–1(d)

§ 54.30–1

apply to welded pressure vessels and non-pressure vessel type tanks of quenched and tempered steels other than 9-percent nickel.

(b) [Reserved]

[CGFR 68–82, 33 FR 18828, Dec. 18, 1968, as amended by USCG–2003–16330, 73 FR 65171, Oct. 31, 2008]

Subpart 54.30—Mechanical Stress Relief

§ 54.30–1 Scope.

(a) Certain pressure vessels may be mechanically stress relieved in accordance with the requirements in this subpart.

(b) [Reserved]

§ 54.30–3 Introduction.

(a) Large conventional pressure vessels used to transport liquefied petroleum and natural gases, at "low temperatures" may often be difficult to thermally stress relieve. Where no other problem, such as corrosion exists, mechanical stress relief will be permitted for Class II-L pressure vessels.

(b) Mechanical stress relief serves to cause small flaws, particularly in the weld zone, to yield plastically at the flaw tip resulting in a local relief of stress and a blunting of the crack tip. To achieve the maximum benefit from mechanical stress relief, it is necessary that the stresses so imposed be more severe than those expected in normal service life. At the same time, it is necessary that the stresses which are imposed are not so high as to result in appreciable deformation or general yielding.

(c) The weld joint efficiencies as listed in table UW–12 of section VIII of the ASME Boiler and Pressure Vessel Code (incorporated by reference; see 46 CFR 54.01–1) shall apply except that a minimum of spot radiography will be required. UW–12(c) of section VIII of the ASME Boiler and Pressure Vessel Code that permits omitting all radiography does not apply. Spot examination shall follow UW–52 of section VIII of the ASME Boiler and Pressure Vessel Code and, in addition, these vessels will be required to have radiographic examination of intersecting circumferential and longitudinal joints for a distance of at least 20 times the plate thickness from the junction. See 46 CFR 54.25–8 on spot radiography.

(d) Severe cold forming will not be permitted unless thermal stress relief is used. For example, parts of the vessels which are individually cold formed, such as heads, must be thermally stress relieved, where the extreme fiber strain measured at the surface exceeds 5 percent as determined by:

Percent strain=$(65t/R_f)[1-(R_f/R_o)]$

where:

t=Plate thickness.
R_f=Final radius.
R_o=Original radius (equals infinity for flat plate).

[CGFR 68–82, 33 FR 18828, Dec. 18, 1968, as amended by USCG–2000–7790, 65 FR 58460, Sept. 29, 2000; USCG–2003–16330, 73 FR 65171, Oct. 31, 2008]

§ 54.30–5 Limitations and requirements.

(a) Class II-L pressure vessels which require stress relief (see table 54.01–5(b)) may be mechanically stress relieved provided:

(1) The steels from which they are fabricated do not specifically require thermal stress relief in UCS–56 of section VIII of the ASME Boiler and Pressure Vessel Code (incorporated by reference; see 46 CFR 54.01–1) and have a ratio of yield to ultimate tensile strength not greater than 0.8. For example: A–537 steels could be mechanically stress relieved.

(2) Pressure difference across the shell is not greater than 100 pounds per square inch, thickness of shell is not greater than 1 inch, and the design temperature is not greater than 115 °F.

(3) It will carry liquids of specific gravity no greater than 1.05.

(4) Design details are sufficient to eliminate stress concentrators: Mechanical stress relief is not acceptable in designs involving the following types of welded connections shown in UW–16.1 of section VIII of the ASME Boiler and Pressure Vessel Code:

(i) Types l, m, n, and p because of nonintegral reinforcement. Type o will be acceptable provided the plate, nozzle, and reinforcement assembly are furnace stress relieved and the reinforcement is at least 6 inches or 10t, whichever is larger, from the plate head.

(ii) Types d, e, and f because expansion and contraction stresses are concentrated at the junction points.

(5) That no slip-on flanges in sizes greater than 2 inches are used.

(6) The categories A and B joints are type one as described in table UW–12 of section VIII of the ASME Boiler and Pressure Vessel Code and all categories C and D joints are full penetration welds. See UW–3 of the ASME Code for definition of categories.

(b) When a pressure vessel is to be mechanically stress relieved in accordance with §54.30–10(a)(1), its maximum allowable working pressure will be 40 percent of the value which would otherwise be determined. However, an increase of this 40 percent factor may be permitted if the stress relief is carried out at a pressure higher than that required by §54.30–10(a)(1) and an experimental strain analysis is carried out during stress relief. This evaluation should provide information as to the strains at the saddles, welded seams and nozzles as well as the body of the vessel. The hydrostatic pressure applied during stress relief should be such that, except in the case of welds, the stresses in the vessel shall closely approach but not exceed 90 percent of the yield stress of the material at the test temperature. The proposed experimental program should be submitted to the Commandant for approval prior to its use. Photo-elastic coating, strain gaging, or a brittle coating technique is suggested for the experimental analysis.

[CGFR 68–82, 33 FR 18828, Dec. 18, 1968, as amended by USCG–2003–16630, 73 FR 65171, Oct. 31, 2008]

§54.30–10 Method of performing mechanical stress relief.

(a) The mechanical stress relief shall be carried out in accordance with the following stipulations using water as the pressurizing medium:

(1) At a hydrostatic pressure (measured at the tank top) of 1½ times the design pressure. (See UA–60(e) of section VIII of the ASME Boiler and Pressure Vessel Code.)

(2) At a temperature of 70 °F. or the service temperature plus 50 °F., whichever is higher. Where the ambient temperature is below 70 °F., and use of water at that temperature is not practical, the minimum temperature for mechanical stress relief may be below 70 °F. but shall not be less than 50 °F. above service temperature.

(3) The stress relief shall be at the required temperature and pressure and held for a period not less than 2 hours per inch of metal thickness, but in no case less than 2 hours.

(b) It is considered preferable that mechanical stress relief be accomplished with the tanks in place on their saddles or supporting structure in the barge or ship in which they will be utilized. In any case, it is considered mandatory that the tank be supported only by its regular saddles or supporting structure, without any auxiliary or temporary supports.

[CGFR 68–82, 33 FR 18828, Dec. 18, 1968, as amended by USCG–2003–16630, 73 FR 65171, Oct. 31, 2008]

§54.30–15 Requirement for analysis and computation.

(a) A stress analysis shall be performed to determine if the tank may be exposed to excessive loadings during the mechanical stress relief process. This analysis should include consideration of the local stresses in way of saddles or other supporting structure and additional bending stresses due to the weight of the pressurizing liquid particularly in areas of high stress concentration. While it is necessary that the general stress level during the process be in excess of the normal working level, the calculated maximum stress during test shall not exceed 90 percent of the yield strength of the material at test temperature. The supporting structure shall be analyzed to verify its adequacy.

(b) In all cases where the tanks are mechanically stress relieved in place in the ship or barge and the tanks are designed to carry cargoes with a specific gravity less than 1.05, the ship or barge shall be shown to have adequate stability and buoyancy, as well as strength to carry the excess weight of the tank during the stress relief procedure.

PART 56—PIPING SYSTEMS AND APPURTENANCES

Subpart 56.01—General

Sec.
56.01–1 Scope (replaces 100.1).
56.01–2 Incorporation by reference.
56.01–3 Power boilers, external piping and appurtenances (Replaces 100.1.1, 100.1.2, 122.1, 132 and 133).
56.01–5 Adoption of ASME B31.1 for power piping, and other standards.
56.01–10 Plan approval.

Subpart 56.04—Piping Classification

56.04–1 Scope.
56.04–2 Piping classification according to service.
56.04–10 Other systems.

Subpart 56.07—Design

56.07–5 Definitions (modifies 100.2).
56.07–10 Design conditions and criteria (modifies 101–104.7).

Subpart 56.10—Components

56.10–1 Selection and limitations of piping components (replaces 105 through 108).
56.10–5 Pipe.

Subpart 56.15—Fittings

56.15–1 Pipe joining fittings.
56.15–5 Fluid-conditioner fittings.
56.15–10 Special purpose fittings.

Subpart 56.20—Valves

56.20–1 General.
56.20–5 Marking (modifies 107.2).
56.20–7 Ends.
56.20–9 Valve construction.
56.20–15 Valves employing resilient material.
56.20–20 Valve bypasses.

Subpart 56.25—Pipe Flanges, Blanks, Flange Facings, Gaskets, and Bolting

56.25–5 Flanges.
56.25–7 Blanks.
56.25–10 Flange facings.
56.25–15 Gaskets (modifies 108.4).
56.25–20 Bolting.

Subpart 56.30—Selection and Limitations of Piping Joints

56.30–1 Scope (replaces 110 through 118).
56.30–3 Piping joints (reproduces 110).
56.30–5 Welded joints.
56.30–10 Flanged joints (modifies 104.5.1 (a)).
56.30–15 Expanded or rolled joints.
56.30–20 Threaded joints.
56.30–25 Flared, flareless, and compression fittings.
56.30–27 Caulked joints.
56.30–30 Brazed joints.
56.30–35 Gasketed mechanical couplings.
56.30–40 Flexible pipe couplings of the compression or slip-on type.

Subpart 56.35—Expansion, Flexibility and Supports

56.35–1 Pipe stress calculations (replaces 119.7).
56.35–10 Nonmetallic expansion joints (replaces 119.5.1).
56.35–15 Metallic expansion joints (replaces 119.5.1).

Subpart 56.50—Design Requirements Pertaining to Specific Systems

56.50–1 General (replaces 122).
56.50–10 Special gauge requirements.
56.50–15 Steam and exhaust piping.
56.50–20 Pressure relief piping.
56.50–25 Safety and relief valve escape piping.
56.50–30 Boiler feed piping.
56.50–35 Condensate pumps.
56.50–40 BBlowoff piping (replaces 122.1.4).
56.50–45 Circulating pumps.
56.50–50 Bilge and ballast piping.
56.50–55 Bilge pumps.
56.50–57 Bilge piping and pumps, alternative requirements.
56.50–60 Systems containing oil.
56.50–65 Burner fuel-oil service systems.
56.50–70 Gasoline fuel systems.
56.50–75 Diesel fuel systems.
56.50–80 Lubricating-oil systems.
56.50–85 Tank-vent piping.
56.50–90 Sounding devices.
56.50–95 Overboard discharges and shell connections.
56.50–96 Keel cooler installations.
56.50–97 Piping for instruments, control, and sampling (modifies 122.3).
56.50–103 Fixed oxygen-acetylene distribution piping.
56.50–105 Low-temperature piping.
56.50–110 Diving support systems.

Subpart 56.60—Materials

56.60–1 Acceptable materials and specifications (replaces 123 and table 126.1 in ASME B31.1).
56.60–2 Limitations on materials.
56.60–3 Ferrous materials.
56.60–5 Steel (High temperature applications).
56.60–10 Cast iron and malleable iron.
56.60–15 Ductile iron.
56.60–20 Nonferrous materials.
56.60–25 Nonmetallic materials.

Coast Guard, Dept. of Homeland Security

Subpart 56.65—Fabrication, Assembly and Erection

56.65-1 General (replaces 127 through 135).

Subpart 56.70—Welding

56.70-1 General.
56.70-3 Limitations.
56.70-5 Material.
56.70-10 Preparation (modifies 127.3).
56.70-15 Procedure.
56.70-20 Qualification, general.

Subpart 56.75—Brazing

56.75-5 Filler metal.
56.75-10 Joint clearance
56.75-15 Heating
56.75-20 Brazing qualification.
56.75-25 Detail requirements.
56.75-30 Pipe joining details.

Subpart 56.80—Bending and Forming

56.80-5 Bending.
56.80-10 Forming (reproduces 129.2).
56.80-15 Heat treatment of bends and formed components.

Subpart 56.85—Heat Treatment of Welds

56.85-5 Heating and cooling method
56.85-10 Preheating.
56.85-15 Postheat treatment.

Subpart 56.90—Assembly

56.90-1 General.
56.90-5 Bolting procedure.
56.90-10 Threaded piping (modifies 135.5).

Subpart 56.95—Inspection

56.95-1 General (replaces 136).
56.95-5 Rights of access of marine inspectors.
56.95-10 Type and extent of examination required.

Subpart 56.97—Pressure Tests

56.97-1 General (replaces 137).
56.97-5 Pressure testing of nonstandard piping system components.
56.97-25 Preparation for testing (reproduces 137.2).
56.97-30 Hydrostatic tests (modifies 137.4).
56.97-35 Pneumatic tests (replaces 137.5).
56.97-38 Initial service leak test (reproduces 137.7).
56.97-40 Installation tests.

AUTHORITY: 33 U.S.C. 1321(j), 1509; 43 U.S.C. 1333; 46 U.S.C. 3306, 3703; E.O. 12234, 45 FR 58801, 3 CFR, 1980 Comp., p. 277; E.O. 12777, 56 FR 54757, 3 CFR, 1991 Comp., p. 351; Department of Homeland Security Delegation No. 0170.1.

SOURCE: CGFR 68-82, 33 FR 18843, Dec. 18, 1968, unless otherwise noted.

Subpart 56.01—General

[CGFR 68-82, 33 FR 18843, Dec. 18, 1968, as amended by USCG-2003-16630, 73 FR 65171, Oct. 31, 2008]

§ 56.01-1 Scope (replaces 100.1).

(a) This part contains requirements for the various ships' and barges' piping systems and appurtenances.

(b) The respective piping systems installed on ships and barges shall have the necessary pumps, valves, regulation valves, safety valves, relief valves, flanges, fittings, pressure gages, liquid level indicators, thermometers, etc., for safe and efficient operation of the vessel.

(c) Piping for industrial systems on mobile offshore drilling units need not fully comply with the requirements of this part but must meet subpart 58.60 of this subchapter.

[CGFR 68-82, 33 FR 18843, Dec. 18, 1968, as amended by CGD 73-251, 43 FR 56799, Dec. 4, 1978]

§ 56.01-2 Incorporation by reference.

(a) Certain material is incorporated by reference into this part with the approval of the Director of the Federal Register under 5 U.S.C. 552(a) and 1 CFR part 51. To enforce any edition other than that specified in this section, the Coast Guard must publish notice of change in the FEDERAL REGISTER and the material must be available to the public. All approved material is available for inspection at the National Archives and Records Administration (NARA). For information on the availability of this material at NARA, call 202-741-6030 or go to *http://www.archives.gov/federal_register/code_of_federal_regulations/ibr_locations.html.* The material is also available for inspection at the Coast Guard Headquarters. Contact Commandant (CG-ENG), Attn: Office of Design and Engineering Systems, U.S. Coast Guard Stop 7509, 2703 Martin Luther King Jr. Avenue SE., Washington, DC 20593-7509. The material is also available from the sources listed below.

§ 56.01-2

(b) *American National Standards Institute (ANSI)*, 25 West 43rd Street, New York, NY 10036:

(1) ANSI/ASME B1.1–1982 Unified Inch Screw Threads (UN and UNR Thread Form) (1982) ("ANSI/ASME B1.1"), 56.25–20; 56.60–1;

(2) ANSI/ASME B1.20.1–1983 Pipe Threads, General Purpose (Inch) (1983) ("ANSI/ASME B1.20.1"), 56.60–1;

(3) ANSI/ASME B1.20.3–1976 (Reaffirmed 1982) Dryseal Pipe Threads (Inch) ("ANSI/ASME B1.20.3"), 56.60–1;

(4) ANSI/ASME B16.15–1985 [Reaffirmed 1994] Cast Bronze Threaded Fittings, Classes 125 and 250 (1985) ("ANSI/ASME B16.15"), 56.60–1;

(c) *American Petroleum Institute (API)*, 1220 L Street, NW., Washington, DC 20005–4070:

(1) API Standard 607, Fire Test for Soft-Seated Quarter-Turn Valves, Manufacturing, Distribution and Marketing Department, Fourth Edition (1993) ("API 607"), 56.20–15; and

(2) [Reserved]

(d) *American Society of Mechanical Engineers (ASME) International*, Three Park Avenue, New York, NY 10016–5990:

(1) 2001 ASME Boiler and Pressure Vessel Code, Section I, Rules for Construction of Power Boilers (July 1, 2001) ("Section I of the ASME Boiler and Pressure Vessel Code"), 56.15–1; 56.15–5; 56.20–1; 56.60–1; 56.70–15; 56.95–10;

(2) ASME Boiler and Pressure Vessel Code, Section VIII, Division 1, Rules for Construction of Pressure Vessels (1998 with 1999 and 2000 addenda) ("Section VIII of the ASME Boiler and Pressure Vessel Code"), 56.15–1; 56.15–5; 56.20–1; 56.25–5; 56.30–10; 56.30–30; 56.60–1; 56.60–2; 56.60–15; 56.95–10;

(3) 1998 ASME Boiler & Pressure Vessel Code, Section IX, Welding and Brazing Qualifications (1998) ("Section IX of the ASME Boiler and Pressure Vessel Code"), 56.70–5; 56.70–20; 56.75–20;

(4) ASME B16.1–1998 Cast Iron Pipe Flanges and Flanged Fittings, Classes 25, 125, 250 (1998) ("ASME B16.1"), 56.60–1; 56.60–10;

(5) ASME B16.3–1998 Malleable Iron Threaded Fittings, Classes 150 and 300 (1998) ("ASME B16.3"), 56.60–1;

(6) ASME B16.4–1998 Gray Iron Threaded Fittings, Classes 125 and 250 (1998) ("ASME B16.4"), 56.60–1;

(7) ASME B16.5–2003 Pipe Flanges and Flanged Fittings NPS ½ Through NPS 24 Metric/Inch Standard (2003) ("ASME B16.5"), 56.25–20; 56.30–10; 56.60–1;

(8) ASME B16.9–2003 Factory-Made Wrought Steel Buttwelding Fittings (2003) ("ASME B16.9"), 56.60–1;

(9) ASME B16.10–2000 Face-to-Face and End-to-End Dimensions of Valves (2000) ("ASME B16.10"), 56.60–1;

(10) ASME B16.11–2001 Forged Fittings, Socket-Welding and Threaded (2001) ("ASME B16.11"), 56.30–5; 56.60–1;

(11) ASME B16.14–1991 Ferrous Pipe Plugs, Bushings, and Locknuts with Pipe Threads (1991) ("ASME B16.14"), 56.60–1;

(12) ASME B16.18–2001 Cast Copper Alloy Solder Joint Pressure Fittings (2001) ("ASME B16.18"), 56.60–1;

(13) ASME B16.20–1998 (Revision of ASME B16.20 1993), Metallic Gaskets for Pipe Flanges: Ring-Joint, Spiral-Wound, and Jacketed (1998) ("ASME B16.20"), 56.60–1;

(14) ASME B16.21–2005 (Revision of ASME B16.21–1992) Nonmetallic Flat Gaskets for Pipe Flanges (May 31, 2005) ("ASME B16.21"): 56.60–1;

(15) ASME B16.22–2001 (Revision of ASME B16.22–1995) Wrought Copper and Copper Alloy Solder Joint Pressure Fittings (Aug. 9, 2002) ("ASME B16.22"): 56.60–1;

(16) ASME B16.23–2002 (Revision of ASME B16.23–1992) Cast Copper Alloy Solder Joint Drainage Fittings: DWV (Nov. 8, 2002) ("ASME B16.23"): 56.60–1;

(17) ASME B16.24–2001 Cast Copper Alloy Pipe Flanges and Flanged Fittings, Class 150, 300, 400, 600, 900, 1500, and 2500 (2001) ("ASME B16.24"), 56.60–1;

(18) ASME B16.25–2003 Buttwelding Ends (2003) ("ASME B16.25"), 56.30–5; 56.60–1; 56.70–10;

(19) ASME B16.28–1994 Wrought Steel Buttwelding Short Radius Elbows and Returns (1994) ("ASME B16.28"), 56.60–1;

(20) ASME B16.29–2007 (Revision of ASME B16.29–2001) Wrought Copper and Wrought Copper Alloy Solder-Joint Drainage Fittings—DWV (Aug. 20, 2007) ("ASME B16.29"), 56.60–1;

(21) ASME B16.34–1996 Valves—Flanged, Threaded, and Welding End (1996) ("ASME B16.34"), 56.20–1; 56.60–1;

(22) ASME B16.42–1998 Ductile Iron Pipe Flanges and Flanged Fittings,

Coast Guard, Dept. of Homeland Security §56.01-2

Classes 150 and 300 (1998) ("ASME B16.42"), 56.60-1;

(23) ASME B18.2.1-1996 Square and Hex Bolts and Screws (Inch Series) (1996) ("ASME B18.2.1"), 56.25-20; 56.60-1;

(24) ASME/ANSI B18.2.2-1987 Square and Hex Nuts (Inch Series) (1987) ("ASME/ANSI B18.2.2"), 56.25-20; 56.60-1;

(25) ASME B31.1-2001 Power Piping ASME Code for Pressure Piping, B31 (2001) ("ASME B31.1"), 56.01-3; 56.01-5; 56.07-5; 56.07-10; 56.10-1; 56.10-5; 56.15-1; 56.15-5; 56.20-1; 56.25-7; 56.30-1; 56.30-5; 56.30-10; 56.30-20; 56.35-1; 56.50-1; 56.50-15; 56.50-40; 56.50-65; 56.50-70; 56.50-97; 56.60-1; 56.65-1; 56.70-10; 56.70-15; 56.80-5; 56.80-15; 56.95-1; 56.95-10; 56.97-1;

(26) ASME B36.10M-2004 Welded and Seamless Wrought Steel Pipe (2004) ("ASME B36.10M"), 56.07-5; 56.30-20; 56.60-1; and

(27) ASME B36.19M-2004 Stainless Steel Pipe (2004) ("ASME B36.19M"), 56.07-5; 56.60-1.

(28) ASME SA-675 (1998), Specification for Steel Bars, Carbon, Hot-Wrought, Special Quality, Mechanical Properties ("ASME SA-675"), 56.60-2.

(e) *ASTM International*, 100 Barr Harbor Drive, P.O. Box C700, West Conshohocken, PA 19428-2959, 877-909-2786, *http://www.astm.org:*

(1) ASTM A 36/A 36M-97a, Standard Specification for Carbon Structural Steel ("ASTM A 36"), 56.30-10;

(2) ASTM A 47-90 (1995), Standard Specification for Ferritic Malleable Iron Castings ("ASTM A 47"), 56.60-1;

(3) ASTM A 53-98, Standard Specification for Pipe, Steel, Black and Hot-Dipped, Zinc-Coated, Welded and Seamless ("ASTM Specification A 53" or "ASTM A 53"), 56.10-5; 56.60-1;

(4) ASTM A 106-95, Standard Specification for Seamless Carbon Steel Pipe for High-Temperature Service ("ASTM A 106"), 56.60-1;

(5) ASTM A 126-95, Standard Specification for Gray Iron Castings for Valves, Flanges, and Pipe Fittings ("ASTM A 126"), 56.60-1;

(6) ASTM A134-96 (Reapproved 2012), Standard Specification for Pipe, Steel, Electric-Fusion (Arc)-Welded (Sizes NPS 16 and Over) ("ASTM A 134"), (approved March 1, 2012), incorporation by reference approved for §56.60-1;

(7) ASTM A 135-97c, Standard Specification for Electric-Resistance-Welded Steel Pipe ("ASTM A 135"), 56.60-1;

(8) ASTM A 139-96, Standard Specification for Electric-Fusion (Arc)-Welded Steel Pipe (NPS 4 and Over) ("ASTM A 139"), 56.60-1;

(9) ASTM A 178/A 178M-95, Standard Specification for Electric-Resistance-Welded Carbon Steel and Carbon-Manganese Steel Boiler and Superheater Tubes ("ASTM A 178"), 56.60-1;

(10) ASTM A179/A179M-90a (Reapproved 2012), Standard Specification for Seamless Cold-Drawn Low-Carbon Steel Heat-Exchanger and Condenser Tubes ("ASTM A 179"), (approved March 1, 2012), incorporation by reference approved for §56.60-1;

(11) ASTM A 182/A 182M-97c, Standard Specification for Forged or Rolled Alloy-Steel Pipe Flanges, Forged Fittings, and Valves and Parts for High-Temperature Service ("ASTM A-182"), 56.50-105;

(12) ASTM A 192/A 192M-91 (1996), Standard Specification for Seamless Carbon Steel Boiler Tubes for High-Pressure Service ("ASTM A 192"), 56.60-1;

(13) ASTM A 194/A 194M-98b, Standard Specification for Carbon and Alloy Steel Nuts for Bolts for High Pressure or High Temperature Service, or Both ("ASTM A-194"), 56.50-105;

(14) ASTM A 197-87 (1992), Standard Specification for Cupola Malleable Iron ("ASTM A 197"), 56.60-1;

(15) ASTM A 210/A 210M-96, Standard Specification for Seamless Medium-Carbon Steel Boiler and Superheater Tubes ("ASTM A 210"), 56.60-1;

(16) ASTM A 213/A 213M-95a, Standard Specification for Seamless Ferritic and Austenitic Alloy-Steel Boiler, Superheater, and Heat-Exchanger Tubes ("ASTM A 213"), 56.60-1;

(17) ASTM A214/A214M-96 (Reapproved 2012), Standard Specification for Electric-Resistance-Welded Carbon Steel Heat-Exchanger and Condenser Tubes ("ASTM A 214"), (approved March 1, 2012), incorporation by reference approved for §56.60-1;

(18) ASTM A 226/A 226M-95, Standard Specification for Electric-Resistance-Welded Carbon Steel Boiler and Superheater Tubes for High-Pressure Service ("ASTM A 226"), 56.60-1;

§ 56.01-2

(19) ASTM A 234/A 234M-97, Standard Specification for Piping Fittings of Wrought Carbon Steel and Alloy Steel for Moderate and High Temperature Service ("ASTM A 234"), 56.60-1;

(20) ASTM A 249/A 249M-96a, Standard Specification for Welded Austenitic Steel Boiler, Superheater, Heat-Exchanger, and Condenser Tubes ("ASTM A 249"), 56.60-1;

(21) ASTM A 268/A 268M-96, Standard Specification for Seamless and Welded Ferritic and Martensitic Stainless Steel Tubing for General Service ("ASTM A 268"), 56.60-1;

(22) ASTM A 276-98, Standard Specification for Stainless Steel Bars and Shapes ("ASTM A 276"), 56.60-2;

(23) ASTM A 307-97, Standard Specification for Carbon Steel Bolts and Studs, 60,000 PSI Tensile Strength ("ASTM A 307"), 56.25-20;

(24) ASTM A 312/A 312M-95a, Standard Specification for Seamless and Welded Austenitic Stainless Steel Pipes ("ASTM A-312" or "ASTM A 312"), 56.50-105; 56.60-1;

(25) ASTM A 320/A 320M-97, Standard Specification for Alloy/Steel Bolting Materials for Low-Temperature Service ("ASTM A-320"), 56.50-105;

(26) ASTM A 333/A 333M-94, Standard Specification for Seamless and Welded Steel Pipe for Low-Temperature Service ("ASTM A-333" or "ASTM A 333"), 56.50-105; 56.60-1;

(27) ASTM A 334/A 334M-96, Standard Specification for Seamless and Welded Carbon and Alloy-Steel Tubes for Low-Temperature Service ("ASTM A-334" or "ASTM A 334"), 56.50-105; 56.60-1;

(28) ASTM A 335/A 335M-95a, Standard Specification for Seamless Ferritic Alloy-Steel Pipe for High-Temperature Service ("ASTM A 335"), 56.60-1;

(29) ASTM A 350/A 350M-97, Standard Specification for Carbon and Low-Alloy Steel Forgings, Requiring Notch; Toughness Testing for Piping Components ("ASTM A-350"), 56.50-105;

(30) ASTM A 351/A 351M-94a, Standard Specification for Castings, Austenitic, Austenitic-Ferritic (Duplex), for Pressure-Containing Parts ("ASTM A-351"), 56.50-105;

(31) ASTM A 352/A 352M-93 (1998), Standard Specification for Steel Castings, Ferritic and Martensitic, for Pressure-Containing Parts, Suitable for Low-Temperature Service ("ASTM A-352"), 56.50-105;

(32) ASTM A 358/A 358M-95a, Standard Specification for Electric-Fusion-Welded Austenitic Chromium-Nickel Alloy Steel Pipe for High-Temperature Service ("ASTM A 358"), 56.60-1;

(33) ASTM A 369/A 369M-92, Standard Specification for Carbon and Ferritic Alloy Steel Forged and Bored Pipe for High-Temperature Service ("ASTM A 369"), 56.60-1;

(34) ASTM A 376/A 376M-96, Standard Specification for Seamless Austenitic Steel Pipe for High-Temperature Central-Station Service ("ASTM A 376"), 56.60-1; 56.60-2;

(35) ASTM A 395/A 395M-98, Standard Specification for Ferritic Ductile Iron Pressure-Retaining Castings for Use at Elevated Temperatures ("ASTM A 395"), 56.50-60; 56.60-1; 56.60-15;

(36) ASTM A 403/A 403M-98, Standard Specification for Wrought Austenitic Stainless Steel Piping Fittings ("ASTM A 403"), 56.60-1;

(37) ASTM A 420/A 420M-96a, Standard Specification for Piping Fittings of Wrought Carbon Steel and Alloy Steel for Low-Temperature Service ("ASTM A-420" or "ASTM A 420"), 56.50-105; 56.60-1;

(38) ASTM A 520-97, Standard Specification for Supplementary Requirements for Seamless and Electric-Resistance-Welded Carbon Steel Tubular Products for High-Temperature Service Conforming to ISO Recommendations for Boiler Construction ("ASTM A 520"), 56.60-1;

(39) ASTM A 522/A 522M-95b, Standard Specification for Forged or Rolled 8 and 9% Nickel Alloy Steel Flanges, Fittings, Valves, and Parts for Low-Temperature Service ("ASTM A-522"), 56.50-105;

(40) ASTM A 536-84 (Reapproved 2009), Standard Specification for Ductile Iron Castings ("ASTM A 536"), (approved May 1, 2009), incorporation by reference approved for § 56.60-1;

(41) ASTM A 575-96 (Reapproved 2007), Standard Specification for Steel Bars, Carbon, Merchant Quality, M-Grades ("ASTM A 575"), (approved September 1, 2005), incorporation by reference approved for § 56.60-2;

(42) ASTM A576-90b (Reapproved 2012), Standard Specification for Steel

Coast Guard, Dept. of Homeland Security §56.01-2

Bars, Carbon, Hot-Wrought, Special Quality ("ASTM A576"), (approved March 1, 2012), incorporation by reference approved for §56.60–2;

(43) ASTM B 16–92, Standard Specification for Free-Cutting Brass Rod, Bar, and Shapes for Use in Screw Machines ("ASTM B 16"), 56.60–2;

(44) ASTM B 21–96, Standard Specification for Naval Brass Rod, Bar, and Shapes ("ASTM B 21"), 56.60–2;

(45) ASTM B 26/B 26M–97, Standard Specification for Aluminum-Alloy Sand Castings ("ASTM B 26"), 56.60–2;

(46) ASTM B 42–96, Standard Specification for Seamless Copper Pipe, Standard Sizes ("ASTM B 42"), 56.60–1;

(47) ASTM B 43–96, Standard Specification for Seamless Red Brass Pipe, Standard Sizes ("ASTM B 43"), 56.60–1;

(48) ASTM B 68–95, Standard Specification for Seamless Copper Tube, Bright Annealed ("ASTM B 68"), 56.60–1;

(49) ASTM B 75–97, Standard Specification for Seamless Copper Tube ("ASTM B 75"), 56.60–1;

(50) ASTM B 85–96, Standard Specification for Aluminum-Alloy Die Castings ("ASTM B 85"), 56.60–2;

(51) ASTM B 88–96, Standard Specification for Seamless Copper Water Tube ("ASTM B 88"), 56.60–1;

(52) ASTM B 96–93, Standard Specification for Copper-Silicon Alloy Plate, Sheet, Strip, and Rolled Bar for General Purposes and Pressure Vessels ("ASTM B 96"), 56.60–2;

(53) ASTM B 111–95, Standard Specification for Copper and Copper-Alloy Seamless Condenser Tubes and Ferrule Stock ("ASTM B 111"), 56.60–1;

(54) ASTM B 124–96, Standard Specification for Copper and Copper Alloy Forging Rod, Bar, and Shapes ("ASTM B 124"), 56.60–2;

(55) ASTM B 134–96, Standard Specification for Pipe, Steel, Electric-Fusion (Arc)-Welded (Sizes NPS 16 and Over) ("ASTM B 134"), 56.60–1;

(56) ASTM B 161–93, Standard Specification for Nickel Seamless Pipe and Tube ("ASTM B 161"), 56.60–1;

(57) ASTM B 165–93, Standard Specification of Nickel-Copper Alloy (UNS N04400) Seamless Pipe and Tube ("ASTM B 165"), 56.60–1;

(58) ASTM B 167–97a, Standard Specification for Nickel-Chromium-Iron Alloys (UNS N06600, N06601, N06603, N06690, N06025, and N06045) Seamless Pipe and Tube ("ASTM B 167"), 56.60–1;

(59) ASTM B 171–95, Standard Specification for Copper-Alloy Plate and Sheet for Pressure Vessels, Condensers, and Heat Exchangers ("ASTM B 171"), 56.60–2;

(60) ASTM B 210–95, Standard Specification for Aluminum and Aluminum-Alloy Drawn Seamless Tubes ("ASTM B 210"), 56.60–1;

(61) ASTM B 234–95, Standard Specification for Aluminum and Aluminum-Alloy Drawn Seamless Tubes for Condensers and Heat Exchangers ("ASTM B 234"), 56.60–1;

(62) ASTM B 241/B 241M–96, Standard Specification for Aluminum and Aluminum-Alloy Seamless Pipe and Seamless Extruded Tube ("ASTM B 241"), 56.60–1;

(63) ASTM B 280–97, Standard Specification for Seamless Copper Tube for Air Conditioning and Refrigeration Field Service ("ASTM B 280"), 56.60–1;

(64) ASTM B 283–96, Standard Specification for Copper and Copper-Alloy Die Forgings (Hot-Pressed) ("ASTM B 283"), 56.60–2;

(65) ASTM B 315–93, Standard Specification for Seamless Copper Alloy Pipe and Tube ("ASTM B 315"), 56.60–1;

(66) ASTM B 361–95, Standard Specification for Factory-Made Wrought Aluminum and Aluminum-Alloy Welding Fittings ("ASTM B 361"), 56.60–1;

(67) ASTM B 858M–95, Standard Test Method for Determination of Susceptibility to Stress Corrosion Cracking in Copper Alloys Using an Ammonia Vapor Test ("ASTM B 858M"), 56.60–2;

(68) ASTM E 23–96, Standard Test Methods for Notched Bar Impact Testing of Metallic Materials ("ASTM E 23"), 56.50–105;

(69) ASTM F682–82a (Reapproved 2008), Standard Specification for Wrought Carbon Steel Sleeve-Type Pipe Couplings ("ASTM F 682"), (approved November 1, 2008), incorporation by reference approved for §56.60–1;

(70) ASTM F1006–86 (Reapproved 2008), Standard Specification for Entrainment Separators for Use in Marine Piping Applications ("ASTM F 1006"), (approved November 1, 2008), incorporation by reference approved for §56.60–1;

(71) ASTM F1007-86 (Reapproved 2007), Standard Specification for Pipeline Expansion Joints of the Packed Slip Type for Marine Application ("ASTM F 1007"), (approved December 1, 2007), incorporation by reference approved for § 56.60-1;

(72) ASTM F1020-86 (Reapproved 2011), Standard Specification for Line-Blind Valves for Marine Applications ("ASTM F 1020"), (approved April 1, 2011), incorporation by reference approved for § 56.60-1;

(73) ASTM F1120-87 (Reapproved 2010), Standard Specification for Circular Metallic Bellows Type Expansion Joints for Piping Applications ("ASTM F 1120"), (approved May 1, 2010), incorporation by reference approved for § 56.60-1;

(74) ASTM F1123-87 (Reapproved 2010), Standard Specification for Non-Metallic Expansion Joints ("ASTM F 1123"), (approved March 1, 2010), incorporation by reference approved for § 56.60-1;

(75) ASTM F1139-88 (Reapproved 2010), Standard Specification for Steam Traps and Drains ("ASTM F 1139"), (approved March 1, 2010), incorporation by reference approved for § 56.60-1;

(76) ASTM F1172-88 (Reapproved 2010), Standard Specification for Fuel Oil Meters of the Volumetric Positive Displacement Type ("ASTM F 1172"), (approved March 1, 2010), incorporation by reference approved for § 56.60-1;

(77) ASTM F 1173-95, Standard Specification for Thermosetting Resin Fiberglass Pipe and Fittings to be Used for Marine Applications ("ASTM F 1173"), 56.60-1;

(78) ASTM F1199-88 (Reapproved 2010), Standard Specification for Cast (All Temperatures and Pressures) and Welded Pipe Line Strainers (150 psig and 150 °F Maximum) ("ASTM F 1199"), (approved March 1, 2010), incorporation by reference approved for § 56.60-1;

(79) ASTM F1200-88 (Reapproved 2010), Standard Specification for Fabricated (Welded) Pipe Line Strainers (Above 150 psig and 150 °F) ("ASTM F 1200"), (approved March 1, 2010), incorporation by reference approved for § 56.60-1;

(80) ASTM F1201-88 (Reapproved 2010), Standard Specification for Fluid Conditioner Fittings in Piping Applications above 0 °F ("ASTM F 1201"), (approved May 1, 2010), incorporation by reference approved for § 56.60-1;

(81) ASTM F 1387-93, Standard Specification for Performance of Mechanically Attached Fittings ("ASTM F 1387"), 56.30-25;

(82) ASTM F 1476-95a, Standard Specification for Performance of Gasketed Mechanical Couplings for Use in Piping Applications ("ASTM F 1476"), 56.30-35; and

(83) ASTM F 1548-94, Standard Specification for the Performance of Fittings for Use with Gasketed Mechanical Couplings, Used in Piping Applications ("ASTM F 1548"), 56.30-35.

(f) *Expansion Joint Manufacturers Association Inc. (EJMA)*, 25 North Broadway, Tarrytown, NY 10591:

(1) Standards of the Expansion Joint Manufacturers Association, 1980, 56.60-1; and

(2) [Reserved]

(g) *Fluid Controls Institute Inc. (FCI)*, 31 South Street, Suite 303, Morristown, NJ 07960:

(1) FCI 69-1 Pressure Rating Standard for Steam Traps ("FCI 69-1"), 56.60-1; and

(2) [Reserved]

(h) *International Maritime Organization (IMO)*, Publications Section, 4 Albert Embankment, London, SE1 7SR United Kingdom:

(1) Resolution A.753(18) Guidelines for the Application of Plastic Pipes on Ships ("IMO Resolution A.753(18)"), 56.60-25; and

(2) [Reserved]

(i) *International Organization for Standardization (ISO)*, Case Postal 56, CH-1211 Geneva 20 Switzerland:

(1) ISO 15540 Ships and Marine Technology-Fire Resistance of Hose Assemblies-Test Methods, First Edition (Aug. 1, 1999) ("ISO 15540"), 56.60-25; and

(2) [Reserved]

(j) *Instrument Society of America (ISA)*, 67 Alexander Drive, Research Triangle Park, NC 27709:

(1) ISA-S75.02 (1996) ("ISA-S75.02"), 56.20-15; and

(2) [Reserved]

(k) *Manufacturers Standardization Society of the Valve and Fittings Industry, Inc. (MSS)*, 127 Park Street NE, Vienna, VA 22180:

(1) SP–6–2001 Standard Finishes for Contact Faces of Pipe Flanges and Connecting-End Flanges of Valves and Fittings (2001) ("MSS SP–6"), 56.25–10; 56.60–1;

(2) SP–9–2001 Spot Facing for Bronze, Iron and Steel Flanges (2001) ("MSS SP–9"), 56.60–1;

(3) SP–25–1998 Standard Marking System for Valves, Fittings, Flanges and Unions (1998) ("MSS SP–25"), 56.15–1; 56.20–5; 56.60–1;

(4) SP–44–1996 Steel Pipe Line Flanges (Reaffirmed 2001) ("MSS SP–44"), 56.60–1;

(5) SP–45–2003 Bypass and Drain Connections (2003) ("MSS SP–45"), 56.20–20; 56.60–1;

(6) SP–51–2003 Class 150LW Corrosion Resistant Cast Flanges and Flanged Fittings (2003) ("MSS SP–51"), 56.60–1;

(7) SP–53–95 Quality Standard for Steel Castings and Forgings for Valves, Flanges and Fittings and Other Piping Components–Magnetic Particle Examination Method (1995) ("MSS SP–53"), 56.60–1;

(8) SP–55–2001 Quality Standard for Steel Castings for Valves, Flanges and Fittings and Other Piping Components–Visual Method (2001) ("MSS SP–55"), 56.60–1;

(9) SP–58 Pipe Hangers and Supports–Materials, Design and Manufacture (1993) ("MSS SP–58"), 56.60–1;

(10) SP–61–2003 Pressure Testing of Steel Valves (2003) ("MSS SP–61"), 56.60–1;

(11) SP–67 Butterfly Valves (1995) ("MSS SP–67"), 56.60–1;

(12) SP–69 Pipe Hangers and Supports–Selection and Application (1996) ("MSS SP–69"), 56.60–1;

(13) SP–72 Ball Valves with Flanged or Butt-Welding Ends for General Service (1987) ("MSS SP–72"), 56.60–1;

(14) SP–73 (R 96) Brazing Joints for Copper and Copper Pressure Fittings (1991) ("MSS SP–73"), 56.60–1; and

(15) SP–83 Class 3000 Steel Pipe Unions, Socket Welding and Threaded (1995) ("MSS SP–83"), 56.60–1;

(l) *Society of Automotive Engineers (SAE)*, 400 Commonwealth Drive, Warrendale, PA 15096:

(1) J1475 (1996) Surface Vehicle Hydraulic Hose Fittings for Marine Applications (June 1996) ("SAE J1475"), 56.60–25; and

(2) J1942 (1997) Standards Hose and Hose Assemblies for Marine Applications (May 1997) ("SAE J1942"), 56.60–25.

[USCG–2003–16630, 73 FR 65171, Oct. 31, 2008, as amended by USCG–2009–0702, 74 FR 49228, Sept. 25, 2009; USCG–2012–0832, 77 FR 59777, Oct. 1, 2012; USCG–2012–0866, 78 FR 13250, Feb. 27, 2013; USCG 2013–0671, 78 FR 60148, Sept. 30, 2013]

§ 56.01–3 Power boilers, external piping and appurtenances (Replaces 100.1.1, 100.1.2, 122.1, 132 and 133).

(a) Power boiler external piping and components must meet the requirements of this part and §§ 52.01–105, 52.01–110, 52.01–115, and 52.01–120 of this chapter.

(b) Specific requirements for external piping and appurtenances of power boilers, as defined in §§ 100.1.1 and 100.1.2, appearing in the various paragraphs of ASME B31.1 (incorporated by reference; see 46 CFR 56.01–2), are not adopted unless specifically indicated elsewhere in this part.

[CGD 77–140, 54 FR 40602, Oct. 2, 1989; 55 FR 39968, Oct. 1, 1990; USCG–2003–16630, 73 FR 65174, Oct. 31, 2008]

§ 56.01–5 Adoption of ASME B31.1 for power piping, and other standards.

(a) Piping systems for ships and barges must be designed, constructed, and inspected in accordance with ASME B31.1 (incorporated by reference; see 46 CFR 56.01–2), as limited, modified, or replaced by specific requirements in this part. The provisions in the appendices to ASME B31.1 are adopted and must be followed when the requirements of ASME B31.1 or the rules in this part make them mandatory. For general information, table 56.01–5(a) lists the various paragraphs and sections in ASME B31.1 that are limited, modified, replaced, or reproduced by rules in this part.

TABLE 56.01–5(a)—LIMITATIONS AND MODIFICATIONS IN THE ADOPTION OF ASME B31.1 FOR PRESSURE AND POWER PIPING

Section or paragraph in ASME B31.1 and disposition	Unit in this part
100.1 replaced by	56.01–1.
100.2 modified by	56.07–5.
101 through 104.7 modified by.	56.07–10.
101.2 modified by	56.07–10(a), (b).

§ 56.01-10

TABLE 56.01–5(a)—LIMITATIONS AND MODIFICATIONS IN THE ADOPTION OF ASME B31.1 FOR PRESSURE AND POWER PIPING—Continued

Section or paragraph in ASME B31.1 and disposition	Unit in this part
101.5 replaced by	56.07–10(c).
102.2 modified by	56.07–10(d).
102.3 and 104.1.2 modified by.	56.07–10(e).
104.3 modified by	56.07–10(f).
104.4 modified by	56.07–10(e).
104.5.1 modified by	56.30–10.
105 through 108 replaced by	56.10–1 through 56.25–20.
110 through 118 replaced by	56.30–1 through 56.30–35.
119.5.1 replaced by	56.35–10, 56.35–15.
119.7 replaced by	56.35–1.
122.1.4 replaced by	56.50–40.
122.3 modified by	56.50–97.
122.6 through 122.10 replaced by.	56.50–1 through 56.50–80.
123 replaced by	56.60–1.
Table 126.1 is replaced by	56.30–5(c)(3), 56.60–1.
127 through 135 replaced by	56.65–1, 56.70–10 through 56.90–10.
136 replaced by	56.95–1 through 56.95–10.
137 replaced by	56.97–1 through 56.97–40.

(viii) (b) When a section or paragraph of the regulations in this part relates to material in ASME B31.1, the relationship with ASME B31.1 will appear immediately after the heading of the section or at the beginning of the paragraph as follows:

(1) (Modifies ___.) This indicates that the material in ASME B31.1 so numbered for identification is generally applicable but is being altered, amplified, or augmented.

(2) (Replaces ___.) This indicates that the material in ASME B31.1 so numbered for identification does not apply.

(3) (Reproduces ___.) This indicates that the material in ASME B31.1 so numbered for identification is being identically reproduced for convenience, not for emphasis.

(c) As stated in § 56.01-2 of this chapter, the standards of the American National Standards Institute (ANSI) and ASME specifically referred to in this part must be the governing requirements for the matters covered unless specifically limited, modified, or replaced by other rules in this subchapter. See 46 CFR 56.60–1(b) for the other adopted commercial standards applicable to piping systems that also constitute this subchapter.

[USCG–2003–16630, 73 FR 65175, Oct. 31, 2008]

§ 56.01-10 Plan approval.

(a) Plans and specifications for new construction and major alterations showing the respective piping systems shall be submitted, as required by subpart 50.20 of this subchapter.

(b) Piping materials and appliances, such as pipe, tubing, fittings, flanges, and valves, except safety valves and safety relief valves covered in part 162 of subchapter Q (Specifications) of this chapter, are not required to be specifically approved by the Commandant, but shall comply with the applicable requirements for materials, construction, markings, and testing. These materials and appliances shall be certified as described in part 50 of this subchapter. Drawings listing material specifications and showing details of welded joints for pressure-containing appurtenances of welded construction shall be submitted in accordance with paragraph (a) of this section.

(c)(1) Prior to installation aboard ship, diagrams of the following systems shall be submitted for approval:

(i) Steam and exhaust piping.
(ii) Boiler feed and blowoff piping.
(iii) Safety valve escape piping.
(iv) Fuel oil service, transfer and filling piping. (Service includes boiler fuel and internal combustion engine fuel piping.)
(v) Fire extinguishing systems including fire main and sprinkler piping, inert gas and foam.
(vi) Bilge and ballast piping.
(vii) Tank cleaning piping.
(viii) Condenser circulating water piping.
(ix) Vent, sound and overflow piping.
(x) Sanitary drains, soil drains, deck drains, and overboard discharge piping.
(xi) Internal combustion engine exhaust piping. (Refer to part 58 of this subchapter for requirements.)
(xii) Cargo piping.
(xiii) Hot water heating systems if the temperature is greater than 121 °C(250 °F).
(xiv) Compressed air piping.
(xv) Fluid power and control systems (hydraulic, pneumatic). (Refer to subpart 58.30 of this subchapter for specific requirements.)
(xvi) Lubricating oil piping.

(xvii) Refrigeration and air conditioning piping. (Refer to part 58 of this subchapter for specific requirements.)

(2) Arrangement drawings of the following systems shall also be submitted prior to installation:

(i) All Classes I, I-L, and II-L systems.

(ii) All Class II firemain, foam, sprinkler, bilge and ballast, vent sounding and overflow systems.

(iii) Other Class II systems only if specifically requested or required by regulations in this subchapter.

(d)(1) The drawings or diagrams shall include a list of material, furnishing pipe diameters, wall thicknesses, design pressure, fluid temperature, applicable ASTM material or ANSI component specification, type, size, design standard, and rating of valves, flanges, and fittings.

(2) Pump rated capacity and pump shutoff head shall appear on piping diagrams. Pump characteristic curves shall be submitted for all pumps in the firemain and foam systems. These curves need not be submitted if the following information is shown on the drawing:

(i) Rated capacity and head at rated capacity.

(ii) Shutoff head.

(iii) Head at 150 percent rated capacity.

(3) Standard drawings of the following fabrication details shall be submitted:

(i) Welding details for piping connections.

(ii) Welding details for nonstandard fittings (when appropriate).

(d-1) Plans of piping for industrial systems on mobile offshore drilling units must be submitted under subpart 58.60 of this subchapter.

(e) Where piping passes through watertight bulkheads and/or fire boundaries, plans of typical details of piping penetrations shall be submitted.

(f) Arrangement drawings specified in paragraph (c)(2) of this section are not required if—

(1) The location of each component for which there is a location requirement (i.e., shell penetration, fire station, foam monitor, etc.) is indicated on the piping diagram;

(2) The diagram includes, or is accompanied by and makes reference to, a material schedule which describes components in sufficient detail to substantiate their compliance with the regulations of this subchapter;

(3) A thermal stress analysis is not required; and

(4) A dynamic analysis is neither required nor elected in lieu of allowable stress reduction.

[CGFR 68–82, 33 FR 18843, Dec. 18, 1968, as amended by CGFR 69–127, 35 FR 9978, June 17, 1970; CGFR 72–59R, 37 FR 6189, Mar. 25, 1972; CGD 73–251, 43 FR 56799, Dec. 4, 1978, CGD 77–140, 54 FR 40602, Oct. 2, 1989; CGD 95–012, 60 FR 48049, Sept. 18, 1995]

Subpart 56.04—Piping Classification

§ 56.04–1 Scope.

Piping shall be classified as shown in table 56.04–1.

TABLE 56.04–1—PIPING CLASSIFICATIONS

Service	Class	Section in this part
Normal	I, II	56.04–2
Low temperature	I-L, II-L	56.50–105

[CGD 72–206R, 38 FR 17229, June 29, 1973, as amended by CGD 77–140, 54 FR 40602, Oct. 2, 1989; CGD 95–012, 60 FR 48049, Sept. 18, 1995]

§ 56.04–2 Piping classification according to service.

The designation of classes according to service is found in table 56.04–2.

TABLE 56.04–2—PRESSURE PIPING CLASSIFICATION

Service	Class [1]	Pressure (p.s.i.g.)		Temp. (°F)
Class B and C poisons [2]	I	any	and	0 and above.
	I-L	any	and	below 0.
	II	([3])	([3])	([3])
	II-L	([3])	([3])	([3])
Gases and vapors [2]	I	above 150	or	above 650.

§ 56.04-10

TABLE 56.04-2—PRESSURE PIPING CLASSIFICATION—Continued

Service	Class [1]	Pressure (p.s.i.g.)		Temp. (°F)
Liquefied flammable gases [2]	I-L	above 150	and	below 0.
	II	150 and below	and	0 to 650.
	II-L	150 and below	and	below 0.
	I	above 150	and	0 and above. [1]
	I-L	above 150	and	below 0.
	II	150 and below	and	0 and above.
	II-L	150 and below	and	below 0.
Molten sulphur	I	above 225	or	above 330.
	II	225 and below	and	330 and below.
Cargo liquids Grades A through D [2]	I	above 225	or	above 150.
	I-L	above 225	and	below 0.
	II	225 and below	and	0 to 150.
	II-L	225 and below	and	below 0.
Cargo liquids Grade E	I	above 225	or	above 400.
	I-L	above 225	and	below 0.
	II	225 and below	and	0 to 400.
	II-L	225 and below	and	below 0.
Water	I	above 225	or	above 350.
	II	225 and below	and	350 and below.
Fuels (Bunker, diesel, gasoline, etc.)	I	above 150	or	above 150.
	II	150 and below	and	150 and below.
Lubricating oil	I	above 225	or	above 400.
	II	225 and below	and	400 and below.
Asphalt	I	above 225	or	above 400.
	II	225 and below	and	400 and below.
Heat transfer oil	I	above 225	or	above 400.
	II	225 and below	and	400 and below.
Hydraulic fluid	I	above 225	or	above 400.
	II	225 and below	and	400 and below.
Flammable or combustible dangerous cargoes.	Refer to specific requirements of part 40 of this chapter.			
Other dangerous cargoes.	Refer to specific requirements of part 98 of this chapter.			

[1] Where doubt exists as to proper classification, refer to the Commandant for resolution.
[2] For definitions, see 46 CFR parts 30, 151, and 154. Note that the category "B and C" poisons is not used in the rules applying to self-propelled vessels (46 CFR part 153).
[3] Not permitted except inside cargo tanks approved for Class B and C poisons.

[CGFR 68–82, 33 FR 18843, Dec. 18, 1968, as amended by CGD 73–254, 40 FR 40164, Sept. 2, 1975; CGD 73–96, 42 FR 49024, Sept. 26, 1977]

§ 56.04-10 Other systems.

Piping systems and appurtenances not requiring plan approval may be accepted by the marine inspector if:

(a) The system is suitable for the service intended,

(b) There are guards, shields, insulation and similar devices where needed for protection of personnel,

(c) Failure of the systems would not hazard the vessel, personnel or vital systems, and

(d) The system is not manifestly unsafe.

[CGD 77–140, 54 FR 40602, Oct. 2, 1989]

Subpart 56.07—Design

§ 56.07-5 Definitions (modifies 100.2).

(a) *Piping.* The definitions contained in 100.2 of ASME B31.1 (incorporated by reference; see 46 CFR 56.01–2) apply, as well as the following:

(1) The word *piping* within the meaning of the regulations in this subchapter refers to fabricated pipes or tubes with flanges and fittings attached, for use in the conveyance of vapors, gases or liquids, regardless of whether the diameter is measured on the inside or the outside.

(b) *Nominal diameter.* The term *nominal diameter* or *diameter* as used in this part, means the commercial diameter of the piping, i.e., pipe size.

(c) *Schedule.* The word *Schedule* when used in this part refers to specific values as given in ASME B36.10M and B36.19M (both incorporated by reference; see 46 CFR 56.01–2).

(d) *Fittings and appurtenances.* The word *fitting* and the phrase *fittings and appurtenances* within the meaning of the regulations in this subchapter refer to pressure containing piping system components other than valves and pipe. This includes piping system components whose function is to join branches of the system (such as tees, wyes, elbows, unions, bushings, etc.) which are referred to as pipe joining fittings, as well as components which operate on the fluid contained in the system (such as traps, drains, strainers, separators, filters, meters, etc.), which are referred to as "fluid conditioner" fittings. Thermometer wells and other similar fittings which form part of the pressure barrier of any system are included under this heading. Expansion joints, slip joints, rotary joints, quick disconnect couplings, etc., are referred to as special purpose fittings, and may be subject to such special design and testing requirements as prescribed by the Commandant. Refer to subpart 56.15 for design requirements for fittings.

(e) *Nonstandard fittings.* "Nonstandard fitting" means a component of a piping system which is not fabricated under an adopted industry standard.

(f) *Vital systems.* (1) Vital systems are those systems that are vital to a vessel's survivability and safety. For the purpose of this subchapter, the following are vital systems:

(i) Systems for fill, transfer, and service of fuel oil;

(ii) Fire-main systems;

(iii) Fixed gaseous fire-extinguishing systems;

(iv) Bilge systems;

(v) Ballast systems;

(vi) Steering systems and steering-control systems;

(vii) Propulsion systems and their necessary auxiliaries and control systems;

(viii) Ship's service and emergency electrical-generation systems and their auxiliaries vital to the vessel's survivability and safety;

(ix) Any other marine-engineering system identified by the cognizant OCMI as crucial to the survival of the vessel or to the protection of the personnel aboard.

(2) For the purpose of this subchapter, a system not identified by paragraph (1) of this definition is a non-vital system.

(g) *Plate flange.* The term *plate flange,* as used in this subchapter, means a flange made from plate material, and may have a raised face and/or a raised hub.

[CGFR 68–82, 33 FR 18843, Dec. 18, 1968, as amended by CGFR 69–127, 35 FR 9978, June 17, 1970; CGD 77–140, 54 FR 40602, Oct. 2, 1989; USCG–2003–16630, 73 FR 65175, Oct. 31, 2008]

§ 56.07–10 **Design conditions and criteria (modifies 101–104.7).**

(a) *Maximum allowable working pressure.* (1) The maximum allowable working pressure of a piping system must not be greater than the internal design pressure defined in 104.1.2 of ASME B31.1 (incorporated by reference; see 46 CFR 56.01–2).

(2) Where the maximum allowable working pressure of a system component, such as a valve or a fitting, is less than that computed for the pipe or tubing, the system pressure shall be limited to the lowest of the component maximum allowable working pressures.

(b) *Relief valves. (modifies 101.2).* (1) Every system which may be exposed to pressures higher than the system's maximum allowable working pressure shall be safeguarded by appropriate relief devices. (See § 52.01–3 of this subchapter for definitions.) Relief valves are required at pump discharges except for centrifugal pumps so designed and applied that a pressure in excess of the maximum allowable working pressure for the system cannot be developed.

(2) The relief valve setting shall not exceed the maximum allowable working pressure of the system. Its relieving capacity shall be sufficient to prevent the pressure from rising more than 20 percent above the system maximum allowable working pressure. The rated relieving capacity of safety and relief valves used in the protection of piping systems only shall be based on actual flow test data and the capacity shall be certified by the manufacturer at 120 percent of the set pressure of the valve.

(3) Relief valves shall be certified as required in part 50 of this subchapter for valves, and shall also meet the requirements of § 54.15–10 of this subchapter.

(c) *Ship motion dynamic effects (replaces 101.5.3).* Piping system designs

§ 56.10-1

shall account for the effects of ship motion and flexure, including weight, yaw, sway, roll, pitch, heave, and vibration.

(d) *Ratings for pressure and temperature (modifies 102.2).* The material in 102.2 of ASME B31.1 applies, with the following exceptions:

(1) The details of components not having specific ratings as described in 102.2.2 of ASME B31.1 must be furnished to the Marine Safety Center for approval.

(1) The details of components not having specific ratings as described in 102.2.2 of ANSI B31.1 must be furnished to the Marine Safety Center for approval.

(2) Boiler blowoff piping must be designed in accordance with § 56.50-40 of this part.

(e) *Pressure design (modifies 102.3, 104.1.2, and 104.4).* (1) Materials for use in piping must be selected as described in § 56.60-1(a) of this part. Tabulated values of allowable stress for these materials must be measured as indicated in 102.3.1 of ASME B31.1 and in tables 56.60-1 and 56.60-2(a) of this part.

(2) Allowable stress values, as found in the ASME Code, which are restricted in application by footnote or are italicized shall not be used. Where multiple stresses are listed for a material, the lowest value of the listing shall be used unless otherwise approved by the Commandant. In all cases the temperature is understood to be the actual temperature of the component.

(3) Where the operator desires to use a material not listed, permission must be obtained from the Commandant. Requirements for testing found in § 56.97-40(a)(2) and § 56.97-40(a)(4) may affect design and should be considered. Special design limitations may be found for specific systems. Refer to subpart 56.50 for specific requirements.

(f) *Intersections (modifies 104.3).* The material in 104.3 of ASME B31.1 is applicable with the following additions:

(1) Reinforcement calculations where applicable shall be submitted.

(2) Wherever possible the longitudinal joint of a welded pipe should not be pierced.

[CGFR 68–82, 33 FR 18843, Dec. 18, 1968, as amended by CGFR 69–127, 35 FR 9978, June 17, 1970; 37 FR 16803, Aug. 19, 1972; CGD 73–254, 40 FR 40164, Sept. 2, 1975; CGD 77–140, 54 FR 40602, Oct. 2, 1989; CGD 95–012, 60 FR 48050, Sept. 18, 1995; CGD 95–028 62 FR 51200, Sept. 30, 1997; USCG–1998–4442, 63 FR 52190, Sept. 30, 1998; USCG–2003–16630, 73 FR 65175, Oct. 31, 2008]

Subpart 56.10—Components

§ 56.10-1 Selection and limitations of piping components (replaces 105 through 108).

(a) Pipe, tubing, pipe joining fittings, and piping system components, shall meet material and standard requirements of subpart 56.60 and shall meet the certification requirements of part 50 of this subchapter.

(b) The requirements in this subpart and in subparts 56.15 through 56.25 must be met instead of those in 105 through 108 in ASME B31.1 (incorporated by reference; see 46 CFR 56.01-2); however, certain requirements are marked "reproduced."

[CGFR 68–82, 33 FR 18843, Dec. 18, 1968, as amended by CGFR 69–127, 35 FR 9978, June 17, 1970; USCG–2003–16630, 73 FR 65175, Oct. 31, 2008]

§ 56.10-5 Pipe.

(a) *General.* Pipe and tubing shall be selected as described in table 56.60-1(a).

(b) *Ferrous pipe.* ASTM Specification A 53 (incorporated by reference, see § 56.01-2) furnace welded pipe shall not be used for combustible or flammable liquids within machinery spaces. (See §§ 30.10-15 and 30.10-22 of this chapter.)

(c) *Nonferrous pipe.* (See also § 56.60-20.) (1) Copper and brass pipe for water and steam service may be used for design pressures up to 250 pounds per square inch and for design temperatures to 406 °F.

(2) Copper and brass pipe for air may be used in accordance with the allowable stresses found from table 56.60-1(a).

(3) Copper-nickel alloys may be used for water and steam service within the design limits of stress and temperature

indicated in ASME B31.1 (incorporated by reference; see 46 CFR 56.01–2).

(4) Copper tubing may be used for dead-end instrument service up to 1,000 pounds per square inch.

(5) Copper, brass, or aluminum pipe or tube shall not be used for flammable fluids except where specifically permitted by this part.

(6) Aluminum-alloy pipe or tube along with similar junction equipment may be used within the limitation stated in 124.7 of ASME B31.1 and paragraph (c)(5) of this section.

(d) *Nonmetallic pipe.* Plastic pipe may be used subject to the conditions described in §56.60–25.

[CGFR 68–82, 33 FR 18843, Dec. 18, 1968, as amended by CGFR 69–127, 35 FR 9978, June 17, 1970; CGFR 72–59R, 37 FR 6189, Mar. 25, 1972; CGD 77–140, 54 FR 40602, Oct. 2, 1989; CGD 95–028, 62 FR 51200, Sept. 30, 1997; USCG–2000–7790, 65 FR 58460, Sept. 29, 2000; USCG–2003–16630, 73 FR 65175, Oct. 31, 2008]

Subpart 56.15—Fittings

SOURCE: CGD 77–140, 54 FR 40602, Oct. 2, 1989, unless otherwise noted.

§56.15–1 Pipe joining fittings.

(a) Pipe joining fittings certified in accordance with subpart 50.25 of this subchapter are acceptable for use in piping systems.

(b) Threaded, flanged, socket-welding, buttwelding, and socket-brazing pipe joining fittings, made in accordance with the applicable standards in tables 56.60–1(a) and 56.60–1(b) of this part and of materials complying with subpart 56.60 of this part, may be used in piping systems within the material, size, pressure, and temperature limitations of those standards and within any further limitations specified in this subchapter. Fittings must be designed for the maximum pressure to which they may be subjected, but in no case less than 50 pounds per square inch gage.

(c) Pipe joining fittings not accepted for use in piping systems in accordance with paragraph (b) of this section must meet the following:

(1) All pressure-containing materials must be accepted in accordance with §56.60–1 of this part.

(2) Fittings must be designed so that the maximum allowable working pressure does not exceed one-fourth of the burst pressure or produce a primary stress greater than one-fourth of the ultimate tensile strength of the material for Class II systems and for all Class I, I-L, and II-L systems receiving ship motion dynamic analysis and nondestructive examination. For Class I, I-L, or II-L systems not receiving ship motion dynamic analysis and nondestructive examination under §56.07–10(c) of this part, the maximum allowable working pressure must not exceed one-fifth of the burst pressure or produce a primary stress greater than one-fifth of the ultimate tensile strength of the material. The maximum allowable working pressure may be determined by—

(i) Calculations comparable to those of ASME B31.1 (incorporated by reference; see 46 CFR 56.01–2) or section VIII of the ASME Boiler and Pressure Vessel Code (incorporated by reference; see 46 CFR 56.01–2);

(ii) Subjecting a representative model to a proof test or experimental stress analysis described in paragraph A–22 of section I of the ASME Boiler and Pressure Vessel Code (incorporated by reference; see 46 CFR 56.01–2); or

(iii) Other means specifically accepted by the Marine Safety Center.

(3) Fittings must be tested in accordance with §56.97–5 of this part.

(4) If welded, fittings must be welded in accordance with subpart 56.70 of this part and part 57 of this chapter or by other processes specifically approved by the Marine Safety Center. In addition, for fittings to be accepted for use in piping systems in accordance with this paragraph, the following requirements must be met:

(i) For fittings sized three inches and below—

(A) The longitudinal joints must be fabricated by either gas or arc welding;

(B) One fitting of each size from each lot of 100 or fraction thereof must be flattened cold until the opposite walls meet without the weld developing any cracks;

(C) One fitting of each size from each lot of 100 or fraction thereof must be hydrostatically tested to the pressure required for a seamless drawn pipe of

§ 56.15-5

the same size and thickness produced from equivalent strength material, as determined by the applicable pipe material specification; and

(D) If a fitting fails to meet the test in paragraph (c)(4)(i)(B) or (c)(4)(i)(C) of this section, no fitting in the lot from which the test fitting was chosen is acceptable.

(ii) For fittings sized above three inches—

(A) The longitudinal joints must be fabricated by arc welding;

(B) For pressures exceeding 150 pounds per square inch, each fitting must be radiographically examined as specified in section VIII of the ASME Boiler and Pressure Vessel Code;

(C) For pressures not exceeding 150 pounds per square inch, the first fitting from each size in each lot of 20 or fraction thereof must be examined by radiography to ensure that the welds are of acceptable quality;

(D) One fitting of each size from each lot of 100 or fraction thereof must be hydrostatically tested to the pressure required for a seamless drawn pipe of the same size and thickness produced from equivalent strength material, as determined by the applicable pipe material specification; and

(E) If a fitting fails to meet the test in paragraph (c)(4)(ii)(C) or (c)(4)(ii)(D) of this section, no fitting in the lot from which the test fitting was chosen is acceptable.

(d) Single welded butt joints without the use of backing strips may be employed in the fabrication of pipe joining fittings of welded construction provided radiographic examination indicates that complete penetration is obtained.

(e) Each pipe joining fitting must be marked in accordance with MSS SP-25 (incorporated by reference; see 46 CFR 56.01-2).

[CGFR 68-82, 33 FR 18843, Dec. 18, 1968, as amended by USCG-2003-16630, 73 FR 65176, Oct. 31, 2008]

§ 56.15-5 Fluid-conditioner fittings.

(a) Fluid conditioner fittings certified in accordance with subpart 50.25 of this subchapter are acceptable for use in piping systems.

(b) Fluid conditioner fittings, not containing hazardous materials as defined in § 150.115 of this chapter, which are made in accordance with the applicable standards listed in table 56.60-1(b) of this part and of materials complying with subpart 56.60 of this part, may be used within the material, size, pressure, and temperature limitations of those standards and within any further limitations specified in this subchapter.

(c) The following requirements apply to nonstandard fluid conditioner fittings which do not contain hazardous materials as defined in § 150.115 of this chapter:

(1) The following nonstandard fluid conditioner fittings must meet the applicable requirements in § 54.01-5 (c)(3), (c)(4), and (d) of this chapter or the remaining provisions in part 54 of this chapter, except that Coast Guard shop inspection is not required:

(i) Nonstandard fluid conditioner fittings that have a net internal volume greater than 0.04 cubic meters (1.5 cubic feet) and that are rated for temperatures and pressures exceeding those specified as minimums for Class I piping systems.

(ii) Nonstandard fluid-conditioner fittings that have an internal diameter exceeding 15 centimeters (6 inches) and that are rated for temperatures and pressures exceeding those specified as minimums for Class I piping systems.

(2) All other nonstandard fluid conditioner fittings must meet the following:

(i) All pressure-containing materials must be accepted in accordance with § 56.60-1 of this part.

(ii) Nonstandard fluid conditioner fittings must be designed so that the maximum allowable working pressure does not exceed one-fourth of the burst pressure or produce a primary stress greater than one-fourth of the ultimate tensile strength of the material for Class II systems and for all Class I, I-L, and II-L systems receiving ship motion dynamic analysis and nondestructive examination. For Class I, I-L, or II-L systems not receiving ship motion dynamic analysis and nondestructive examination under § 56.07-10(c) of this part, the maximum allowable working pressure must not exceed one-fifth of the burst pressure or produce a primary stress greater than one-fifth of the ultimate tensile strength of the material. The maximum allowable working pressure may be determined by—

(A) Calculations comparable to those of ASME B31.1 (incorporated by reference; see 46 CFR 56.01–2) or section VIII of the ASME Boiler and Pressure Vessel Code (incorporated by reference; see 46 CFR 56.01–2);

(B) Subjecting a representative model to a proof test or experimental stress analysis described in paragraph A–22 of section I of the ASME Boiler and Pressure Vessel Code (incorporated by reference, see 46 CFR 56.01–2); or

(C) Other means specifically accepted by the Marine Safety Center.

(iii) Nonstandard fluid conditioner fittings must be tested in accordance with § 56.97–5 of this part.

(iv) If welded, nonstandard fluid conditioner fittings must be welded in accordance with subpart 56.70 of this part and part 57 of this chapter or by other processes specifically approved by the Marine Safety Center.

(d) All fluid conditioner fittings that contain hazardous materials as defined in § 150.115 of this chapter must meet the applicable requirements of part 54 of this chapter, except subpart 54.10.

(e) Heat exchangers having headers and tubes and brazed boiler steam air heaters are not considered fluid conditioner fittings and must meet the requirements in part 54 of this chapter regardless of size. For brazed boiler steam air heaters, see also § 56.30–30(b)(1) of this part.

[CGD 77–140, 54 FR 40602, Oct. 2, 1989, as amended by CGD 83–043, 60 FR 24772, May 10, 1995; USCG–2003–16630, 73 FR 65176, Oct. 31, 2008]

§ 56.15–10 Special purpose fittings.

(a) Special purpose fittings certified in accordance with subpart 50.25 of this subchapter are acceptable for use in piping systems.

(b) Special purpose fittings made in accordance with the applicable standards listed in table 56.60–1(b) of this part and of materials complying with subpart 56.60 of this part, may be used within the material, size, pressure, and temperature limitations of those standards and within any further limitations specified in this subchapter.

(c) Nonstandard special purpose fittings must meet the requirements of §§ 56.30–25, 56.30–40, 56.35–10, 56.35–15, or 56.35–35 of this part, as applicable.

Subpart 56.20—Valves

§ 56.20–1 General.

(a) Valves certified in accordance with subpart 50.25 of this subchapter are acceptable for use in piping systems.

(b) Non-welded valves complying with the standards listed in § 56.60–1 of this part may be used within the specified pressure and temperature ratings of those standards, provided the limitations of § 56.07–10(c) of this part are applied. Materials must comply with subpart 56.60 of this part. Welded valves complying with the standards and specifications listed in § 56.60–1 of this part may be used in Class II systems only unless they meet paragraph (c) of this section.

(c) All other valves must meet the following:

(1) All pressure-containing materials must be accepted in accordance with § 56.60–1 of this part.

(2) Valves must be designed so that the maximum allowable working pressure does not exceed one-fourth of the burst pressure or produce a primary stress greater than one-fourth of the ultimate tensile strength of the material for Class II systems and for all Class I, I-L, and II-L systems receiving ship motion dynamic analysis and nondestructive examination. For Class I, I-L, or II-L systems not receiving ship motion dynamic analysis and nondestructive examination under § 56.07–10(c) of this part, the maximum allowable working pressure must not exceed one-fifth of the burst pressure or produce a primary stress greater than one-fifth of the ultimate tensile strength of the material. The maximum allowable working pressure may be determined by—

(i) Calculations comparable to those of ASME B31.1 (incorporated by reference; see 46 CFR 56.01–2) or section VIII of the ASME Boiler and Pressure Vessel Code (incorporated by reference; see 46 CFR 56.01–2), if the valve shape permits this;

§ 56.20-5

(ii) Subjecting a representative model to a proof test or experimental stress analysis described in paragraph A-22 of section I the ASME Boiler and Pressure Vessel Code (incorporated by reference; see 46 CFR 56.01-2); or

(iii) Other means specifically accepted by the Marine Safety Center.

(3) Valves must be tested in accordance with § 56.97-5 of this part.

(4) If welded, valves must be welded in accordance with subpart 56.70 of this part and part 57 of this chapter or by other processes specifically approved by the Marine Safety Center.

(d) Where liquid trapped in any closed valve can be heated and an uncontrollable rise in pressure can result, means must be provided in the design, installation, and operation of the valve to ensure that the pressure in the valve does not exceed that allowed by this part for the attained temperature. (For example, if a flexible wedge gate valve with the stem installed horizontally is closed, liquid from testing, cleaning, or condensation can be trapped in the bonnet section of the closed valve.) Any resulting penetration of the pressure wall of the valve must meet the requirements of this part and those for threaded and welded auxiliary connections in ASME B16.34 (incorporated by reference; see 46 CFR 56.01-2).

[CGD 77-140, 54 FR 40604, Oct. 2, 1989; 55 FR 39968, Oct. 1, 1990; USCG-2003-16630, 73 FR 65176, Oct. 31, 2008]

§ 56.20-5 Marking (modifies 107.2).

Each valve shall bear the manufacturer's name or trademark and reference symbol to indicate the service conditions for which the manufacturer guarantees the valve. The marking shall be in accordance with MSS SP-25 (incorporated by reference; see 46 CFR 56.01-2).

[USCG-2003-16630, 73 FR 65176, Oct. 31, 2008]

§ 56.20-7 Ends.

(a) Valves may be used with flanged, threaded, butt welding, socket welding or other ends in accordance with applicable standards as specified in subpart 56.60.

§ 56.20-9 Valve construction.

(a) Each valve must close with a right-hand (clockwise) motion of the handwheel or operating lever as seen by one facing the end of the valve stem. Each gate, globe, and angle valve must generally be of the rising-stem type, preferably with the stem threads external to the valve body. Where operating conditions will not permit such installations, the use of a nonrising-stem valve will be acceptable. Each nonrising-stem valve, lever-operated valve, or other valve where, because of design, the position of the disc or closure mechanism is not obvious must be fitted with an indicator to show whether the valve is opened or closed, except as provided for in § 56.50-1(g)(2)(iii) of this part. No such indicator is required for any valve located in a tank or similar inaccessible space when indicators are available at accessible sites. The operating levers of each quarter-turn (rotary) valve must be parallel to the fluid flow when open and perpendicular to the fluid flow when closed.

(b) Valves of Class I piping systems (for restrictions in other classes refer to sections on low temperature service), having diameters exceeding 2 inches must have bolted, pressure seal, or breech lock bonnets and flanged or welding ends, except that socket type welding ends shall not be used where prohibited by § 56.30-5(c) of this part, § 56.30-10(b)(4) of this part for the same pressure class, or elsewhere in this part. For diameters not exceeding 2 inches, screwed union bonnet or bolted bonnet, or bonnetless valves of a type which will positively prevent the stem from screwing out of the body may be employed. Outside screw and yoke design must be used for valves 3 inches and larger for pressures above 600 pounds per square inch gage. Cast iron valves with screwed-in or screwed-over bonnets are prohibited. Union bonnet type cast iron valves must have the bonnet ring made of steel, bronze, or malleable iron.

(c) Valves must be designed for the maximum pressure to which they may be subjected, but in no case shall the design pressure be less than 50 pounds per square inch gage. The use of wafer type resilient seated valves is not permitted for shell connections unless they are so arranged that the piping immediately inboard of the valve can be removed without affecting the watertight integrity of the shell connection. Refer also to §56.20–15(b)(2)(iii) of this part. Large fabricated ballast manifold connecting lines exceeding 8 inches nominal pipe size must be designed for a pressure of not less than 25 pounds per square inch gage.

(d) Disks or disk faces, seats, stems and other wearing parts of valves shall be made of material possessing corrosion and heat-resisting qualities suitable for the service conditions to which they may be subjected.

(e) Plug cocks shall be constructed with satisfactory and positive means of preventing the plug from becoming loosened or removed from the body when the plug is operated. Cocks having plug locking arrangements depending on cotter pins are prohibited.

(f) Cocks shall be marked in a straight line with the body to indicate whether they are open or closed.

(g) Materials forming a portion of the pressure barrier shall comply with the applicable provisions of this part.

[CGFR 68–82, 33 FR 18843, Dec. 18, 1968, as amended by CGD 77–140, 54 FR 40604, Oct. 2, 1989; CGD 95–012, 60 FR 48050, Sept. 18, 1995; USCG–2004–18884, 69 FR 58346, Sept. 30, 2004; USCG–2003–16630, 73 FR 65176, Oct. 31, 2008]

§56.20–15 Valves employing resilient material.

(a) A valve in which the closure is accomplished by resilient nonmetallic material instead of a metal to metal seat shall comply with the design, material, construction and testing for valves specified in this part.

(b) Valves employing resilient material shall be divided into three categories, Positive shutoff, Category A, and Category B, and shall be tested and used as follows:

(1) *Positive shutoff valves.* The closed valve must pass less than 10 ml/hr (0.34 fluid oz/hr) of liquid or less than 3 l/hr (0.11 cubic ft/hr) of gas per inch nominal pipe size through the line after removal of all resilient material and testing at full rated pressure. Packing material must be fire resistant. Piping subject to internal head pressure from a tank containing oil must be fitted with positive shutoff valves located at the tank in accordance with §56.50–60(d). Otherwise positive shutoff valves may be used in any location in lieu of a required Category A or Category B valve.

(2) *Category A valves.* The closed valve must pass less than the greater of 5 percent of its fully open flow rate or 15 percent divided by the square root of the nominal pipe size (NPS) of its fully open flow rate through the line after complete removal of all resilient seating material and testing at full rated pressure; as represented by the formula: (15% / SQRT × (NPS)) (Fully open flow rate). Category A valves may be used in any location except where positive shutoff valves are required by §56.50–60(d). Category A valves are required in the following locations:

(i) Valves at vital piping system manifolds;

(ii) Isolation valves in cross-connects between two piping systems, at least one of which is a vital system, where failure of the valve in a fire would prevent the vital system(s) from functioning as designed.

(iii) Valves providing closure for any opening in the shell of the vessel.

(3) *Category B valves.* The closed valve will not provide effective closure of the line or will permit appreciable leakage from the valve after the resilient material is damaged or destroyed. Category B valves are not required to be tested and may be used in any location except where a Category A or positive shutoff valve is required.

(c) If a valve designer elects to use either a calculation or actual fire testing instead of material removal and pressure testing, the calculation must employ ISA–S75.02 (incorporated by reference; see 46 CFR 56.01–2) to determine the flow coefficient (C_v), or the fire testing must be conducted in accordance with API 607 (incorporated by reference; see 46 CFR 56.01–2).

[CGD 95–028, 62 FR 51200, Sept. 30, 1997, as amended by USCG–2003–16630, 73 FR 65176, Oct. 31, 2008]

§56.20–20 Valve bypasses.

(a) Sizes of bypasses shall be in accordance with MSS SP–45 (incorporated by reference; see 46 CFR 56.01–2).

§ 56.25-5

(b) Pipe for bypasses should be at least Schedule 80 seamless, and of a material of the same nominal chemical composition and physical properties as that used for the main line. Lesser thickness may be approved depending on the installation and service conditions.

(c) Bypasses may be integral or attached.

[CGFR 68-82, 33 FR 18843, Dec. 18, 1968, as amended by USCG-2003-16630, 73 FR 65176, Oct. 31, 2008]

Subpart 56.25—Pipe Flanges, Blanks, Flange Facings, Gaskets, and Bolting

§ 56.25-5 Flanges.

Each flange must conform to the design requirements of either the applicable standards of table 56.60-1(b) of this part, or of those of appendix 2 of section VIII of the ASME Boiler and Pressure Vessel Code (incorporated by reference; see 46 CFR 56.01-2). Plate flanges must meet the requirements of § 56.30-10(b)(5) of this part and the material requirements of § 56.60-1(a) of this part. Flanges may be integral or may be attached to pipe by threading, welding, brazing, or other means within the applicable standards specified in table 56.60-1(b) of this part and the requirements of this subpart. For flange facing gasket combinations other than those specified above, calculations must be submitted indicating that the gaskets will not result in a higher bolt loading or flange moment than for the acceptable configurations.

[CGD 77-140, 54 FR 40605, Oct. 2, 1989, as amended by USCG-2002-13058, 67 FR 61278, Sept. 30, 2002; USCG-2003-16630, 73 FR 65176, Oct. 31, 2008]

§ 56.25-7 Blanks.

Each blank must conform to the design requirements of 104.5.3 of ASME B31.1 (incorporated by reference; see 46 CFR 56.01-2).

[USCG-2003-16630, 73 FR 65176, Oct. 31, 2008]

§ 56.25-10 Flange facings.

(a) Flange facings shall be in accordance with the applicable standards listed in table 56.60-1(b) and MSS SP-6 (incorporated by reference; see 46 CFR 56.01-2).

(b) When bolting class 150 standard steel flanges to flat face cast iron flanges, the steel flange must be furnished with a flat face, and bolting must be in accordance with § 56.25-20 of this part. Class 300 raised face steel flanges may be bolted to class 250 raised face cast iron flanges with bolting in accordance with § 56.25-20(b) of this part.

[CGFR 68-82, 33 FR 18843, Dec. 18, 1968, as amended by CGD 77-140, 54 FR 40605, Oct. 2, 1989; USCG-2003-16630, 73 FR 65176, Oct. 31, 2008]

§ 56.25-15 Gaskets (modifies 108.4).

(a) Gaskets shall be made of materials which are not injuriously affected by the fluid or by temperature.

(b) Each gasket must conform to the design requirements of the applicable standards of table 56.60-1(b) of this part.

(c) Only metallic and suitable asbestos-free nonmetallic gaskets may be used on flat or raised face flanges if the expected normal operating pressure exceeds 720 pounds per square inch or the operating temperature exceeds 750 °F.

(d) The use of metal and nonmetallic gaskets is not limited as to pressure provided the gasket materials are suitable for the maximum fluid temperatures.

[CGFR 68-82, 33 FR 18843, Dec. 18, 1968, as amended by CGD 86-035, 54 FR 36316, Sept. 1, 1989; USCG-2003-16630, 73 FR 65176, Oct. 31, 2008]

§ 56.25-20 Bolting.

(a) *General.* (1) Bolts, studs, nuts, and washers must comply with applicable standards and specifications listed in 46 CFR 56.60-1. Unless otherwise specified, bolting must be in accordance with ASME B16.5 (incorporated by reference; see 46 CFR 56.01-2).

(2) Bolts and studs must extend completely through the nuts.

(3) See § 58.30-15(c) of this chapter for exceptions on bolting used in fluid power and control systems.

(b) Carbon steel bolts or bolt studs may be used if expected normal operating pressure does not exceed 300 pounds per square inch gauge and the expected normal operating temperature does not exceed 400 °F. Carbon steel bolts must have heavy hexagon heads in accordance with ASME B18.2.1 (incorporated by reference, see 46 CFR 56.01–2) and must have heavy semi-finished hexagonal nuts in accordance with ASME/ANSI B18.2.2 (incorporated by reference, see 46 CFR 56.01–2), unless the bolts are tightly fitted to the holes and flange stress calculations taking the bolt bending stresses into account are submitted. When class 250 cast iron flanges are used or when class 125 cast iron flanges are used with ring gaskets, the bolting material must be carbon steel conforming to ASTM A 307 (incorporated by reference, see 46 CFR 56.01–2), Grade B.

(c) Alloy steel stud bolts must be threaded full length or, if desired, may have reduced shanks of a diameter not less than that at the root of the threads. They must have heavy semi-finished hexagonal nuts in accordance with ANSI B18.2.2.

(d) All alloy bolts or studs and accompanying nuts are to be threaded in accordance with ANSI/ASME B1.1 (incorporated by reference; see 46 CFR 56.01–2), Class 2A external threads, and Class 2B internal threads (8-thread series 8UN for one inch and larger).

(e) (*Reproduces 108.5.1*) Washers, when used under nuts, shall be of forged or rolled material with steel washers being used under steel nuts and bronze washers under bronze nuts.

[CGFR 68–82, 33 FR 18843, Dec.18, 1968, as amended by CGD 77–140, 54 FR 40605, Oct. 2, 1989; USCG–2000–7790, 65 FR 58460, Sept. 29, 2000; USCG–2003–16630, 73 FR 65176, Oct. 31, 2008]

Subpart 56.30—Selection and Limitations of Piping Joints

§ 56.30–1 Scope (replaces 110 through 118).

The selection and limitation of piping joints must be as required by this subpart rather than as required by 110 through 118 of ASME B31.1 (incorporated by reference; see 46 CFR 56.01–2); however, certain requirements are marked "reproduced" in this subpart.

[USCG–2003–16630, 73 FR 65177, Oct. 31, 2008]

§ 56.30–3 Piping joints (reproduces 110).

The type of piping joint used shall be suitable for the design conditions and shall be selected with consideration of joint tightness, mechanical strength and the nature of the fluid handled.

§ 56.30–5 Welded joints.

(a) *General.* Welded joints may be used for materials for which welding procedures, welders, and welding machine operators have been qualified in accordance with part 57 of this subchapter.

(b) *Butt welds—general.* Butt welds may be made with or without backing or insert rings within the limitations established in § 56.70–15. When the use of backing rings will result in undesirable conditions such as severe stress concentrations, corrosion or erosion, then:

(1) The backing rings shall be removed and the inside of the joint ground smooth, or

(2) The joint shall be welded without backing rings, or

(3) Consumable insert rings must be used. Commonly used types of butt welding end preparations are shown in ASME B16.25 (incorporated by reference; see 46 CFR 56.01–2).

(4) Restrictions as to the use of backing rings appear for the low temperature piping systems and should be checked when designing for these systems.

(c) *Socket welds (Modifies 127.3.3A.).*

(1) Each socket weld must conform to ASME B16.11 (incorporated by reference; see 46 CFR 56.01–2), to applicable standards listed in 46 CFR 56.60–1, table 56.60–1(b), and to Figure 127.4.4C in ASME B31.1 (incorporated by reference; see 46 CFR 56.01–2) as modified by § 56.30–10(b)(4) of this part. A gap of approximately one-sixteenth inch between the end of the pipe and the bottom of the socket must be provided before welding. This may best be provided by bottoming the pipe and backing off slightly before tacking.

(2) Socket welds must not be used where severe erosion or crevice corrosion is expected to occur. Restrictions on the use of socket welds appear in § 56.70–15(d)(3) of this part for Class I service and in § 56.50–105 of this part for

§ 56.30–10

low temperature service. These sections should be checked when designing for these systems. See § 56.70–15(d)(4) of this part for Class II service.

(3) (*Reproduces 111.3.4.*) Drains and bypasses may be attached to a fitting or valve by socket welding provided the socket depth, bore diameter and shoulder thickness conform to ASME B16.11.

(d) *Fillet welds.* A fillet weld may vary from convex to concave. The size of a fillet weld is determined as shown in Figure 127.4.4A of ASME B31.1. Fillet-weld details for socket-welding components must meet § 56.30–5(c). Fillet-weld details for flanges must meet § 56.30–10 of this part (see also § 56.70–15(d)(3) and (4) of this part for applications of fillet welds).

(e) *Seal welds.* Seal welds may be used but shall not be considered as contributing any strength to the joint.

[CGFR 68–82, 33 FR 18843, Dec. 18, 1968, as amended by CGFR 69–127, 35 FR 9978, June 17, 1970; CGD 77–140, 54 FR 40605, Oct. 2, 1989; CGD 95–012, 60 FR 48050, Sept. 18, 1995; USCG–2003–16630, 73 FR 65177, Oct. 31, 2008]

§ 56.30–10 Flanged joints (modifies 104.5.1(a)).

(a) Flanged or butt-welded joints are required for Classes I and I-L piping for nominal diameters exceeding 2 inches, except as otherwise specified in this subchapter.

(b) Flanges may be attached by any method shown in Figure 56.30–10(b) or by any additional means that may be approved by the Marine Safety Center. Pressure temperature ratings of the appropriate ANSI/ASME standard must not be exceeded.

(1) *Figure 56.30–10(b), Method 1.* Flanges with screw threads may be used in accordance with 46 CFR 56.30–20, table 56.30–20(c).

(2) *Figure 56.30–10(b), Method 2.* ASME B16.5 (incorporated by reference; see 46 CFR 56.01–2) Class 150 and Class 300 low-hubbed flanges with screw threads, plus the addition of a strength fillet weld of the size as shown, may be used in Class I systems not exceeding 750 °F or 4 NPS, in Class II systems without diameter limitations, and in Class II–L systems not exceeding 1 NPS. If 100 percent radiography is required by 46 CFR 56.95–10 for the class, diameter, wall thickness, and material of pipe being joined, the use of the threaded flanges is not permitted and buttwelding flanges must be provided. For Class II piping systems, the size of the strength fillet may be limited to a maximum of 0.525 inch instead of 1.4T.

(3) *Figure 56.30–10(b), Method 3.* Slip-on flanges meeting ASME B16.5 may be used in piping systems of Class I, Class II, or Class II–L not to exceed the service pressure-temperature ratings for flanges of class 300 and lower, within the temperature limitations of the material selected for use, and not to exceed 4-inch Nominal Pipe Size (NPS) in systems of Class I and Class II–L. If 100 percent radiography is required by 46 CFR 56.95–10 for the class, diameter, wall thickness, and material of the pipe being joined, then slip-on flanges are not permitted and butt-welding flanges are required. The configuration in Figure 127.4.4B(b) of ASME B31.1 (incorporated by reference; see 46 CFR 56.01–2), using a face and backweld, may be preferable where eliminating void spaces is desirable. For systems of Class II, the size of the strength fillet may be limited to a maximum of 0.525 inch instead of 1.4T, and the distance from the face of the flange to the end of the pipe may be a maximum of three-eighths of an inch. Restrictions on the use of slip-on flanges appear in 46 CFR 56.50–105 for low-temperature piping systems.

(4) *Figure 56.30–10(b), Method 4.* ASME B16.5 socket welding flanges may be used in Class I or II–L systems not exceeding 3 NPS for class 600 and lower class flanges and 2 1/2 NPS for class 900 and class 1500 flanges within the service pressure-temperature ratings of the standard. Whenever full radiography is required by 46 CFR 56.95–10 for the class, diameter, and wall thickness of the pipe being joined, the use of socket welding flanges is not permitted and a butt weld type connection must be provided. For Class II piping, socket welding flanges may be used without diameter limitation, and the size of the fillet weld may be limited to a maximum of 0.525 inch instead of 1.4T. Restrictions on the use of socket welds appear in 46 CFR 56.50–105 for low temperature piping systems.

(5) *Figure 56.30–10(b), Method 5.* Flanges fabricated from steel plate

Coast Guard, Dept. of Homeland Security §56.30-10

meeting the requirements of part 54 of this chapter may be used for Class II piping for pressures not exceeding 150 pounds per square inch and temperatures not exceeding 450 °F. Plate material listed in UCS-6(b) of section VIII of the ASME Boiler and Pressure Vessel Code (incorporated by reference; see 46 CFR 56.01-2) may not be used in this application, except that material meeting ASTM A 36 (incorporated by reference, see 46 CFR 56.01-2) may be used. The fabricated flanges must conform at least to the ASME B16.5 class 150 flange dimensions. The size of the strength fillet weld may be limited to a maximum of 0.525 inches instead of 1.4T and the distance from the face of the flange to the end of the pipe may be a maximum of three-eighths inch.

(6) *Figure 56.30-10 (b), Method 6.* Steel plate flanges meeting the material and construction requirements listed in paragraph (b)(5) of this section may be used for Class II piping for pressures not exceeding 150 pounds per square inch or temperatures not exceeding 650 °F. The flange shall be attached to the pipe as shown by Figure 56.30-10(b). Method 6. The pressure shall not exceed the American National Standard Service pressure temperature rating. The size of the strength fillet weld may be limited to a maximum of 0.525 inch instead of 1.4T and the distance from the face of the flange to the end of the pipe may be a maximum of three-eighths inch.

(7) *Figure 56.30-10 (b), Method 7.* Lap joint flanges (Van Stone) may be used for Class I and Class II piping. The Van Stone equipment must be operated by competent personnel. The ends of the pipe must be heated from 1,650° to 1,900 °F. dependent on the size of the pipe prior to the flanging operation. The foregoing temperatures must be carefully adhered to in order to prevent excess scaling of the pipe. The extra thickness of metal built up in the end of the pipe during the forming operation must be machined to restore the pipe to its original diameter. The machined surface must be free from surface defects and the back of the Van Stone lap must be machined to a fine tool finish to furnish a line contact with the mating surface on the flange for the full circumference as close as possible to the fillet of the flange. The number of heats to be used in forming a flange must be determined by the size of the pipe and not more than two pushups per heat are permitted. The width of the lap flange must be at least three times the thickness of the pipe wall and the end of the pipe must be properly stress relieved after the flanging operation is completed. Manufacturers desiring to produce this type of joint must demonstrate to a marine inspector that they have the proper equipment and personnel to produce an acceptable joint.

(8) *Figure 56.30-10 (b), Method 8.* Welding neck flanges may be used on any piping provided the flanges are butt-welded to the pipe. The joint must be welded as indicated by Figure 56.30-10(b), Method 8, and a backing ring employed which will permit complete penetration of the weld metal. If a backing ring is not used, refer to 46 CFR 56.30-5(b) for requirements.

(9) *Figure 56.30-10 (b), Method 9.* Welding neck flanges may also be attached to pipe by a double-welded butt joint as shown by Figure 56.30-10(b), Method 9.

(10) *Figure 56.30-10 (b), Method 10.* Flanges may be attached by shrinking the flange on to the end of the pipe and flaring the end of the pipe to an angle of not less than 20° A fillet weld of the size shown by Figure 56.30-10(b), Method 10, must be used to attach the hub to the pipe. This type of flange is limited to a maximum pressure of 300 pounds per square inch at temperatures not exceeding 500 °F.

(11) *Figure 56.30-10(b), Method 11.* The flange of the type described and illustrated by Figure 56.30-10(b), Method 10, except with the fillet weld omitted, may be used for Class II piping for pressures not exceeding 150 pounds per square inch and temperatures not exceeding 450 °F.

(12) *Figure 56.30-10(b), Method 12.* High-hub bronze flanges may be used for temperatures not exceeding 425 °F. The hub of the flange must be bored to a depth not less than that required for a threaded connection of the same diameter leaving a shoulder for the pipe to butt against. A preinserted ring of silver brazing alloy having a melting

point not less than 1,000 °F and of sufficient quantity to fill the annular clearance between the flange and the pipe must be inserted in the groove. The pipe must then be inserted in the flange and sufficient heat applied externally to melt the brazing alloy until it completely fills the clearance between the hub and the flange of the pipe. A suitable flux must be applied to the surfaces to be joined to produce a satisfactory joint.

(13) *Figure 56.30–10(b), Method 13.* The type of flange as described for Figure 56.30–10(b), Method 12, may be employed and in lieu of an annular groove being machined in the hub of the flange for the preinserted ring of silver brazing alloy, a bevel may be machined on the end of the hub and the silver brazing alloy introduced from the end of the hub to attach the pipe to the flange.

(14) *Figure 56.30–10(b), Method 14.* Flanges may be attached to nonferrous pipe by inserting the pipe in the flange and flanging the end of the pipe into the recess machined in the face of the flange to receive it. The width of the flange must be not less than three times the pipe wall thickness. In addition, the pipe must be securely brazed to the wall of the flange.

(15) *Figure 56.30–10(b), Method 15.* The flange of the type described and illustrated by Figure 56.30–10(b), Method 14, except with the brazing omitted, may be used for Class II piping and where the temperature does not exceed 250 °F.

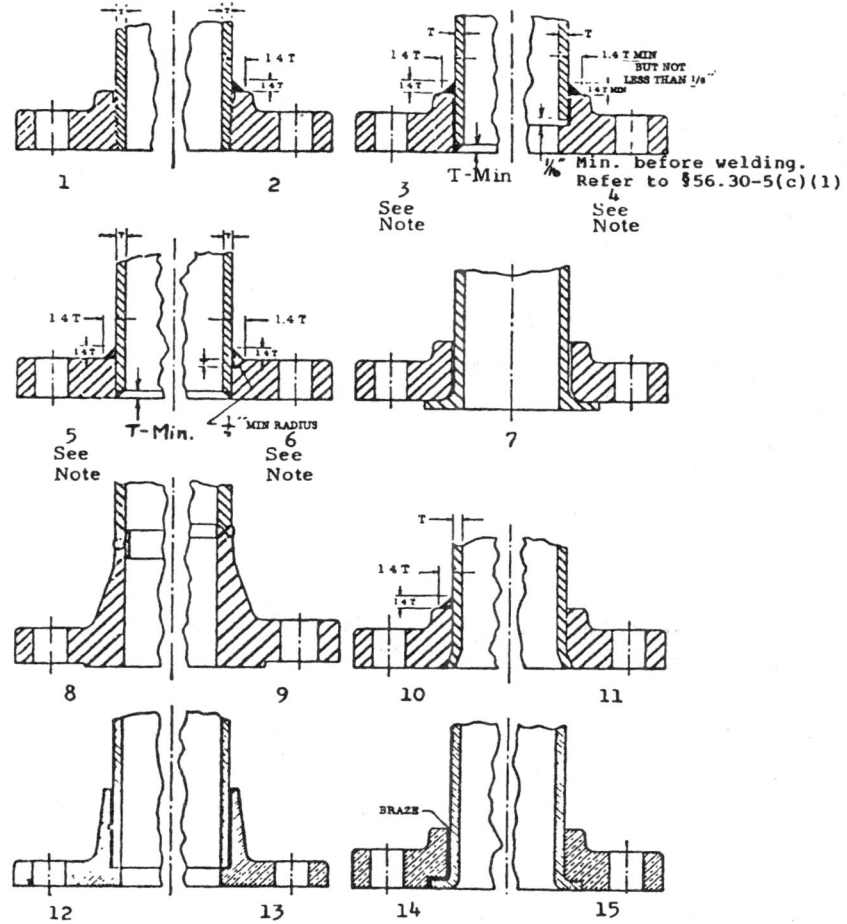

Figure 56.30–10(b)—Methods of Attachment

NOTE TO FIG. 56.30–10(b): "T" is the nominal pipe wall thickness used. Consult the text of paragraph (b) for modifications on Class II piping systems. Fillet weld leg size need not exceed the thickness of the applicable ASME hub.

[CGFR 68–82, 33 FR 18843, Dec. 18, 1968, as amended by CGFR 69–127, 35 FR 9978, June 17, 1970; CGD 77–140, 54 FR 40605, Oct. 2, 1989; USCG–2000–7790, 65 FR 58460, Sept. 29, 2000; USCG–2003–16630, 73 FR 65177, Oct. 31, 2008; 73 FR 76247, Dec. 16, 2008]

§ 56.30–15 Expanded or rolled joints.

(a) Expanded or rolled joints may be used where experience or test has demonstrated that the joint is suitable for the design conditions and where adequate provisions are made to prevent separation of the joint. Specific application for use must be made to the Commandant.

(b) [Reserved]

§ 56.30–20 Threaded joints.

(a) Threaded joints may be used within the limitations specified in subpart 56.15 of this chapter and within other limitations specified in this section.

(b) (*Reproduces 114.1.*) All threads on piping components must be taper pipe threads in accordance with the applicable standard listed in 46 CFR 56.60–1, table 56.60–1(b). Threads other than taper pipe threads may be used for piping components where tightness of the joint depends on a seal weld or a seating surface other than the threads, and where experience or test has demonstrated that such threads are suitable.

(c) Threaded joints may not be used where severe erosion, crevice corrosion, shock, or vibration is expected to occur; or at temperatures over 925 °F. Size limitations are given in table 56.30–20(c) of this section.

TABLE 56.30–20(c)—THREADED JOINTS [1] [2]

Maximum nominal size, inches	Maximum pressure, p.s.i.g.
Above 2″	(Not permitted in Class I piping service.)
Above 1″ up to 2″	600.
Above ¾″ up to 1″	1,200.
¾″ and below	1,500.

[1] Further restrictions on the use of threaded joints appear in the low temperature piping section.

[2] Threaded joints in hydraulic systems are permitted above the pressures indicated for the nominal sizes shown when commercially available components such as pumps, valves and strainers may only be obtained with threaded connections.

(d) No pipe with a wall thickness less than that of standard weight of ASME B36.10M (incorporated by reference; see 46 CFR 56.01–2) steel pipe may be threaded regardless of service. For restrictions on the use of pipe in steam service more than 250 pounds per square inch or water service over 100 pounds per square inch and 200 °F (938C), see part 104.1.2(c)(1) of ASME B31.1 (incorporated by reference; see 46 CFR 56.01–2). Restrictions on the use of threaded joints apply for low-temperature piping and must be checked when designing for these systems.

[CGFR 68–82, 33 FR 18843, Dec. 18, 1968, as amended by CGFR 69–127, 35 FR 9978, June 17, 1970; CGD 73–254, 40 FR 40164, Sept. 2, 1975; CGD 77–140, 54 FR 40606, Oct. 2, 1989; USCG–2003–16630, 73 FR 65178, Oct. 31, 2008]

§ 56.30–25 Flared, flareless, and compression fittings.

(a) This section applies to pipe fittings that are mechanically connected to pipe by such means as ferrules, flared ends, swaging, elastic strain preload, crimping, bite-type devices, and shape memory alloys. Fittings to which this section applies must be designed, constructed, tested, and marked in accordance with ASTM F 1387 (incorporated by reference, see § 56.01–2). Previously approved fittings may be retained as long as they are maintained in good condition to the satisfaction of the Officer in Charge, Marine Inspection.

(b) Flared, flareless and compression fittings may be used within the service limitations of size, pressure, temperature, and vibration recommended by the manufacturer and as specified in this section.

(c) Flared, flareless, and compression type tubing fittings may be used for tube sizes not exceeding 50 millimeters (2 inches) outside diameter within the limitations of applicable standards and specifications listed in this section and § 56.60–1 of this part.

(d) Flareless fittings must be of a design in which the gripping member or sleeve must grip or bite into the outer surface of the tube with sufficient strength to hold the tube against pressure, but without appreciably distorting the inside tube diameter or reducing the wall thickness. The gripping member must also form a pressure seal against the fitting body.

(e) For fluid services, other than hydraulic systems, using a combustible fluid as defined in § 30.10–15 of this chapter and for fluid services using a flammable fluid as defined in § 30.10–22 of this chapter, flared fittings must be used; except that flareless fittings of the nonbite type may be used when the tubing system is of steel, nickel copper or copper nickel alloy. When using copper or copper zinc alloy, flared fittings are required. (See also § 56.50–70 for gasoline fuel systems, § 56.50–75 for diesel fuel systems, and § 58.25–20 for hydraulic systems for steering gear.)

[CGD 95–027, 61 FR 26000, May 23, 1996; 61 FR 35138, July 5, 1996, as amended by USCG–1999–5151, 64 FR 67180, Dec. 1, 1999; USCG–2000–7790, 65 FR 58460, Sept. 29, 2000]

§ 56.30-27 Caulked joints.

Caulked joints may not be used in marine installations.

[CGD 77-140, 54 FR 40606, Oct. 2, 1989]

§ 56.30-30 Brazed joints.

(a) *General (refer also to subpart 56.75)*. Brazed socket-type joints shall be made with suitable brazing alloys. The minimum socket depth shall be sufficient for the intended service. Brazing alloy shall either be end-fed into the socket or shall be provided in the form of a preinserted ring in a groove in the socket. The brazing alloy shall be sufficient to fill completely the annular clearance between the socket and the pipe or tube.

(b) *Limitations*. (1) Brazed socket-type joints shall not be used on systems containing flammable or combustible fluids in areas where fire hazards are involved or where the service temperature exceeds 425 °F. When specifically approved by the Commandant, brazed construction may be used for service temperatures up to 525 °F. in boiler steam air heaters provided the requirements of UB-12 of section VIII ASME Boiler and Pressure Vessel Code (incorporated by reference; see 46 CFR 56.01-2) are satisfied at the highest temperature desired.

(2) Brazed joints depending solely upon a fillet, rather than primarily upon brazing material between the pipe and socket are not acceptable.

[CGFR 68-82, 33 FR 18843, Dec. 18, 1968, as amended by USCG-2003-16630, 73 FR 65178, Oct. 31, 2008]

§ 56.30-35 Gasketed mechanical couplings.

(a) This section applied to pipe fittings that form a seal by compressing a resilient gasket onto the pipe joint primarily by threaded fasteners and where joint creep is only restricted by such means as machined grooves, centering pins, or welded clips. Fittings to which this section applies must be designed, constructed, tested, and marked in accordance with ASTM F 1476 (incorporated by reference, see § 56.01-2) and ASTM F 1548 (incorporated by reference, see § 56.01-2). Previously approved fittings may be retained as long as they are maintained in good condition to the satisfaction of the Officer in Charge, Marine Inspection.

(b) Gasketed mechanical couplings may be used within the service limitations of pressure, temperature and vibration recommended by the manufacturer, except that gasketed mechanical couplings must not be used in—

(1) Any location where leakage, undetected flooding or impingement of liquid on vital equipment may disable the vessel; or

(2) In tanks where the liquid conveyed in the piping system is not chemically compatible with the liquid in the tank.

(c) Gasketed mechanical couplings must not be used as expansion joints. Positive restraints must be included, where necessary, to prevent the coupling from creeping on the pipe and uncovering the joint. Bite-type devices do not provide positive protection against creep and are generally not accepted for this purpose. Machined grooves, centering pins, and welded clips are considered positive means of protection against creep.

[CGD 95-027, 61 FR 26001, May 23, 1996, as amended by USCG-1999-5151, 64 FR 67180, Dec. 1, 1999]

§ 56.30-40 Flexible pipe couplings of the compression or slip-on type.

(a) Flexible pipe couplings of the compression or slip-on type must not be used as expansion joints. To ensure that the maximum axial displacement (approximately $3/8''$ maximum) of each coupling is not exceeded, positive restraints must be included in each installation.

(b) Positive means must also be provided to prevent the coupling from "creeping" on the pipe and uncovering the joint. Bite type devices do not provide positive protection against creeping and are not generally accepted for this purpose unless other means are also incorporated. Machined grooves or centering pins are considered positive means, and other positive means will be considered.

(c) Couplings which employ a solid sleeve with welded attachments on both pipes will require the removal of one set of attachments before dismantling. Rewelding of the attachments may require gas freeing of the line.

§ 56.35-1

(d) The installation shall be such as to preclude appreciable difference in the vibration magnitudes of the pipes joined by the couplings. The couplings shall not be used as a vibration damper. The vibration magnitude and frequency should not exceed that recommended by the coupling manufacturer.

(e) Flexible couplings made in accordance with the applicable standards listed in table 56.60-1(b) of this part and of materials complying with subpart 56.60 of this part may be used within the material, size, pressure, and temperature limitations of those standards and within any further limitations specified in this subchapter. Flexible couplings fabricated by welding must also comply with part 57 of this chapter.

(f) Flexible couplings must not be used in cargo holds or in any other space where leakage, undetected flooding, or impingement of liquid on vital equipment may disable the ship, or in tanks where the liquid conveyed in the piping system is not compatible with the liquid in the tank. Where flexible couplings are not allowed by this subpart, joints may be threaded, flanged and bolted, or welded.

(g) Damaged or deteriorated gaskets shall not be reinstalled.

(h) Each coupling shall be tested in accordance with § 56.97-5.

[CGFR 68-82, 33 FR 18843, Dec. 18, 1968, as amended by CGD 77-140, 54 FR 40606, Oct. 2, 1989]

Subpart 56.35—Expansion, Flexibility and Supports

§ 56.35-1 Pipe stress calculations (replaces 119.7).

(a) A summary of the results of pipe stress calculations for the main and auxiliary steam piping where the design temperatures exceed 800 °F shall be submitted for approval. Calculations shall be made in accordance with one of the recognized methods of stress analysis acceptable to the Marine Safety Center to determine the magnitude and direction of the forces and movements at all terminal connections, anchor and junction points, as well as the resultant bending stress, longitudinal pressure stress, torsional stress, and combined expansion stress at all such points. The location of the maximum combined stress shall be indicated in each run of pipe between anchor points.

(b) The Marine Safety Center (MSC) will give special consideration to the use of the full tabulated value of "S" in computing S_h and S_c where all material used in the system is subjected to further nondestructive testing specified by the MSC, and where the calculations prescribed in 119.6.4 and 102.3.2 of ASME B31.1 (incorporated by reference; see 46 CFR 56.01-2) and 46 CFR 56.07-10 are performed. The procedures for nondestructive testing and the method of stress analysis must be approved by the MSC before the submission of computations and drawings for approval.

[CGD 77-140, 54 FR 40607, Oct. 2, 1989, as amended by USCG-2003-16630, 73 FR 65178, Oct. 31, 2008]

§ 56.35-10 Nonmetallic expansion joints (replaces 119.5.1).

(a) Nonmetallic expansion joints certified in accordance with subpart 50.25 of this subchapter are acceptable for use in piping systems.

(b) Nonmetallic expansion joints must conform to the standards listed in table 56.60-1(b) of this part. Nonmetallic expansion joints may be used within their specified pressure and temperature rating in vital and nonvital machinery sea connections inboard of the skin valve. These joints must not be used to correct for improper piping workmanship or misalignment. Joint movements must not exceed the limits set by the joint manufacturer.

[CGD 77-140, 54 FR 40607, Oct. 2, 1989]

§ 56.35-15 Metallic expansion joints (replaces 119.5.1).

(a) Metallic expansion joints certified in accordance with subpart 50.25 of this subchapter are acceptable for use in piping systems.

(b) Metallic expansion joints must conform to the standards listed in table 56.60-1(b) of this part and may be used within their specified pressure and temperature rating.

[CGD 77-140, 54 FR 40607, Oct. 2, 1989]

Subpart 56.50—Design Requirements Pertaining to Specific Systems

§ 56.50-1 General (replaces 122).

The requirements in this subpart for piping systems apply instead of those in section 122 of ASME B31.1 (incorporated by reference; see 46 CFR 56.01-2). Installation requirements applicable to all systems:

(a) Where pipes and scuppers are carried through watertight or oiltight bulkheads, decks or tank tops, or are carried through fire control bulkheads and decks, the integrity of the structure shall be maintained. Lead or other heat sensitive materials shall not be used in piping systems which make such bulkhead or deck penetrations where the deterioration of such systems in the event of fire would impair the integrity of the bulkheads or decks. (For plastic pipe installations, see § 56.60–25(a).) Where plate insert pads are used, bolted connections shall have threads tapped into the plate to a depth of not less than the diameter of the bolt. If welded, the pipe or flange shall be welded to both sides of the plating. Openings in structure through which pipes pass shall be reinforced where necessary. Flanges shall not be bolted to bulkheads so that the plate forms a part of the joint. Metallic materials having a melting point of 1,700 °F. or less are considered heat sensitive and if used must be suitably insulated.

(b)(1) Pipes piercing the collision bulkhead shall be fitted with screwdown valves operable from above the bulkhead deck and the valve shall be fitted inside the forepeak tank adjacent to the collision bulkhead. The pipe penetrating the collision bulkhead shall be welded to the bulkhead on both sides. On new installations or replacement in vessels of 150 gross tons and over, the valve body shall be of steel or ductile cast iron.

(2) Passenger vessels shall not have the collision bulkhead pierced below the margin line by more than one pipe conveying liquids in the forepeak tank except that if the forepeak tank is divided to hold two different kinds of liquids, the collision bulkhead may be pierced below the margin line by two pipes, provided there is no practical alternative to the fitting of the second pipe and further provided the safety of the vessel is maintained.

(c) Valves and cocks not forming part of a piping system are not permitted in watertight subdivision bulkheads, however, sluice valves or gates in oiltight bulkheads of tankships may be used if approved by the Marine Safety Center.

(d) Piping shall not be run over or in the vicinity of switchboards or other electrical equipment if avoidable. When such leads are necessary, welded joints only shall be used and provision shall be made to prevent leakage from damaging the equipment.

(e) Stuffing boxes shall not be used on deep tank bulkheads, double bottoms or in any position where they cannot be easily examined. This requirement does not apply to ore carriers operating on the Great Lakes or cargo lines of oil tankers.

(f) Piping systems shall be installed so that under no condition will the operation of safety or relief valves be impaired.

(g)(1) Power actuated valves in systems other than as specified in § 56.50-60 of this part may be used if approved for the system by the Marine Safety Center. All power actuated valves required in an emergency to operate the vessel's machinery, to maintain its stability, and to operate the bilge and firemain systems must have a manual means of operation.

(2)(i) Remote valve controls that are not readily identifiable as to service must be fitted with nameplates.

(ii) Remote valve controls must be accessible under service conditions.

(iii) Remote valve controls, except reach rods, must be fitted with indicators that show whether the valves they control are open or closed. Valve position indicating systems must be independent of valve control systems.

(iv) Valve reach rods must be adequately protected.

(v) Solid reach rods must be used in tanks containing liquids, except that tank barges having plug cocks inside cargo tanks may have reach rods of extra-heavy pipe with the annular space between the lubricant tube and the pipe wall sealed with a nonsoluble to prevent penetration of the cargo.

(3) Air operated remote control valves must be provided with self-indicating lines at the control boards which indicate the desired valve positions, i.e., open or closed.

(h) Suitable drains shall be provided at low points of piping systems.

(i) Valves and cocks shall be located so as to be easily accessible and valves or cocks attached to the shell of the vessel or to sea chests located below the floorplating shall be operable from above the floorplates.

(j) When welded fabrication is employed, a sufficient number of detachable joints shall be provided to facilitate overhauling and maintenance of machinery and appurtenances. The joints shall be located so that adequate space is provided for welding, and the location of the welds shall be indicated on the plans.

(k) Piping, including valves, pipe fittings and flanges, conveying vapors, gases or liquids whose temperature exceeds 150 °F., shall be suitably insulated where necessary to preclude injury to personnel.

(l) Where pipes are run through dry cargo spaces they must be protected from mechanical injury by a suitable enclosure or other means.

[CGFR 68–82, 33 FR 18843, Dec. 18, 1968, as amended by CGFR 69–127, 35 FR 9978, June 17, 1970; CGD 77–140, 54 FR 40607, Oct. 2, 1989; USCG–2003–16630, 73 FR 65178, Oct. 31, 2008]

§ 56.50–10 Special gauge requirements.

(a) Where pressure-reducing valves are employed, a pressure gauge must be provided on the low-pressure side of the reducing station.

(b) Fuel oil service, fire, cargo and fuel oil transfer and boiler feed pumps must be provided with a pressure gage on the discharge side of the pump. Additional information pertaining to fire pumps is in § 34.10–5 of subchapter D (Tank Vessels), § 76.10–5 of subchapter H (Passenger Vessels), § 95.10–5 of subchapter I (Cargo and Miscellaneous Vessels), and § 108.417 of subchapter IA (Mobile Offshore Drilling Units) of this chapter.

[CGFR 68–82, 33 FR 18843, Dec. 18, 1968, as amended by CGFR 69–127, 35 FR 9978, June 17, 1970; CGD 73–251, 43 FR 56799, Dec. 4, 1978; USCG–2003–16630, 73 FR 65178, Oct. 31, 2008]

§ 56.50–15 Steam and exhaust piping.

(a) The design pressures of the steam piping connected to the boiler drum or to the superheater inlet header shall not be less than the lowest pressure setting of any drum safety valve. The value of allowable stress for the material shall not exceed that corresponding to the saturated steam temperature at drum pressure and shall be selected as described in § 56.07–10(e).

(b) Main superheater outlet piping systems, desuperheated piping systems, and other auxiliary superheater piping systems led directly from the boiler superheater shall be designed for a pressure not less than the pressure at which the superheater safety valve is set. In the case of a superheated safety valve which is drum pilot actuated, the design pressure of such piping systems shall not be less than the pressure setting of the actuator valve on the drum. Where it can be shown that the limitations set forth in 102.2.4 of ASME B31.1 (incorporated by reference; see 46 CFR 56.01–2) will not be exceeded, the design pressure of such piping systems may be reduced but shall not be less than the pressure setting of the actuator valve on the drum less the pressure drop through the superheater, including associated piping and a control desuperheater if fitted, at the normal rated operating condition. In both cases, the value of allowable stress shall be selected using a temperature not less than that of the steam at the superheater outlet at the normal rated operating conditions in accordance with § 56.07–10(e). Valves and fittings shall be selected for the above temperature and pressure from the accepted standards in 46 CFR 56.60–1, Table 56.60–1(b), using the pressure-temperature rating in the standard.

(c) Steam stop valves in sizes exceeding 6 inches shall be fitted with by-passes for heating the line and equalizing the pressure before the valve is opened.

(d) In multiple boiler installations each boiler's main, auxiliary and desuperheated steam lines shall be fitted with two valves, one a stop valve and one a stop check valve.

(e) Main and auxiliary steam stop valves must be readily accessible, operable by one person and arranged to seat against boiler pressure.

(f) The auxiliary steam piping of each vessel equipped with more than one boiler must be so arranged that steam for the whistle and other vital auxiliary systems, such as the electrical-generation plant, may be supplied from any power boiler.

(g) Steam and exhaust pipes shall not be led through coal bunkers or dry cargo spaces unless approved by the Commandant.

(h)(1) Steam piping, with the exception of the steam heating system, must not be led through passageways, accommodation spaces, or public spaces unless the arrangement is specifically approved by the Marine Safety Center.

(2) Steam pressure in steam heating systems must not exceed 150 pounds per square inch gage, except that steam pressure for accommodation and public space heating must not exceed 45 pounds per square inch gage.

(3) Steam lines and registers in non-accommodation and non-public spaces must be suitably located and/or shielded to minimize hazards to any personnel within the space. Where hazards in a space cannot be sufficiently minimized, the pressure in the steam line to that space must be reduced to a maximum of 45 pounds per square inch gage.

(4) High temperature hot water for heating systems may not exceed 375 °F.

(i) Where positive shutoff valves are fitted in the exhaust lines of machinery, and the exhaust side, including engine steam cylinders and chests, turbine casings, exhaust piping and shutoff valves, is not designed for the full inlet pressure, the exhaust side must be protected from over pressure by one of the following means:

(1) A full flow relief valve in the exhaust side so set and of sufficient capacity to prevent the exhaust side from being accidentally or otherwise subjected to a pressure in excess of its maximum allowable pressure.

(2) A sentinel relief valve or other warning device fitted on the exhaust side together with a back pressure trip device which will close the inlet valve prior to the exhaust side pressure exceeding the maximum allowable pressure. A device that will throttle the inlet valve, so that the exhaust side does not exceed the maximum allowable pressure, may be substituted for the back pressure trip.

(j) Shore steam connections shall be fitted with a relief valve set at a pressure not exceeding the design pressure of the piping.

(k) Means must be provided for draining every steam pipe in which dangerous water hammer might otherwise occur.

[CGFR 68–82, 33 FR 18843, Dec. 18, 1968, as amended by CGFR 69–127, 35 FR 9978, June 17, 1970; CGFR 72–59R, 37 FR 6189, Mar. 25, 1972; CGD 73–254, 40 FR 40165, Sept. 2, 1975; CGD 77–140, 54 FR 40607, Oct. 2, 1989; CGD 83–043, 60 FR 24772, May 10, 1995; USCG–2003–16630, 73 FR 65178, Oct. 31, 2008]

§ 56.50–20 Pressure relief piping.

(a) *General.* There must be no intervening stop valves between the vessel or piping system being protected and its protective device or devices, except as specifically provided for in other regulations or as specifically authorized by the Marine Safety Center.

(b) *Discharge lines (reproduces 122.6.2(d)).* Discharge lines from pressure-relieving safety devices shall be designed to facilitate drainage.

(c) *Stop valves.* Stop valves between the safety or relief valve and the point of discharge are not permitted, except as specifically provided for in other regulations or as specifically approved by the Marine Safety Center.

(d) *Reference.* See also § 56.07–10(a) and (b) for specific requirements.

[CGFR 68–82, 33 FR 18843, Dec. 18, 1968, as amended by CGFR 69–127, 35 FR 9979, June 17, 1970; CGD 77–140, 54 FR 40607, Oct. 2, 1989]

§ 56.50–25 Safety and relief valve escape piping.

(a) Escape piping from unfired steam generator, boiler, and superheater safety valves shall have an area of not less than that of the combined areas of the outlets of all valves discharging thereto and shall be led as near vertically as practicable to the atmosphere.

(b) Expansion joints or flexible pipe connections shall be fitted in escape piping. The piping shall be adequately supported and installed so that no

§ 56.50-30

stress is transmitted to the safety valve body.

(c) Safety or relief valve discharges, when permitted to terminate in the machinery space, shall be led below the floorplates or to a remote position to minimize the hazardous effect of the escaping steam.

(d) The effect of the escape piping on the operation of the relief device shall be considered. The back pressure in the escape piping from the main propulsion steam generator should not exceed 10 percent of the relief device setting unless a compensated relief device is used. Back pressure must be calculated with all relief valves which discharge to a common escape pipe relieving simultaneously at full capacity.

[CGFR 68–82, 33 FR 18843, Dec. 18, 1968, as amended by CGD 77–140, 54 FR 40608, Oct. 2, 1989; CGD 95–012, 60 FR 48050, Sept. 18, 1995]

§ 56.50-30 Boiler feed piping.

(a) *General requirements.* (1) Steam vessels, and motor vessels fitted with steam driven electrical generators shall have at least two separate means of supplying feed water for the boilers. All feed pumps shall be fitted with the necessary connections for this purpose. The arrangement of feed pumps shall be in accordance with paragraph (d) or (e) of this section.

(2) Feed pump supply to power boilers may utilize the group feed system or the unit feed system.

(3) Feed discharge piping from the pump up to, but not including the required stop and stop-check valves, shall be designed for either the feed pump relief valve setting or the shutoff head of the pump if a relief valve is not fitted. (Refer to § 56.07–10(b) for specific requirements.) Feed piping from the boiler, to and including the required stop and stop-check valves (see paragraph (b) of this section), shall have a design pressure which exceeds the maximum allowable working pressure of the boiler by either 25 percent or 225 pounds per square inch whichever is less. The value of allowable stress for design purposes shall be selected as described in § 56.07–10(e) at a temperature not below that for saturated steam at the maximum allowable working pressure of the boiler.

(4) Feed pumps for water tube boilers shall have fresh water connections only. Care shall be taken to prevent the accidental contamination of feed water from salt water or oil systems.

(b) *Feed valves.* (1) Stop and stop-check valves must be fitted in the main feed line and must be attached as closely as possible to drum inlets or to the economizer inlet on boilers fitted with integral economizers.

(2) Where the installation will not permit the feed stop valve to be attached directly to the drum inlet nozzle on boilers not fitted with economizers, a distance piece may be installed between the stop valve and the inlet nozzle.

(3) Feed stop or stop-check valves may be located near the operating platform on boilers fitted with economizers provided the piping between the valves and the economizer, exclusive of the feed valves and the economizer inlet nozzles, is installed with a minimum of intervening flanged connections.

(4) Auxiliary feed lines shall be fitted with stop valves and stop-check valves. Boilers not having auxiliary feed water nozzles, or where independent auxiliary feed lines are not installed, shall have the auxiliary feed line to the drum or economizer connected to the main feed line as close as possible to the main feed stop valves; and the valves in the auxiliary feed line shall be fitted as close as possible to the junction point.

(5) Boilers fitted with economizers shall have a check valve fitted in the economizer discharge and located as close as possible to the drum fed inlet nozzle. When economizer bypasses are fitted, a stop-check valve shall be installed in lieu of the aforementioned check valve.

(6) A sentinel valve is not required for vessels constructed after September 30, 1997, and for other vessels to which it has been shown to the satisfaction of the cognizant Officer in Charge, Marine Inspection or the Coast Guard Marine Safety Center, that a sentinel valve is not necessary for the safe operation of the particular boiler.

(c) *Feed water regulators, heaters, and grease extractors.* (1) Where feed water regulators, tubular feed water heaters, and grease extractors are installed, an alternate means of operation with

Coast Guard, Dept. of Homeland Security § 56.50-40

these devices bypassed shall be provided.

(2) Feed water regulators designed with a built-in bypass for emergency use need not be fitted with an external bypass when installed in a feed system provided with an auxiliary feed line. All feed water regulators installed in a unit feed system shall be fitted with an external bypass. Feed water regulators bypasses shall be so arranged that the regular feed valves are in operation while the bypass is in use.

(3) A feed water regulator may be interposed between the stop and stop-check valves in the feed lines.

(d) *Group feed system.* Group feed systems shall be provided with pumps and piping as follows:

(1) Oceangoing and Great Lakes steam vessels, having a feed pump attached to the main propelling unit, shall be provided with at least one independently driven feed pump. Each of these pumps shall be used exclusively for feed purposes and shall be capable of supplying the operating boilers at their normal capacity. In addition, a second independently driven pump, capable of supplying such boilers at 75 percent of their normal capacity, shall be provided for emergency use. This second pump may be used for other purposes.

(2) If two independently driven pumps are provided, each capable of supplying the boilers at their normal required operating capacity, and neither of which is used for other purposes, the third or emergency feed pump is not required. Where more than two independently driven feed pumps are provided, their aggregate capacity shall not be less than 200 percent of that demanded by the boilers at their required normal operating capacity.

(3) River or harbor steam vessels shall have at least two means for feeding the boilers; one of which shall be an independently driven pump, the other may be an attached pump, an additional independently driven pump, or an injector.

(e) *Unit feed system.* Unit feed systems shall be provided with pumps and piping as follows:

(1) The unit feed system may be used on vessels having two or more boilers. When the unit feed system is employed each boiler shall have its own independently driven main feed pump capable of supplying the boiler at its normal operating capacity. In addition these shall be an auxiliary independently driven feed pump of the same capacity which can be operated in place of and in conjunction with the main feed pump. In vessels with three or more boilers, not more than two boilers may be served by any one auxiliary pump. The auxiliary pump may be so interconnected that any pump can feed any boiler.

(2) In the unit feed system, a separate feed line shall be provided for each boiler from its pumps. A separate auxiliary feed line is not required. The discharge from each pump and the feed supply to each boiler shall be automatically controlled by the level of the water in that boiler. In addition to the automatic control, manual control shall be provided.

(f) *Feedwater.* The feedwater shall be introduced into a boiler as required by § 52.01–105(b) of this subchapter.

[CGFR 68–82, 33 FR 18843, Dec. 18, 1968, as amended by CGD 95–028, 62 FR 51201, Sept. 30, 1997; USCG–2002–13058, 67 FR 61278, Sept. 30, 2002; USCG–2003–16630, 73 FR 65178, Oct. 31, 2008]

§ 56.50-35 Condensate pumps.

Two means shall be provided for discharging the condensate from the main condenser, one of which shall be mechanically independent of the main propelling machinery. If one of the independent feed pumps is fitted with a direct suction from the condenser and a discharge to the feed tank, it may be accepted as an independent condensate pump. On vessels operating on lakes (including Great Lakes), bays, sounds, or rivers, where provision is made to operate noncondensing, only one condensate unit will be required.

§ 56.50-40 Blowoff piping (replaces 122.1.4).

(a)(1) The owner or operator of a vessel must follow the requirements for blowoff piping in this section instead of the requirements in 122.1.4 of ASME B31.1 (incorporated by reference; see 46 CFR 56.01–2).

(2) Where blowoff valves are connected to a common discharge from

two or more boilers, a nonreturn valve shall be provided in the line from each boiler to prevent accidental blowback in the event the boiler blowoff valve is left open.

(b) Blowoff piping external to the boiler shall be designed for not less than 125 percent of the maximum allowable working pressure of the boiler, or the maximum allowable working pressure of the boiler plus 225 pounds per square inch, whichever is less. When the required blowoff piping design pressure exceeds 100 pounds per square inch gage, the wall thickness of the piping shall not be less than Schedule 80. The value of allowable stress for design purposes shall be selected as described in §56.07–10(e) at a temperature not below that of saturated steam at the maximum allowable working pressure of the boiler.

(c) Boiler blowoff piping which discharges above the lightest loadline of a vessel shall be arranged so that the discharge is deflected downward.

(d) Valves such as the globe type so designed as to form pockets in which sediment may collect shall not be used for blowoff service.

[CGFR 68–82, 33 FR 18843, Dec. 18, 1968, as amended by CGFR 69–127, 35 FR 9978, June 17, 1970; CGD 73–254, 40 FR 40165, Sept. 2, 1975; USCG–2003–16630, 73 FR 65178, Oct. 31, 2008]

§ 56.50–45 Circulating pumps.

(a) A main circulating pump and emergency means for circulating water through the main condenser shall be provided. The emergency means may consist of a connection from an independent power pump fitted between the main circulating pump and the condenser.

(b) Independent sea suctions shall be provided for the main circulating and the emergency circulating pumps.

(c) A cross connection between the circulating pumps in the case of multiple units will be acceptable in lieu of an independent power pump connection.

(d) On vessels operating on lakes (including Great Lakes), bays, sounds, or rivers, where provision is made to operate noncondensing, only one circulating unit will be required.

§ 56.50–50 Bilge and ballast piping.

(a)(1) All vessels except unmanned barges shall be provided with a satisfactory bilge pumping plant capable of pumping from and draining any watertight compartment except for ballast, oil and water tanks which have acceptable means for filling and emptying independent of the bilge system. The bilge pumping system shall be capable of operation under all practicable conditions after a casualty whether the ship is upright or listed. For this purpose wing suctions will generally be necessary except in narrow compartments at the ends of the vessel where one suction may be sufficient. In compartments of unusual form, additional suctions may be required.

(2) Arrangements shall be made whereby water in the compartments will drain to the suction pipes. Efficient means shall be provided for draining water from all tank tops, other watertight flats and insulated holds. Peak tanks, chain lockers and decks over peak tanks may be drained by eductors, ejectors, or hand pumps. Where piping is led through the forepeak, see § 56.50–1(b).

(3) Where drainage from particular compartments is considered undesirable, the provisions for such drainage may be omitted, provided it can be shown by calculations that the safety of the vessel will not be impaired.

(4) Where the vessel is to carry Class 3 flammable liquids with a flashpoint below 23 °C (74 °F), Class 6, Division 6.1, poisonous liquids, or Class 8 corrosive liquids with a flashpoint below 23 °C (74 °F) as defined in 49 CFR part 173, in enclosed cargo spaces, the bilge-pumping system must be designed to ensure against inadvertent pumping of such liquids through machinery-space piping or pumps.

(5) For each vessel constructed on or after June 9, 1995, and on an international voyage, arrangements must be made to drain the enclosed cargo spaces on either the bulkhead deck of a passenger vessel or the freeboard deck of a cargo vessel.

(i) If the deck edge, at the bulkhead deck of a passenger vessel or the freeboard deck of a cargo vessel, is immersed when the vessel heels 5° or less, the drainage of the enclosed cargo spaces must discharge to a space, or spaces, of adequate capacity, each of which has a high-water-level alarm and a means to discharge overboard. The number, size and arrangement of the drains must prevent unreasonable accumulation of water. The pumping arrangements must take into account the requirements for any fixed manual or automatic sprinkling system. In enclosed cargo spaces fitted with carbon-dioxide extinguishing systems, the drains must have traps or other means to prevent escape of the smothering gas. The enclosed cargo spaces must not drain to machinery spaces or other spaces where sources of ignition may be present if water may be contaminated with Class 3 flammable liquids; Class 6, Division 6.1, poisonous liquids; or Class 8 corrosive liquids with a flashpoint below 23 °C (74 °F).

(ii) If the deck edge, at the bulkhead deck of a passenger vessel or the freeboard deck of a cargo vessel, is immersed only when the vessel heels more than 5°, the drainage of the enclosed cargo spaces may be by means of a sufficient number of scuppers discharging overboard. The installation of scuppers must comply with § 42.15-60 of this chapter.

(b) Passenger vessels shall have provision made to prevent the compartment served by any bilge suction piping from being flooded in the event the pipe is severed or otherwise damaged by collision or grounding in any other compartment. Where the piping is located within one-fifth of the beam of the side of the vessel (measured at right angles to the centerline at the level of the deepest subdivision loadline or deepest loadline where a subdivision loadline is not assigned) or is in a ductkeel, a nonreturn valve shall be fitted to the end of the pipe in the compartment which it serves.

(c)(1) Each bilge suction must lead from a manifold except as otherwise approved by the Commanding Officer, Marine Safety Center. As far as practicable, each manifold must be in, or be capable of remote operation from, the same space as the bilge pump that normally takes suction on that manifold. In either case, the manifold must be capable of being locally controlled from above the floorplates and must be easily accessible at all times. As far as practicable, each overboard-discharge valve for a bilge system must comply with the requirements governing location and accessibility for suction manifolds. Except as otherwise permitted by paragraph (c)(4) of this section for a vessel employing a common-rail bilge system, each bilge-manifold valve controlling a bilge suction from any compartment must be of the stop-check type.

(2) Each passenger vessel on an international voyage must comply with the provisions of SOLAS II–1/21.

(3) A common-rail bilge system may be installed as an acceptable alternative to the system required by paragraph (c)(1) of this section, provided it satisfies all of the following criteria:

(i) The common-rail main runs inboard at least one-fifth of the beam of the vessel.

(ii) A stop-check valve or both a stop valve and a check valve are provided in each branch line and located inboard at least one-fifth of the beam of the vessel.

(iii) The stop valve or the stop-check valve is power-driven, is capable of remote operation from the space where the pump is, and, regardless of the status of the power system, is capable of manual operation to both open and close the valve.

(iv) The stop valve or the stop-check valve is accessible for both manual operation and repair under all operating conditions, and the space used for access contains no expansion joint or flexible coupling that, upon failure, would cause flooding and prevent access to the valve.

(v) A port and a starboard suction serve each space protected unless, under the worst conditions of list and trim and with liquid remaining after pumping, the vessel's stability remains acceptable, in accordance with subchapter S of this chapter.

(vi) For each vessel designed for the carriage of combinations of both liquid and dry bulk cargoes (O/B/O), no bilge pump or piping is located in a machinery space other than in a pump room for cargo, and no liquid and other cargoes are carried simultaneously.

§ 56.50-50

(vii) For each cargo vessel in Great Lakes service, each common-rail piping for the bilge and ballast system serving cargo spaces, if installed and if connected to a dedicated common-rail bilge system, must lead separately from a valved manifold located at the pump.

(d) The internal diameter of bilge suction pipes including strainers shall be determined by formulas (1) and (2), except that the nearest commercial size not more than one-fourth inch under the required diameter may be used. Bilge suction pipes shall be suitably faired to pump inlets.

(1) For suctions to each main bilge pump:

$$d = 1 + \sqrt{\frac{L(B+D)}{2500}} \quad (1) \quad (4) \quad (5)$$

(2) For branch suctions to cargo and machinery spaces:

$$d = 1 + \sqrt{\frac{c(B+D)}{1500}} \quad (2) \quad (3) \quad (5)$$

where:
L=Length of vessel on loadwater line, in feet.
B=Breadth of vessel, in feet. (5)
D=Molded depth (in feet) to the bulkhead deck. (6)
c=Length of compartment, in feet.
d=Required internal diameter of suction pipe, in inches.

NOTE 1. For tank vessels, "L" may be reduced by the combined length of the cargo oil tanks.

NOTE 2. For bulk carriers with full depth wing tanks served by a ballast system where the beam of the vessel is not representative of the breadth of the compartment, "B" may be appropriately modified to the breadth of the compartment.

NOTE 3. In the calculation for a vessel with more than one hull, such as a catamaran, the breadth of the unit is the breadth of one hull.

NOTE 4. In the calculation for a mobile offshore drilling unit, "L" is reducible by the combined length of spaces that can be pumped by another piping system meeting §§ 56.50-50 and 56.50-55, where "L" is the length of the unit at the waterline.

NOTE 5. For mobile offshore drilling units employing unusual hull forms, "B" may be modified to the average breadth rather than the maximum breadth.

NOTE 6. For each passenger vessel constructed on or after June 9, 1995, and being on an international voyage, D must be measured to the next deck above the bulkhead deck if an enclosed cargo space on the bulkhead deck that is internally drained in accordance with paragraph (a)(4) of this section extends the entire length of the vessel. Where the enclosed cargo space extends a lesser length, D must be taken as the sum of the molded depth (in feet) to the bulkhead deck plus lh/L where l and h are the aggregate length and height (in feet) of the enclosed cargo space.

(3) For vessels of 150 gross tons and over, no main suction piping shall be less than 2½ inches internal diameter. Branch piping need not be more than 4 inches and shall not be less than 2 inches in diameter except for drainage of small pockets or spaces in which case 1½-inch diameter may be used. For vessels less than 150 gross tons no bilge suction shall be less than 1½ inches internal diameter and no branch piping shall be less than 1 inch nominal pipe size.

(4) For vessels of 65 feet in length or less and not engaged on an international voyage, the bilge pipe sizes computed by Formulas (1) and (2) of this paragraph are not mandatory, but in no case shall the size be less than 1 inch nominal pipe size.

(5) The number, location, and size of bilge suctions in the boiler and machinery compartments shall be determined when the piping plans are submitted for approval and shall be based upon the size of the compartments and the drainage arrangements.

(e) *Independent bilge suction.* One of the independent bilge pumps must have a suction of a diameter not less than that given by Formula (2) in paragraph (d) of this section that is led directly from the engine room bilge entirely independent of the bilge main, and on passenger vessels each independent bilge pump located in the machinery spaces must have such direct suctions from these spaces, except that not more than two pumps are required to have direct suctions from any one space. A suction that is led directly from a suitably located pump manifold may be considered to be independent of the bilge main. Where two direct suctions are required in any one compartment on passenger vessels, one suction must be located on each side of the compartment. If watertight bulkheads separate the engine and boiler rooms, a direct suction or suctions must be fitted to each compartment unless the pumps available for bilge service are distributed throughout these compartments, in which case at least one pump in each such compartment must be fitted with direct suction in its compartment. In a vessel with more than one hull, there must be one bilge pump that has an independent bilge suction in each hull. In a column stabilized mobile offshore drilling unit, the independent bilge suction must be from the pumproom bilge.

(f) *Emergency bilge suctions.* In addition to the independent bilge suction(s) required by paragraph (e) of this section, an emergency bilge suction must be provided in the machinery space for all self-propelled vessels as described in the following subparagraphs. Emergency suctions must be provided from pumps other than those required by § 56.50–55(a) of this part. Such suctions must have nonreturn valves, and must meet the following criteria as appropriate:

(1) On passenger vessels propelled by steam and operating on an international voyage or on ocean, coastwise, or Great Lakes routes, the main circulating pump is to be fitted with a direct bilge suction for the machinery space. The diameter of such suctions shall not be less than two-thirds the diameter of the main sea injection. When it can be shown to the satisfaction of the Commandant that the main circulating pump is not suitable for emergency bilge service, a direct emergency bilge suction is to be led from the largest available independent power driven pump to the drainage level of the machinery space. The suction is to be of the same diameter as the main inlet of the pump used and the capacity of the pump shall exceed that of a required main bilge pump.

(2) On passenger vessels propelled by internal combustion engines and operating on an international voyage or on ocean, coastwise, or Great Lakes routes, the largest available pump in the engine room is to be fitted with the direct bilge suction in the machinery space except that a required bilge pump may not be used. The area of the suction pipe is to be equal to the full suction inlet of the pump. The discharge capacity of the pump selected shall exceed the capacity of the required main bilge pump.

(3) Vessels over 180 feet in length which are not passenger vessels and which operate on international voyages or in ocean, coastwise, or Great Lakes service, must be provided with a direct emergency bilge suction from any pump in the machinery space, except that a required bilge pump may not be used. The discharge capacity of the pump selected must exceed the capacity of the required main bilge pump and the area of the suction inlet is to be equal to the full suction inlet of the pump.

(4) Vessels under 180 feet in length need not provide an emergency bilge suction, except that passenger vessels shall comply with the requirements of paragraphs (f) (1) and (2) of this section.

(5) Each vessel with more than one hull must have an emergency bilge suction in each hull.

(6) Each column stabilized mobile offshore drilling unit must have—

(i) An emergency bilge suction in each hull; and

(ii) A remote control for the emergency pump and associated valves that can be operated from the ballast control room.

(g) Each individual bilge suction shall be fitted with a suitable bilge strainer having an open area of not less than three times at of the suction pipe. In addition a mud box or basket strainer shall be fitted in an accessible position between the bilge suction manifold and the pump.

(h) Pipes for draining cargo holds or machinery spaces must be separate from pipes which are used for filling or emptying tanks where water or oil is carried. Bilge and ballast piping systems must be so arranged as to prevent oil or water from the sea or ballast spaces from passing into cargo holds or machinery spaces, or from passing from one compartment to another, whether from the sea, water ballast, or oil tanks, by the appropriate installation of stop and non-return valves. The bilge and ballast mains must be fitted with separate control valves at the pumps. Except as allowed by paragraph (c)(4)(vii) of this section, piping for

§ 56.50-55

draining a cargo hold or machinery space must be separate from piping used for filling or emptying any tank where water or oil is carried. Piping for bilge and ballast must be arranged so as to prevent, by the appropriate installation of stop and non-return valves, oil or water from the sea or ballast spaces from passing into a cargo hold or machinery space, or from passing from one compartment to another, regardless of the source. The bilge and ballast mains must be fitted with separate control valves at the pumps.

(i) Ballast piping shall not be installed to any hull compartment of a wood vessel. Where the carriage of liquid ballast in such vessels is necessary, suitable ballast tanks, structurally independent of the hull, shall be provided.

(j) When dry cargo is to be carried in deep tanks, arrangement shall be made for disconnecting or blanking-off the oil and ballast lines, and the bilge suctions shall be disconnected or blanked-off when oil or ballast is carried. Blind flanges or reversible pipe fittings may be employed for this purpose.

(k) Where bilge and ballast piping is led through tanks, except ballast piping in ballast tanks, means must be provided to minimize the risk of flooding of other spaces due to pipe failure within the tanks. In this regard, such piping may be in an oiltight or watertight pipe tunnel, or the piping may be of Schedule 80 pipe wall thickness, fitted with expansion bends, and all joints within the tanks are welded. Alternative designs may be installed as approved by the Marine Safety Center. Where a pipe tunnel is installed, the watertight integrity of the bulkheads must be maintained. No valve or fitting may be located within the tunnel if the pipe tunnel is not of sufficient size to afford easy access. These requirements need not be met provided the contents of the tank and piping system are chemically compatible and strength and stability calculations are submitted showing that crossflooding resulting from a pipe, the tank, and the spaces through which the piping passes will not seriously affect the safety of the ship, including the launching of lifeboats due to the ship's listing. Bilge lines led through tanks without a pipe tunnel must be fitted with nonreturn valves at the bilge suctions.

(l) When bilge pumps are utilized for other services, the piping shall be so arranged that under any condition at least one pump will be available for drainage of the vessel through an overboard discharge, while the other pump(s) are being used for a different service.

(m) All bilge pipes used in or under fuel storage tanks or in the boiler or machinery space, including spaces in which oil settling tanks or oil pumping units are located, shall be of steel or other acceptable material.

(n) Oil pollution prevention requirements for bilge and ballast systems are contained in subpart B of part 155, title 33, Code of Federal Regulations.

NOTE: For the purposes of this section, a pumproom is a machinery space on a column stabilized mobile offshore drilling unit.

[CGFR 68–82, 33 FR 18843, Dec. 18, 1968, as amended by CGFR 69–127, 35 FR 9979, June 17, 1970; CGD 73–58R, 39 FR 18767, May 30, 1974; 79–165a, 45 FR 64188, Sept. 29, 1980; CGD 77–140, 54 FR 40608, Oct. 2, 1989; 55 FR 39968, Oct. 1, 1990; CGD 83–043, 60 FR 24772, May 10, 1995; CGD 95–028, 62 FR 51201, Sept. 30, 1997]

§ 56.50-55 Bilge pumps.

(a) *Self-propelled vessels.* (1) Each self-propelled vessel must be provided with a power-driven pump or pumps connected to the bilge main as required by table 56.50–55(a).

TABLE 56.50–55(a)—POWER BILGE PUMPS REQUIRED FOR SELF-PROPELLED VESSELS

Vessel length, in feet	Passenger vessels [1]			Dry-cargo vessels [2]		Tank vessels	Mobile offshore drilling units	
	International voyages [3]	Ocean, coastwise and Great Lakes	All other waters	Ocean, coastwise and Great Lakes	All waters		All waters	All waters
180′ or more	[4]3	[4]3	2	2	2	2	2	
Below 180′ and exceeding 65′	[4]3	[5]2	[5]2	[5]2	[5]2	2	2	

202

Coast Guard, Dept. of Homeland Security § 56.50–55

TABLE 56.50–55(a)—POWER BILGE PUMPS REQUIRED FOR SELF-PROPELLED VESSELS—Continued

Vessel length, in feet	Passenger vessels [1]			Dry-cargo vessels [2]		Tank vessels	Mobile offshore drilling units
	International voyages [3]	Ocean, coastwise and Great Lakes	All other waters	Ocean, coastwise and Great Lakes	All waters	All waters	All waters
65′ or less	3	1	1	1	1	1	....

[1] Small passenger vessels under 100 gross tons refer to subpart 182.520 of subchapter T (Small Passenger Vessel) of this chapter.
[2] Dry-bulk carriers having ballast pumps connected to the tanks outside the engineroom and to the cargo hold may substitute the appropriate requirements for tank vessels.
[3] Not applicable to passenger vessels which do not proceed more than 20 mile from the nearest land, or which are employed in the carriage of large numbers of unberthed passengers in special trades.
[4] When the criterion numeral exceeds 30, an additional independent power-driven pump is required. (See part 171 of this chapter for determination of criterion numeral.)
[5] Vessels operating on lakes (including Great Lakes), bays, sounds, or rivers where steam is always available, or where a suitable water supply is available from a power-driven pump of adequate pressure and capacity, may substitute siphons or eductors for one of the required power-driven pumps, provided a siphon or eductor is permanently installed in each hold or compartment.

(b) *Nonself-propelled vessels.* (1) Ocean going sailing vessels and barges shall be provided with pumps connected to the bilge main as required in table 56.50–55(b)(1).

TABLE 56.50–55(b)(1)—BILGE PUMPS REQUIRED FOR NONSELF-PROPELLED VESSELS

Type of vessel	Waters navigated	Power pumps [1]	Hand pumps
Sailing	Ocean and coastwise	Two	[2]
Manned barges	.....do	Two	[2]
Manned barges	Other than ocean and coastwise	[3]	[3]
Unmanned barges	All waters	[3]	[3]
Mobile offshore drilling units	All waters	Two	None.

[1] Where power is always available, independent power bilge pumps shall be installed as required and shall be connected to the bilge main.
[2] Efficient hand pumps connected to the bilge main may be substituted for the power pumps. Where there is no common bilge main, one hand pump will be required for each compartment.
[3] Suitable hand or power pumps or siphons, portable or fixed, carried either on board the barge or on the towing vessel shall be provided.

(2) The pumps and source of power for operation on oceangoing sailing vessels and barges shall be located above the bulkhead deck or at the highest convenient level which is always accessible.

(3) Each hull of a vessel with more than one hull, such as a catamaran, must meet Table 56.50–55(b).

(c) *Capacity of independent power bilge pump.* Each power bilge pump must have the capacity to develop a suction velocity of not less than 400 feet per minute through the size of bilge main piping required by § 56.50–50(d)(1) of this part under ordinary conditions; except that, for vessels of less than 65 feet in length not engaged on international voyages, the pump must have a minimum capacity of 25 gallons per minute and need not meet the velocity requirement of this paragraph.

(d) *Priming.* Suitable means shall be provided for priming centrifugal pumps which are not of the self-priming type.

(e) *Location.* (1) For self-propelled vessels, if the engines and boilers are in two or more watertight compartments, the bilge pumps must be distributed throughout these compartments. On other self-propelled vessels and mobile offshore drilling units, the bilge pumps must be in separate compartments to the extent practicable. When the location of bilge pumps in separate watertight compartments is not practicable, alternative arrangements may be submitted for consideration by the Marine Safety Center.

(2) For nonself-propelled vessels requiring two bilge pumps, these pumps, insofar as practicable, shall be located in separate watertight machinery spaces. When the location of bilge

§ 56.50–57

pumps in separate watertight compartments is not possible, the Commandant will consider alternate arrangements of the bilge pumps.

(3) The emergency bilge pumps shall not be installed in a passenger ship forward of the collision bulkhead.

(4) Each hull of a vessel with more than one hull must have at least two means for pumping the bilges in each hull. No multi-hulled vessel may operate unless one of these means is available to pump each bilge.

(f) *Other pumps.* Sanitary, ballast, and general service pumps having the required capacity may be accepted as independent power bilge pumps if fitted with the necessary connections to the bilge pumping system.

[CGFR 68–82, 33 FR 18843, Dec. 18, 1968, as amended by CGD 79–023, 48 FR 51007, Nov. 4, 1983; CGD 77–140, 54 FR 40608, Oct. 2, 1989; 55 FR 39968, Oct. 1, 1990; CGD 83–043, 60 FR 24773, May 10, 1995; USCG–2004–18884, 69 FR 58346, Sept. 30, 2004]

§ 56.50–57 **Bilge piping and pumps, alternative requirements.**

(a) If a passenger vessel complies with §§ 171.075 and 171.082 of this chapter, its bilge pumping and piping systems must meet §§ 56.50–50 and 56.50–55, except as follows:

(1) Each bilge pumping system must comply with—

(i) Regulation 19(b) of the Annex to IMCO Resolution A.265 (VIII) in place of §§ 56.50–55(a)(1), 56.50–55(a)(3), and 56.50–55(f);

(ii) Regulation 19(d) of the Annex to IMCO Resolution A.265 (VIII) in place of § 56.50–55(a)(2).

(2) Each bilge main must comply with Regulation 19(i) of the Annex to IMCO Resolution A.265 (VIII) in place of § 56.50–50(d) except—

(i) The nearest commercial pipe size may be used if it is not more than one-fourth inch under the required diameter; and

(ii) Each branch pipe must comply with § 56.50–50(d)(2).

(b) The standards referred to in this section, which are contained in the Inter-governmental Maritime Consultative Organization (IMCO) Resolution A.265 (VIII), dated December 10, 1973, are incorporated by reference. This document is available from the National Technical Information Service, Springfield, Virginia, 22151, under the title "Regulations on Subdivision and Stability of Passenger Ships as Equivalent to part B of chapter II of the International Convention for the Safety of Life at Sea, 1960" (Volume IV of the U.S. Coast Guard's "Commandant's International Technical Series", USCG CITS–74–1–1.)

[CGD 76–053, 47 FR 37553, Aug. 26, 1982, as amended by CGD 79–023, 48 FR 51007, Nov. 4, 1983]

§ 56.50–60 **Systems containing oil.**

(a)(1) Oil-piping systems for the transfer or discharge of cargo or fuel oil must be separate from other piping systems as far as practicable, and positive means shall be provided to prevent interconnection in service.

(2) Fuel oil and cargo oil systems may be combined if the cargo oil systems contain only Grade E oils and have no connection to cargo systems containing grades of oil with lower flash points or hazardous substances.

(3) Pumps used to transfer oil must have no discharge connections to fire mains, boiler feed systems, or condensers unless approved positive means are provided to prevent oil from being accidentally discharged into any of the aforementioned systems.

(b) When oil needs to be heated to lower its viscosity, heating coils must be properly installed in each tank.

(1) Each drain from a heating coil as well as each drain from an oil heater must run to an open inspection tank or other suitable oil detector before returning to the feed system.

(2) As far as practicable, no part of the fuel-oil system containing heated oil under pressure exceeding 180 KPa (26 psi) may be placed in a concealed position so that defects and leakage cannot be readily observed. Each machinery space containing a part of the system must be adequately illuminated.

(c) Filling pipes may be led directly from the deck into the tanks or to a manifold in an accessible location permanently marked to indicate the tanks to which they are connected. A shutoff valve must be fitted at each filling end. Oil piping must not be led through accommodation spaces, except that low pressure fill piping not normally used at sea may pass through accommodation spaces if it is of steel construction, all welded, and not concealed.

(d) Piping subject to internal head pressure from oil in the tank must be fitted with positive shutoff valves located at the tank.

(1) Valves installed on the outside of the oil tanks must be made of steel, ductile cast iron ASTM A 395 (incorporated by reference; see 46 CFR 56.01–2), or a ductile nonferrous alloy having a melting point above 1,700 °F and must be arranged with a means of manual control locally at the valve and remotely from a readily accessible and safe location outside of the compartment in which the valves are located.

(i) In the special case of a deep tank in any shaft tunnel, piping tunnel, or similar space, one or more valves must be fitted on the tank, but control in the event of fire may be effected by means of an additional valve on the piping outside the tunnel or similar space. Any such additional valve installed inside a machinery space must be capable of being operated from outside this space.

(ii) [Reserved]

(2) If valves are installed on the inside of the tank, they may be made of cast iron and arranged for remote control only. Additional valves for local control must be located in the space where the system exits from the tank or adjacent tanks. Valves for local control outside the tanks must be made of steel, ductile cast iron ASTM A 395 , or a ductile nonferrous alloy having a melting point above 1,700 °F.

(3) Power operated valves installed to comply with the requirements of this section must meet the following requirements:

(i) Valve actuators must be capable of closing the valves under all conditions, except during physical interruption of the power system (e.g., cable breakage or tube rupture). Fluid power actuated valves, other than those opened against spring pressure, must be provided with an energy storage system which is protected, as far as practicable, from fire and collision. The storage system must be used for no other purpose and must have sufficient capacity to cycle all connected valves from the initial valve position to the opposite position and return. The cross connection of this system to an alternate power supply will be given special consideration by the Marine Safety Center.

(ii) The valve shall have a local power actuator to both open and close the valve unless local manual opening operation will not prevent remote closing of the valve.

(iii) The positioning of the valve by either the local or remote actuators shall not void the ability of the other actuator to close the valve.

(iv) The valve shall be provided with a means of emergency manual operation to both open and close the valve regardless of the status of the power operating system. Such manual operation may interfere with the power operation, and if so, shall be protected from causal use by means of covers, locking devices, or other suitable means. Instructions and warnings regarding the emergency system shall be conspicuously posted at the valve.

(4) Remote operation for shutoff valves on small independent oil tanks will be specially considered in each case where the size of tanks and their location may warrant the omission of remote operating rods.

(e) Fuel oil tanks overhanging boilers are prohibited.

(f) Valves for drawing fuel or draining water from fuel are not permitted in fuel oil systems except that a single valve may be permitted in the case of diesel driven machinery if suitably located within the machinery space away from any potential source of ignition. Such a valve shall be fitted with a cap or a plug to prevent leakage.

(g) Test cocks must not be fitted to fuel oil or cargo oil tanks.

(h) Oil piping must not run through feed or potable water tanks. Feed or potable water piping must not pass through oil tanks.

(i) Where flooding equalizing cross-connections between fuel or cargo tanks are required for stability considerations, the arrangement must be approved by the Marine Safety Center.

(j) Piping conveying oil must be run well away from hot surfaces wherever possible. Where such leads are unavoidable, only welded joints are to be used, or alternatively, suitable shields are to be fitted in the way of flanged or mechanical pipe joints when welded joints are not practicable. Piping that conveys fuel oil or lubricating oil to equipment and is in the proximity of equipment or lines having an open flame or having parts operating above 500 °F must be of seamless steel. (See § 56.50–65 of this part.)

(k) Oil piping drains, strainers and other equipment subject to normal oil leakage must be fitted with drip pans or other means to prevent oil draining into the bilge.

(l) Where oil piping passes through a non-oil tank without stop valves complying with paragraph (d) of this section installed at all tank penetrations, the piping must comply with § 56.50–50(k).

(m) Each arrangement for the storage, distribution, and use of oil in a pressure-lubrication system must—

(1) As well as comply with § 56.50–80, be such as to ensure the safety of the vessel and all persons aboard; and

(2) In a machinery space, meet the applicable requirements of §§ 56.50–60 (b)(2) and (d), 56.50–85(a)(11), 56.50–90 (c) and (d), and 58.01–55(f) of this subchapter. No arrangement need comply with § 56.50–90 (c)(1) and (c)(3) of this subchapter if the sounding pipe is fitted with an effective means of closure, such as a threaded cap or plug or other means acceptable to the Officer in Charge, Marine Inspection. The use of flexible piping or hose is permitted in accordance with the applicable requirements of §§ 56.35–10, 56.35–15, and 56.60–25(c).

(n) Each arrangement for the storage, distribution, and use of any other flammable oil employed under pressure in a power transmission-system, control and activating system, or heating system must be such as to ensure the safety of the vessel and all persons aboard by—

(1) Complying with subpart 58.30 of this subchapter; and,

(2) Where means of ignition are present, meeting the applicable requirements of §§ 56.50–85(a)(11), 56.50–90 (c) and (d), and 58.01–55(f) of this subchapter. Each pipe and its valves and fittings must be of steel or other approved material, except that the use of flexible piping or hose is permitted in accordance with the applicable requirements of §§ 56.35–10, 56.35–15, and 56.60–25(c).

[CGFR 68–82, 33 FR 18843, Dec. 18, 1968, as amended by CGFR 69–127, 35 FR 9979, June 17, 1970; CGD 73–254, 40 FR 40165, Sept. 2, 1975; CGD 77–140, 54 FR 40609, Oct. 2, 1989; 55 FR 39968, Oct. 1, 1990; CGD 83–043, 60 FR 24774, May 10, 1995; USCG–2000–7790, 65 FR 58460, Sept. 29, 2000; USCG–2004–18884, 69 FR 58346, Sept. 30, 2004; USCG–2003–16630, 73 FR 65178, Oct. 31, 2008]

§ 56.50–65 Burner fuel-oil service systems.

(a) All discharge piping from the fuel oil service pumps to burners must be seamless steel with a thickness of at least Schedule 80. If required by § 56.07–10(e) of this part or paragraph 104.1.2 of ASME B31.1 (incorporated by reference; see 46 CFR 56.01–2), the thickness must be greater than Schedule 80. Short lengths of steel, or annealed copper nickel, nickel copper, or copper pipe and tubing may be used between the fuel oil burner front header manifold and the atomizer head to provide flexibility. All material used must meet the requirements of subpart 56.60 of this part. The use of non-metallic materials is prohibited. The thickness of the short lengths must not be less than the larger of 0.9 mm (0.35 inch) or that required by § 56.07–10(e) of this part. Flexible metallic tubing for this application may be used when approved by the Marine Safety Center. Tubing fittings must be of the flared type except that flareless fittings of the nonbite type may be used when the tubing is steel, nickel copper or copper nickel.

(b)(1) All vessels having oil fired boilers must have at least two fuel service pumps, each of sufficient capacity to supply all the boilers at full power, and arranged so that one may be overhauled while the other is in service. At least two fuel oil heaters of approximately equal capacity must be installed and so arranged that any heater may be overhauled while the other(s) is (are) in service. Suction and discharge strainers must be of the duplex or other type capable of being cleaned without interrupting the oil supply.

(2) All auxiliary boilers, except those furnishing steam for vital equipment and fire extinguishing purposes other

than duplicate installations, may be equipped with a single fuel oil service pump and a single fuel oil heater. Such pumps need not be fitted with discharge strainers.

(3) Strainers must be located so as to preclude the possibility of spraying oil on the burner or boiler casing, or be provided with spray shields. Coamings, drip pans, etc., must be fitted under fuel oil service pumps, heaters, etc., where necessary to prevent oil drainage to the bilge.

(4) Boilers burning fuel oils of low viscosity need not be equipped with fuel oil heaters, provided acceptable evidence is furnished to indicate that satisfactory combustion will be obtained without the use of heaters.

(c) Piping between service pumps and burners shall be located so as to be readily observable, and all bolted flange joints shall be provided with a wrap around deflector to deflect spray in case of a leak. The relief valve located at the pump and the relief valves fitted to the fuel oil heaters shall discharge back into the settling tank or the suction side of the pump. The return line from the burners shall be so arranged that the suction piping cannot be subjected to discharge pressure.

(d) If threaded-bonnet valves are employed, they shall be of the union-bonnet type capable of being packed under pressure.

(e) Unions shall not be used for pipe diameters of 1 inch and above.

(f) Boiler header valves of the quick closing type shall be installed in the fuel supply lines as close to the boiler front header as practicable. The location is to be accessible to the operator or remotely controlled.

(g) Bushings and street ells are not permitted in fuel oil discharge piping.

(h) Each fuel-oil service pump must be equipped with controls as required by § 58.01–25 of this subchapter.

[CGFR 68–82, 33 FR 18843, Dec. 18, 1968, as amended by CGFR 69–127, 35 FR 9978, June 17, 1970; CGD 77–140, 54 FR 40609, Oct. 2, 1989; CGD 83–043, 60 FR 24774, May 10, 1995; USCG–2003–16630, 73 FR 65178, Oct. 31, 2008]

§ 56.50–70 Gasoline fuel systems.

(a) *Material.* (1) Fuel supply piping to the engines shall be of seamless drawn annealed copper pipe or tubing, nickel copper, or copper nickel pipe or tubing meeting the requirements of subpart 56.60.

(2) Thicknesses of tubing walls must not be less than the larger of that shown in Table 56.50–70(a) of this section or that required by 46 CFR 56.07–10(e) and 104.1.2 of ASME B31.1 (incorporated by reference; see 46 CFR 56.01–2).

(3) Tubing fittings shall be of nonferrous drawn or forged metal and of the flared type except that the flareless fittings of the nonbite type may be used when the tubing system is of nickel copper or copper nickel. Tubing shall be cut square and flared by suitable tools. Tube ends shall be annealed before flaring. Pipe fittings shall be of nonferrous material. Pipe thread joints shall be made tight with a suitable compound.

(4) Valves for fuel lines shall be of nonferrous material of the union bonnet type with ground seats except that cocks may be used if they are the solid bottom type with tapered plugs and union bonnets.

TABLE 56.50–70(a)—TUBING WALL THICKNESS

Outside diameter of tubing in inches	Thickness	
	B.W.G.	Inch
⅛, ³⁄₁₆, ¼	#21	0.032
⁵⁄₁₆, ⅜	#20	.035
⁷⁄₁₆, ½	#19	.042

(b) *Installation.* (1) All fuel pipes, pipe connections, and accessories shall be readily accessible. The piping shall run in sight wherever practicable, protected against mechanical injury, and effectively secured against excessive movement and vibration by the use of soft nonferrous metal liners or straps without sharp edges. Where passing through steel decks or bulkheads, fuel lines shall be protected by close fitting ferrules or stuffing boxes. Refer to § 56.30–25 for tubing joint installations.

(2) Either a short length of suitable metallic or nonmetallic flexible tubing or hose or a loop of annealed copper tubing must be installed in the fuel-supply line at or near the engine to prevent damage by vibration.

(i) If nonmetallic flexible hose is used, it must meet the requirements of 46 CFR 56.60–25(b) for fuel service.

(ii) Flexible hose connections should maintain metallic contact between the sections of the fuel-supply lines; however, if they do not, the fuel tank must be grounded.

(3) Valves in fuel lines shall be installed to close against the flow.

(c) *Shutoff valves.* Shutoff valves of a suitable type shall be installed in the fuel supply lines, one as close to each tank as practicable, and one as close to each carburetor as practicable. Where fuel tanks are installed below the weather deck, arrangements shall be provided for operating all shutoff valves at the tanks from outside the compartments in which they are located, preferably from an accessible position on the weather deck. The operating gear for the shutoff valves at the tanks shall be accessible at all times and shall be suitably marked.

(d) *Strainers.* A suitable twin strainer shall be fitted in the fuel supply line in the engine compartment. Strainers shall be of the type opening on top for cleaning screens. A drip pan shall be fitted under the strainer.

(e) *Outlets and drains.* Outlets in fuel lines for drawing gasoline for any purpose are prohibited. Valved openings in the bottom of fuel tanks are prohibited; however, openings fitted with threaded plug or cap can be used for cleaning purposes.

(f) *Fuel suction connections.* All fuel suction and return lines shall enter the top of the fuel tanks and connections shall be fitted into spuds. Such lines shall extend nearly to the bottom of the tank.

(g) *Filling and sounding pipes.* Filling and sounding pipes shall be so arranged that vapors or possible overflow when filling cannot escape to the inside of the vessel but will discharge overboard. Such pipes shall terminate on the weather deck clear of any coamings and shall be fitted with suitable shutoff valves or deck plugs. Filling and sounding pipes shall extend to within one-half of their diameter from the bottom of the tank or from the surface of the striking plate in case of a sounding pipe. A flame screen of noncorrodible wire mesh shall be fitted in the throat of the filling pipe. Sounding pipes shall be kept closed at all times except during sounding.

(h) *Vent pipes.* Each tank shall be fitted with a vent, the cross-sectional area of which shall not be less than that of the filling pipe. The vent pipes shall terminate at least 2 feet above the weather deck and not less than 3 feet from any opening into living quarters or other below deck space. The ends of vent pipes shall terminate with U-bends and shall be fitted with flame screens or flame arresters. The flame screens shall consist of a single screen of corrosion resistant wire of at least 30 by 30 mesh.

(i) *Gasoline tanks.* For requirements pertaining to independent gasoline fuel tanks see subpart 58.50 of this subchapter.

(j) *Fuel pumps.* Each fuel pump must be equipped with controls as required by § 58.01-25 of this subchapter.

[CGFR 68-82, 33 FR 18843, Dec. 18, 1968, as amended by CGFR 69-127, 35 FR 9978, June 17, 1970; CGFR 72-59R, 37 FR 6189, Mar. 25, 1972; CGD 83-043, 60 FR 24774, May 10, 1995; USCG-2002-13058, 67 FR 61278, Sept. 30, 2002; USCG-2003-16630, 73 FR 65178, Oct. 31, 2008]

§ 56.50-75 **Diesel fuel systems.**

(a) *Vessels greater than 100 gross tons.* (1) The diesel fuel system shall comply with §§ 56.50-60, 56.50-85, and 56.50-90. The fuel supply piping to engines shall be of seamless steel, annealed seamless copper or brass pipe or tubing, or of nickel copper or copper nickel alloy meeting the requirements of subpart 56.60 for materials and § 56.50-70(a)(2) for thickness. Fuel oil service or unit pumps shall be equipped with controls to comply with § 58.01-25 of this subchapter.

(2) The installation shall comply with § 56.50-70(b).

(3) Tubing connections and fittings shall be drawn or forged metal of the flared type except that flareless fittings of the nonbite type may be used when the tubing system is steel, nickel-copper, or copper-nickel. When making flared tube connections the tubing shall be cut square and flared by suitable tools. Tube ends shall be annealed before flaring.

(b) *Vessels of 100 gross tons and less and tank barges*—(1) *Materials.* Fuel supply piping shall be of copper, nickel copper or copper nickel having a minimum wall thickness of 0.035 inch except that piping of other materials such as seamless steel pipe or tubing which provides equivalent safety may be used.

(2) *Tubing connections and fittings.* Tubing connections shall comply with the provisions of § 56.50–75(a)(3).

(3) *Installation.* The installation of diesel fuel piping shall comply with the requirements of § 56.50–70(b).

(4) *Shutoff valves.* Shutoff valves shall be installed in the fuel supply lines, one as close to each tank as practicable, and one as close to each fuel pump as practicable. Valves shall be accessible at all times.

(5) *Outlets and drains.* Valves for removing water or impurities from fuel oil systems will be permitted in the machinery space provided such valves are fitted with caps or plugs to prevent leakage.

(6) *Filling pipe.* Tank filling pipes on motorboats and motor vessels of less than 100 gross tons and tank barges shall terminate on an open deck and shall be fitted with suitable shutoff valves, deck plugs, or caps.

(7) *Vent pipes.* Each tank shall be fitted with a vent pipe complying with § 56.50–85.

(8) *Independent diesel fuel tanks.* See subpart 58.50 of this subchapter for specific requirements.

[CGFR 68–82, 33 FR 18843, Dec. 18, 1968, as amended by CGD 77–140, 54 FR 40610, Oct. 2, 1989]

§ 56.50–80 **Lubricating-oil systems.**

(a) The lubricating oil system shall be designed to function satisfactorily when the vessel has a permanent 15° list and a permanent 5° trim.

(b) When pressure or gravity-forced lubrication is employed for the steam driven main propelling machinery, an independent auxiliary lubricating pump shall be provided.

(c) Oil coolers on steam driven machinery shall be provided with two separate means of circulating water through the coolers.

(d) For internal combustion engine installations, the requirements of paragraphs (b) and (c) of this section shall be met, but they do not apply to vessels in river and harbor service, nor to any vessel below 300 gross tons. Where the size and design of an engine is such that lubrication before starting is not necessary and an attached pump is normally used, the independent auxiliary pump is not required if a duplicate of the attached pump is carried as spare. In meeting the requirements of paragraph (c) of this section in the case of internal combustion engines, two separate means are to be provided for circulating coolant on those engines on which oil coolers are fitted. One of those means must be independently driven and may consist of a connection from a pump of adequate size normally used for other purposes utilizing the required coolant. Where the design of an engine will not readily accommodate an independent pump connection, the independent auxiliary pump will not be required if a duplicate of the attached pump is carried as a spare. Oil filters shall be provided on all internal combustion engine installations. On main propulsion engines which are fitted with full-flow type filters, the arrangement shall be such that the filters may be cleaned without interrupting the oil supply except that such an arrangement is not required on vessels having more than a single main propulsion engine.

(e) The lubricating oil piping shall be independent of other piping systems and shall be provided with necessary coolers, heaters, filters, etc., for proper operation. Oil heaters shall be fitted with bypasses.

(f) Diesel engine lubrication systems shall be so arranged that vapors from the sump tank may not be discharged back into the engine crank case of engines of the dry sump type.

(g) Steam turbine driven propulsion and auxiliary generating machinery depending on forced lubrication shall be arranged to shut down automatically upon failure of the lubricating system.

(h) Sight-flow glasses may be used in lubricating-oil systems provided it has been demonstrated, to the satisfaction of the Commanding Officer, Marine Safety Center, that they can withstand exposure to a flame at a temperature of 927 °C (1700 °F) for one hour, without failure or appreciable leakage.

§ 56.50-85

(i) Steam driven propulsion machinery must be provided with an emergency supply of lubricating oil that must operate automatically upon failure of the lubricating oil system. The emergency oil supply must be adequate to provide lubrication until the equipment comes to rest during automatic shutdown.

[CGFR 68–82, 33 FR 18843, Dec. 18, 1968, as amended by CGFR 69–127, 35 FR 9979, June 17, 1970; CGD 81–030, 53 FR 17837, May 18, 1988; CGD 83–043, 60 FR 24774, May 10, 1995]

§ 56.50-85 Tank-vent piping.

(a) This section applies to vents for all independent, fixed, non-pressure tanks or containers or for spaces in which liquids, such as fuel, ship's stores, cargo, or ballast, are carried.

(1) The structural arrangement in double bottom and other tanks shall be such as to permit the free passage of air and gases from all parts of the tanks to vent pipes.

(2) Tanks having a comparatively small surface, such as fuel oil settling tanks, need be fitted with only one vent pipe, but tanks having a comparatively large surface shall be fitted with at least two vent pipes. The vents shall be located so as to provide venting of the tanks under any service condition.

(3) Vent pipes for fuel oil tanks shall, wherever possible, have a slope of no less than 30°. Header lines, where both ends are adequately drained to a tank, are excluded from this requirement.

(4) Tank vents must extend above the weather deck, except vents from fresh water tanks, bilge oily-water holding tanks, bilge slop tanks, and tanks containing Grade E combustible liquids, such as lubricating oil, may terminate in the machinery space, provided—

(i) The vents are arranged to prevent overflow on machinery, electrical equipment, and hot surfaces;

(ii) Tanks containing combustible liquids are not heated; and

(iii) The vents terminate above the deep load waterline if the tanks have boundaries in common with the hull.

(5) Vents from oil tanks must terminate not less than three feet from any opening into living quarters.

(6) Vents extending above the freeboard deck or superstructure deck from fuel oil and other tanks must be at least Schedule 40 in wall thickness. Except for barges in inland service and for Great Lakes vessels, the height from the deck to any point where water may gain access through the vent to below deck must be at least 30 inches (760mm) on the freeboard deck and 17½ inches (450mm) on the superstructure deck. On Great Lakes vessels, the height from the deck to any point where water may gain access through the vent to below deck must be at least 30 inches (760mm) on the freeboard deck, 24 inches (610mm) on the raised quarterdeck, and 12 inches (305mm) on other superstructure decks. Where the height of vents on Great Lakes vessels may interfere with the working of the vessel, a lower height may be approved by the Marine Safety Center provided the vent cap is properly protected from mechanical damage. For barges in inland service, the vents must extend at least six inches above the deck. A lesser amount may be approved by the Marine Safety Center if evidence is provided that a particular vent has proven satisfactory in service.

(7) Satisfactory means, permanently attached, shall be provided for closing the openings of all vents, except that barges in inland service may be exempted. Acceptable means of closure are:

(i) A ball check valve where the ball float, normally in the open position, will float up and close under the action of a submerging wave. The valve shall be designed so that the effective clear discharge area through the valve with the float in the open position is not less than the inlet area of the vent pipe to which the valve is connected.

(ii) A hinged closure normally open on the outlet of the return bend, which must close automatically by the force of a submerging wave; or

(iii) Another suitable device acceptable to the Commanding Officer, Marine Safety Center.

(8) Vent outlets from all tanks which may emit flammable or combustible vapors, such as bilge slop tanks and contaminated drain tanks, must be fitted with a single screen of corrosion-resistant wire of at least 30 by 30 mesh, or two screens of at least 20 by 20 mesh spaced not less than one-half inch

(13mm) nor more than 1½ inches (38mm) apart. The clear area through the mesh must not be less than the internal unobstructed area of the required pipe.

(9) Where vents are provided with flame screens, the closure device shall be situated so as not to damage these screens.

(10) The diameter of each vent pipe must not be less than 1½ inches nominal pipe size for fresh water tanks, 2 inches nominal pipe size for water ballast tanks, and 2½ inches nominal pipe size for fuel oil tanks, except that small independent tanks need not have a vent more than 25% greater in cross-sectional area than the fill line.

(11)(i) If a tank may be filled by a pressure head exceeding that for which the tank is designed, the aggregate cross-sectional area of the vents in each tank must be not less than the cross-sectional area of the filling line unless the tank is protected by overflows, in which case the aggregate cross-sectional area of the overflows must be not less than the cross-sectional area of the filling line.

(ii) Provision must be made to guard against liquids rising in the venting system to a height that would exceed the design head of a cargo tank or fuel-oil tank. It may be made by high-level alarms or overflow-control systems or other, equivalent means, together with gauging devices and procedures for filling cargo tanks.

(12) Where deep tanks are intended for the occasional carriage of dry or liquid cargo, a "spectacle" or ring and blank flange may be fitted in the overflow pipe so arranged as not to interfere with venting when the tanks contain oil.

(13) Vents from fresh water or water ballast tanks shall not be connected to a common header with vents from oil or oily ballast tanks.

(b) Tank vents must remain within the watertight subdivision boundaries in which the tanks they vent are located. Where the structural configuration of a vessel makes meeting this requirement impracticable, the Marine Safety Center may permit a tank vent to penetrate a watertight subdivision bulkhead. All tank vents which penetrate watertight subdivision bulkheads must terminate above the weather deck.

[CGFR 68–82, 33 FR 18843, Dec. 18, 1968, as amended by CGD 77–140, 54 FR 40610, Oct. 2, 1989; CGD 83–043, 60 FR 24774, May 10, 1995; CGD 95–012, 60 FR 48050, Sept. 18, 1995]

§ 56.50–90 Sounding devices.

(a) Each tank must be provided with a suitable means of determining liquid level. Except for a main cargo tank on a tank vessel, each integral hull tank and compartment, unless at all times accessible while the vessel is operating, must be fitted with a sounding pipe.

(b) Where sounding pipes terminate below the freeboard deck on cargo vessels, they shall be fitted with gate valves. On passenger vessels, where sounding pipes terminate below the bulkhead deck, they shall be fitted with self-closing gate valves.

(c) Except as allowed by this paragraph, on each vessel constructed on or after June 9, 1995, no sounding pipe used in a fuel-oil tank may terminate in any space where the risk of ignition of spillage from the pipe might arise. None may terminate in a space for passengers or crew. When practicable, none may terminate in a machinery space. When the Commanding Officer, Marine Safety Center, determines it impracticable to avoid terminating a pipe in a machinery space, a sounding pipe may terminate in a machinery space if all the following requirements are met:

(1) In addition to the sounding pipe, the fuel-oil tank has an oil-level gauge complying with paragraph (d) of this section.

(2) The pipe terminates in a place remote from ignition hazards unless precautions are taken such as fitting an effective screen (shield) to prevent the fuel oil, in case of spillage through the end of the pipe, from coming into contact with a source of ignition.

(3) The end of the pipe is fitted with a self-closing blanking device and a small-diameter, self-closing control cock located below the blanking device for the purpose of ascertaining before the blanking device is opened that no fuel oil is present. Provision must be made to ensure that no spillage of fuel oil through the control cock involves an ignition hazard.

(d) On each vessel constructed on or after June 9, 1995, other oil-level gauges may be used instead of sounding pipes if all the following requirements are met:

(1) In a passenger vessel, no such gauge may require penetration below the top of the tank, and neither the failure of a gauge nor an overfilling of the tank may permit release of fuel into the space.

(2) In a cargo vessel, neither the failure of such a gauge nor an overfilling of the tank may permit release of fuel into the space. The use of cylindrical gauge-glasses is prohibited. The use of oil-level gauges with flat glasses and self-closing valves between the gauges and fuel tanks is acceptable.

(e) The upper ends of sounding pipes terminating at the weather deck shall be closed by a screw cap or plug. Great Lakes dry cargo carriers may have the sounding pipes which service ballast water tanks terminate at least 4 inches above the deck if closure is provided by a tight fitting hinged cover making metal-to-metal contact with the hinge on the forward side. Positive means to secure these caps in the closed position shall be provided. Provision shall be made to prevent damage to the vessels' plating by the striking of the sounding rod.

(f) On mobile offshore drilling units where installation of sounding pipes may not be practicable for some tanks, alternate means of determining liquid level may be used if approved by the Commandant.

[CGFR 68–82, 33 FR 18843, Dec. 18, 1968, as amended by CGD 73–251, 43 FR 56800, Dec. 4, 1978; CGD 83–043, 60 FR 24774, May 10, 1995; CGD 95–028, 62 FR 51201, Sept. 30, 1997]

§ 56.50–95 Overboard discharges and shell connections.

(a)(1) All inlets and discharges led through the vessel's side shall be fitted with efficient and accessible means, located as close to the hull penetrations as is practicable, for preventing the accidental admission of water into the vessel either through such pipes or in the event of fracture of such pipes.

(2) The number of scuppers, sanitary discharges, tank overflows, and other similar openings in the vessel's side shall be reduced to a minimum, either by making each discharge serve for as many as possible of the sanitary and other pipes, or in any other satisfactory manner.

(3) In general, when the bulkhead deck is above the freeboard deck, the requirements of this section apply relative to the bulkhead deck. For vessels not assigned load lines, such as certain inland vessels and barges, the weather deck shall be taken as the freeboard deck.

(b)(1) Scuppers and discharge pipes originating at any level and penetrating the shell either more than 17½ inches (450mm) below the freeboard deck or less than 23½ inches (600mm) above the summer load waterline must be provided with an automatic nonreturn valve at the shell. This valve, unless required by paragraph (b)(2) of this section, may be omitted if the piping is not less than Schedule 80 in wall thickness for nominal pipe sizes through 8 inches, Schedule 60 for nominal pipe sizes above 8 inches and below 16 inches, and Schedule 40 for nominal pipe sizes 16 inches and above.

(2) Discharges led through the shell originating either from spaces below the freeboard deck or from within enclosed superstructures and equivalent deckhouses on the freeboard deck as defined in § 42.13–15(i) of subchapter E (Load Lines) of this chapter, shall be fitted with efficient and accessible means for preventing water from passing inboard. Normally each separate discharge shall have one automatic nonreturn valve with a positive means of closing it from a position above the freeboard deck. Where, however, the vertical upward distance from the summer load line to the inboard end of the discharge pipe through which flooding can take place exceed 0.01L, the discharge may have two automatic nonreturn valves without positive means of closing, provided that the inboard valve is always accessible for examination under service conditions. Where that vertical distance exceeds 0.02L a single automatic nonreturn valve without positive means of closing is acceptable. In an installation where the two automatic nonreturn valves are used, the inboard valve must be above the tropical load line. The means for operating the positive action valve shall be

readily accessible and provided with an indicator showing whether the valve is open or closed. A suitable arrangement shall be made to insure the valve is not closed by unauthorized persons, and a notice shall be posted in a conspicuous place at the operating station to the effect that the valve shall not be closed except as required in an emergency.

(3) Where scuppers and drains are installed in superstructures or deckhouses not enclosed as defined in § 42.13–15(j) of subchapter E (Load Lines) of this chapter, they shall be led overboard. Refer to paragraph (b)(1) of this section for any nonreturn valve requirement.

(4) Sanitary pump discharges leading directly overboard or via a holding tank must meet the standards prescribed by this paragraph. The location of the sanitary system openings within the vessel determines whether the requirements of paragraph (b)(2) or (3) of this section are applicable.

(c) Overflow pipes which discharge through the vessel's side must be located as far above the deepest load line as practicable and fitted with valves as required by paragraph (b) of this section. Two automatic nonreturn valves must be used unless it is impracticable to locate the inboard valve in an accessible position, in which case a nonreturn valve with a positive means of closure from a position above the freeboard deck will be acceptable. Overflows which extend at least 30 inches above the freeboard deck before discharging overboard may be fitted with a single automatic nonreturn valve at the vessel's side. Overflow pipes which serve as tank vents must not be fitted with positive means of closure without the specific approval of the Marine Safety Center. Overflow pipes may be vented to the weather.

(d)(1) Sea inlets and discharges, such as used in closed systems required for the operation of main and auxiliary machinery, as in pump connections or scoop injection heat exchanger connections, need not meet the requirements of paragraphs (b) (1) and (2) of this section but instead shall be fitted with a shutoff valve located as near the shell plating as practicable, and may be locally controlled if the valve is located in a manned machinery space. These controls shall be readily accessible above the floor plates and shall be provided with indication showing whether the valve is opened or closed. Manned machinery spaces include the main machinery space and are either attended by the crew or are automated in accordance with part 62 of this subchapter to be comparable to an attended space.

(2) In unmanned machinery spaces, all machinery inlets and discharges as described in paragraph (d)(1) of this section shall be remotely operable from a position above the freeboard deck unless otherwise approved and shall meet the access and marking requirements of paragraph (b)(2) of this section.

(e)(1) Pipes terminating at the shell plating shall be fitted with bends or elbows between the outboard openings and the first rigid connection inboard. In no case shall such pipes be fitted in a direct line between the shell opening and the first inboard connection.

(2) Seachests and other hull fittings shall be of substantial construction and as short as possible. They shall be located as to minimize the possibility of being blocked or obstructed.

(3) The thickness of inlet and discharge connections outboard of the shutoff valves, and exclusive of seachests, must be not less than that of Schedule 80 for nominal pipe sizes through 8 inches, Schedule 60 for nominal pipe sizes above 8 inches and below 16 inches, and Schedule 40 for nominal pipe sizes 16 inches and above.

(f) Valves required by this section and piping system components outboard of such required valves on new vessel installations or replacements in vessels of 150 gross tons and over shall be of a steel, bronze, or ductile cast iron specification listed in Table 56.60–1(a). Lead or other heat sensitive materials having a melting point of 1,700 °F. or less shall not be used in such service, or in any other application where the deterioration of the piping system in the event of fire would give rise to danger of flooding. Brittle materials such as cast iron shall not be used in such service. Where nonmetallic materials are used in a piping system, and shell closures are required by this section, a positive closure metallic valve is required (see also § 56.60–25).

(g) The inboard openings of ash and rubbish-chute discharges shall be fitted with efficient covers. If the inboard opening is located below the freeboard deck, the cover shall be watertight, and in addition, an automatic non-return valve shall be fitted in the chute in any easily accessible position above the deepest load line. Means shall be provided for securing both the cover and the valve when the chute is not in use. When ash-ejectors or similar expelling devices located in the boiler-room have the inboard openings below the deepest load line, they shall be fitted with efficient means for preventing the accidental admission of water. The thickness of pipe for ash ejector discharge shall be not less than Schedule 80.

(h) Where deck drains, soil lines, and sanitary drains discharge through the shell in way of cargo tanks on tank vessels, the valves required by this section shall be located outside the cargo tanks. These valves shall meet the material requirements of paragraph (f) of this section. The piping led through such tanks shall be fitted with expansion bends where required, and shall be of steel pipe having a wall thickness of not less than five-eighths inch, except that the use of suitable corrosion-resistant material of lesser thickness will be given special consideration by the Commandant. All pipe joints within the tanks shall be welded. Soil lines and sanitary drains which pass through cargo tanks shall be provided with non-return valves with positive means of closing or other suitable means for preventing the entrance of gases into living quarters.

(i) Except as provided for in § 58.20–20(c) of this chapter, sea valves must not be held open with locks. Where it is necessary to hold a discharge or intake closed with a lock, either a locking valve may be located inboard of the sea valve, or the design must be such that there is sufficient freedom of motion to fully close the locked sea valve after an event, such as fire damage to the seat, causes significant leakage through the valve. Valves which must be opened in and emergency, such as bilge discharges or fire pump suctions must not be locked closed, whether they are sea valves or not.

[CGFR 68–82, 33 FR 18843; Dec. 18, 1968, as amended by CGFR 69–127, 35 FR 9979, June 17, 1970; CGFR 72–59R, 37 FR 6189, Mar. 25, 1972; CGD 81–030, 53 FR 17837, May 18, 1988; CGD 77–140, 54 FR 40610, Oct. 2, 1989]

§ 56.50–96 Keel cooler installations.

(a) Keel cooler installations shall meet the requirements of § 56.50–95(d)(1) and (2), and (e)(3), and (f) except that shutoff or isolation valves will not be required for the inlet and discharge connections if:

(1) The installation is forward of the collision bulkhead; or,

(2) The installation is integral with the ship's hull such that the cooler tubes are welded directly to the hull of the vessel with the hull forming part of the tube and satisfies all of the following:

(i) The cooler structure is fabricated from material of the same thickness and quality as the hull plating to which it is attached except that in the case of half round pipe lesser thickness may be used if specifically approved by the Commandant. In any case the structure, with the exception of the hull proper, need not exceed three-eighths inch in thickness.

(ii) The flexible connections and all openings internal to the vessel, such as expansion tank vents and fills, in the installation are above the deepest load line and all piping components are Schedule 80 or thicker below the deepest load line.

(iii) Full penetration welds are employed in the fabrication of the structure and its attachment to the hull.

(iv) The forward end of the structure must be faired to the hull such that the horizontal length of the fairing is no less than four times the height of the structure, or be in a protected location such as inside a bow thruster trunk.

[CGFR 68–82, 33 FR 18843, Dec. 18, 1968, as amended by CGFR 72–59R, 37 FR 6189, Mar. 25, 1972; CGD 77–140, 54 FR 40611, Oct. 2, 1989]

§ 56.50-97 Piping for instruments, control, and sampling (modifies 122.3).

(a) Piping for instruments, control, and sampling must comply with paragraph 122.3 of ASME B31.1 (incorporated by reference; see 46 CFR 56.01-2) except that:

(1) Soldered type fittings may not be used.

(2) The outside diameter of takeoff connections may not be less than 0.840 inches for service conditions up to 900 psi or 800 °F., and 1.050 inches for conditions that exceed either of these limits.

[CGFR 68-82, 33 FR 18843, Dec. 18, 1968, as amended by CGFR 69-127, 35 FR 9978, June 17, 1970; CGD 73-254, 40 FR 40165, Sept. 2, 1975; USCG-2003-16630, 73 FR 65178, Oct. 31, 2008]

§ 56.50-103 Fixed oxygen-acetylene distribution piping.

(a) This section applies to fixed piping installed for the distribution of oxygen and acetylene carried in cylinders as vessels stores.

(b) The distribution piping shall be of at least standard wall thickness and shall include a means, located as close to the supply cylinders as possible, of regulating the pressure from the supply cylinders to the suitable pressure at the outlet stations.

(c) Acetylene distribution piping and pipe fittings must be seamless steel. Copper alloys containing less than 65 percent copper may be used in connection with valves, regulators, gages, and other equipment used with acetylene.

(d) Oxygen distribution piping and pipe fittings must be seamless steel or copper.

(e) When more than two cylinders are connected to a manifold, the supply pipe between each cylinder and manifold shall be fitted with a non-return valve.

(f) Except for the cylinder manifolds, acetylene is not to be piped at a pressure in excess of 100 kPa (14.7 psi).

(g) Pipe joints on the low pressure side of the regulators shall be welded.

(h) Branch lines shall not run through unventilated spaces or accommodation spaces.

(i) Relief valves or rupture discs shall be installed as relief devices in the piping system if the maximum design pressure of the piping system can be exceeded. The relief device set pressure shall not exceed the maximum design pressure of the piping system. Relief devices shall discharge to a location in the weather at least 3 m (10 ft) from sources of ignition or openings to spaces or tanks.

(j) Outlet stations are to be provided with suitable protective devices which will prevent the back flow of gas into the supply lines and prevent the passage of flame into the supply lines.

(k) Shutoff valves shall be fitted at each outlet.

[CGD 95-028, 62 FR 51201, Sept. 30, 1997]

§ 56.50-105 Low-temperature piping.

(a) *Class I-L.* Piping systems designated to operate at temperatures below 0 °F. and pressures above 150 pounds per square inch gage shall be of Class I-L. Exceptions to this rule may be found in the individual requirements for specific commodities in subchapters D, I, and O of this chapter. The following requirements for Class I-L piping systems shall be satisfied:

(1) *Materials.* All materials used in low temperature piping systems shall be selected from among those specifications listed in Table 56.50-105 and shall satisfy all of the requirements of the specifications, except that:

(i) The minimum service temperature as defined in § 54.25-10(a)(2) of this subchapter shall not be colder than that shown in Table 56.50-105; and

(ii) The material shall be tested for low temperature toughness using the Charpy V-notch specimen of ASTM E 23 (incorporated by reference, see § 56.01-2), "Notched Bar Impact Testing of Metallic Materials", Type A, Figure 4. The toughness testing requirements of subpart 54.05 of this subchapter shall be satisfied for each particular product form. Charpy V-notch tests shall be conducted at temperatures not warmer than 10 °F. below the minimum service temperature of the design, except that for service temperatures of −320 °F. and below, the impact test may be conducted at the service temperature. The minimum average energy shall not be less than that shown in Table 56.50-105. In the case of steels conforming to the specifications of Table 54.25-20(a) of this subchapter the minimum lateral expansion shall not be less than that required in § 54.25-20 of this subchapter.

§ 56.50-105

The minimum energy permitted for a single specimen and the minimum subsize energies shall be those obtained by multiplying the average energy shown in Table 56.50–105 by the applicable fraction shown in Table 56.50–105(a).

TABLE 56.50–105(a)—CHARPY V-NOTCH ENERGY MULTIPLYING FACTORS

Charpy V-notch specimen size [1]	Factor for minimum energy, average of 3 specimens [1]	Factor for minimum energy single specimen [1]
10×10 mm	1	2/3
10×7.5 mm	5/6	5/9
10×5.0 mm	2/3	4/9
10×2.5 mm	1/2	1/3

[1] Straight line interpolation for intermediate values is permitted.

(iii) Steels equivalent to those listed in Table 56.50–105 of this part, but not produced according to a particular ASTM specification, may be used only with the prior consent of the Marine Safety Center. Steels differing in chemical composition, mechanical properties or heat treatments from those specified may be specially approved by the Marine Safety Center. Similarly, aluminum alloys and other nonferrous materials not covered in Table 56.50–105 of this part may be specifically approved by the Marine Safety Center for service at any low temperature. There are restrictions on the use of certain materials in this part and in subchapter O of this chapter.

(2) *Piping weldments.* Piping weldments shall be fabricated to satisfy the requirements of § 57.03–1(b) of this subchapter in addition to subpart 56.70. Toughness testing of production weldments for low temperature piping systems and assemblies is not required.

(3) *Postweld heat treatment.* All piping weldments shall be postweld heat treated for stress relief in accordance with the procedures of subpart 56.85. The only exceptions to this requirement are for materials which do not require postweld heat treatment as shown in Table 56.85–10. Relief from postweld heat treatment shall not be dependent upon pipe thickness or weld joint type.

(4) *Nonacceptable joints.* Single welded butt joints with backing ring left in place, socket welds, slip-on flanges, pipe joining sleeves, and threaded joints shall not be used, except in small diameter instrument lines.

(5) *Other requirements.* All other requirements of this part for Class I piping apply to Class I-L piping. Pressure testing must comply with subpart 56.97 of this part, and nondestructive testing of circumferentially welded joints must comply with § 56.95–10. Seamless tubular products must be used except that, when the service pressure does not exceed 1724 KPa (250 psi), the Commanding Officer, Marine Safety Center, may give special consideration to appropriate grades of piping and tubing that are welded without the addition of filler metal in the root pass. Each production procedure and quality-control program for welded products must be acceptable to the Officer in Charge, Marine Inspection.

(b) *Class II-L.* Piping systems designed to operate at temperatures below 0 °F. and pressures not higher than 150 pounds per square inch gage shall be of Class II-L. Exceptions to this rule may be found in the individual requirements for specific commodities in subchapter D (Tank Vessels) and I (Cargo and Miscellaneous Vessels) of this chapter. The following requirements for Class II-L piping systems shall be satisfied:

(1) Materials must be the same as those required by paragraph (a)(1) of this section except that pipe and tubing of appropriate grades welded without the addition of a filler metal may be used. The Commandant may give special consideration to tubular products welded with the addition of filler metal.

(2) Piping weldments shall be fabricated to satisfy the requirements of § 57.03–1(b) of this subchapter in addition to subpart 56.70. Toughness testing of production weldments for low temperature piping systems and assemblies is not required.

(3) All piping weldments shall be postweld heat treated for stress relief in accordance with the procedures of subpart 56.85. The only exceptions to this requirement are for materials which do not require postweld heat treatment as shown in Table 56.85–10 and for socket weld joints and slip-on flange weld attachments where the

Coast Guard, Dept. of Homeland Security § 56.50-105

weld thickness does not exceed that exempted by this table. Otherwise, relief from post-weld heat treatment shall not be dependent upon pipe thickness or weld joint type.

(4) Socket welds in nominal sizes above 3 inches, slip-on flanges in nominal sizes above 4 inches, and threaded joints in sizes above 1 inch shall not be used.

(5) Pressure testing must comply with subpart 56.97, and nondestructive testing of welded joints must comply with § 56.95–10.

(6) All other requirements contained in this part for Class II piping shall be applicable to Class II-L systems, except that § 56.70–15(b)(3)(iv) shall not apply.

TABLE 56.50–105—ACCEPTABLE MATERIALS AND TOUGHNESS TEST CRITERIA [2]

Product form	ASTM specification [3]	Grade [4]	Minimum service temperature	Minimum avg Charpy V notch energy
Pipe		1	−30 °F	20 ft. lb.
		3	−150 °F	25 ft. lb.
Tube (carbon and low alloy steels).	A–333 and A–334	4 (A–333 only)	−100 °F	25 ft. lb.
		6	−30 °F	20 ft. lb.
		7	−100 °F	25 ft. lb.
		8	−320 °F	Refer to § 54.25–20 of this subchapter.
Pipe (Austenitic stainless steel).	A–312	All Grades	No limit	Austenitic stainless steel piping need be impact tested only when toughness tests are specified in subpart 54.25 of this subchapter for plating of the same alloy designation. When such toughness tests are required, the minimum average energy is 25 ft. lb.
Wrought welding fittings (carbon and low alloy steels).	A–420	WPL1	−30 °F	20 ft. lb.
		WPL3	−150 °F	25 ft. lb.
		WPL4	−100 °F	25 ft. lb.
Forged or rolled flanges, forged fittings, valves and pressure parts (carbon and low alloy steels).	A–350 [1]	LF1	−30 °F	20 ft. lb.
		LF2	−30 °F	20 ft. lb.
		LF3	−150 °F	25 ft. lb.
		LF4	−100 °F	25 ft. lb.
Forged or rolled flanges, forged fittings, valves and pressure parts (high alloy steels).	A–182	Austenitic grades only (304, 304H, 304L, 310, 316, 316H, 316L, 321, 321H, 347, 347H, 348, 348H).	No limit	These products need be impact tested only when toughness tests are specified in subpart 54.25 of this subchapter for plating of the same alloy designation. When such toughness tests are required, the minimum average energy is 25 ft. lb.
Forged flanges, fittings, and valves (9% nickel).	A–522	9% Ni	−320 °F	Refer to § 54.25–20 of this subchapter.
Castings for valves and pressure parts (carbon and low alloy steels).	A–352 [1]	LCB	−30 °F	20 ft. lb.
		LC1	−50 °F	20 ft. lb.
		LC2	−100 °F	25 ft. lb.
		LC3	−150 °F	25 ft. lb.
Castings for valves and pressure parts (high alloy steel).	A–351	Austenitic grades CF3, CF3A, CF8, CF8A, CF3M, CF8M, CF8C, CK20 only.	No limit, except −325 °F for grades CF8C and CK20.	No toughness testing required except for service temperatures colder than −425 °F for grades CF3, CF3A, CF8, CF8A, CF3M, and CF8M. 25 ft. lb.

§ 56.50-110

TABLE 56.50–105—ACCEPTABLE MATERIALS AND TOUGHNESS TEST CRITERIA [2]—Continued

Product form	ASTM specification [3]	Grade [4]	Minimum service temperature	Minimum avg Charpy V notch energy
Bolting	A-320	L7, L9, L10, L43	-150 °F	average must be attained in these tests. 20 ft. lb.
		B8D, B8T, B8F, B8M	-325 °F	No test required.
		2B8, B8C	No limit	No test required, except for service temperatures colder than -425 °F. In such case the minimum average energy is 25 ft. lb.
Nuts, bolting	A-194	4	-150 °F	20 ft. lb.
		8T, 8F	-325 °F	No test required.
		8, 8C	No limit	Same requirement as comparable grades (B8, B8C) of bolting listed above.

[1] Quench and temper heat treatment may be permitted when specifically authorized by the Commandant. In those cases the minimum average Charpy V-notch energy shall be specially designated by the Commandant.
[2] Other material specifications for product forms acceptable under part 54 for use at low temperatures may also be used for piping systems provided the applicable toughness requirements of this Table are also met.
[3] Any repair method must be acceptable to the Commandant CG-ENG, and welding repairs, as well as fabrication welding must be in accordance with part 57 of this chapter.
[4] The acceptability of several alloys for low temperature service is not intended to suggest acceptable resistance to marine corrosion. The selection of alloys for any particular shipboard location must take corrosion resistance into account and be approved by the Marine Safety Center.

NOTE: The ASTM standards listed in table 56.50–105 are incorporated by reference; see 46 CFR 56.01–2.

[CGFR 68–82, 33 FR 18843, Dec. 18, 1968, as amended by CGFR 72–59R, 37 FR 6189, 6190, Mar. 25, 1972; CGD 73–254, 40 FR 40165, Sept. 2, 1975; CG 79–108, 43 FR 46545, Oct. 10, 1978; CGD 74–289, 44 FR 26008, May 3, 1979; CGD 77–140, 54 FR 40611, Oct. 2, 1989; CGD 83–043, 60 FR 24775, May 10, 1995; USCG–2000–7790, 65 FR 58460, Sept. 29, 2000; USCG–2003–16630, 73 FR 65178, Oct. 31, 2008; USCG–2009–0702, 74 FR 49228, Sept. 25, 2009; USCG–2012–0832, 77 FR 59777, Oct. 1, 2012]

§ 56.50–110 Diving support systems.

(a) In addition to the requirements of this part, piping for diving installations which is permanently installed on the vessel must meet the requirements of subpart B (Commercial Diving Operations) of part 197 of this chapter.

(b) Piping for diving installations which is not permanently installed on the vessel need not meet the requirements of this part, but must meet the requirements of subpart B of part 197 of this chapter.

(c) Piping internal to a pressure vessel for human occupancy (PVHO) need not meet the requirements of this part, but must meet the requirements of subpart B of part 197 of this chapter.

[CGD 76–009, 43 FR 53683, Nov. 16, 1978]

Subpart 56.60—Materials

§ 56.60–1 Acceptable materials and specifications (replaces 123 and Table 126.1 in ASME B31.1).

(a)(1) The material requirements in this subpart shall be followed in lieu of those in 123 in ASME B31.1 (incorporated by reference; see 46 CFR 56.01–2).

(2) Materials used in piping systems must be selected from the specifications that appear in Table 56.60–1(a) of this section or 46 CFR 56.60–2, Table 56.60–2(a), or they may be selected from the material specifications of sections I or VIII of the ASME Boiler and Pressure Vessel Code (both incorporated by reference; see 46 CFR 56.01–2) if not prohibited by a regulation of this subchapter dealing with the particular

Coast Guard, Dept. of Homeland Security §56.60-1

section of the ASME Boiler and Pressure Vessel Code. Table 56.60–1(a) of this section contains only pipe, tubing, and fitting specifications. Determination of acceptability of plate, forgings, bolting, nuts, and castings may be made by reference to the ASME Boiler and Pressure Vessel Code as previously described. Additionally, accepted materials for use as piping system components appear in 46 CFR 56.60–2, Table 56.60–2(a). Materials conforming to specifications not described in this subparagraph must receive the specific approval of the Marine Safety Center before being used. Materials listed in Table 126.1 of ASME B31.1 are not accepted unless specifically permitted by this paragraph.

(b) Components made in accordance with the commercial standards listed in Table 56.60–1(b) of this section and made of materials complying with paragraph (a) this section may be used in piping systems within the limitations of the standards and within any further limitations specified in this subchapter.

NOTE: Table 56.60–1(a) replaces Table 126.1 in ASME B31.1 and sets forth specifications of pipes, tubing, and fittings intended for use in piping-systems. The first column lists acceptable standards from ASTM (all incorporated by reference; see 46 CFR 56.01–2); the second lists those from ASME (all incorporated by reference; see 46 CFR 56.01–2). The Coast Guard will consider use of alternative pipes, tubing, and fittings when it receives certification of their mechanical properties. Without this certification it will restrict use of such alternatives to piping-systems inside heat exchangers that ensure containment of the material inside pressure shells.

TABLE 56.60–1(a)—ADOPTED SPECIFICATIONS AND STANDARDS

ASTM standards	ASME standards	Notes
Pipe, seamless:		
A 106 Carbon steel	ASME B31.1.	
A 335 Ferritic alloys	ASME B31.1.	
A 376 Austenitic alloys	ASME B31.1	([1]).
Pipe, seamless and welded:		
A 53 Types S, F, and E steel pipe	ASME B31.1	([2 3 4]).
A 312 Austenitic steel (welded with no filler metal).	ASME B31.1	([1 4]).
A 333 Low temperature steel pipe	Sec. VIII of the ASME Boiler and Pressure Vessel Code.	([5]).
Pipe, welded:		
A 134 Fusion welded steel plate pipe	See footnote 7	([7]).
A 135 ERW pipe	ASME B31.1	([3]).
A 139 Grade B only, fusion welded steel pipe.	ASME B31.1	([8]).
A 358 Electric fusion welded pipe, high temperature, austenitic.	ASME B31.1	([1 4 9]).
Pipe, forged and bored:		
A 369 Ferritic alloy	ASME B31.1.	
Pipe, centrifugally cast:	(None applicable)	([1 9])
Tube, seamless:		
A 179 Carbon steel heat exchanger and condenser tubes.	UCS23, Sec. VIII of the ASME Boiler and Pressure Vessel Code.	([11]).
A 192 Carbon steel boiler tubes	PG23.1, Sec. I of the ASME Boiler and Pressure Vessel Code.	([10]).
A 210 Medium carbon boiler tubes	PG23.1, Sec. I of the ASME Boiler and Pressure Vessel Code.	
A 213 Ferritic and austenitic boiler tubes.	PG23.1, Sec. I of the ASME Boiler and Pressure Vessel Code.	([1]).
Tube, seamless and welded:		
A 268 Seamless and ERW ferritic stainless tubing.	PG23.1, Sec. I of the ASME Boiler and Pressure Vessel Code.	([4]).
A 334 Seamless and welded (no added filler metal) carbon and low alloy tubing for low temperature.	UCS23, Sec. VIII of the ASME Boiler and Pressure Vessel Code.	([4 5]).
Tube, welded:		
A 178 (Grades A and C only) ERW boiler tubes.	PG23.1, Sec. I of the ASME Boiler and Pressure Vessel Code.	([10] Grade A) ([4]).
A 214 ERW heat exchanger and condenser tubes.	UCS27, Sec. VIII of the ASME Boiler and Pressure Vessel Code.	
A 226 ERW boiler and superheater tubes.	PG23.1, Sec. I of the ASME Boiler and Pressure Vessel Code.	([4 10]).
A 249 Welded austenitic boiler and heat exchanger tubes (no added filler metal).	PG23.1, Sec. I of the ASME Boiler and Pressure Vessel Code.	([1 4]).

§ 56.60-1

TABLE 56.60–1(a)—ADOPTED SPECIFICATIONS AND STANDARDS—Continued

ASTM standards	ASME standards	Notes
Wrought fittings (factory made):		
A 234 Carbon and ferritic alloys	Conforms to applicable American National Standards (ASME B16.9 and ASME B16.11).	([12]).
A 403 Austenitic alloys	......do	([12]).
A 420 Low temperature carbon and steel alloy.	......do	([12]).
Castings,[13] iron:		
A 47 Malleable iron	Conform to applicable American National Standards or refer to UCI–23 or UCD–23, Sec. VIII of the ASME Boiler and Pressure Vessel Code.	([14]).
A 126 Gray iron	......do	([14]).
A 197 Malleable iron	......do	([14]).
A 395 Ductile iron	UCD–23, Sec. VIII of the ASME Boiler and Pressure Vessel Code.	([14]).
A 536 Ductile iron	See footnote 20	([20]).
Nonferrous Materials [15]		
Pipe, seamless:		
B 42 Copper	UNF23, Sec. VIII of the ASME Boiler and Pressure Vessel Code.	([16]).
B 43 Red brass	......do.	
B 241 Aluminum alloy	......do.	
Pipe and tube, seamless:		
B 161 Nickel	......do.	
B 165 Nickel-copper	......do.	
B 167 Ni-Cr-Fe	......do.	
B 315 Copper-silicon	......do.	
Tube, seamless:		
B 68 Copper	See footnote 17	([16 17 18]).
B 75 Copper	UNF23, Sec. VIII of the ASME Boiler and Pressure Vessel Code.	([16]).
B 88 Copper	See footnote 17	([16 17]).
B 111 Copper and copper alloy	UNF23, Sec. VIII of the ASME Boiler and Pressure Vessel Code.	
B 210 Aluminum alloy, drawn	......do.	
B 234 Aluminum alloy, drawn	......do.	
B 280 Copper tube for refrigeration service.	See footnote 17	([16 17]).
Welding fittings:		
B 361 Wrought aluminum welding fittings.	Shall meet ASME Standards.	

ASTM specification	Minimum tensile	Longitudinal joint efficiency	P No.	Allowable stresses (p.s.i.)
A 134:				
Grade 285A	45,000	0.80	1	$11,250 \times 0.8 = 9,000$.
Grade 285B	50,000	0.80	1	$12,500 \times 0.8 = 10,000$.
Grade 285C	55,000	0.80	1	$13,750 \times 0.8 = 11,000$.

Note: When using 104.1.2 in ASME B31.1 to compute wall thickness, the stress shown here shall be applied as though taken from the stress tables. An additional factor of 0.8 may be required by § 56.07–10(c) and (e).

[1] For austenitic materials where two sets of stresses appear, use the lower values.

[2] Type F (Furnace welded, using open hearth, basic oxygen, or electric furnace only) limited to Class II applications with a maximum service temperature of 450 °F. Type E (ERW grade) limited to maximum service temperature of 650 °F, or less.

[3] Electric resistance welded pipe or tubing of this specification may be used to a maximum design pressure of 350 pounds per square inch gage.

[4] Refer to limitations on use of welded grades given in § 56.60–2(b).

[5] Use generally considered for Classes I–L and II–L applications. For Class I–L service only, the seamless grade is permitted. For other service refer to footnote 4 and to § 56.50–105.

[6] Furnace lap or furnace butt grades only. Limited to Class II applications only where the maximum service temperature is 450 °F, or less.

[7] Limited to Grades 285A, 285B, and 285C only (straight and spiral seam). Limited to Class II applications only where maximum service temperature is 300 °F or less for straight seam, and 200 °F or less for spiral seam.

[8] Limited to Class II applications where the maximum service temperature is 300 °F or less for straight seam and 200 °F or less for spiral seam.

[9] For Class I applications only the Class I Grade of the specification may be used.

[10] When used in piping systems, a certificate shall be furnished by the manufacturer certifying that the mechanical properties at room temperature specified in ASTM A 520 (incorporated by reference; see 46 CFR 56.01–2) have been met. Without this certification, use is limited to applications within heat exchangers.

[11] When used in piping systems, a certificate shall be furnished by the manufacturer certifying that the mechanical properties for A192 in ASTM A 520 have been met. Without this certification, use is limited to applications within heat exchangers.

[12] Hydrostatic testing of these fittings is not required but all fittings shall be capable of withstanding without failure, leakage, or impairment of serviceability, a hydrostatic test of 1½ times the designated rating pressure.

Coast Guard, Dept. of Homeland Security § 56.60-1

[13] Other acceptable iron castings are in UCI–23 and UCD–23 of section VIII of the ASME Boiler and Pressure Vessel Code. (See also §§ 56.60–10 and 56.60–15.) Acceptable castings of materials other than cast iron may be found in sections I or VIII of the ASME Boiler and Pressure Vessel Code.

[14] Acceptable when complying with American National Standards Institute standards. Ductile iron is acceptable for temperatures not exceeding 650 °F. For pressure temperature limitations refer to UCD–3 of section VIII of the ASME Boiler and Pressure Vessel Code. Other grades of cast iron are acceptable for temperatures not exceeding 450 °F. For pressure temperature limitations refer to UCI–3 of section VIII of the ASME Boiler and Pressure Vessel Code.

[15] For limitations in use refer to §§ 56.10–5(c) and 56.60–20.

[16] Copper pipe must not be used for hot oil systems except for short flexible connections at burners. Copper pipe must be annealed before installation in Class I piping systems. See also §§ 56.10–5(c) and 56.60–20.

[17] The stress values shall be taken from UNF23 of section VIII of the ASME Boiler and Pressure Vessel Code for B75 annealed and light drawn temper as appropriate.

[18] B68 shall be acceptable if provided with a mill hydrostatic or eddy current test.

[19] Centrifugally cast pipe must be specifically approved by the Marine Safety Center.

[20] Limited to pipe fittings and valves. See 46 CFR 56.60–15(d) for additional information.

TABLE 56.60–1(b)—ADOPTED STANDARDS APPLICABLE TO PIPING SYSTEMS (REPLACES TABLE 126.1)

American National Standards Institute (all incorporated by reference; see 46 CFR 56.01–2)	
ANSI/ASME B1.1	1982 Unified Inch Screw Threads (UN and UNR Thread Form).
ANSI/ASME B1.20.1	1983 Pipe Threads, General Purpose (Inch).
ANSI/ASME B1.20.3	1976 (Reaffirmed 1982) Dryseal Pipe Threads (Inch).
ANSI/ASME B16.15	1985 [Reaffirmed 1994] Cast Bronze Threaded Fittings, Classes 125 and 250.

American Society of Mechanical Engineers (ASME) International (all incorporated by reference; see 46 CFR 56.01–2)	
ASME B16.1	1998 Cast Iron Pipe Flanges and Flanged Fittings, Classes 25, 125, 250.
ASME B16.3	1998 Malleable Iron Threaded Fittings, Classes 150 and 300.
ASME B16.4	1998 Gray Iron Threaded Fittings, Classes 125 and 250.
ASME B16.5	2003 Pipe Flanges and Flanged Fittings NPS ½ Through NPS 24 Metric/Inch Standard.[3]
ASME B16.9	2003 Factory-Made Wrought Steel Buttwelding Fittings.
ASME B16.10	2000 Face-to-Face and End-to-End Dimensions of Valves.
ASME B16.11	2001 Forged Fittings, Socket-Welding and Threaded.
ASME B16.14	1991 Ferrous Pipe Plugs, Bushings, and Locknuts with Pipe Threads.
ASME B16.18	2001 Cast Copper Alloy Solder Joint Pressure Fittings.[4]
ASME B16.20	1998 (Revision of ASME B16.20 1993) Metallic Gaskets for Pipe Flanges: Ring-Joint, Spiral-Wound, and Jacketed.
ASME B16.21	2005 Nonmetallic Flat Gaskets for Pipe Flanges.
ASME B16.22	2001 Wrought Copper and Copper Alloy Solder Joint Pressure Fittings.[4]
ASME B16.23	2002 Cast Copper Alloy Solder Joint Drainage Fittings: DWV.[4]
ASME B16.24	2001 Cast Copper Alloy Pipe Flanges and Flanged Fittings: Class 150, 300, 400, 600, 900, 1500, and 2500.[3]
ASME B16.25	2003 Buttwelding Ends.
ASME B16.28	1994 Wrought Steel Buttwelding Short Radius Elbows and Returns.[4]
ASME B16.29	2007 Wrought Copper and Wrought Copper Alloy Solder Joint Drainage Fittings-DWV.[4]
ASME B16.34	1996 Valves—Flanged, Threaded, and Welding End.[3]
ASME B16.42	1998 Ductile Iron Pipe Flanges and Flanged Fittings, Classes 150 and 300.
ASME B18.2.1	1996 Square and Hex Bolts and Screws (Inch Series).
ASME/ANSI B18.2.2	1987 Square and Hex Nuts (Inch Series).

§ 56.60-1

TABLE 56.60-1(b)—ADOPTED STANDARDS APPLICABLE TO PIPING SYSTEMS (REPLACES TABLE 126.1)—Continued

ASME B31.1	2001 Power Piping ASME Code for Pressure Piping, B31.
ASME B36.10M	2004 Welded and Seamless Wrought Steel Pipe.
ASME B36.19M	2004 Stainless Steel Pipe.

American Society for Testing and Materials (ASTM) (all incorporated by reference; see 46 CFR 56.01–2)

ASTM F 682	Standard Specification for Wrought Carbon Steel Sleeve-Type Pipe Couplings.
ASTM F 1006	Standard Specification for Entrainment Separators for Use in Marine Piping Applications.[4]
ASTM F 1007	Standard Specification for Pipe-Line Expansion Joints of the Packed Slip Type for Marine Application.
ASTM F 1020	Standard Specification for Line-Blind Valves for Marine Applications.
ASTM F 1120	Standard Specification for Circular Metallic Bellows Type Expansion Joints for Piping Applications.[4]
ASTM F 1123	Standard Specification for Non-Metallic Expansion Joints.
ASTM F 1139	Standard Specification for Steam Traps and Drains.
ASTM F 1172	Standard Specification for Fuel Oil Meters of the Volumetric Positive Displacement Type.
ASTM F 1173	Standard Specification for Thermosetting Resin Fiberglass Pipe and Fittings to be Used for Marine Applications.
ASTM F 1199	Standard Specification for Cast (All Temperature and Pressures) and Welded Pipe Line Strainers (150 psig and 150 Degrees F Maximum).
ASTM F 1200	Standard Specification for Fabricated (Welded) Pipe Line Strainers (Above 150 psig and 150 Degrees F.)
ASTM F 1201	Standard Specification for Fluid Conditioner Fittings in Piping Applications above 0 Degrees F.

Expansion Joint Manufacturers Association Inc. (incorporated by reference; see 46 CFR 56.01–2)

Standards of the Expansion Joint Manufacturers Association, 1980

Fluid Controls Institute Inc. (incorporated by reference; see 46 CFR 56.01–2)

FCI 69–1	Pressure Rating Standard for Steam Traps.

Manufacturers' Standardization Society of the Valve and Fittings Industry, Inc. (all incorporated by reference; see 46 CFR 56.01–2)[4]

SP–6	Standard Finishes for Contact Faces of Pipe Flanges and Connecting-End Flanges of Valves and Fittings.
SP–9	Spot Facing for Bronze, Iron and Steel Flanges.
SP–25	Standard Marking System for Valves, Fittings, Flanges and Unions.
SP–44	Steel Pipe Line Flanges.[4]
SP–45	Bypass and Drain Connection Standard.
SP–51	Class 150LW Corrosion Resistant Cast Flanges and Flanged Fittings.[4]
SP–53	Quality Standard for Steel Castings and Forgings for Valves, Flanges and Fittings and Other Piping Components—Magnetic Particle Examination Method.

Coast Guard, Dept. of Homeland Security §56.60–2

TABLE 56.60–1(b)—ADOPTED STANDARDS APPLICABLE TO PIPING SYSTEMS (REPLACES TABLE 126.1)—Continued

SP–55	Quality Standard for Steel Castings for Valves, Flanges and Fittings and Other Piping Components—Visual Method.
SP–58	Pipe Hangers and Supports—Materials, Design and Manufacture.
SP–61	Pressure Testing of Steel Valves.
SP–67	Butterfly Valves.[2][4]
SP–69	Pipe Hangers and Supports—Selection and Application.
SP–72	Ball Valves with Flanged or Butt-Welding Ends for General Service.[4]
SP–73	Brazing Joints for Copper and Copper Pressure Fittings.
SP–83	Class 3000 Steel Pipe Unions, Socket-Welding and Threaded.

[1] [Reserved]
[2] In addition, for bronze valves, adequacy of body shell thickness shall be satisfactory to the Marine Safety Center. Refer to §56.60–10 of this part for cast-iron valves.
[3] Mill or manufacturer's certification is not required, except where a needed portion of the required marking is deleted because of size or is absent because of age of existing stocks.
[4] Because this standard offers the option of several materials, some of which are not generally acceptable to the Coast Guard, compliance with the standard does not necessarily indicate compliance with these rules. The marking on the component or the manufacturer or mill certificate must indicate the specification or grade of the materials as necessary to fully identify the materials. The materials must comply with the requirements in this subchapter governing the particular application.

[USCG–2003–16630, 73 FR 65179, Oct. 31, 2008]

§56.60–2 Limitations on materials.

Welded pipe and tubing. The following restrictions apply to the use of welded pipe and tubing specifications when utilized in piping systems, and not when utilized in heat exchanger, boiler, pressure vessel, or similar components:

(a) *Longitudinal joint.* Wherever possible, the longitudinal joint of a welded pipe shall not be pierced with holes for branch connections or other purposes.

(b) *Class II.* Use unlimited except as restricted by maximum temperature or pressure specified in Table 56.60–1(a) or by the requirements contained in §56.10–5(b) of this chapter.

(c) *Class I.* (1) For those specifications in which a filler metal is used, the following applies to the material as furnished prior to any fabrication:

(i) For use in service above 800 °F. full welding procedure qualifications by the Coast Guard are required. See part 57 of this subchapter.

(ii) Ultrasonic examination as required by item S–6 in ASTM A 376 (incorporated by reference; see 46 CFR 56.01–2) shall be certified as having been met in all applications except where 100 percent radiography is a requirement of the particular material specification.

(2) For those specifications in which no filler material is used in the welding process, the ultrasonic examination as required by item S–6 in ASTM A–376 shall be certified as having been met for service above 800 °F.

TABLE 56.60–2(a)—ADOPTED SPECIFICATIONS NOT LISTED IN THE ASME BOILER AND PRESSURE VESSEL CODE*

ASTM specifications	Source of allowable stress	Notes
Ferrous Materials [1]		
Bar stock:		
A 276	See footnote 4	([4]).
(Grades 304–A, 304L–A, 310–A, 316–A, 316L–A, 321–A, 347–A, and 348–A).		
A 575 and A 576.		
(Grades 1010–1030)	See footnote 2	([2][3]).

§ 56.60-3

TABLE 56.60-2(a)—ADOPTED SPECIFICATIONS NOT LISTED IN THE ASME BOILER AND PRESSURE VESSEL CODE *—Continued

ASTM specifications	Source of allowable stress	Notes
Nonferrous Materials		
Bar stock:		
B 16 (soft and half hard tempers)	See footnote 5	([5] [7]).
B 21 (alloys A, B, and C)	See footnote 8	([8]).
B 124:		
Alloy 377	See footnotes 5 and 9	([5] [9]).
Alloy 464	See footnote 8	([8] [10]).
Alloy 655	See footnote 11	([11]).
Alloy 642	See footnote 12	([7] [12]).
Alloy 630	See footnote 13	([7] [13]).
Alloy 485	See footnote 8	([8] [10]).
Forgings:		
B 283 (forging brass)	See footnotes 5 and 9	([5] [9]).
Castings:		
B 26	See footnotes 5, 14, and 15	([5] [14,15]).
B 85	See footnotes 5, 14, and 15	([5] [14,15]).

*Note: Table 56.60–2(a) is a listing of adopted bar stock and nonferrous forging and casting specifications not listed in the ASME Boiler and Pressure Vessel Code. Particular attention should be given to the supplementary testing requirements and service limitations contained in the footnotes. All ASTM standards referred to in Table 56.60–2(a) and its footnotes are incorporated by reference (see 46 CFR 56.01–2).

[1] For limitations in use refer to 46 CFR 56.60–5.

[2] Allowable stresses shall be the same as those listed in UCS23 of section VIII of the ASME Boiler and Pressure Vessel Code (incorporated by reference; see 46 CFR 56.01–2) for SA–675 material of equivalent tensile strength.

[3] Physical testing shall be performed as for material manufactured to ASME SA–675 (incorporated by reference, see 46 CFR 56.01–2), except that the bend test shall not be required.

[4] Allowable stresses shall be the same as those listed in UCS23 of section VIII of the ASME Boiler and Pressure Vessel Code for the corresponding SA–182 material.

[5] Limited to air and hydraulic service with a maximum design temperature of 150 °F. The material must not be used for salt water service or other fluids that may cause dezincification or stress corrosion cracking.

[6] [Reserved]

[7] An ammonia vapor test, in accordance with ASTM B 858M–95 shall be performed on a representative model of each finished product design.

[8] Allowable stresses shall be the same as those listed in UNF23 of section VIII of the ASME Boiler and Pressure Vessel Code for SB–171, naval brass.

[9] An ammonia vapor test, in accordance with ASTM B 858M, shall be performed on a representative model for each finished product design. Tension tests shall be performed to determine tensile strength, yield strength, and elongation. Minimum values shall be those listed in Table 3 of ASTM B 283.

[10] Physical testing, including mercurous nitrate test, shall be performed as for material manufactured to ASTM B 21.

[11] Physical testing shall be performed as for material manufactured to ASTM B 96. Allowable stresses shall be the same as those listed in UNF23 of section VIII of the ASME Boiler and Pressure Vessel Code for SB–96 and shall be limited to a maximum allowable temperature of 212 °F.

[12] Physical testing shall be performed as for material manufactured to ASTM B 171, alloy D. Allowable stresses shall be the same as those listed in UNF23 of section VIII of the ASME Boiler and Pressure Vessel Code for SB–171, aluminum bronze D.

[13] Physical testing shall be performed as for material manufactured to ASTM B 171, alloy E. Allowable stresses shall be the same as those listed in UNF23 of section VIII of the ASME Boiler and Pressure Vessel Code for SB–171, aluminum bronze, alloy E.

[14] Tension tests shall be performed to determine tensile strength, yield strength, and elongation. Minimum values shall be those listed in table X–2 of ASTM B 85.

[15] Those alloys with a maximum copper content of 0.6 percent or less shall be acceptable under this specification. Cast aluminum shall not be welded or brazed.

[CGFR 68–82, 33 FR 18843, Dec. 18, 1968, as amended by CGFR 69–127, 35 FR 9978, June 17, 1970; CGD 72–104R, 37 FR 14233, July 18, 1972; CGD 73–248, 39 FR 30839, Aug. 26, 1974; CGD 73–254, 40 FR 40165, Sept. 2, 1975; CGD 77–140, 54 FR 40612, Oct. 2, 1989; CGD 95–012, 60 FR 48050, Sept. 18, 1995; CGD 95–027, 61 FR 26001, May 23, 1996; CGD 95–028, 62 FR 51201, Sept. 30, 1997; USCG–1998–4442, 63 FR 52190, Sept. 30, 1998; USCG–1999–5151, 64 FR 67180, Dec. 1, 1999; USCG–2003–16630, 73 FR 65182, Oct. 31, 2008]

§ 56.60-3 Ferrous materials.

(a) Ferrous pipe used for salt water service must be protected against corrosion by hotdip galvanizing or by the use of extra heavy schedule material.

(b) (Reproduces 124.2.C) Carbon or alloy steel having carbon content of more than 0.35 percent shall not be used in welded construction, nor be shaped by oxygen-cutting process or other thermal-cutting process.

[CGD 73–254, 40 FR 40165, Sept. 2, 1975, as amended by USCG–2003–16630, 73 FR 65183, Oct. 31, 2008]

§ 56.60-5 Steel (High temperature applications).

(a) (Reproduces 124.2.A.) Upon prolonged exposure to temperatures above 775 °F (412 °C), the carbide phase of plain carbon steel, plain nickel-alloy steel, carbon-manganese-alloy steel, manganese-vanadium-alloy steel, and carbon-silicon steel may convert to graphite.

(b) (Reproduces 124.2.B.) Upon prolonged exposure to temperatures above 875 °F (468 °C), the carbide phase of alloy steels, such as carbon-molybdenum, manganese-molybdenum-vanadium, manganese-chromium-vanadium, and chromium-vanadium, may convert to graphite.

(c) [Reserved]

(d) The design temperature of a piping system employing one or more of the materials listed in paragraphs (a), (b), and (c) of this section shall not exceed the lowest graphitization temperature specified for materials used.

[CGFR 68–82, 33 FR 18843, Dec. 18, 1968, as amended by CGFR 69–127, 35 FR 9978, June 17, 1970; CGD 72–104R, 37 FR 14233, July 18, 1972; CGD 73–248, 39 FR 30839, Aug. 26, 1974; CGD 73–254, 40 FR 40165, Sept. 2, 1975; USCG–2003–16630, 73 FR 65183, Oct. 31, 2008]

§ 56.60-10 Cast iron and malleable iron.

(a) The low ductility of cast iron and malleable iron should be recognized and the use of these metals where shock loading may occur should be avoided. Cast iron and malleable iron components shall not be used at temperatures above 450 °F. Cast iron and malleable iron fittings conforming to the specifications of 46 CFR 56.60–1, Table 56.60–1(a) may be used at pressures not exceeding the limits of the applicable standards shown in that table at temperatures not exceeding 450 °F. Valves of either of these materials may be used if they conform to the standards for class 125 and class 250 flanges and flanged fittings in ASME B16.1 (incorporated by reference; see 46 CFR 56.01–2) and if their service does not exceed the rating as marked on the valve.

(b) Cast iron and malleable iron shall not be used for valves or fittings in lines carrying flammable or combustible fluids[1] which are directly connected to, or in the proximity of, equipment or other lines having open flame, or any parts operating at temperatures above 500 °F. Cast iron shall not be used for hull fittings, or in systems conducting lethal products.

(c) Malleable iron and cast iron valves and fittings, designed and marked for Class 300 refrigeration service, may be used for such service provided the pressure limitation of 300 pounds per square inch is not exceeded. Malleable iron flanges of this class may also be used in sizes 4 inches and smaller (oval and square design).

[CGFR 68–82, 33 FR 18843, Dec. 18, 1968, as amended by CGFR 69–127, 35 FR 9978, June 17, 1970; CGD 73–254, 40 FR 40165, Sept. 2, 1975; CGD 77–140, 54 FR 40612, Oct. 2, 1989; CGD 95–027, 61 FR 26001, May 23, 1996; USCG–2003–16630, 73 FR 65183, Oct. 31, 2008]

§ 56.60-15 Ductile iron.

(a) Ductile cast iron components made of material conforming to ASTM A 395 (incorporated by reference, see 46 CFR 56.01–2) may be used within the service restrictions and pressure-temperature limitations of UCD–3 of section VIII of the ASME Boiler and Pressure Vessel Code (incorporated by reference; see 46 CFR 56.01–2).

(b) Ductile iron castings conforming to ASTM A 395 (incorporated by reference, see § 56.01–2) may be used in hydraulic systems at pressures in excess of 7500 kilopascals (1000 pounds per square inch) gage, provided the following:

(1) The castings receive a ferritizing anneal when the as-cast thickness does not exceed one inch;

(2) Large castings for components, such as hydraulic cylinders, are examined as specified for a casting quality factor of 90 percent in accordance with UG–24 of section VIII of the ASME Boiler and Pressure Vessel Code; and

(3) The castings are not welded, brazed, plugged, or otherwise repaired.

(c) After machining, ductile iron castings must be hydrostatically tested to twice their maximum allowable working pressure and must show no leaks.

(d) Ductile iron castings exhibiting less than 12 percent elongation in 50 millimeters (2 inches) when subjected

---

[1] For definitions of flammable or combustible fluids, see §§ 30.10–15 and 30.10–22 of subchapter D (Tank Vessels) of this chapter.

§ 56.60-20

to a tensile test must meet the requirements for cast iron in this part.

[CGD 77-140, 54 FR 40612, Oct. 2, 1989, as amended by CGD 95-027, 61 FR 26001, May 23, 1996; USCG-2000-7790, 65 FR 58460, Sept. 29, 2000; USCG-2003-16630, 73 FR 65183, Oct. 31, 2008]

§ 56.60-20 Nonferrous materials.

Nonferrous materials listed in this subpart may be used in piping systems under the following conditions (see also § 56.10-5(c)):

(a) The low melting points of many nonferrous metals and alloys, such as aluminum and aluminum alloys, must be recognized. These types of heat sensitive materials must not be used to conduct flammable, combustible, or dangerous fluids, or for vital systems unless approved by the Marine Safety Center.

NOTE: For definitions of flammable or combustible fluids, see §§ 30.10-15 and 30.10-22 or parts 151-154 of this chapter. Dangerous fluids are those covered by regulations in part 98 of this chapter.

(b) The possibility of galvanic corrosion due to the relative solution potentials of copper and aluminum and their alloys should be considered when used in conjunction with each other or with steel or with other metals and their alloys when an electrolyte is present.

(c) A suitable thread compound must be used in making up threaded joints in aluminum pipe to prevent seizing which might cause leakage and perhaps prevent disassembly. Pipe in the annealed temper should not be threaded.

(d) The corrosion resistance of copper bearing aluminum alloys in a marine atmosphere is poor and alloys with copper contents exceeding 0.6 percent should not be used. Refer to Table 56.60-2(a) of this part for further guidance.

[CGFR 68-82, 33 FR 18843, Dec. 18, 1968, as amended by CGD 77-140, 54 FR 40612, Oct. 2, 1989; CGD 95-027, 61 FR 26001, May 23, 1996]

§ 56.60-25 Nonmetallic materials.

(a) Plastic pipe installations shall be in accordance with IMO Resolution A.753(18) (incorporated by reference; see 46 CFR 56.01-2) and the following supplemental requirements:

(1) Materials used in the fabrication of plastic pipe shall comply with the appropriate standards listed in § 56.01-2 of this chapter.

(2) Plastic pipe is not permitted in a concealed space in an accommodation or service area, such as behind ceilings or linings or between double bulkheads, unless—

(i) Each trunk or duct containing such piping is completely surrounded by "A"-class divisions; or

(ii) An approved smoke-detection system is fitted in the concealed space and each penetration of a bulkhead or deck and each installation of a draft stop is made in accordance with IMO resolution A.753(18) to maintain the integrity of fire divisions.

(3) Plastic pipe used outboard of the required metallic shell valve in any piping system penetrating the vessel's shell (see § 56.50-95(f)) shall have the same fire endurance as the metallic shell valve. Where the shell valve and the plastic pipe are in the same unmanned space, the valve shall be operable from above the freeboard deck.

(4) Pipe that is to be used for potable water shall bear the seal of approval or NSF mark of the National Sanitation Foundation Testing Laboratory, Incorporated, School of Public Health, University of Michigan, Ann Arbor, MI 48103.

(b) *Nonmetallic flexible hose.* (1) Nonmetallic flexible hose must be in accordance with SAE J1942 (incorporated by reference; see 46 CFR 56.01-2) and may be installed only in vital and nonvital fresh and salt water systems, nonvital pneumatic systems, lube oil and fuel systems, and fluid power systems.

(2) Nonmetallic flexible hose may be used in vital fresh and salt water systems at a maximum service pressure of 1,034 kPa (150 psi). Nonmetallic flexible hose may be used in lengths not exceeding 76 cm (30 inches) where flexibility is required, subject to the limits in paragraphs (a)(1) through (4) of this section. Nonmetallic flexible hose may be used for plastic pipe in duplicate installations in accordance with this paragraph (b).

(3) Nonmetallic flexible hose may be used for plastic pipe in non-vital fresh and salt water systems and non-vital

pneumatic systems, subject to the limits of paragraphs (a)(1) through (4) of this section. Unreinforced hoses are limited to a maximum service pressure of 345 kPa (50 psi); reinforced hoses are limited to a maximum service pressure of 1,034 kPa (150 psi).

(4) Nonmetallic flexible hose may be used in lube oil, fuel oil and fluid power systems only where flexibility is required and in lengths not exceeding 30 inches.

(5) Nonmetallic flexible hose must be complete with factory-assembled end fittings requiring no further adjustment of the fittings on the hose, except that field attachable type fittings may be used. Hose end fittings must comply with SAE J1475 (incorporated by reference; see 46 CFR 56.01–2). Field attachable fittings must be installed following the manufacturer's recommended practice. If special equipment is required, such as crimping machines, it must be of the type and design specified by the manufacturer. A hydrostatic test of each hose assembly must be conducted in accordance with § 56.97–5 of this part.

(6) The fire-test procedures of ISO 15540 (incorporated by reference; see 46 CFR 56.01–2) are an acceptable alternative to those procedures of SAE J1942. All other tests of SAE J1942 are still required.

(c) Plastic valves, fittings, and flanges may be used in systems employing plastic pipe. Such valves, fittings, and flanges shall be designed, fabricated, tested, and installed so as to satisfy the intent of the requirements for plastic pipe contained in this section.

(d) If it is desired to use nonmetallic materials other than those specified in this section, a request furnishing the chemical and physical properties of the material shall be submitted to the Commandant for consideration.

[CGFR 68–82, 33 FR 18843, Dec. 18, 1968, as amended by CGFR 69–127, 35 FR 9979, June 17, 1970; CGD 72–104R, 37 FR 14234, July 18, 1972; CGD 73–254, 40 FR 40165, Sept. 2, 1975; CGD 77–140, 54 FR 40613, Oct. 2, 1989; CGD 88–032, 56 FR 35822, July 29, 1991; CGD 83–043, 60 FR 24775, May 10, 1995; CGD 95–072, 60 FR 50462, Sept. 29, 1995; CGD 96–041, 61 FR 50728, Sept. 27, 1996; CGD 95–028, 62 FR 51201, Sept. 30, 1997; USCG–2002–13058, 67 FR 61278, Sept. 30, 2002; USCG–2003–16630, 73 FR 65183, Oct. 31, 2008]

Subpart 56.65—Fabrication, Assembly and Erection

§ 56.65–1 General (replaces 127 through 135).

The requirements for fabrication, assembly and erection in subparts 56.70 through 56.90 shall apply in lieu of 127 through 135.4 of ASME B31.1 (incorporated by reference; see 46 CFR 56.01–2). Those paragraphs reproduced are so noted.

[USCG–2003–16630, 73 FR 65184, Oct. 31, 2008]

§ 56.70–1 General.

(a) The following generally applies to all types of welding, such as stud welding, casting repair welding and all processes of fabrication welding. Where the detailed requirements are not appropriate to a particular process, alternatives must be approved by the Marine Safety Center.

[CGD 77–140, 54 FR 40614, Oct. 2, 1989]

§ 56.70–3 Limitations.

Backing rings. Backing strips used at longitudinal welded joints must be removed.

[CGD 73–254, 40 FR 40165, Sept. 2, 1975]

§ 56.70–5 Material.

(a) *Filler metal.* All filler metal, including consumable insert material, must comply with the requirements of section IX of the ASME Boiler and Pressure Vessel Code (incorporated by reference; see 46 CFR 56.01–2) and 46 CFR 57.02–5.

(b) *Backing rings.* When metallic backing rings are used they shall be made from material of weldable quality compatible with the base metal,

§ 56.70–10

whether subsequently removed or not. When nonmetallic backing rings are used they shall be of material which does not deleteriously affect either base or weld metal, and shall be removed after welding is completed. Backing rings may be of the consumable insert type, removable ceramic type, of solid or split band type. A ferrous backing ring which becomes a permanent part of the weld shall not exceed 0.05 percent sulphur. If two abutting surfaces are to be welded to a third member used as a backing ring and one or two of the three members are ferritic and the other member or members are austenitic, the satisfactory use of such materials shall be determined by procedure qualifications.

[CGFR 68–82, 33 FR 18843, Dec. 18, 1968, as amended by CGD 73–254, 40 FR 40165, Sept. 2, 1975; USCG–2002–13058, 67 FR 61278, Sept. 30, 2002; USCG–2003–16630, 73 FR 65184, Oct. 31, 2008]

§ 56.70–10 Preparation (modifies 127.3).

(a) *Butt welds (reproduces 127.3)*(1)— *End preparation.* (i) Oxygen or arc cutting is acceptable only if the cut is reasonably smooth and true, and all slag is cleaned from the flame cut surfaces. Discoloration which may remain on the flame cut surface is not considered to be detrimental oxidation.

(ii) Butt-welding end preparation dimensions contained in ASME B16.25 (incorporated by reference; see 46 CFR 56.01–2) or any other end preparation that meets the procedure qualification requirements are acceptable.

(iii) If piping component ends are bored, such boring shall not result in the finished wall thickness after welding being less than the minimum design thickness. Where necessary, weld metal of the appropriate analysis may be deposited on the inside or outside of the piping component to provide sufficient material for machining to insure satisfactory fitting of rings.

(iv) If the piping component ends are upset they may be bored to allow for a completely recessed backing ring, provided the remaining net thickness of the finished ends is not less than the minimum design thickness.

(2) *Cleaning.* Surfaces for welding shall be clean and shall be free from paint, oil, rust, scale, or other material which is detrimental to welding.

(3) *Alignment.* The inside diameters of piping components to be joined must be aligned as accurately as practicable within existing commercial tolerances on diameters, wall thicknesses, and out of roundness. Alignment must be preserved during welding. Where ends are to be joined and the internal misalignment exceeds $\frac{1}{16}$-inch, it is preferred that the component with the wall extending internally be internally trimmed (see Fig. 127.3) so that adjoining internal surfaces are approximately flush. However, this trimming must not reduce a piping component wall thickness below the minimum design thickness and the change in the contour may not exceed 30°.

(4) *Spacing.* The root opening of the joint shall be as given in the procedure specification.

(b) *Fillet welds (modifies 127.4.4).* In making fillet welds, the weld metal must be deposited in such a way as to obtain adequate penetration into the base metal at the root of the weld. Piping components that are to be joined utilizing fillet welds must be prepared in accordance with applicable provisions and requirements of this section. For typical details, see Figures 127.4.4A and 127.4.4C of ASME B31.1 (incorporated by reference; see 46 CFR 56.01–2) and 46 CFR 56.30–10(b). See 46 CFR 56.30–5(d) for additional requirements.

[CGFR 68–82, 33 FR 18843, Dec. 18, 1968, as amended by CGFR 69–127, 35 FR 9978, June 17, 1970; CGD 73–254, 40 FR 40165, Sept. 2, 1975; CGD 77–140, 54 FR 40614, Oct. 2, 1989; USCG–2003–16630, 73 FR 65184, Oct. 31, 2008]

§ 56.70–15 Procedure.

(a) *General.* (1) Qualification of the welding procedures to be used, and of the performance of welders and operators, is required, and shall comply with the requirements of part 57 of this subchapter.

(2) No welding shall be done if there is direct impingement of rain, snow, sleet, or high wind on the piping component weldment.

(3) Sections of pipe shall be welded insofar as possible in the fabricating shop. Prior to welding Class I piping or low temperature piping, the fabricator shall request a marine inspector to

visit his plant to examine his fabricating equipment and to witness the qualification tests required by part 57 of this subchapter. One test specimen shall be prepared for each process and welding position to be employed in the fabrication.

(1) Girth butt welds must be complete penetration welds and may be made with a single vee, double vee, or other suitable type of groove, with or without backing rings or consumable inserts.

(2) Girth butt welds in Class I, I-L, and II-L piping systems shall be double welded butt joints or equivalent single welded butt joints for pipe diameters exceeding three-fourth inch nominal pipe size. The use of a single welded butt joint employing a backing ring (note restrictions in paragraph (b)(3)(iv) of this section) on the inside of the pipe is an acceptable equivalent for Class I and Class II-L applications, but not permitted for Class I-L applications. Single welded butt joints employing either an inert gas for first pass backup or a consumable insert ring may be considered the equivalent of a double welded butt joint for all classes of piping and is preferable for Class I-L and II-L systems where double butt welds cannot be used. Appropriate welding procedure qualification tests shall be conducted as specified in part 57 of this subchapter. A first pass inert gas backup is intended to mean that the inside of the pipe is purged with inert gas and that the root is welded with the inert gas metal arc (mig) or inert gas tungsten arc (tig) processes. Classes I, I-L, and II-L piping are required to have the inside of the pipe machined for good fit up if the misalignment exceeds that specified in §56.70–10(a)(3). In the case of Class II piping the machining of the inside of the pipe may be omitted. For single welded joints, where possible, the inside of the joint shall be examined visually to assure full penetration. Radiographic examination of at least 20 percent of single welded joints to check for penetration is required for all Class I and Class I-L systems regardless of size following the requirements of §56.95–10. Ultrasonic testing may be utilized in lieu of radiographic examination if the procedures are approved.

(3) For Class II piping, the type of joints shall be similar to Class I piping, with the following exceptions:

(i) Single-welded butt joints may be employed without the use of backing rings in all sizes provided that the weld is chipped or ground flush on the root side of the weld.

(ii) For services such as vents, overflows, and gravity drains, the backing ring may be eliminated and the root of the weld need not be ground.

(iii) Square-groove welds without edge preparation may be employed for butt joints in vents, overflows, and gravity drains where the pipe wall thickness does not exceed three-sixteenth inch.

(iv) The crimped or forged backing ring with continuous projection around the outside of the ring is acceptable only for Class II piping. The projection must be completely fused.

(4) Tack welds which become part of the finished weld, shall be made by a qualified welder. Tack welds made by an unqualified welder shall be removed. Tack welds which are not removed shall be made with an electrode which is the same as or equivalent to the electrode to be used for the first pass. Their stopping and starting ends must be properly prepared by grinding or other suitable means so that they may be satisfactorily incorporated into the final weld. Tack welds which have cracked shall be removed.

(5) When components of different outside diameters are welded together, the weld joint must be filled to the outside surface of the component having the larger diameter. There must be a gradual transition, not exceeding a slope of 1:3, in the weld between the two surfaces. To avoid unnecessary weld deposit, the outside surface of the component having the larger diameter must be tapered at an angle not to exceed 30 degrees with the axis of the pipe. (See Fig. 127.4.2 of ASME B31.1 (incorporated by reference; see 46 CFR 56.01–2).)

(6) As-welded surfaces are permitted; however, the surface of the welds must be sufficiently free from coarse ripple, grooves, overlaps, abrupt ridges and valleys to meet the following:

(i) The surface condition of the finished welds must be suitable for the proper interpretation of radiographic and other nondestructive examinations when nondestructive examinations are required by §56.95–10. In those cases where there is a question regarding the surface condition on the interpretation of a radiographic film, the film must be compared to the actual weld surface for interpretation and determination of acceptability.

(ii) Reinforcements are permitted in accordance with Table 56.70–15.

(iii) Undercuts must not exceed $\frac{1}{32}$-inch and must not encroach on the minimum required section thickness.

(iv) If the surface of the weld requires grinding to meet the above criteria, care must be taken to avoid reducing the weld or base material below the minimum required thickness.

(7) The type and extent of examination required for girth butt welds is specified in §56.95–10.

(8) Sections of welds that are shown by radiography or other examination to have any of the following type of imperfections shall be judged unacceptable and shall be repaired as provided in paragraph (f) of this section:

(i) Any type of crack or zone of incomplete fusion or penetration.

(ii) Any slag inclusion or porosity greater in extent than those specified as acceptable set forth in PW–51 of section I of the ASME Boiler and Pressure Vessel Code (incorporated by reference; see 46 CFR 56.01–2).

(iii) Undercuts in the external surfaces of butt welds which are more than $\frac{1}{32}$-inch deep.

(iv) Concavity on the root side of full penetration girth butt welds where the resulting weld thickness is less than the minimum pipe wall thickness required by this subchapter. Weld reinforcement up to a maximum of $\frac{1}{32}$-inch thickness may be considered as pipe wall thickness in such cases.

(c) *Longitudinal butt welds.* Longitudinal butt welds in piping components not made in accordance with the standards and specifications listed in 56.60–1 (a) and (b) must meet the requirements of paragraph 104.7 of ASME B31.1 (incorporated by reference; see 46 CFR 56.01–2) and may be examined nondestructively by an acceptable method. Imperfections shall not exceed the limits established for girth butt welds except that no undercutting shall be permitted in longitudinal butt welds. See also §56.60–2(b).

(d) *Fillet welds.* (1) Fillet welds may vary from convex to concave. The size of a fillet weld is determined as shown in Figure 127.4.4A in ASME B31.1. Fillet weld details for socket-welding components must meet §56.30–5(c) of this part. Fillet weld details for flanges must meet §56.30–10(c) of this part. Fillet weld details for flanges must meet §56.30–10 of this part.

(2) The limitations on cracks and undercutting set forth in paragraph (b)(8) of this section for girth welds are also applicable to fillet welds.

(3) Class I piping not exceeding 3 inches nominal pipe size and not subject to full radiography by §56.95–10 of this part may be joined by sleeves fitted over pipe ends or by socket type joints. Where full radiography is required, only butt type joints may be used. The inside diameter of the sleeve must not exceed the outside diameter of the pipe or tube by more than 0.080 inch. Fit between socket and pipe must conform to applicable standards for socket weld fittings. Depth of insertion of pipe or tube within the socket or sleeve must not be less than three-eighths inch. The fillet weld must be deposited in a minimum of two passes, unless specifically approved otherwise in a special procedure qualification. Requirements for joints employing socket weld and slip-on flanges are in §56.30–10 of this part.

(4) Sleeve and socket type joints may be used in Class II piping systems without restriction as to size of pipe or tubing joined. Applicable standards must be followed on fit. The fillet welds must be deposited in a minimum of two passes, unless specifically approved otherwise in a special procedure qualification. Requirements for joints employing socket weld and slip-on flanges are in §56.30–10 of this part.

(e) *Seal welds (reproduces 127.4.5).* (1) Where seal welding of threaded joints is performed, threads shall be entirely covered by the seal weld. Seal welding shall be done by qualified welders.

(2) The limitation on cracks and undercutting set forth in §56.70–15(b)(8) for girth welds are also applicable to seal welds.

Coast Guard, Dept. of Homeland Security § 56.70-15

(f) *Weld defect repairs.* (1) All defects in welds requiring repair must be removed by a flame or arc-gouging, grinding, chipping, or machining. Repair welds must be made in accordance with the same procedures used for original welds, or by another welding process if it is a part of a qualified procedure, recognizing that the cavity to be repaired may differ in contour and dimensions from the original joint. The types, extent, and method of examination and limits of imperfections of repair welds shall be the same as for the original weld.

(2) Preheating may be required for flame-gouging or arc-gouging certain alloy materials of the air hardening type in order to prevent surface checking or cracking adjacent to the flame or arc-gouged surface.

(g) *Welded branch connections.* (1) Figure 127.4.8A, Figure 127.4.8B, and Figure 127.4.8C of ASME B31.1 show typical details of branch connections with and without added reinforcement. However, no attempt has been made to show all acceptable types of construction and the fact that a certain type of construction is illustrated does not indicate that it is recommended over other types not illustrated. See also Figure 56.70-15(g) for additional pipe connections.

(2) Figure 127.4.8D of ASME B31.1 shows basic types of weld attachments used in the fabrication of branch connections. The location and minimum size of these attachment welds shall conform to the requirements of this paragraph. Weld sizes shall be calculated in accordance with 104.3.1 of ASME B31.1, but shall not be less than the sizes shown in Figure 127.4.8D and F of ASME B31.1.

(3) The notations and symbols used in this paragraph and in Figure 127.4.8D and F of ASME B31.1 are as follows:

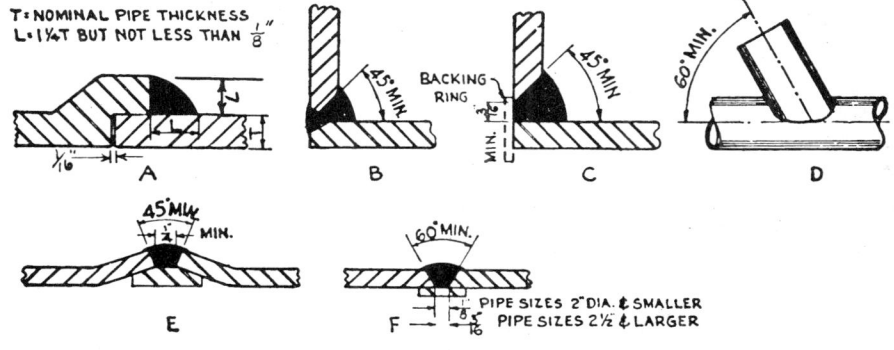

FIGURE 56.70-15(G)—ACCEPTABLE TYPES OF WELDED PIPE CONNECTIONS

t_n=nominal thickness of branch wall less corrosion allowance, inches.
t_c=the smaller of ¼ inch or $0.7t_n$.
t_e=nominal thickness of reinforcing element (ring or saddle), inches (t_e=0 if there is no added reinforcement).
t_{min}=the smaller of t_n or t_e.
t_w=dimension of partial penetration weld, inches.

(4) Branch connections (including specially made, integrally reinforced branch connection fittings) that abut the outside surface of the run wall, or that are inserted through an opening cut in the run wall, shall have opening and branch contour to provide a good fit and shall be attached by means of full penetration groove welds except as otherwise permitted in paragraph (g)(7) of this section. The full penetration groove welds shall be finished with cover fillet welds having a minimum throat dimension not less than $2t_c$. The limitation as to imperfection of these groove welds shall be as set forth in

127.4.2(C) of ASME B31.1 for girth welds.

(5) In branch connections having reinforcement pads or saddles, the reinforcement shall be attached by welds at the outer edge and at the branch periphery as follows:

(i) If the weld joining the added reinforcement to the branch is a full penetration groove weld, it shall be finished with a cover fillet weld having a minimum throat dimension not less than t_c the weld at the outer edge, joining the added reinforcement to the run, shall be a fillet weld with a minimum throat dimension of 0.5 t_e.

(ii) If the weld joining the added reinforcement to the branch is a fillet weld, the throat dimension shall not be less than 0.7 t_{min}. The weld at the outer edge joining the outer reinforcement to the run shall also be a fillet weld with a minimum throat dimension of 0.5 t_e.

(6) When rings or saddles are used, a vent hole shall be provided (at the side and not at the crotch) in the ring or saddle to reveal leakage in the weld between branch and main run and to provide venting during welding and heat treating operations. Rings or saddles may be made in more than one piece if the joints between the pieces have strength equivalent to ring or saddle parent metal and if each piece is provided with a vent hole. A good fit shall be provided between reinforcing rings or saddles and the parts to which they are attached.

(7) Branch connections 2 in. NPS and smaller that do not require reinforcement may be constructed as shown in Fig. 127.4.8F of ASME B31.1. This construction is limited to use in Class I and II piping systems at a maximum design temperature of 750 °F. or a maximum pressure of 1025 psi.

(h) *Heat treatment.* Heat treatment for welds shall be in accordance with subpart 56.85.

TABLE 56.70–15—REINFORCEMENT OF GIRTH AND LONGITUDINAL BUTT WELDS

Thickness (in inches) of base metal	Maximum thickness (in inches) of reinforcement for design temperature		
	Below 0 °F or above 750 °F	350° to 750 °F	0 °F and above but less than 350 °F
Up to ⅛, inclusive	¹⁄₁₆	³⁄₃₂	³⁄₁₆
Over ⅛ to ³⁄₁₆, inclusive	¹⁄₁₆	⅛	³⁄₁₆
Over ³⁄₁₆ to ½, inclusive	¹⁄₁₆	⁵⁄₃₂	³⁄₁₆
Over ½ to 1, inclusive	³⁄₃₂	³⁄₁₆	³⁄₁₆
Over 1 to 2, inclusive	⅛	¼	¼
Over 2	⁵⁄₃₂	(¹)	(¹)

[1] The greater of ¼ in. or ⅛ times the width of the weld in inches.

NOTES: 1. For double welded butt joints, this limitation on reinforcement given above applies separately to both inside and outside surfaces of the joint.
2. For single welded butt joints, the reinforcement limits given above apply to the outside surface of the joint only.
3. The thickness of weld reinforcement is based on the thickness of the thinner of the materials being joined.
4. The weld reinforcement thicknesses must be determined for the higher of the abutting surfaces involved.
5. For boiler external piping use the column titled "Below 0 °F. or above 750 °F." for weld reinforcement thicknesses.

[CGFR 68–82, 33 FR 18843, Dec. 18, 1968, as amended by CGFR 69–127, 35 FR 9978, June 17, 1970; CGD 73–254, 40 FR 40165, Sept. 2, 1975; CGD 77–140, 54 FR 40614, Oct. 2, 1989; 55 FR 39969, Oct. 1, 1990; CGD 95–012, 60 FR 48050, Sept. 18, 1995; USCG–2003–16630, 73 FR 65184, Oct. 31, 2008]

§ 56.70–20 Qualification, general.

(a) Qualification of the welding procedures to be used, and of the performance of welders and welding operators, is required, and shall comply with the requirements of section IX of the ASME Boiler and Pressure Vessel Code (incorporated by reference; see 46 CFR 56.01–2) except as modified by part 57 of this subchapter.

(b) Each butt-welded joint of Class I of Class I-L piping shall be marked with the welder's identification symbol. Dies shall not be used to mark the pipe where the pressure exceeds 600

Coast Guard, Dept. of Homeland Security § 56.75-30

pounds per square inch or the temperature exceeds 750 °F. or in Class I-L systems.

[CGFR 68-82, 33 FR 18843, Dec. 18, 1968, as amended by USCG-2003-16630, 73 FR 65184, Oct. 31, 2008]

Subpart 56.75—Brazing

§ 56.75-5 Filler metal.

(a) The filler metal used in brazing must be a nonferrous metal or alloy having a melting point above 1,000 °F. and below that of the metal being joined. The filler metal must meet and flow freely within the desired temperature range and, in conjunction with a suitable flux or controlled atmosphere, must wet and adhere to the surfaces to be joined. Prior to using a particular brazing material in a piping system, the requirements of § 56.60-20 of this part should be considered.

(b) The brazing material used shall have a shearing strength of at least 10,000 pounds per square inch. The maximum allowable working pressure for brazing piping shall be determined by this part.

(c) Fluxes that are fluid and chemically active at the brazing temperature must be used when necessary to prevent oxidation of the filler metal and of the surfaces to be joined and to promote free flowing of the filler metal.

[CGFR 68-82, 33 FR 18843, Dec. 18, 1968, as amended by CGD 77-140, 54 FR 40615, Oct. 2, 1989; USCG-2003-16630, 73 FR 65184, Oct. 31, 2008]

§ 56.75-10 Joint clearance.

(a) The clearance between surfaces to be joined shall be no larger than is necessary to insure complete capillary distribution of the filler metal; between 0.002-inch minimum and 0.006-inch maximum.

(b) [Reserved]

[CGFR 68-82, 33 FR 18843, Dec. 18, 1968, as amended by USCG-2003-16630, 73 FR 65184, Oct. 31, 2008]

§ 56.75-15 Heating

(a) The joint shall be brought to brazing temperature in as short a time as possible to minimize oxidation.

(b) [Reserved]

[CGFR 68-82, 33 FR 18843, Dec. 18, 1968, as amended by USCG-2003-16630, 73 FR 65184, Oct. 31, 2008]

§ 56.75-20 Brazing qualification.

(a) The qualification of the performance of brazers and brazing operators shall be in accordance with the requirements of part C, section IX of the ASME Boiler and Pressure Vessel Code (incorporated by reference; see 46 CFR 56.01-2) and part 57 of this subchapter.

(b) Manufacturers shall perform those tests required by paragraph (a) of this section prior to performing production brazing.

[CGFR 68-82, 33 FR 18343, Dec. 18, 1968, as amended by USCG-2003-16630, 73 FR 65184, Oct. 31, 2008]

§ 56.75-25 Detail requirements.

(a) Pipe may be fabricated by brazing when the temperature to which such connections may be subjected does not exceed 425 °F. (For exception refer to § 56.30-30(b)(1).)

(b) The surfaces to be brazed must be clean and free from grease, oxides, paint, scale, and dirt of any kind. Any suitable chemical or mechanical cleaning method may be used to provide a clean, wettable surface for brazing.

(c) After the parts to be joined have been thoroughly cleaned the edges to be brazed shall be given an even coating of flux prior to heating the joint as a protection against oxidation.

[CGFR 68-82, 33 FR 18843, Dec. 18, 1968, as amended by USCG-2003-16630, 73 FR 65184, Oct. 31, 2008]

§ 56.75-30 Pipe joining details.

(a) *Silver brazing.* (1) Circumferential pipe joints may be either of the socket or butt type. When butt joints are employed the edges to be joined shall be cut or machined square and the edges shall be held closely together to insure a satisfactory joint.

(b) *Copper-alloy brazing.* (1) Copper-alloy brazing may be employed to join pipe, valves, and fittings. Circumferential joints may be either of the butt or socket type. Where butt joints are employed, the included angle shall be not less than 90° where the wall thickness

§ 56.80-5

is three-sixteenths of an inch or greater. The annular clearance of socket joints shall be held to small clearances which experience indicates is satisfactory for the brazing alloy to be employed, method of heating, and material to be joined. The annular clearance shall be shown on drawings submitted for approval of socket joints.

(2) Copper pipe fabricated with longitudinal joints for pressures not exceeding that permitted by the regulations in this subchapter may have butt, lapped, or scarfed joints. If of the latter type, the kerf of the material shall be not less than 60°.

(c) *Brazing, general.* (1) Heat shall be applied evenly and uniformly to all parts of the joint in order to prevent local overheating.

(2) The members to be joined shall be held firmly in place until the brazing alloy has set so as to prevent any strain on the joint until the brazing alloy has thoroughly solidified. The brazing shall be done by placing the flux and brazing material on one side of the joint and applying heat until the brazing material flows entirely through the lap and shows uniformly along the seam on the other side of the joint. Sufficient flux shall be used to cause the brazing material to appear promptly after reaching the brazing temperature.

Subpart 56.80—Bending and Forming

§ 56.80-5 Bending.

Pipe may be bent by any hot or cold method and to any radius which will result in a bend surface free of cracks, as determined by a method of inspection specified in the design, and substantially free of buckles. Such bends shall meet the design requirements of 102.4.5 and 104.2.1 of ASME B31.1 (incorporated by reference; see 46 CFR 56.01-2). This shall not prohibit the use of bends designed as creased or corrugated. If doubt exists as to the wall thickness being adequate, Class I piping having diameters exceeding 4 inches shall be nondestructively examined by the use of ultrasonics or other acceptable method. Alternatively, the pipe may be drilled, gaged, and fitted with a screwed plug extending outside the pipe covering. The nondestructive method shall be employed where the design temperature exceeds 750 °F. Prior to the use of nondestructive method of examination by the above procedure, it shall be demonstrated by the user, in the presence of a marine inspector on specimens similar to those to be examined, that consistent results, having an accuracy of plus or minus 3 percent, can be obtained.

[CGFR 68-82, 33 FR 18843, Dec. 18, 1968, as amended by CGFR 69-127, 35 FR 9979, June 17, 1970; USCG-2003-16630, 73 FR 65185, Oct. 31, 2008]

§ 56.80-10 Forming (reproduces 129.2).

(a) Piping components may be formed (swaging, lapping, or upsetting of pipe ends, extrusion of necks, etc.) by any suitable hot or cold working method, providing such processes result in formed surfaces which are uniform and free of cracks or other defects, as determined by methods of inspection specified in the design.

§ 56.80-15 Heat treatment of bends and formed components.

(a) Carbon-steel piping that has been heated to at least 1,650 °F (898 °C) for bending or other forming requires no subsequent heat treatment.

(b) Ferritic alloy steel piping which has been heated for bending or other forming operations shall receive a stress relieving treatment, a full anneal, or a normalize and temper treatment, as specified by the design specification before welding.

(c) Cold bending and forming of carbon steel having a wall thickness of three-fourths of an inch and heavier, and all ferritic-alloy pipe in nominal pipe sizes of 4 inches and larger, or one-half-inch wall thickness or heavier, will require a stress-relieving treatment.

(d) Cold bending of carbon-steel and ferritic-alloy steel pipe in sizes and wall thicknesses less than specified in 129.3.3 of ASME B31.1 (incorporated by reference; see 46 CFR 56.01-2) may be used without a postheat treatment.

(e) For other materials the heat treatment of bends and formed components must be such as to ensure pipe properties that are consistent with the original pipe specification.

(f) All scale shall be removed from heat treated pipe prior to installation.

(g) Austenitic stainless-steel pipe that has been heated for bending or other forming may be used in the "as-bent" condition unless the design specification requires post-bending heat treatment.

[CGFR 68–62, 33 FR 18843, Dec. 18, 1968, as amended by CGFR 69–127, 35 FR 9979, June 17, 1970; CGD 73–254, 40 FR 40166, Sept. 2, 1975; USCG–2003–16630, 73 FR 65185, Oct. 31, 2008]

Subpart 56.85—Heat Treatment of Welds

§ 56.85-5 Heating and cooling method.

Heat treatment may be accomplished by a suitable heating method that will provide the desired heating and cooling rates, the required metal temperature, metal temperature uniformity, and temperature control.

[USCG–2003–16630, 73 FR 65185, Oct. 31, 2008]

§ 56.85-10 Preheating.

(a) The minimum preheat temperatures listed in Table 56.85–10 for P-number materials groupings are mandatory minimum pre-heat temperatures. Preheat is required for Class I, I-L, I-N, II-N and II-L piping when the ambient temperature is below 50 °F.

(b) During the welding of dissimilar materials, the minimum preheat temperature may not be lower than either the highest temperature listed in Table 56.85–10 for any of the materials to be welded or the temperature established in the qualified welding procedure.

(c) The preheat temperature shall be checked by use of temperature-indicating crayons, thermocouples, pyrometers, or other suitable methods to ensure that the required preheat temperature is obtained before, and uniformly maintained during the welding.

TABLE 56.85–10—PREHEAT AND POSTHEAT TREATMENT OF WELDS

ASME Sec IX Nos.	Preheat required			Post heat treatment requirement (1)(2)		
	Minimum wall (3)(4) (inch)	Minimum temperature (5)(6)(°F)	Minimum wall and other (3)(4)(17)(inch)	Temperature (7)(8)(9)(10)(11)(12)(°F)(inch)	Time cycle	
					Hour per inch of wall (3)(4)	Minimum time within range (hour)
P–1(16)	All	50 (for .30 C. maximum or less) (13).	Over ¾ in	1,100 to 1,200 (minimum) (maximum).	1	1
P–1(16)	All	175 (for over .30 C.) (13) and wall thickness over 1 in.	......do	......do	1	1
P–3(15)	All walls	175	Over ½ in	1,200 to 1,350 (minimum) (maximum).	1	1
P–4(15)	Up to ¾ in inclusive.	300	Over ½ in or over 4 in nom. size or.	1,330 to 1,400 (minimum) (maximum).	1	1
	Over ¾ in	400	Over .15 C. maximum.			
P–5(15) (less than 5 cr.).	Up to ¾ in inclusive.	300	Over ½ in or over 4 in. nom. size or.	1,300 to 1,425 (minimum) (maximum).	1	1
	Over ¾ in	400	Over 0.15 C. maximum.			
P–5(15) (5 cr. and higher).	Up to ¾ inclusive.	300	All walls	......do	1	2
	Over ¾ in	400	Over 0.15 C. maximum.			
P–6	All walls	300 (14).	All walls	1,400 to 1,500 (minimum) (maximum).	1	2
P–8	......do	None required	......do	None required.		

For P–7, P–9A, P–9B, P–10C and other materials not listed the Preheat and Postheat Treatment is to be in accordance with the qualified procedure.

§ 56.85-15

Notes Applicable to Table 56.85-10:

(1) Not applicable to dissimilar metal welds.

(2) When postheat treatment by annealing or normalizing is used, the postheat treatment temperatures must be in accordance with the qualified welding procedure.

(3) Wall thickness of a butt weld is defined as the thicker of the two abutting ends after end preparation including I.D. machining.

(4) The thickness of socket, fillet, and seal welds is defined as the throat thicknesses for pressure and nonpressure retaining welds.

(5) Preheat temperatures must be checked by use of temperature indicating crayons, thermocouple pyrometers, or other suitable method.

(6) For inert gas tungsten arc root pass welding lower preheat in accordance with the qualified procedure may be used.

(7) The maximum postheat treatment temperature listed for each P number is a recommended maximum temperature.

(8) Postheat treatment temperatures must be checked by use of thermocouple pyrometers or other suitable means.

(9) Heating rate for furnace, gas, electric resistance, and other surface heating methods must not exceed: (i) 600 °F per hour for thicknesses 2 inches and under.

(ii) 600 °F per hour divided by ½ the thickness in inches for thickness over 2 inches.

(10) Heating route for induction heating must not exceed:

(i) 600 °F per hour for thickness less than 1½ inches (60 and 400 cycles).

(ii) 500 °F per hour when using 60 cycles and 400 °F per hour when using 400 cycles for thicknesses 1½ inches and over.

(11) When local heating is used, the weld must be allowed to cool slowly from the postheat treatment temperature. A suggested method of retarding cooling is to wrap the weld with asbestos and allow to cool in still air. When furnace cooling is used, the pipe sections must be cooled in the furnace to 1000 °F and may then be cooled further in still air.

(12) Local postheat treatment of butt welded joints must be performed on a circumferential band of the pipe. The minimum width of this band, centered on the weld, must be the width of the weld plus 2 inches.

Local postheat treatment of welded branch connections must be performed by heating a circumferential band of the pipe to which the branch is welded. The width of the heated band must extend at least 1 inch beyond the weld joining the branch.

(13) 0.30 C. max applies to specified ladle analysis.

(14) 600 °F maximum interpass temperature.

(15) Welding on P-3, P-4, and P-5 with 3 Cr max. may be interrupted only if—

(i) At least ⅜ inch thickness of weld is deposited or 25 percent of welding groove is filled, whichever is greater;

(ii) The weld is allowed to cool slowly to room temperature; and

(iii) The required preheat is resumed before welding is continued.

(16) When attaching welding carbon steel non-pressure parts to steel pressure parts and the throat thickness of the fillet or partial or full penetration weld is ½ in. or less, postheat treatment of the fillet weld is not required for Class I and II piping if preheat to a minimum temperature of 175 °F is applied when the thickness of the pressure part exceeds ¾ in.

(17) For Class I-L and II-L piping systems, relief from postweld heat treatment may not be dependent upon wall thickness. See also §§ 56.50–105(a)(3) and 56.50–105(b)(3) of this chapter.

[CGFR 68–82, 33 FR 18843, Dec. 18, 1968, as amended by CGFR 69–127, 35 FR 9980, June 17, 1970; CGD 72–104R, 37 FR 14234, July 18, 1972; CGD 72–206R, 38 FR 17229, June 29, 1973; CGD 73–254, 40 FR 40166, Sept. 2, 1975; CGD 77–140, 54 FR 40615, Oct. 2, 1989; USCG–2003–16630, 73 FR 65185, Oct. 31, 2008]

§ 56.85-15 Postheat treatment.

(a) Where pressure retaining components having different thicknesses are welded together as is often the case when making branch connections, the preheat and postheat treatment requirements of Table 56.85–10 apply to the thicker of the components being joined. Postweld heat treatment is required for Classes I, I-L, II-L, and systems. It is not required for Class II piping. Refer to § 56.50–105(a)(3) for exceptions in Classes I-L and II-L systems and to paragraph (b) of this section for Class I systems.

(b) All buttwelded joints in Class I piping shall be postweld heated as required by Table 56.85–10. The following exceptions are permitted:

(1) High pressure salt water piping systems used in tank cleaning operations; and,

(2) Gas supply piping of carbon or carbon molybdenum steel used in gas turbines.

(c) All complicated connections including manifolds shall be stress-relieved in a furnace as a whole as required by Table 56.85–10 before being taken aboard ship for installation.

(d) The postheating treatment selected for parts of an assembly must not adversely affect other components.

Heating a fabricated assembly as a complete unit is usually desirable; however, the size or shape of the unit or the adverse effect of a desired treatment on one or more components where dissimilar materials are involved may dictate alternative procedures. For example, it may be heated as a section of the assembly before the attachment of others or local circumferential-band heating of welded joints in accordance with 46 CFR 56.85–10, Table 56.85–10 Note (12) and 46 CFR 56.85–15(j)(3).

(e) Postheating treatment of welded joints between dissimilar metals having different postheating requirements must be established in the qualified welding procedure.

(f)–(h) [Reserved]

(i) For those materials listed under P–1, when the wall thickness of the thicker of the two abutting ends, after their preparation, is less than three-fourths inch, the weld needs no postheating treatment. In all cases, where the nominal wall thickness is three-fourths inch or less, postheating treatment is not required.

(j) (1)–(2) [Reserved]

(3) In local postheat treatment the entire band must be brought up to uniform specified temperature over the complete circumference of the pipe section, with a gradual diminishing of the temperature outward from the edges of the band.

[CGFR 68–82, 33 FR 18843, Dec. 18, 1968, as amended by CGD 72–206R, 38 FR 17229, June 29, 1973; CGD 73–254, 40 FR 40167, Sept. 2, 1975; USCG–2003–16630, 73 FR 65185, Oct. 31, 2008]

Subpart 56.90—Assembly

§ 56.90–1 General.

(a) The assembly of the various piping components, whether done in a shop or as field erection, shall be done so that the completely erected piping conforms with the requirements of the regulations in this subchapter and with the specified requirements of the engineering design.

§ 56.90–5 Bolting procedure.

(a) All flanged joints shall be fitted up so that the gasket contact faces bear uniformly on the gasket and then shall be made up with relatively uniform bolt stress. Bolt loading and gasket compression need only be verified by touch and visual observation.

(b) When bolting gasketed flanged joints, the gasket must be properly compressed in accordance with the design principles applicable to the type of gasket used.

(c) Steel to cast iron flanged joints shall be assembled with care to prevent damage to the cast iron flange in accordance with § 56.25–10.

(d) All bolts must be engaged so that there is visible evidence of complete threading through the nut or threaded attachment.

[CGFR 68–82, 33 FR 18843, Dec. 18, 1968, as amended by USCG–2003–16630, 73 FR 65185, Oct. 31, 2008]

§ 56.90–10 Threaded piping (modifies 135.5).

(a) Any compound or lubricant used in threaded joints shall be suitable for the service conditions and shall not react unfavorably with either the service fluid or the piping materials.

(b) Threaded joints which are to be seal welded shall be made up without any thread compound.

(c) Backing off to permit alignment of pipe threaded joints shall not be permitted.

[CGFR 68–82, 33 FR 18843, Dec. 18, 1968, as amended by USCG–2003–16630, 73 FR 65185, Oct. 31, 2008]

Subpart 56.95—Inspection

§ 56.95–1 General (replaces 136).

(a) The provisions in this subpart shall apply to inspection in lieu of 136 of ASME B31.1 (incorporated by reference; see 46 CFR 56.01–2).

(b) Prior to initial operation, a piping installation shall be inspected to the extent necessary to assure compliance with the engineering design, and with the material, fabrication, assembly and test requirements of ASME B31.1, as modified by this subchapter. This inspection is the responsibility of the owner and may be performed by employees of the owner or of an engineering organization employed by the

§ 56.95-5

owner, together with the marine inspector.

[CGFR 68-82, 33 FR 18843, Dec. 18, 1968, as amended by CGFR 69-127, 35 FR 9979, June 17, 1970; USCG-2003-16630, 73 FR 65185, Oct. 31, 2008]

§ 56.95-5 Rights of access of marine inspectors.

Marine inspectors shall have rights of access to any place where work concerned with the piping is being performed. This includes manufacture, fabrication, assembly, erection, and testing of the piping or system components. Marine inspectors shall have access to review all certifications or records pertaining to the inspection requirements of § 56.95-1, including certified qualifications for welders, welding operators, and welding procedures.

§ 56.95-10 Type and extent of examination required.

(a) *General.* The types and extent of nondestructive examinations required for piping must be in accordance with this section and Table 136.4 of ASME B31.1 (incorporated by reference; see 46 CFR 56.01-2). In addition, a visual examination shall be made.

(1) 100 percent radiography[1] is required for all Class I, I-L, and II-L piping with wall thickness equal to or greater than 10 mm (.375 in.).

(2) Nondestructive examination is required for all Class II piping equal to or greater than 18 inches nominal diameter regardless of wall thickness. Any test method acceptable to the Officer in Charge, Marine Inspection may be used.

(3) Appropriate nondestructive examinations of other piping systems are required only when deemed necessary by the Officer in Charge, Marine Inspection. In such cases a method of testing satisfactory to the Officer in Charge, Marine Inspection must be selected from those described in this section.

(b) *Visual examination.* Visual examination consists of observation by the marine inspector of whatever portions of a component or weld are exposed to such observation, either before, during, or after manufacture, fabrication, assembly or test. All welds, pipe and piping components shall be capable of complying with the limitations on imperfections specified in the product specification under which the pipe or component was purchased, or with the limitations on imperfections specified in § 56.70-15(b) (7) and (8), and (c), as applicable.

(c) *Nondestructive types of examinations*—(1) *100 Percent radiography.* Where 100 percent radiography[1] is required for welds in piping, each weld in the piping shall be completely radiographed. If a butt weld is examined by radiography, for either random or 100 percent radiography, the method used shall be as follows:

(i) X-ray or gamma ray method of radiography may be used. The selection of the method shall be dependent upon its adaptability to the work being radiographed. The procedure to be followed shall be as indicated in PW-51 of section I of the ASME Boiler and Pressure Vessel Code (incorporated by reference; see 46 CFR 56.01-2).

(ii) If a piping component or a weld other than a butt weld is radiographed, the method used shall be in accordance with UW-51 of section VIII of the ASME Boiler and Pressure Vessel Code (incorporated by reference; see 46 CFR 56.01-2).

(2) *Random radiography.* Where random radiography[1] is required, one or more welds may be completely or partially radiographed. Random radiography is considered to be a desirable means of spot checking welder performance, particularly in field welding where conditions such as position, ambient temperatures, and cleanliness are not as readily controlled as in shop welding. It is to be employed whenever an Officer in Charge, Marine Inspection questions a pipe weld not otherwise required to be tested. The standards of acceptance are the same as for 100 percent radiography.

(3) *Ultrasonic.* Where 100 percent ultrasonic testing is specified, the entire surface of the weld being inspected shall be covered using extreme care and careful methods to be sure that a true representation of the actual conditions is obtained. The procedures to be

---

[1] Where for some reason, such as joint configuration, radiography is not applicable, another approved examination may be utilized.

used shall be submitted to the Commandant for approval.

(4) *Liquid penetrant.* Where liquid penetrant examination is required, the entire surface of the weld being examined shall be covered. The examination shall be performed in accordance with appendix VIII to section VIII of the ASME Boiler and Pressure Vessel Code. The following standards of acceptance shall be met:

(i) All linear discontinuities and aligned penetrant indications revealed by the test shall be removed. Aligned penetrant indications are those in which the average of the center-to-center distances between any one indication and the two adjacent indications in any straight line is less than three-sixteenths inch. All other discontinuities revealed on the surface need not be removed unless the discontinuities are also revealed by radiography, in which case the pertinent radiographic specification shall apply.

(5) *Magnetic particle.* Where magnetic particle testing is required, the entire surface of the weld being examined shall be covered. The testing shall be performed in accordance with appendix VI to section VIII of the ASME Boiler and Pressure Vessel Code. The following standards of acceptance are required for welds. All linear discontinuities and aligned indications revealed by the test shall be removed. Aligned indications are those in which the average of the center-to-center distances between any one indication and the two adjacent indications in any straight line is less than three-sixteenths inch. All other revealed discontinuities need not be removed unless the discontinuities are also revealed by radiography, in which case the requirements of paragraph (c)(1) of this section shall be met.

[CGFR 68–82, 33 FR 18843, Dec. 18, 1968, as amended by CGD 72–206R, 38 FR 17229, June 29, 1973; CGD 78–108, 43 FR 46546, Oct. 10, 1978; CGD 77–140, 54 FR 40615, Oct. 2, 1989; CGD 95–028, 62 FR 51202, Sept. 30, 1997; USCG–2000–7790, 65 FR 58460, Sept. 29, 2000; USCG–2003–16630, 65185, Oct. 31, 2008]

Subpart 56.97—Pressure Tests

§ 56.97–1 General (replaces 137).

(a) *Scope.* The requirements in this subpart apply to pressure tests of piping in lieu of 137 of ASME B31.1 (incorporated by reference; see 46 CFR 56.01–2). Those paragraphs reproduced are so noted.

(b) *Leak tightness.* It is mandatory that the design, fabrication and erection of piping constructed under the regulations in this subchapter demonstrate leak tightness. Except where otherwise permitted in this subpart, this requirement must be met by a hydrostatic leak test prior to initial operations. Where a hydrostatic test is not practicable, a pneumatic test (§ 56.97–35) or initial service leak test (§ 56.97–38) may be substituted if approved by the Commandant.

(1) At no time during the hydrostatic test may any part of the piping system be subjected to a stress greater than 90 percent of its yield strength (0.2 percent offset) at test temperature.

(2) Pneumatic tests may be used in lieu of the required hydrostatic test (except as permitted in paragraph (b)(3) of this section), only when—

(i) Piping subassemblies or systems are so designed or supported that they cannot be safely filled with water;[1] or

(ii) Piping subassemblies or systems are to be used in services where traces of the testing medium cannot be tolerated and, whenever possible, the piping subassemblies or system have been previously hydrostatically tested to the pressure required in § 56.97–30(e).

(3) A pneumatic test at a pressure not to exceed 25 psig may be applied before a hydrostatic or a pneumatic test as a means of locating major leaks. The preliminary pneumatic test must be carried out in accordance with the requirements of § 56.97–35.

NOTE: Compressed gas is hazardous when used as a testing medium. It is, therefore, recommended that special precautions for protection of personnel be taken whenever gas under pressure is used as the test medium.

---

[1] These tests may be made with the item being tested partially filled with water, if desired.

(4) The hydrostatic test of the piping system, when conducted in accordance with the requirements of this part, is acceptable as the test for piping subassemblies and may also be used in lieu of any such test required by the material specification for material used in the piping subassembly or system provided the minimum test pressure required for the piping system is met, except where the installation would prevent performing any nondestructive examination required by the material specification to be performed subsequent to the hydrostatic or pneumatic test.

[CGD 73–254, 40 FR 40167, Sept. 2, 1975, as amended by USCG–2003–16630, 73 FR 65185, Oct. 31, 2008]

§ 56.97–5 Pressure testing of nonstandard piping system components.

(a) All nonstandard piping system components such as welded valves and fittings, nonstandard fittings, manifolds, seacocks, and other appurtenances must be hydrostatically tested to twice the rated pressure stamped thereon, except that no component should be tested at a pressure causing stresses in excess of 90 percent of its yield strength.

(b) Items for which an accepted standard appears in Table 56.60–1(b) need not be tested as described in paragraph (a) of this section, but need only meet the test required in the applicable standard.

[CGFR 68–82, 33 FR 18843, Dec. 18, 1968, as amended by CGD 77–140, 54 FR 40615, Oct. 2, 1989]

§ 56.97–25 Preparation for testing (reproduces 137.2).

(a) *Exposure of joints.* All joints including welds must be left uninsulated and exposed for examination during the test.

(b) *Addition of temporary supports.* Piping systems designed for vapor or gas may be provided with additional temporary supports, if necessary, to support the weight of the test liquid.

(c) *Restraint or isolation of expansion joints.* Expansion joints must be provided with temporary restraint, if required for the additional pressure load under test, or they must be isolated from the test.

(d) *Isolation of equipment not subjected to pressure test.* Equipment that is not to be subjected to the pressure test must be either disconnected from the piping subassembly or system or isolated by a blank flange or similar means. Valves may be used if the valve with its closure is suitable for the proposed test pressure.

(e) *Treatment of flanged joints containing blinds.* Flanged joints at which blinds are inserted to blank off other equipment during the test need not be tested.

(f) *Precautions against test medium expansion.* If a pressure test is to be maintained for a period of time and the test medium in the system is subject to thermal expansion, precautions must be taken to avoid excessive pressure. A small relief valve set to $1\frac{1}{3}$ times the test pressure is recommended during the pressure test.

[CGD 73–254, 40 FR 40167, Sept. 2, 1975]

§ 56.97–30 Hydrostatic tests (modifies 137.4).

(a) *Provision of air vents at high points.* Vents must be provided at all high points of the piping subassembly or system in the position in which the test is to be conducted to purge air pockets while the component or system is filling.

(b) *Test medium and test temperature.* (1) Water will be used for a hydrostatic leak test unless another medium is approved by the Commandant.

(2) The temperature of the test medium will be that of the available source unless otherwise approved by the Commandant upon review of the metallurgical aspects of the piping materials with respect to its brittle fracture properties.

(c) *Check of test equipment before applying pressure.* The test equipment must be examined before pressure is applied to ensure that it is tight and that all low-pressure filling lines and other items that should not be subjected to the test pressure have been disconnected or isolated by valves or other suitable means.

(d) *Examination for leakage after application of pressure.* Following the application of the hydrostatic test pressure for a minimum of 10 minutes (see § 56.97–30(g)), examination for leakage must be made of all joints, connections and of all regions of high stress, such as regions around openings and thickness-transition sections.

(e) *Minimum required hydrostatic test pressure.* Except as otherwise permitted in § 56.97–30(f) or § 56.97–40, piping systems must be subjected to a hydrostatic test pressure that at every point in the system is not less than 1.5 times the maximum allowable working pressure.

(f) *Maximum permissible hydrostatic test pressure.* (1) When a system is tested hydrostatically, the test pressure must not exceed the maximum test pressure of any component such as vessels, pumps, or valves in the system.

(2) At no time during the hydrostatic test may any part of the piping system be subjected to a stress greater than 90 percent of its yield strength (0.2 percent offset) at test temperature.

(g) *Hydrostatic test pressure holding time.* The hydrostatic test pressure must be maintained for a minimum total time of 10 minutes and for such additional time as may be necessary to conduct the examination for leakage required by § 56.97–30(d).

[CGD 73–254, 40 FR 40167, Sept. 2, 1975, as amended by USCG–2003–16630, 73 FR 65185, Oct. 31, 2008]

§ 56.97–35 Pneumatic tests (replaces 137.5).

(a) *General Requirements.* When a pneumatic test is performed, it must be conducted in accordance with the requirements of this section.

(b) *Test medium and test temperature.* (1) The gas used as the test medium must not be flammable.

(2) The temperature of the test medium will be that of the available source unless otherwise approved by the Commandant upon review of the metallurgical aspects of the piping materials with respect to its brittle fracture properties.

(c) *Check of test equipment before applying pressure.* The test equipment must be examined before pressure is applied to ensure that it is tight and that all items that should not be subjected to the test pressure have been disconnected or isolated by valves or other suitable means.

(d) *Procedure for applying pressure.* The pressure in the system must gradually be increased to not more than one-half of the test pressure, after which the pressure is increased in steps of approximately one-tenth of the test pressure until the required test pressure has been reached.

(e) *Examination for leakage after application of pressure.* Following the application of pressure for the time specified in § 56.97–35(h), examination for leakage in accordance with 56.97–30(d) must be conducted.

(f) *Minimum required pneumatic test pressure.* Except as provided in § 56.97–35(g) or § 56.97–40, the pneumatic test pressure may not be less than 1.20 nor more than 1.25 times the maximum allowable working pressure of the piping subassembly system.

(g) *Maximum permissible pneumatic test pressure.* When a system is tested pneumatically, the test pressure may not exceed the maximum test pressure of any component such as vessels, pumps or valves in the system.

(h) *Pneumatic test pressure holding time.* The pneumatic test pressure must be maintained for a minimum total time of 10 minutes and for such additional time as may be necessary to conduct the examination for leakage required in § 56.97–30(d).

[CGD 73–254, 40 FR 40168, Sept. 2, 1975]

§ 56.97–38 Initial service leak test (reproduces 137.7).

(a) An initial service leak test and inspection is acceptable when other types of test are not practical or when leak tightness is conveniently demonstrable due to the nature of the service. One example is turbine extraction piping where shut-off valves are not available for isolating a line and where temporary closures are impractical. Others may be systems for service water, low pressure condensate, plant and instrument air, etc., where checking out of pumps and compressors afford ample opportunity for leak tightness inspection prior to fullscale operation.

(b) The piping system must be gradually brought up to design pressure. After inspection of the piping system has proven that the installation is

§ 56.97-40

complete and all joints are leak-tight, the piping has met the requirements of § 56.97-1.

[CGD 73-254, 40 FR 40168, Sept. 2, 1975]

§ 56.97-40 Installation tests.

(a) The following piping systems shall be hydrostatically leak tested in the presence of a marine inspector at a pressure of 1½ times the maximum allowable working pressure of the system:

(1) Class I steam, feedwater, and blowoff piping. Where piping is attached to boilers by welding without practical means of blanking off for testing, the piping shall be subjected to the same hydrostatic pressure to which the boiler is tested. The maximum allowable working pressures of boiler feedwater and blowoff piping shall be the design pressures specified in §§ 56.50-30(a)(3) and 56.50-40(b), respectively.

(2) Fuel oil discharge piping between the pumps and the burners, but not less than 500 pounds per square inch.

(3) High-pressure piping for tank cleaning operations.

(4) Flammable or corrosive liquids and compressed gas cargo piping, but not less than 150 pounds per square inch.

(5) Any Class I, I-L, II-L piping.

(6) Cargo oil piping.

(7) Firemains, but not less than 150 pounds per square inch.

(8) Fuel oil transfer and filling piping.

(9) Class I compressed air piping.

(10) Fixed oxygen-acetylene system piping.

(b) Installation testing requirements for refrigeration, fluid power, and liquefied petroleum gas cooking and heating systems may be found in part 58 of this subchapter.

(c) Class II piping systems shall be tested under working conditions as specified in the section on initial service leak test, § 56.97-38.

[CGFR 68-82, 33 FR 18843, Dec. 18, 1968, as amended by CGFR 69-127, 35 FR 9900, June 17, 1970; CGD 72-206R, 38 FR 17229, June 29, 1973 CGD 73-254, 40 FR 40168, Sept. 2, 1975; CGD 95-028, 62 FR 51202, Sept. 30, 1997]

PART 57—WELDING AND BRAZING

Subpart 57.01—Scope

Sec.
57.01-1 Qualifications and production tests.

Subpart 57.02—General Requirements

57.02-1 Incorporation by reference.
57.02-2 Adoption of section IX of the ASME Code.
57.02-3 Performance qualifications issued by other agencies.
57.02-4 Fabricator's responsibility.
57.02-5 Filler metals.

Subpart 57.03—Procedure Qualifications

57.03-1 General requirements.

Subpart 57.04—Procedure Qualification Range

57.04-1 Test specimen requirements and definition of ranges (modifies QW 202, QW 210, QW 451, and QB 202).

Subpart 57.05—Performance Qualifications

57.05-1 General.
57.05-2 Transfer of performance qualifications.
57.05-3 Limited space qualifications.
57.05-4 Welder qualification by procedure tests.
57.05-5 Low temperature application.

Subpart 57.06—Production Tests

57.06-1 Production test plate requirements.
57.06-2 Production test plate interval of testing.
57.06-3 Method of performing production testing.
57.06-4 Production testing specimen requirements.
57.06-5 Production toughness testing.

AUTHORITY: 46 U.S.C. 3306, 3703, E.O. 12234, 45 FR 58801, 3 CFR, 1980 Comp., p. 277; 49 CFR 1.46.

SOURCE: CGFR 68-82, 33 FR 18872, Dec. 18, 1968, unless otherwise noted.

Subpart 57.01—Scope

§ 57.01-1 Qualifications and production tests.

(a) (*Replaces QW 101 and QB 101.*) The regulations in this part shall apply to the qualification of welding procedures, welders, and brazers, and to production tests for all types of manual and machine arc and gas welding and brazing processes.

Coast Guard, Dept. of Homeland Security § 57.02-2

(b) (*Modifies QW 305 and QB 305.*) Operators of fully automatic welding and brazing machines are specifically exempt from performance qualification tests.

[CGFR 68–82, 33 FR 18872, Dec. 18, 1968, as amended by CGD 74–102, 40 FR 27460, June 30, 1975]

Subpart 57.02—General Requirements

§ 57.02-1 Incorporation by reference.

(a) Certain material is incorporated by reference into this part with the approval of the Director of the Federal Register in accordance with 5 U.S.C. 552(a). To enforce any edition other than that specified in paragraph (b) of this section, the Coast Guard must publish notice of change in the FEDERAL REGISTER and make the material available to the public. All approved material is on file at the Coast Guard Headquarters. Contact Commandant (CG–ENG), Attn: Office of Design and Engineering Systems, U.S. Coast Guard Stop 7509, 2703 Martin Luther King Jr. Avenue SE., Washington, DC 20593–7509. The material is also and is available from the sources indicated in paragraph (b) of this section or at the National Archives and Records Administration (NARA). For information on the availability of this material at NARA, call 202–741–6030, or go to: *http://www.archives.gov/federal_register/code_of_federal_regulations/ibr_locations.html*.

(b) The material approved for incorporation by reference in this part and the sections affected are:

American Society of Mechanical Engineers (ASME) International

Three Park Avenue, New York, NY 10016–5990
Boiler and Pressure Vessel Code, section IX, Welding and Brazing Qualifications, July 1989 with 1989 addenda......57.01–1; 57.02–2; 57.02–3; 57.02–4; 57.03–1; 57.04–1; 57.05–1; 57.06–1; 57.06–3; 57.06–4

[CGD 88–032, 56 FR 35823, July 29, 1991, as amended by CGD 95–072, 60 FR 50462, Sept. 29, 1995; 60 FR 54106, Oct. 19, 1995; CGD 96–041, 61 FR 50728, Sept. 27, 1996; USCG–1999–6216, 64 FR 53224, Oct. 1, 1999; USCG–2009–0702, 74 FR 49229, Sept. 25, 2009; USCG–2012–0832, 77 FR 59778, Oct. 1, 2012; USCG 2013–0671, 78 FR 60148, Sept. 30, 2013]

§ 57.02-2 Adoption of section IX of the ASME Code.

(a) The qualifications for all types of welders and brazers, the qualification of welding procedures, and the production tests for all types of manual and machine arc and gas welding and brazing processes shall be in accordance with section IX of the ASME (American Society of Mechanical Engineers) Code, as limited, modified, or replaced by specific requirements in this part. For general information Table 57.02–1(a) lists the various paragraphs in section IX of the ASME Code which are limited, modified, or replaced by regulations in this part.

TABLE 57.02–1(a)—LIMITATIONS AND MODIFICATIONS TO THE ADOPTION OF SECTION IX OF THE ASME CODE

Paragraphs in section IX ASME code, and Disposition	Unit of this part
QW–101 replaced by	57.01–1(a).
QW–103 replaced by	57.02–3(a).
QW–201 modified by	57.03–1(a).
QW–202 modified by	57.04–1
QW–202.1 modified by	57.03–1(b)
QW–210 modified by	57.04–1.
QW–211 modified by	57.02–4.
QW–253 modified by	57.03–1(g).
QW–254 modified by	57.03–1(g).
QW–255 modified by	57.03–1(g).
QW–305 modified by	57.01–1(b).
QW–451 modified by	57.03–1(b) and 57.04–1.
QB–101 replaced by	57.01–1(a).
QB–103 replaced by	57.02–3(a).
QB–201 modified by	57.03–1(a).
QB–202 modified by	57.04–1.
QB–305 modified by	57.01–1(b).

(1) As stated in § 50.15–5 of this subchapter, section IX of the ASME Code is adopted and shall be the governing requirements for the qualification of all types of welders and brazers, the qualification of all types of welding procedures, and the production tests for all types of manual and machine arc and gas welding and brazing processes used in fabricating power boilers, heating boilers, pressure vessels and piping unless specifically limited, modified or replaced by other regulations in this part.

(b) References to the ASME Code, like paragraph QW–131.1 indicate:

Q=Section IX, Welding and Brazing Qualifications, ASME Code.

§ 57.02–3

W=Part containing requirements for welding procedure, welder, and welding operator qualifications.
131=Major division within the part.
131.1=Specific subparagraph within the part.

(c) When a paragraph or a section of the regulations in this part relates to material in section IX of the ASME Code, the relationship with the code will be shown immediately following the heading of the section or at the beginning of the paragraph as follows:

(1) (Modifies Q___.) This indicates that the material in Q___ is generally applicable but is being altered, amplified or augmented.

(2) (Replaces Q___.) This indicates that Q___ does not apply.

(3) (Reproduces Q___.) This indicates that Q___ is being identically reproduced for convenience, not for emphasis.

[CGFR 68–82, 33 FR 18872, Dec. 18, 1968, as amended by CGFR 69–127, 35 FR 9980, June 17, 1970; CGD 74–102, 40 FR 27460, June 30, 1975. Redesignated by CGD 88–032, 56 FR 35823, July 29, 1991; CGD 95–012, 60 FR 48050, Sept. 18, 1995]

§ 57.02–3 Performance qualifications issued by other agencies.

(a) Within the limits of the qualification tests passed, the Officer in Charge, Marine Inspection, may accept welders who have been qualified by other agencies of the Federal Government; by the American Bureau of Shipping; or by the fabricator concerned, provided the fabricator's tests have been certified by an authorized Code inspector as defined in paragraphs PG–91, N–612, HG–515.2, or UG–91 of the ASME Code.

[CGFR 68–82, 33 FR 18872, Dec. 18, 1968. Redesignated by CGD 88–032, 56 FR 35832, July 29, 1991]

§ 57.02–4 Fabricator's responsibility.

(a) (*Replaces QW 103 and QB 103*). Each manufacturer or contractor is responsible for the welding and brazing done by his organization and shall conduct tests required in this part to qualify the welding and brazing procedures used and the performance of welders and brazers who apply these procedures. The manufacturer shall bear the expense of conducting the tests. Each manufacturer shall maintain a record of the test results obtained in welding and brazing procedure and welder and brazer performance qualifications. These required records, together with identification data, shall be maintained by the manufacturer or contractor on the recommended forms illustrated in QW 480 and QB 480 of section IX, ASME Code, or on any other form acceptable to the Officer in Charge, Marine Inspection. Upon request, duplicate forms shall be furnished by the manufacturer or contractor to the marine inspector.

(b) Except as otherwise provided for in § 57.02–2, the fabricator shall notify the Officer in Charge, Marine Inspection, prior to conducting performance or procedure qualification tests, and arrange a suitable time and place for conducting the tests, so that a marine inspector may be present.

[CGFR 68–82, 33 FR 18872, Dec. 18, 1968, as amended by CGD 74–102, 40 FR 27460, June 30, 1975. Redesignated by CGD 88–032, 56 FR 35823, July 29, 1991]

§ 57.02–5 Filler metals.

(a) Except as provided for in paragraph (b) of this section, when filler metal is used in a welded fabrication that is required to meet the requirements of this part the filler metal must be one that has been approved by the American Bureau of Shipping.

(b) In instances where a fabricator desires to use a filler metal which has not been approved by the American Bureau of Shipping the approval of the filler metal can be made by the Officer in Charge, Marine Inspection on the basis of the fabricator passing the weld procedure qualification tests as outlined in this part. This alternate means of approval applies to wire-gas and wire-flux combinations as well as to stick electrodes. Filler metal approvals given in this manner will extend only to the specific fabricator to whom they are granted.

[CGD 74–102, 40 FR 27460, June 30, 1975. Redesignated by CGD 88–032, 56 FR 35823, July 29, 1991]

Coast Guard, Dept. of Homeland Security §57.03-1

Subpart 57.03—Procedure Qualifications

§57.03-1 General requirements.

(a) (*Modifies QW 201 and QB 201*). In order to obtain Coast Guard approval of a weld procedure to be used on welded fabrication that is required to meet the requirements of this part each manufacturer or contractor must do the following:

(1) Each manufacturer or contractor must submit to the cognizant Officer in Charge, Marine Inspection, for approval, a welding or brazing procedure specification for the particular welding or brazing process to be used. The welding or brazing procedure specification must include a sketch showing joint preparation. Suggested forms showing the information which is required in the welding or brazing procedure specification are in QW 480 and QB 480 of section IX of the ASME Code.

(2) Each manufacturer or contractor must submit to the cognizant Officer in Charge, Marine Inspection, for approval, the results of the physical tests required by section IX of the ASME Code.

(b) (*Modifies QW 202.1 and QW 451*). To obtain approval of the welding procedure, fabricators desiring to use any welding process for applications involving temperatures below −18 °C (approx. 0 °F) must conduct a procedure qualification test in accordance with the requirements of paragraph (a) of this section and the following additional requirements:

(1) The test piece must be large enough so that sufficient material is available for the tests prescribed in QW 451 of the ASME Code, plus toughness tests and a macro-etch specimen.

(2) To obtain approval the fabricator must conduct toughness tests and qualify in accordance with §54.05 of the subchapter. Results of toughness tests must be submitted for approval to the cognizant Officer in Charge, Marine Inspection.

(3) The macro-etch specimen must be submitted with the test results required by paragraph (a) of this section. Macro-etch specimens must not be obtained by flame or arc cutting from the test piece. Weld reinforcement must remain in place unless the production welds are to be machined or ground. Backing rings must also be left in place unless they are to be removed in production.

(4) Low temperature procedure qualification thickness ranges are as indicated in Table 57.03-1(b).

TABLE 57.03-1(b)—LOW TEMPERATURE WELD PROCEDURE QUALIFICATION THICKNESS RANGES

Thickness, "t" of test plate or pipe as welded (inches)	Range of thickness of materials qualified by test plate or pipe (inches)	
	Minimum	Maximum
1/16 to 3/8, inclusive	1/16	3/8
Over 3/8 but less than 3/4	*3/8	3/4
3/4 to 3, inclusive	3/4	**t

*For thicknesses less than 5/8 inch, the thickness of the test plate or pipe is the minimum thickness qualified.
**Where "t" is the thickest material over 3/4 inch to be used in production.

(5) The limits for heat input production, as measured in Joules/inch, must be at or below the maximum heat input applied to the procedure test plate. The word "maximum" must not be interpreted as either nominal or average.

(c) [Reserved]

(d) For quenched and tempered steels, the Commandant may prescribe special testing to assure that the welding procedure produces weldments which are not prone to low energy fracture through the heat affected zone.

(e) Welding procedures that utilize type E 6012, E 6013, E 6014, E 6024, E 7014, or E 7024 electrode will be approved only for the specific type, size, and brand electrode used. If a different type, size, or brand of electrode is used, a new procedure qualification test must be conducted.

(f) Welding or brazing procedure approvals cannot be transferred from one plant to another plant of the same company or from one company to another.

(g) (*Modifies QW 253, QW 254, and QW 255*). Item QW 402.4 is an essential variable for all procedure specifications.

[CGD 74-102, 40 FR 27461, June 30, 1975]

Subpart 57.04—Procedure Qualification Range

§ 57.04-1 Test specimen requirements and definition of ranges (modifies QW 202, QW 210, QW 451, and QB 202).

The type and number of specimens that must be tested to qualify an automatic, semiautomatic, or manual procedure specification shall be in accordance with QW 202, QW 210, or QB 202 of the ASME Code as applicable, except as supplemented by §§ 57.03–1(b) and 57.03–1(d).

[CGD 74–102, 40 FR 27461, June 30, 1975]

Subpart 57.05—Performance Qualifications

§ 57.05-1 General.

(a) This subpart supplements the various paragraphs in section IX of the Code dealing with Performance Qualifications (see § 57.02–2).

[CGFR 69–127, 35 FR 9980, June 17, 1970]

§ 57.05-2 Transfer of performance qualifications.

(a) The performance qualification records of a welder may be transferred from one plant to another of the same company or from one company to another company provided the following requirements are met:

(1) The transfer is authorized by the cognizant Officer in Charge, Marine Inspection;

(2) A copy of the qualification test records of each welder together with employment records and identification data are transferred by the plant or company which qualified the welder to the new plant or company; and,

(3) The new plant or company accepts the welder as qualified.

§ 57.05-3 Limited space qualifications.

When a welder is to be qualified for welding or torch brazing of piping on board ship in a limited or restricted space, the space restrictions shown in connection with Figure 57.05–3(a) or (b) shall be used when welding and brazing the test joint.

Coast Guard, Dept. of Homeland Security §57.05-3

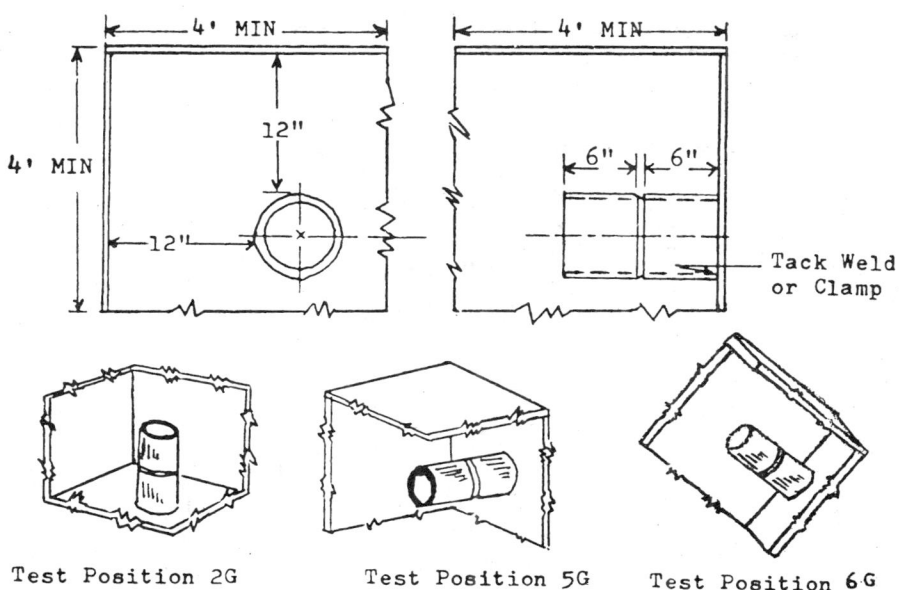

Figure 57.05-3(a)—Limited space restriction for pipe welding performance qualification

§ 57.05-4

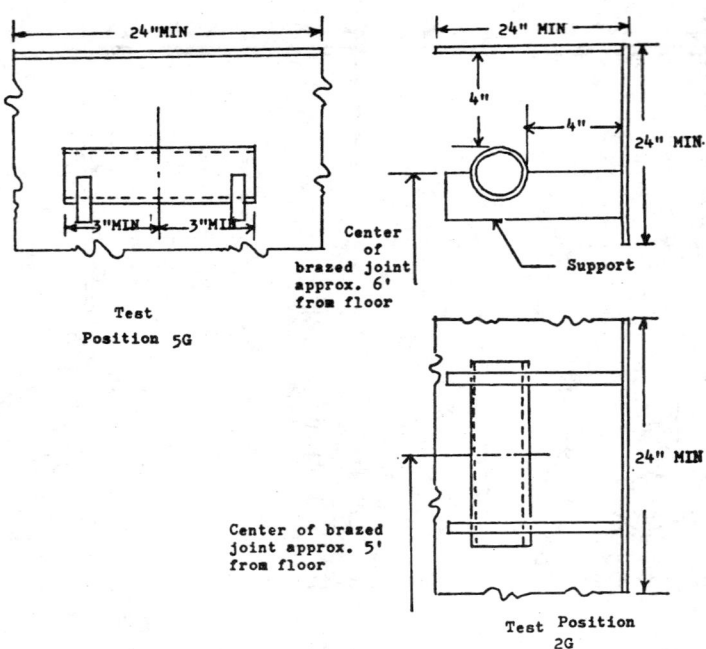

FIGURE 57.05-3(B)—LIMITED SPACE RESTRICTION FOR PIPE BRAZING PERFORMANCE QUALIFICATION

[CGFR 68–82, 33 FR 118872, Dec. 18, 1968, as amended by CGD 74–102, 40 FR 27461, June 30, 1975]

§ 57.05-4 Welder qualification by procedure tests.

Qualification tests of welders may be omitted for welders who weld satisfactory procedure qualification test assemblies as required by subpart 57.03.

§ 57.05-5 Low temperature application.

For low temperature application, each welder shall demonstrate his ability to weld satisfactorily in accordance with procedures qualified in accordance with § 57.03–1(b). Manual welding shall be qualified in the position prescribed by the procedure.

Subpart 57.06—Production Tests

§ 57.06-1 Production test plate requirements.

(a) Production test plates shall be provided for Class I, Class I-L, Class II, and Class II-L pressure vessels are specified in this section.

(b) Main power boilers shall meet the test plate requirements for Class I pressure vessels.

(c) Test plates are not required for heating boilers or Class III pressure vessels. Test plates are not required for main power boilers or pressure vessels constructed of P–1 material as listed in QW 422 of the ASME Code whose welded joints are fully radiographed as required by part 52 or 54 of this subchapter as applicable except when toughness tests are required in accordance with § 57.06–5. When toughness tests are required all prescribed production tests shall be performed.

[CGFR 68–82, 33 FR 18872, Dec. 18, 1968, as amended by CGFR 69–127, 35 FR 9980, June 17, 1970; CGD 72–206R, 38 FR 17229, June 29, 1973; CGD 74–102, 40 FR 27461, June 30, 1975; CGD 95–012, 60 FR 48050, Sept. 18, 1995]

Coast Guard, Dept. of Homeland Security

§ 57.06-2 Production test plate interval of testing.

(a) At least one set of production test plates shall be welded for each Class I or Class I-L pressure vessel except as follows:

(1) When the extent of welding on a single vessel exceeds 50 lineal feet of either or both longitudinal and circumferential joints, at least one set of test plates shall be welded for each 50 feet of joint.

(2) When the extent of welding on vessels welded in succession exceeds 50 lineal feet of either or both longitudinal and circumferential joints, at least one set of test plates shall be welded for each 50 feet of aggregate joint of the same material where the plate thicknesses fall within a range of one-fourth inch. For each 50-foot increment of weld, test plates shall be prepared at the time of fabrication of the first vessel involving that increment.

(b) Production test plates for Class II-L pressure vessels shall be prepared as for Classes I and I-L vessels except that the provisions of paragraphs (a)(1) and (2) of this section are applicable to each 150 lineal feet of welded joint in lieu of each 50 lineal feet.

(c) In the case of Class II pressure vessels no more than one set of production test plates need be prepared for each 300 lineal feet of either or both longitudinal and circumferential joints. In the case of single vessel fabrication a set of test plates is required for each 300 lineal feet of weld or fraction thereof. In the case of multiple vessel fabrication where each increment of 300 lineal feet of weld involves more than one pressure vessel, the set of test plates shall be prepared at the time of fabrication of the first vessel involving that increment.

§ 57.06-3 Method of performing production testing.

(a) Except as otherwise specified in this section a test plate shall be attached to the shell plate on one end of the longitudinal joint of each vessel as shown in Figure 57.06-3, so that the edges of the test plate to be welded are a continuation of and duplication of the corresponding edges of the longitudinal joint. For attached test plates, the weld metal shall be deposited in the test plate welding groove continuously with the weld metal deposited in the groove of the longitudinal joint. As an alternate method, the marine inspector may permit the use of separate test plates, provided the same welding process, procedure, and technique employed in the fabrication of the longitudinal joint are used in welding the test plates.

(b) All test plates, whether attached to the shell or separate in accordance with paragraphs (a) and (d) of this section, shall be prepared from material of the same specification, thickness, and heat treatment and, for Class I-L and Class II-L vessels, the same heat as that of the vessel for which they are required. However, except when required to be from a specific heat, test plates may be prepared from material of a different product form, such as plate in lieu of a forging, provided the chemical composition is within the vessel material specification limits and the melting practice is the same.

(c) Test plates are not required for welded nozzle attachments.

(d) In the case of vessels having no longitudinal welded joints, at least one set of test plates shall be welded for each vessel, using the circumferential joint process, procedure and technique, except that the provisions of § 57.06-2(a) shall also apply for Classes I and I-L vessels, and that the provisions of § 57.06-2 (a) and (c) shall also apply for Classes II and II-L vessels.

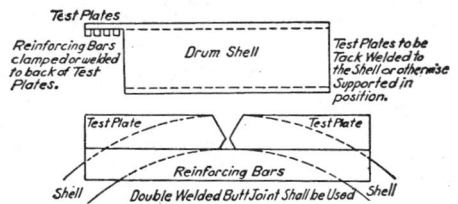

FIGURE 57.06-3—(PW-53.2) METHOD OF FORMING LONGITUDINAL TEST PLATES

(e) Test plates shall be made by the same welder producing the longitudinal and circumferential joints. If more than one welder is employed in the welding of the pressure vessel(s), the test plates shall be made by the welder designated by the marine inspector. The test plates shall be of the same thickness as the material being welded and shall be of sufficient size to provide two specimens of each type required, except that in the case of pressure vessels having no longitudinal seams, the test plate need be only of sufficient length to provide one set of test specimens, and if a retest is necessary, an additional set of test plates may be welded separately.

§ 57.06-4 Production testing specimen requirements.

(a) For test plates three-fourths inch or less in thickness one reduced section tensile specimen and two free-bend specimens shall be tested. For plates exceeding three-fourths inch in thickness one reduced section tensile specimen, one free-bend specimen and one guided side bend specimen shall be tested. In addition boiler drums of thickness five-eighths inch or greater shall have a tension test specimen of the weld metal as required by paragraph (f)(2) of this section. Toughness tests are required for Classes I-L and II-L pressure vessels as specified in § 57.06-5.

(b) The test plates shall be so supported that the warping due to welding shall not throw the finished test plate out of line by an angle of over 5°.

(c) Where the welding has warped the test plates, the plates shall be straightened before being stress-relieved. The test plates shall be subjected to the same stress-relieving operation as required by this subchapter for the pressure vessel itself. At no time shall the test plates be heated to a temperature higher than that used for stress-relieving the vessel.

(d) The bend specimens shall be taken from opposite sides of the reduced-section tensile specimen in their respective test plates as shown in Figures 57.06-4(d)(1) and 57.06-4(d)(2).

Coast Guard, Dept. of Homeland Security § 57.06-4

DISCARD	THIS PIECE
FREE BEND	SPECIMEN
REDUCED SECTION	TENSION TEST SPECIMEN
FREE BEND	SPECIMEN
TOUGHNESS TEST OR ALL WELD METAL (IF REQUIRED)	SPECIMEN [1] TENSION SPECIMEN
FREE BEND	SPECIMEN
REDUCED SECTION	TENSION TEST SPECIMEN
FREE BEND	SPECIMEN
DISCARD	THIS PIECE

Figure 57.06-4(d)(1)—Workmanship test plates for material three-fourths inch or less in thickness

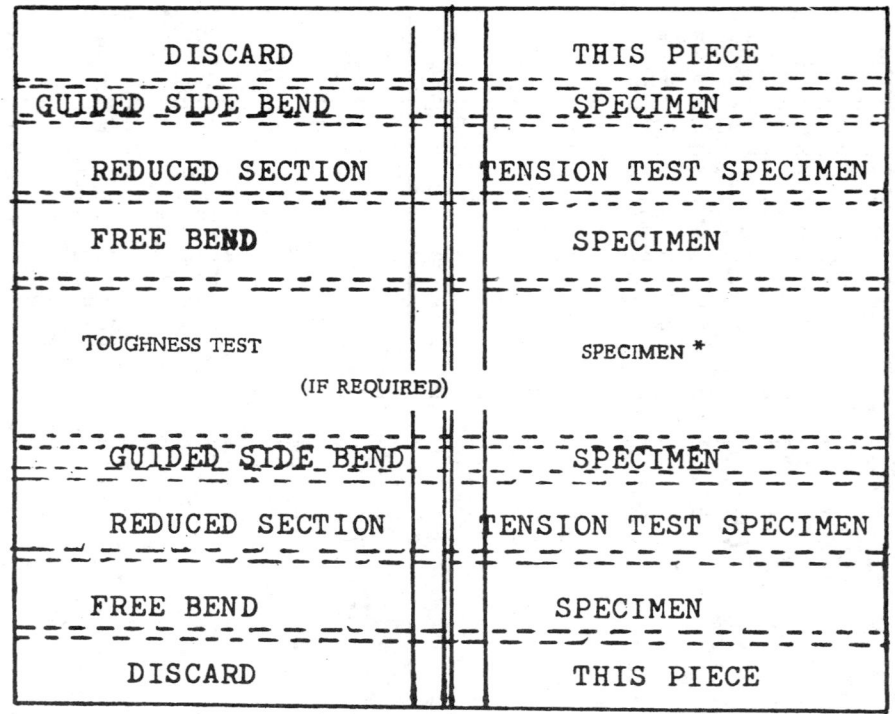

*WHEN CHARPY V NOTCH IMPACT SPECIMENS ARE REQUIRED, THE TEST PLATES SHALL BE NO SMALLER THAN TWO FEET ON A SIDE

FIGURE 57.06–4(D)(2)—WORKMANSHIP TEST PLATES FOR MATERIAL THREE-FOURTHS INCH OR LESS IN THICKNESS

(e) In submitting the samples for test the manufacturer shall state the minimum and maximum tensile range of the base metal.

(f) The external appearances of the welds and the amount of weld reinforcement shall conform to the requirements for fabrication, and the maximum reinforcement for the test plates shall not exceed the maximum permitted for construction.

(1) The tension-test specimen of the joint shall be transverse to the welded joint and shall be of the full thickness of the plate after the weld reinforcement has been machined flush. The form and dimensions shall be as shown in Figure 57.06–4(f)(1)(i). When the capacity of the available testing machine does not permit testing a specimen of the full thickness of the welded plate, the specimen may be cut with a thin saw into as many portions of the thickness as necessary, as shown in Figure 57.06–4(f)(1)(ii) each of which shall meet the requirements. The tensile strength of the joint specimen when it breaks in the weld shall not be less than the minimum of the specified tensile range of the plate used. If the specimen breaks in the plate at not less than 95 percent of the minimum specified tensile range

Coast Guard, Dept. of Homeland Security §57.06-4

of the plate and the weld shows no sign of weakness, the test is considered acceptable.

(2) Boiler drums fabricated of plate of thicknesses of five-eighths inch or greater shall have a tension-test specimen of the weld metal machined to form as shown in Figure 57.06-4(f)(2) taken entirely from the deposited metal. The all-weld tension test specimen shall have a tensile strength of not less than the minimum of the range of the plate which is welded and shall have a minimum elongation in 2 inches of not less than 20 percent.

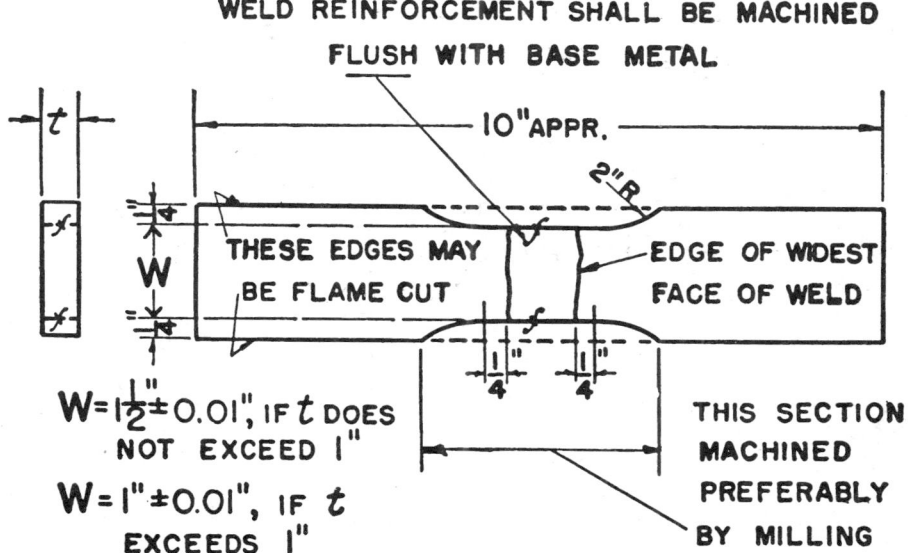

FIGURE 57.06-4(F)(1)(I)—(PW-53.1) REDUCED-SECTION TEST SPECIMEN FOR TENSION TEST OF WELDED JOINT

§ 57.06-4

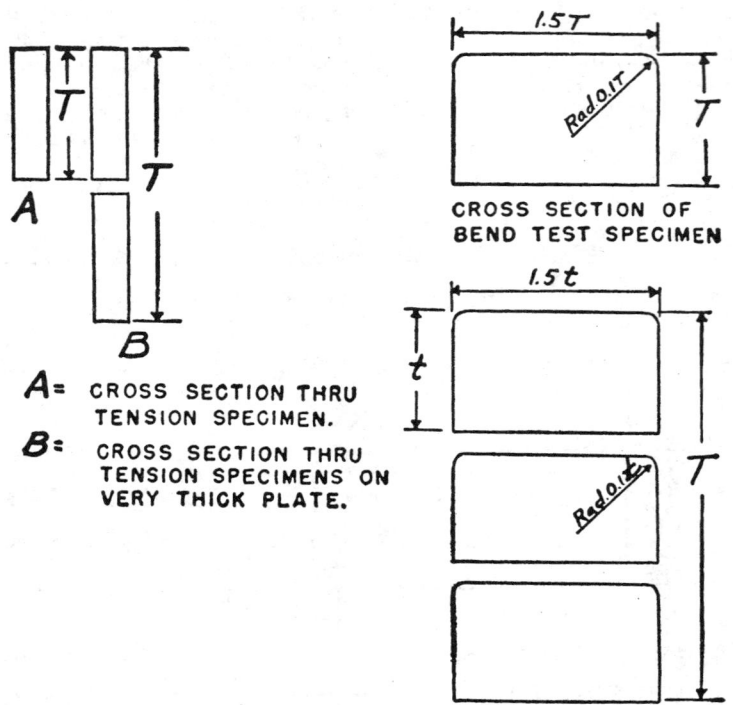

FIGURE 57.06-4(F)(1)(II)—(PW-53.3) CROSS SECTION OF BEND-TEST SPECIMENS FROM VERY THICK PLATE

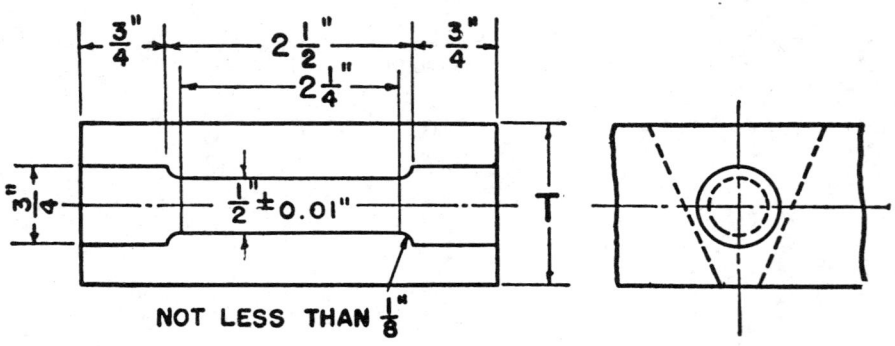

FIGURE 57.06-4(F)(2)—(PW-53.3) ALL WELD METAL TENSION-TEST SPECIMEN

(g) The freebend specimens shall be of the form and dimensions shown in Figure 57.06-4(g). For plates of three-fourths inch or less in thickness one of the specimens shall be bent with the face of the weld in tension. Each

Coast Guard, Dept. of Homeland Security § 57.06-4

freebend specimen shall be bent cold under freebending conditions until the elongation measured within or across approximately the entire weld on the outer surface of the bend is at least 30 percent, except that for Class II and Class II-L pressure vessels, the minimum elongation shall be 20 percent. When the capacity of the available testing machine will not permit testing a full thickness specimen, the specimen may be cut with a thin saw into as many portions of the thickness as necessary as shown in Figure 57.06-4(f)(1)(ii), provided each such piece retains the proportion of 1½ to 1, width to thickness, each of which shall meet the requirements. Cracks at the corners of the specimens or small defects in the convex surface, the greatest dimensions of which do not exceed one-sixteenth inch need not be considered as failures.

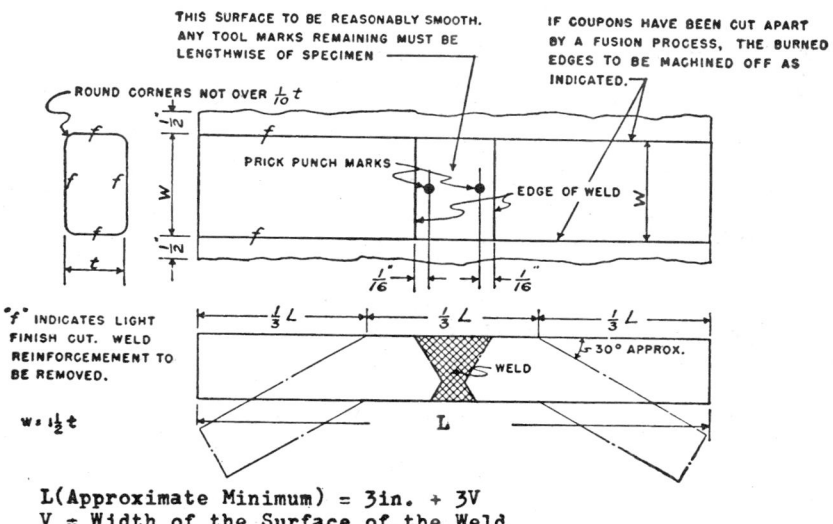

L(Approximate Minimum) = 3in. + 3V
V = Width of the Surface of the Weld

The Length of the Bend Specimen is Immaterial provided the Bend occurs at the Weld. The Minimum Length indicated is only Suggestive and is Not Mandatory.

FIGURE 57.06-4(G)—(PW-53.8) SPECIMEN FOR FREE-BEND TEST

(h) The guided-bend specimen shall be bent with the side of the weld in tension, its width shall be equal to the full thickness of the plate and its thickness, after machining, shall be 0.350 inch to 0.380 inch to permit bending in a jig having the contour of the standard jig as shown in Figure QW 466.1, QW 466.2, or QW 466.3 of the ASME Code. The specimen shall withstand being bent cold to the full capacity of the jig without developing any crack exceeding one-eighth inch in any direction. Where the plate thickness exceeds two inches, the specimen shall be cut in two so that each portion does not exceed 2 inches in width. Each such portion shall be tested and shall meet the requirements.

(i) One retest shall be made for each of the original specimens which fails to meet the requirements. Should the retests fail to meet the requirements, the welds which they represent shall be

§ 57.06-5

chipped out, rewelded and new test plates provided.

[CGFR 68-82, 33 FR 18872, Dec. 18, 1968, as amended by CGFR 69-127R, 35 FR 9980, June 17, 1970; CGD 74-102, 40 FR 27461, June 30, 1975; CGD 80-004, 45 FR 10796, Feb. 19, 1980; CGD 95-012, 60 FR 48050, Sept. 18, 1995]

§ 57.06-5 Production toughness testing.

(a) In addition to the test specimens required by § 57.06-4(a), production toughness test plates shall be prepared for Classes I-L and II-L pressure vessels in accordance with subpart 54.05 of this subchapter.

(b) For nonpressure vessel type cargo tanks and associated secondary barriers as defined in § 38.05-4 of subchapter D (Tank Vessels) of this chapter, production toughness test plates shall be prepared in accordance with subpart 54.05 of this subchapter.

[CGD 68-82, 33 FR 18872, Dec. 18, 1968, as amended by CGD 72-206R, 38 FR 17229, June 29, 1973; CGD 95-012, 60 FR 48050, Sept. 18, 1995]

PART 58—MAIN AND AUXILIARY MACHINERY AND RELATED SYSTEMS

Subpart 58.01—General Requirements

Sec.
58.01-1 Scope.
58.01-5 Applicable standards.
58.01-10 Fuel oil.
58.01-20 Machinery guards.
58.01-25 Means of stopping machinery.
58.01-30 Trial-trip observance.
58.01-35 Main propulsion auxiliary machinery.
58.01-40 Machinery, angles of inclination.
58.01-45 Machinery space, ventilation.
58.01-50 Machinery space, noise.
58.01-55 Tanks for flammable and combustible oil.

Subpart 58.03—Incorporation of Standards

58.03-1 Incorporation by reference.

Subpart 58.05—Main Propulsion Machinery

58.05-1 Material, design and construction.
58.05-5 Astern power.
58.05-10 Automatic shut-off.

Subpart 58.10—Internal Combustion Engine Installations

58.10-5 Gasoline engine installations.
58.10-10 Diesel engine installations.
58.10-15 Gas turbine installations.

Subpart 58.16—Liquefied Petroleum Gases for Cooking and Heating

58.16-1 Scope.
58.16-5 Definition.
58.16-7 Use of liquefied petroleum gas.
58.16-10 Approvals.
58.16-15 Valves and safety relief devices.
58.16-16 Reducing regulators.
58.16-17 Piping and fittings.
58.16-18 Installation.
58.16-19 Tests.
58.16-20 Ventilation of compartments containing gas-consuming appliances.
58.16-25 Odorization.
58.16-30 Operating instructions.
58.16-35 Markings.

Subpart 58.20—Refrigeration Machinery

58.20-1 Scope.
58.20-5 Design.
58.20-10 Pressure relieving devices.
58.20-15 Installation of refrigerating machinery.
58.20-20 Refrigeration piping.
58.20-25 Tests.

Subpart 58.25—Steering Gear

58.25-1 Applicability.
58.25-5 General.
58.25-10 Main and auxiliary steering gear.
58.25-15 Voice communications.
58.25-20 Piping for steering gear.
58.25-25 Indicating and alarm systems.
58.25-30 Automatic restart.
58.25-35 Helm arrangements.
58.25-40 Arrangement of the steering-gear compartment.
58.25-45 Buffers.
58.25-50 Rudder stops.
58.25-55 Overcurrent protection for steering-gear systems.
58.25-60 Non-duplicated hydraulic rudder actuators.
58.25-65 Feeder circuits.
58.25-70 Steering-gear control systems.
58.25-75 Materials.
58.25-80 Automatic pilots and ancillary steering gear.
58.25-85 Special requirements for tank vessels.

Subpart 58.30—Fluid Power and Control Systems

58.30-1 Scope.
58.30-5 Design requirements.
58.30-10 Hydraulic fluid.
58.30-15 Pipe, tubing, valves, fittings, pumps, and motors.
58.30-20 Fluid power hose and fittings.
58.30-25 Accumulators.
58.30-30 Fluid power cylinders.

Coast Guard, Dept. of Homeland Security § 58.01-25

58.30-35 Testing.
58.30-40 Plans.
58.30-50 Requirements for miscellaneous fluid power and control systems.

Subpart 58.50—Independent Fuel Tanks

58.50-1 General requirements.
58.50-5 Gasoline fuel tanks.
58.50-10 Diesel fuel tanks.
58.50-15 Alternate material for construction of independent fuel tanks.

Subpart 58.60—Industrial Systems and Components on Mobile Offshore Drilling Units (MODU)

58.60-1 Applicability.
58.60-2 Alternatives and substitutions.
58.60-3 Pressure vessel.
58.60-5 Industrial systems: Locations.
58.60-7 Industrial systems: Piping.
58.60-9 Industrial systems: Design.
58.60-11 Analyses, plans, diagrams and specifications: Submission.
58.60-13 Inspection.

AUTHORITY: 43 U.S.C. 1333; 46 U.S.C. 3306, 3703; E.O. 12234, 45 FR 58801, 3 CFR, 1980 Comp., p. 277; Department of Homeland Security Delegation No. 0170.1.

SOURCE: CGFR 68-82, 33 FR 18878, Dec. 18, 1968, unless otherwise noted.

Subpart 58.01—General Requirements

§ 58.01-1 Scope.

The regulations in this part contain requirements for the design and construction of main and auxiliary machinery installed on vessels.

§ 58.01-5 Applicable standards.

The applicable standards established by the ABS Steel Vessel Rules (incorporated by reference, see 46 CFR 58.03-1), may be used as the standard for the design, construction, and testing of main and auxiliary machinery except as modified in this subchapter.

[CGFR 68-82, 33 FR 18878, Dec. 18, 1968, as amended by USCG-2003-16630, 73 FR 65185, Oct. 31, 2008]

§ 58.01-10 Fuel oil.

(a) The following limits apply to the use of oil as fuel:

(1) Except as otherwise permitted by this section, no fuel oil with a flashpoint of less than 60 °C (140 °F) may be used.

(2) Except as otherwise permitted by § 58.50-1(b), fuel oil with a flashpoint of not less than 43 °C (110 °F) may be used in emergency generators.

(3) Subject to such further precautions as the Commanding Officer, Marine Safety Center, considers necessary, and provided that the ambient temperature of the space in which such fuel oil is stored or used does not rise to within 18 °F (10 °C) below the flashpoint of the fuel oil, fuel oil having a flashpoint of less than 140 °F (60 °C) but not less than 110 °F (43 °C) may be used.

(4) In a cargo vessel, fuel having a lower flashpoint than otherwise specified in this section—for example, crude oil—may be used provided that such fuel is not stored in any machinery space and that the Commanding Officer, Marine Safety Center, approves the complete installation.

(b) The flashpoint of oil must be determined by the Pensky-Martens Closed Tester, ASTM D 93 (incorporated by reference, see § 58.03-1).

[CGD 83-043, 60 FR 24775, May 10, 1995, as amended by USCG-1999-5151, 64 FR 67180, Dec. 1, 1999; USCG-2003-16630, 73 FR 65186, Oct. 31, 2008]

§ 58.01-20 Machinery guards.

Gears, couplings, flywheels and all machinery capable of injuring personnel shall be provided with adequate covers or guards.

§ 58.01-25 Means of stopping machinery.

Machinery driving forced-draft and induced-draft fans, fuel-oil transfer pumps, fuel-oil unit and service pumps, and similar fuel-oil pumps must be fitted with remote controls from a readily accessible position outside the space concerned so that the fans or pumps may be stopped in case of fire in the compartment in which they are located. The controls must be suitably protected against accidental operation and against tampering and must be suitably marked.

[CGD 83-043, 60 FR 24775, May 10, 1995]

§ 58.01-30 Trial-trip observance.

The operation of main and auxiliary engines, boilers, steering gear, and auxiliaries shall be observed on the trial trip of each new vessel and all deficiencies which affect the safety of the vessel shall be corrected to the satisfaction of the Officer in Charge, Marine Inspection.

§ 58.01-35 Main propulsion auxiliary machinery.

Auxiliary machinery vital to the main propulsion system must be provided in duplicate unless the system served is provided in independent duplicate, or otherwise provides continued or restored propulsion capability in the event of a failure or malfunction of any single auxiliary component.

NOTE: Partial reduction of normal propulsion capability as a result of malfunction or failure is acceptable if the reduced capability is not below that necessary for the vessel to run ahead at 7 knots or half speed, whichever is less, and is adequate to maintain control of the ship.

[CGD 81–030, 53 FR 17837, May 18, 1988]

§ 58.01-40 Machinery, angles of inclination.

(a) Propulsion machinery and all auxiliary machinery essential to the propulsion and safety of the vessel must be designed to operate when the vessel is upright, when the vessel is inclined under static conditions at any angle of list up to and including 15°, and when the vessel is inclined under dynamic conditions (rolling) at any angle of list up to and including 22.5° and, simultaneously, at any angle of trim (pitching) up to and including 7.5° by bow or stern.

(b) Deviations from these angles of inclination may be permitted by the Commanding Officer, Marine Safety Center, considering the type, size, and service of the vessel.

[CGD 83–043, 60 FR 24775, May 10, 1995]

§ 58.01-45 Machinery space, ventilation.

Each machinery space must be ventilated to ensure that, when machinery or boilers are operating at full power in all weather including heavy weather, an adequate supply of air is maintained for the operation of the machinery and for the safety, efficiency, and comfort of the crew.

[CGD 83–043, 60 FR 24775, May 10, 1995]

§ 58.01-50 Machinery space, noise.

(a) Each machinery space must be designed to minimize the exposure of personnel to noise in accordance with IMO A.468(XII) (incorporated by reference, see 46 CFR 58.03–1). No person may encounter a 24-hour effective noise level greater than 82 dB(A) when noise is measured using a sound-level meter and an A-weighting filter.

(b) Except as allowed by paragraph (c) of this section, no machinery space may exceed the following noise levels:
(1) Machinery control room—75 dB(A)
(2) Manned machinery space—90 dB(A)
(3) Unmanned machinery space—110 dB(A)
(4) Periodically unattended machinery space—110 dB(A)
(5) Workshop—85 dB(A)
(6) Any other work space around machinery—90 dB(A)

(c) If adding a source of noise would cause a machinery space to exceed the noise level permitted by paragraph (b) of this section, the new source must be suitably insulated or isolated so that the space does not exceed that noise level. If the space is manned, a refuge from noise must be provided within the space.

(d) Ear protection must be provided for any person entering any space with a noise level greater than 85 dB(A).

(e) Each entrance to a machinery space with a noise level greater than 85 dB(A) must have a warning sign stating that each person entering the space must wear ear protection.

[CGD 83–043, 60 FR 24776, May 10, 1995, as amended by USCG–2003–16630, 73 FR 65186, Oct. 31, 2008]

§ 58.01-55 Tanks for flammable and combustible oil.

(a) For the purposes of this section, a machinery space of category A is a space that contains any of the following:
(1) Internal-combustion machinery used for main propulsion.
(2) Internal-combustion machinery used for other than main propulsion,

Coast Guard, Dept. of Homeland Security § 58.03-1

whose power output is equal to or greater than 500 HP (375 kw).

(3) Any oil-fired boiler.

(4) Any equipment used to prepare fuel oil for delivery to an oil-fired boiler, or equipment used to prepare heated oil for delivery to an internal-combustion engine, including any oil-pressure pumps, filters, and heaters dealing with oil pressures above 26 psi.

(b) As far as practicable, each fuel-oil tank must be part of the vessel's structure and be located outside a machinery space of category A.

(c) If a fuel-oil tank, other than a double-bottom tank, must be located adjacent to or within a machinery space of category A—

(1) At least one of its vertical sides must be contiguous to the boundary of the machinery space;

(2) The tank must have a common boundary with the double-bottom tanks; and

(3) The area of the tank boundary common with the machinery spaces must be kept as small as practicable.

(d) If a fuel-oil tank must be located within a machinery space of category A, it must not contain fuel oil with a flashpoint of less than 60 °C (140 °F).

(e) In general, no freestanding fuel-oil tank is permitted in any machinery space of Category A on a passenger vessel. A freestanding fuel-oil tank is permitted in other spaces only if authorized by the Commanding Officer, Marine Safety Center. If so authorized, each freestanding fuel-oil tank must—

(i) Comply with subpart 58.50 of this subchapter; and

(ii) Be placed in an oil-tight spill tray with a drain pipe leading to a spill-oil tank.

(f) No fuel-oil tank may be located where spillage or leakage from it can constitute a hazard by falling on heated surfaces. The design must also prevent any oil that may escape under pressure from any pump, filter, or heater from coming into contact with heated surfaces.

[CGD 83-043, 60 FR 24776, May 10, 1995]

Subpart 58.03—Incorporation of Standards

§ 58.03-1 Incorporation by reference.

(a) Certain material is incorporated by reference into this part with the approval of the Director of the Federal Register under 5 U.S.C. 552(a) and 1 CFR part 51. To enforce any edition other than that specified in this section, the Coast Guard must publish notice of change in the FEDERAL REGISTER and the material must be available to the public. All approved material is available for inspection at the National Archives and Records Administration (NARA). For information on the availability of this material at NARA, call 202–741–6030 or go to *http://www.archives.gov/federal_register/code_of_federal_regulations/ibr_locations.html*. This material is also available for inspection at the Coast Guard Headquarters. Contact Commandant (CG–ENG), Attn: Office of Design and Engineering Systems, U.S. Coast Guard Stop 7509, 2703 Martin Luther King Jr. Avenue SE., Washington, DC 20593–7509. The material is also available from the sources listed below.

(b) *American Boat and Yacht Council (ABYC)*, 613 Third Street, Suite 10, Annapolis, MD 21403:

(1) P–1–73, Safe Installation of Exhaust Systems for Propulsion and Auxiliary Machinery, 1973 ("ABYC P–1"), 58.10–5; and

(2) [Reserved]

(c) *American Bureau of Shipping (ABS)*, ABS Plaza, 16855 Northchase Drive, Houston, TX 77060.

(1) Rules for Building and Classing Steel Vessels, Part 4 Vessel Systems and Machinery (2003) ("ABS Steel Vessel Rules"), 58.01–5; 58.05–1; 58.10–15; 58.20–5; 58.25–5; and

(2) [Reserved]

(d) *American National Standards Institute (ANSI)*, 11 West 42nd Street, New York, NY 10036:

(1) ANSI B31.3, Chemical Plant and Petroleum Refinery Piping, 1987 ("ANSI B31.3"), 58.60–7;

(2) ANSI B31.5, Refrigeration Piping, 1987 ("ANSI B31.5"), 58.20–5; 58.20–20; and

(3) ANSI B93.5, Recommended practice for the use of Fire Resistant Fluids

for Fluid Power Systems, 1979 ("ANSI B93.5"), 58.30–10.

(e) *American Petroleum Institute (API)*, 1220 L Street, NW., Washington, DC 20005–4070:

(1) API RP 14C, Analysis, Design, Installation and Testing of Basic Surface Safety Systems for Offshore Production Platforms, 1986 ("API RP 14C"), 58.60–9; and

(2) API RP 53, Recommended Practice for Blowout Prevention Equipment Systems for Drilling Wells, 1984 ("API RP 53"), 58.60–7.

(f) *American Society of Mechanical Engineers (ASME) International*, Three Park Avenue, New York, NY 10016–5990:

(1) 2001 ASME Boiler and Pressure Vessel Code, Section I, Rules for Construction of Power Boilers (July 1, 2001) ("Section I of the ASME Boiler and Pressure Vessel Code"), 58.30–15; and

(2) ASME Boiler and Pressure Vessel Code, Section VIII, Division 1, Rules for Construction of Pressure Vessels (1998 with 1999 and 2000 addenda) ("Section VIII of the ASME Boiler and Pressure Vessel Code"), 58.30–15.

(g) *ASTM International (formerly American Society for Testing and Materials) (ASTM)*, 100 Barr Harbor Drive, West Conshohocken, PA 19428–2959:

(1) ASTM A 193/A 193M–98a, Standard Specification for Alloy-Steel and Stainless Steel Bolting Materials for High-Temperature Service ("ASTM A 193"), 58.30–15;

(2) ASTM B 96–93, Standard Specification for Copper-Silicon Alloy Plate, Sheet, Strip, and Rolled Bar for General Purposes and Pressure Vessels ("ASTM B 96"), 58.50–5;

(3) ASTM B 122/B 122M–95, Standard Specification for Copper-Nickel-Tin Alloy, Copper-Nickel-Zinc Alloy (Nickel Silver), and Copper-Nickel Alloy Plate, Sheet, Strip, and Rolled Bar ("ASTM B 122"), 58.50–5;

(4) ASTM B 127–93a, Standard Specification for Nickel-Copper Alloy (UNS N04400) Plate, Sheet, and Strip ("ASTM B 127"), 58.50–5; 58.50–10;

(5) ASTM B 152–97a, Standard Specification for Copper Sheet, Strip, Plate, and Rolled Bar ("ASTM B 152"), 58.50–5;

(6) ASTM B 209–96, Standard Specification for Aluminum and Aluminum Alloy Sheet and Plate ("ASTM B 209"), 58.50–5; 58.50–10;

(7) ASTM D 92–97, Standard Test Method for Flash and Fire Points by Cleveland Open Cup ("ASTM D 92"), 58.30–10;

(8) ASTM D 93–97, Standard Test Methods for Flash Point by Pensky-Martens Closed Cup Tester ("ASTM D 93"), 58.01–10; and

(9) ASTM D 323–94, Standard Test Method for Vapor Pressure of Petroleum Products (Reid Method) ("ASTM D 323"), 58.16–5.

(h) *International Maritime Organization (IMO)*, Publications Section, 4 Albert Embankment, London SE1 7SR, United Kingdom:

(1) A.467(XII), Guidelines for Acceptance of Non-Duplicated Rudder Actuators for Tankers, Chemical Tankers and Gas Carriers of 10,000 Tons Gross Tonnage and Above But Less Than 100,000 Tonnes Deadweight, 1981 ("IMO A.467(XII)"), 58.25–60; and

(2) A.468(XII), Code on Noise Levels on Board Ships, 1981 ("IMO A.468(XII)"), 58.01–50.

(i) *National Fire Protection Association (NFPA)*, 1 Batterymarch Park, Quincy, MA 02169:

(1) NFPA 302, Fire Protection Standard for Pleasure and Commercial Craft, 1989 ("NFPA 302"), 58.10–5; and

(2) [Reserved]

(j) *Society of Automotive Engineers (SAE)*, 400 Commonwealth Drive, Warrendale, PA 15096:

(1) SAE J–1928, Devices Providing Backfire Flame Control for Gasoline Engines in Marine Applications, 1989 ("SAE J–1928"), 58.10–5; and

(2) SAE J429, Mechanical and Material Requirements for Externally Threaded Fasteners (Aug. 1983) ("SAE J429"), 58.30–15.

(k) *Underwriters Laboratories, Inc. (UL)*, 12 Laboratory Drive, Research Triangle Park, NC 27709:

(1) UL 1111, Marine Carburetor Flame Arresters, 1988 ("UL 1111"), 58.10–5; and

(2) [Reserved]

[USCG–2003–16630, 73 FR 65186, Oct. 31, 2008, as amended by USCG–2009–0702, 74 FR 49229, Sept. 25, 2009; USCG–2012–0832, 77 FR 59778, Oct. 1, 2012; USCG 2013–0671, 78 FR 60148, Sept. 30, 2013]

Subpart 58.05—Main Propulsion Machinery

§ 58.05-1 Material, design and construction.

(a) The material, design, construction, workmanship, and arrangement of main propulsion machinery and of each auxiliary, directly connected to the engine and supplied as such, must be at least equivalent to the standards established by the ABS Steel Vessel Rules (incorporated by reference, see 46 CFR 58.03-1), except as otherwise provided by this subchapter.

(b) When main and auxiliary machinery is to be installed without classification society review, the builder shall submit in quadruplicate to the cognizant Officer in Charge, Marine Inspection, such drawings and particulars of the installation as are required by the American Bureau of Shipping Rules for Building and Classing Steel Vessels, Part 4 Vessel Systems and Machinery (2003) for similar installations on classed vessels.

[USCG–2003–16630, 73 FR 65186, Oct. 31, 2008]

§ 58.05-5 Astern power.

(a) All vessels shall have sufficient power for going astern to secure proper control of the ship in all normal circumstances.

§ 58.05-10 Automatic shut-off.

Main propulsion machinery must be provided with automatic shut-off controls in accordance with part 62 of this subchapter. These controls must shut down main propulsion machinery in case of a failure, such as failure of the lubricating-oil supply, that could lead rapidly to complete breakdown, serious damage, or explosion.

[CGD 83–043, 60 FR 24776, May 10, 1995]

Subpart 58.10—Internal Combustion Engine Installations

§ 58.10-5 Gasoline engine installations.

(a) *Engine design.* All installations shall be of marine type engines suitable for the intended service, designed and constructed in conformance with the requirements of this subchapter.

(b) *Carburetors.* (1) Drip collectors shall be fitted under all carburetors, except the down-draft type, to prevent fuel leakage from reaching the bilges and so arranged as to permit ready removal of such fuel leakage. Drip collectors shall be covered with flame screens.

NOTE: It is recommended that drip collectors be drained by a device for automatic return of all drip to engine air intakes.

(2) All gasoline engines must be equipped with an acceptable means of backfire flame control. Installations of backfire flame arresters bearing basic Approval Nos. 162.015 or 162.041 or engine air and fuel induction systems bearing basic Approval Nos. 162.015 or 162.042 may be continued in use as long as they are serviceable and in good condition. New installations or replacements must meet the applicable requirements of this section.

(3) The following are acceptable means of backfire flame control for gasoline engines:

(i) A backfire flame arrester complying with SAE J–1928 (incorporated by reference; see 46 CFR 58.03–1) or UL 1111 (incorporated by reference; see 46 CFR 58.03–1) and marked accordingly. The flame arrester must be suitably secured to the air intake with a flametight connection.

(ii) An engine air and fuel induction system which provides adequate protection from propagation of backfire flame to the atmosphere equivalent to that provided by an acceptable backfire flame arrester. A gasoline engine utilizing an air and fuel induction system, and operated without an approved backfire flame arrester, must either include a reed valve assembly or be installed in accordance with SAE J–1928.

(iii) An arrangement of the carburetor or engine air induction system that will disperse any flames caused by engine backfire. The flames must be dispersed to the atmosphere outside the vessel in such a manner that the flames will not endanger the vessel, persons, on board, or nearby vessels and structures. Flame dispersion may be achieved by attachments to the carburetor or location of the engine air induction system. All attachments must be of metallic construction with flametight connections and firmly secured to withstand vibration, shock, and engine backfire. Such installations do not require formal approval and labeling but must comply with this subpart.

(c) *Exhaust manifold.* The exhaust manifold shall either be water-jacketed and cooled by discharge from a pump which operates whenever the engine is running, or woodwork within nine inches shall be protected by ¼-inch asbestos board covered with not less than No. 22 USSG (U.S. standard gage) galvanized sheet iron or nonferrous metal. A dead air space of ¼-inch shall be left between the protecting asbestos and the wood, and a clearance of not less than two inches maintained between the manifold and the surface of such protection.

(d) *Exhaust pipe.* (1) Exhaust pipe installations must conform to the requirements of ABYC P–1 and part 1, section 23 of NFPA 302 (both incorporated by reference; see 46 CFR 58.03–1) and the following additional requirements:

(i) All exhaust installations with pressures in excess of 15 pounds per square inch gage or employing runs passing through living or working spaces shall meet the material requirements of part 56 of this subchapter.

(ii) Horizontal dry exhaust pipes are permitted only if they do not pass through living or berthing spaces, they terminate above the deepest load waterline and are so arranged as to prevent entry of cold water from rough or boarding seas, and they are constructed of corrosion resisting material "at the hull penetration."

[CGFR 68–82, 33 FR 18878, Dec. 18, 1968, as amended by CGD 88–032, 56 FR 35824, July 29, 1991; USCG–2003–16630, 73 FR 65187, Oct. 31, 2008]

§ 58.10–10 Diesel engine installations.

(a) The requirements of § 58.10–5 (a), (c), and (d) shall apply to diesel engine installations.

(b) A diesel engine air intake on a mobile offshore drilling unit must not be in a classified location.[1]

(c) A diesel engine exhaust on a mobile offshore drilling unit must not discharge into a classified location.[1]

[CGFR 68–82, 33 FR 18878, Dec. 18, 1968, as amended by CGD 73–251, 43 FR 56801, Dec. 4, 1978; CGD 95–028, 62 FR 51202, Sept. 30, 1997]

§ 58.10–15 Gas turbine installations.

(a) *Standards.* The design, construction, workmanship and tests of gas turbines and their associated machinery shall be at least equivalent to the standards of the ABS Steel Vessel Rules (incorporated by reference, see 46 CFR 58.03–1).

(b) *Materials.* The materials used for gas turbine installations shall have properties suitable for the intended service. When materials not conforming to standard ASTM specifications are employed, data concerning their properties, including high temperature strength data, where applicable, shall be furnished.

(c) *Exhausts.* (1) Where piping is used for gas turbine exhaust lines, Class II is required as a minimum. (See subpart 56.04 of this subchapter.) Where the exhaust pressure exceeds 150 pounds per square inch, such as in closed cycle systems, Class I shall be used. Where ducting other than pipe is employed, the drawings and design data shall be submitted to substantiate suitability and safety for the intended service.

(2) Where considered necessary, gas turbines and associated exhaust systems shall be suitably insulated or cooled, by means of lagging, water spray, or a combination thereof.

(3) Gas turbine exhausts shall not be interconnected with boiler uptakes except for gas turbines used for emergency power and lighting or for emergency propulsion. Dampers or other suitable means shall be installed to prevent backflow of boiler exhaust gases through the turbine. Interconnected exhausts must be specifically approved by the Commandant.

(4) A gas turbine exhaust on a mobile offshore drilling unit must not discharge in a classified location.[1]

(d) *Air inlets.* Air inlets must be designed as follows:

[1] Sections 108.171 to 108.175 of this chapter define classified locations for mobile offshore drilling units.

Coast Guard, Dept. of Homeland Security § 58.16-5

(1) Each air inlet must have means to protect the safety of life and to prevent the entrance of harmful foreign material, including water, into the system.

(2) A gas turbine air inlet must not be in a classified location.[1]

(e) *Cooling and ventilation.* Means shall be provided for circulating air, either natural or forced, through the engine compartment for cooling and ventilation.

(f) *Automatic shutdown.* (1) The control system shall be designed for automatic shutdown of the engine with actuation of audible and visible alarms at shutdown. The visible malfunction indicator shall indicate what condition caused the shutdown and remain visible until reset. Automatic shutdown shall occur under the following conditions:

(i) Overspeed.

(ii) Low lubricating oil pressure. Consideration will be given providing alarm only (without shutdown) in those cases where suitable antifriction bearings are fitted.

(2) Audible or visible alarms shall also be provided for:

(i) Excessive gas temperature, measured at the turbine inlet, gas generator, interstage turbine or turbine exhaust.

(ii) Excessive lubricating oil temperature.

(iii) Excessive speed.

(iv) Reduced lubricating oil pressure.

(3) A remote, manually operated shutdown device shall be provided. Such device may be totally mechanical or may be electrical with a manually actuated switch.

(g) *Drawings and design data.* Drawings and design data of the following components shall be submitted to substantiate their suitability and safety for the service intended:

(1) Combustion chamber.

(2) Regenerator or recuperator.

(3) Casing or piping conveying the gas from the combustion device to the gas turbine.

(h) *Fuel systems.* Gas turbine fuel systems shall meet the requirements of part 56 of this subchapter.

(i) *Fire extinguishing systems.* A special local fire extinguishing system may be required for gas turbine installations if considered necessary by the Commandant. Such a system would be in addition to any other required in the compartment in which the gas turbine is located.

[CGFR 68-82, 33 FR 18878, Dec. 18, 1968, as amended by CGFR 72-59R, 37 FR 6190, Mar. 25, 1972; CGD 73-251, 43 FR 56801, Dec. 4, 1978; CGD 83-043, 60 FR 24776, May 10, 1995; USCG-2003-16630, 73 FR 65187, Oct. 31, 2008]

Subpart 58.16—Liquefied Petroleum Gases for Cooking and Heating

§ 58.16-1 Scope.

(a) This subpart prescribes standards for the use of liquefied petroleum gas for heating and cooking on inspected vessels, except ferries.

(b) It is the intent of the regulations in this subpart to permit liquefied petroleum gas systems of the vapor withdrawal type only. Cylinders designed to admit liquid gas into any other part of the system are prohibited.

(c) Except as provided by § 58.16-7(b), all component parts of the system, except cylinders, appliances, and low pressure tubing, shall be designed to withstand a pressure of 500 pounds per square inch without failure.

[CGFR 68-82, 33 FR 18878, Dec. 18, 1968, as amended by CGD 83-013, 54 FR 6402, Feb. 10, 1989]

§ 58.16-5 Definition.

For the purpose of this subpart the term "liquefied petroleum gas" means any liquefied flammable gas which is composed predominantly of hydrocarbons or mixtures of hydrocarbons, such as propane, propylene, butane, butylene, or butadiene, and which has a Reid ASTM D 323 (incorporated by reference, see § 58.03-1). Method of test for Vapor Pressure of Petroleum Products (Reid Method)) vapor pressure exceeding 40 pounds per square inch absolute at 100 °F.

[CGFR 68-82, 33 FR 18878, Dec. 18, 1968, as amended by USCG-2000-7790, 65 FR 58460, Sept. 29, 2000]

---

[1] Sections 108.171 to 108.175 of this chapter define classified locations for mobile offshore drilling units.

§ 58.16-7 Use of liquefied petroleum gas.

(a) Cooking equipment using liquefied petroleum gas on vessels of 100 gross tons or more that carry passengers for hire must meet the requirements of this subpart.

(b) Cooking equipment using liquefied petroleum gas on vessels of less than 100 gross tons that carry passengers for hire must meet the requirements of 46 CFR 25.45-2 or 184.05, as applicable.

(c) Systems using liquefied petroleum gas for cooking or heating on any other vessels subject to inspection by the Coast Guard must meet the requirements of this subpart.

[CGD 83-013, 54 FR 6402, Feb. 10, 1989]

§ 58.16-10 Approvals.

(a) *Gas appliances.* (1) All gas-consuming appliances used for cooking and heating shall be of a type approved by the Commandant, and shall be tested, listed and labeled by an acceptable laboratory, such as:

(i) The American Gas Association Testing Laboratories.

(ii) The Marine Department, Underwriters' Laboratories, Inc. (formerly Yacht Safety Bureau).

(2) Continuous-burning pilot flames are prohibited for use on gas appliances when installed below the weather deck.

(3) Printed instructions for proper installation, operation, and maintenance of each gas-consuming appliance shall be furnished by the manufacturer.

(1) Cylinders in which liquefied petroleum gas is stored and handled must be constructed, tested, marked, maintained, and retested in accordance with 49 CFR part 178.

(2) All liquefied petroleum gas cylinders in service shall bear a test date marking indicating that they have been retested in accordance with the regulations of the Department of Transportation.

(3) Regardless of the date of the previous test, a cylinder shall be rejected for further service when it leaks; when it is weakened appreciably by corrosion, denting, bulging or other evidence of rough usage; when it has lost more than 5 percent of its tare weight; or when it has been involved in a fire.

(c) *Safety-relief devices.* All required safety-relief devices must be approved as to type, size, pressure setting, and location by the Commandant (CG-521) as being in accordance with 49 CFR part 178.

(d) *Valves, regulators, and vaporizers.* All component parts of the system, other than cylinders and low pressure distribution tubing between regulators and appliances, shall be tested and approved by and bear the label of the Underwriters Laboratories, Inc., or other recognized testing laboratory.

(e) *Plan approval.* Drawings in triplicate, showing the location and installation of all piping, gas-consuming appliances, cylinders, and other component parts of the system shall be submitted for approval.

[CGFR 68-82, 33 FR 18878, Dec. 18, 1968, as amended by CGFR 69-127, 35 FR 9980 June 17, 1970; USCG-2003-16630, 73 FR 65187, Oct. 31, 2008]

§ 58.16-15 Valves and safety relief devices.

(a) Each cylinder shall have a manually operated screw-down shutoff valve fitted with a handwheel installed directly at the cylinder outlet.

(b) All cylinders shall be protected by one or more safety relief devices complying with the requirements of § 58.16-10(a). The safety relief device shall be a shutoff valve with an integral spring-loaded safety relief valve and supplementary fusible plug, the latter designed to yield when the cylinder has been emptied of liquid gas by the relief valve under conditions of exposure to excessive heat.

(c) Cylinder valves and safety relief devices shall have direct communication with the vapor space of the cylinder.

(d) In addition to the cylinder valve, a multiple cylinder system shall be provided with a two-way positive shutoff manifold valve of the manually operated type. The manifold valve shall be so arranged that the replacement of empty cylinders can be made without shutting down the flow of gas in the system.

(e) A master packless shutoff valve controlling all burners simultaneously shall be installed at the manifold of all gas-consuming appliances.

§ 58.16-16 Reducing regulators.

(a) All systems shall be provided with a regulating device so adjusted as to release gas to the distribution tubing at a pressure not in excess of 18 inches water column, or approximately 10.5 ounces per square inch.

(b) The low pressure side of all regulators shall be protected against excessive pressure by means of a suitable relief valve which shall be integral with the regulator. The relief valve shall be set to start to discharge at a pressure not less than two times and not more than three times the delivery pressure.

(c) All reducing regulators shall be fitted with a pressure gage located on the high pressure side of the regulator.

§ 58.16-17 Piping and fittings.

(a) The piping between the cylinders and the appliances shall be seamless annealed copper tubing or such other seamless tubing as may be approved by the Commandant.

(b) All high pressure tubing between the cylinders and the regulators shall have a minimum wall thickness of 0.049 inch. All low-pressure tubing between the regulator and appliances shall have a minimum wall thickness of 0.032 inch.

(c) Tubing connecting fittings shall be of the flare type; or connections may be soldered or brazed with material having a melting point in excess of 1,000 °F.

§ 58.16-18 Installation.

(a) *Cylinders, regulating and safety equipment.* (1) Cylinders, regulating and safety equipment shall be installed in a substantially constructed and firmly fixed metal enclosure located on or above the weather deck. The cylinder enclosure shall have access from the weather deck only. The enclosure shall be provided with top and bottom ventilation consisting of a fresh air inlet pipe and an exhaust pipe both entering through the top of the cylinder housing. The enclosure shall be constructed so that when the access opening is closed, no gas can escape except through the ventilation system.

(2) Cylinders, regulating and safety devices shall be securely fastened and supported within the metal enclosure. The cylinders and high pressure equipment shall be so mounted as to be readily accessible and capable of easy removal for refilling and inspection. The stowage of high pressure equipment in the housing shall be such that the cylinder valves can be readily operated and the pressure gage dial be easily visible. Where possible cylinders shall be mounted in an upright position.

(3) Stowage of unconnected spare cylinders, filled or empty, shall comply with the requirements for cylinders.

(4) All valves, manifolds and regulators shall be securely mounted in locations readily accessible for inspection, maintenance and testing, and shall be adequately protected.

(5) Discharge of the safety relief valves shall be vented away from the cylinder, and insofar as practicable, upward into the open atmosphere, but in all cases so as to prevent impingement of the escaping gas onto a cylinder.

(b) *Piping.* (1) All piping shall be installed so as to provide minimum interior runs and adequate flexibility. The piping at the cylinder outlets shall be fitted with flexible metallic connections to minimize the effect of cylinder movement on the outlet piping.

(2) Distribution lines shall be protected from physical damage and be readily accessible for inspection. Lines shall be substantially secured against vibration by means of soft nonferrous metal clips without sharp edges in contact with the tubing. When passing through decks or bulkheads, the lines shall be protected by ferrules of nonabrasive material. The distribution lines shall be continuous length of tubes from the regulator to the shutoff valve at the appliance manifold.

(c) *Gas-consuming appliances.* All gas-consuming appliances shall be permanently and securely fastened in place.

(d) *Electrical.* No electrical connections shall be made within the cylinder housing.

§ 58.16-19 Tests.

(a) *Installation.* (1) After installation, the distribution tubing shall be tested prior to its connection to the regulator and appliance by an air pressure of not less than 5 pounds per square inch.

(2) After satisfactory completion of the tests prescribed in paragraph (a)(1) of this section, the distribution tubing

§ 58.16-20

shall be connected to the regulator and appliance and the entire system subjected to a leak test as required by § 58.16-30(j).

(b) *Periodic.* Leak tests as required by § 58.16-30(j) shall be conducted at least once each month and at each regular annual or biennial inspection. The tests required at monthly intervals shall be conducted by a credentialed officer of the vessel or qualified personnel acceptable to the Officer in Charge, Marine Inspection. The owner, master, or person in charge of the vessel shall keep records of such tests showing the dates when performed and the name(s) of the person(s) and/or company conducting the tests. Such records shall be made available to the marine inspector upon request and shall be kept for the period of validity of the vessel's current certificate of inspection. Where practicable, these records should be kept in or with the vessel's logbook.

[CGFR 68–82, 33 FR 18878, Dec. 18, 1968, as amended by USCG 2006–24371, 74 FR 11265, Mar. 16, 2009]

§ 58.16-20 Ventilation of compartments containing gas-consuming appliances.

(a) Compartments containing gas-consuming appliances which are located above the weather deck shall be fitted with at least two natural ventilator ducts led from the atmosphere with one extending to the floor level and the other extending to the overhead of the compartment. Powered ventilation may be used provided the motor is outside the compartment.

(b) Compartments in which gas-consuming appliances are located entirely below the weather deck shall be provided with powered ventilation of sufficient capacity to effect a change of air at least once every 6 minutes. The motor for the powered ventilation shall be located outside the compartment.

§ 58.16-25 Odorization.

(a) All liquefied petroleum gases shall be effectively odorized by an agent of such character as to indicate positively by a distinctive odor, the presence of gas down to concentration in air of not over one-fifth the lower limit of combustibility.

§ 58.16-30 Operating instructions.

(a) Before opening a cylinder valve, the outlet of the cylinder shall be connected tightly to system; and in the case where only a single cylinder is used in the system, all appliance valves and pilots shall be shut off before the cylinder valve is opened.

(b) Before opening cylinder valve after connecting it to system, the cylinder shall be securely fastened in place.

(c) When cylinders are not in use their outlet valves shall be kept closed.

(d) Cylinders when exhausted shall have their outlet valves closed.

(e) Nothing shall be stored in the metal enclosure except liquefied petroleum gas cylinders and permanently fastened parts of the system.

(f) Valve protecting caps, if provided, shall be firmly fixed in place on all cylinders not attached to the system. Caps for cylinders in use may remain in the cylinder enclosure if rigidly fastened thereto.

(g) The opening to the cylinder enclosure shall be closed at all times except when access is required to change cylinders or maintain equipment.

(h) Close master valve whenever gas-consuming appliance is not in use.

(i) No smoking is permitted in the vicinity of the cylinder enclosure when access to enclosure is open.

(j) Test system for leakage in accordance with the following procedure: With appliance valve closed, the master shutoff valve on the appliance open, and with one cylinder valve open, note pressure in the gage. Close cylinder valve. The pressure should remain constant for at least 10 minutes. If the pressure drops, locate leakage by application of liquid detergent or soapy water solution at all connections. Never use flame to check for leaks. Repeat test for each cylinder in a multicylinder system.

(k) Report any presence of gas odor to

§ 58.16-35 Markings.

(a) The outside of the cylinder enclosure housing liquefied petroleum gas cylinders, valves and regulators shall be marked as follows:

Liquefied Petroleum Gas
Keep Open Fires Away.
Operating Instructions
Inside and In

(b) A durable and permanently legible instruction sign covering safe operation and maintenance of the gas-consuming appliance shall be installed adjacent to the appliance.

(c) "Operating Instructions" as listed in § 58.16-30 shall be framed under glass, or other equivalent, clear, transparent material, in plainly visible locations on the outside of the metal enclosure and near the most frequently used gas-consuming appliance, so they may be easily read.

Subpart 58.20—Refrigeration Machinery

§ 58.20-1 Scope.

(a) The regulations in this subpart apply to fixed refrigeration systems for air conditioning, refrigerated spaces, cargo spaces, and reliquefaction of low temperature cargo installed on vessels.

(b) The regulations in this subpart shall not apply to small self-contained units.

§ 58.20-5 Design.

(a) Refrigeration machinery may be accepted for installation provided the design, material, and fabrication comply with the applicable requirements of the ABS Steel Vessel Rules (incorporated by reference, see 46 CFR 58.03–1). The minimum pressures for design of all components must be those listed for piping in Table 501.2.4 of ANSI B31.5 (incorporated by reference; see 46 CFR 58.03–1). In no case may pressure components be designed for a pressure less than that for which the safety devices of the system are set. Pressure vessels must be designed in accordance with part 54 of this subchapter.

(b) For refrigeration systems other than those for reliquefaction of cargo, only those refrigerants under § 147.90 of this chapter are allowed.

[CGFR 68–82, 33 FR 18878, Dec. 18, 1968, as amended by CGFR 69–127, 35 FR 9980, June 17, 1970; CGD 84–044, 53 FR 7748, Mar. 10, 1988; USCG–2003–16630, 73 FR 65187, Oct. 31, 2008]

§ 58.20-10 Pressure relieving devices.

(a) Each pressure vessel containing refrigerants, which may be isolated, shall be protected by a relief valve set to relieve at a pressure not exceeding the maximum allowable working pressure of the vessel. When a pressure vessel forms an integral part of a system having a relief valve, such vessel need not have an individual relief valve.

(b) Relief valves fitted on the high pressure side may discharge to the low pressure side before relieving to atmosphere. When relieving to atmosphere, a relief valve shall be fitted in the atmospheric discharge connection from the receivers and condensers. The relief valve from the receivers may relieve to the condenser which in turn may relieve either to the low side or to atmosphere. It shall be set to relieve at a pressure not greater than the maximum allowable working pressure. A rupture disk may be fitted in series with the relief valve, provided the bursting pressure of the rupture disk is not in excess of the relief valve set pressure. Where a rupture disk is fitted on the downstream side of the relief valve, the relief valve shall be of the type not affected by back pressure.

§ 58.20-15 Installation of refrigerating machinery.

(a) Where refrigerating machines are installed in which anhydrous ammonia is used as a refrigerant, such machines shall be located in a well-ventilated, isolated compartment preferably on the deck, but in no case shall it be permissible to install such machines in the engineroom space unless the arrangement is such as to eliminate any hazard from gas escaping to the engineroom. Absorption machines using a solution of aqua ammonia or machines using carbon dioxide are exempt from this requirement, provided the maximum charges that might be released in the event of breakage do not exceed 300 pounds.

(b) Machinery compartments containing equipment for ammonia shall be fitted with a sprinkler system providing an effective water spray and having a remote control device located outside the compartment.

(c) All refrigeration compressor spaces shall be effectively ventilated

§ 58.20–20

and drained and shall be separated from the insulated spaces by a watertight bulkhead, unless otherwise approved.

[CGFR 68–82, 33 FR 18878, Dec. 18, 1968, as amended by USCG–2004–18884, 69 FR 58346, Sept. 30, 2004]

§ 58.20–20 Refrigeration piping.

(a) All piping materials shall be suitable for handling the primary refrigerant, brine, or fluid used, and shall be of such chemical and physical properties as to remain ductile at the lowest operating temperature.

(b) Piping systems shall be designed in accordance with ANSI B31.5 (incorporated by reference; see 46 CFR 58.03–1). Piping used for cargo reliquefaction systems shall also comply with the applicable requirements found in low temperature piping, § 56.50–105 of this subchapter.

(c) A relief valve shall be fitted on or near the compressor on the gas discharge side between the compressor and the first stop valve with the discharge therefrom led to the suction side. A check valve shall be fitted in the atmospheric discharge line if it is led through the side of the vessel below the freeboard deck, or a shutoff valve may be employed if it is locked in the open position.

[CGFR 68–82, 33 FR 18878, Dec. 18, 1968, as amended by CGFR 69–127, 35 FR 9980, June 17, 1970; USCG–2003–16630, 73 FR 65187, Oct. 31, 2008]

§ 58.20–25 Tests.

(a) All pressure vessels, compressors, piping, and direct expansion cooling coils shall be leak tested after installation to their design pressures, hydrostatically or pneumatically.

(b) No pneumatic tests in refrigeration systems aboard ships shall be made at pressures exceeding the design pressure of the part of the system being tested. Pneumatic tests may be made with the refrigerant in the system or if the refrigerant has been removed, oil-pumped dry nitrogen or bone dry carbon dioxide with a detectable amount of the refrigerant added, should be used as a testing medium. (Carbon dioxide should not be used to leak test an ammonia system.) In no case should air, oxygen, any flammable gas or any flammable mixture of gases be used for testing.

Subpart 58.25—Steering Gear

SOURCE: CGD 83–043, 60 FR 24776, May 10, 1995, unless otherwise noted

§ 58.25–1 Applicability.

(a) Except as specified otherwise, this subpart applies to—

(1) Each vessel or installation of steering gear contracted for on or after June 9, 1995; and

(2) Each vessel on an international voyage with an installation of steering gear contracted for on or after September 1, 1984.

(b) Each vessel not on an international voyage with an installation of steering gear contracted for before June 9, 1995, and each vessel on an international voyage with such an installation contracted for before September 1, 1984, may meet either the requirements of this subpart or those in effect on the date of the installation.

§ 58.25–5 General.

(a) *Definitions.*

Ancillary steering equipment means steering equipment, other than the required control systems and power actuating systems, that either is not required, such as automatic pilot or nonfollowup control from the pilothouse, or is necessary to perform a specific required function, such as the automatic detection and isolation of a defective section of a tanker's hydraulic steering gear.

Auxiliary steering gear means the equipment, other than any part of the main steering gear, necessary to steer the vessel in case of failure of the main steering gear, not including a tiller, quadrant, or other component serving the same purpose. *Control system* means the equipment by which orders for rudder movement are transmitted from the pilothouse to the steering-gear power units. A control system for steering gear includes, but is not limited to, one or more—

(1) Transmitters;

(2) Receivers;

(3) Feedback devices;

Coast Guard, Dept. of Homeland Security § 58.25–5

(4) Hydraulic servo-control pumps, with associated motors and motor controllers;

(5) Differential units, hunting gear, and similar devices;

(6) All gearing, piping, shafting, cables, circuitry, and ancillary devices for controlling the output of power units; and

(7) Means of bringing steering-gear power units into operation.

Fast-acting valve, as used in this subpart, means a ball, plug, spool, or similar valve with a handle connected for quick manual operation.

Followup control means closed-loop (feedback) control that relates the position of the helm to a specific rudder angle by transmitting the helm-angle order to the power actuating system and, by means of feedback, automatically stopping the rudder when the angle selected by the helm is reached.

Main steering gear means the machinery, including power actuating systems, and the means of applying torque to the rudder stock, such as a tiller or quadrant, necessary for moving the rudder to steer the vessel in normal service.

Maximum ahead service speed means the greatest speed that a vessel is designed to maintain in service at sea at the deepest loadline draft.

Maximum astern speed means the speed that it is estimated the vessel can attain at the maximum designed power astern at the deepest loadline draft.

Power actuating system means the hydraulic equipment for applying torque to the rudder stock. It includes, but is not limited to—

(1) Rudder actuators;

(2) Steering-gear power units; and

(3) Pipes, valves, fittings, linkages, and cables for transmitting power from the power unit or units to the rudder actuator or actuators.

Speedily regained, as used in this subpart, refers to the time it takes one qualified crewmember, after arriving in the steering-gear compartment, and without the use of tools, to respond to a failure of the steering gear and take the necessary corrective action.

Steering capability means steering equivalent to that required of auxiliary steering gear by § 58.25–10(c)(2).

Steering gear means the machinery, including power actuating systems, control systems, and ancillary equipment, necessary for moving the rudder to steer the vessel.

Steering-gear power unit means:

(1) In the case of electric steering gear, an electric motor and its associated electrical equipment, including motor controller, disconnect switch, and feeder circuit.

(2) In the case of an electro-hydraulic steering gear, an electric motor, connected pump, and associated electrical equipment such as the motor controller, disconnect switch, and feeder circuit.

(3) In the case of hydraulic steering gear, the pump and its prime mover.

Tank vessel, as used in this subpart, means a self-propelled vessel, including a chemical tanker or a gas carrier, defined either as a tanker by 46 U.S.C. 2101(38) or as a tank vessel by 46 U.S.C. 2101(39).

(b) Unless it otherwise complies with this subpart, each self-propelled vessel must be provided with a main steering gear and an auxiliary steering gear. These gear must be arranged so that—

(1) The failure of one will not render the other inoperative; and

(2) Transfer from the main to the auxiliary can be effected quickly.

(c) Each substantial replacement of steering-gear components or reconfiguration of steering-gear arrangements on an existing vessel must comply with the requirements of this subpart for new installations to the satisfaction of the cognizant Officer in Charge, Marine Inspection.

(d) Each non-pressure-containing steering-gear component and each rudder stock must be of sound and reliable construction, meet the minimum material requirements of § 58.25–75, and be designed to standards at least equal to those established by the ABS Steel Vessel Rules (incorporated by reference, see 46 CFR 58.03–1).

(e) The suitability of any essential steering-gear component not duplicated must be specifically approved by the Commanding Officer, Marine Safety Center. Where a steering-gear component is shared by—

(1) A control system (e.g., a control-system transfer switch located in the steering-gear compartment);

(2) The main and auxiliary steering gear (e.g., an isolation valve); or

(3) A power actuating system and its control system (e.g., a directional control valve)—the requirements for both systems apply, to provide the safest and most reliable arrangement.

(f) Steering gear must be separate and independent of all other shipboard systems, except—

(1) Electrical switchboards from which they are powered;

(2) Automatic pilots and similar navigational equipment; and

(3) Propulsion machinery for an integrated system of propulsion and steering.

(g) Except on a vessel with an integrated system of propulsion and steering, no thruster may count as part of a vessel's required steering capability.

(h) Except for a tank vessel subject to § 58.25–85(e), each oceangoing vessel required to have power-operated steering gear must be provided with arrangements for steadying the rudder both in an emergency and during a shift from one steering gear to another. On hydraulic steering gear, a suitable arrangement of stop valves in the main piping is an acceptable means of steadying the rudder.

(i) General arrangement plans for the main and auxiliary steering gear and their piping must be submitted for approval in accordance with subpart 50.20 of this subchapter.

[CGD 83–043, 60 FR 24776, May 10, 1995, as amended by USCG–2003–16630, 73 FR 65187, Oct. 31, 2008]

§ 58.25–10 Main and auxiliary steering gear.

(a) Power-operated main and auxiliary steering gear must be separate systems that are independent throughout their length. Other systems and arrangements of steering gear will be acceptable if the Commanding Officer, Marine Safety Center, determines that they comply with, or exceed the requirements of, this subpart.

(b) The main steering gear and rudder stock must be—

(1) Of adequate strength for and capable of steering the vessel at maximum ahead service speed, which must be demonstrated to the satisfaction of the cognizant Officer in Charge, Marine Inspection;

(2) Capable of moving the rudder from 35° on either side to 35° on the other with the vessel at its deepest loadline draft and running at maximum ahead service speed, and from 35° on either side to 30° on the other in not more than 28 seconds under the same conditions;

(3) Operated by power when necessary to comply with paragraph (b)(2) of this section or when the diameter of the rudder stock is over 12 centimeters (4.7 inches) in way of the tiller, excluding strengthening for navigation in ice; and

(4) Designed so that they will not be damaged when operating at maximum astern speed; however, this requirement need not be proved by trials at maximum astern speed and maximum rudder angle.

(c) The auxiliary steering gear must be—

(1) Of adequate strength for and capable of steering the vessel at navigable speed and of being brought speedily into action in an emergency;

(2) Capable of moving the rudder from 15° on either side to 15° on the other in not more than 60 seconds with the vessel at its deepest loadline draft and running at one-half maximum ahead service speed or 7 knots, whichever is greater; and

(3) Operated by power when necessary to comply with paragraph (c)(2) of this section or when the diameter of the rudder stock is over 23 centimeters (9 inches) in way of the tiller, excluding strengthening for navigation in ice.

(d) No auxiliary means of steering is required on a double-ended ferryboat with independent main steering gear fitted at each end of the vessel.

(e) When the main steering gear includes two or more identical power units, no auxiliary steering gear need be fitted, if—

(1) In a passenger vessel, the main steering gear is capable of moving the rudder as required by paragraph (b)(2) of this section while any one of the power units is not operating;

Coast Guard, Dept. of Homeland Security § 58.25-25

(2) In a cargo vessel, the main steering gear is capable of moving the rudder as required by paragraph (b)(2) of this section while all the power units are operating;

(3) In a vessel with an installation completed on or after September 1, 1984, and on an international voyage, and in any other vessel with an installation completed after June 9, 1995, the main steering gear is arranged so that, after a single failure in its piping system (if hydraulic), or in one of the power units, the defect can be isolated so that steering capability can be maintained or speedily regained in less than ten minutes; or

(4) In a vessel with an installation completed before September 1, 1986, and on an international voyage, with steering gear not complying with paragraph (e)(3) of this section, the installed steering gear has a proved record of reliability and is in good repair.

NOTE: The place where isolation valves join the piping system, as by a flange, constitutes a single-failure point. The valve itself need not constitute a single-failure point if it has a double seal to prevent substantial loss of fluid under pressure. Means to purge air that enters the system as a result of the piping failure must be provided, if necessary, so that steering capability can be maintained or speedily regained in less than ten minutes.

(f) In each vessel of 70,000 gross tons or over, the main steering gear must have two or more identical power units complying with paragraph (e) of this section.

§ 58.25-15 Voice communications.

Each vessel must be provided with a sound-powered telephone system, complying with subpart 113.30 of this chapter, to communicate between the pilothouse and the steering-gear compartment, unless an alternative means of communication between them has been approved by the Commanding Officer, Marine Safety Center.

§ 58.25-20 Piping for steering gear.

(a) Pressure piping must comply with subpart 58.30 of this part.

(b) Relief valves must be fitted in any part of a hydraulic system that can be isolated and in which pressure can be generated from the power units or from external forces such as wave action. The valves must be of adequate size, and must be set to limit the maximum pressure to which the system may be exposed, in accordance with § 56.07-10(b) of this subchapter.

(c) Each hydraulic system must be provided with—

(1) Arrangements to maintain the cleanliness of the hydraulic fluid, appropriate to the type and design of the hydraulic system; and

(2) For a vessel on an ocean, coastwise, or Great Lakes voyage, a fixed storage tank having sufficient capacity to recharge at least one power actuating system including the reservoir. The storage tank must be permanently connected by piping so that the hydraulic system can be readily recharged from within the steering-gear compartment and must be fitted with a device to indicate liquid level that complies with § 56.50-90 of this subchapter.

(d) Neither a split flange nor a flareless fitting of the grip or bite type, addressed by § 56.30-25 of this subchapter, may be used in hydraulic piping for steering gear.

§ 58.25-25 Indicating and alarm systems.

(a) Indication of the rudder angle must be provided both at the main steering station in the pilothouse and in the steering-gear compartment. The rudder-angle indicator must be independent of control systems for steering gear.

(b) Each electric-type rudder-angle indicator must comply with § 113.40-10 of this chapter and, in accordance with § 112.15-5(h) of this chapter, draw its power from the source of emergency power.

(c) On each vessel of 1,600 gross tons or over, a steering-failure alarm must be provided in the pilothouse in accordance with §§ 113.43-3 and 113.43-5 of this chapter.

(d) An audible and a visible alarm must activate in the pilothouse upon—

(1) Failure of the electric power to the control system of any steering gear;

(2) Failure of that power to the power unit of any steering gear; or

§ 58.25-30

(3) Occurrence of a low oil level in any oil reservoir of a hydraulic, power-operated steering-gear system.

(e) An audible and a visible alarm must activate in the machinery space upon—

(1) Failure of any phase of a three-phase power supply;

(2) Overload of any motor described by § 58.25-55(c); or

(3) Occurrence of a low oil level in any oil reservoir of a hydraulic, power-operated steering-gear system.

NOTE: See § 62.50-30(f) of this subchapter regarding extension of alarms to the navigating bridge on vessels with periodically unattended machinery spaces.

(f) Each power motor for the main and auxiliary steering gear must have a "motor running" indicator light in the pilothouse, and in the machinery space, that activates when the motor is energized.

§ 58.25-30 Automatic restart.

Each control system for main and auxiliary steering gear and each power actuating system must restart automatically when electrical power is restored after it has failed.

§ 58.25-35 Helm arrangements.

(a) The arrangement of each steering station, other than in the steering-gear compartment, must be such that the helmsman is abaft the wheel. The rim of the wheel must be plainly marked with arrows and lettering for right and left rudder, or a suitable notice indicating these directions must be posted directly in the helmsman's line of sight.

(b) Each steering wheel must turn clockwise for "right rudder" and counterclockwise for "left rudder." When the vessel is running ahead, after clockwise movement of the wheel the vessel's heading must change to the right.

(c) If a lever-type control is provided, it must be installed and marked so that its movement clearly indicates both the direction of the rudder's movement and, if followup control is also provided, the amount of the rudder's movement.

(d) Markings in the pilothouse must not interfere with the helmsman's vision, but must be clearly visible at night.

NOTE: See § 113.40-10 of this chapter for the arrangement of rudder-angle indicators at steering stations.

§ 58.25-40 Arrangement of the steering-gear compartment.

(a) The steering-gear compartment must—

(1) Be readily accessible and, as far as practicable, separated from any machinery space;

(2) Ensure working access to machinery and controls in the compartment; and

(3) Include handrails and either gratings or other non-slip surfaces to ensure a safe working environment if hydraulic fluid leaks.

NOTE: Where practicable, all steering gear should be located in the steering-gear compartment.

(b) [Reserved]

§ 58.25-45 Buffers.

For each vessel on an ocean, coastwise, or Great Lakes voyage, steering gear other than hydraulic must be designed with suitable buffering arrangements to relieve the gear from shocks to the rudder.

§ 58.25-50 Rudder stops.

(a) Power-operated steering gear must have arrangements for cutting off power to the gear before the rudder reaches the stops. These arrangements must be synchronized with the rudder stock or with the gear itself rather than be within the control system for the steering gear, and must work by limit switches that interrupt output of the control system or by other means acceptable to the Commanding Officer, Marine Safety Center.

(b) Strong and effective structural rudder stops must be fitted; except that, where adequate positive stops are provided within the steering gear, such structural stops need not be fitted.

§ 58.25-55 Overcurrent protection for steering-gear systems.

(a) Each feeder circuit for steering must be protected by a circuit breaker on the switchboard that supplies it and

Coast Guard, Dept. of Homeland Security § 58.25-65

must have an instantaneous trip set at a current of at least—

(1) 300% and not more than 375% of the rated full-load current of one steering-gear motor for a direct-current motor; or

(2) 175% and not more than 200% of the locked-rotor current of one steering-gear motor for an alternating-current motor.

(b) No feeder circuit for steering may have any overcurrent protection, except that required by paragraph (a) of this section.

(c) Neither a main or an auxiliary steering-gear motor, nor a motor for a steering-gear control system, may be protected by an overload protective device. The motor must have a device that activates an audible and a visible alarm at the main machinery-control station if there is an overload that would cause overheating of the motor.

(d) No control circuit of a motor controller, steering-gear control system, or indicating or alarm system may have overcurrent protection except short-circuit protection that is instantaneous and rated at 400% to 500% of—

(1) The current-carrying capacity of the conductor; or

(2) The normal load of the system.

(e) The short-circuit protective device for each steering-gear control system must be in the steering-gear compartment and in the control circuit immediately following the disconnect switch for the system.

(f) When, in a vessel of less than 1,600 gross tons, an auxiliary steering gear, which §58.25-10(c)(3) requires to be operated by power, is not operated by electric power or is operated by an electric motor primarily intended for other service, the main steering gear may be fed by one circuit from the main switchboard. When such an electric motor is arranged to operate an auxiliary steering gear, neither §58.25-25(e) nor paragraphs (a) through (c) of this section need be complied with if both the overcurrent protection and compliance with §§58.25-25(d), 58.25-30, and 58.25-70 (j) and (k) satisfy the Commanding Officer, Marine Safety Center.

§ 58.25-60 Non-duplicated hydraulic rudder actuators.

Non-duplicated hydraulic rudder actuators may be installed in the steering-gear control systems on each vessel of less than 100,000 deadweight tons. These actuators must meet IMO A.467(XII) (incorporated by reference, see 46 CFR 58.03-1) and be acceptable to the Commanding Officer, Marine Safety Center. Also, the piping for the main gear must comply with 46 CFR 58.25-10(e)(3).

[USCG-2003-16630, 73 FR 65187, Oct. 31, 2008]

§ 58.25-65 Feeder circuits.

(a) Each vessel with one or more electric-driven steering-gear power units must have at least two feeder circuits, which must be separated as widely as practicable. One or more of these circuits must be supplied from the vessel's service switchboard. On a vessel where the rudder stock is over 23 centimeters (9 inches) in diameter in way of the tiller, excluding strengthening for navigation in ice, and where a final source of emergency power is required by §112.05-5(a) of this chapter, one or more of these circuits must be supplied from the emergency switchboard, or from an alternative source of power that—

(1) Is available automatically within 45 seconds of loss of power from the vessel's service switchboard;

(2) Comes from an independent source of power in the steering-gear compartment;

(3) Is used for no other purpose; and

(4) Has a capacity for one half-hour of continuous operation, to move the rudder from 15° on either side to 15° on the other in not more than 60 seconds with the vessel at its deepest loadline draft and running at one-half maximum ahead service speed or 7 knots, whichever is greater.

(b) Each vessel that has a steering gear with multiple electric-driven power units must be arranged so that each power unit is supplied by a separate feeder.

(c) Each feeder circuit must have a disconnect switch in the steering-gear compartment.

(d) Each feeder circuit must have a current-carrying capacity of—

(1) 125% of the rated full-load current rating of the electric steering-gear motor or power unit; and

(2) 100% of the normal current of one steering-gear control system including all associated motors.

§ 58.25–70 Steering-gear control systems.

(a) Each power-driven steering-gear system must be provided with at least one steering-gear control system.

(b) The main steering gear must be operable from the pilothouse by mechanical, hydraulic, electrical, or other means acceptable to the Commanding Officer, Marine Safety Center. This gear and its components must give full followup control of the rudder. Supplementary steering-gear control not giving full followup may also be provided from the pilothouse.

(c) Each steering-gear control system must have in the pilothouse a switch arranged so that one operation of the switch's lever automatically supplies power to a complete system and its associated power unit or units. This switch must be—

(1) Operated by one lever;

(2) Arranged so that not more than one control system and its associated power unit or units can be energized from the pilothouse at any one time;

(3) Arranged so that the lever passes through "off" during transfer of control from one control system to another; and

(4) Arranged so that the switches for each control system are in separate enclosures or are separated by fire-resistant barriers.

(d) Each steering-gear control system must receive its power from—

(1) The feeder circuit supplying power to its steering-gear power unit or units in the steering-gear compartment; or

(2) A direct connection to the busbars supplying the circuit for its steering-gear power unit or units from a point on the switchboard adjacent to that supply.

(e) Each steering-gear control system must have a switch that—

(1) Is in the steering-gear compartment; and

(2) Disconnects the system from its power source and from the steering gear that the system serves.

(f) Each motor controller for a steering gear must be in the steering-gear compartment.

(g) A means of starting and stopping each motor for a steering gear must be in the steering-gear compartment.

(h) When the main steering gear is arranged in accordance with § 58.25–10(e), two separate and independent systems for full followup control must be provided in the pilothouse; except that—

(1) The steering wheel or lever need not be duplicated; and

(2) If the system consists of a hydraulic telemotor, no second separate and independent system need be provided other than on each tank vessel subject to § 58.25–85.

(i) When only the main steering gear is power-driven, two separate and independent systems for full followup control must be provided in the pilothouse; except that the steering wheel or lever need not be duplicated.

(j) When the auxiliary steering gear is power-driven, a control system for the auxiliary steering gear must be provided in the pilothouse that is separate and independent from the control system for the main steering gear; except that the steering wheel or lever need not be duplicated.

(k) On a vessel of 500 gross tons or above, each main steering gear and auxiliary steering gear must be arranged so that its power unit or units are operable by controls from the steering-gear compartment. These controls must not be rendered inoperable by failure of the controls in the pilothouse.

§ 58.25–75 Materials.

(a) Materials used for the mechanical or hydraulic transmission of power to the rudder stock must have an elongation of at least 15% in 5 centimeters (2 inches); otherwise, components used for this purpose must be shock-tested in accordance with subpart 58.30 of this part.

(b) No materials with low melting-points, including such materials as aluminum and nonmetallic seals, may be used in control systems for steering gear or in power actuating systems unless—

(1) The materials are within a compartment having little or no risk of fire;

(2) Because of redundancy in the system, damage by fire to any component would not prevent immediate restoration of steering capability; or

(3) The materials are within a steering-gear power actuating system.

§ 58.25-80 Automatic pilots and ancillary steering gear.

(a) Automatic pilots and ancillary steering gear, and steering-gear control systems, must be arranged to allow immediate resumption of manual operation of the steering-gear control system required in the pilothouse. A switch must be provided, at the primary steering position in the pilothouse, to completely disconnect the automatic equipment from the steering-gear controls.

(b) Automatic pilots and ancillary steering gear must be arranged so that no single failure affects proper operation and independence of the main or auxiliary steering gear, required controls, rudder-angle indicators, or steering-failure alarm.

§ 58.25-85 Special requirements for tank vessels.

(a) Each tank vessel must meet the applicable requirements of §§ 58.25-1 through 58.25-80.

(b) On each tank vessel of 10,000 gross tons or over, the main steering gear must comprise two or more identical power units that comply with § 58.25-10(e)(2).

(c) Each tank vessel of 10,000 gross tons or over constructed on or after September 1, 1984, must comply with the following:

(1) The main steering gear must be arranged so that, in case of loss of steering capability due to a single failure in any part of the power actuating system of the main steering gear, excluding seizure of a rudder actuator or failure of the tiller, quadrant, or components serving the same purpose, steering capability can be regained not more than 45 seconds after the loss of one power actuating system.

(2) The main steering gear must include either—

(i) Two separate and independent power actuating systems, complying with § 58.25-10(b)(2); or

(ii) At least two identical hydraulic-power actuating systems, which, acting simultaneously in normal operation, must comply with § 58.25-10(b)(2). (When they must so comply, these systems must be connected. Loss of hydraulic fluid from one system must be capable of being detected, and the defective system automatically isolated, so the other system or systems remain fully operational.)

(3) Steering gear other than hydraulic must meet equivalent standards to the satisfaction of the Commanding Officer, Marine Safety Center.

(d) On each tank vessel of 10,000 gross tons or over, but less than 100,000 deadweight tons, the main steering gear need not comply with paragraph (c) of this section if the rudder actuator or actuators installed are non-duplicated hydraulic and if—

(1) The actuators comply with § 58.25-60; and

(2) In case of loss of steering capability due to a single failure either of any part of the piping systems or in one of the power units, steering capability can be regained in not more than 45 seconds.

(e) On each tank vessel of less than 70,000 deadweight tons, constructed before, and with a steering-gear installation before, September 1, 1986, and on an international voyage, the steering gear not complying with paragraph (c) (1), (2), or (3) of this section, as applicable, may continue in service if the steering gear has a proved record of reliability and is in good repair.

(f) Each tank vessel of 10,000 gross tons or over, constructed before, and with a steering-gear installation before, September 1, 1984, must—

(1) Meet the applicable requirements in §§ 58.25-15, 58.25-20(c), 58.25-25 (a), (d), and (e), and 58.25-70 (e), (h), (i), and (j);

(2) Ensure working access to machinery and controls in the steering-gear compartment (which must include handrails and either gratings or other non-slip surfaces to ensure a safe working environment in case hydraulic fluid leaks);

(3) Have two separate and independent steering-gear control systems,

§ 58.30-1

each of which can be operated from the pilothouse; except that it need not have separate steering wheels or steering levers;

(4) Arrange each system required by paragraph (f)(3) of this section so that, if the one in operation fails, the other can be operated from the pilothouse immediately; and

(5) Supply each system required by paragraph (f)(3) of this section, if electric, with power by a circuit that is—

(i) Used for no other purpose; and either—

(ii) Connected in the steering-gear compartment to the circuit supplying power to the power unit or units operated by that system; or

(iii) Connected directly to the busbars supplying the circuit for its steering-gear power unit or units at a point on the switchboard adjacent to that supply.

(g) Each tank vessel of 40,000 gross tons or over, constructed before, and with a steering-gear installation before, September 1, 1984, and on an international voyage, must have the steering gear arranged so that, in case of a single failure of the piping or of one of the power units, either steering capability equivalent to that required of the auxiliary steering gear by § 58.25–10(c)(2) can be maintained or the rudder's movement can be limited so that steering capability can be speedily regained in less than 10 minutes. This arrangement must be achieved by—

(1) An independent means of restraining the rudder;

(2) Fast-acting valves that may be manually operated to isolate the actuator or actuators from the external hydraulic piping, together with a means of directly refilling the actuators by a fixed, independent, power-operated pump and piping; or

(3) An arrangement such that, if hydraulic-power actuating systems are connected, loss of hydraulic fluid from one system must be detected and the defective system isolated either automatically or from within the pilothouse so that the other system remains fully operational.

NOTE: The term "piping or * * * one of the power units" in paragraph (g) of this section refers to the pressure-containing components in hydraulic or electro-hydraulic steering gear. It does not include rudder actuators or hydraulic-control servo piping and pumps used to stroke the pump or valves of the power unit, unless their failure would result in failure of the unit or of the piping to the actuator.

Subpart 58.30—Fluid Power and Control Systems

§ 58.30-1 Scope.

(a) This subpart contains requirements for fluid power transmission and control systems and appurtenances. Except as otherwise provided for in this section, these requirements are applicable to the following fluid power and control systems:

(1) Steering apparatus, main and auxiliary, including bow thruster systems.

(2) Cargo hatch operating systems unless fitted with an alternate mechanical means of operation and approved by the Commandant as hydraulically or pneumatically fail-safe. A system is considered to be fail-safe if a component failure will result in a slow and controlled release of the loading so as not to endanger personnel.

(3) Watertight door operating system.

(4) Automatic propulsion boiler system.

(5) Starting systems for internal combustion engines used for main propulsion, main or auxiliary power, as the prime mover for any required emergency apparatus, or as the source of propulsion power in ship maneuvering thruster systems.

(6) Centralized control system of main propulsion and auxiliary machinery.

(7) Lifeboat handling equipment.

(8) Controllable pitch propeller system.

(9) Installations used to remotely control components of piping systems listed in § 56.01–10(c)(1) of this subchapter.

(10) All systems containing a pneumatic or hydropneumatic accumulator. In the case of hydropneumatic accumulators where it can be shown to the satisfaction of the Commandant that due to friction losses, constriction, or other design features, the hazard of explosive rupture does not exist downstream of a certain point in the hydraulic system, the requirements of this subpart will

Coast Guard, Dept. of Homeland Security § 58.30–15

apply only to the accumulator and the system upstream of this point.

(11) Materials and/or personnel handling equipment systems, i.e. cranes, hydraulic elevators, etc., not approved by the Commandant as fail-safe as defined in paragraph (a)(2) of this section.

(12) Any fluid power or control system installed in the cargo area of pump rooms on a tank vessel, or in spaces in which cargo is handled on a liquefied flammable gas carrier.

(13) All pneumatic power and control systems having a maximum allowable working pressure in excess of 150 pounds per square inch.

(14) Any other hydraulic or pneumatic system on board that, in the judgment of the Commandant, constitutes a hazard to the seaworthiness of the ship or the safety of personnel either in normal operation or in case of failure.

(b) Other fluid power and control systems do not have to comply with the detailed requirements of this subpart but must meet the requirements of § 58.30–50.

[CGFR 68–82, 33 FR 18878, Dec. 18, 1968, as amended by CGD 73–254, 40 FR 40168, Sept. 2, 1975]

§ 58.30–5 Design requirements.

(a) The requirements of part 56 are also applicable to piping and fittings in fluid power and control systems listed in § 58.30–1 of this part, except as modified herein. The designer should consider the additional pressure due to hydraulic shock and should also consider the rate of pressure rise caused by hydraulic shock.

(b) The system shall be so designed that proper functioning of any unit shall not be affected by the back pressure in the system. The design shall be such that malfunctioning of any unit in the system will not render any other connected or emergency system inoperative because of back pressure.

(c) Pneumatic systems with a maximum allowable working pressure in excess of 150 pounds per square inch shall be designed with a surge tank or other acceptable means of pulsation dampening.

(d) Each pneumatic system must minimize the entry of oil into the system and must drain the system of liquids.

[CGFR 68–82, 33 FR 18878, Dec. 18, 1968, as amended by CGFR 69–127, 35 FR 9980, June 17, 1970; CGD 73–254, 40 FR 40168, Sept. 2, 1975; CGD 83–043, 60 FR 24781, May 10, 1995; CGD 95–027, 61 FR 26001, May 23, 1996]

§ 58.30–10 Hydraulic fluid.

(a) The requirements of this section are applicable to all fluid power transmission and control systems installed on vessels subject to inspection.

(b) The fluid used in hydraulic power transmission systems shall have a flashpoint of not less than 200 °F. for pressures below 150 pounds per square inch and 315 °F. for pressures 150 pounds per square inch and above, as determined by ASTM D 92 (incorporated by reference, see § 58.03–1), Cleveland "Open Cup" test method.

(c) The chemical and physical properties of the hydraulic fluid shall be suitable for use with any materials in the system or components thereof.

(d) The hydraulic fluid shall be suitable for operation of the hydraulic system through the entire temperature range to which it may be subjected in service.

(e) The recommendations of the system component manufacturers and ANSI B93.5 (incorporated by reference; see 46 CFR 58.03–1) shall be considered in the selection and use of hydraulic fluid.

[CGFR 68–82, 33 FR 18878, Dec. 18, 1968, as amended by CGFR 69–127, 35 FR 9980, June 17, 1970; USCG–1999–5151, 64 FR 67180, Dec. 1, 1999; USCG–2003–16630, 73 FR 65187, Oct. 31, 2008]

§ 58.30–15 Pipe, tubing, valves, fittings, pumps, and motors.

(a) The requirements of this section are applicable to those hydraulic and pneumatic systems listed in § 58.30–1.

(b) Materials used in the manufacture of tubing, pipes, valves, flanges, and fittings shall be selected from those specifications that appear in 46 CFR 56.60–1, Table 56.60–1(a) or 46 CFR 56.60–2, Table 56.60–2(a); or they may be selected from the material specifications of section I or section VIII of the ASME Boiler and Pressure Vessel Code (both incorporated by reference; see 46 CFR 58.03–1) if not prohibited by the section of this subchapter dealing with

§ 58.30-20

the particular section of the ASME Boiler and Pressure Vessel Code. Materials designated by other specifications shall be evaluated on the basis of physical and chemical properties. To assure these properties, the specifications shall specify and require such physical and chemical testing as considered necessary by the Commandant. All tubing and pipe materials shall be suitable for handling the hydraulic fluid used and shall be of such chemical and physical properties as to remain ductile at the lowest operating temperature.

(c) Bolting shall meet the requirements of 46 CFR 56.25-20 except that regular hexagon bolts conforming to SAE J429, grades 2 through 8 (incorporated by reference, see 46 CFR 58.03-1), or ASTM A 193 (incorporated by reference, see 46 CFR 58.03-1) may be used in sizes not exceeding 1½ inches.

(d) The maximum allowable working pressure and minimum thickness shall be calculated as required by § 56.07-10(e) of this subchapter when the outside diameter to wall thickness ratio is greater than 6. Where the ratio is less than 6, the wall thickness may be established on the basis of an applicable thick-wall cylinder equation acceptable to the Commandant using the allowable stress values specified in § 56.07-10(e) of this subchapter.

(e) All flared, flareless and compression type joints shall be in accordance with § 56.30-25 of this subchapter.

(f) Fluid power motors and pumps installed on vessels subject to inspection shall be certified by the manufacturer as suitable for the intended use. Such suitability shall be demonstrated by operational tests conducted aboard the vessel which shall be witnessed by a marine inspector.

[CGFR 68-82, 33 FR 18878, Dec. 18, 1968, as amended by CGD 73-254, 40 FR 40168, Sept. 2, 1975; CGD 95-027, 61 FR 26001, May 23, 1996; USCG-2000-7790, 65 FR 58460, Sept. 29, 2000;]

§ 58.30-20 Fluid power hose and fittings.

(a) The requirements of this section are applicable to those hydraulic and pneumatic systems listed in § 58.30-1.

(b) Hose and fittings shall meet the requirements of subpart 56.60 of this subchapter.

(c) Hose assemblies may be installed between two points of relative motion but shall not be subjected to torsional deflection (twisting) under any conditions of operation and shall be limited, in general, to reasonable lengths required for flexibility. Special consideration may be given to the use of longer lengths of flexible hose where required for proper operation of machinery and components in the hydraulic system.

(d) Sharp bends in hoses shall be avoided.

§ 58.30-25 Accumulators.

(a) An accumulator is an unfired pressure vessel in which energy is stored under high pressure in the form of a gas or a gas and hydraulic fluid. Accumulators must meet the applicable requirements in § 54.01-5 (c)(3), (c)(4), and (d) of this chapter or the remaining requirements in part 54.

(b) If the accumulator is of the gas and fluid type, suitable separators shall be provided between the two media, if their mixture would be dangerous, or would result in contamination of the hydraulic fluid and loss of gas through absorption.

(c) Each accumulator which may be isolated, shall be protected on the gas and fluid sides by relief valves set to relieve at pressures not exceeding the maximum allowable working pressures. When an accumulator forms an integral part of systems having relief valves, the accumulator need not have individual relief valves.

[CGFR 68-82, 33 FR 18878, Dec. 18, 1968 as amended by CGD 77-147, 47 FR 21811, May 20, 1982]

§ 58.30-30 Fluid power cylinders.

(a) The requirements of this section are applicable to those hydraulic and pneumatic systems listed in § 58.30-1 and to all pneumatic power transmission systems.

(b) Fluid power cylinders consisting of a container and a movable piston rod extending through the containment vessel, not storing energy but converting a pressure to work, are not considered to be pressure vessels and need not be constructed under the provisions of part 54 of this subchapter.

(c) Cylinders shall be designed for a bursting pressure of not less than 4 times the maximum allowable working pressure. Drawings and calculations or a certified burst test report shall be submitted to show compliance with this requirement.

(d) Piston rods, except steering gear rams, shall either be of corrosion resistant material or shall be of steel protected by a plating system acceptable to the Commandant.

(e) Materials selection shall be in accordance with the requirements of §58.30–15(b).

§58.30–35 Testing.

(a) All fluid power and control systems and components thereof shall be tested as required by this section.

(b) Accumulators constructed as pressure vessels under the provisions of part 54 of this subchapter shall be tested and retested as required by parts 54 and 61 of this subchapter.

(c) Fluid power and control systems and piping assemblies shall be given an installation test as follows:

(1) Fluid power and control systems and piping assemblies and associated equipment components, including hydraulic steering gear, in lieu of being tested at the time of installation, may be shop tested by the manufacturer to 1½ times the maximum allowable pressure of the system. The required test pressure shall be maintained for a sufficient amount of time to check all components for strength and porosity and to permit an inspection to be made of all connections.

(2) Fluid power and control systems and associated hydraulic equipment components which have been tested in conformance with paragraph (c)(1) of this section and so certified by the manufacturer, may be tested after installation as a complete assembly by stalling the driven unit in a safe and satisfactory manner and by blowing the relief valves. Otherwise, these systems shall be hydrostatically tested in the presence of a marine inspector at a pressure of 1½ times the maximum allowable pressure.

(3) Fluid power and control systems incorporating hydropneumatic accumulators containing rupture discs may be tested at the maximum allowable working pressure of the system in lieu of 1½ times this value as prescribed in paragraphs (c)(1) and (2) of this section provided the accumulators have been previously tested in accordance with paragraph (b) of this section and welded or brazed piping joints are not employed in the system. If welded or brazed joints are employed, the system shall be tested in accordance with the requirements of paragraphs (c)(1) and (2) of this section except that the accumulators may be isolated from the remainder of the system.

(d) Fluid power and control systems shall be purged with an inert gas or with the working fluid and all trapped air bled from the system prior to any shipboard testing. In no case shall air, oxygen, any flammable gas, or any flammable mixture of gases be used for testing fluid power systems.

(e) Fluid control systems, such as boiler combustion controls, containing components with internal parts, such as bellows or other sensing elements, which would be damaged by the test pressure prescribed in paragraphs (c)(1) and (2) of this section may be tested at the maximum allowable working pressure of the system. In addition, all fluid control systems may be tested using the system working fluid.

§58.30–40 Plans.

(a) Diagrammatic plans and lists of materials must be submitted for each of the fluid power and control systems listed in §58.30–1(a) that is installed on the vessel. Plan submission must be in accordance with subpart 50.20 of this subchapter and must include the following:

(1) The purpose of the system.
(2) Its location on the vessel.
(3) The maximum allowable working pressure.
(4) The fluid used in the system.
(5) The velocity of the fluid flow in the system.
(6) Details of the system components in accordance with §56.01–10(d) of this subchapter.

[CGD 73–254, 40 FR 40168, Sept. 2, 1975]

§58.30–50 Requirements for miscellaneous fluid power and control systems.

(a) All fluid power and control systems installed on a vessel, except those

§ 58.50-1

listed in § 58.30-1(a), must meet the following requirements:

(1) Diagrams of the system providing the information required by § 58.30-40(a)(1) through (4) must be submitted. These are not approved but are needed for records and for evaluation of the system in accordance with § 58.30-1(a)(14).

(2) The hydraulic fluid used in the system must comply with § 58.30-10.

(3) The installed system must be tested in accordance with § 58.30-35(c)(2).

(4) All pneumatic cylinders must comply with § 58.30-30.

(5) Additional plans may be required for "fail-safe" equipment and for cargo hatch systems with alternate means of operation.

[CGD 73-254, 40 FR 40168, Sept. 2, 1975]

Subpart 58.50—Independent Fuel Tanks

§ 58.50-1 General requirements.

(a) The regulations in this subpart contain requirements for independent fuel tanks.

(b) Passenger vessels exceeding 100 gross tons constructed prior to July 1, 1935, may carry gasoline as fuel not exceeding 40 gallons to supply the emergency electrical system. Passenger vessels exceeding 100 gross tons constructed on or after July 1, 1935, and all emergency systems converted on or after July 1, 1935, shall use fuel which has a flashpoint exceeding 110 °F.

(PMCC) for internal combustion engine units. Such vessels shall carry a sufficient quantity of fuel to supply the emergency electrical system. Refer to § 112.05-5 of subchapter J (Electrical Engineering), of this chapter.

(c) An outage of 2 percent shall be provided on all fuel tanks containing petroleum products.

[CGFR 68-82, 33 FR 18878, Dec. 18, 1968, as amended by CGD 73-254, 40 FR 40169, Sept. 2, 1975]

§ 58.50-5 Gasoline fuel tanks.

(a) *Construction*—(1) *Shape*. Tanks may be of either cylindrical or rectangular form, except that tanks for emergency electrical systems shall be of cylindrical form.

(2) *Materials and construction*. The material used and the minimum thickness allowed shall be as indicated in Table 58.50-5(a) except that consideration will be given to other materials which provide equivalent safety as indicated in § 58.50-15.

(3) *Prohibited types*. Tanks with flanged-up top edges that may trap and hold moisture shall not be used.

(4) *Openings*. Openings for fill, vent and fuel pipes, and openings for fuel level gages where used, shall be on the topmost surface of tanks. Tanks shall have no openings in bottoms, sides, or ends, except that an opening fitted with threaded plug or cap may be used for tank cleaning purposes.

TABLE 58.50-5(a)

Material	ASTM specification (all incorporated by reference; see 46 CFR 58.03-1)	Thickness in inches and gage numbers [1] vs. tank capacities for—		
		1- through 80-gallon tanks	More than 80- and not more than 150-gallon tanks	Over 150-gallon tanks [2]
Aluminum [5]	B 209, Alloy 5086 [6]	0.250 (USSG 3)	0.250 (USSG 3)	0.250 (USSG 3).
Nickel-copper	B 127, Hot rolled sheet or plate	0.037 (USSG 20).[3]	0.050 (USSG 18)	0.107 (USSG 12).
Copper-nickel	B 122, Alloy No. 5	0.045 (AWG 17)	0.057 (AWG 15)	0.128 (AWG 8).
Copper	B 152, Type ETP	0.057 (AWG 15)	0.080 (AWG 12)	0.182 (AWG 5).
Copper-silicon	B 96, alloys C65400 and C65500.	0.050 (AWG 16)	0.064 (AWG 14)	0.144 (AWG 7).
Steel or iron [4]	0.0747 (MfgStd 14)	0.1046 (MfgStd 12)	0.179 (MfgStd 7)..	

[1] Gauges used are U.S. standard "USSG" for aluminum and nickel-copper; "AWG" for copper, copper-nickel and copper-silicon; and "MfgStd" for steel.
[2] Tanks over 400 gallons shall be designed with a factor of safety of four on the ultimate strength of the material used with a design head of not less than 4 feet of liquid above the top of the tank.
[3] Nickel-copper not less than 0.031 inch (USSG 22) may be used for tanks up to 30-gallon capacity.
[4] Fuel tanks constructed of iron or steel, which is less than 3/16-inch thick shall be galvanized inside and outside by the hot dip process.
[5] Anodic to most common metals. Avoid dissimilar metal contact with tank body.
[6] And other alloys acceptable to the Commandant.

(5) *Joints.* All metallic tank joints shall be welded or brazed.

(6) *Fittings.* Nozzles, flanges, or other fittings for pipe connections shall be welded or brazed to the tank. The tank openings in way of pipe connections shall be properly reinforced where necessary. Where fuel level gages are used, the flange to which gage fittings are attached shall be welded or brazed to the tank. No tubular gage glasses or trycocks shall be fitted to the tanks.

(7) *Baffle plates.* All tanks exceeding 30 inches in any horizontal dimension shall be fitted with vertical baffle plates where necessary for strength or for control of excessive surge. In general, baffle plates installed at intervals not exceeding 30 inches will be considered as meeting this requirement.

(8) *Baffle plate details.* Baffle plates, where required, shall be of the same material and not less than the minimum thickness required in the tank walls and shall be connected to the tank walls by welding or brazing. Limber holes at the bottom and air holes at the top of all baffles shall be provided.

(b) *Installation.* (1) Gasoline fuel tanks used for propulsion shall be located in water-tight compartments separate from, but adjacent to the engineroom or machinery space. Fuel tanks for auxiliaries shall be located on or above the weather deck outside of the engine housing or compartment and as close to the engine as practicable. All tanks shall be so installed as to provide a free circulation of air around the tanks.

(2) Cylindrical tanks with longitudinal seams shall be arranged horizontally where practicable so that such seams are located as near the top as possible.

(3) Fuel tanks shall be so installed as to permit examination, testing, or removal for cleaning.

(4) Fuel tanks shall be adequately supported and braced to prevent movement. Portable fuel tanks are not permitted.

(5) All fuel tanks shall be electrically bonded to the common ground.

(c) *Testing.* (1) Prior to installation, tanks vented to atmosphere shall be tested to, and must withstand, a pressure of 5 pounds per square inch or 1½ times the maximum head to which they may be subjected in service, whichever is greater. A standpipe of 11½ feet in height attached to the tank may be filled with water to accomplish the 5 pounds per square inch test. Permanent deformation of the tank will not be cause for rejection unless accompanied by leakage.

(2) After installation of the fuel tank on a vessel the complete installation shall be tested in the presence of a marine inspector to a head not less than that to which the tank may be subjected in service. Fuel may be used as a testing medium.

(3) All tanks not vented to atmosphere shall be constructed and tested in accordance with part 54 of this subchapter.

[CGFR 68–82, 33 FR 18878, Dec. 18, 1968, as amended by CGFR 72–59R, 37 FR 6190, Mar. 25, 1972; USCG–1999–5151, 64 FR 67180, Dec. 1, 1999; USCG–2003–16630, 73 FR 65187, Oct. 31, 2008]

§ 58.50–10 Diesel fuel tanks.

(a) *Construction.* (1) Tanks may be of either cylindrical or rectangular form.

(2) The materials used and the minimum thickness allowed in the construction of independent fuel tanks shall be as indicated in Table 58.50–10(a), except that consideration will be given to other materials which provide equivalent safety as indicated in § 58.50–15.

(3) Tanks with flanged-up top edges, that may trap and hold moisture, shall not be used.

TABLE 58.50–10(a)

Material	ASTM specification (all incorporated by reference; see 46 CFR 58.03–1)	Thickness in inches and gage numbers [1] vs. tank capacities for—		
		1- through 80-gallon tanks	More than 80- and not more than 150-gallon tanks	Over 150-gallon tanks [2]
Aluminum [5]	B 209, Alloy 5086 [6]	0.250 (USSG 3)	0.250 (USSG 3)	0.250 (USSG 3).
Nickel-copper	B 127, Hot rolled sheet or plate	0.037 (USSG 20).[3]	0.050 (USSG 18)	0.107 (USSG 12).

Table 58.50–10(a)—Continued

Material	ASTM specification (all incorporated by reference; see 46 CFR 58.03–1)	Thickness in inches and gage numbers[1] vs. tank capacities for—		
		1- through 80-gallon tanks	More than 80- and not more than 150-gallon tanks	Over 150-gallon tanks[2]
Steel or iron[4]	0.0747 (MfgStd 14)	0.1046 (MfgStd 12)	0.179 (MfgStd 7)	

[1] Gauges used are U.S. standard "USSG" for aluminum and nickel-copper and "MfgStd" for steel or iron.
[2] Tanks over 400 gallons shall be designed with a factor of safety of four on the ultimate strength of the material used with design head of not less than 4 feet of liquid above the top of the tank.
[3] Nickel-copper not less than 0.031 inch (USSG 22) may be used for tanks up to 30-gallon capacity.
[4] For diesel tanks the steel or iron shall not be galvanized on the interior.
[5] Anodic to most common metals. Avoid dissimilar metal contact with tank body.
[6] And other alloys acceptable to the Commandant.

(4) Openings for fill and vent pipes must be on the topmost surface of a tank. There must be no openings in the bottom, sides, or ends of a tank except as follows:

(i) The opening for the fuel supply piping is not restricted to the top of the tank.

(ii) An opening fitted with threaded plug or cap may be used on the bottom of the tank for tank cleaning purposes.

(iii) Liquid level gages must penetrate at a point that is more than 2 inches from the bottom of the tank.

(5) All tank joints shall be welded.

(6) Nozzles, flanges, or other fittings for pipe connections shall be welded or brazed to the tank. The tank opening in way of pipe connections shall be properly reinforced where necessary. Where liquid level indicating devices are attached to the tank, they shall be of heat resistant materials adequately protected from mechanical damage and provided at the tank connections with devices which will automatically close in the event of rupture of the gage or gage lines.

(7) All tanks exceeding 30 inches in any horizontal dimension shall be fitted with vertical baffle plates where necessary for strength or for control of excessive surge. In general, baffle plates installed at intervals not exceeding 30 inches will be considered as meeting this requirement.

(8) Baffle plates, where required, shall be of the same material and not less than the minimum thickness required in the tank walls and shall be connected to the tank walls by welding or brazing. Limber holes at the bottom and air holes at the top of all baffle plates shall be provided.

(9) Iron or steel tanks shall not be galvanized on the interior. Galvanizing paint or other suitable coating shall be used to protect the outside of iron and steel tanks.

(b) *Installation.* (1) Tanks containing fuel for emergency lighting units shall be located on an open deck or in an adequately ventilated metal compartment. No tank shall be located in a compartment where the temperature may exceed 150 °F.

(2) When cylindrical tanks are installed, longitudinal seams shall be located as near the top of the tank as possible. Fuel tanks shall be located in, or as close as practicable, to the machinery space which is served.

(3) Fuel tanks shall be so installed as to permit examination, testing, or removal for cleaning.

(4) Fuel tanks shall be adequately supported and braced to prevent movement. Portable tanks are not permitted.

(5) All fuel tanks shall be electrically bonded to the common ground.

(c) *Tests.* (1) Prior to installation, tanks vented to the atmosphere shall be tested to and must withstand a pressure of 5 pounds per square inch or 1½ times the maximum head to which they may be subjected in service, whichever is greater. A standpipe of 11½ feet in height attached to the tank may be filled with water to accomplish the 5 pounds per square inch test. Permanent deformation of the tank will not be cause for rejection unless accompanied by leakage.

(2) After installation of the fuel tank on a vessel the complete installation shall be tested in the presence of a marine inspector to a head not less than

Coast Guard, Dept. of Homeland Security §58.60–9

that to which the tank may be subjected in service. Fuel may be used as a testing medium.

(3) All tanks not vented to atmosphere shall be constructed and tested in accordance with part 54 of this subchapter.

[CGFR 68–82, 33 FR 18878, Dec. 18, 1968, as amended by CGFR 69–127, 35 FR 9980, June 17, 1970; CGFR 72–59R, 37 FR 6190, Mar. 25, 1972; USCG–1999–5151, 64 FR 67180, Dec. 1, 1999; USCG–2003–16630, 73 FR 65188, Oct. 31, 2008]

§58.50–15 Alternate material for construction of independent fuel tanks.

(a) Materials other than those specifically listed in 46 CFR 58.50–5, Table 58.50–5(a) and in 46 CFR 58.50–10, Table 58.50–10(a) may be used for fuel tank construction only if the tank as constructed meets material and testing requirements approved by the Commandant (CG–ENG). Approved testing may be accomplished by any acceptable laboratory, such as the Marine Department, Underwriters' Laboratories, Inc., or may be done by the fabricator if witnessed by a marine inspector.

(b) [Reserved]

[USCG–2003–16630, 73 FR 65188, Oct. 31, 2008, as amended by USCG–2012–0832, 77 FR 59778, Oct, 1, 2012]

Subpart 58.60—Industrial Systems and Components on Mobile Offshore Drilling Units (MODU)

SOURCE: CGD 73–251, 43 FR 56801, Dec. 4, 1978, unless otherwise noted.

§58.60–1 Applicability.

This subpart applies to the following industrial systems on board a mobile offshore drilling unit (MODU):

(a) Cementing systems.

(b) Circulation systems, including—

(1) Pipes and pumps for mud;

(2) Shale shakers;

(3) Desanders; and

(4) Degassers.

(c) Blow out preventor control systems.

(d) Riser and guideline tensioning systems.

(e) Motion compensation systems.

(f) Bulk material storage and handling systems.

(g) Other pressurized systems designed for the MODU's industrial operations.

§58.60–2 Alternatives and substitutions.

(a) The Coast Guard may accept substitutes for fittings, material, apparatus, equipment, arrangements, calculations, and tests required in this subpart if the substitute provides an equivalent level of safety.

(b) In any case where it is shown to the satisfaction of the Commandant that the use of any particular equipment, apparatus, arrangement, or test is unreasonable or impracticable, the Commandant may permit the use of alternate equipment, apparatus, arrangement, or test to such an extent and upon such condition as will insure, to his satisfaction, a degree of safety consistent with the minimum standards set forth in this subpart.

§58.60–3 Pressure vessel.

A pressure vessel that is a component in an industrial system under this subpart must meet the applicable requirements in §54.01–5 of this chapter.

[CGD 73–251, 43 FR 56601, Dec. 4, 1978, as amended by CGD 77–147, 47 FR 21811, May 20, 1982]

§58.60–5 Industrial systems: Locations.

An industrial system under this subpart must not be in a space that is—

(a) Concealed; or

(b) Inaccessible to industrial personnel.

§58.60–7 Industrial systems: Piping.

The piping for industrial systems under this subpart must meet ANSI B31.3 (incorporated by reference, see 46 CFR 58.03–1), except that blow out preventor control systems must also meet API RP 53 (incorporated by reference, see 46 CFR 58.03–1).

[USCG–2003–16630, 73 FR 65188, Oct. 31, 2008]

§58.60–9 Industrial systems: Design.

Each system under this subpart must be designed and analyzed in accordance with the principles of API RP 14C (incorporated by reference, see 46 CFR 58.03–1).

[USCG–2003–16630, 73 FR 65188, Oct. 31, 2008]

§ 58.60–11 Analyses, plans, diagrams and specifications: Submission.

(a) Each industrial system must be analyzed by a registered professional engineer to certify that the system has been designed in accordance with applicable standards.

(b) The certification must—
(1) Appear on all diagrams and analyses; and
(2) Be submitted under § 50.20–5 of this chapter.

(c) Standards or specifications for non-pressurized, mechanical or structural systems, and components such as derricks, drawworks, and rotary tables which comply with standards or specifications not referenced in this subchapter must be referenced on the plans or in the specifications of the unit.

§ 58.60–13 Inspection.

An industrial system is accepted by the Coast Guard if the inspector finds—
(a) The system meets this subpart;
(b) There are guards, shields, insulation or similar devices for protection of personnel; and
(c) The system is not manifestly unsafe.

PART 59—REPAIRS TO BOILERS, PRESSURE VESSELS AND APPURTENANCES

Subpart 59.01—General Requirements

Sec.
59.01–1 Scope.
59.01–2 Incorporation by reference.
59.01–5 Repairs, replacements, or alterations.

Subpart 59.10—Welding Repairs to Boilers and Pressure Vessels in Service

59.10–1 Scope.
59.10–5 Cracks.
59.10–10 Corroded surfaces.
59.10–15 Rivets and staybolts.
59.10–20 Patches in shells and tube sheets.
59.10–25 Stayed areas.
59.10–30 Seal welding.
59.10–35 Wrapper plates and back heads.

Subpart 59.15—Miscellaneous Boiler Repairs

59.15–1 Furnace repairs.
59.15–5 Stayed furnaces and combustion chambers.
59.15–10 Bagged or blistered shell plates.

Subpart 59.20—Welding Repairs to Castings

59.20–1 Carbon-steel or alloy-steel castings.

AUTHORITY: 46 U.S.C. 3306, 3703; E.O. 12234, 45 FR 58801, 3 CFR, 1980 Comp., p. 227; Department of Homeland Security Delegation No. 0170.1.

SOURCE: CGFR 68–82, 33 FR 18887, Dec. 18, 1968, unless otherwise noted.

Subpart 59.01—General Requirements

§ 59.01–1 Scope.

The regulations in this part apply to the repairs of all boilers, appurtenances and pressure vessels subject to inspection by the Coast Guard.

§ 59.01–2 Incorporation by reference.

(a) Certain material is incorporated by reference into this part with the approval of the Director of the Federal Register under 5 U.S.C. 552(a) and 1 CFR part 51. To enforce any edition other than that specified in this section, the Coast Guard must publish notice of change in the FEDERAL REGISTER and the material must be available to the public. All approved material is available for inspection at the National Archives and Records Administration (NARA). For information on the availability of this material at NARA, call 202–741–6030 or go to *http://www.archives.gov/federal_register/code_of_federal_regulations/ibr_locations.html.* The material is also available for inspection at the Coast Guard Headquarters. Contact Commandant (CG–ENG), Attn: Office of Design and Engineering Systems, U.S. Coast Guard Stop 7509, 2703 Martin Luther King Jr. Avenue SE., Washington, DC 20593–7509. The material is also available from the sources listed below.

(b) *American Society of Mechanical Engineers (ASME) International*, Three Park Avenue, New York, NY 10016–5990:

(1) 2001 ASME Boiler and Pressure Vessel Code, Section I, Rules for Construction of Power Boilers (July 1, 2001) ("Section I of the ASME Boiler and Pressure Vessel Code"), 59.10–5;

(2) ASME Boiler and Pressure Vessel Code, Section VII, Recommended

Coast Guard, Dept. of Homeland Security § 59.10-5

Guidelines for the Care of Power Boilers (July 1, 2001) ("Section VII of the ASME Boiler and Pressure Vessel Code"), 59.01-5;

(3) ASME Boiler and Pressure Vessel Code, Section VIII, Division 1, Rules for Construction of Pressure Vessels (1998 with 1999 and 2000 addenda) ("Section VIII of the ASME Boiler and Pressure Vessel Code"), 59.10-5; 59.10-10; and

(4) ASME Boiler and Pressure Vessel Code, Section IX, Welding and Brazing Qualifications (1998) ("Section IX of the ASME Boiler and Pressure Vessel Code"), 59.10-5.

[USCG-2003-16630, 73 FR 65188, Oct. 31, 2008, as amended by USCG-2009-0702, 74 FR 49229, Sept. 25, 2009; USCG-2012-0832, 77 FR 59778, Oct. 1, 2012; USCG 2013-0671, 78 FR 60148, Sept. 30, 2013]

§ 59.01-5 Repairs, replacements, or alterations.

(a) No repairs, replacements, or alterations, except emergency repairs, shall be made to boilers, pressure vessels, their mountings or internal fittings, safety valves, piping systems, or pressure appliances without prior approval by the Officer in Charge, Marine Inspection.

(b) Emergency repairs, replacements, or alterations shall be reported as soon as practicable to the Officer in Charge, Marine Inspection, at or nearest the first port where the vessel may call after such repairs are made.

(c) Plan approval shall be obtained from the Officer in Charge, Marine Inspection, for all alterations to systems in service as listed in § 56.01-10(c) of this subchapter and those items listed in paragraph (a) of this section.

(d) Repairs, replacements, or alterations to machinery or items not covered by other sections of this part shall be made in a manner consistent with the part of this subchapter containing the construction standards for the item in question.

(e) Where applicable, manufacturers' instruction books, manuals, and the like, and section VII of the ASME Boiler and Pressure Vessel Code (incorporated by reference; see 46 CFR 59.01-2) must be used for guidance.

[CGFR 68-82, 33 FR 18887, Dec. 18, 1968, as amended by USCG-2003-16630, 73 FR 65189, Oct. 31, 2008]

Subpart 59.10—Welding Repairs to Boilers and Pressure Vessels in Service

§ 59.10-1 Scope.

(a) Repairs to boilers or pressure vessels in service may be performed by welding provided the welding meets the applicable requirements of part 57 of this subchapter.

(b) No repairs by welding shall be made except temporary emergency repairs without prior approval of the Officer in Charge, Marine Inspection. Emergency repairs shall be replaced with permanent repairs meeting the requirements of this subchapter when the vessel returns to a port in which an Officer in Charge, Marine Inspection, is located except in the case of minor repairs which in the opinion of the Officer in Charge, Marine Inspection, do not materially affect the safety of the boiler or pressure vessel.

(c) Repair welding of power boilers, not meeting the requirements of subpart 52.05 of this subchapter, is prohibited unless the stress is carried by such other type(s) of construction complying with the requirements of this subchapter, and where the adequacy of the boiler design is not solely dependent upon the strength of the welds.

(d) Only welded repairs as specified in this subchapter are permitted on boilers and pressure vessels. The welding repairs allowed by this subpart apply only to boilers and pressure vessels fabricated of carbon steel. Welding repairs to boilers and pressure vessels fabricated of alloy steel will be given special consideration by the Commandant. Such other method of repairs by means of welding not covered in this subchapter shall be referred to the Commandant and may be authorized by him, if in his opinion, it meets the intent of this subchapter.

§ 59.10-5 Cracks.

(a) Cracks extending from the calking edge of plates to the rivet holes of

§ 59.10-5

circumferential joints may be welded provided the cracks are veed out so that complete penetration of the weld metal is secured.

(b) Circumferential cracks from rivet hole to rivet hole in girth joints may be welded provided there are not more than three consecutive cracked ligaments nor more than a total of six cracked ligaments in any one girth joint.

(c) Cracks in staybolted plates may be welded provided they are located entirely within staybolted areas and the total length of any crack or series of consecutive cracks does not exceed two staybolt pitches.

(d) Cracks in plain, circular or Adamson ring or similar type furnaces may be welded provided any one crack does not exceed 12 inches in length and after completion the weld is stress-relieved. Cracks in corrugated furnaces may be repaired by welding provided any one crack does not exceed 20 inches in length.

(e) Fire cracks may be welded at riveted door openings extending from the edge of the plate, but not more than 2 inches beyond the centerline of the rivet holes.

(f) Cracks may be welded between tube holes in the shell of water tube boiler drums, provided there are not more than two cracks in any one row in any direction, nor more than a total of four cracks in a drum, and further provided the welding meets the requirements of this subchapter for Class I welded pressure vessels and is approved by the Commandant.

(g) Cracks that occur in superheater manifolds, water wallheaders, water drums, sectional headers, and other appurtenances including steam manifolds of water tube boilers may be repaired in accordance with paragraph (h) of this section if the repair is approved.

(h) All cracks permitted to be repaired under this subpart shall be excavated to sound metal by grinding, flame or arc gouging or chipping out the defective metal to form a clean welding groove. The first two methods of excavation are preferable. Either a V groove or U groove wherein complete penetration of the weld metal is secured may be used. After excavation is completed and prior to welding, the excavated area shall be examined by magnetic particle, dye penetrant, or other acceptable test method. When the reverse side of the weld is accessible the root of the weld shall be chipped or ground out to insure a clean surface of the originally deposited metal and the resultant groove welded to obtain a sound weld having complete penetration. When the weld cannot be back chipped because the reverse side is inaccessible, a backing strip or other approved means of assuring full penetration shall be employed.

(i) During welding of cracks a preheat shall be maintained by controlled temperatures. The degree of preheat shall be determined by the rules listed in accordance with the materials P-number groupings of PW-38, section I, appendix R, section VIII and Table Q. 11.1, section IX of the ASME Boiler and Pressure Vessel Code (all incorporated by reference; see 46 CFR 59.01-2). For thicknesses exceeding three-fourths inch, suitable U grooves should be employed. A welding sequence shall be used so as to equalize welding stresses.

(j) Postweld heat treatment of repaired cracks shall be performed in accordance with the rules specified in PW-39, section I and UW-40, section VIII of the ASME Boiler and Pressure Vessel Code for boilers and pressure vessels respectively.

(k) Welded repairs of cracks shall be nondestructively tested in accordance with the rules specified in PW-40, section I, and UW-51, section VIII of the ASME Boiler and Pressure Vessel Code for boilers and pressure vessels respectively.

(l) After cracks originating in tube or rivet holes are repaired by welding, the holes shall be properly reamed and the weld reinforcing ground flush with the plate in way of rivet heads.

(m) Flat tube sheets in fire-tube boilers which have corroded or where cracks exist in the ligaments may be repaired by welding.

(n) Welding repairs to drums of power boilers, except as otherwise permitted in this subpart, are prohibited.

[CGFR 68-82, 33 FR 18887, Dec. 18, 1968, as amended by USCG-2003-16630, 73 FR 65189, Oct. 31, 2008]

§ 59.10-10 Corroded surfaces.

(a) Corroded surfaces in the calking edges of circumferential seams may be built up by welding to the original thickness under the following conditions:

(1) The thickness of the original metal to be built up between the rivet holes and the calking edge shall not be less than one-fourth of the diameter of the rivet hole, and the portion of the calking edge to be thus reinforced shall not exceed 30 inches in length in a circumferential direction.

(2) In all repairs to circumferential seams by welding, the rivets shall be removed over the portions to be welded for a distance of at least 6 inches beyond the repaired portion.

(3) After repairs are made the rivet holes shall be reamed before the rivets are redriven.

(b) It is not permissible to build up or reinforce a grooved or corroded area of unstayed internal surfaces by means of welding, except that widely scattered pit holes may be built up by welding.

(c) Where external corrosion has reduced the thickness of flat plates around hand holes to an extent of not more than 40 percent of the original thickness and for a distance not exceeding 2 inches from the edge of the hole, the plate may be built up by welding.

(d) Where stayed sheets have corroded to a depth not exceeding 40 percent of their original thickness, they may be reinforced or built up by welding. Where the staybolts are fitted with riveted heads, the staybolts in the reinforced area shall be renewed in accordance with the provisions of § 52.20-15 of this subchapter, but where the staybolts are fitted with nuts, the nuts may be removed and after reinforcing has been applied, collars may be welded around the staybolts in lieu of the nuts. Such reinforced areas shall not exceed 400 square inches nor more than 30 inches in one direction. Two such areas in any one plate may be reinforced: Provided, that the distance between the reinforced surfaces is not less than 30 inches.

(e) When the corroded portion of a staybolted surface exceeds 400 square inches, it is permissible to make repairs by cutting out the defective portion and replacing it with a new plate, the edges of the new plate to be welded in position. In such cases, new staybolts shall be fitted in accordance with the requirements of § 52.20-15 of this subchapter and where welding is performed through a line of staybolts, welded collars as required by Figure 52.01-3 of this subchapter shall be used to attach the staybolts.

(f) Eroded seams of welded pressure vessels may be repaired by rewelding the wasted portion. The wasted section of the seam shall be excavated sufficiently by grinding, flame or arc gouging or chipping to ensure proper weld penetration. Rewelded seams shall be nondestructively tested in accordance with section VIII of the ASME Boiler and Pressure Vessel Code (incorporated by reference, see 46 CFR 59.01-2).

[CGFR 68-82, 33 FR 18887, Dec. 18, 1968, as amended by USCG-2003-16630, 73 FR 65189, Oct. 31, 2008]

§ 59.10-15 Rivets and staybolts.

(a) It is not permitted to reinforce or build up by welding the heads of rivets or staybolts that have deteriorated. Such rivets or staybolts shall be replaced. The seal welding of rivet heads to secure tightness is prohibited.

(b) Where leaks develop around staybolts which are otherwise in good condition, the nuts may be replaced with a beveled collar formed around the end of the stay by means of welding. In such cases, the depth of collar measured on the stay and the width measured on the plate, shall be equal to one-half the diameter of the staybolt.

§ 59.10-20 Patches in shells and tube sheets.

(a) Unreinforced openings in the shells or drums of boilers or pressure vessels, the diameter of which does not exceed the maximum diameter of an unreinforced opening in accordance with § 52.01-100 of this subchapter may be closed by the use of a patch or plate inside the drum or shell and sealed against leakage by welding. Such plates shall have a diameter of at least 2 inches larger than the diameter of the hole and shall have a thickness equal to the thickness of the plate to

§ 59.10-25

which it is attached. It is not permissible to insert such patches in the shell or head flush with the surrounding plate unless the requirements of this subchapter for Class I welded pressure vessels are met.

(b) Portions of tube sheets which have deteriorated may be renewed by replacing the wasted portion with a new section. The ligaments between the tube holes may be joined by means of welding and staytubes. Other acceptable means of lowering the stress on the repaired section may be used if in the judgment of the Officer in Charge, Marine Inspection, it is necessary.

§ 59.10-25 Stayed areas.

Welding repairs are permitted in staybolted areas or areas adequately stayed by other means so that should failure of the welds occur the stress will be carried by the stays. The welds shall be located entirely within staybolted areas and shall not pass through the outer row of stays.

§ 59.10-30 Seal welding.

Where leaks occur in riveted joints or connections, they shall be carefully investigated to determine the cause. Such leaks may be made tight by seal welding the edge, if, in the opinion of the Officer in Charge, Marine Inspection, this will make a satisfactory repair.

§ 59.10-35 Wrapper plates and back heads.

Wrapper plates and back heads may be renewed in whole or repaired as follows:

(a) Wrapper plates or backs heads shall be cut between two rows of staybolts or on a line of staybolts where the thickness is approximately the same as the original construction. If welding is employed on a line of staybolts, the staybolts shall be fitted with a welded collar as required by Figure 52.01-3 of this subchapter.

(b) The edges of wrapper plates riveted to tube sheets and back heads shall be removed by cutting out the rivets.

(c) The edges of existing plates and new plates shall be beveled by chipping, flame cutting or grinding so as to form a suitable groove whereby complete penetration of the weld metal will be obtained. The edge preparation and preheat shall comply with the requirements of § 59.10-5(h).

(d) The edges of the new plate shall be buttwelded and the plate shall be riveted to the flanges of the tube sheet and back heads and the staybolts renewed.

(e) Sections of wrapper plates of combustion chambers outside of stayed areas may be repaired by welding provided the welded joints are stress-relieved by means of controlled heat and the joints are nondestructively tested.

Subpart 59.15—Miscellaneous Boiler Repairs

§ 59.15-1 Furnace repairs.

(a) Where corrugated or plain furnaces or flues are distorted by 1½ inches or more, they shall be repaired by either of the following methods:

(1) The furnace shall be forced back to a true circular shape, and the Officer in Charge, Marine Inspection, may require strongbacks or other acceptable means of support to hold the furnace from future collapse, if in his opinion such support is necessary; or,

(2) The furnace shall be adequately stayed as found necessary in the judgment of the Officer in Charge, Marine Inspection.

(b) Distortion means the difference between any single measured diameter of the furnace and the diameter of a true circle at the same location. The diameter of the true circle may be taken as the original furnace diameter or may be determined by a means acceptable to the Officer in Charge, Marine Inspection.

(c) Where the distortion does not exceed 1½ inches it will not be necessary to force the furnace back to a true circle if the allowable pressure is reduced in the ratio of 1½ percent for each one-tenth of an inch of distortion. However, if the maximum distortion does not exceed 1 inch and the length of the distorted area is not more than three corrugations, or, if the maximum distortion does not exceed three-fourths inch for a length greater than three corrugations of distorted area, the repairs

Coast Guard, Dept. of Homeland Security § 59.15-10

or reduction in pressure will not be required unless considered necessary by the marine inspector.

(d) When it becomes necessary to rivet a patch to a furnace or other part of the heating surface, the riveted patch shall be placed on the waterside of the plate in order not to form a pocket in which sediment may collect.

(e) Furnace crowns which have become distorted, not in excess of the limitations provided in paragraph (c) of this section, may be repaired by pumping back the distorted section to as nearly a true circle as possible and reinforcing the same by means of a ring, arc- or gas-welded to the distorted corrugation as shown in Figure 59.15–1, the welding to be done by welders and welding processors qualified in accordance with part 57 of this subchapter using acceptable welding electrodes in accordance with § 57.02–4 of this subchapter.

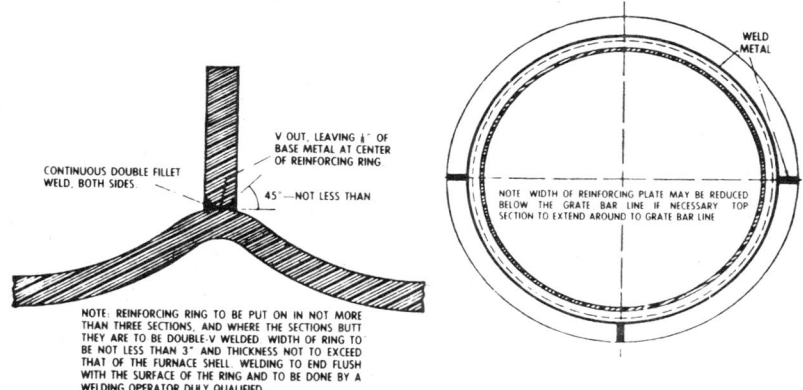

FIGURE 59.15–1—APPROVED METHOD OF REINFORCING FURNACES BY MEANS OF ARC OR GAS WELDING

§ 59.15-5 Stayed furnaces and combustion chambers.

(a) Where the plate forming the walls of stayed furnaces or combustion chambers become bulged between staybolts, repairs may be made by inserting an additional staybolt in the center of such space supported by the four staybolts.

(b) Where it is desired to rivet a patch to the wall of a stayed furnace or combustion chamber, the defective portion of the plate shall be cut away until solid material is reached, the patch shall be riveted on the waterside, and the staybolts renewed, and extended through the new plate.

§ 59.15-10 Bagged or blistered shell plates.

(a) When the shell plates of cylindrical boilers which are exposed to the radiant heat of the fire become bagged or blistered, it shall be the duty of the chief engineer in charge of the vessel to notify the Officer in Charge, Marine Inspection, for examination before raising steam on the boiler.

(b) Where the shell plate is bagged due to overheating, the Officer in Charge, Marine Inspection, may, if in his judgment it is practicable, permit the same to be driven back to its original position.

(c) Where the shell plate has blistered, bagged, or bulged to such an extent that there is an appreciable thinning of the plate, the Officer in Charge, Marine Inspection, shall require the defective portion to be cut away and the shell repaired by fitting a patch of steel plate conforming to the

§ 59.20-1

requirements of § 52.01-90 of this subchapter in place of the defective portion. Care shall be taken that the riveting schedule of the patch is so arranged as to give the plate sufficient strength to withstand the stress placed on it in service.

Subpart 59.20—Welding Repairs to Castings

§ 59.20-1 Carbon-steel or alloy-steel castings.

Defects in carbon-steel or alloy-steel castings may be repaired by welding. The repairs shall be performed in accordance with the material specification to which the casting was originally supplied.

PART 60 [RESERVED]

PART 61—PERIODIC TESTS AND INSPECTIONS

Subpart 61.01—General

Sec.
61.01-1 Scope.

Subpart 61.03—Incorporation of Standards

61.03-1 Incorporation by reference.

Subpart 61.05—Tests and Inspections of Boilers

61.05-1 Scope.
61.05-5 Preparation of boilers for inspection and test.
61.05-10 Boilers in service.
61.05-15 Boiler mountings and attachments.
61.05-20 Boiler safety valves.

Subpart 61.10—Tests and Inspections of Pressure Vessels

61.10-1 Scope.
61.10-5 Pressure vessels in service.

Subpart 61.15—Periodic Tests of Piping Systems

61.15-1 Scope.
61.15-5 Steam piping.
61.15-10 Liquefied-petroleum-gas piping for heating and cooking.
61.15-12 Nonmetallic expansion joints.
61.15-15 Other piping.

Subpart 61.20—Periodic Tests of Machinery and Equipment

61.20-1 Steering gear.
61.20-3 Main and auxiliary machinery and associated equipment, including fluid control systems.
61.20-5 Drydock examination.
61.20-15 Tailshaft examination.
61.20-17 Examination intervals.
61.20-18 Examination requirements.
61.20-21 Extension of examination interval.
61.20-23 Tailshaft clearance; bearing weardown.

Subpart 61.30—Tests and Inspections of Fired Thermal Fluid Heaters

61.30-1 Scope.
61.30-5 Preparation of thermal fluid heater for inspection and test.
61.30-10 Hydrostatic test.
61.30-15 Visual inspection.
61.30-20 Automatic control and safety tests.

Subpart 61.35—Design Verification and Periodic Testing for Automatic Auxiliary Boilers

61.35-1 General.
61.35-3 Required tests and checks.

Subpart 61.40—Design Verification and Periodic Testing of Vital System Automation

61.40-1 General.
61.40-3 Design verification testing.
61.40-6 Periodic safety tests.
61.40-10 Test procedure details.

AUTHORITY: 43 U.S.C. 1333; 46 U.S.C. 2103, 3306, 3307, 3703; E.O. 12234, 45 FR 58801, 3 CFR 1980 Comp., p. 277; Department of Homeland Security Delegation No. 0170.1.

SOURCE: CGFR 68-82, 33 FR 18890, Dec. 18, 1968, unless otherwise noted.

Subpart 61.01—General

§ 61.01-1 Scope.

(a) Periodic tests and inspection shall be made of the main and auxiliary machinery, boilers, and other equipment as prescribed in this part.

(b) The inspections and tests shall insure that the equipment and associated structure are in satisfactory operating conditions and fit for the service for which they are intended.

[CGFR 68-82, 33 FR 18890, Dec. 18, 1968, as amended by CGD 95-012, 60 FR 48050, Sept. 18, 1995]

Subpart 61.03—Incorporation of Standards

§ 61.03-1 Incorporation by reference.

(a) Certain material is incorporated by reference into this part with the approval of the Director of the Federal Register under 5 U.S.C. 552(a) and 1 CFR part 51. To enforce any edition other than that specified in paragraph (b) of this section, the Coast Guard must publish a notice of change in the FEDERAL REGISTER and the material must be available to the public. All approved material is available for inspection at the Coast Guard Headquarters. Contact Commandant (CG–ENG), Attn: Office of Design and Engineering Systems, U.S. Coast Guard Stop 7509, 2703 Martin Luther King Jr. Avenue SE., Washington, DC 20593–7509. The material is also available from the sources indicated in paragraph (b) of this section or at the National Archives and Records Administration (NARA). For information on the availability of this material at NARA, call 202–741–6030, or go to: *http://www.archives.gov/federal_register/code_of_federal_regulations/ibr_locations.html.*

(b) The material approved for incorporation by reference in this part and the sections affected are as follows:

American Society for Testing and Materials (ASTM)

100 Barr Harbor Drive, West Conshohocken, PA 19428–2959.

ASTM D 665–98, Standard Test Method for Rust-Preventing Characteristics of Inhibited Mineral Oil in the Presence of Water 61.20–17

[CGD 95–027, 61 FR 26001, May 23, 1996, as amended by CGD 96–041, 61 FR 50728, Sept. 27, 1996; 97–057, 62 FR 51044, Sept. 30, 1997; USCG–1999–6216, 64 FR 53225, Oct. 1, 1999; USCG–1999–5151, 64 FR 67180, Dec. 1, 1999; USCG–2009–0702, 74 FR 49229, Sept. 25, 2009; USCG–2012–0832, 77 FR 59778, Oct. 1, 2012; USCG 2013–0671, 78 FR 60149, Sept. 30, 2013]

Subpart 61.05—Tests and Inspections of Boilers

§ 61.05-1 Scope.

The term *boiler* as used in this subpart includes power boilers subject to part 52 and heating boilers subject to part 53 of this subchapter.

[CGD 80–064, 49 FR 32193, Aug. 13, 1984]

§ 61.05-5 Preparation of boilers for inspection and test.

(a) For internal inspection, manhole and handhold plates, and washout plugs shall be removed as required by the marine inspector and the furnace and combustion chambers shall be thoroughly cooled and cleaned. Portable obstructions shall be removed as necessary for proper access.

(b) In preparing the boilers for the hydrostatic test, they shall be filled with water at not less than 70 °F. and not more than 160 °F. for watertube boilers, and not more than 100 °F. for firetube boilers. The safety valves shall be secured by means of gags or clamps.

[CGFR 68–82, 33 FR 18890, Dec. 18, 1968, as amended by CGD 95–027, 61 FR 26001, May 23, 1996]

§ 61.05-10 Boilers in service.

(a) Each boiler, including superheater, reheater, economizer, auxiliary boiler, low-pressure heating boiler, and unfired steam boiler, must be available for examination by the marine inspector at intervals specified by Table 61.05–10, and more often if necessary, to determine that the complete unit is in a safe and satisfactory condition. When a hydrostatic test is required, the marine inspector may examine all accessible parts of the boiler while it is under pressure.

(b) The owner, master, or person in charge of the vessel shall give ample notice to the cognizant Officer in Charge, Marine Inspection, so that a marine inspector may witness the tests and make the required inspections.

(c) Firetube boilers which cannot be entered or which cannot be satisfactorily examined internally, all boilers of lap seam construction and all boilers to which extensive repairs have been made or the strength of which the marine inspector has any reason to question, shall be subjected to a hydrostatic test of 1½ times the maximum allowable working pressure. All other boilers shall be subjected to a hydrostatic test of 1¼ times the maximum allowable working pressure.

(d) In applying hydrostatic pressure to boilers, arrangements shall be made to prevent main and auxiliary stop valves from being simultaneously subjected to the hydrostatic pressure on one side and steam pressure on the other side.

(e) If the marine inspector has reason to believe that the boiler has deteriorated to any appreciable extent under the bottom where it rests on saddles or foundations, he shall cause the boiler to be lifted to such position that it can be thoroughly examined, provided the examination cannot be made otherwise.

(f) The marine inspector may require any boiler to be drilled or gaged to determine actual thickness any time its safety is in doubt. At the first inspection for certification after a firetube or flue boiler has been installed for 10 years, it shall be gaged to determine the extent of deterioration. Thickness will be measured at or near the waterline, at the bottom and at such other places deemed necessary by the marine inspector. Examination may be by drilling or a nondestructive means acceptable to the marine inspector. Prior to the use of a nondestructive method of examination, the user shall demonstrate to the marine inspector that results having an accuracy within plus or minus 5 percent are consistently obtainable when using specimens similar to those to be examined on the boiler.

(g) If the thickness is found to be less than the original thickness upon which the maximum allowable working pressure was based, it shall be recalculated. The thickness of the thinnest measured portion shall be used in this calculation. Either the design formulas given in this subchapter or the ones in effect when the boiler was contracted for or built may normally be used in this recalculation. In no case will an increase in the pressure allowed be made.

TABLE 61.05-10—INSPECTION INTERVALS FOR BOILERS [1] [2] [3]

	Firetube boiler ≥150 psi	Watertube boiler	Any firetube boiler for propulsion	Firetube boiler <150 psi
Hydro Test:				
Passenger Vessel	2.5	2.5	1	2.5
Other Vessel	2.5	5	1	5
Fireside Inspection	1	2.5	1	2.5
Waterside Inspection	1	2.5	1	2.5
Boiler Safety-Valve Test	1	2.5	1	1
Valves Inspection	5	5	5	5
Studs and Bolts Inspection	10	10	10	10
Mountings Inspection	10	10	10	10
Steam Gauge Test	2.5	2.5	2.5	2.5
Fusible Plug Inspection	2.5		2.5	2.5

[1] All intervals are in years.
[2] Where the 2.5-year interval is indicated: two tests or inspections must occur within any five-year period, and no more than three years may elapse between any test or inspection and its immediate predecessor.
[3] Intervals for hybrid boilers are the same as for firetube boilers.

[CGFR 68–82, 33 FR 18890, Dec. 18, 1968, as amended by CGD 80–064, 49 FR 32193, Aug. 13, 1984; CGD 83–043, 60 FR 24781, May 10, 1995; USCG–1999–4976, 65 FR 6500, Feb. 9, 2000]

§ 61.05-15 Boiler mountings and attachments.

(a) Each valve shall be opened and examined by the marine inspector at the interval specified in Table 61.05–10.

(b) Each stud or bolt for each boiler mounting that paragraph (c) of this section requires to be removed may be examined by the marine inspector.

(c)(1) Each boiler mounting may be removed from the boiler and be examined by the marine inspector at the interval specified by Table 61.05–10 when any of the following conditions exist:

(2) Where boiler mountings or valves are attached to boiler nozzles and a satisfactory internal examination of these mountings or valves and their attaching studs, bolts, or other means of attachment, can be performed by opening up the valves, such mountings or valves need not be removed from the

Coast Guard, Dept. of Homeland Security § 61.10–5

boiler unless in the opinion of the Officer in Charge, Marine Inspection, such action is necessary.

(d) The Officer in Charge, Marine Inspection, may require the examinations prescribed in this section to be made at more frequent intervals, if in his opinion such action is necessary to be assured of the safety of the boiler and its attachments.

(e) Water columns, gage glasses, and gage cocks shall be examined to determine that they are in satisfactory working order.

(f) Each steam gauge for a boiler or a main steam line may be examined and checked for accuracy by the marine inspector at the interval specified by Table 61.05–10.

(g) Each fusible plug may be examined by the marine inspector at the interval specified by Table 61.05–10.

[CGFR 68–82, 33 FR 18890, Dec. 18, 1968, as amended by CGFR 69–127, 35 FR 9980, June 17, 1970; CGD 83–043, 60 FR 24782, May 10, 1995]

§ 61.05–20 Boiler safety valves.

Each safety valve for a drum, superheater, or reheater of a boiler shall be tested at the interval specified by table 61.05–10.

[CGD 95–028, 62 FR 51202, Sept. 30, 1997]

Subpart 61.10—Tests and Inspections of Pressure Vessels

§ 61.10–1 Scope.

All pressure vessels aboard ships, mobile offshore drilling units, and barges are subject to periodic inspection.

[CGD 68–82, 33 FR 18890, Dec. 18, 1968, as amended by CGD 73–251, 43 FR 56801, Dec. 4, 1978; CGD 95–012, 60 FR 48050, Sept. 18, 1995]

§ 61.10–5 Pressure vessels in service.

(a) *Basic requirements.* Each pressure vessel must be examined or tested every 5 years. The extent of the test or examination should be that necessary to determine that the pressure vessel's condition is satisfactory and that the pressure vessel is fit for the service intended.

(b) *Internal and external tests and inspections.* (1) Each pressure vessel listed on the Certificate of Inspection must be thoroughly examined externally every 5 years.

(2) In addition, each pressure vessel listed on the Certificate of Inspection that is fitted with a manhole or other inspection opening so it can be satisfactorily examined internally, must be opened for internal examination every 5 years.

(3) No pressure vessel need be hydrostatically tested except when a defect is found that, in the marine inspector's opinion, may affect the safety of the pressure vessel. In this case, the pressure vessel should be hydrostatically tested at a pressure of $1\frac{1}{2}$ times the maximum allowable working pressure.

(c) *Special purpose vessels.* (1) If your vessel's Certificate of Inspection is renewed annually, the following must be examined under operating conditions at each inspection for certification: all tubular heat exchangers, hydraulic accumulators, and all pressure vessels used in refrigeration service.

(2) If your vessel's Certificate of Inspection is renewed less often than annually, the following must be examined under operating conditions twice every 5 years: all tubular heat exchangers, hydraulic accumulators, and all pressure vessels used in refrigeration service.

(3) No more than 3 years may elapse between any examination and its immediate predecessor.

(d) *Hydrostatic tests under pressure.* Each pressure vessel, other than one exempted by this section, must be subjected to a hydrostatic test at a pressure of $1\frac{1}{4}$ times the maximum allowable working pressure twice within any five-year period, except that no more than three years may elapse between any test and its immediate predecessor.

(e) *Exemptions from hydrostatic tests.* The following pressure vessels will not normally be subjected to a hydrostatic test:

(1) Tubular heat exchangers.

(2) Pressure vessels used in refrigeration service.

(3) Hydraulic accumulators.

(4) Pressure vessels which have been satisfactorily examined internally by a marine inspector and in which no defects have been found which impair the safety of the pressure vessel.

§ 61.15-1

(5) Pressure vessels which were initially pneumatically tested in accordance with part 54 of this subchapter.

(6) Pressure vessels not stamped with the Coast Guard Symbol.

(f) *Compressed gas or hazardous liquid pressure vessel tests.* Cargo tanks of pressure vessel configuration containing liquefied, compressed gases or hazardous liquids must be inspected and tested as required by the applicable regulations published in subchapter D or subchapter I of this chapter.

(g) *Bulk storage tanks.* Each bulk storage tank containing refrigerated liquefied CO_2 for use aboard a vessel as a fire-extinguishing agent shall be subjected to a hydrostatic test of 1½ times the maximum allowable working pressure in the tenth year of the installation and at ten-year intervals thereafter. After the test, the tank should be drained and an internal examination made. Parts of the jacket and lagging on the underside of the tank designated by the marine inspector must be removed at the time of the test so the marine inspector may determine the external condition of the tank.

(h) *Pneumatic tests.* (1) Pressure vessels that were pneumatically tested before being stamped with the Coast Guard Symbol must be examined internally twice every 5 years and examined externally at each Inspection for Certification. No more than 3 years may elapse between any external examination and its immediate predecessor.

(2) For tanks whose design precludes a thorough internal or external examination, the thickness must be determined by a nondestructive method acceptable to the Officer in Charge, Marine Inspection.

(3) If (due to the product carried) your vessel's inspection intervals are prescribed in subchapter D (Tank Vessels), subchapter I (Cargo and Miscellaneous Vessels), or subchapter I-A (Mobile Offshore Drilling Units), you must comply with the pneumatic test regulations there, instead of the ones in this section.

(i) *Safety or relief valves on pressure vessels.* (1) If your vessel's Certificate of Inspection is renewed annually, the marine inspector must check the settings of the safety or relief valves on all pressure vessels, except cargo tanks, at each inspection for certification.

(2) If your vessel's Certificate of Inspection is renewed less often than annually, the marine inspector must check the settings of the safety or relief valves on all pressure vessels, except cargo tanks, twice every 5 years. No more than 3 years may elapse between any check and its immediate predecessor.

(3) Cargo tank safety or relief valves must be checked at the interval required in subchapter D (Tank Vessels) or subchapter I (Cargo and Miscellaneous Vessels) of this chapter.

[CGFR 68-82, 33 FR 18890, Dec. 18, 1968, as amended by CGFR 69-127, 35 FR 9980, June 17, 1970; CGD 73-251, 43 FR 56801, Dec. 4, 1978; CGD 77-147, 47 FR 21811, May 20, 1982; CGD 86-033, 53 FR 36024, Sept. 16, 1988; CGD 83-043, 60 FR 24782, May 10, 1995; CGD 95-028, 62 FR 51202, Sept. 30, 1997; USCG-1999-6216, 64 FR 53225, Oct. 1, 1999; USCG-1999-4976, 65 FR 6500, Feb. 9, 2000]

Subpart 61.15—Periodic Tests of Piping Systems

§ 61.15-1 Scope.

In conducting hydrostatic tests on piping, the required test pressure shall be maintained for a sufficient length of time to permit an inspection to be made of all joints and connections. The setting of the relief valve or safety valve will be considered as establishing the maximum allowable working pressure of the system.

[CGFR 68-82, 33 FR 18890, Dec. 18, 1968, as amended by CGD 95-012, 60 FR 48050, Sept. 18, 1995]

§ 61.15-5 Steam piping.

(a) Main steam piping shall be subjected to a hydrostatic test equal to 1¼ times the maximum allowable working pressure at the same periods prescribed for boilers in § 61.05-10. The hydrostatic test shall be applied from the boiler drum to the throttle valve. If the covering of the piping is not removed, the test pressure shall be maintained on the piping for a period of ten minutes. If any evidence of moisture or leakage is detected, the covering shall be removed and the piping thoroughly examined.

Coast Guard, Dept. of Homeland Security §61.20–1

(b) All steam piping subject to pressure from the main boiler should be subjected to a hydrostatic test at a pressure of 1¼ times the maximum allowable working pressure of the boiler after every five years of service except as otherwise provided for in paragraph (a) of this section. Unless the covering of the piping is removed, the test pressure must be maintained on the piping for ten minutes. If any evidence of moisture or leakage is detected, the covering should be removed and the piping thoroughly examined. No piping with a nominal size of 3 inches or less need be hydrostatically tested.

(c) The setting of safety and relief valves installed in piping systems shall be checked by the marine inspector at each inspection for certification for vessels whose Certificates of Inspection are renewed each year. For other vessels, the setting must be checked twice within any 5-year period, and no more than 3 years may elapse between any check and its immediate predecessor.

[CGFR 68–82, 33 FR 18890, Dec. 18, 1968, as amended by CGD 73–248, 39 FR 30839, Aug. 26, 1974; CGD 83–043, 60 FR 24782, May 10, 1995; USCG–1999–4976, 65 FR 6500, Feb. 9, 2000]

§61.15–10 Liquefied-petroleum-gas piping for heating and cooking.

(a) Leak tests as described in paragraph (b) of this section shall be conducted at least once each month, at each inspection for certification, and at each periodic inspection. The tests required at monthly intervals shall be conducted by an appropriately credentialed officer of the vessel or qualified personnel acceptable to the Officer in Charge, Marine Inspection. The owner, master, or person in charge of the vessel shall keep records of such tests showing the dates when performed and the name(s) of the person(s) and/or company conducting the tests. Such records shall be made available to the marine inspector upon request and shall be kept for the period of validity of the vessel's current certificate of inspection. Where practicable, these records should be kept in or with the vessel's logbook.

(b) Test the system for leakage in accordance with the following procedure: With the appliance valve closed, the master shutoff valve on the appliance open, and one cylinder valve open, note pressure in gauge.

[CGFR 68–82, 33 FR 18890, Dec. 18, 1968, as amended by USCG–1999–4976, 65 FR 6500, Feb. 9, 2000; USCG–2003–16630, 73 FR 65189, Oct. 31, 2008; USCG–2006–24371, 74 FR 11265, Mar. 16, 2009]

§61.15–12 Nonmetallic expansion joints.

(a) Nonmetallic expansion joints must be examined externally at each inspection for certification and periodic inspection for signs of excessive wear, fatigue, deterioration, physical damage, misalignment, improper flange-to-flange spacing, and leakage. A complete internal examination must be conducted when an external examination reveals excessive wear or other signs of deterioration or damage.

(b) A nonmetallic expansion joint must be replaced 10 years after it has been placed into service if it is located in a system which penetrates the side of the vessel and both the penetration and the nonmetallic expansion joint are located below the deepest load waterline. The Officer in Charge, Marine Inspection may grant an extension of the ten year replacement to coincide with the vessel's next drydocking.

[CGD 77–140, 54 FR 40615, Oct. 2, 1989, as amended by CGD 95–028, 62 FR 51202, Sept. 30, 1997; USCG–1999–4976, 65 FR 6501, Feb. 9, 2000]

§61.15–15 Other piping.

(a) All other piping systems shall be examined under working conditions as required by the marine inspector.

Subpart 61.20—Periodic Tests of Machinery and Equipment

§61.20–1 Steering gear.

(a) The marine inspector must inspect the steering gear at each inspection for certification for vessels whose Certificate of Inspections are renewed each year. For other vessels, the marine inspector must inspect the steering gear twice within a 5-year period, and no more than 3 years may elapse between any inspection and its immediate predecessor. The marine inspector may inspect the steering gear more often, if necessary.

§ 61.20-3

(b) All devices employed in the change-over from automatic to manual operation shall be examined and tested.

[CGFR 68–82, 33 FR 18890, Dec. 18, 1968, as amended by USCG–1999–4976, 65 FR 6501, Feb. 9, 2000]

§ 61.20-3 Main and auxiliary machinery and associated equipment, including fluid control systems.

(a) At each inspection for certification and periodic inspection the marine inspector shall conduct such tests and inspections of the main propulsion and auxiliary machinery and of its associated equipment, including the fluid control systems, as he feels necessary to check safe operation.

(b) Remote control for the means of stopping machinery driving forced and induced draft fans, fuel oil transfer pumps, fuel oil unit pumps, and fans in the ventilation systems serving machinery and cargo spaces shall be tested at each regular inspection for certification and periodic inspection.

[CGFR 68–82, 33 FR 18890, Dec. 18, 1968, as amended by USCG–1999–4976, 65 FR 6501, Feb. 9, 2000]

§ 61.20-5 Drydock examination.

(a) When any vessel is drydocked, examination shall be made of the propeller, stern bushing, sea connection, and fastenings if deemed necessary by the marine inspector.

(b) Sea chests, sea valves, sea strainers, and valves for the emergency bilge suction shall be opened up for examination every 5 years at the time of drydocking.

[CGFR 68–82, 33 FR 18890, Dec. 18, 1968, as amended by CGD 84–024, 53 FR 32231, Aug. 24, 1988; CGD 95–028, 62 FR 51202, Sept. 30, 1997]

§ 61.20-15 Tailshaft examination.

The rules in §§ 61.20–15 through 61.20–23 apply only to vessels in ocean and coastwise service. Each examination, inspection and test prescribed by these sections must be conducted in the presence of a marine inspector.

[CGD 78–153, 45 FR 52388, Aug. 7, 1980]

§ 61.20-17 Examination intervals.

(a) A lubricant that demonstrates the corrosion inhibiting properties of oil when tested in accordance with ASTM D 665 (incorporated by reference, see § 61.03–1) is considered to be equivalent to oil for the purposes of the tailshaft examination interval.

(b) Except as provided in paragraphs (c) through (f) of this section, each tailshaft on a vessel must be examined twice within any 5 year period. No more than 3 years may elapse between any 2 tailshaft examinations.

(c) Tailshafts on vessels fitted with multiple shafts must be examined once every 5 years.

(d) Tailshafts with inaccessible portions fabricated of materials resistant to corrosion by sea water, or fitted with a continuous liner or a sealing gland which prevents sea water from contacting the shaft, must be examined once every 5 years if they are constructed or fitted with a taper, keyway, and propeller designed in accordance with the American Bureau of Shipping standards to reduce stress concentrations or are fitted with a flanged propeller. Accessible portions of tailshafts must be examined visually during each drydock examination.

(e) Tailshafts with oil lubricated bearings, including bearings lubricated with a substance considered to be equivalent to oil under the provisions of paragraph (a) of this section need not be drawn for examination—

(1) If tailshaft bearing clearance readings are taken whenever the vessel undergoes a drydock examination or underwater survey;

(2) If the inboard seal assemblies are examined whenever the vessel undergoes a drydock examination or underwater survey;

(3) If an analysis of the tailshaft bearing lubricant is performed semiannually in accordance with the lubrication system manufacturer's recommendations to determine bearing material content or the presence of other contaminants; and

(4) If—

(i) For tailshafts with a taper, the propeller is removed and the taper and the keyway (if fitted) are nondestructively tested at intervals not to exceed 5 years; or

(ii) For tailshafts with a propeller fitted to the shaft by means of a coupling flange, the propeller coupling

Coast Guard, Dept. of Homeland Security §61.30–5

bolts and flange radius are nondestructively tested whenever they are removed or made accessible in connection with overhaul or repairs.

(f) Tailshafts on mobile offshore drilling units are not subject to examination intervals under paragraphs (b) through (d) of this section if they are—
(1) Examined during each regularly scheduled drydocking; or
(2) Regularly examined in a manner acceptable to the Commandant CG–CVC.

[CGD 95–027, 61 FR 26001, May 23, 1996, as amended by CGD 96–041, 61 FR 50728, Sept. 27, 1996; 61 FR 52497, Oct. 7, 1996; USCG–1999–5151, 64 FR 67180, Dec. 1, 1999; USCG–2009–0702, 74 FR 49229, Sept. 25, 2009; USCG–2012–0832, 77 FR 59778, Oct. 1, 2012]

§61.20–18 Examination requirements.

(a) Each tailshaft must be drawn and visually inspected at each examination.

(b) On tailshafts with a taper, keyway, (if fitted) and propeller designed in accordance with American Bureau of Shipping standards to reduce stress concentrations, the forward 1/3 of the shaft's taper section must be nondestructively tested in addition to a visual inspection of the entire shaft.

(c) On tailshafts with a propeller fitted to the shaft by means of a coupling flange, the flange, the fillet at the propeller end, and each coupling bolt must be nondestructively tested in addition to a visual inspection of the entire shaft.

[CGD 84–024, 52 FR 39652, Oct. 23, 1987, as amended by CGD 84–024, 53 FR 32231, Aug. 24, 1988]

§61.20–21 Extension of examination interval.

The Commandant CG–CVC may authorize extensions of the interval between tailshaft examinations.

[CGD 84–024, 52 FR 39652, Oct. 23, 1987, as amended by CGD 95–072, 60 FR 50463, Sept. 29, 1995; CGD 96–041, 61 FR 50728, Sept. 27, 1996; USCG–2009–0702, 74 FR 49229, Sept. 25, 2009; USCG–2012–0832, 77 FR 59778, Oct. 1, 2012]

§61.20–23 Tailshaft clearance; bearing weardown.

(a) Water lubricated bearings, other than rubber, must be rebushed as follows:

(1) Where the propelling machinery is located amidship, the after stern tube bearing must be rebushed when it is worn down to 6.4 mm (0.25 in) clearance for shafts of 229 mm (9 in) or less in diameter, 7.95 mm (0.3125 in) clearance for shafts exceeding 229 mm (9 in) but not exceeding 305 mm (12 in) in diameter, and 9.53 mm (0.375 in) clearance for shafts exceeding 305 mm (12 in) in diameter.

(2) Where the propelling machinery is located aft, the after stern tube bearing must be rebushed when weardown is 1.6 mm (.0625 in) less than the applicable clearance for propelling machinery located amidship.

(b) Water lubricated rubber bearings must be rebushed when any water groove is half the original depth.

(c) Oil lubricated bearings must be rebushed when deemed necessary by the Officer in Charge, Marine Inspection. The manufacturer's recommendation shall be considered in making this determination.

[CGD 78–153, 45 FR 52388, Aug. 7, 1980]

Subpart 61.30—Tests and Inspections of Fired Thermal Fluid Heaters

Source: CGD 80–064, 49 FR 32193, Aug. 13, 1984, unless otherwise noted.

§61.30–1 Scope.

The term *thermal fluid heater* as used in this part includes any fired automatic auxiliary heating unit which uses a natural or synthetic fluid in the liquid phase as the heat exchange medium and whose operating temperature and pressure do not exceed 204 °C (400 °F) and 225 psig, respectively. Thermal fluid heaters having operating temperatures and pressures higher than 204 °C (400 °F) and 225 psig, respectively, are inspected under subpart 61.05—Tests and Inspections of Boilers.

§61.30–5 Preparation of thermal fluid heater for inspection and test.

For visual inspection, access plates and manholes shall be removed as required by the marine inspector and the

§ 61.30-10

heater and combustion chambers shall be thoroughly cooled and cleaned.

[CGD 80-064, 49 FR 32193, Aug. 13, 1984, as amended by CGD 95-027, 61 FR 26002, May 23, 1996]

§ 61.30-10 Hydrostatic test.

All new installations of thermal fluid heaters must be given a hydrostatic test of 1½ times the maximum allowable working pressure. The test must be conducted in the presence of a marine inspector. No subsequent hydrostatic tests are required unless, in the opinion of the Officer in Charge Marine Inspection, the condition of the heater warrants such a test. Where hydrostatic tests are required, an inspection is made of all accessible parts under pressure. The thermal fluid may be used as the hydrostatic test medium.

§ 61.30-15 Visual inspection.

Thermal fluid heaters are examined by a marine inspector at the inspection for certification, periodic inspection and when directed by the Officer in Charge Marine Inspection, to determine that the complete unit is in a safe and satisfactory condition. The visual examination includes, but is not limited to, the combustion chamber, heat exchanger, refractory, exhaust stack, and associated pumps and piping.

[CGD 80-064, 49 FR 32193, Aug. 13, 1984, as amended by USCG-1999-4976, 65 FR 6501, Feb. 9, 2000]

§ 61.30-20 Automatic control and safety tests.

Operational tests and checks of all safety and limit controls, combustion controls, programming controls, and safety relief valves must be conducted by the owner, chief engineer, or person in charge at the inspection for certification, periodic inspection, and when directed by the Officer in Charge, Marine Inspection, to determine that the control components and safety devices are functioning properly and are in satisfactory operating condition. These tests and checks must be conducted in the presence of a marine inspector and must include the following: proper prepurge, burner ignition sequence checks, operation of the combustion controls, limit controls, fluid flow controls, fluid level controls, high temperature control, proper postpurge control, and verification of the flame safeguard.

[CGD 88-057, 55 FR 24237, June 15, 1990, as amended by USCG-1999-4976, 65 FR 6501, Feb. 9, 2000]

NOTE: Sections 63.05-90 and 63.10-90 of this chapter may be referenced concerning operating tests.

Subpart 61.35—Design Verification and Periodic Testing for Automatic Auxiliary Boilers

SOURCE: CGD 88-057, 55 FR 24237, June 15, 1990, unless otherwise noted.

§ 61.35-1 General.

(a) All automatic auxiliary boilers except fired thermal fluid heaters must be tested and inspected in accordance with this subpart and subpart 61.05 of this part.

(b) Fired thermal fluid heaters must be tested and inspected in accordance with subpart 61.30 of this part.

(c) All controls, safety devices, and other control system equipment must be tested and inspected to verify their proper design, construction, installation, and operation.

(d) All tests must be performed after installation of the automatic auxiliary boiler and its control system(s) aboard the vessel.

(e) As far as practicable, test techniques must not simulate monitored system conditions by misadjustment, artificial signals, improper wiring, tampering, or revision of the system tested. The use of a synthesized signal or condition applied to a sensor is acceptable if the required test equipment is maintained in good working order and is periodically calibrated. Proper operation and proper calibration of test equipment must be demonstrated to the Officer in Charge, Marine Inspection.

§ 61.35-3 Required tests and checks.

(a) Tests and checks must include the following:

(1) *Safety (Programming) controls.* Safety controls must control and cycle the unit in the proper manner and sequence. Proper prepurge, ignition, postpurge, and modulation must be

Coast Guard, Dept. of Homeland Security § 61.40-6

verified. All time intervals must be verified.

(2) *Flame safeguard.* The flame safeguard system must be tested by causing flame and ignition failures. Operation of the audible alarm and visible indicator must be verified. The shutdown times must be verified.

(3) *Fuel supply controls.* Satisfactory shutdown operation of the two fuel control solenoid valves must be verified. No visible leakage from the valves into the burner(s) must be verified.

(4) *Fuel oil pressure limit control.* A safety shutdown must be initiated by lowering the fuel oil pressure below the value required for safe combustion. System shutdown and the need for manual reset prior to automatic start-up must be verified.

(5) *Fuel oil temperature limit control.* (Units designed to burn heavy fuel oil.) A safety shutdown must be initiated by lowering the fuel oil temperature below the designed temperature. System shutdown and the need for manual reset prior to automatic startup must be verified.

(6) *Combustion controls.* Smooth and stable operation of the combustion controls must be verified.

(7) *Draft limit control.* The draft loss interlock switch must be tested to ensure proper operation. The draft limit control must cause burner shutdown and prevent startup when an inadequate air volume is supplied to the burner(s).

(8) *Limit controls.* Shutdown caused by the limit controls must be verified.

(9) *Water level controls.* Water level controls must be tested by slowly lowering the water level in the boiler. Each operating water level control must be individually tested. The upper low water cutoff and the lower low water cutoff must each be tested. The audible alarm and visible indicator associated with the lower low water cutoff must be tested. The manual reset device must be tested after the lower low water cutoff has been activated.

(10) *Feed water flow controls.* The feed water flow limit device (found on steam boilers and water heaters without water level controls) must be tested by interrupting the feed water supply. Manual reset must be required prior to restarting the boiler.

(11) *Low voltage test.* The fuel supply to the burners must automatically shut off when the supply voltage is lowered.

(12) *Switches.* All switches must be tested to verify satisfactory operation.

Subpart 61.40—Design Verification and Periodic Testing of Vital System Automation

SOURCE: CGD 81-030, 53 FR 17837, May 18, 1988, unless otherwise noted.

§ 61.40-1 General.

(a) All automatically or remotely controlled or monitored vital systems addressed by part 62 of this subchapter must be subjected to tests and inspections to evaluate the operation and reliability of controls, alarms, safety features, and interlocks. Test procedures must be submitted to the Coast Guard for approval.

(b) Persons designated by the owner of the vessel shall conduct all tests and the Design Verification and Periodic Safety tests shall be witnessed by the Coast Guard.

(c) Design Verification and Periodic Safety test procedure documents approved by the Coast Guard must be retained aboard the vessel.

§ 61.40-3 Design verification testing.

(a) Tests must verify that automated vital systems are designed, constructed, and operate in accordance with all applicable requirements of part 62 of this subchapter. The tests must be based upon the failure analysis, if required by § 62.20-3(b) of this subchapter, functional performance requirements, and the Periodic Safety tests of § 61.40-6.

(b) Tests must be performed immediately after the installation of automated equipment or before the issuance of the initial Certificate of Inspection.

§ 61.40-6 Periodic safety tests.

(a) Periodic Safety tests must demonstrate the proper operation of the primary and alternate controls,

§ 61.40-10

alarms, power sources, transfer override arrangements, interlocks, and safety controls. Systems addressed must include fire detection and extinguishing, flooding safety, propulsion, maneuvering, electric power generation and distribution, and emergency internal communications.

(b) Tests must be conducted at periodic intervals specified by the Coast Guard to confirm that vital systems and safety features continue to operate in a safe, reliable manner.

NOTE: Normally, these tests are conducted annually.

§ 61.40-10 Test procedure details.

(a) Test procedure documents must be in a step-by-step or checkoff list format. Each test instruction must specify equipment status, apparatus necessary to perform the tests, safety precautions, safety control and alarm setpoints, the procedure to be followed, and the expected test result.

(b) Test techniques must not simulate monitored system conditions by mis-adjustment, artificial signals, improper wiring, tampering, or revision of the system unless the test would damage equipment or endanger personnel. In the latter case, the use of a synthesized signal or condition applied to the sensor is acceptable if test equipment is maintained in good working order and is periodically calibrated to the satisfaction of the Officer in Charge, Marine Inspection. Other test techniques must be approved by the Commandant CG–ENG.

[CGD 80–064, 49 FR 32193, Aug. 13, 1984, as amended by CGD 95–072, 60 FR 50463, Sept. 29, 1995; CGD 96–041, 61 FR 50728, Sept. 27, 1996; USCG–2009–0702, 74 FR 49229, Sept. 25, 2009; USCG–2012–0832, 77 FR 59778, Oct. 1, 2012]

PART 62—VITAL SYSTEM AUTOMATION

Subpart 62.01—General Provisions

Sec.
62.01-1 Purpose, preemptive effect.
62.01-3 Scope.
62.01-5 Applicability.

Subpart 62.05—Reference Specifications

62.05-1 Incorporation by reference.

Subpart 62.10—Terms Used

62.10-1 Definitions.

Subpart 62.15—Equivalents

62.15-1 Conditions under which equivalents may be used.

Subpart 62.20—Plan Submittal

62.20-1 Plans for approval.
62.20-3 Plans for information.
62.20-5 Self-certification.

Subpart 62.25—General Requirements for All Automated Vital Systems

62.25-1 General.
62.25-5 All control systems.
62.25-10 Manual alternate control systems.
62.25-15 Safety control systems.
62.25-20 Instrumentation, alarms, and centralized stations.
62.25-25 Programable systems and devices.
62.25-30 Environmental design standards.

Subpart 62.30—Reliability and Safety Criteria, All Automated Vital Systems

62.30-1 Failsafe.
62.30-5 Independence.
62.30-10 Testing.

Subpart 62.35—Requirements for Specific Types of Automated Vital Systems

62.35-1 General.
62.35-5 Remote propulsion-control systems.
62.35-10 Flooding safety.
62.35-15 Fire safety.
62.35-20 Oil-fired main boilers.
62.35-35 Starting systems for internal-combustion engines.
62.35-40 Fuel systems.
62.35-35 Tabulated monitoring and safety control requirements for specific systems.

Subpart 62.50—Automated Self-propelled Vessel Manning

62.50-1 General.
62.50-20 Additional requirements for minimally attended machinery plants.
62.50-30 Additional requirements for periodically unattended machinery plants.

AUTHORITY: 46 U.S.C. 3306, 3703, 8105; E.O. 12234, 45 FR 58801, 3 CFR, 1980 Comp., p. 277; Department of Homeland Security Delegation No. 0170.1.

SOURCE: CGD 81–030, 53 FR 17838, May 18, 1988, unless otherwise noted.

Coast Guard, Dept. of Homeland Security § 62.05-1

Subpart 62.01—General Provisions

§ 62.01-1 Purpose, preemptive effect.

The purpose of this part is to make sure that the safety of a vessel with automated vital systems, in maneuvering and all other sailing conditions, is equal to that of the vessel with the vital systems under direct manual operator supervision. The regulations in this part have preemptive effect over State or local regulations in the same field.

[CGD 81-030, 53 FR 17838, May 18, 1988, as amended by USGD-2006-24797, 77 FR 33874, June 7, 2012]

§ 62.01-3 Scope.

(a) This part contains the minimum requirements for vessel automated vital systems. Specifically, this part contains—

(1) In subpart 62.25, the general requirements for all vital system automation;

(2) In subpart 62.30, the criteria used to evaluate the designed reliability and safety of all automated vital systems;

(3) In subpart 62.35, the minimum additional equipment, configuration, and functional requirements necessary when certain vital systems are automated; and

(4) In subpart 62.50, the minimum additional requirements when automated systems are provided to replace specific personnel or to reduce overall crew requirements.

§ 62.01-5 Applicability.

(a) *Vessels.* This part applies to self-propelled vessels of 500 gross tons and over that are certificated under subchapters D, I, or U and to self-propelled vessels of 100 gross tons and over that are certificated under subchapter H.

(b) *Systems and equipment.* Except as noted in § 62.01-5(c), this part applies to automation of vital systems or equipment that—

(1) Is automatically controlled or monitored;

(2) Is remotely controlled or monitored; or

(3) Utilizes automation for the purpose of replacing specific personnel or to reduce overall crew requirements.

(c) *Exceptions.* This part does not apply to the following systems and equipment unless they are specifically addressed or unless their failure would degrade the safety and reliability of the systems required by this part:

(1) Automatic auxiliary heating equipment (see part 63 of this subchapter).

(2) Steering systems (see subparts 58.25 and 111.93 of this chapter).

(3) Non-vital and industrial systems.

(4) The communication and alarm systems in part 113 of this chapter.

(d) *Central control rooms.* The requirements of subpart 62.50 only apply to vessels automated to replace specific personnel or to reduce overall crew requirements, except where the main propulsion or ship service electrical generating plants are automatically or remotely controlled from a control room. In this case, § 62.50-20(a)(3) (except the provision in paragraph 62.50-20(a)(3)(ii) relating to electrical power distribution), (b)(3), (c), (e)(1), (e)(2), (e)(4), and (f)(2) apply, regardless of manning.

[CGD 81-030, 53 FR 17838, May 18, 1988, as amended by USCG-2000-7790, 65 FR 58460, Sept. 29, 2000]

Subpart 62.05—Reference Specifications

§ 62.05-1 Incorporation by reference.

(a) Certain material is incorporated by reference into this part with the approval of the Director of the Federal Register under 5 U.S.C. 552(a) and 1 CFR part 51. To enforce any edition other than that specified in this section, the Coast Guard must publish notice of change in the FEDERAL REGISTER and the material must be available to the public. All approved material is available for inspection at the National Archives and Records Administration (NARA). For information on the availability of this material at NARA, call 202-741-6030 or go to *http://www.archives.gov/federal_register/code_of_federal_regulations/ibr_locations.html.* The material is also available for inspection at the Coast Guard Headquarters. Contact Commandant (CG-ENG), Attn: Office of Design and Engineering Systems, U.S. Coast Guard Stop 7509, 2703 Martin Luther King Jr. Avenue SE., Washington, DC 20593-7509. The material is also

§ 62.10-1

from the sources in paragraph (b) of this section.

(b) *American Bureau of Shipping (ABS)*, ABS Plaza, 16855 Northchase Drive, Houston, TX 77060:

(1) Rules for Building and Classing Steel Vessels, Part 4 Vessel Systems and Machinery (2003) ("ABS Steel Vessel Rules"), 62.25–30; 62.35–5; 62.35–35; 62.35–40; 62.35–50; 62.50–30; and

(2) [Reserved]

[USCG–2003–16630, 73 FR 65189, Oct. 31, 2008, as amended by USCG–2009–0702, 74 FR 49229, Sept. 25, 2009; USCG–2012–0832, 77 FR 59778, Oct. 1, 2012; USCG 2013–0671, 78 FR 60149, Sept. 30, 2013]

Subpart 62.10—Terms Used

§ 62.10-1 Definitions.

(a) For the purpose of this part:

Alarm means an audible and visual indication of a hazardous or potentially hazardous condition that requires attention.

Automated means the use of automatic or remote control, instrumentation, or alarms.

Automatic control means self-regulating in attaining or carrying out an operator-specified equipment response or sequence.

Boiler low-low water level is the minimum safe level in the boiler, in no case lower than that visible in the gage glass (see § 52.01–110 of this chapter, Water Level Indicators).

Engineering Control Center (ECC) means the centralized engineering control, monitoring, and communications location.

Failsafe means that upon failure or malfunction of a component, subsystem, or system, the output automatically reverts to a pre-determined design state of least critical consequence. Typical failsafe states are listed in Table 62.10–1(a).

TABLE 62.10-1(a)—TYPICAL FAILSAFE STATES

System or component	Preferred failsafe state
Cooling water valve	As is or open.
Alarm system	Annunciate.
Safety system	Shut down, limited, or as is & alarm.
Burner valve	Closed.
Propulsion speed control	As is.
Feedwater valve	As is or open.
Controllable pitch propeller	As is.
Propulsion safety trip	As is & alarm.
Fuel tank valve	See § 56.50–60(d).

Flooding safety refers to flooding detection, watertight integrity, and dewatering systems.

Independent refers to equipment arranged to perform its required function regardless of the state of operation, or failure, of other equipment.

Limit control means a function of an automatic control system to restrict operation to a specified operating range or sequence without stopping the machinery.

Local control means operator control from a location where the equipment and its output can be directly manipulated and observed, e.g., at the switchboard, motor controller, propulsion engine, or other equipment.

Manual control means operation by direct or power-assisted operator intervention.

Monitor means the use of direct observation, instrumentation, alarms, or a combination of these to determine equipment operation.

Remote control means non-local automatic or manual control.

Safety trip control system means a manually or automatically operated system that rapidly shuts down another system or subsystem.

System means a grouping or arrangement of elements that interact to perform a specific function and typically includes the following, as applicable:
A fuel or power source.
Power conversion elements.
Control elements.
Power transmission elements.
Instrumentation.
Safety control elements.
Conditioning elements.

Vital system or equipment is essential to the safety of the vessel, its passengers and crew. This typically includes, but is not limited to, the following:
Fire detection, alarm, and extinguishing systems.
Flooding safety systems.
Ship service and emergency electrical generators, switchgear, and motor control circuits serving vital electrical loads.

Coast Guard, Dept. of Homeland Security § 62.20–5

The emergency equipment and systems listed in § 112.15 of this chapter.

Propulsion systems, including those provided to meet § 58.01–35.

Steering systems.

Subpart 62.15—Equivalents

§ 62.15–1 Conditions under which equivalents may be used.

(a) The Coast Guard accepts a substitute or alternate for the requirements of this part if it provides an equivalent level of safety and reliability. Demonstration of functional equivalence must include comparison of a qualitative failure analysis based on the requirements of this part with a comparable analysis of the proposed substitute or alternate.

Subpart 62.20—Plan Submittal

§ 62.20–1 Plans for approval.

(a) The following plans must be submitted to the Coast Guard for approval in accordance with § 50.20–5 and § 50.20–10 of this chapter:

(1) A general arrangement plan of control and monitoring equipment, control locations, and the systems served.

(2) Control and monitoring console, panel, and enclosure layouts.

(3) Schematic or logic diagrams including functional relationships, a written description of operation, and sequences of events for all modes of operation.

(4) A description of control or monitoring system connections to non-vital systems.

(5) A description of programable features.

(6) A description of built-in test features and diagnostics.

(7) Design Verification and Periodic Safety test procedures described in subpart 61.40 of this chapter.

(8) Control system normal and emergency operating instructions.

§ 62.20–3 Plans for information.

(a) One copy of the following plans must be submitted to the Officer in Charge, Marine Inspection, for use in the evaluation of automated systems provided to replace specific personnel or to reduce overall crew requirements:

(1) Proposed manning, crew organization and utilization, including routine maintenance, all operational evolutions, and emergencies.

(2) A planned maintenance program for all vital systems.

(b) One copy of a qualitative failure analysis must be submitted in accordance with § 50.20–5 of this chapter for the following:

(1) Propulsion controls.

(2) Microprocessor-based system hardware.

(3) Safety controls.

(4) Automated electric power management.

(5) Automation required to be independent that is not physically separate.

(6) Any other automation that, in the judgement of the Commandant, potentially constitutes a safety hazard to the vessel or personnel in case of failure.

NOTE: The qualitative failure analysis is intended to assist in evaluating the safety and reliability of the design. It should be conducted to a level of detail necessary to demonstrate compliance with applicable requirements and should follow standard qualitative analysis procedures. Assumptions, operating conditions considered, failures considered, cause and effect relationships, how failures are detected by the crew, alternatives available to the crew, and possible design verification tests necessary should be included. Questions regarding failure analysis should be referred to the Marine Safety Center at an early stage of design.

§ 62.20–5 Self-certification.

(a) The designer or manufacturer of an automated system shall certify to the Coast Guard, in writing, that the automation is designed to meet the environmental design standards of § 62.25–30. Plan review, shipboard testing, or independent testing to these standards is not required.

(b) [Reserved]

NOTE: Self-certification should normally accompany plan submittal.

Subpart 62.25—General Requirements for All Automated Vital Systems

§ 62.25-1 General.

(a) Vital systems that are automatically or remotely controlled must be provided with—
(1) An effective primary control system;
(2) A manual alternate control system;
(3) A safety control system, if required by § 62.25-15;
(4) Instrumentation to monitor system parameters necessary for the safe and effective operation of the system; and
(5) An alarm system if instrumentation is not continuously monitored or is inappropriate for detection of a failure or unsafe condition.

(b) Automation systems or subsystems that control or monitor more than one safety control, interlock, or operating sequence must perform all assigned tasks continuously, i.e., the detection of unsafe conditions must not prevent control or monitoring of other conditions.

(c) Each console for a vital control or alarm system and any similar enclosure that relies upon forced cooling for proper operation of the system must have a backup means of providing cooling. It must also have an alarm activated by the failure of the temperature-control system.

[CGD 81-030, 53 FR 17838, May 18, 1988, as amended by USCG-2003-16630, 73 FR 65189, Oct. 31, 2008]

§ 62.25-5 All control systems.

(a) Local and remote starting for any propulsion engine or turbine equipped with a jacking or turning gear must be prevented while the turning gear is engaged.

(b) Automatic control systems must be stable over the entire range of normal operation.

(c) Inadvertent grounding of an electrical or electronic safety control system must not cause safety control operation or safety control bypassing.

[CGD 81-030, 53 FR 17838, May 18, 1988, as amended by USCG-2003-16630, 73 FR 65189, Oct. 31, 2008]

§ 62.25-10 Manual alternate control systems.

(a) Manual alternate control systems must—
(1) Be operable in an emergency and after a remote or automatic primary control system failure;
(2) Be suitable for manual control for prolonged periods;
(3) Be readily accessible and operable; and
(4) Include means to override automatic controls and interlocks, as applicable.

(b) Permanent communications must be provided between primary remote control locations and manual alternate control locations if operator attendance is necessary to maintain safe alternate control.

NOTE: Typically, this includes main boiler fronts and local propulsion control.

§ 62.25-15 Safety control systems.

(a) Minimum safety trip controls required for specific types of automated vital systems are listed in Table 62.35-50.

NOTE: Safety control systems include automatic and manual safety trip controls and automatic safety limit controls.

(b) Safety trip controls must not operate as a result of failure of the normal electrical power source unless it is determined to be the failsafe state.

(c) Automatic operation of a safety control must be alarmed in the machinery spaces and at the cognizant remote control location.

(d) Local manual safety trip controls must be provided for all main boilers, turbines, and internal combustion engines.

(e) Automatic safety trip control systems must—
(1) Be provided where there is an immediate danger that a failure will result in serious damage, complete breakdown, fire, or explosion;
(2) Require manual reset prior to renewed operation of the equipment; and
(3) Not be provided if safety limit controls provide a safe alternative and trip would result in loss of propulsion.

§ 62.25-20 Instrumentation, alarms, and centralized stations.

(a) *General.* Minimum instrumentation and alarms required for specific types of automated vital systems are listed in Table 62.35–50.

(b) *Instrumentation Location.* (1) Manual control locations, including remote manual control and manual alternate control, must be provided with the instrumentation necessary for safe operation from that location.

NOTE: Typically, instrumentation includes means to monitor the output of the monitored system.

(2) Systems with remote instrumentation must have provisions for the installation of instrumentation at the monitored system equipment.

(3) The status of automatically or remotely controlled vital auxiliaries, power sources, switches, and valves must be visually indicated in the machinery spaces or the cognizant remote control location, as applicable.

NOTE: Status indicators include run, standby, off, open, closed, tripped, and on, as applicable. Status indicators at remote control locations other than the ECC, if provided, may be summarized. Equipment normally provided with status indicators are addressed in Table 62.35–50 and subparts 58.01, 56.50, and 112.45.

(4) Sequential interlocks provided in control systems to ensure safe operation, such as boiler programing control or reversing of propulsion diesels, must have summary indicators in the machinery spaces and at the cognizant control location to show if the interlocks are satisfied.

(5) Instrumentation listed in Table 62.35–50 must be of the continuous display type or the demand display type. Displays must be in the ECC or in the machinery spaces if an ECC is not provided.

(c) *Instrumentation details.* Demand instrumentation displays must be clearly readable and immediately available to the operator.

(d) *Alarms.* (1) All alarms must clearly distinguish among—

(i) Normal, alarm, and acknowledged alarm conditions; and

(ii) Fire, general alarm, carbon dioxide/Halon 1301/clean agent fire extinguishing system, vital machinery, flooding, engineers' assistance-needed, and non-vital alarms.

(2) Required alarms in high ambient noise areas must be supplemented by visual means, such as rotating beacons, that are visible throughout these areas. Red beacons must only be used for general or fire alarm purposes.

(3) Automatic transfer to required backup or redundant systems or power sources must be alarmed in the machinery spaces.

(4) Flooding safety, fire, loss of power, and engineers' assistance-needed alarms extended from the machinery spaces to a remote location must not have a duty crewmember selector.

NOTE: Other alarms may be provided with such a selector, provided there is no off position.

(5) Automation alarms must be separate and independent of the following:

(i) The fire detection and alarm systems.

(ii) The general alarm.

(iii) CO_2/halon release alarms.

(6) Failure of an automatic control, remote control, or alarm system must be immediately alarmed in the machinery spaces and at the ECC, if provided.

(e) *Alarm details.* (1) All alarms must—

(i) Have a manual acknowledgement device (No other means to reduce or eliminate the annunciated signal may be provided except dimmers described in paragraph (g)(2) of this section);

(ii) Be continuously powered;

(iii) Be provided with a means to test audible and visual annunciators;

(iv) Provide for normal equipment starting and operating transients and vessel motions, as applicable, without actuating the alarm;

(v) Be able to simultaneously indicate more than one alarm condition, as applicable;

(vi) Visually annunciate until the alarm is manually acknowledged and the alarm condition is cleared;

(vii) Audibly annunciate until manually acknowledged;

(viii) Not prevent annunciation of subsequent alarms because of previous alarm acknowledgement; and

(ix) Automatically reset to the normal operating condition only after the

§ 62.25-25

alarm has been manually acknowledged and the alarm condition is cleared.

(2) Visual alarms must initially indicate the equipment or system malfunction without operator intervention.

(3) Power failure alarms must monitor on the load side of the last supply protective device.

(f) *Summarized and grouped alarms.* Visual alarms at a control location that are summarized or grouped by function, system, or item of equipment must—

(1) Be sufficiently specific to allow any necessary action to be taken; and

(2) Have a display at the equipment or an appropriate control location to identify the specific alarm condition or location.

(g) *Central control locations.* (1) Central control locations must—

(i) Be arranged to allow the operator to safely and efficiently communicate, control, and monitor the vital systems under normal and emergency conditions, with a minimum of operator confusion and distraction;

(ii) Be on a single deck level; and

(iii) Co-locate control devices and instrumentation to allow visual assessment of system response to control input.

(2) Visual alarms and instruments on the navigating bridge must not interfere with the crew's vision. Dimmers must not eliminate visual indications.

(3) Alarms and instrumentation at the main navigating bridge control location must be limited to those that require the attention or action of the officer on watch, are required by this chapter, or that would result in increased safety.

[CGD 81–030, 53 FR 17838, May 18, 1988, as amended by USCG– 2006–24797, 77 FR 33874, June 7, 2012]

§ 62.25-25 Programable systems and devices.

(a) Programable control or alarm system logic must not be altered after Design Verification testing without the approval of the cognizant Officer in Charge, Marine Inspection (OCMI). (See subpart 61.40 of this subchapter, Design Verification Tests). Safety control or automatic alarm systems must be provided with means, acceptable to the cognizant OCMI, to make sure setpoints remain within the safe operating range of the equipment.

(b) Operating programs for microprocessor-based or computer-based vital control, alarm, and monitoring systems must be stored in non-volatile memory and automatically operate on supply power resumption.

(c) If a microprocessor-based or computer-based system serves both vital and non-vital systems, hardware and software priorities must favor the vital systems.

(d) At least one copy of all required manuals, records, and instructions for automatic or remote control or monitoring systems required to be aboard the vessel must not be stored in electronic or magnetic memory.

[CGD 81–030, 53 FR 17838, May 18, 1988; 53 FR 19090, May 26, 1988]

§ 62.25-30 Environmental design standards.

(a) All automation must be suitable for the marine environment and must be designed and constructed to operate indefinitely under the following conditions:

(1) Ship motion and vibration described in Table 9 of section 4-9-7 of the ABS Steel Vessel Rules (incorporated by reference; see 46 CFR 62.05–1); note that inclination requirements for fire and flooding safety systems are described in 46 CFR 112.05–5(c).

(2) Ambient air temperatures described in Table 9 of part 4-9-7 of the ABS Steel Vessel Rules.

(3) Electrical voltage and frequency tolerances described in Table 9 of part 4-9-7 of the ABS Steel Vessel Rules.

(4) Relative humidity of 0 to 95% at 45 °C.

(5) Hydraulic and pneumatic pressure variations described in Table 9 of part 4-9-7 of the ABS Steel Vessel Rules.

NOTE: Considerations should include normal dynamic conditions that might exceed these values, such as switching, valve closure, power supply transfer, starting, and shutdown.

(b) Low voltage electronics must be designed with due consideration for static discharge, electromagnetic interference, voltage transients, fungal growth, and contact corrosion.

[CGD 81-030, 53 FR 17838, May 18, 1988, as amended by USCG-2003-16630, 73 FR 65189, Oct. 31, 2008]

Subpart 62.30—Reliability and Safety Criteria, All Automated Vital Systems

§ 62.30-1 Failsafe.

(a) The failsafe state must be evaluated for each subsystem, system, or vessel to determine the least critical consequence.

(b) All automatic control, remote control, safety control, and alarm systems must be failsafe.

§ 62.30-5 Independence.

(a) Single non-concurrent failures in control, alarm, or instrumentation systems, and their logical consequences, must not prevent sustained or restored operation of any vital system or systems.

(b)(1) Except as provided in paragraphs (b)(2) and (b)(3) of this section, primary control, alternate control, safety control, and alarm and instrumentation systems for any vital system must be independent of each other.

(2) Independent sensors are not required except that sensors for primary speed, pitch, or direction of rotation control in closed loop propulsion control systems must be independent and physically separate from required safety control, alarm, or instrumentation sensors.

(3) The safety trip control of § 62.35-5(b)(2) must be independent and physically separate from all other systems.

(c) Two independent sources of power must be provided for all primary control, safety control, instrumentation and alarm systems. Failure of the normal source of power must actuate an alarm in the machinery spaces. One source must be from the emergency power source (see part 112 of this chapter, Emergency Lighting and Power Systems) unless one of the sources is—

(1) Derived from the power supply of the system being controlled or monitored;

(2) A power take-off of that system; of

(3) An independent power source equivalent to the emergency power source.

§ 62.30-10 Testing.

(a) Automated vital systems must be tested in accordance with subpart 61.40 of this chapter.

(b) On-line built-in test equipment must not lock out or override safety trip control systems. This equipment must indicate when it is active.

Subpart 62.35—Requirements for Specific Types of Automated Vital Systems

§ 62.35-1 General.

(a) Minimum instrumentation, alarms, and safety controls required for specific types of automated vital systems are listed in Table 62.35-50.

(b) Automatic propulsion systems, automated electric power management systems, and all associated subsystems and equipment must be capable of meeting load demands from standby to full system rated load, under steady state and maneuvering conditions, without need for manual adjustment or manipulation.

§ 62.35-5 Remote propulsion-control systems.

(a) *Manual propulsion control.* All vessels having remote propulsion control from the navigating bridge, an ECC or maneuvering platform, or elsewhere must have a manual alternate propulsion control located at the equipment.

NOTE: Separate local control locations may be provided for each independent propeller.

(b) *Centralized propulsion control equipment.* Navigating bridge, ECC, maneuvering platform, and manual alternate control locations must include—

(1) Control of the speed and direction of thrust for each independent propeller controlled;

(2) A guarded manually actuated safety trip control (which stops the propelling machinery) for each independent propeller controlled;

(3) Shaft speed and thrust direction indicators for each independent propeller controlled;

§ 62.35-10

(4) The means to pass propulsion orders required by § 113.30-5 and § 113.35-3 of this chapter; and

(5) The means required by paragraph (d) of this section to achieve control location transfer and independence.

(c) *Main navigating bridge propulsion control.* (1) Navigating bridge remote propulsion control must be performed by a single control device for each independent propeller. Control must include automatic performance of all associated services, and must not permit rate of movement of the control device to overload the propulsion machinery.

(2) On vessels propelled by steam turbines, the navigation bridge primary control system must include safety limit controls for high and low boiler water levels and low steam pressure. Actuation of these limits must be alarmed on the navigating bridge and at the maneuvering platform or ECC.

(3) On vessels propelled by internal combustion engines, an alarm must annunciate on the navigating bridge and at the maneuvering platform or ECC, if provided, to indicate starting capability less than 50% of that required by § 62.35-35. If the primary remote control system provides automatic starting, the number of automatic consecutive attempts that fail to produce a start must be limited to reserve 50% of the required starting capability.

(d) *Transfer of control location.* Transfer of control location must meet section 4-9-2/5.11 of the ABS Steel Vessel Rules (incorporated by reference; see 46 CFR 62.05-1). Manual alternative-propulsion-control locations must be capable of overriding, and of operating independent of, all remote and automatic propulsion-control locations.

(e) *Control system details.* (1) Each operator control device must have a detent at the zero thrust position.

(2) Propulsion machinery automatic safety trip control operation must only occur when continued operation could result in serious damage, complete breakdown, or explosion of the equipment. Other than the overrides mentioned in § 62.25-10(a)(4) and temporary overrides located at the main navigating bridge control location, overrides of these safety trip controls are prohibited. Operation of permitted overrides must be alarmed at the navigating bridge and at the maneuvering platform or ECC, as applicable, and must be guarded against inadvertent operation.

(3) Remote propulsion control systems must be failsafe by maintaining the preset (as is) speed and direction of thrust until local manual or alternate manual control is in operation, or the manual safety trip control operates. Failure must activate alarms on the navigating bridge and in the machinery spaces.

[CGD 81-030, 53 FR 17838, May 18, 1988; 53 FR 19090, May 26, 1988; as amended by USCG-2003-16630, 73 FR 65189, Oct. 31, 2008; USCG-2011-0618, 76 FR 60754, Sept. 30, 2011]

§ 62.35-10 Flooding safety.

(a) Automatic bilge pumps must—

(1) Be provided with bilge high level alarms that annunciate in the machinery spaces and at a manned control location and are independent of the pump controls;

(2) Be monitored to detect excessive operation in a specified time period; and

(3) Meet all applicable pollution control requirements.

(b) Remote controls for flooding safety equipment must remain functional under flooding conditions to the extent required for the associated equipment by § 56.50-50 and § 56.50-95 of this chapter.

(c) Remote bilge level sensors, where provided, must be located to detect flooding at an early stage and to provide redundant coverage.

§ 62.35-15 Fire safety.

(a) All required fire pump remote control locations must include the controls necessary to charge the firemain and—

(1) A firemain pressure indicator; or

(2) A firemain low pressure alarm.

§ 62.35-20 Oil-fired main boilers.

(a) *General.* (1) All main boilers, regardless of intended mode of operation, must be provided with the automatic safety trip control system(s) of paragraphs (h)(1), (h)(2)(i), (h)(2)(ii), and (i) of this section to prevent unsafe conditions after light off.

(2) Manual alternate control of boilers must be located at the boiler front.

Coast Guard, Dept. of Homeland Security § 62.35-20

(3) A fully automatic main boiler must include—
(i) Automatic combustion control;
(ii) Programing control;
(iii) Automatic feedwater control;
(iv) Safety controls; and
(v) An alarm system.

(4) Following system line-up and starting of auxiliaries, fully automatic main boilers must only require the operator to initiate the following sequences:
(i) Boiler pre-purge.
(ii) Trial for ignition of burners subsequent to successful initial burner light-off.
(iii) Normal shutdown.
(iv) Manual safety trip control operation.
(v) Adjustment of primary control setpoints.

(5) All requirements for programing control subsystems and safety control systems must be met when a boiler—
(i) Automatically sequences burners;
(ii) Is operated from a location remote from the boiler front; or
(iii) Is fully automatic.

(6) Where light oil pilots are used, the programing control and burner safety trip controls must be provided for the light oil system. Trial for ignition must not exceed 15 seconds and the main burner trial for ignition must not proceed until the pilot flame is proven.

(b) *Feedwater control.* Automatic feedwater control subsystems must sense, at a minimum, boiler water level and steam flow.

(c) *Combustion control.* Automatic combustion control subsystems must provide—
(1) An air/fuel ratio which ensures complete combustion and stable flame with the fuel in use, under light off, steady state, and transient conditions; and
(2) Stable boiler steam pressure and outlet temperatures under steady state and transient load conditions; and
(3) A low fire interlock to prevent high firing rates and superheater damage during boiler warm up.

(d) *Programing control.* The programing control must provide a programed sequence of interlocks for the safe ignition and normal shutdown of the boiler burners. The programing control must prevent ignition if unsafe conditions exist and must include the following minimum sequence of events and interlocks:

(1) *Prepurge.* Boilers must undergo a continuous purge of the combustion chamber and convecting spaces to make sure of a minimum of 5 changes of air. The purge must not be less than 15 seconds in duration, and must occur immediately prior to the trial for ignition of the initial burner of a boiler. All registers and dampers must be open and an air flow of at least 25 percent of the full load volumetric air flow must be proven before the purge period commences. The prepurge must be complete before trial for ignition of the initial burner.

NOTE: A pre-purge is not required immediately after a complete post-purge.

(2) *Trial for ignition and ignition.* (i) Only one burner per boiler is to be in trial for ignition at any time.
(ii) Total boiler air flow during light off must be sufficient to prevent pocketing and explosive accumulations of combustible gases.
(iii) The burner igniter must be in position and proven energized before admission of fuel to the boiler. The igniter must remain energized until the burner flame is established and stable, or until the trial for ignition period ends.
(iv) The trial for ignition period must be as short as practical for the specific installation, but must not exceed 15 seconds.
(v) Failure of the burner to ignite during a trial for ignition must automatically actuate the burner safety trip controls.

(3) *Post-purge.* (i) Immediately after normal shutdown of the boiler, an automatic purge of the boiler equal to the volume and duration of the prepurge must occur.
(ii) Following boiler safety trip control operation, the air flow to the boiler must not automatically increase. Post purge in such cases must be under manual control.

(e) *Burner fuel oil valves.* Each burner must be provided with a valve that is—
(1) Automatically closed by the burner or boiler safety trip control system; and

§ 62.35-35

(2) Operated by the programming control or combustion control subsystems, as applicable.

(f) *Master fuel oil valves.* Each boiler must be provided with a master fuel oil valve to stop fuel to the boiler automatically upon actuation by the boiler safety trip control system.

(g) *Valve closure time.* The valves described in paragraphs (e) and (f) of this section must close within 4 seconds of automatic detection of unsafe trip conditions.

(h) *Burner safety trip control system.* (1) Each burner must be provided with at least one flame detector.

(2) The burner valve must automatically close when—

(i) Loss of burner flame occurs;

(ii) Actuated by the boiler safety trip control system;

(iii) The burner is not properly seated or in place; or

(iv) Trial for ignition fails, if a programing control is provided.

(i) *Boiler safety trip control system.* (1) Each boiler must be provided with a safety trip control system that automatically closes the master and all burner fuel oil valves upon—

(i) Boiler low-low water level;

(ii) Inadequate boiler air flow to support complete combustion;

(iii) Loss of boiler control power;

(iv) Manual safety trip operation; or

(v) Loss of flame at all burners.

(2) The low-low water level safety trip control must account for normal vessel motions and operating transients.

[CGD 81–030, 53 FR 17838, May 18, 1988, as amended by USCG–2002–13058, 67 FR 61278, Sept. 30, 2002]

§ 62.35-35 Starting systems for internal-combustion engines.

The starting systems for propulsion engines and for prime movers of ships' service generators required to start automatically must meet sections 4–6–5/9.5 and 4–8–2/11.11 of the ABS Steel Vessel Rules (incorporated by reference; see 46 CFR 62.05–1).

[USCG–2003–16630, 73 FR 65189, Oct. 31, 2008]

§ 62.35-40 Fuel systems.

(a) *Level alarms.* Where high or low fuel tank level alarms are required, they must be located to allow the operator adequate time to prevent an unsafe condition.

(b) *Coal fuels.* (1) Controls and instrumentation for coal systems require special consideration by the Commandant CG–521.

(2) Interlocks must be provided to ensure a safe transfer of machinery operation from one fuel to another.

(c) *Automatic fuel heating.* Automatic fuel heating must meet section 4–9–3/15.1 of the ABS Steel Vessel Rules (incorporated by reference; see 46 CFR 62.05–1).

(d) *Overflow prevention.* Fuel oil day tanks, settlers, and similar fuel oil service tanks that are filled automatically or by remote control must be provided with a high level alarm that annunciates in the machinery spaces and either an automatic safety trip control or an overflow arrangement.

[CGD 81–030, 53 FR 17838, May 18, 1988, as amended by CGD 95–072, 60 FR 50463, Sept. 29, 1995; CGD 96–041, 61 FR 50728, Sept. 27, 1996; USCG–2003–16630, 73 FR 65190, Oct. 31, 2008; USCG–2009–0702, 74 FR 49229, Sept. 25, 2009]

§ 62.35-50 Tabulated monitoring and safety control requirements for specific systems.

The minimum instrumentation, alarms, and safety controls required for specific types of systems are listed in Table 62.35–50.

TABLE 62.35–50—MINIMUM SYSTEM MONITORING AND SAFETY CONTROL REQUIREMENTS FOR SPECIFIC SYSTEMS (NOTE 1)

System	Service	Instrumentation	Alarm	Safety control	Notes
Main (Propulsion) boiler	(¹)	(¹)	(¹)	....	(2)
	Supply casing and uptakes.	....	Fire.		
	Burner flame	Status	Failure	Burner auto trip	(3)
	Burner seating	....	Failure	......ditto	(3)
	Trial for ignition	Status	Failure	......ditto.	
	Control power	Available (pressure)	Failure (low)	......ditto	(3)
				Manual trip	(3)

Coast Guard, Dept. of Homeland Security § 62.35–50

TABLE 62.35–50—MINIMUM SYSTEM MONITORING AND SAFETY CONTROL REQUIREMENTS FOR SPECIFIC SYSTEMS (NOTE 1)—Continued

System	Service	Instrumentation	Alarm	Safety control	Notes
Main (Propulsion steam) turbine.	Burner valve .... Low fire interlock ...... Program control interlock. (^{2})	Open/closed. Status. Status. (^{2})	 (^{2})		(4, 5)
Main propulsion, diesel	(^{1})	(^{1})	(^{1})	Manual trip.	(4, 5)
Main propulsion, remote control.			Failure	Manual trip. ......ditto.	
	Auto safety trip override.		Activated.		
	Starting power	Pressure (voltage)	Low	Limit	(2)
	Location in control	Status	Override		(6)
	Shaft speed/direction/pitch.	(^{3})	(^{3})	(^{3}).	
	Clutch fluid	Pressure	Low.		
Main propulsion, electric	(^{4})	(^{4})	(^{4})	(^{4})	(7)
Main propulsion, shafting.	Stern tube oil tank level.		Low.		
	Line shaft bearing	Temperature .... Forced lubrication Pressure.	High. Low.		
Main propulsion, controllable pitch propeller.	Hydraulic oil	Pressure	High, Low.		
Generators	Ship service	Temperature .... (^{1}) .... Starting pressure/voltage.	High. (^{1}). Low.		
	Emergency	(^{5})	Tripped. (^{5})	(^{5}). (^{6}).	
	Turbogenerator	($^{1\ 6}$)	($^{1\ 6}$)	Manual trip.	
	Diesel	($^{1\ 7}$)	($^{1\ 7}$)	(^{7})	(5)
Auxiliary boiler		Run	Trip	Manual trip.	(12)
Gas turbine	(^{8})	(^{8})	(^{8})	(^{8})	(5)
Engines and turbines	Jacking/turning gear	Engaged			(8)
Fuel oil	(^{9})	(^{9})	(^{9}).		
	Remote/auto fill level		High	Auto trip or overflow arrangement.	
	Hi. press. leakage level.		High.		
Bilge	Pump remote control Pump auto control .... Level	Run. Run .... Open/closed.	Excessive operations. High/location.		
Machinery space CL.3 W.T. doors.					
Fire detection	Machinery spaces		Space on fire		(9)
Fire main		Pressure	Low.		
Personnel	Deadman		Fail to acknowledge		(10)
General, control and alarm systems.	Power supply	Available (pressure)	Failure (low).		
	System function ...... Console air conditioning.		Failure .... Failure.		(11)
	Built in test equipment.	Active.			
	Sequential interlock .. Safety control	Activated.	 Activated	 Auto trip/limit	(11)
Redundant auxiliary, system, power supply.		Status	Auto transfer.		

^{1} See the ABS Steel Vessel Rules (incorporated by reference; see 46 CFR 62.05–1) Part 4–9–4, tables 7A and 8.
^{2} See ABS Steel Vessel Rules Part 4–9–4, tables 7A and 8.
^{3} See § 113.37 of this chapter.
^{4} See subparts 111.33 and 111.35 of this chapter.
^{5} See subparts 112.45 and 112.50 of this chapter.
^{6} See § 111.12–1(c) of this chapter.
^{7} See § 111.12–1 (b), (c) of this chapter.
^{8} See ABS Steel Vessel Rules Part 4–9–4, Table 8; and 46 CFR 58.10–15(f).

§ 62.50-1

⁹See ABS Steel Vessel Rules Part 4–9–4, tables 7A and 8.

NOTES ON TABLE 62.35–50:

1. The monitoring and controls listed in this table are applicable if the system listed is provided or required.
2. Safety limit controls must be provided in navigating bridge primary propulsion control systems. See § 62.35–5(c).
3. Safety trip controls and alarms must be provided for all main boilers, regardless of mode of operation. See § 62.35–20(a).
4. Loss of forced lubrication safety trip controls must be provided, as applicable.
5. Override of overspeed and loss of forced lubrication pressure safety trip controls must not be provided. See § 62.35–5(e)(2).
6. Transfer interlocks must be provided.
7. Semiconductor controlled rectifiers must have current limit controls.
8. Interlocks must be provided. See § 62.25–5(a).
9. Main and remote control stations, including the navigational bridge, must provide visual and audible alarms in the event of a fire in the main machinery space.
10. See § 62.50–20(b)(1).
11. Alarms and controls must be failsafe. See § 62.30–1.
12. Vital auxiliary boilers only. Also see part 63.

[CGD 81–030, 53 FR 17838, May 18, 1988; 53 FR 19090, May 26, 1988, as amended by USCG–2000–7790, 65 FR 58461, Sept. 29, 2000; USCG–2003–16630, 73 FR 65190, Oct. 31, 2008]

Subpart 62.50—Automated Self-propelled Vessel Manning

§ 62.50-1 General.

(a) Where automated systems are provided to replace specific personnel in the control and observation of the engineering plant and spaces, or reduce overall crew requirements, the arrangements must make sure that under all sailing conditions, including maneuvering, the safety of the vessel is equal to that of the same vessel with the entire plant under fully attended direct manual supervision.

(b) Coast Guard acceptance of automated systems to replace specific personnel or to reduce overall crew requirements is predicated upon—
(1) The capabilities of the automated systems;
(2) The combination of the personnel, equipment, and systems necessary to ensure the safety of the vessel, personnel, and environment in all sailing conditions, including maneuvering;
(3) The ability of the crew to perform all operational evolutions, including emergencies such as fire or control or monitoring system failure;
(4) A planned maintenance program including routine maintenance, inspection, and testing to ensure the continued safe operation of the vessel; and
(5) The automated system's demonstrated reliability during an initial trial period, and its continuing reliability.

NOTE: The cognizant Officer in Charge, Marine Inspection, (OCMI) also determines the need for more or less equipment depending on the vessel characteristics, route, or trade.

(c) Equipment provided to replace specific personnel or to reduce overall crew requirements that proves unsafe or unreliable in the judgment of the cognizant Officer in Charge, Marine Inspection, must be immediately replaced or repaired or vessel manning will be modified to compensate for the equipment inadequacy.

§ 62.50-20 Additional requirements for minimally attended machinery plants.

NOTE: Minimally attended machinery plants include vessel machinery plants and spaces that are automated, but not to a degree where the plant could be left unattended. Emphasis is placed on the centralized remote control and monitoring of the machinery plant and machinery spaces.

(a) *General.* (1) Navigating bridge propulsion control must be provided.

(2) An ECC must be provided and must include the automatic and remote control and monitoring systems necessary to limit the operator's activity to monitoring the plant, initiating programed control system sequences, and taking appropriate action in an emergency.

(3) The ECC must include control and monitoring of all vital engineering systems, including—
(i) The propulsion plant and its auxiliaries;
(ii) Electrical power generation and distribution;

Coast Guard, Dept. of Homeland Security § 62.50–20

(iii) Machinery space fire detection, alarm, and extinguishing systems; and

(iv) Machinery space flooding safety systems, except the valves described in paragraph (e)(4) of this section.

(4) ECC control of vital systems must include the ability to place required standby systems, auxiliaries, and power sources in operation, unless automatic transfer is provided, and to shut down such equipment when necessary.

NOTE: ECC remote control need not include means for a single operator to bring the plant to standby from a cold plant or dead ship condition or controls for non-vital systems or equipment.

(b) *Alarms and instrumentation.* (1) A personnel alarm must be provided and must annunciate on the bridge if not routinely acknowledged at the ECC or in the machinery spaces.

(2) Continuous or demand instrumentation displays must be provided at the ECC to meet the system and equipment monitoring requirements of this part if the ECC is to be continuously attended. If the watchstander's normal activities include maintenance, a roving watch, or similar activities in the machinery spaces but not at the ECC, both alarms and instrumentation must be provided.

(3) All required audible alarms must annunciate throughout the ECC and machinery spaces.

(c) *Fire detection and alarms.* An approved automatic fire detection and alarm system must be provided to monitor all machinery spaces. The system must activate all alarms at the ECC, the navigating bridge, and throughout the machinery spaces and engineers' accommodations. The ECC and bridge alarms must visually indicate which machinery space is on fire, as applicable.

NOTE: For purposes of this part, the specific location of fires that are not in machinery spaces need not be indicated.

(d) *Fire pumps.* (1) The ECC must include control of the main machinery space fire pumps.

(2) Remote control of a required fire pump must be provided from the navigating bridge. Where one or more fire pumps is required to be independent of the main machinery space, at least one such pump must be controlled from the navigating bridge.

(e) *Flooding safety.* (1) Machinery space bilges, bilge wells, shaft alley bilges, and other minimally attended locations where liquids might accumulate must be monitored from the ECC to detect flooding angles from vertical of up to 15° heel and 5° trim.

(2) The ECC must include the controls necessary to bring at least one independent bilge pump and independent bilge suction required by § 56.50–50(e) of this chapter into operation to counter flooding.

(3) Where watertight doors in subdivision bulkheads are required in the machinery spaces, they must be Class 3 watertight doors and must be controllable from the ECC and the required navigating bridge control location.

(4) Controls must be provided to operate the sea inlet and discharge valves required by § 56.50–95(d) of this chapter and the emergency bilge suction required by § 56.50–50(f). These controls must be arranged to allow time for operation in the event of flooding with the vessel in the fully loaded condition. Time considerations must include detection, crew response, and control operation time.

(f) *Communications.* (1) A means must be provided at the ECC to selectively summon any engineering department member from the engineering accommodations to the ECC.

(2) The voice communications system required by § 113.30–5(a) of this chapter must also include the engineering officers' accommodations.

(g) *Electrical systems.* (1) The ECC must include the controls and instrumentation necessary to place the ship service and propulsion generators in service in 30 seconds.

(2) The main distribution and propulsion switchboards and generator controls must either be located at the ECC, if the ECC is within the boundaries of the main machinery space, or the controls and instrumentation required by part 111 of this chapter must be duplicated at the ECC. Controls at the switchboard must be able to override those at the ECC, if separate. Also see § 111.12–11(g) and § 111.30–1 regarding switchboard location.

313

§ 62.50-30

(h) *Maintenance program.* (1) The vessel must have a planned maintenance program to ensure continued safe operation of all vital systems. Program content and detail is optional, but must include maintenance and repair manuals for work to be accomplished by maintenance personnel and checkoff lists for routine inspection and maintenance procedures.

(2) The planned maintenance program must be functioning prior to the completion of the evaluation period for reduced manning required by § 62.50-1(b)(5).

(3) Maintenance and repair manuals must include details as to what, when, and how to troubleshoot, repair and test the installed equipment and what parts are necessary to accomplish the procedures. Schematic and logic diagrams required by § 62.20-1 of this part must be included in this documentation. Manuals must clearly delineate information that is not applicable to the installed equipment.

[CGD 81-030, 53 FR 17838, May 18, 1988; 53 FR 19090, May 26, 1988; 53 FR 24270, June 28, 1988; USCG-2004-18884, 69 FR 58346, Sept. 30, 2004]

§ 62.50-30 Additional requirements for periodically unattended machinery plants.

NOTE: Periodically unattended machinery plants include machinery plants and spaces that are automated to the degree that they are self-regulating and self-monitoring and could safely be left periodically unattended. Emphasis is placed on providing systems that act automatically until the crew can take action in the event of a failure or emergency. Requirements are in addition to those of a minimally attended machinery plant.

(a) *General.* The requirements of this section must be met in addition to those of § 62.50-20 of this part.

(b) *Automatic transfer.* Redundant vital auxiliaries and power sources must automatically transfer to the backup units upon failure of operating units.

(c) *Fuel systems.* Each system for the service or treatment of fuel must meet section 4-6-4/13.5 of the ABS Steel Vessel Rules (incorporated by reference; see 46 CFR 62.05-1).

(d) *Starting systems.* Automatic or remote starting system receivers, accumulators, and batteries must be automatically and continuously charged.

(e) *Assistance-needed alarm.* The engineer's assistance-needed alarm (see subpart 113.27 of this chapter) must annunciate if—

(1) An alarm at the ECC is not acknowledged in the period of time necessary for an engineer to respond at the ECC from the machinery spaces or engineers' accommodations; or

(2) An ECC alarm system normal power supply fails.

(f) *Remote alarms.* ECC alarms for vital systems that require the immediate attention of the bridge watch officer for the safe navigation of the vessel must be extended to the bridge. All ECC alarms required by this part must be extended to the engineers' accommodations. Other than fire or flooding alarms, this may be accomplished by summarized visual alarm displays.

(g) *ECC alarms.* All requirements of this part for system or equipment monitoring must be met by providing both displays and alarms at the ECC.

(h) *Fire control station.* A control station for fire protection of the machinery spaces must be provided outside the machinery spaces. At least one access to this station must be independent of category A machinery spaces, and any boundary shared with these spaces must have an A-60 fire classification as defined in § 72.05 of this chapter. Except where such an arrangement is not possible, control and monitoring cables and piping for the station must not adjoin or penetrate the boundaries of a category A machinery space, uptakes, or casings. The fire control station must include—

(1) Annunciation of which machinery space is on fire;

(2) Control of a fire pump required by this chapter to be independent of the main machinery spaces;

(3) Controls for machinery space fixed gas fire extinguishing systems;

(4) Control of oil piping positive shut-off valves located in the machinery spaces and required by § 56.50-60(d);

(5) Controls for machinery space fire door holding and release systems, skylights and similar openings;

(6) The remote stopping systems for the machinery listed in § 111.103 of this chapter; and

(7) Voice communications with the bridge.

(i) *Oil leakage.* Leakages from high pressure fuel oil pipes must be collected and high levels must be alarmed at the ECC.

(j) *Maintenance program.* The maintenance program of § 62.50–20(h) must include a checkoff list to make sure that routine daily maintenance has been performed, fire and flooding hazards have been minimized, and plant status is suitable for unattended operation. Completion of this checkoff list must be logged before leaving the plant unattended.

(k) *Continuity of electrical power.* The electrical plant must meet sections 4–8–2/3.11 and 4.8.2/9.9 of the ABS Steel Vessel Rules, and must:

(1) Not use the emergency generator for this purpose;

(2) Restore power in not more than 30 seconds; and

(3) Account for loads permitted by § 111.70–3(f) of this chapter to automatically restart.

[CGD 81–030, 53 FR 17838, May 18, 1988; 53 FR 19090, May 26, 1988; as amended by USCG–2003–16630, 73 FR 65190, Oct. 31, 2008]

PART 63—AUTOMATIC AUXILIARY BOILERS

Subpart 63.01—General Provisions

Sec.
63.01–1 Purpose.
63.01–3 Scope and applicability.

Subpart 63.05—Reference Specifications

63.05–1 Incorporation by reference.

Subpart 63.10—Miscellaneous Submittals

63.10–1 Test procedures and certification report.

Subpart 63.15—General Requirements

63.15–1 General.
63.15–3 Fuel system.
63.15–5 Strainers.
63.15–7 Alarms.
63.15–9 Inspections and tests.

Subpart 63.20—Additional Control System Requirements

63.20–1 Specific control system requirements.

Subpart 63.25—Requirements for Specific Types of Automatic Auxiliary Boilers

63.25–1 Small automatic auxiliary boilers.
63.25–3 Electric hot water supply boilers.
63.25–5 Fired thermal fluid heaters.
63.25–7 Exhaust gas boilers.
63.25–9 Incinerators.

AUTHORITY: 46 U.S.C. 3306, 3703; E.O. 12234, 45 FR 58801, 3 CFR, 1980 Comp., p. 277; Department of Homeland Security Delegation No. 0170.1.

SOURCE: CGD 88–057, 55 FR 24238, June 15, 1990, unless otherwise noted.

Subpart 63.01—General Provisions

§ 63.01–1 Purpose.

This part specifies the minimum requirements for safety for each automatic auxiliary boiler, including its design, construction, testing, and operation.

§ 63.01–3 Scope and applicability.

(a) This part contains the requirements for automatic auxiliary boilers, including their controls, control system components, electrical devices, safety devices, and accessories. Types of automatic auxiliary boilers which are covered include large and small automatic auxiliary boilers, automatic heating boilers, automatic waste heat boilers, donkey boilers, miniature boilers, electric boilers, fired thermal fluid heaters, automatic incinerators, and electric hot water supply boilers. Automatic auxiliary boilers are classified by their service, control systems, pressure and temperature boundaries, heat input ratings, and firing mediums as follows:

(1) Automatic auxiliary boilers listed in Table 54.01–5(A) of this chapter which reference this part for regulation of their automatic controls.

(2) Automatic control systems for automatic auxiliary boilers having a heat input rating of less than 12,500,000 Btu/hr. (3.66 megawatts).

(3) Electric hot water supply boilers (heaters) containing electric heating elements rated at 600 volts or less.

(4) Exhaust gas boilers, and their controls and accessories used to heat water and/or generate steam.

(5) Incinerators (and their control systems) used for the generation of steam and/or oxidation of ordinary

§ 63.05-1

waste materials and garbage. This part also includes incinerators which serve as automatic auxiliary boilers.

(6) Fired thermal fluid heaters and their controls.

(b) *Exceptions.* Automatic boilers having heat input ratings of 12,500,000 Btu/hr. (3.66 megawatts) and above must meet the requirements of part 52 of this chapter. Their control systems must meet the requirements of part 62 of this chapter. Electric cooking equipment must comply with § 111.77-3 of this chapter. Electric oil immersion heaters must comply with part 111, subpart 111.85 of this chapter. Electric air heating equipment must comply with part 111, subpart 111.87 of this chapter.

[CGD 88–057, 55 FR 24238, June 15, 1990, as amended by USCG–2002–13058, 67 FR 61278, Sept. 30, 2002; USCG–2004–18884, 69 FR 58346, Sept. 30, 2004]

Subpart 63.05—Reference Specifications

§ 63.05-1 Incorporation by reference.

(a) Certain material is incorporated by reference into this part with the approval of the Director of the Federal Register under 5 U.S.C. 552(a) and 1 CFR part 51. To enforce any edition other than that specified in this section, the Coast Guard must publish notice of change in the FEDERAL REGISTER and the material must be available to the public. All approved material is available for inspection at the National Archives and Records Administration (NARA). For information on the availability of this material at NARA, call 202–741–6030 or go to *http://www.archives.gov/federal_register/code_of_federal_regulations/ibr_locations.html*. The material is also available for inspection at the Coast Guard Headquarters. Contact Commandant (CG–ENG), Attn: Office of Design and Engineering Systems, U.S. Coast Guard Stop 7509, 2703 Martin Luther King Jr. Avenue SE., Washington, DC 20593–7509. The material is also available from the sources listed in paragraphs (b) through (g) of this section.

(b) *American Gas Association*, 1515 Wilson Boulevard, Arlington, VA 22209:

(1) ANSI/AGA Z21.22–86 Relief Valves and Automatic Shutoff Devices for Hot Water Supply Systems, March 28, 1986 ("ANSI/AGA Z21.22"), 63.25–3; and

(2) [Reserved]

(c) *American Society of Mechanical Engineers (ASME) International*, Three Park Avenue, New York, NY 10016–5990:

(1) ASME CSD–1–2004, Controls and Safety Devices for Automatically Fired Boilers (2004) ("ASME CSD–1"), 63.10–1; 63.15–1; 63.20–1; and

(2) [Reserved]

(d) *ASTM International (formerly American Society for Testing and Materials) (ASTM)*, 100 Barr Harbor Drive, West Conshohocken, PA 19428–2959:

(1) ASTM F 1323–2001, Standard Specification for Shipboard Incinerators (2001) ("ASTM F 1323"), 63.25–9; and

(2) [Reserved]

(e) *International Maritime Organization (IMO)*, Publications Section, 4 Albert Embankment, London, SE1 7SR United Kingdom:

(1) Resolution MEPC.76(40), Standard Specification for Shipboard Incinerators (Sep. 25, 1997) ("IMO MEPC.76(40)"), 63.25–9; and

(2) The International Convention for the Prevention of Pollution from Ships (MARPOL 73/78), Annexes I, II, III, and V (1978) ("IMO MARPOL 73/78"), 63.25–9

(f) *International Organization for Standardization (ISO)*, Case postale 56, CH–1211 Geneva 20, Switzerland:

(1) ISO 9096, Stationary source emissions—Manual determination of mass concentration of particulate matter, Second edition (Feb. 1, 2003) ("ISO 9096"), 63.25–9;

(2) ISO 10396, Stationary source emissions—Sampling for the automated determination of gas emission concentrations for permanently-installed monitoring systems, Second edition (Feb. 1, 2007) ("ISO 10396"), 63.25–9; and

(3) ISO 13617, Shipbuilding-Shipboard Incinerators—Requirements, Second Edition (Nov. 15, 2001) ("ISO 13617"), 63.25–9.

(g) *Underwriters' Laboratories, Inc. (UL)*, 12 Laboratory Drive, Research Triangle Park, NC 27709–3995:

(1) UL 174, Standard for Household Electric Storage Tank Water Heaters, Tenth Edition, Feb. 28, 1996 (Revisions through and including Nov. 10, 1997) ("UL 174"), 63.25–3;

(2) UL 296, Oil Burners (1993) ("UL 296"), 63.15–5;

(3) UL 343, Pumps for Oil-Burning Appliances, Eighth Edition (May 27, 1997) ("UL 343"), 63.15–3; and

(4) UL 1453, Standard for Electric Booster and Commercial Storage Tank Water Heaters, Fourth Edition (Sep. 1, 1995) ("UL 1453"), 63.25–3.

[USCG–2003–16630, 73 FR 65190, Oct. 31, 2008, as amended by USCG–2009–0702, 74 FR 49229, Sept. 25, 2009; USCG–2012–0832, 77 FR 59778, Oct. 1, 2012; USCG 2013–0671, 78 FR 60149, Sept. 30, 2013]

Subpart 63.10—Miscellaneous Submittals

§ 63.10–1 Test procedures and certification report.

Two copies of the following items must be submitted. Visitors may deliver them to the Commanding Officer, Marine Safety Center, U.S. Coast Guard, 4200 Wilson Boulevard Suite 400, Arlington, VA 22203, or they may be transmitted by mail to the Commanding Officer (MSC), Attn: Marine Safety Center, U.S. Coast Guard Stop 7410, 4200 Wilson Boulevard Suite 400, Arlington, VA 20598–7410, in a written or electronic format. Information for submitting the VSP electronically can be found at http://www.uscg.mil/HQ/MSC.

(a) Detailed instructions for operationally testing each automatic auxiliary boiler, its controls, and safety devices.

(b) A certification report for each automatic auxiliary boiler that:

(1) Meets paragraph CG–510 of ASME CSD–1 (incorporated by reference, see 46 CFR 63.05–1); and

(2) Certifies that each automatic auxiliary boiler, its controls, and safety devices comply with the additional requirements of this part.

[CGD 88–057, 55 FR 24238, June 15, 1990, as amended by USCG–2007–29018, 72 FR 53965, Sept. 21, 2007; USCG–2003–16630, 73 FR 65190, Oct. 31, 2008; USCG–2009–0702, 74 FR 49229, Sept. 25, 2009; USCG 2013–0671, 78 FR 60149, Sept. 30, 2013]

Subpart 63.15—General Requirements

§ 63.15–1 General.

(a) Each automatic auxiliary boiler must be designed and constructed for its intended service according to the requirements of the parts referenced in § 54.01–5, Table 54.01–5(A) of this chapter.

(b) Controls and safety devices for automatic auxiliary boilers must meet the applicable requirements of ASME CSD–1 (incorporated by reference, see 46 CFR 63.05–1), except Paragraph CG–310.

(c) All devices and components of an automatic auxiliary boiler must satisfactorily operate within the marine environment. The boiler must satisfactorily operate with a momentary roll of 30°, a list of 15°, and a permanent trim of 5° with it installed in a position as specified by the manufacturer.

(d) An electrical control used to shut down the automatic auxiliary boiler must be installed in accordance with § 58.01–25 of this chapter. This device must stop the fuel supply to the fuel burning equipment.

(e) Mercury tube actuated controls are prohibited from being installed and used on automatic auxiliary boilers.

[CGD 88–057, 55 FR 24238, June 15, 1990, asd amended by USCG–2003–16630, 73 FR 65191, Oct. 31, 2008]

§ 63.15–3 Fuel system.

(a) Firing of an automatic auxiliary boiler by natural gas is prohibited unless specifically approved by the Marine Safety Center.

(b) Heated heavy fuel oil may be used provided the heaters are equipped with a high temperature limiting device that shuts off the heating source at a temperature below the flashpoint of the oil and is manually reset. When a thermostatically-controlled electric oil heater and a level device is used, it must meet the requirements of part 111, subpart 111.85 of this chapter.

NOTE: An auxiliary boiler may be safely ignited from the cold condition using unheated diesel or light fuel oil and subsequently shifted to heated heavy fuel.

§ 63.15-5

(c) The fuel oil service pump and its piping system must be designed in accordance with § 56.50-65 of this chapter. All materials must meet the requirements of part 56, subpart 56.60 of this chapter. The use of cast iron or malleable iron is prohibited.

(d) The fuel oil service system (including the pump) must meet the pressure classification and design criteria found in § 56.04-2, Table 56.04-2 of this chapter.

(e) When properly selected for the intended service, fuel pumps meeting the performance and test requirements of UL 343 (incorporated by reference, see 46 CFR 63.05-1) meet the requirements of this section.

[CGD 88-057, 55 FR 24238, June 15, 1990, asd amended by USCG-2003-16630, 73 FR 65191, Oct. 31, 2008]

§ 63.15-5 Strainers.

(a) Strainers must be installed in the fuel supply line. Each strainer must be self-cleaning, fitted with a bypass, or be capable of being cleaned without interrupting the fuel oil supply.

(b) The strainer must not allow a quantity of air to be trapped inside which would affect the rate of fuel flow to the burner or reduce the effective area of the straining element.

(c) The strainer must meet the requirements for strainers found in UL 296 (incorporated by reference, see 46 CFR 63.05-1) and the requirements for fluid conditioner fittings found in 46 CFR 56.15-5.

[CGD 88-057, 55 FR 24238, June 15, 1990, asd amended by USCG-2003-16630, 73 FR 65191, Oct. 31, 2008]

§ 63.15-7 Alarms.

(a) An audible alarm must automatically sound when a flame safety system shutdown occurs. A visible indicator must indicate that the shutdown was caused by the flame safety system.

(b) Means must be provided to silence the audible alarm. The visible indicators must require manual reset.

(c) For steam boilers, operation of the lower low water cutoff must automatically sound an audible alarm. A visual indicator must indicate that the shutdown was caused by low water.

(d) For a periodically unattended machinery space, the auxiliary boiler trip alarm required by 46 CFR 62.35-50, Table 62.35-50 satisfies the requirements for the audible alarms specified in this section.

§ 63.15-9 Inspections and tests.

All automatic auxiliary boilers must be inspected and tested in accordance with the requirements of part 61 of this chapter.

Subpart 63.20—Additional Control System Requirements

§ 63.20-1 Specific control system requirements.

In addition to the requirements found in ASME CSD-1 (incorporated by reference; see 46 CFR 63.05-1), the following requirements apply for specific control systems:

(a) *Primary safety control system.* Following emergency safety trip control operation, the air flow to the boiler must not automatically increase. For this condition, postpurge must be accomplished manually.

(b) *Combustion control system.* A low fire interlock must ensure low fire start when variable firing rates are used.

(c) *Water level controls and low water cutoff controls.* Water level controls must be constructed and located to minimize the effects of vessel roll and pitch. Float chamber low water cutoff controls using stuffing boxes to transmit the motion of the float from the chamber to the external switches are prohibited. No outlet connection other than pressure controls, water columns, drains, and steam gages may be installed on the float chamber or on the pipes connecting the float chamber to the boiler. The water inlet valve must not feed water into the boiler through the float chamber. The boiler feed piping must comply with the applicable requirements of § 56.50-30 of this chapter.

[CGD 88-057, 55 FR 24238, June 15, 1990, asd amended by USCG-2003-16630, 73 FR 65191, Oct. 31, 2008]

Subpart 63.25—Requirements for Specific Types of Automatic Auxiliary Boilers

§ 63.25-1 Small automatic auxiliary boilers.

Small automatic auxiliary boilers defined as having heat-input ratings of 400,000 Btu/hr. or less (117 kilowatts or less) must also meet the following requirements.

(a) Small automatic auxiliary boilers must be equipped with a visual indicator which indicates when the low water cutoff has activated.

(b) A prepurge period of a sufficient duration to ensure at least four changes of air in the combustion chamber and stack, but not less than 15 seconds must be provided. Ignition must occur only before or simultaneously with the opening of the fuel oil valve.

[CGD 88–057, 55 FR 24238, June 15, 1990, asd amended by USCG–2003–16630, 73 FR 65191, Oct. 31, 2008]

§ 63.25-3 Electric hot water supply boilers.

(a) Electric hot water supply boilers that have a capacity not greater than .454 liters (120 U.S. gallons), a heat input rate not greater than 200,000 Btu/hr. (58.6 kilowatts), meet the requirements of UL 174 or UL 1453 (both incorporated by reference, see 46 CFR 63.05–1), and are protected by the relief device(s) required in 46 CFR 53.05–2 do not have to meet any other requirements of this section except the periodic testing required by paragraph (j) of this section. Electric hot water supply boilers that meet the requirements of UL 174 may have temperature-pressure relief valves that meet the requirements of ANSI/AGA Z21.22 (incorporated by reference, see 46 CFR 63.05–1) in lieu of 46 CFR subpart 53.05.

(b) Each hot water supply boiler must be constructed in accordance with the applicable requirements of part 52 or part 53 of this chapter.

(c) Branch circuit conductors for hot water supply boilers which have a capacity not greater than 454 liters (120 U.S. gallons) must have a current carrying capacity of not less than 125 percent of the current rating of the appliance. Branch circuit conductors for hot water supply boilers with capacities of more than 454 liters (120 U.S. gallons) must have a current carrying capacity of not less than 100 percent of the current rating of the appliance. Wiring materials and methods must comply with part 111, subpart 111.60 of this chapter. A hot water supply boiler having a current rating of more than 48 amperes and employing resistance type heating elements must have the heating elements on subdivided circuits. Each subdivided load, except for an electric hot water supply boiler employing a resistance type immersion electric heating element, must not exceed 48 amperes, and it must be protected at not more than 60 amperes. An electric hot water supply boiler employing a resistance type immersion electric heating element may be subdivided into circuits not exceeding 120 amperes and protected at not more than 150 amperes. Overcurrent protection devices must comply with part 111, subpart 111.50 of this chapter.

(d) Heating elements must be insulated electrically from the water being heated, guarded against mechanical injury and contact with outside objects, and securely supported. Consideration must be given to sagging, opening, and other adverse conditions of the elements resulting from continuous heating, and flexion of supports and wiring due to alternate heating and cooling. Wrap-around elements must be secured in a manner which prevents loosening.

(e) Iron and steel parts must be protected against corrosion by enameling, galvanizing, or plating. Iron and steel storage tanks having a wall thickness less than 6.4mm (¼-inch) must have the inside surface protected against corrosion.

(f) Each heating element must have a temperature regulating device. The device must limit the water from obtaining a temperature greater than 90 °C (194 °F). If the control has a marked off position, the control must disconnect the heating element from all ungrounded conductors, and it must not respond to temperature when placed in the off position.

(g) An independent temperature limiting device must prevent the water in the upper 25 percent of the tank from attaining a temperature higher than 99 °C (210 °F). This device must require

§ 63.25-5

manual resetting, be trip free from the operating means, open all ungrounded power supply conductors to the heater, and be readily accessible.

(h) Electric hot water supply boilers must have pressure and temperature relieving valves. The valve temperature setting must not be more than 99 °C (210 °F). The pressure relief setting must not be higher than the marked working pressure of the boiler. The pressure and temperature relief valves must meet part 53, subpart 53.05 of this chapter. The pressure and temperature relief valves may be combined into a pressure-temperature relief valve.

(i) Electric hot water supply boilers must be marked in a visible location with the manufacturer's name, model or other identification number, water capacity, and the electrical ratings of each heating element. When two or more heating elements are installed, the maximum wattage or current consumption must be indicated. The cold water inlet and the hot water outlet must each be clearly distinguished or marked for identification purposes.

(j) All electric hot water supply boilers must have their pressure relief devices tested as required by 46 CFR part 52 or part 53, as applicable. Electric hot water supply boilers that meet the requirements of UL 174 or UL 1453 and have heating elements, temperature regulating controls, and temperature limiting controls are satisfactory for installation and service without further installation testing. All electric hot water supply boilers not meeting the requirements of UL 174 or UL 1453 must have their heating elements, temperature regulating controls, and temperature limiting controls tested by the marine inspector at the time of installation.

[CGD 88–057, 55 FR 24238, June 15, 1990, as amended by CGD 95–028, 62 FR 51202, Sept. 30, 1997; USCG–2003–16630, 73FR 65191, Oct. 31, 2008]

§ 63.25-5 Fired thermal fluid heaters.

(a) *Construction.* Fired thermal fluid heaters must meet the requirements of part 52 of this chapter, as applicable.

(b) *Controls.* Fired thermal fluid heaters must have a low fluid level cutout device or a low flow device. When the rate of fluid flow through the heating coils is insufficient to ensure proper heat transfer, the device must cut off the fuel supply to the burner. If the fluid temperature exceeds the designed maximum operating temperature, a high temperature limit device must cut off the fuel supply to the burner. These devices must be of the manual reset type.

§ 63.25-7 Exhaust gas boilers.

(a) *Construction.* An auxiliary exhaust gas boiler must meet the applicable construction requirements of part 52 or part 53 of this chapter as determined from § 54.01-5, Table 54.01-5(A) of this chapter.

(b) *Controls.* Each drum type exhaust gas steam boiler must have a feed water control system. The system must automatically supply the required amount of feed water and maintain it at the proper level. For boilers without a fixed water level, the control system must supply the feed water at a rate sufficient to ensure proper heat transfer. The system must adequately fill the boiler when cold.

(c) *Alarms.* When a condition arises which results in inadequate heat transfer, a high temperature alarm or low flow alarm must be activated. An audible alarm must automatically sound, and a visual indicator must indicate when the fluid temperature exceeds the maximum operating temperature or when the fluid/steam flowing through the heat exchanger is insufficient to ensure proper heat transfer. Additionally, an audible alarm must automatically sound, and a visual indicator must indicate when a soot fire is present in the exhaust gas boiler's uptake.

§ 63.25-9 Incinerators.

(a) *General.* Incinerators installed on or after March 26, 1998, must meet the requirements of IMO MEPC.76(40) (incorporated by reference; see 46 CFR 63.05–1). Incinerators in compliance with ISO 13617 (incorporated by reference; see 46 CFR 63.05–1), are considered to meet IMO MEPC.76(40). Incinerators in compliance with both ASTM F 1323 (incorporated by reference; see 46 CFR 63.05–1) and Annexes A1–A3 of IMO MEPC.76(40) are considered to meet IMO MEPC.76(40). An application for type approval of shipboard incinerators must be sent to the Commanding Officer, Marine Safety Center, U.S. Coast Guard, 4200 Wilson Boulevard Suite 400, Arlington, VA 22203, or they may be transmitted by mail to the Commanding Officer (MSC), Attn: Marine Safety Center, U.S. Coast Guard Stop 7410, 4200 Wilson Boulevard Suite 400, Arlington, VA 20598–7410..

(b) *Testing.* Before type approval is granted, the manufacturer must have tests conducted, or submit evidence that such tests have been conducted by an independent laboratory acceptable to the Commandant (CG–521). The laboratory must:

(1) Have the equipment and facilities for conducting the inspections and tests required by this section;

(2) Have experienced and qualified personnel to conduct the inspections and tests required by this section;

(3) Have documentary proof of the laboratory's qualifications to perform the inspections and tests required by this section; and

(4) Not be owned or controlled by a manufacturer, supplier, or vendor of shipboard incinerators.

(c) *Prohibited substances.* Shipboard incineration of the following substances is prohibited:

(1) Annex I, II, and III cargo residues of IMO MARPOL 73/78 (incorporated by reference; see 46 CFR 63.05–1) and related contaminated packing materials.

(2) Polychlorinated biphenyls (PCBs).

(3) Garbage, as defined in Annex V of IMO MARPOL 73/78, containing more than traces of heavy metals.

(4) Refined petroleum products containing halogen compounds.

(d) *Operating manual.* Each ship with an incinerator subject to this rule must possess a manufacturer's operating manual, which must specify how to operate the incinerator within the limits described in Annex A1.5 of IMO MEPC.76(40).

(e) *Training.* Each person responsible for operating any incinerator must be trained and be capable of implementing the guidance provided in the manufacturer's operating manual.

(f) *Acceptable methods and standards for testing emissions.* The methods and standards for testing emissions that the laboratory may use in determining emissions-related information described in Annex A1.5 of IMO MEPC.76(40) are:

(1) 40 CFR part 60 Appendix A, Method 1–Sample and velocity traverses for stationary sources;

(2) 40 CFR part 60 Appendix A, Method 3A–Determination of oxygen and carbon dioxide concentrations in emissions from stationary sources (instrumental-analyzer procedure);

(3) 40 CFR part 60 Appendix A, Method 5–Determination of particulate emissions from stationary sources;

(4) 40 CFR part 60 Appendix A, Method 9–Visual determination of the opacity of emissions from stationary sources;

(5) 40 CFR part 60 Appendix A, Method 10–Determination of carbon-monoxide emissions from stationary sources;

(6) ISO 9096 (incorporated by reference; see 46 CFR 63.05–1); and

(7) ISO 10396 (incorporated by reference; see 46 CFR 63.05–1).

[USCG–2003–16630, 73FR 65191, Oct. 31, 2008, as amended by USCG–2009–0702, 74 FR 49229, Sept. 25, 2009; USCG 2013–0671, 78 FR 60149, Sept. 30, 2013]

PART 64—MARINE PORTABLE TANKS AND CARGO HANDLING SYSTEMS

Subpart A—General

Sec.
64.1 Purpose.
64.2 Incorporation by reference.
64.3 Applicability.
64.5 Definitions.
64.9 Maintenance, repair, and alteration of MPTs.

Subpart B—Standards for an MPT

64.11 Design of MPTs.
64.13 Allowable stress; tank.
64.15 Allowable stress; framework.
64.17 Minimum tank thickness.
64.19 External pressure.
64.21 Material.
64.23 Gasket and lining.
64.25 Cross section.
64.27 Base.
64.29 Tank saddles.
64.31 Inspection opening.
64.33 Pipe connection.
64.35 Bottom filling or discharge connection.
64.37 Valve and fitting guard.

§ 64.1

64.39   Valve securing device.
64.41   Stop valve closure.
64.43   Lifting fittings.
64.45   Securing devices.
64.47   Type of relief devices.
64.49   Labeling openings.
64.51   Tank parts marking.
64.53   Information plate for MPTs.
64.55   Relief device location.

Subpart C—Pressure Relief Devices and Vacuum Relief Devices for MPTs

64.57   Acceptance of pressure relief devices.
64.59   Spring loaded pressure relief valve.
64.61   Rupture disc.
64.63   Minimum emergency venting capacity.
64.65   Vacuum relief device.
64.67   Shutoff valve.
64.69   Location of the pressure relief device.
64.71   Marking of pressure relief devices.

Subpart D [Reserved]

Subpart E—Periodic Inspections and Tests of MPTs

64.77   Inspection and test.
64.79   Inspection of pressure and vacuum relief device.
64.81   30-month inspection of an MPT.
64.83   Hydrostatic test.

Subpart F—Cargo Handling System

64.87   Purpose.
64.88   Plan approval, construction, and inspection of cargo-handling systems.
64.89   Cargo pump unit.
64.91   Relief valve for the cargo pump discharge.
64.93   Pump controls.
64.95   Piping.
64.97   Cargo hose.

AUTHORITY: 46 U.S.C. 3306, 3703; 49 U.S.C. App. 1804; Department of Homeland Security Delegation No. 0170.1.

SOURCE: CGD 73–172, 39 FR 22950, June 25, 1974, unless otherwise noted.

Subpart A—General

§ 64.1   Purpose.

This part contains the requirements for—

(a) Design, construction, repair, alteration, and marking of marine portable tanks (MPTs) authorized by this chapter to be carried on inspected vessels;

(b) Periodic inspections and tests of MPTs; and

(c) Design and construction of cargo-handling systems for MPTs and other portable tanks authorized under subparts 98.30 and 98.33 of this chapter.

[CGD 84–043, 55 FR 37409, Sept. 11, 1990; 55 FR 47477, Nov. 14, 1990]

§ 64.2   Incorporation by reference.

(a) Certain material is incorporated by reference into this part with the approval of the Director of the Federal Register in accordance with 5 U.S.C. 552(a). To enforce any edition other than the one listed in paragraph (b) of this section, the Coast Guard must publish notice of the change in the FEDERAL REGISTER and make the material available to the public. All approved material is on file at the Coast Guard Headquarters. Contact Commandant (CG–DCO–D), Attn: Deputy for Operations Policy and Capabilities, U.S. Coast Guard Stop 7318, 2703 Martin Luther King Jr. Avenue SE., Washington, DC 20593–7318. The material is also available from the source indicated in paragraph (b) of this section or at the National Archives and Records Administration (NARA). For information on the availability of this material at NARA, call 202–741–6030, or go to: *http://www.archives.gov/ federal_register/ code_of_federal_regulations/ ibr_locations.html*.

(b) The material approved for incorporation by reference in this part, and the sections affected, are:

American Society of Mechanical Engineers (ASME) International

Three Park Avenue, New York, NY 10016–5990.

ASME Boiler and Pressure Vessel Code, Section VIII, Division 1, Pressure Vessels, 1989, with Addenda issued December 31, 1989 ("ASME Code").........64.5, 64.7, 64.11, 64.13, 64.21, 64.25, 64.31

[CGD 84–043, 55 FR 37409, Sept. 11, 1990; 55 FR 47477, Nov. 14, 1990, as amended by CGD 96–041, 61 FR 50728, Sept. 27, 1996; CGD 97–057, 62 FR 51044, Sept. 30, 1997; USCG–1999–6216, 64 FR 53225, Oct. 1, 1999; USCG–2012–0832, 77 FR 59778, Oct. 1, 2012; USCG 2013–0671, 78 FR 60149, Sept. 30, 2013]

§ 64.3   Applicability.

(a) This part applies to each MPT for which the Commanding Officer, U.S.

Coast Guard Marine Safety Center, receives an application for approval on or before May 1, 1991.

(b) Subpart F of this part also applies to portable tanks and to cargo-handling systems for portable tanks authorized under subparts 98.30 and 98.33 of this chapter.

[CGD 84–043, 55 FR 37409, Sept. 11, 1990]

§ 64.5 Definitions.

As used in this part:

(a) *Marine portable tank* or *MPT* means a liquid-carrying tank that—

(1) Has a capacity of 110 gallons or more;

(2) Is designed to be carried on a vessel;

(3) Can be lifted full or empty onto and off a vessel, and can be filled and discharged while on a vessel;

(4) Is not permanently attached to the vessel; and

(5) Was inspected and stamped by the Coast Guard on or before September 30, 1992.

(b) *Tank* means the pressure vessel and the associated fittings of an MPT that come in contact with the product being carried.

(c) *Total containment pressure* means the minimum pressure for total product containment under normal operating conditions at a gauge pressure consisting of the absolute vapor pressure of the product at 122 °F added to the dynamic pressure, based on the tank dimensions and the location of the relief devices, of not less than 5 pounds per square inch gauge (psig) at the top of the tank in the operating position.

(d) *Maximum allowable working pressure* means the maximum gauge pressure at the top of the tank in the operating position at 122 °F, equal to or greater than the total containment pressure as defined in paragraph (c) of this section. The maximum allowable working pressure is used in the calculation of the minimum thickness of each element of the tank, excluding the allowance for corrosion and the thickness for loadings other than pressure, as provided for in the ASME Code.

(e) *Test pressure* means a hydrostatic pressure of at least one and one-half times the maximum allowable working pressure.

(f) *Dynamic loading conditions* means the following:

(1) A loading in the vertical down direction equal to 2 times the weight of the tank and the heaviest product carried.

(2) A loading in the transverse direction equal to the weight of the tank and the heaviest product carried.

(3) A loading in the longitudinal direction equal to the weight of the tank and the heaviest product carried.

(g) *Owner* means the person, corporation, company, partnership, or organization in which is vested the ownership, dominion, or title of a portable tank.

[CGD 73–172, 39 FR 22950, June 25, 1974, as amended by CGD 84–043, 55 FR 37409, Sept. 11, 1990]

§ 64.9 Maintenance, repair, and alteration of MPTs.

(a) Each MPT must be maintained in accordance with the approved plans, this part, and subpart 98.30 of this chapter.

(b) Repair of an MPT is authorized, provided that each repair is in accordance with the approved plans.

(c) No MPT may be altered, except with the written approval of the Commanding Officer, U.S. Coast Guard Marine Safety Center.

(d) After each welded repair or alteration, an MPT must be hydrostatically pressure-tested in accordance with paragraph (a) of § 64.83 of this part.

[CGD 84–043, 55 FR 37409, Sept. 11, 1990]

Subpart B—Standards for an MPT

§ 64.11 Design of MPTs.

An MPT must be designed—

(a) In accordance with the ASME Code and this subpart;

(b) With a maximum gross weight of 55,000 pounds;

(c) To hold a liquid cargo that has a vapor pressure of 43 pounds per square inch absolute (psia) or less at a temperature of 122 °F;

(d) With a minimum service temperature of 0 °F or higher;

(e) With a maximum allowable working pressure of not less than 20 pounds per square inch gauge (psig) but not more than 48 psig; and

§ 64.13

(f) To withstand dynamic loading conditions applied simultaneously.

[CGD 84-043, 55 FR 37410, Sept. 11, 1990; 55 FR 40755, Oct. 4, 1990]

§ 64.13 Allowable stress; tank.

(a) The calculated stress in the tank under design conditions, including dynamic loading conditions applied simultaneously, must not exceed the allowable stress listed in Division 1 of section VIII of the ASME Code, for a design temperature of 122 °F.

(b) The calculated stress in the tank at test pressure must not exceed 75 percent of the minimum yield stress,[1] or 37.5 percent of the minimum tensile stress[1] of the material, whichever is less.

[CGD 73-172, 39 FR 22950, June 25, 1974, as amended by CGD 84-043, 55 FR 37410, Sept. 11, 1990]

§ 64.15 Allowable stress; framework.

The calculated stress for the framework must be 80 percent or less of the minimum yield stress of the framework material under the dynamic loading conditions that are applied simultaneously.

§ 64.17 Minimum tank thickness.

(a) Except as allowed in paragraph (b) of this section, a tank with a diameter of—

(1) 6 feet or less must have a shell and head of 3/16 inch thickness or more; or

(2) More than 6 feet must have a shell and head of 1/4 inch thickness or more.

(b) If the tank has additional framework to guard against accidental puncturing of the tank, the shell and head thickness must be 1/8 inch or more.

§ 64.19 External pressure.

(a) A tank without a vacuum breaker must be designed to withstand an external pressure of 7½ psig or more.

(b) A tank with a vacuum breaker must be designed to withstand an external pressure of 3 psig or more.

---

[1] Listed in Division 1 of section VIII of the ASME Code.

§ 64.21 Material.

The material for a tank must meet the requirements in Division 1 of section VIII of the ASME Code.

[CGD 73-172, 39 FR 22950, June 25, 1974, as amended by CGD 84-043, 55 FR 37410, Sept. 11, 1990]

§ 64.23 Gasket and lining.

Each gasket and lining must be made of material that is—

(a) Chemically compatible with the product for which the tank is approved; and

(b) Resistant to deterioration from the product for which the tank is approved.

§ 64.25 Cross section.

A tank must have a cross section design that is—

(a) Circular; or

(b) Other than circular and stress analyzed experimentally by the method contained in UG-101 of the ASME Code.

[CGD 73-172, 39 FR 22950, June 25, 1974, as amended by CGD 84-043, 55 FR 37410, Sept. 11, 1990]

§ 64.27 Base.

The base of an MPT must be as wide and as long as the tank.

§ 64.29 Tank saddles.

If a tank is not completely supported by a framework, it must be supported by two or more external saddles, each of which extends to 120 degrees or more of the shell circumference.

§ 64.31 Inspection opening.

An MPT must have an inspection opening that is designed in accordance with Division 1 of section VIII of the ASME Code.

[CGD 73-172, 39 FR 22950, June 25, 1974, as amended by CGD 84-043, 55 FR 37410, Sept. 11, 1990]

§ 64.33 Pipe connection.

Each pipe connection that is not a pressure relief device must be fitted with a manually operated stop valve or closure located as close to the tank as practicable.

§ 64.35 Bottom filling or discharge connection.

If an MPT is designed with a filling or discharge connection in the bottom, the connection must be fitted with a bolted blank flange, threaded cap, or similar device to protect against leakage of the product, and a manually operated valve that is located—
(a) Inside the tank and operated outside the tank; or
(b) Outside the tank but as close to it as practicable.

§ 64.37 Valve and fitting guard.

Each valve and fitting must be protected from mechanical damage by—
(a) The tank;
(b) A tank saddle;
(c) The framework; or
(d) A guard.

§ 64.39 Valve securing device.

Each filling and discharge valve must have a securing device to prevent unintentional opening.

§ 64.41 Stop valve closure.

A stop valve that operates by a screwed spindle must close in a clockwise direction.

§ 64.43 Lifting fittings.

Each MPT must have attached lifting fittings so that the tank remains horizontal and stable while being moved.

§ 64.45 Securing devices.

An MPT or its framework must have sufficient number of positive action securing devices, including hooks, lugs, or padeyes, to attach the unit to the vessel so that—
(a) The stress does not exceed the standard contained in § 64.15; and
(b) Additional lashing is not needed.

§ 64.47 Type of relief devices.

(a) An MPT with an internal capacity of more than 550 U.S. gallons must have one or more spring loaded relief valves. In addition, a rupture disc may be attached.
(b) An MPT with an internal capacity of 550 U.S. gallons or less must have a rupture disc or a spring loaded relief valve.

§ 64.49 Labeling openings.

Each opening of a tank must be labeled to identify the function such as "suction", "discharge", "heating coil".

§ 64.51 Tank parts marking.

Any part of a tank furnished by an outside supplier may not be used in a tank unless it bears—
(a) The Coast Guard symbol;
(b) The Marine Inspection Office identification letters;
(c) The word "part";
(d) The manufacturer's name and serial number; and
(e) The design pressure.

§ 64.53 Information plate for MPTs.

(a) A corrosion-resistant metal plate containing the information in paragraph (b) of this section must be permanently attached to each MPT.
(b) Each information plate required in paragraph (a) of this section must bear the following information in legible letters 3/16 inch or more in height:
(1) Owner's name.
(2) Manufacturer's name.
(3) Date of manufacture.
(4) Serial number of tank.
(5) Maximum allowable working pressure in psig.
(6) Test pressure in psig.
(7) External-pressure rating in psig.
(8) Total capacity in gallons.
(9) Maximum net weight in long tons.
(10) Maximum gross weight in long tons.
(11) Percent ullage at 122 °F.
(12) Date of hydrostatic test.

[CGD 84-043, 55 FR 37410, Sept. 11, 1990]

§ 64.55 Relief device location.

A pressure relief device must be located on an MPT in a place that—
(a) Is the highest practical point of the tank; and
(b) Allows direct communication with the vapor space.

Subpart C—Pressure Relief Devices and Vacuum Relief Devices for MPTs

§ 64.57 Acceptance of pressure relief devices.

A pressure relief device for an MPT must be—

§ 64.59

(a) From a supplier[2] accepted under chapter I of title 46, Code of Federal Regulations; or

(b) Accepted by the Coast Guard in accordance with the procedures in § 50.25–10 of this chapter.

[CGD 84–043, 55 FR 37410, Sept. 11, 1990]

§ 64.59 Spring loaded pressure relief valve.

A spring loaded pressure relief valve must—

(a) Be set at a nominal pressure of 125 percent of the maximum allowable working pressure;

(b) Have a minimum normal venting capacity that is sufficient to prevent the tank pressure from exceeding 137.5 percent of the maximum allowable working pressure;

(c) Close after discharge of a pressure not lower than 115 percent of the maximum allowable working pressure; and

(d) If closed, remain closed at any pressure less than 115 percent of the maximum allowable working pressure.

§ 64.61 Rupture disc.

If a rupture disc is the only pressure relief device on the tank, the rupture disc must—

(a) Rupture at a pressure of 125 percent of the maximum allowable working pressure; and

(b) Have a minimum normal venting capacity that is sufficient to prevent the tank pressure from exceeding 137.5 percent of the maximum allowable working pressure.

§ 64.63 Minimum emergency venting capacity.

(a) The total emergency venting capacity (Q) of the relief devices of an uninsulated MPT must be in accordance with Table 1 or the following formula based upon the pressure relief device operating at a pressure not to exceed the test pressure:

$$Q = 633{,}000 \left(\frac{A^{0.82}}{LC}\right)\sqrt{\frac{ZT}{M}}$$

where:

---
[2] Accepted suppliers are listed in CG–190, *Equipment list*.

Q=Minimum required rate of discharge in cubic feet per minute of free air at standard conditions (60 °F and 14.7 psia).

M=Molecular weight of the product, or 86.7.

T=Temperature, degrees Rankine (460° + temperature in degrees F of gas at relieving temperature), or 710° Rankine.

A=Total external surface area of the tank compartment in square feet.

L=Latent heat of the product being vaporized at relieving conditions in Btu per pound, or 144 Btu per pound.

Z=Compressibility factor of the gas at relieving conditions, or 1.0.

C=Constant based on relation of specific heats, in accordance with appendix J of division 1 of section VIII of the ASME Code, 1974 edition, or 315.

(b) The total emergency venting capacity (Q) of an insulated portable tank may have a reduction if—

(1) It is shown to the Coast Guard that the insulation reduces the heat transmission to the tank;

(2) The present reduction of the emergency venting capacity (Q) is limited to the percent reduction of the heat transmission to the tank or 50 percent, whichever is less; and

(3) The insulation is sheathed.

TABLE 1—MINIMUM EMERGENCY VENTING CAPACITY IN CUBIC FEET: FREE AIR/HOUR (14.7 LB/IN²A AND 60 °F)

Exposed area square feet[1]	Cubic feet free air per hour	Exposed area square feet[1]	Cubic feet free air per hour
20	27,600	275	237,000
30	38,500	300	256,000
40	48,600	350	289,500
50	58,600	400	322,100
60	67,700	450	355,900
70	77,000	500	391,000
80	85,500	550	417,500
90	94,800	600	450,000
100	104,000	650	479,000
120	121,000	700	512,000
140	136,200	750	540,000
160	152,100	800	569,000
180	168,200	850	597,000
200	184,000	900	621,000
225	199,000	950	656,000
250	219,500	1,000	685,000

[1] Interpolate for intermediate sizes.

[CGD 73–172, 39 FR 22950, June 25, 1974, as amended by CGD 84–043, 55 FR 37410, Sept. 11, 1990; 55 FR 47477, Nov. 14, 1990]

§ 64.65 Vacuum relief device.

(a) Each MPT that is designed for an external pressure of less than 7.5 psig must have a vacuum relief device.

(b) A vacuum relief device for an MPT must—
(1) Open at an external pressure of not less than 3 psig; and
(2) Have an opening with a cross-section of 0.44 square inch or more.

[CGD 84–043, 55 FR 37410, Sept. 11, 1990]

§ 64.67   Shutoff valve.

A shutoff valve may not be located—
(a) Between the tank opening and pressure relief device; or
(b) On the discharge side of the pressure relief device.

§ 64.69   Location of the pressure relief device.

A pressure relief device must be—
(a) Accessible for inspection and repair before stowage of the tank; and
(b) Attached so that escaping gas does not impinge on the tank or framework.

§ 64.71   Marking of pressure relief devices.

A pressure relief device must be plainly and permanently marked with the—
(a) Set pressure rating;
(b) Rated flow capacity expressed as cubic feet of standard air (60 °F 14.7 psia) per minute and the pressure at which the flow capacity is determined;
(c) Manufacturer's name and identifying number; and
(d) Pipe size of inlet.

Subpart D [Reserved]

Subpart E—Periodic Inspections and Tests of MPTs

§ 64.77   Inspection and test.

For the handling and stowage requirements in § 98.30–3 of this chapter, each MPT must pass the following inspections and tests conducted by the owner or the owner's representative:
(a) Pressure relief and vacuum relief devices must be inspected one time or more during each 12 month period of service in accordance with § 64.79.
(b) An MPT must be inspected during the 30 months before any month in which it is in service in accordance with § 64.81.

(c) An MPT must pass a hydrostatic test in accordance with § 64.83 during the 60 months before any month in which it is in service.
(d) After each welded repair, an MPT must pass a hydrostatic test in accordance with § 64.83.

[CGD 73–172, 39 FR 22950, June 25, 1974, as amended by CGD 84–043, 55 FR 37410, Sept. 11, 1990]

§ 64.79   Inspection of pressure and vacuum relief device.

(a) The inspection of the pressure and vacuum relief device required in § 64.77(a) must include—
(1) Disassembling;
(2) A visual inspection for defective parts; and
(3) A test of the accuracy of the pressure setting.
(b) If the pressure and vacuum relief valve passes the inspection required in paragraph (a) of this section, the owner or his representative may attach to the device a metal tag containing the date of the inspection.

§ 64.81   30-month inspection of an MPT.

(a) The 30-month inspection of an MPT required in § 64.77(b) must include—
(1) An internal and external examination for—
(i) Corrosion;
(ii) Cracking of base material; and
(iii) Weld defects; and
(2) A visual inspection for defective parts and a manual operation of the gauging device, remote operating mechanism, and each valve, except the pressure relief device.
(b) If the tank passes the inspection required in paragraph (a) of this section, the owner or his representative may stencil the date of the inspection on the MPT near the metal identification plate that is required in § 64.53 in durable and legible letters that are 1¼ inch in height or larger.

§ 64.83   Hydrostatic test.

(a) The hydrostatic test required in § 64.77(c) includes—
(1) Closing each manhole and other openings by normal means of closure;
(2) Using wrenches or other tools that are used during normal operations to close the manhole and other openings;

§ 64.87

(3) Using the same type of gaskets as used in service;

(4) If required for the inspection, removing tank insulation;

(5) Filling the tank with water and pressurizing to the test pressure indicated on the metal identification plate without leaking; and

(6) If fitted with an internal heating coil, the heating coil passing a hydrostatic test at a pressure of 200 psig or more or 50 percent or more above the rated pressure of the coil, whichever is greater.

(b) If the tank passes the hydrostatic test required in paragraph (a) of this section, the owner or his representative may stamp the date of the test and his initials on the metal identification plate required in § 64.53.

Subpart F—Cargo Handling System

§ 64.87 Purpose.

Each cargo-handling system required to satisfy § 98.30–25 or § 98.33–13 of this chapter must meet the requirements of this subpart.

[CGD 84–043, 55 FR 37410, Sept. 11, 1990]

§ 64.88 Plan approval, construction, and inspection of cargo-handling systems.

Plans for the cargo-handling system of a portable tank authorized under subpart 98.30 of this chapter must be approved by the Coast Guard in accordance with the requirements of § 56.01–10 of this subchapter. In addition, the cargo-handling system must be constructed and inspected in accordance with part 56 of this subchapter.

[CGD 84–043, 55 FR 37410, Sept. 11, 1990]

§ 64.89 Cargo pump unit.

(a) A cargo pump unit that fills or discharges a portable tank must be—

(1) Constructed of materials that are compatible with the product to be pumped; and

(2) Designed to be compatible with the hazard associated with the product to be pumped.

(b) The cargo pump power unit must be—

(1) Diesel;

(2) Hydraulic;

(3) Pneumatic; or

(4) Electric.

(c) The starting system for a cargo pump power unit must be designed to be compatible with the hazard associated with the product to be pumped.

(d) A diesel engine that is used to drive a cargo pump must have a spark arrestor on the exhaust system.

§ 64.91 Relief valve for the cargo pump discharge.

The cargo pump discharge must have a relief valve that is—

(a) Fitted between the cargo pump discharge and the shut-off valve, with the relief valve discharge piped back to the cargo pump suction or returned to the tank; and

(b) Set at the maximum design pressure of the piping and discharge hose, or less.

§ 64.93 Pump controls.

(a) A pressure gauge must be installed—

(1) On the pump discharge;

(2) Near the pump controls; and

(3) Visible to the operator.

(b) A pump must have a remote, quick acting, manual shutdown that is conspicuously labeled and located in an easily accessible area away from the pump. The quick acting, manual shutdown for remote operation must provide a means of stopping the pump power unit.

§ 64.95 Piping.

(a) Piping, valves, flanges, and fittings used in the pumping system must be designed in accordance with part 56 of this chapter.

(b) A cargo loading and discharge header or manifold must—

(1) Have stop valves to prevent cargo leakage; and

(2) Be visible to the operator at the cargo pump controls.

(c) Each pipe and valve in the pumping system that has an open end must have a plug or cap to prevent leakage.

(d) Each hose connection must be threaded or flanged except for a quick connect coupling that may be specifically accepted by the U.S. Coast Guard in accordance with the procedures in § 50.25–10 of this chapter.

(e) A non-return valve must be in the pump discharge if a backflow condition may occur during pumping.

(f) Any non-metallic flexible hose that is used in the piping system must comply with § 56.60–25(c) of this chapter.

[CGD 73–172, 39 FR 22950, June 25, 1974, as amended by USCG–2004–18884, 69 FR 58346, Sept. 30, 2004]

§ 64.97 Cargo hose.

Each hose assembly, consisting of couplings and a hose that has an inside diameter—

(a) Larger than three inches, must meet the requirements in 33 CFR 154.500; or

(b) Three inches or less, must be designed to withstand the pressure of the shutoff head of the cargo pump or pump discharge relief valve setting, but not less than 100 pounds per square inch.

SUBCHAPTER G—DOCUMENTATION AND MEASUREMENT OF VESSELS

PART 66 [RESERVED]

PART 67—DOCUMENTATION OF VESSELS

Subpart A—General

Sec.
67.1 Purpose.
67.3 Definitions.
67.5 Vessels eligible for documentation.
67.7 Vessels requiring documentation.
67.9 Vessels excluded from or exempt from documentation.
67.11 Restriction on transfer of an interest in documented vessels to foreign persons; foreign registry or operation.
67.12 Right of appeal.
67.13 Incorporation by reference.
67.14 OMB control numbers assigned pursuant to the Paperwork Reduction Act.

Subpart B—Forms of Documentation; Endorsements; Eligibility of Vessel

67.15 Form of document—all endorsements.
67.17 Registry endorsement.
67.19 Coastwise endorsement.
67.21 Fishery endorsement.
67.23 Recreational endorsement.

Subpart C—Citizenship Requirements for Vessel Documentation

67.30 Requirement for citizen owner.
67.31 Stock or equity interest requirements.
67.33 Individual.
67.35 Partnership.
67.36 Trust.
67.37 Association or joint venture.
67.39 Corporation.
67.41 Governmental entity.
67.43 Evidence of citizenship.
67.47 Requirement for Maritime Administration approval.

Subpart D—Title Requirements for Vessel Documentation

67.50 Requirement for title evidence.
67.53 Methods of establishing title.
67.55 Requirement for removal from foreign registry.
67.57 Extent of title evidence required for initial documentation.
67.59 Extent of title evidence required for change in ownership of a documented vessel.
67.61 Extent of title evidence required for vessels returning to documentation.
67.63 Extent of title evidence required for captured, forfeited, special legislation, and wrecked vessels.

Subpart E—Acceptable Title Evidence; Waiver

67.70 Original owner.
67.73 Transfers prior to documentation.
67.75 Transfers by sale or donation subsequent to documentation.
67.77 Passage of title by court action.
67.79 Passage of title without court action following death of owner.
67.81 Passage of title in conjunction with a corporate merger or similar transaction.
67.83 Passage of title by extra-judicial repossession and sale.
67.85 Change in general partners of partnership.
67.87 Change of legal name of owner.
67.89 Waiver of production of a bill of sale eligible for filing and recording.
67.91 Passage of title pursuant to operation of State law.

Subpart F—Build Requirements for Vessel Documentation

67.95 Requirement for determination.
67.97 United States built.
67.99 Evidence of build.
67.101 Waiver of evidence of build.

Subpart G—Tonnage and Dimension Requirements for Vessel Documentation

67.105 Requirement for determination.
67.107 System of measurement; evidence.

Subpart H—Assignments and Designations Required for Vessel Documentation

67.111 Assignment of official number.
67.113 Managing owner designation; address; requirement to report change of address.
67.117 Vessel name designation.
67.119 Hailing port designation.

Subpart I—Marking Requirements for Vessel Documentation

67.120 General requirement.
67.121 Official number marking requirement.
67.123 Name and hailing port marking requirements.
67.125 Disputes.

Coast Guard, Dept. of Homeland Security Pt. 67

Subpart J—Application for Special Qualifications for Vessel Documentation

67.130 Submission of applications.
67.131 Forfeited vessels.
67.132 Special legislation.
67.133 Wrecked vessels.
67.134 Captured vessels.

Subpart K—Application for Documentation, Exchange or Replacement of Certificate of Documentation, or Return to Documentation; Mortgagee Consent; Validation

67.141 Application procedure; all cases.
67.142 Penalties.
67.143 Restriction on withdrawal of application.
67.145 Restrictions on exchange; requirement and procedure for mortgagee consent.
67.149 Exchange of Certificate of Documentation; vessel at sea.
67.151 Replacement of Certificate of Documentation; special procedure for wrongfully withheld document.

Subpart L—Validity of Certificates of Documentation; Renewal of Endorsement; Requirement for Exchange, Replacement, Deletion, Cancellation

67.161 Validity of Certificate of Documentation.
67.163 Renewal of endorsement.
67.165 Deposit of Certificate of Documentation.
67.167 Requirement for exchange of Certificate of Documentation.
67.169 Requirement for replacement of Certificate of Documentation.
67.171 Deletion; requirement and procedure.
67.173 Cancellation; requirement and procedure.

Subpart M—Miscellaneous Applications

67.175 Application for new vessel determination.
67.177 Application for foreign rebuilding determination.

Subpart N [Reserved]

Subpart O—Filing and Recording of Instruments—General Provisions

67.200 Instruments eligible for filing and recording.
67.203 Restrictions on filing and recording.
67.205 Requirement for vessel identification.
67.207 Requirement for date and acknowledgment.
67.209 No original instrument requirement.
67.211 Requirement for citizenship declaration.
67.213 Place of filing and recording.
67.215 Date and time of filing.
67.217 Termination of filing and disposition of instruments.
67.218 Optional filing of instruments in portable document format as attachments to electronic mail.
67.219 Optional filing of instruments by facsimile.

Subpart P—Filing and Recording of Instruments—Bills of Sale and Related Instruments

67.220 Requirements.
67.223 Filing limitation.

Subpart Q—Filing and Recording of Instruments—Mortgages, Preferred Mortgages, and Related Instruments

67.231 General requirements; optional application for filing and recording.
67.233 Restrictions on recording mortgages, preferred mortgages, and related instruments.
67.235 Requirements for mortgages.
67.237 Requirements for assignments of mortgages.
67.239 Requirements for assumptions of mortgages.
67.241 Requirements for amendments of or supplements to mortgages.
67.243 Requirements for instruments subordinating mortgages.
67.245 Requirements for interlender agreements.

Subpart R—Filing and Recording of Instruments—Notices of Claim of Lien and Supplemental Instruments

67.250 General requirements.
67.253 Requirements for notices of claim of lien.
67.255 Restrictions on filing and recording.
67.257 Requirements for assignments of notices of claim of lien.
67.259 Requirements for amendments to notice of claim of lien.

Subpart S—Removal of Encumbrances

67.261 General requirements.
67.263 Requirement for removal of encumbrances by court order, affidavit, or Declaration of Forfeiture.
67.265 Requirements for instruments evidencing satisfaction or release.

Subpart T—Abstracts of Title, and Certificates of Ownership

67.301 Issuance of Abstract of Title.
67.303 Issuance of Certificate of Ownership.

Subpart U—Special Provisions

67.311 Alteration of Certificate of Documentation.
67.313 Requirement to have Certificate of Documentation on board.
67.315 Requirement to produce Certificate of Documentation.
67.317 Requirement to renew endorsements on the Certificate of Documentation.
67.319 Requirement to report change in vessel status and surrender Certificate of Documentation.
67.321 Requirement to report change of address of managing owner.
67.323 Operation without documentation.
67.325 Violation of endorsement.
67.327 Operation under Certificate of Documentation with invalid endorsement.
67.329 Unauthorized name change.
67.331 Improper markings.

Subpart V—Exception From Fishery Endorsement Requirements Due to Conflict With International Agreements

67.350 Conflicts with international agreements.
67.352 Applicability.

Subparts W–X [Reserved]

Subpart Y—Fees

67.500 Applicability.
67.501 Application for Certificate of Documentation.
67.503 Application for exchange or replacement of a Certificate of Documentation.
67.505 Application for return of vessel to documentation.
67.507 Application for replacement of lost or mutilated Certificate of Documentation.
67.509 Application for approval of exchange of Certificate of Documentation requiring mortgagee consent.
67.511 Application for trade endorsement(s).
67.513 Application for evidence of deletion from documentation.
67.515 [Reserved]
67.517 Application for late renewal.
67.519 Application for waivers.
67.521 Application for new vessel determination.
67.523 Application for wrecked vessel determination.
67.525 Application for determination of rebuild.
67.527 Application for filing and recording bills of sale and instruments in the nature of a bill of sale.
67.529 Application for filing and recording mortgages and related instruments.
67.531 Application for filing and recording notices of claim of lien.
67.533 Application for Certificate of Compliance.
67.535 Issuance of Abstract of Title.
67.537 Issuance of Certificate of Ownership.
67.539 Copies of instruments and documents.
67.550 Fee table.

AUTHORITY: 14 U.S.C. 664; 31 U.S.C. 9701; 42 U.S.C. 9118; 46 U.S.C. 2103, 2107, 2110, 12106, 12120, 12122; 46 U.S.C. app. 841a, 876; Department of Homeland Security Delegation No. 0170.1.

SOURCE: CGD 89–007, CGD 89–007a, 58 FR 60266, Nov. 15, 1993, unless otherwise noted.

Subpart A—General

§ 67.1 Purpose.

A Certificate of Documentation is required for the operation of a vessel in certain trades, serves as evidence of vessel nationality, and permits a vessel to be subject to preferred mortgages.

§ 67.3 Definitions.

The following definitions are for terms used in this part.

Acknowledgment means:

(a) An acknowledgment or notarization in any form which is in substantial compliance with the Uniform Acknowledgments Act, the Uniform Recognition of Acknowledgments Act, the Uniform Law on Notarial Acts, or the statutes of the State within which it is taken, made before a notary public or other official authorized by a law of a State or the United States to take acknowledgment of deeds;

(b) An acknowledgment or notarization before a notary or other official authorized to take acknowledgments of deeds by the law of a foreign nation which is a party to the Hague Convention Abolishing the Requirement for Legalisation of Public Documents, 1961, provided that the acknowledgment or notarization is accompanied by the certificate described in Article 3 of that Convention; or

(c) Any attestation which is substantially in the following form:

State:
County:

On [date] the person(s) named above acknowledged execution of the foregoing instrument in their stated capacity(ies) for the purpose therein contained.
Notary Public
My commission expires: [date]

Captured vessel means a vessel which has been taken by citizens of the

Coast Guard, Dept. of Homeland Security §67.3

United States during a period of war and is thereafter condemned as a prize by a court of competent jurisdiction.

Certification of Documentation means form CG–1270.

Citizen, unless expressly provided otherwise, means a person meeting the applicable citizenship requirements of subpart C of this part as a United States citizen.

Coastwise trade includes the transportation of passengers or merchandise between points embraced within the coastwise laws of the United States.

Commandant means the Commandant of the United States Coast Guard.

Documentation officer means the Coast Guard official who is authorized to process and approve applications made under this part, and record instruments authorized to be filed and recorded under this part.

Documented vessel means a vessel which is the subject of a valid Certificate of Documentation.

Endorsement means an entry which may be made on a Certificate of Documentation, and which, except for a recreational endorsement, is conclusive evidence that a vessel is entitled to engage in a specified trade.

NOTE: Rulings and interpretations concerning what activities constitute coastwise trade and the fisheries can be obtained from the U.S. Customs and Border Protection, 799 9th Street NW., Washington DC 20001 (Cargo Security, Carriers and Immigration Branch).

Exclusive Economic Zone (EEZ) means the zone established by Presidential Proclamation Numbered 5030, dated March 10, 1983 (48 FR 10105, 3 CFR, 1983 Comp., p. 22).

Fisheries includes processing, storing, transporting (except in foreign commerce), planting, cultivating, catching, taking, or harvesting fish, shellfish, marine animals, pearls, shells, or marine vegetation in the navigable waters of the United States or in the Exclusive Economic Zone.

Forfeited vessel means a vessel:

(1) Which has been adjudged forfeited by a Federal District Court to the Federal Government of the United States for a breach of its laws; or

(2) Which has been forfeited under an administrative forfeiture action to the Federal Government of the United States for a breach of its laws; or

(3) Which has been seized by the Federal Government of the United States for a breach of its laws and which has been sold at an interlocutory sale, the proceeds of which have been adjudged forfeited by a Federal District Court to the Federal Government of the United States. A vessel is considered forfeited within the meaning of this definition even if the proceeds, though adjudged forfeited to the United States, do not actually accrue to the United States.

Hull means the shell, or outer casing, and internal structure below the main deck which provide both the flotation envelope and structural integrity of the vessel in its normal operations. In the case of a submersible vessel, the term includes all structural members of the pressure envelope.

Manufacturer's Certificate of Origin means a certificate issued under the law or regulation of a State, evidencing transfer of a vessel from the manufacturer as defined in 33 CFR part 181 to another person.

National Vessel Documentation Center means the organizational unit designated by the Commandant to process vessel documentation transactions and maintain vessel documentation records. The address is: National Vessel Documentation Center, 792 T.J. Jackson Drive, Falling Waters, WV 25419. Telephone: (800) 799-VDOC (8362).

New vessel means a vessel:

(1) The hull and superstructure of which are constructed entirely of new materials; or

(2) Which is constructed using structural parts of an existing vessel, which parts have been torn down so that they are no longer advanced to a degree which would commit them to use in the building of a vessel.

Officer in Charge, Marine Inspection (OCMI) means the Coast Guard official designated as such by the Commandant, under the superintendence and direction of a Coast Guard District Commander, who is in charge of an inspection zone in accordance with regulations set forth in 46 CFR part 1.

Person means an individual; corporation; partnership; limited liability partnership; limited liability company; association; joint venture; trust arrangement; and the government of the United States, a State, or a political

333

§ 67.5

subdivision of the United States or a State; and includes a trustee, beneficiary, receiver, or similar representative of any of them.

Registration means a certificate of number issued pursuant to rules in 33 CFR part 173, a record under the maritime laws of a foreign country, or a certificate issued by a political subdivision of a foreign country.

Secretary means the Secretary of Homeland Security.

State means a State of the United States or a political subdivision thereof, Guam, Puerto Rico, the Virgin Islands, American Samoa, the District of Columbia, the Northern Mariana Islands, and any other territory or possession of the United States.

Superstructure means the main deck and any other structural part above the main deck.

United States, when used in a geographic sense means the States of the United States, Guam, Puerto Rico, the Virgin Islands, American Samoa, the District of Columbia, the Northern Mariana Islands, and any other territory or possession of the United States, except that for purposes of § 67.19(d)(3) trust territories are not considered to be part of the United States.

Vessel includes every description of watercraft or other contrivance capable of being used as a means of transportation on water, but does not include aircraft.

Wrecked vessel, under the provisions of 46 U.S.C. app. 14, means a vessel which:

(1) Has incurred substantial damage to its hull or superstructure as a result of natural or accidental causes which occurred in the United States or its adjacent waters; and

(2) Has undergone, in a shipyard in the United States or its possessions, repairs equaling three times the appraised salved value of the vessel.

[CGD 89–007, CGD 89–007a, 58 FR 60266, Nov. 15, 1993, as amended by CGD 95–014, 60 FR 31603, June 15, 1995; CDG 94–070, 60 FR 40241, Aug. 7, 1995; CGD 95–012, 60 FR 48050, Sept. 18, 1995; USCG–1998–4442, 63 FR 52190, Sept. 30, 1998; USCG–2001–8825, 69 FR 5400, Feb. 4, 2004; USCG–2004–18884, 69 FR 58346, Sept. 30, 2004; USCG–2005–20258, 71 FR 61417, Oct. 18, 2006; USCG–2012–0832, 77 FR 59778, Oct. 1, 2012]

§ 67.5 Vessels eligible for documentation.

Any vessel of at least five net tons wholly owned by a citizen or citizens of the United States is eligible for documentation under this part. This includes, but is not limited to, vessels used exclusively for recreational purposes and vessels used in foreign trade.

§ 67.7 Vessels requiring documentation.

Any vessel of at least five net tons which engages in the fisheries on the navigable waters of the United States or in the Exclusive Economic Zone, or coastwise trade, unless exempt under § 67.9(c), must have a Certificate of Documentation bearing a valid endorsement appropriate for the activity in which engaged.

[CGD 89–007, CGD 89–007a, 58 FR 60266, Nov. 15, 1993, as amended by USCG–2009–0702, 74 FR 49230, Sept. 25, 2009]

§ 67.9 Vessels excluded from or exempt from documentation.

(a) A vessel of less than five net tons is excluded from documentation.

(b) A vessel which does not operate on the navigable waters of the United States or in the fisheries in the Exclusive Economic Zone is exempt from the requirement to have a Certificate of Documentation.

(c) A non-self-propelled vessel, qualified to engage in the coastwise trade is exempt from the requirement to be documented with a coastwise endorsement when engaged in coastwise trade:

(1) Within a harbor;

(2) On the rivers or lakes (except the Great Lakes) of the United States; or

(3) On the internal waters or canals of any State.

(d) A vessel exempt from the requirement to be documented by paragraph (b) or (c) of this section may be documented at the option of the owner, provided it meets the other requirements of this part.

§ 67.11 Restriction on transfer of an interest in documented vessels to foreign persons; foreign registry or operation.

(a) Unless approved by the Maritime Administration—

(1) A documented vessel or a vessel last documented under the laws of the United States may not be placed under foreign registry or operated under the authority of a foreign country.

(2) A documented vessel or a vessel last documented under the laws of the United States owned by a citizen of the United States as defined in section 2 of the Shipping Act, 1916 (46 U.S.C. app. 802), may not be sold, mortgaged, leased, chartered, delivered, or otherwise transferred to any person who is not a citizen of the United States as defined in section 2 of the Shipping Act, 1916 (46 U.S.C. app. 802).

(b) The restrictions in paragraph (a)(2) of this section do not apply to a vessel that has been operated only as:

(1) A fishing vessel, fish processing vessel, or fish tender vessel as defined in 46 U.S.C. 2101;

(2) A recreational vessel; or

(3) Both.

NOTE: For purposes of carrying out its responsibilities under the provisions of this part only, the Coast Guard will deem a vessel which has been documented exclusively with a fishery or recreational endorsement or both from the time it was first documented, or for a period of not less than one year prior to foreign transfer or registry, to qualify for the exemption granted in paragraph (b) of this section.

(c) The exemption in paragraph (b) of this section does not relieve all vessels from meeting the fishery endorsement requirements of this part. If your vessel is less than 100 feet in length and is a fishing vessel, fish processing vessel, or fish tender vessel as defined in 46 U.S.C. 2101, you must meet the fishery endorsement requirements set out in this part. Each vessel 100 feet and greater in length applying for a fishery endorsement is regulated by the Maritime Administration requirements found in 46 CFR part 356.

[CGD 89–007, CGD 89–007a, 58 FR 60266, Nov. 15, 1003, as amended by USCG–1999–6095, 65 FR 76575, Dec. 7, 2000]

§ 67.12 Right of appeal.

Any person directly affected by a decision or action taken under this part by or on behalf of the Coast Guard may appeal therefrom in accordance with subpart 1.03 of this chapter.

§ 67.13 Incorporation by reference.

(a) Certain material is incorporated by reference into this part with the approval of the Director of the Federal Register under 5 U.S.C. 552(a) and 1 CFR part 51. To enforce any edition other than that specified in paragraph (b) of this section, the Coast Guard must publish notice of change in the FEDERAL REGISTER and the material must be available to the public. All approved material may be inspected at the U.S. Coast Guard, National Vessel Documentation Center, 792 T.J. Jackson Drive, Falling Waters, WV 25419 and is available from the source indicated in paragraph (b) of this section or at the National Archives and Records Administration (NARA). For information on the availability of this material at NARA, call 202–741–6030, or go to: http://www.archives.gov/federal_register/code_of_federal_regulations/ibr_locations.html.

(b) The material approved for incorporation by reference in this part and the section affected is as follows:

U.S. Department of Commerce, National Technical Information Service, Springfield, VA 22181

Federal Information Processing Standards Publication 55DC, Guideline: Codes For Named Populated Places, Primary County Divisions, And Other Locational Entities of the United States and Outlying Areas (1987)—67.119

[CGD 89–007, CGD 89–007a, 58 FR 60266, Nov. 15, 1993, as amended by CGD 95–070, 60 FR 40241, Aug. 7, 1995; USCG–2004–18884, 69 FR 58346, Sept. 30, 2004]

§ 67.14 OMB control numbers assigned pursuant to the Paperwork Reduction Act.

(a) *Purpose.* This section collects and displays the control numbers assigned to information collection and record-keeping requirements in this subchapter by the Office of Management and Budget (OMB) pursuant to the Paperwork Reduction Act of 1980 (44 U.S.C. 3501 *et seq.*). The Coast Guard intends that this section comply with the requirements of 44 U.S.C. 3507(f) which requires that agencies display a current control number assigned by the Director of the OMB for each approved

§ 67.15

agency information collection requirement.

(b) *Display.*

46 CFR part or section where identified or described	Current OMB control No.
Part 67	1625-0027
Part 68	1625-0027

[CGD 89-007, CGD 89-007a, 58 FR 60266, Nov. 15, 1993, as amended by USCG-2004-18884, 69 FR 58346, Sept. 30, 2004]

Subpart B—Forms of Documentation; Endorsements; Eligibility of Vessel

§ 67.15 Form of document—all endorsements.

(a) The form of document is a Certificate of Documentation, form CG-1270.

(b) Upon application in accordance with subpart K of this part and determination of qualification by the Director, National Vessel Documentation Center, a Certificate of Documentation may be issued with a registry, coastwise, fishery, or recreational endorsement.

(c) A Certificate of Documentation may bear simultaneous endorsements for recreation and more than one trade, including operation under 46 CFR part 68.

NOTE: Where a vessel possesses a Certificate of Documentation bearing more than one endorsement, the actual use of the vessel determines the endorsement under which it is operating.

[CGD 89-007, CGD 89-007a, 58 FR 60266, Nov. 15, 1993; 58 FR 65131, Dec. 13, 1993, as amended by CGD 95-014, 60 FR 31604, June 15, 1995; USCG-1999-6216, 64 FR 53225, Oct. 1, 1999; USCG-2009-0702, 74 FR 49230, Sept. 25, 2009]

§ 67.17 Registry endorsement.

(a) A registry endorsement entitles a vessel to employment in the foreign trade; trade with Guam, American Samoa, Wake, Midway, or Kingman Reef; and any other employment for which a coastwise, or fishery endorsement is not required.

(b) Any vessel eligible for documentation under § 67.5 is eligible for a registry endorsement.

(c) A vessel otherwise eligible for a registry endorsement for which the Maritime Administration has not given approval for unrestricted transfer pursuant to 46 CFR part 221 loses that eligibility during any period in which it is mortgaged to a person not identified in § 67.233(b).

[CGD 89-007, CGD 89-007a, 58 FR 60266, Nov. 15, 1993, as amended by USCG-2009-0702, 74 FR 49230, Sept. 25, 2009]

§ 67.19 Coastwise endorsement.

(a) A coastwise endorsement entitles a vessel to employment in unrestricted coastwise trade, dredging, towing, and any other employment for which a registry or fishery endorsement is not required.

(b) If eligible for documentation and not restricted from coastwise trade by paragraph (c) or (d) of this section, the following vessels are eligible for a coastwise endorsement:

(1) Vessels built in the United States (§ 67.97);

(2) Forfeited vessels (§ 67.131);

(3) Vessels granted coastwise trading privileges by special legislation (§ 67.132);

(4) Wrecked vessels (§ 67.133);

(5) Captured vessels (§ 67.134); and

(6) Vessels purchased, chartered, or leased from the Secretary of Transportation by persons who are citizens of the United States (46 U.S.C. app. 808).

(c) A vessel otherwise eligible for a coastwise endorsement under paragraph (b) of this section permanently loses that eligibility if:

(1) It is thereafter sold in whole or in part to an owner:

(i) Not a citizen as defined in subpart C of this part, or

(ii) Not a person permitted to document vessels pursuant to 46 CFR part 68;

(2) It is thereafter registered under the laws of a foreign country;

(3) It undergoes rebuilding as defined in § 67.177 outside of the United States; or

(4) It is a crude oil tanker of 20,000 deadweight tons or above, and after October 17, 1978, has segregated ballast tanks, a crude oil washing system, or an inert gas system installed outside of the United States as defined in § 67.3.

(d) A vessel otherwise eligible for a coastwise endorsement under paragraph (b) of this section loses that eligibility, except as provided in paragraph (e) of this section, during any period in which it is:

(1) Owned by a corporation which does not meet the citizenship requirements of § 67.39(c);

(2) Owned by a partnership which does not meet the citizenship requirements of § 67.35(a); or

(3) Mortgaged to a person not identified in § 67.233(b).

(e) The restriction imposed by paragraph (d)(2) of this section does not apply to any vessel for which the Maritime Administration has given approval for unrestricted transfer pursuant to regulations set forth in 46 CFR part 221.

[CGD 89–007, CGD 89–007a, 58 FR 60266, Nov. 15, 1993; 58 FR 65131, Dec. 13, 1993, as amended by CGD 94–008, 59 FR 49846, Sept. 30, 1994; CGD 94–040, 61 FR 17815, Apr. 22, 1996; USCG–2002–13058, 67 FR 61278, Sept. 30, 2002; USCG–2009–0702, 74 FR 49230, Sept. 25, 2009]

§ 67.21 Fishery endorsement.

(a) A fishery endorsement entitles a vessel to employment in the fisheries as defined in § 67.3, subject to Federal and State laws regulating the fisheries, and in any other employment for which a registry or coastwise endorsement is not required. A fishery endorsement entitles a vessel to land its catch, wherever caught, in the United States.

(b) If eligible for documentation and not restricted from the fisheries by paragraph (c) of this section, the following vessels are eligible for a fishery endorsement:

(1) Vessels built in the United States (§ 67.97);

(2) Forfeited vessels (§ 67.131);

(3) Vessels granted fisheries privileges by special legislation(§ 67.132);

(4) Wrecked vessels (§ 67.133); and

(5) Captured vessels (§ 67.134).

(c) A vessel otherwise eligible for a fishery endorsement under paragraph (b) of this section permanently loses that eligibility if it undergoes rebuilding as defined in § 67.177 outside of the United States.

(d) A vessel otherwise eligible for a fishery endorsement under paragraph (b) of this section loses that eligibility during any period in which it is:

(1) Owned by a partnership which does not meet the requisite citizenship requirements of § 67.35(b);

(2) Owned by a corporation which does not meet the citizenship requirements of § 67.39(b); or

(3) Chartered or leased to an individual who is not a citizen of the United States or to an entity that is not eligible to own a vessel with a fishery endorsement, except that time charters, voyage charters and other charters that are not a demise of the vessel may be entered into with Non-Citizens for the charter of dedicated Fish Tender Vessels and Fish Processing Vessels that are not engaged in the harvesting of fish or fishery resources without the vessel losing its eligibility for a fishery endorsement.

(e) A vessel operating with a fishery endorsement on October 1, 1998, under the authority of the Western Pacific Fishery Management Council, or a purse seine vessel engaged in tuna fishing outside of the EEZ of the United States or pursuant to the South Pacific Regional Fisheries Treaty may continue to operate as set out in 46 U.S.C. 12102(c)(5), provided that the owner of the vessel continues to comply with the fishery endorsement requirements that were in effect on October 1, 1998.

(f) An individual or entity that is otherwise eligible to own a vessel with a fishery endorsement shall be ineligible if an instrument or evidence of indebtedness, secured by a mortgage of the vessel, to a trustee eligible to own a vessel with a fishery endorsement is issued, assigned, transferred, or held in trust for a person not eligible to own a vessel with a fishery endorsement, unless the Commandant determines that the issuance, assignment, transfer, or trust arrangement does not result in an impermissible transfer of control of the vessel and that the trustee:

(1) Is organized as a corporation that meets § 67.39(b) of this part, and is doing business under the laws of the United States or of a State;

(2) Is authorized under those laws to exercise corporate trust powers which meet § 67.36(b) of this part;

§67.23

(3) Is subject to supervision or examination by an official of the United States Government or a State;

(4) Has a combined capital and surplus (as stated in its most recent published report of condition) of at least $3,000,000; and

(5) Meets any other requirements prescribed by the Commandant.

For vessels greater than or equal to 100 feet in length, approval of such an arrangement from the Maritime Administration will be accepted as evidence that the above conditions are met and will be approved by the Commandant. For vessels less than 100 feet, a standard loan and mortgage agreement that has received general approval under 46 CFR 356.21 will be accepted as evidence that the above conditions are met and will be approved by the Commandant.

[CGD 89-007, CGD 89-007A, 58 FR 60266, Nov. 15, 1993, as amended by CGD 94-040, 61 FR 17815, Apr. 22, 1996; USCG-1999-6095, 65 FR 76575, Dec. 7, 2000; USCG-2009-0702, 74 FR 49230, Sept. 25, 2009]

§67.23 Recreational endorsement.

(a) A recreational endorsement entitles a vessel to pleasure use only.

(b) Any vessel eligible for documentation under §67.5 is eligible for a recreational endorsement.

NOTE: A vessel having a Certificate of Documentation endorsed only for recreation may be bareboat chartered only for recreational use. Guidance on the elements of a valid bareboat charter should be obtained through private legal counsel.

Subpart C—Citizenship Requirements for Vessel Documentation

§67.30 Requirement for citizen owner.

Certificates of Documentation may be issued under this part only to vessels which are wholly owned by United States citizens. Pursuant to extraordinary legislation at 46 U.S.C. app. 883-1 (Bowater Amendment) and 46 U.S.C. 12106(d) (Oil Pollution Act of 1990), Certificates of Documentation with limited endorsements may be issued in accordance with part 68 of this chapter to vessels owned by certain persons who are not citizens as defined in this part.

§67.31 Stock or equity interest requirements.

(a) The stock or equity interest requirements for citizenship under this subpart encompass: title to all classes of stock; title to voting stock; and ownership of equity. An otherwise qualifying corporation or partnership may fail to meet stock or equity interest requirements because: Stock is subject to trust or fiduciary obligations in favor of non-citizens; non-citizens exercise, directly or indirectly, voting power; or non-citizens, by any means, exercise control over the entity. The applicable stock or equity interest requirement is not met if the amount of stock subject to obligations in favor of non-citizens, non-citizen voting power, or non-citizen control exceeds the percentage of the non-citizen interest permitted.

(b) For the purpose of stock or equity interest requirements for citizenship under this subpart, control of non-fishing industry vessels includes an absolute right to: Direct corporate or partnership business; limit the actions of or replace the chief executive officer, a majority of the board of directors, or any general partner; direct the transfer or operations of any vessel owned by the corporation or partnership; or otherwise exercise authority over the business of the corporation or partnership. Control does not include the right to simply participate in these activities or the right to receive a financial return, e.g., interest or the equivalent of interest on a loan or other financing obligations.

(c) For the purpose of this section, control of a fishing industry vessel means having:

(1) The right to direct the business of the entity that owns the vessel;

(2) The right to limit the actions of or to replace the chief executive officer, the majority of the board of directors, any general partner, or any person serving in a management capacity of the entity that owns the vessel;

(3) The right to direct the transfer, the operation, or the manning of a vessel with a fishery endorsement.

(d) For purposes of meeting the stock or equity interest requirements for citizenship under this subpart where title to a vessel is held by an entity comprised, in whole or in part, of other entities which are not individuals, each entity contributing to the stock or equity interest qualifications of the entity holding title must be a citizen eligible to document vessels in its own right with the trade endorsement sought.

[CGD 89–007, CGD 89–007a, 58 FR 60266, Nov. 15, 1003, as amended by USCG–1999–6095, 65 FR 76575, Dec. 7, 2000; USCG–2004–18884, 69 FR 58346, Sept. 30, 2004]

§ 67.33 Individual.

An individual is a citizen if native-born, naturalized, or a derivative citizen of the United States, or otherwise qualifies as a United States citizen.

§ 67.35 Partnership.

A partnership meets citizenship requirements if all its general partners are citizens, and:

(a) For the purpose of obtaining a registry or recreational endorsement, at least 50 percent of the equity interest in the partnership is owned by citizens.

(b) For the purpose of obtaining a fishery endorsement, at least 75 percent of the equity interest in the partnership, at each tier of the partnership and in the aggregate, is owned by citizens.

(c) For the purpose of obtaining a coastwise endorsement at least 75 percent of the equity interest in the partnership is owned by citizens or the vessel qualifies under § 68.60 or § 68.105 of this chapter.

[CGD 94–008, 59 FR 49846, Sept. 30, 1994, as amended by USCG–1999–6095, 65 FR 76575, Dec. 7, 2000; USCG–2001–8825, 69 FR 5401, Feb. 4, 2004; USCG–2005–20258, 71 FR 61417, Oct. 18, 2006; USCG–2009–0702, 74 FR 49230, Sept. 25, 2009]

§ 67.36 Trust.

(a) For the purpose of obtaining a registry or recreational endorsement, a trust arrangement meets citizenship requirements if:

(1) Each of its trustees is a citizen; and

(2) Each beneficiary with an enforceable interest in the trust is a citizen.

(b) For the purpose of obtaining a fishery endorsement, a trust arrangement meets citizenship requirements if:

(1) It meets all the requirements of paragraph (a) of this section; and

(2) At least 75 percent of the equity interest in the trust, at each tier of the trust and in the aggregate, is owned by citizens.

(c) For the purpose of obtaining a coastwise endorsement a trust arrangement meets citizenship requirements if:

(1) It meets the requirements of paragraph (a) of this section and at least 75 percent of the equity interest in the trust is owned by citizens; or

(2) It meets the requirements of § 68.60 or § 68.105 of this chapter.

[CGD 94–008, 59 FR 49846. Sept. 30, 1994, as amended by USCG–1999–6095, 65 FR 76576, Dec. 7, 2000; USCG–2001–8825, 69 FR 5401, Feb. 4, 2004; USCG–2005–20258, 71 FR 61417, Oct. 18, 2006; USCG–2009–0702, 74 FR 49230, Sept. 25, 2009]

§ 67.37 Association or joint venture.

(a) An association meets citizenship requirements if each of its members is a citizen.

(b) A joint venture meets citizenship requirements if each of its members is a citizen.

[USCG–1999–6095, 65 FR 76576, Dec. 7, 2000]

§ 67.39 Corporation.

(a) For the purpose of obtaining a registry or a recreational endorsement, a corporation meets citizenship requirements if:

(1) It is incorporated under the laws of the United States or of a State;

(2) Its chief executive officer, by whatever title, is a citizen;

(3) Its chairman of the board of directors is a citizen; and

(4) No more of its directors are non-citizens than a minority of the number necessary to constitute a quorum.

(b) For the purpose of obtaining a fishery endorsement, a corporation meets citizenship requirements if:

(1) It meets all the requirements of paragraph (a) of this section; and

(2) At least 75 percent of the stock interest in the corporation, at each tier of the corporation and in the aggregate, is owned by citizens.

§ 67.41

(c) For the purpose of obtaining a coastwise endorsement a corporation meets citizenship requirements if:
(1) It meets the requirements of paragraph (a) of this section and at least 75 percent of the stock interest in the corporation is owned by citizens; or
(2) It meets the requirements of § 68.60 or § 68.105 of this chapter.

(d) A corporation which does not meet the stock interest requirement of paragraph (c) of this section may qualify for limited coastwise trading privileges by meeting the requirements of part 68 of this chapter.

[CGD 89–007, CGD 89–007a, 58 FR 60266, Nov. 15, 1993, as amended by CGD 94–008, 59 FR 49847, Sept. 30, 1994; USCG–1999–6095, 65 FR 76576, Dec. 7, 2000; USCG–2001–8825, 69 FR 5401, Feb. 4, 2004; USCG–2005–20258, 71 FR 61417, Oct. 18, 2006; USCG–2009–0702, 74 FR 49230, Sept. 25, 2009]

§ 67.41 Governmental entity.

A governmental entity is a citizen for the purpose of obtaining a vessel document if it is an entity of the Federal Government of the United States or of the government of a State as defined in § 67.3.

§ 67.43 Evidence of citizenship.

When received by the Coast Guard, a properly completed original Application for Initial Issue, Exchange, or Replacement of Certificate of Documentation; or Redocumentation (form CG–1258) establishes a rebuttable presumption that the applicant is a United States citizen.

[CGD 89–007, CGD 89–007a, 58 FR 60266, Nov. 15, 1993; 58 FR 65131, Dec. 13, 1993]

§ 67.47 Requirement for Maritime Administration approval.

(a) The following transactions, among others, require approval of the Maritime Administration in accordance with 46 CFR part 221:
(1) Placement of the vessel under foreign registry;
(2) Operation of the vessel under the authority of a foreign country; and
(3) Sale or transfer of an interest in or control of the vessel from a citizen, as defined in section 2 of the Shipping Act, 1916 (46 U.S.C. app. 802), to a person not a citizen within the meaning of section 2 of that act.

(b) A Certificate of Documentation may not be issued for a vessel which subsequent to the last issuance of a Certificate of Documentation has undergone any transaction listed in paragraph (a) of this section, even if the owner meets the citizenship requirements of this subpart, unless evidence is provided that the Maritime Administration approved the transaction.

(c) The restriction imposed by paragraph (b) of this section does not apply to a vessel identified in § 67.11(b).

Subpart D—Title Requirements for Vessel Documentation

§ 67.50 Requirement for title evidence.

The owner of a vessel must present title evidence in accordance with one of the methods specified in this subpart:

(a) When application is made for a coastwise endorsement for a vessel which has not previously been qualified for such endorsement;
(b) For initial documentation of a vessel;
(c) When the ownership of a documented vessel changes in whole or in part;
(d) When the general partners of a partnership owning a documented vessel change by addition, deletion, or substitution, without dissolution of the partnership; or
(e) When a vessel which has been deleted from documentation is returned to documentation and there has been an intervening change in ownership.

[CGD 89–007, CGD 89–007a, 58 FR 60266, Nov. 15, 1993, as amended by USCG–2009–0702, 74 FR 49230, Sept. 25, 2009]

§ 67.53 Methods of establishing title.

Title to a vessel may be established through one of the following methods:

(a) *Simplified method without evidence of build.* The owner must produce a copy of the last registration of the vessel (State, Federal, or foreign) and evidence which establishes chain of title from that registration to the present owner.

(b) *Simplified method with evidence of build.* The owner must produce a copy of the last registration of the vessel

(State, Federal, or foreign) and evidence which establishes chain of title from that registration to the present owner along with evidence of the facts of build in accordance with subpart F of this part.

(c) *Complete chain of title, without evidence of citizenship for each entity in that chain of title.* The owner must provide evidence which establishes:

(1) The facts of build in accordance with subpart F of this part; and

(2) A complete chain of title for the vessel from the person for whom the vessel was built to the present owner.

(d) *Complete chain of title, with evidence of citizenship for each entity in that chain of title.* The owner must provide evidence which establishes:

(1) The facts of build in accordance with subpart F of this part; and

(2) A complete chain of title for the vessel from the person for whom the vessel was built to the present owner, accompanied by competent and persuasive evidence establishing the citizenship of each entity in the chain of title.

§ 67.55 Requirement for removal from foreign registry.

The owner of a vessel must present evidence of removal of the vessel from foreign registry whenever:

(a) The owner applies for initial documentation of a vessel that has at any time been registered under the laws of a foreign country; or

(b) The owner applies for reentry into documentation of a vessel that had been registered under the laws of a foreign country since it was last documented under the laws of the United States.

§ 67.57 Extent of title evidence required for initial documentation.

(a) Vessels never registered under any system:

(1) Where a coastwise endorsement is sought, the only title evidence required for a vessel being documented by the owner for whom it was built is the certification of the builder (form CG–1261) described in § 67.99. Any other applicant must present title evidence in accordance with § 67.53(d).

(2) Where a fishery endorsement is sought, the only title evidence required for a vessel being documented by the owner for whom it was built is the certification of the builder (form CG–1261) described in § 67.99. Any other applicant must present title evidence in accordance with either paragraph (c) or (d) of § 67.53.

(3) Where a registry or recreational endorsement is sought, the only title evidence required for a vessel being documented by the first owner of the vessel is the certification of the builder (form CG–1261) described in § 67.99, or a Manufacturer's Certificate of Origin. Any other applicant must also present title evidence in accordance with either paragraph (c)(2) or (d)(2) of § 67.53.

NOTE: Manufacturer's Certificates of Origin are sometimes used as shipping documents for vessels, and may recite as the first owner a person other than the person for which the vessel was built. Therefore, a chain of title which begins with a Certificate of Origin will be deemed incomplete.

(b) Vessels previously registered under the laws of a State or a foreign government:

(1) Where a coastwise endorsement is sought, title evidence must be presented in accordance with § 67.53(d).

(2) Where a fishery endorsement is sought, title evidence must be presented in accordance with paragraph (b), (c), or (d) of § 67.53.

(3) Where a registry or recreational endorsement is sought, title evidence must be presented in accordance with paragraph (a), (b), (c), or (d) of § 67.53.

[CGD 89–007, CGD 89–007a, 58 FR 60266, Nov. 15, 1993, as amended by USCG–2009–0702, 74 FR 49230, Sept. 25, 2009]

§ 67.59 Extent of title evidence required for change in ownership of a documented vessel.

When the ownership of a documented vessel changes, in whole or in part, the applicant for documentation must present:

(a) Title evidence in accordance with subpart E of this part to reflect all ownership changes subsequent to the last issuance of a Certificate of Documentation; and

(b) Where a registry, fishery, or recreational endorsement is sought, evidence of the citizenship of all owners subsequent to the last owner for whom the vessel was documented except for a vessel:

§67.61

(1) Identified in §67.11(b); or

(2) For which the Maritime Administration has granted approval for transfer or sale under 46 CFR part 221.

(c) Where a coastwise endorsement is sought, evidence establishing the citizenship of all owners subsequent to the last owner for whom the vessel was documented with a coastwise endorsement, if such evidence is not already on file with the Coast Guard. If the vessel has never been documented with a coastwise endorsement, evidence must be presented to establish the citizenship of each owner of the vessel for whom such evidence is not already on file with the Coast Guard.

[CGD 89–007, CGD 89–007a, 58 FR 60266, Nov. 15, 1993, as amended by USCG–2009–0702, 74 FR 49230, Sept. 25, 2009]

§67.61 Extent of title evidence required for vessels returning to documentation.

(a) When the owner of a vessel which has been deleted from documentation applies to have the vessel returned to documentation, the owner must, except as provided in paragraphs (b) and (c) of this section, provide evidence establishing the complete chain of title from the last owner under documentation, and citizenship evidence for all owners in that chain of title.

(b) When a vessel is returned to documentation after having been under foreign registry, the owner must provide a copy of the last foreign registry, the evidence of removal from foreign registry required by §67.55, and evidence establishing the complete chain of title from the last owner under foreign registry. No citizenship evidence need be provided for owners in that chain of title.

(c) The owner of a vessel identified in §67.11(b) or for which the Maritime Administration has granted approval for transfer or sale, either by written order or by general approval in 46 CFR part 221, and which was under a State or Federal registration or titling system, must provide a copy of the last registration or title, the evidence of removal from foreign registry required by §67.55, if applicable, and evidence establishing the complete chain of title from the last owner under such registry or title. No citizenship evidence need be provided for owners in that chain of title.

NOTE: Although vessels returned to documentation without a complete chain of title are not eligible for a coastwise endorsement, this does not preclude such an endorsement if the chain of title, with citizenship evidence, is completed at a later date.

[CGD 89–007, CGD 89–007a, 58 FR 60266, Nov. 15, 1993, as amended by USCG–2009–0702, 74 FR 49230, Sept. 25, 2009]

§67.63 Extent of title evidence required for captured, forfeited, special legislation, and wrecked vessels.

(a) In the case of a captured or forfeited vessel, the owner must provide evidence establishing the chain of title from the judicial decree of capture or decree of forfeiture, or the evidence of administrative forfeiture described in §67.131(b). Citizenship evidence for all owners in the chain of title is required only if a coastwise endorsement is sought.

(b) In the case of a vessel which is the subject of special legislation or a wrecked vessel, the owner must provide:

(1) For initial documentation of a vessel or return to documentation of a vessel deleted from documentation, a copy of the last Federal, State, or foreign registration, the evidence of removal from foreign registry required by §67.55, if applicable, and evidence establishing the chain of title from the last registration. If a coastwise endorsement is sought, the owner must present citizenship evidence for all owners in the chain of title from the grant of special legislation or the determination by the Director, National Vessel Documentation Center that the vessel is eligible for documentation under 46 U.S.C. app. 14.

(2) For a documented vessel, the title evidence reflecting all ownership changes subsequent to the last documented owner of record. In addition, unless the vessel qualifies for exemption under §67.11(b) or the vessel is the

subject of Maritime Administration approval for unrestricted transfer, citizenship evidence must be presented for all owners in that chain of title.

[CGD 89–007, CGD 89–007a, 58 FR 60266, Nov. 15, 1993, 58 FR 65131, Dec. 13, 1993, as amended by CGD 95–014, 60 FR 31604, June 15, 1995; USCG–1998–4442, 63 FR 52191, Sept. 30, 1998; USCG–2009–0702, 74 FR 49230, Sept. 25, 2009]

Subpart E—Acceptable Title Evidence; Waiver

§ 67.70 Original owner.

The builder's certification described in § 67.99 serves as evidence of the original owner's title to a vessel.

§ 67.73 Transfers prior to documentation.

A transfer of vessel title prior to documentation may be evidenced by:

(a) Completion of the transfer information on the reverse of the builder's certification on form CG–1261;

(b) Completion of the transfer information on the reverse of the Manufacturer's Certificate of Origin; or

(c) A bill of sale which meets the criteria for filing and recording set forth in subpart P of this part.

§ 67.75 Transfers by sale or donation subsequent to documentation.

(a) Except as otherwise provided in this subpart, transfers of vessel title must be evidenced by a bill of sale which meets the criteria for filing and recording set forth in subpart P of this part. Except as otherwise provided in subpart O of this part, each bill of sale must be accompanied by a declaration of citizenship from the new owner, executed on the appropriate Maritime Administration form described in § 67.211.

(b) The bill of sale form used may be form CG–1340 or form CG–1356, as appropriate.

(c) An applicant for documentation who cannot produce required title evidence in the form of an instrument eligible for filing and recording in accordance with subpart P of this part may apply for a waiver of that requirement in accordance with the provisions of § 67.89.

§ 67.77 Passage of title by court action.

(a) When title to a vessel has passed by court action, that passage must be established by copies of the relevant court order(s) certified by an official of the court.

(b) When authority to transfer a vessel has been conferred by court action, that authority must be established by copies of the relevant court order(s) certified by an official of the court.

§ 67.79 Passage of title without court action following death of owner.

(a) When title to a vessel formerly owned in whole or in part by an individual now deceased passes without court action, an applicant for documentation must present:

(1) When title passes to a surviving joint tenant or tenants or to a tenant by the entirety, a copy of the death certificate, certified by an appropriate State official; or

(2) Where the laws of cognizant jurisdiction permit passage of title without court action, evidence of compliance with applicable State law.

(b) Passage of title subsequent to devolutions such as those described in paragraph (a) of this section, must be established in accordance with the remainder of this subpart.

§ 67.81 Passage of title in conjunction with a corporate merger or similar transaction.

When the title to a vessel has passed as the result of a corporate merger or similar transaction wherein the assets of one corporation have been transferred to another, the passage of title must be established by:

(a) Materials, such as a resolution of the board of directors or shareholders of the corporation which held title to the vessel before the transaction, which either unequivocally transfers all of the assets of the corporation or which specifically identifies the vessel as being among the assets transferred; and

(b) In jurisdictions where there is an official recognition of corporate mergers and similar transactions, a copy of such official recognition certified by the cognizant official of that jurisdiction.

§ 67.83 Passage of title by extra-judicial repossession and sale.

When title to a documented vessel has passed by reason of an extra-judicial repossession and sale, such passage must be established by:

(a) A copy of the instrument under which foreclosure was made;

(b) An affidavit from the foreclosing party setting forth the reasons for foreclosure, the chronology of foreclosure, the statute(s) under which foreclosure was made, and the steps taken to comply with the relevant instrument and statute(s);

(c) Evidence of substantial compliance with the relevant instrument and statute(s); and

(d) A bill of sale which meets the criteria for filing and recording set forth in subpart P of this part from the foreclosing party as agent for the defaulting owner(s).

§ 67.85 Change in general partners of partnership.

When the general partners of a partnership owning a documented vessel change by addition, deletion, or substitution without dissolution of the partnership, the change must be established by a written statement from a surviving general partner detailing the nature of the change.

§ 67.87 Change of legal name of owner.

(a) When the name of a corporation which owns a documented vessel changes, the corporation must present certification from the appropriate governmental agency evidencing registration of the name change.

(b) When the name of an individual who owns a documented vessel changes for any reason, competent and persuasive evidence establishing the change must be provided.

§ 67.89 Waiver of production of a bill of sale eligible for filing and recording.

(a) When the evidence of title passage required by this subpart is a bill of sale which meets the criteria for filing and recording set forth in subpart P of this part, and the applicant is unable to produce a bill of sale meeting those criteria, the applicant may request that the Director, National Vessel Documentation Center waive that requirement.

(b) No waiver of the requirement to produce a bill of sale eligible for filing and recording may be granted unless the applicant provides:

(1) A written statement detailing the reasons why an instrument meeting the filing and recording criteria of this part cannot be obtained; and

(2) Competent and persuasive evidence of the passage of title.

[CGD 89–007, CGD 89–007a, 58 FR 60266, Nov. 15, 1993; 58 FR 65131, Dec. 13, 1993, as amended by CGD 95–014, 60 FR 31604, June 15, 1995; USCG–1998–4442, 63 FR 52191, Sept. 30, 1998]

§ 67.91 Passage of title pursuant to operation of State law.

When title to a documented vessel has passed by operation of State law for reasons other than those specified in this subpart, such passage must be established by:

(a) A copy of the statute permitting transfer of title to the vessel and setting forth procedures to be followed in disposing of the vessel;

(b) An affidavit from the party acting against the vessel, setting forth the basis for selling the vessel, and the steps taken to comply with the requirements of the statute under which title passes;

(c) Evidence of substantial compliance with the relevant statute(s); and

(d) A bill of sale which meets the criteria for filing and recording set forth in subpart P of this part from the acting party as agent for the owner(s) of record.

NOTE: State law authorizing a marina to dispose of abandoned vessels is an example of passage of title by operation of law contemplated by § 67.91.

Subpart F—Build Requirements for Vessel Documentation

§ 67.95 Requirement for determination.

Evidence that a vessel was built in the United States must be on file for any vessel for which a coastwise or fishery endorsement is sought, unless the vessel is otherwise qualified for

Coast Guard, Dept. of Homeland Security §67.111

those endorsements under subpart J of this part.

[CGD 89–007, CGD 89–007a, 58 FR 60266, Nov. 15, 1993, as amended by USCG–2009–0702, 74 FR 49230, Sept. 25, 2009]

§67.97 United States built.

To be considered built in the United States a vessel must meet both of the following criteria:

(a) All major components of its hull and superstructure are fabricated in the United States; and

(b) The vessel is assembled entirely in the United States.

§67.99 Evidence of build.

(a) Evidence of the facts of build may be either a completed original form CG–1261, or other original document containing the same information, executed by a person having personal knowledge of the facts of build because that person:

(1) Constructed the vessel;

(2) Supervised the actual construction of the vessel; or

(3) Is an officer or employee of the company which built the vessel and has examined the records of the company concerning the facts of build of the vessel.

(b) A vessel owner applying for documentation must file a separate certificate from each builder involved in the construction of the vessel.

(c) A Manufacturer's Certificate of Origin is not evidence of the facts of build.

§67.101 Waiver of evidence of build.

(a) A vessel owner applying for documentation unable to obtain the evidence of build required by §67.99 may apply for a waiver of that requirement to the Director, National Vessel Documentation Center.

(b) No waiver of the requirement in §67.99 to produce evidence of build may be granted unless the applicant provides:

(1) A written request for the waiver, explaining why the evidence required by §67.99 cannot be furnished; and

(2) Competent and persuasive evidence of the facts of build.

[CGD 89–007, CGD 89–007a, 58 FR 60266, Nov. 15, 1993, 58 FR 65131, Dec. 13, 1993, as amended by CGD 95–014, 60 FR 31604, June 15, 1995; USCG–1998–4442, 63 FR 52190, Sept. 30, 1998]

Subpart G—Tonnage and Dimension Requirements for Vessel Documentation

§67.105 Requirement for determination.

The gross and net tonnage and dimensions of a vessel must be determined:

(a) For initial documentation;

(b) Whenever there is a change in the gross or net tonnage or dimensions of a documented vessel; or

(c) When the gross or net tonnage of a vessel returning to documentation has changed since the vessel was last documented.

§67.107 System of measurement; evidence.

(a) The gross and net tonnage and dimensions of a vessel for purposes of this part are determined in accordance with 46 CFR part 69.

(b) A certificate of measurement issued by an authorized official is the only acceptable evidence of the gross and net tonnage of a vessel measured in accordance with subpart B, C, or D of 46 CFR part 69. A certificate of measurement is not issued for vessels measured under subpart E of 46 CFR part 69 since the gross and net tonnage are determined as part of the documentation process.

[CGD 89–007, CGD 89–007a, 58 FR 60266, Nov. 15, 1003, as amended by USCG–2001–10224, 66 FR 48620, Sept. 21, 2001]

Subpart H—Assignments and Designations Required for Vessel Documentation

§67.111 Assignment of official number.

(a) The owner of a vessel must submit an Application for Initial Issue, Exchange, or Replacement of Certificate of Documentation; or Redocumentation (form CG–1258) to the Director, National Vessel Documentation

§ 67.113

Center, to apply for an official number for the vessel when:

(1) Application is made for initial documentation of the vessel; or

(2) An existing vessel has been severed, with two or more vessels resulting. In this case, the official number of the original vessel is retired and the owner of each resulting vessel must apply for designation of a new official number.

(b) Upon receipt of form CG-1258, the Director, National Vessel Documentation Center will have an official number assigned to the vessel and furnish it to the vessel owner.

[CGD 89-007, CGD 89-007a, 58 FR 60266, Nov. 15, 1993, 58 FR 65131, Dec. 13, 1993, as amended by CGD 95-014, 60 FR 31604, June 15, 1995; USCG-1998-4442, 63 FR 52190, Sept. 30, 1998]

§ 67.113 Managing owner designation; address; requirement to report change of address.

The owner of each vessel must designate a managing owner on the Application for Initial Issue, Exchange, or Replacement of Certificate of Documentation; or Redocumentation (CG-1258).

(a) The managing owner of a vessel owned by one person is the owner of the vessel.

(b) The managing owner of a vessel owned by more than one person must be one of the owners. The person designated as managing owner must have an address in the United States except where no owner of the vessel has an address in the United States.

(c) The managing owner of a vessel owned in a trust arrangement must be one of the trustees.

(d) The address of the managing owner must be as follows:

(1) For an individual, any residence of the managing owner.

(2) For a partnership, its address:

(i) In the State under whose laws it is organized; or

(ii) Of its principal place of business.

(3) For a corporation, its address:

(i) For service of process within the State of incorporation; or

(ii) Of its principal place of business.

(e) Whenever the address of the managing owner changes, the managing owner shall notify the Director, National Vessel Documentation Center within 10 days.

[CGD 89-007, CGD 89-007a, 58 FR 60266, Nov. 15, 1993; 58 FR 65131, Dec. 13, 1993, as amended by CGD 95-014, 60 FR 31604, June 15, 1995; USCG-1998-4442, 63 FR 52190, Sept. 30, 1998]

§ 67.117 Vessel name designation.

(a) The owner of a vessel must designate a name for the vessel on the Application for Initial Issue, Exchange, or Replacement of Certificate of Documentation; or Redocumentation (form CG-1258) submitted to the Director, National Vessel Documentation Center:

(1) Upon application for initial documentation of the vessel; or

(2) When the owner elects to change the name of the vessel.

(b) The name designated:

(1) Must be composed of letters of the Latin alphabet or Arabic or Roman numerals;

(2) May not be identical, actually or phonetically, to any word or words used to solicit assistance at sea; and

(3) May not contain nor be phonetically identical to obscene, indecent, or profane language, or to racial or ethnic epithets.

(c) The name of a documented vessel may not be changed without the prior approval of the Director, National Vessel Documentation Center.

(d) Until such time as the owner of a vessel elects to change the name of a vessel, the provisions of paragraph (b) of this section do not apply to vessels validly documented before January 1, 1994.

[CGD 89-007, CGD 89-007a, 58 FR 60266, Nov. 15, 1993; 58 FR 65131, Dec. 13, 1993, as amended by CGD 95-014, 60 FR 31604, June 15, 1995; USCG-1998-4442, 63 FR 52191, Sept. 30, 1998]

§ 67.119 Hailing port designation.

(a) Upon application for any Certificate of Documentation in accordance with subpart K of this part, the owner of a vessel must designate a hailing port to be marked upon the vessel.

(b) The hailing port must be a place in the United States included in the U.S. Department of Commerce's Federal Information Processing Standards Publication 55DC.

(c) The hailing port must include the State, territory, or possession in which it is located.

(d) The Director, National Vessel Documentation Center has final authority to settle disputes as to the propriety of the hailing port designated.

(e) Until such time as the vessel owner elects to designate a new hailing port, the provisions of paragraph (c) of this section do not apply to vessels which were issued a Certificate of Documentation before July 1, 1982.

[CGD 89-007, CGD 89-007a, 58 FR 60266, Nov. 15, 1993, as amended by CGD 95-014, 60 FR 31604, June 15, 1995; USCG-1998-4442, 63 FR 52191, Sept. 30, 1998]

Subpart I—Marking Requirements for Vessel Documentation

§ 67.120 General requirement.

No Certificate of Documentation issued under this part will be deemed valid for operation of the vessel until the vessel is marked in accordance with this subpart.

§ 67.121 Official number marking requirement.

The official number of the vessel, preceded by the abbreviation "NO." must be marked in block-type Arabic numerals not less than three inches in height on some clearly visible interior structural part of the hull. The number must be permanently affixed to the vessel so that alteration, removal, or replacement would be obvious. If the official number is on a separate plate, the plate must be fastened in such a manner that its removal would normally cause some scarring of or damage to the surrounding hull area.

§ 67.123 Name and hailing port marking requirements.

(a) For vessels other than those covered in paragraphs (b) and (c) of this section, the name of the vessel must be marked on some clearly visible exterior part of the port and starboard bow and the stern of the vessel. The hailing port of the vessel must be marked on some clearly visible exterior part of the stern of the vessel.

(b) *Vessels with square bow.* For vessels having a square bow, the name of the vessel must be marked on some clearly visible exterior part of the bow in a manner to avoid obliteration. The name and hailing port must be marked on some clearly visible exterior part of the stern.

(c) *Recreational vessels.* For vessels documented exclusively for recreation, the name and hailing port must be marked together on some clearly visible exterior part of the hull.

(d) The markings required by paragraphs (a), (b), and (c) of this section, which may be made by the use of any means and materials which result in durable markings, must be made in clearly legible letters of the Latin alphabet or Arabic or Roman numerals not less than four inches in height.

§ 67.125 Disputes.

The OCMI for the zone in which the vessel is principally operated has final authority in any disputes concerning the permanence, durability, legibility, or placement of a vessel's markings.

Subpart J—Application for Special Qualifications for Vessel Documentation

§ 67.130 Submission of applications.

All applications made under this subpart and all subsequent filings to effect documentation, except as provided in § 67.133(b), must be submitted to the National Vessel Documentation Center.

[CGD 95-014, 60 FR 31604, June 15, 1995]

§ 67.131 Forfeited vessels.

In addition to any other submissions required by this part, the owner of a forfeited vessel applying for a Certificate of Documentation for that vessel must submit the following:

(a) Where the vessel has been adjudged forfeit, or the proceeds of the sale of the vessel have been adjudged forfeit to the Federal Government of the United States by a Federal District Court, a copy of the court order certified by an official of the court;

(b) Where the vessel was forfeited to the Federal Government of the United States under an administrative forfeiture action, an affidavit from an officer of the agency which performed the forfeiture who has personal knowledge of the particulars of the vessel's

§ 67.132

forfeiture or a Declaration of Forfeiture issued by the agency which performed the forfeiture.

§ 67.132 Special legislation.

(a) Vessels not otherwise entitled to be operated in the coastwise trade or in the fisheries may obtain these privileges as a result of special legislation by the Congress of the United States.

(b) In addition to any other submissions required by this part, the owner of a vessel which is entitled to engage in a specified trade because it is the subject of special legislation must include a copy of the legislation to establish the entitlement.

[CGD 89–007, CGD 89–007a, 58 FR 60266, Nov. 15, 1993, as amended by USCG–2009–0702, 74 FR 49230, Sept. 25, 2009]

§ 67.133 Wrecked vessels.

(a) A vessel owner requesting a determination that the vessel is wrecked within the meaning of 46 U.S.C. app. 14 must submit the following to the Director, National Vessel Documentation Center:

(1) Competent and persuasive evidence of the occasion and location of the casualty. Coast Guard situation or investigation reports are acceptable as casualty evidence. Other competent and persuasive evidence may be accepted in the discretion of the Director, National Vessel Documentation Center.

(2) A writing setting forth the physical location of the vessel, containing a guarantee that the requesting party assumes full responsibility for all costs, liabilities, and other expenses that arise in conjunction with the services performed by the board of appraisers, and stating that at the time of documentation the vessel will be owned by a citizen of the United States.

(b) In addition to other submissions required by this part, a vessel owner applying for a Certificate of Documentation for a vessel accorded privileges by the Wrecked Vessel Statute (46 U.S.C. app. 14) must include a copy of the determination of the Director, National Vessel Documentation Center that the vessel qualifies for documentation under the statute.

NOTE: The determination of the appraised salved value must be made by a board of three appraisers appointed by the Director, National Vessel Documentation Center. The board must determine that the repairs made upon the vessel are equal to three times the appraised salvage value. The determination of the appraised salvage value will include consideration of the fact that if the vessel is found in compliance with the Wrecked Vessel Statute it will attain coastwise and fishery privileges. The cost of the board must be borne by the applicant.

[CGD 89–007, CGD 89–007a, 58 FR 60266, Nov. 15, 1993; 58 FR 65131, Dec. 13, 1993, as amended by CGD 95–014, 60 FR 31604, June 15, 1995; USCG–1998–4442, 63 FR 52191, Sept. 30, 1998]

§ 67.134 Captured vessels.

In addition to other submissions required by this part, a vessel owner applying for a Certificate of Documentation for a vessel which qualifies as a captured vessel must include a copy of the court order stating that the vessel was lawfully captured and condemned as a prize.

Subpart K—Application for Documentation, Exchange or Replacement of Certificate of Documentation, or Return to Documentation; Mortgagee Consent; Validation

§ 67.141 Application procedure; all cases.

The owner of a vessel applying for an initial Certificate of Documentation, exchange or replacement of a Certificate of Documentation, or return of a vessel to documentation after deletion from documentation must:

(a) Submit the following to the National Vessel Documentation Center:

(1) Application for Initial Issue, Exchange, or Replacement of Certificate of Documentation; or Redocumentation (form CG–1258);

(2) Title evidence, if applicable;

(3) Mortgagee consent on form CG–4593, if applicable; and

(4) If the application is for replacement of a mutilated document or exchange of documentation, the outstanding Certificate of Documentation.

(b) Each vessel 100 feet and greater in length applying for a fishery endorsement must meet the requirements of 46 CFR part 356 and must submit materials required in paragraph (a) of this section.

(c) Upon receipt of the Certification of Documentation and prior to operation of the vessel, ensure that the vessel is marked in accordance with the requirements set forth in subpart I of this part.

[CGD 89-007, CGD 89-007a, 58 FR 60266, Nov. 15, 1993; 58 FR 65131, Dec. 13, 1993, as amended by CGD 95-014, 60 FR 31604, June 15, 1995; USCG-1999-6095, 65 FR 76576, Dec. 7, 2000]

§ 67.142 Penalties.

(a) An owner or operator of a vessel with a fishery endorsement who violates chapter 121 of title 46, U.S. Code or any regulation issued thereunder is liable to the United States Government for a civil penalty of not more than $10,000. Each day of a continuing violation is a separate violation.

(b) A fishing vessel and its equipment are liable to seizure and forfeiture to the United States Government—

(1) When the owner of the fishing vessel, or the representative or agent of the owner, knowingly falsifies applicable information or knowingly conceals a material fact during the application process for or application process to renew a fishery endorsement of the vessel;

(2) When the owner of the fishing vessel, or the representative or agent of the owner, knowingly and fraudulently uses a vessel's certificate of documentation;

(3) When the fishing vessel engages in fishing [as such term is defined in section 3 of the Magnuson-Stevens Fishery Conservation and Management Act (16 U.S.C. 1802)] within the Exclusive Economic Zone after its fishery endorsement has been denied or revoked;

(4) When a vessel is employed in a trade without an appropriate trade endorsement;

(5) When a documented vessel with only a recreational endorsement operates as a fishing vessel; or

(6) When a vessel with a fishery endorsement is commanded by a person who is not a citizen of the United States.

(c) In addition to penalties under paragraphs (a) and (b) of this section, the owner of a vessel with a fishery endorsement is liable to the United States Government for a civil penalty of up to $100,000 for each day in which the vessel has engaged in fishing within the Exclusive Economic Zone, if the owner of the fishing vessel, or the representative or agent of the owner, knowingly falsifies applicable information or knowingly conceals a material fact during the application process for or application process to renew a fishery endorsement of the vessel.

[USCG-1999-6095, 65 FR 76576, Dec. 7, 2000]

§ 67.143 Restriction on withdrawal of application.

A vessel owner making application pursuant to § 67.141 may not withdraw that application without mortgagee consent if a mortgage has been filed against the vessel. Consent of the mortgagee is evidenced by filing a properly completed original Application, Consent, and Approval for Withdrawal of Application for Documentation or Exchange of Certificate of Documentation (form CG-4593).

[CGD 89-007, CGD 89-007a, 58 FR 60266, Nov. 15, 1993; 58 FR 65131, Dec. 13, 1993]

§ 67.145 Restrictions on exchange; requirement and procedure for mortgagee consent.

(a) A Certificate of Documentation issued to a vessel which is the subject of an outstanding mortgage recorded pursuant to subpart Q of this part or predecessor regulations, may not be exchanged for a cause arising under §§ 67.167(b) (1) through (5) or 67.167(c) (1) through (8) without the consent of the mortgagee, except as provided in paragraph (b) of this section.

(b) The provisions of paragraph (a) of this section do not apply to a vessel which is subject only to a mortgage filed or recorded before January 1, 1989, which had not attained preferred status as of that date.

(c) When the owner of a vessel applies for a Certificate of Documentation and the consent of the mortgagee is required under paragraph (a) of this section, the applicant must submit a properly completed original Application, Consent, and Approval for Withdrawal of Application for Documentation or

§ 67.149

Exchange of Certificate of Documentation (form CG–4593) signed by or on behalf of the mortgagee to the National Vessel Documentation Center.

[CGD 89–007, CGD 89–007a, 58 FR 60266, Nov. 15, 1993, as amended by CGD 94–008, 59 FR 49847, Sept. 30, 1994; CGD 95–014, 60 FR 31604, June 15, 1995]

§ 67.149 Exchange of Certificate of Documentation; vessel at sea.

(a) When exchange of a Certificate of Documentation issued to a vessel is required pursuant to subpart L of this part and the vessel is at sea, the owner may affect the exchange while the vessel is still at sea by:

(1) Complying with the requirements of § 67.141; and

(2) complying with the requirements of § 67.145, if applicable.

NOTE: A Certificate of Documentation is issued upon compliance with the applicable requirements, however, the requirement to mark the vessel with its new name or hailing port in accordance with subpart I of this part, if applicable, is waived until the vessel reaches its first port of call, wherever that may be.

(b) The documentation officer prepares a new Certificate of Documentation and forwards it for delivery to the vessel's next port of call. If the port of call is in the United States, the Certificate is forwarded to the nearest U.S. Coast Guard Sector Office. If the port of call is in a foreign country, the Certificate is forwarded to the nearest American Consulate. The new Certificate is delivered only upon surrender of the old Certificate, which is then forwarded to the National Vessel Documentation Center.

[CGD 89–007, CGD 89–007a, 58 FR 60266, Nov. 15, 1993, as amended by CGD 95–014, 60 FR 31604, June 15, 1995; USCG–2006–25556, 72 FR 36330, July 2, 2007]

§ 67.151 Replacement of Certificate of Documentation; special procedure for wrongfully withheld document.

When the owner of a documented vessel alleges that the Certificate of Documentation for that vessel is being wrongfully withheld by any person the owner must:

(a) Submit to the Director, National Vessel Documentation Center, a statement setting forth the reasons for the allegation; and

(b) Upon the Director, National Vessel Documentation Center that the Certificate is being wrongfully withheld, apply for replacement of the Certificate in accordance with the requirements of § 67.141.

[CGD 89–007, CGD 89–007a, 58 FR 60266, Nov. 15, 1993; 58 FR 65131, Dec. 13, 1993, as amended by CGD 95–014, 60 FR 31604, June 15, 1995; USCG–1998–4442, 63 FR 52191, Sept. 30, 1998]

Subpart L—Validity of Certificates of Documentation; Renewal of Endorsement; Requirement for Exchange, Replacement, Deletion, Cancellation

§ 67.161 Validity of Certificate of Documentation.

(a) Notwithstanding any other provision of this subpart, except as provided in paragraph (b) of this section, a Certificate of Documentation but no trade endorsement thereon, issued to a vessel which is the subject of an outstanding mortgage filed or recorded in accordance with subpart Q of this part or any predecessor regulations, remains valid for purposes of:

(1) 46 U.S.C. chapter 125;

(2) 46 U.S.C. chapter 313 for an instrument filed or recorded before the date of invalidation, and an assignment or a notice of claim of lien filed after that date;

(3) Sections 9 and 37(b) of the Shipping Act, 1916 (46 U.S.C. app. 808, 835(b)); and

(4) Section 902 of the Merchant Marine Act, 1936 (46 U.S.C. app. 1242).

(b) The provisions of paragraph (a) of this section do not apply to a vessel which is subject only to a mortgage filed or recorded before January 1, 1989, which had not attained preferred status as of that date.

§ 67.163 Renewal of endorsement.

(a) *Requirement for renewal of endorsement.* Endorsements on Certificates of Documentation are valid for one year. Prior to the expiration of that year, the owner of a vessel which is not exempt from the requirement for documentation under paragraph (c) of § 67.9

Coast Guard, Dept. of Homeland Security §67.167

must apply for renewal of the endorsement(s) by complying with paragraph (b) of this section. The owner of a vessel exempt from the requirement for documentation under paragraph (c) of §67.9 must either:

(1) Apply for renewal of the endorsement by complying with paragraph (b) of this section; or

(2) Place the Certificate of Documentation on deposit in accordance with §67.165.

(b) *Renewal application.* The owner of a vessel must apply for renewal of each endorsement by executing an original Notice of Expiration (CG–1280) or Final Notice After Expiration (CG–1280–B) certifying that the information contained in the Certificate of Documentation and any endorsement(s) thereon remains accurate, and that the Certificate has not been lost, mutilated, or wrongfully withheld. The completed CG–1280 or CG–1280–B must be forwarded to the Director, National Vessel Documentation Center.

(c) *Requirement to affix decal.* The owner must affix the renewal decal to the Certificate of Documentation. The presence of a current renewal decal is evidence that the endorsement has been renewed.

NOTE: Renewal of endorsements on a Certificate of Documentation may be denied if the vessel owner is the subject of an outstanding civil penalty assessed by the Coast Guard.

[CGD 89–007, CGD 89–007a, 58 FR 60266, Nov. 15, 1993, as amended by CGD 95–014, 60 FR 31604, June 15, 1995; USCG–1998–4442, 63 FR 52191, Sept. 30, 1998]

§67.165 Deposit of Certificate of Documentation.

(a) *Option for deposit in lieu of renewal of endorsement.* In lieu of renewing the endorsement(s) in accordance with §67.163, the owner of a vessel which is exempt from the requirement for documentation under paragraph (c) of §67.9 may deposit the vessel's outstanding Certificate of Documentation with the National Vessel Documentation Center.

(b) *Reporting requirement.* The owner of a vessel whose Certificate is on deposit in accordance with paragraph (a) of this section must make a written report to the National Vessel Documentation Center when:

(1) Exchange of the Certificate is required upon the occurrence of one or more of the events described in §67.167 (b), (c), or (d); or

(2) The vessel is subject to deletion from the roll of actively documented vessels upon the occurrence of one or more of the events described in §67.171(a)(1) through (8).

(c) *Validity of document on deposit.* A Certificate of Documentation placed on deposit in accordance with paragraph (a) of this section is valid for the purposes of:

(1) 46 U.S.C. chapter 125;

(2) 46 U.S.C. chapter 313;

(3) Sections 9 and 37(b) of the Shipping Act, 1916 (46 U.S.C. app. 808, 835(b)); and

(4) Section 902 of the Merchant Marine Act, 1936 (46 U.S.C. app. 1242).

[CGD 89–007, CGD 89–007a, 58 FR 60266, Nov. 15, 1993; 58 FR 65131, Dec. 13, 1993, as amended by CGD 95–014, 60 FR 31604, June 15, 1995]

§67.167 Requirement for exchange of Certificate of Documentation.

(a) When application for exchange of the Certificate of Documentation is required upon the occurrence of one or more of the events described in paragraphs (b), (c), or (d) of this section, or the owner of the vessel chooses to apply for exchange of the Certificate pursuant to paragraph (e) of this section, the owner must send or deliver the Certificate to the National Vessel Documentation Center, and apply for an exchange of the Certificate in accordance with subpart K of this part.

(b) A Certificate of Documentation together with any endorsement(s) thereon becomes invalid immediately, except as provided in §67.161, when:

(1) The ownership of the vessel changes in whole or in part;

(2) The general partners of a partnership change by addition, deletion, or substitution;

(3) The State of incorporation of any corporate owner of the vessel changes;

(4) The name of the vessel changes;

(5) The hailing port of the vessel changes; or

(6) The vessel is placed under the command of a person who is not a citizen of the United States.

§ 67.169

(c) A Certificate of Documentation together with any endorsement(s) thereon becomes invalid immediately, except as provided in § 67.161 and in paragraph (f) of this section, if the vessel is not a sea, or upon the vessel's next arrival in port anywhere in the world if the vessel is at sea, when:

(1) The gross or net tonnages or dimensions of the vessel change;

(2) Any beneficiary with an enforceable interest in a trust arrangement owning a vessel changes by addition or substitution;

(3) The trustee of a trust arrangement owning a vessel changes by addition, substitution, or deletion;

(4) A tenant by the entirety owning any part of the vessel dies;

(5) The restrictions imposed on the vessel change by addition or substitution;

(6) The legal name of any owner of the vessel changes;

(7) A self-propelled vessel becomes non-self-propelled or a non-self-propelled vessel becomes self-propelled;

(8) The endorsements for the vessel change by addition, deletion, or substitution;

(9) A substantive or clerical error made by the issuing documentation officer is discovered; and

(10) For a vessel with a coastwise endorsement under 46 U.S.C. 12106(e), one of the events in § 68.80 or § 68.111 of this chapter occurs.

(d) Although a Certificate of Documentation and any endorsements thereon remain valid, the owner of a documented vessel must apply for exchange of the Certificate upon an election to designate a new managing owner of the vessel in accordance with § 67.113.

(e) Although a Certificate of Documentation and any endorsement(s) thereon remain valid, the owner may apply for exchange of the Certificate if:

(1) The restrictions imposed on the vessel change by deletion; or

(2) The vessel attains a special entitlement under subpart J of this part.

(f) A Certificate of Documentation which becomes invalid pursuant to paragraph (c) of this section remains valid for the purposes of filing a new mortgage or amendment, assignment, assumption, or subordination agreement for 30 days after the date it would otherwise have become invalid.

[CGD 89–007, CGD 89–007a, 58 FR 60266, Nov. 15, 1993; 58 FR 65131, Dec. 13, 1993, as amended by CGD 95–014, 60 FR 31604, June 15, 1995; USCG–2001–8825, 69 FR 5401, Feb. 4, 2004; USCG–2005–20258, 71 FR 61418, Oct. 18, 2006]

§ 67.169 Requirement for replacement of Certificate of Documentation.

(a) The owner of a documented vessel must make application in accordance with subpart K of this part for replacement of a Certificate of Documentation which is:

(1) Lost;

(2) Mutilated; or

(3) Wrongfully withheld from the vessel owner.

(b) When application for replacement of a Certificate of Documentation is required because the Certificate has been mutilated, the existing Certificate must be physically given up to the National Vessel Documentation Center.

[CGD 89–007, CGD 89–007a, 58 FR 60266, Nov. 15, 1993; 58 FR 65131, Dec. 13, 1993, as amended by CGD 95–014, 60 FR 31605, June 15, 1995]

§ 67.171 Deletion; requirement and procedure.

(a) A Certificate of Documentation together with any endorsement(s) thereon is invalid, except as provided in § 67.161, and the vessel is subject to deletion from the roll of actively documented vessels when:

(1) The vessel is placed under foreign flag;

(2) The vessel is sold or transferred in whole or in part to a person who is not a citizen of the United States within the meaning of subpart C of this part;

(3) Any owner of the vessel ceases to be a citizen of the United States within the meaning of subpart C of this part;

(4) The owner no longer elects to document the vessel;

(5) The vessel no longer measures at least five net tons;

(6) The vessel ceases to be capable of transportation by water;

(7) The owner fails to exchange the Certificate as required by § 67.167;

(8) The owner fails to maintain the markings required by subpart I of this part;

(9) The endorsements on the Certificate are revoked because the vessel

Coast Guard, Dept. of Homeland Security §67.175

owner is the subject of an outstanding civil penalty assessed by the Coast Guard; or

(10) The owner fails to:

(i) Renew the endorsement(s) as required by §67.163; or

(ii) Comply with the provisions of §67.165.

(b) Where a cause for deletion arises for any reason under paragraphs (a)(1) through (6) of this section, the owner must send or deliver the original Certificate of Documentation to the National Vessel Documentation Center together with a statement setting forth the reason(s) deletion is required.

(c) When a Certificate of Documentation is required to be deleted because the vessel has been placed under foreign flag or has been sold or transferred in whole or in part to a non-citizen of the United States, the owner of that vessel must comply with the requirements of paragraph (b) of this section, and file:

(1) Evidence of the sale or transfer, if any; and

(2) Evidence that the Maritime Administration has consented to the sale or transfer, except for vessels identified in §67.11(b) and vessels for which the Maritime Administration has granted approval for unrestricted sale or transfer pursuant to regulations set forth in 46 CFR part 221.

(d) A certificate evidencing deletion from U.S. documentation will be issued upon request of the vessel owner to the National Vessel Documentation Center upon compliance with the applicable requirements of this subpart.

[CGD 89–007, CGD 89–007a, 58 FR 60266, Nov. 15, 1993, as amended by CGD 94–008, 59 FR 49847, Sept. 30, 1994; CGD 95–014, 60 FR 31605, June 15, 1995]

§67.173 Cancellation; requirement and procedure.

A Certificate of Documentation issued to a vessel together with any endorsement(s) thereon is invalid, except as provided in §67.161, and subject to cancellation upon a determination by the Director, National Vessel Documentation Center that the issuance of the Certificate was improper for any reason. When a Certificate is subject to cancellation, the owner of the vessel upon being notified of such requirement must send or deliver the Certificate to a documentation officer at the National Vessel Documentation Center. The vessel owner may submit an application for exchange in accordance with subpart K of this part to correct the error giving rise to cancellation. If the vessel for which the Certificate was cancelled was previously documented, it remains documented under the previous Certificate of Documentation, unless deleted under the provisions of §67.171.

NOTE: Certificates of Documentation which have been canceled are retained at the National Vessel Documentation Center.

[CGD 89–007, CGD 89–007a, 58 FR 60266, Nov. 15, 1993; 58 FR 65131, Dec. 13, 1993, as amended by CGD 95–014, 60 FR 31605, June 15, 1995; USCG–1998–4442, 63 FR 52190, 52191, Sept. 30, 1998]

Subpart M—Miscellaneous Applications

§67.175 Application for new vessel determination.

(a) When a vessel has been constructed entirely of new materials, no application for a new vessel determination need be made under this section. Application for initial documentation must be made in accordance with subpart K of this part.

(b) When parts of an existing vessel have been used in the construction of a vessel and the owner wants a determination that the resulting vessel is new in accordance with this part, the owner must file with the Director, National Vessel Documentation Center;

(1) A builder's certification, as described in §67.99;

(2) A written statement describing the extent to which materials from the existing vessel were used in the construction and the extent to which those materials were torn down; and

(3) Accurate sketches or blueprints of the hull and superstructure which must identify, where practicable, components of the old vessel.

[CGD 89–007, CGD 89–007a, 58 FR 60266, Nov. 15, 1993; 58 FR 65131, Dec. 13, 1993, as amended by CGD 95–014, 60 FR 31605, June 15, 1995; USCG–1998–4442, 63 FR 52191, Sept. 30, 1998]

§ 67.177 Application for foreign rebuilding determination.

A vessel is deemed rebuilt foreign when any considerable part of its hull or superstructure is built upon or substantially altered outside of the United States. In determining whether a vessel is rebuilt foreign, the following parameters apply:

(a) Regardless of its material of construction, a vessel is deemed rebuilt when a major component of the hull or superstructure not built in the United States is added to the vessel.

(b) For a vessel of which the hull and superstructure is constructed of steel or aluminum—

(1) A vessel is deemed rebuilt when work performed on its hull or superstructure constitutes more than 10 percent of the vessel's steelweight, prior to the work, also known as discounted lightship weight.

(2) A vessel may be considered rebuilt when work performed on its hull or superstructure constitutes more than 7.5 percent but not more than 10 percent of the vessel's steelweight prior to the work.

(3) A vessel is not considered rebuilt when work performed on its hull or superstructure constitutes 7.5 percent or less of the vessel's steelweight prior to the work.

(c) For a vessel of which the hull and superstructure is constructed of material other than steel or aluminum—

(1) A vessel is deemed rebuilt when work performed on its hull or superstructure constitutes a quantum of work determined, to the maximum extent practicable, to be comparable to more than 10 percent of the vessel's steelweight prior to the work, calculated as if the vessel were wholly constructed of steel or aluminum.

(2) A vessel may be considered rebuilt when work performed on its hull or superstructure constitutes a quantum of work determined, to the maximum extent practicable, to be comparable to more than 7.5 percent but not more than 10 percent of the vessel's steelweight prior to the work, calculated as if the vessel were wholly constructed of steel or aluminum.

(3) A vessel is not considered rebuilt when work performed on its hull or superstructure constitutes a quantum of work determined, to the maximum extent practicable, to be comparable to 7.5 percent or less of the vessel's steelweight prior to the work, calculated as if the vessel were wholly constructed of steel or aluminum.

(d) For a vessel of mixed construction, such as a vessel the hull of which is constructed of steel or aluminum and the superstructure of which is constructed of fibrous reinforced plastic, the steelweight of the work performed on the portion of the vessel constructed of a material other than steel or aluminum will be determined, to the maximum extent practicable, and aggregated with the work performed on the portion of the vessel constructed of steel or aluminum. The numerical parameters described in paragraph (b) of this section will then be applied to the aggregate of the work performed on the vessel compared to the vessel's steelweight prior to the work, calculated as if the vessel were wholly constructed of steel or aluminum, to determine whether the vessel has been rebuilt.

(e) The owner of a vessel currently entitled to coastwise or fisheries endorsements which is altered outside the United States and the work performed is determined to constitute or be comparable to more than 7.5 percent of the vessel's steelweight prior to the work, or which has a major component of the hull or superstructure not built in the United States added, must file the following information with the National Vessel Documentation Center within 30 days following the earlier of completion of the work or redelivery of the vessel to the owner or owner's representative:

(1) A written statement applying for a rebuilt determination, outlining in detail the work performed and naming the place(s) where the work was performed;

(2) Calculations showing the actual or comparable steelweight of the work performed on the vessel, the actual or comparable steelweight of the vessel, and comparing the actual or comparable steelweight of the work performed to the actual or comparable steelweight of the vessel;

(3) Accurate sketches or blueprints describing the work performed; and

Coast Guard, Dept. of Homeland Security § 67.203

(4) Any further submissions requested by the National Vessel Documentation Center.

(f) Regardless of the extent of actual work performed, the owner of a vessel currently entitled to coastwise or fisheries endorsements may, as an alternative to filing the items listed in paragraph (e) of this section, submit a written statement to the National Vessel Documentation Center declaring the vessel rebuilt outside the United States. The vessel will then be deemed to have been rebuilt outside the United States with loss of trading privileges.

(g) A vessel owner may apply for a preliminary rebuilt determination by submitting:

(1) A written statement applying for a preliminary rebuilt determination, outlining in detail the work planned and naming the place(s) where the work is to be performed;

(2) Calculations showing the actual or comparable steelweight of work to be performed on the vessel, the actual or comparable steelweight of the vessel, and comparing the actual or comparable steelweight of the planned work to the actual or comparable steelweight of the vessel;

(3) Accurate sketches or blueprints describing the planned work; and

(4) Any further submissions requested by the National Vessel Documentation Center.

NOTE: A statement submitted in accordance with paragraph (f) of this section does not constitute an application for a rebuilt determination and does not require payment of a fee.

[CGD 94-040, 61 FR 17815, Apr. 22, 1996, as amended by USCG-2009-0702, 74 FR 49230, Sept. 25, 2009]

Subpart N [Reserved]

Subpart O—Filing and Recording of Instruments—General Provisions

§ 67.200 Instruments eligible for filing and recording.

Only the following listed instruments are eligible for filing and recording:

(a) Bills of sale and instruments in the nature of bills of sale;

(b) Deeds of gift;

(c) Mortgages and assignments, assumptions, supplements, amendments, subordinations, satisfactions, and releases thereof;

(d) Preferred mortgages and assignments, assumptions, supplements, amendments, subordinations, satisfactions, and releases thereof;

(e) Interlender agreements affecting mortgages, preferred mortgages, and related instruments; and

(f) Notices of claim of lien, assignments, amendments, and satisfactions and releases thereof.

§ 67.203 Restrictions on filing and recording.

(a) No instrument will be accepted for filing unless the vessel to which it pertains is the subject of:

(1) A valid Certificate of Documentation; or

(2) An application for initial documentation, exchange of Certificate of Documentation, return to documentation, or for deletion from documentation, which is in substantial compliance with the applicable regulations, submitted to the National Vessel Documentation Center.

(b) An instrument identified as eligible for filing and recording under § 67.200 may not be filed and recorded if it bears a material alteration.

(c) An instrument identified as eligible for filing and recording under § 67.200 (a) or (b) may not be filed and recorded if any vendee or transferee under the instrument is not a citizen of the United States as defined in section 2 of the Shipping Act, 1916, (46 U.S.C. app. 802) unless the Maritime Administration has consented to the grant to a non-citizen made under the instrument.

(d) The restriction imposed by paragraph (c) of this section does not apply to a bill of sale or deed of gift conveying an interest in a vessel which was neither documented nor last documented pursuant to these regulations or any predecessor regulations thereto at the time the instrument was executed, nor to an instrument conveying an interest in a vessel identified in § 67.11(b).

(e) An instrument identified as eligible for filing and recording under § 67.200(c) may not be filed or recorded if the mortgagee or assignee is not a person qualifying as a citizen of the

§ 67.205

United States as defined in the Shipping Act, 1916, as amended, (46 U.S.C. app. chapter 23) or a trustee as defined in 46 U.S.C. 31328, unless the Maritime Administration has consented to the grant to a non-citizen made under the instrument. This restriction does not apply to an instrument conveying an interest in a vessel identified in § 67.11(b).

(f) An instrument identified as eligible for filing and recording under § 67.200(d) may not be filed or recorded if the mortgagee or assignee is not a person described in 46 U.S.C. 31322(a)(1)(D). This restriction does not apply to an instrument conveying an interest in a vessel identified in § 67.11(b).

[CGD 89–007, CGD 89–007a, 58 FR 60266, Nov. 15, 1993; 58 FR 65131, Dec. 13, 1993, as amended by CGD 95–014, 60 FR 31605, June 15, 1995]

§ 67.205 Requirement for vessel identification.

(a) Every instrument presented for filing and recording must contain sufficient information to clearly identify the vessel(s) to which the instrument relates.

(b) Instruments pertaining to vessels which have been documented must contain the vessel's name and official number, or other unique identifier.

(c) Vessels which have never been documented must be identified by one of the following:

(1) The vessel's Hull Identification Number assigned in accordance with 33 CFR 181.25; or

(2) Other descriptive information, which clearly describes the vessel. Such information may include length, breadth, depth, year of build, name of manufacturer, and any numbers which may have been assigned in accordance with 33 CFR part 173.

§ 67.207 Requirement for date and acknowledgment.

(a) Every instrument presented for filing and recording must:

(1) Bear the date of its execution; and

(2) Contain an acknowledgment.

(b) No officer or employee of the Coast Guard is authorized to take such acknowledgments unless the instrument is executed on behalf of the Federal Government of the United States.

§ 67.209 No original instrument requirement.

A copy of the original signed and acknowledged instrument must be presented. The original instrument itself may be presented but is not required. The copy may be delivered to the National Vessel Documentation Center or transmitted by facsimile or in portable document format (.pdf) in accordance with the procedures in §§ 67.218 and 67.219 of this part. Signatures may be affixed manually or digitally.

[USCG–2007–28098, 72 FR 42312, Aug. 2, 2007]

§ 67.211 Requirement for citizenship declaration.

(a) Instruments in the nature of a bill of sale or deed of gift, mortgages, and assignments of mortgages conveying an interest in a documented vessel are ineligible for filing and recording unless accompanied by a declaration of citizenship, except as provided in paragraph (c) and (d) of this section.

(b) Citizenship declarations must be executed on the form prescribed by the Maritime Administration in 46 CFR part 221. These forms are available from the National Vessel Documentation Center and from the Vessel Transfer and Disposal Officer (MAR–745.1), Maritime Administration, United States Department of Transportation, Washington, DC 20590.

(c) The requirement for presentation of a citizenship declaration does not apply to a transaction conveying an interest in a vessel:

(1) Described in 46 CFR 221.11(b)(1) (i) through (iv);

(2) To a person making application for documentation; or

(3) To an entity of the Federal Government of the United States or of a State or political subdivision thereof, or a corporate entity which is an agency of any such government or political subdivision.

(d) The requirement for presentation of a citizenship declaration is waived when the instrument(s) presented for filing effects a transfer for which:

(1) The Maritime Administration has given general approval in 46 CFR part 221; or

(2) Written approval of the Maritime Administrator has been obtained in accordance with 46 CFR part 221.

(e) If the transfer of interest is one which requires written approval of the Maritime Administrator in accordance with rules in 46 CFR part 221, evidence of that approval must be presented for filing with the instrument effecting the transfer of interest.

NOTE: If the grantee(s) of an ownership interest in a vessel described in paragraphs (c)(1) or (d) of this section do(es) not make application for documentation, a declaration of citizenship may be required in order to ensure that the vessel so conveyed retains any coastwise privileges to which it may be entitled.

[CGD 89–007, CGD 89–007a, 58 FR 60266, Nov. 15, 1993; 58 FR 65131, Dec. 13, 1993, as amended by CGD 95–014, 60 FR 31605, June 15, 1995; USCG–2009–0702, 74 FR 49230, Sept. 25, 2009]

§ 67.213 Place of filing and recording.

(a) All instruments submitted for filing and recording must be submitted to the National Vessel Documentation Center.

(b) All instruments are recorded at the National Vessel Documentation Center.

[CGD 95–014, 60 FR 31605, June 15, 1995]

§ 67.215 Date and time of filing.

(a) An instrument is deemed filed at the actual date and time at which the instrument is received by the National Vessel Documentation Center, except as provided in paragraph (b) of this section. Any materials submitted to supplement an instrument after the instrument is filed are deemed part of the original filing and relate back to the date and time of that filing.

(b) If filing of an instrument is subject to termination in accordance with § 67.217(a) and a new instrument is filed as a substitute for the original instrument, the filing of the original instrument will be terminated in accordance with § 67.217(c) and the substitute instrument will be considered a new filing. The substitute instrument will be deemed filed at the actual time and date it is received by the National Vessel Documentation Center.

[CGD 89–007, CGD 89–007a, 58 FR 60266, Nov. 15, 1993; 58 FR 65131, Dec. 13, 1993, as amended by CGD 95–014, 60 FR 31605, June 15, 1995]

§ 67.217 Termination of filing and disposition of instruments.

(a) The filing of an instrument is subject to termination if:

(1) It is determined that the instrument cannot be recorded because the instrument itself is not in substantial compliance with the applicable regulations in this part;

(2) The filing was not made in compliance with the requirements of § 67.213;

(3) The Application for Initial Issue, Exchange, or Replacement of Certificate of Documentation; or Redocumentation (form CG–1258) submitted with the instrument(s) was not made in substantial compliance with the applicable regulations of this part;

(4) The owner of the vessel submits an Application, Consent, and Approval for Withdrawal of Application for Documentation or Exchange of Certificate of Documentation (form CG–4593), with mortgagee consent, if applicable; or

(5) Another instrument is filed evidencing satisfaction or release of the subject instrument and the subject instrument is one described in subpart Q of this part.

(b) Ninety days prior to terminating the filing pursuant to a reason listed in paragraphs (a) (1), (2), or (3) of this section, the National Vessel Documentation Center will send written notice detailing the reasons the filing is subject to termination to the following person(s) and any agent known to be acting on behalf of the same:

(1) The applicant for documentation, if a bill of sale, instrument in the nature of a bill of sale, or a deed of gift;

(2) The mortgagee or assignee, if a mortgage or assignment or amendment thereof;

(3) The claimant, if a notice of claim of lien; or

(4) The lender first named in an interlender agreement affecting a mortgage, preferred mortgage, or related instrument.

(c) If the reason(s) which subject the filing to termination remain uncorrected for a period of 90 days after the notice described in paragraph (b) of this section is sent, or upon receipt of the request for withdrawal described in paragraph (a)(4) of this section, or satisfaction or release as described in

§ 67.218

paragraph (a)(5) of this section, the instrument will be returned to either:

(1) The applicant for documentation, if a bill of sale, instrument in the nature of a bill of sale, or a deed of gift;

(2) The mortgagee or assignee, if a mortgage or assignment or amendment thereof;

(3) The claimant, if a notice of claim of lien;

(4) The lender first named in an interlender agreement affecting a mortgage, preferred mortgage, or related instrument; or

(5) An agent for any appropriate party, provided that the agent has filed with the Coast Guard a writing bearing the original signature of the appropriate party(ies) clearly identifying the instrument(s) being returned and stating that the instrument(s) may be returned to the agent.

[CGD 89–007, CGD 89–007a, 58 FR 60266, Nov. 15, 1993; 58 FR 65131, Dec. 13, 1993, as amended by CGD 95–014, 60 FR 31605, June 15, 1995]

§ 67.218 Optional filing of instruments in portable document format as attachments to electronic mail.

(a) Any instrument identified as eligible for filing and recording under § 67.200 may be submitted in portable document format (.pdf) as an attachment to electronic mail (e-mail) for filing at the National Vessel Documentation Center. The e-mail address to be used for instrument filing may be obtained from the National Vessel Documentation Center Web site. If the instrument submitted for filing in .pdf format pertains to a vessel that is not a currently documented vessel, a completed Application for Initial Issue, Exchange, or Replacement Certificate of Documentation, or Return to Documentation (form CG–1258) or a letter application for deletion from documentation must already be on file with the National Vessel Documentation Center or must be submitted in .pdf format with the instrument being submitted in .pdf format for filing.

(b) All instruments submitted for filing in .pdf format must be clearly legible, be submitted from 8½ inch by 11 inch paper in not less than 10-point type size, and submitted as an attachment to e-mail.

(c) The e-mail required by paragraph (b) should indicate:

(1) The name, address, telephone number, and e-mail address of the person submitting the instrument for filing in .pdf format;

(2) The number of pages submitted for filing in .pdf format; and

(3) The name of the vessel, official number or hull identification number of the vessel(s), and the name(s) of the owner(s) of the vessel(s) to which the instrument relates.

(d) The filing of any instrument submitted for filing in .pdf format is terminated and the instrument will be returned to the submitter if the instrument is subject to termination for any cause under § 67.217(a).

[USCG–2007–28098, 72 FR 42312, Aug. 2, 2007]

§ 67.219 Optional filing of instruments by facsimile.

(a) Any instrument identified as eligible for filing and recording under § 67.200 may be submitted for filing to the National Vessel Documentation Center by facsimile at (304) 271–2405. If the instrument submitted by facsimile for filing pertains to a vessel that is not a currently documented vessel, a completed Application for Initial Issue, Exchange, or Replacement Certificate of Documentation, or Return to Documentation (form CG–1258) or a letter application for deletion from documentation must already be on file with the National Vessel Documentation Center or must be submitted by facsimile with the instrument being submitted by facsimile for filing.

(b) All instruments submitted by facsimile for filing must be clearly legible, be submitted from 8½ inch by 11 inch paper in not less than 10-point type size, and accompanied by a cover sheet.

(c) The cover sheet required by paragraph (b) should indicate:

(1) The name, address, telephone number, and facsimile telephone number of the person submitting the instrument by facsimile;

(2) The number of pages submitted by facsimile; and

(3) The name of the vessel, official number or hull identification number of the vessel(s), and the name(s) of the

Coast Guard, Dept. of Homeland Security § 67.233

owner(s) of the vessel(s) to which the instrument relates.

(d) The filing of any instrument submitted by facsimile is terminated and the instrument will be returned to the submitter if the instrument is subject to termination for any cause under § 67.217(a).

[USCG–2007–28098, 72 FR 42312, Aug. 2, 2007]

Subpart P—Filing and Recording of Instruments—Bills of Sale and Related Instruments

§ 67.220 Requirements.

An instrument in the nature of a bill of sale or a deed of gift must:

(a) Meet all of the requirements of subpart O of this part;

(b) Be signed by or on behalf of all the seller(s) or donor(s); and

(c) Recite the following:

(1) The name(s) and address(es) of the seller(s) or donor(s) and the interest in the vessel held by the seller(s) or donor(s); and

(2) The name(s) and address(es) of the buyer(s) or donee(s) and the interest in the vessel held by each buyer or donee.

§ 67.223 Filing limitation.

An instrument presented for filing and recording under this subpart may be filed only in conjunction with an application for initial documentation or return to documentation of the vessel or with an application for a change to or deletion of the vessel's outstanding Certificate of Documentation.

Subpart Q—Filing and Recording of Instruments—Mortgages, Preferred Mortgages, and Related Instruments

§ 67.231 General requirements; optional application for filing and recording.

(a) A mortgage or related instrument presented for filing and recording must meet all of the requirements of subpart O of this part in addition to the pertinent section(s) of this subpart.

(b) All instruments supplemental to mortgages must recite information which clearly identifies the mortgage to which the supplemental instrument is applicable. Such information will normally consist of the book and page where that mortgage is recorded and the date and time of filing. If the submission of the supplemental instrument is contemporaneous with submission of the mortgage, the information should include the names of all parties to the mortgage, the date of the mortgage, and the amount of the mortgage.

(c) An Optional Application for Filing (CG–5542) may be attached to a mortgage or related instrument. If form CG–5542 is properly completed with all information required for indexing the instrument and the signature(s) specified thereon, the instrument to which it is attached will be filed and recorded with no further review.

§ 67.233 Restrictions on recording mortgages, preferred mortgages, and related instruments.

(a) A mortgage or assumption of mortgage which otherwise meets the requirements of this subpart is nonetheless not eligible for filing and recording if:

(1) The mortgagor or assuming party(ies) did not actually hold legal title to the interest in the vessel being mortgaged or covered by the assumption at the time of filing of the mortgage or assumption; or

(2) If the vessel(s) which the mortgage cover(s) is (are) not documented or not the subject of an application for documentation.

(b) A mortgage of a vessel 100 feet or greater in length applying for a fishery endorsement is eligible for filing and recording as a preferred mortgage only if it meets the requirements of this part and the requirements of 46 CFR 356.19.

(c) The requirements of paragraph (b) of this section do not apply to the mortgagee of a vessel identified in § 67.11(b) or to any other vessel to which the Maritime Administration has given approval for unrestricted transfer pursuant to regulations in 46 CFR part 221.

[CGD 89–007, CGD 89–007a, 58 FR 60266, Nov. 15, 1003, as amended by USCG–1999–6095, 65 FR 76576, Dec. 7, 2000]

§ 67.235 Requirements for mortgages.

(a) A mortgage presented for filing and recording must:

(1) Be signed by or on behalf of each mortgagor; and

(2) Recite the following:

(i) The name and address of each mortgagor and the interest in the vessel held by the mortgagor(s);

(ii) The name and address of each mortgagee and the interest in the vessel granted by the mortgage; and

(iii) The amount of the direct or contingent obligations that is or may become secured by the mortgage, excluding interest, expenses, and fees. The amount may be recited in one or more units of account as agreed to by the parties.

(b) A mortgage submitted for filing and recording as a preferred mortgage must cover the whole of a vessel.

(c) A mortgage which secures more than one vessel may, at the option of the parties, provide for separate discharge of such vessels.

§ 67.237 Requirements for assignments of mortgages.

An assignment of mortgage presented for filing and recording must:

(a) Be signed by or on behalf of each assignor; and

(b) Recite the following:

(1) The name and address of each assignor and the interest in the mortgage held by the assignor(s); and

(2) The name and address of each assignee and the interest in the mortgage granted to the assignee(s).

§ 67.239 Requirements for assumptions of mortgages.

An assumption of mortgage presented for filing and recording must:

(a) Be signed by or on behalf of each original mortgagor, each mortgagee, and each assuming party; and

(b) Recite the following:

(1) The name and address of each original mortgagor and the interest in the vessel mortgaged; and

(2) The name and address of each assuming party and the interest in the mortgage assumed.

§ 67.241 Requirements for amendments of or supplements to mortgages.

An amendment of or supplement to a mortgage presented for filing and recording must:

(a) Be signed by or on behalf of each mortgagor and each mortgagee; and

(b) Recite the following:

(1) The name and address of each mortgagor and mortgagee; and

(2) The nature of the change effected by the instrument.

§ 67.243 Requirements for instruments subordinating mortgages.

An instrument subordinating a mortgage presented for filing and recording must:

(a) Be signed by or on behalf of each mortgagee whose mortgage is being subordinated; and

(b) Recite the following:

(1) The name and address of each mortgagee whose mortgage is being subordinated; and

(2) The name and address of each party holding an interest in the instrument subordinating the mortgage.

§ 67.245 Requirements for interlender agreements.

An interlender agreement between multiple mortgagees must:

(a) Be signed by or on behalf of all mortgagees who are party to the interlender agreement; and

(b) Recite the names and addresses of all parties to the interlender agreement.

Subpart R—Filing and Recording of Instruments—Notices of Claim of Lien and Supplemental Instruments

§ 67.250 General requirements.

(a) A notice of claim of lien or supplemental instrument thereto submitted for filing and recording must meet all of the requirements of subpart O of this part.

(b) An instrument assigning or amending a notice of claim of lien must recite information which clearly identifies the notice of claim of lien being assigned or amended. Such information will normally consist of the book and page where the notice of claim is recorded and the date and time of filing. If the submission of the assignment or amendment is contemporaneous with submission of the notice of claim of lien, the information should include the name of each original claimant, the date of the notice of claim, and the amount of the claim and other information to adequately identify the notice of claim of lien being assigned or amended.

§ 67.253 Requirements for notices of claim of lien.

A notice of claim of lien must:
(a) Be signed by or on behalf of each claimant; and
(b) Recite the following:
(1) The name and address of each claimant;
(2) The nature of the lien claimed;
(3) The date on which the lien was established; and
(4) The amount of the lien claimed.

§ 67.255 Restrictions on filing and recording.

A notice of claim of lien is not entitled to filing and recording unless the vessel against which the lien is claimed is covered by a preferred mortgage filed or recorded in accordance with subpart Q of this part or predecessor regulations thereto and which is outstanding at the time the lien is filed and recorded.

§ 67.257 Requirements for assignments of notices of claim of lien.

An assignment of a notice of claim of lien must:
(a) Be signed by or on behalf of each original claimant or last assignee of record; and
(b) Recite the following:
(1) The name and address of each claimant; and
(2) The name and address of each assignee and the interest in the claim being assigned.

§ 67.259 Requirements for amendments to notice of claim of lien.

An amendment to notice of claim of lien presented for filing and recording must:
(a) Be signed by or on behalf of each original claimant or last assignee of record; and

(b) Recite the nature of the change being effected by the instrument.

Subpart S—Removal of Encumbrances

§ 67.261 General requirements.

The filing of an instrument against a vessel in accordance with subparts Q or R of this part may be terminated and, if recorded, removed from the record of that vessel by the filing of:
(a) A court order, affidavit, or Declaration of Forfeiture described in § 67.263; or
(b) A satisfaction or release instrument described in § 67.265 which meets the requirements of this part for filing and recording.

§ 67.263 Requirement for removal of encumbrances by court order, affidavit, or Declaration of Forfeiture.

The encumbrances described in subparts Q and R of this part are removed from the record upon filing of:
(a) A copy of the order from a court of competent jurisdiction certified by an official of the court declaring title to the vessel to be free and clear, or declaring the encumbrance to be of no effect, or ordering the removal of the encumbrance from the record;
(b) A copy of the order from a Federal District Court in an *in rem* action certified by an official of the court requiring the free and clear sale of the vessel at a Marshal's sale and, where issued under local judicial procedures, a copy of the order confirming such sale certified by an official of the court;
(c) A copy of an order from a Federal District Court certified by an official of the court declaring the vessel itself or the proceeds of its sale to be forfeited to the Federal Government of the United States for a breach of its laws; or
(d) Where the vessel was forfeited under an administrative forfeiture action to the Federal Government of the United States, either an affidavit from an officer of the agency which performed the forfeiture, who has personal knowledge of the particulars of the vessel's forfeiture, or a Declaration of Forfeiture issued by the agency which performed the forfeiture.

§ 67.265 Requirements for instruments evidencing satisfaction or release.

An instrument satisfying or releasing a mortgage, a notice of claim of lien, or a preferred mortgage presented for filing and recording must:

(a) Meet all the requirements of subpart O of this part;

(b) Be signed by or on behalf of:

(1) Each mortgagee if a mortgage; or

(2) Each claimant if a notice of claim of lien; and

(c) Recite the following:

(1) The name of each mortgagor, if any, and the name of each mortgagee or claimant;

(2) The amount of the mortgage or claim of lien; and

(3) Information which clearly identifies the mortgage or claim of lien being satisfied or released. Such information will normally consist of the book and page where that mortgage or claim of lien is recorded. If the recording information cannot be provided because the satisfaction or release is being submitted prior to recording of the mortgage or claim of lien, the instrument must recite other information sufficient to clearly identify the encumbrance being satisfied or released.

Subpart T—Abstracts of Title and Certificates of Ownership

SOURCE: CGD 95–014, 60 FR 31605, June 15, 1995, unless otherwise noted.

§ 67.301 Issuance of Abstract of Title.

Any person may request the National Vessel Documentation Center to issue a General Index or Abstract of Title (form CG–1332) for a vessel.

§ 67.303 Issuance of Certificate of Ownership.

Any person may request the National Vessel Documentation Center to issue a Certificate of Ownership (form CG–1330) for a vessel.

Subpart U—Special Provisions

§ 67.311 Alteration of Certificate of Documentation.

Except for affixing a new address label in accordance with the direction of a documentation officer or a renewal decal issued in accordance with § 67.163, no person other than a documentation officer shall intentionally alter a Certificate of Documentation.

§ 67.313 Requirement to have Certificate of Documentation on board.

(a) The person in command of a documented vessel must have on board that vessel the original Certificate of Documentation currently in effect for that vessel.

(b) The requirement of paragraph (a) of this section does not apply:

(1) To non-self-propelled vessels not engaged in foreign trade;

(2) When the Certificate of Documentation has been submitted to the National Vessel Documentation Center for exchange in accordance with § 67.167 (d) or (e); or

(3) When the vessel is in storage or out of the water.

[CGD 89–007, CGD 89–007a, 58 FR 60266, Nov. 15, 1993; 58 FR 65131, Dec. 13, 1993, as amended by CGD 95–014, 60 FR 31605, June 15, 1995]

§ 67.315 Requirement to produce Certificate of Documentation.

(a) The person in command of a documented vessel must produce the original Certificate of Documentation currently in effect for that vessel upon the demand of any person acting in an official public capacity.

(b) The requirement of paragraph (a) of this section does not apply:

(1) To non-self-propelled vessels not engaged in foreign trade;

(2) When the Certificate of Documentation has been submitted to the National Vessel Documentation Center for exchange in accordance with § 67.167 (d) or (e); or

(3) When the vessel is in storage or out of the water.

[CGD 89–007, CGD 89–007a, 58 FR 60266, Nov. 15, 1993; 58 FR 65131, Dec. 13, 1993, as amended by CGD 95–014, 60 FR 31605, June 15, 1995]

§ 67.317 Requirement to renew endorsements on the Certificate of Documentation.

(a) Except as provided in paragraph (b) of this section, the owner of a documented vessel must annually renew each endorsement upon the current Certificate of Documentation for that vessel in accordance with § 67.163.

(b) The requirement of paragraph (a) of this section does not apply to Certificates of Documentation placed on deposit in accordance with § 67.165.

§ 67.319 Requirement to report change in vessel status and surrender Certificate of Documentation.

The owner of a documented vessel must immediately report any change in vessel status which causes any Certificate of Documentation to become invalid under subpart L of this part and which must be exchanged, replaced, deleted, or canceled, to the National Vessel Documentation Center. The outstanding Certificate must be surrendered in accordance with the requirements of subparts K and L of this part.

[CGD 89–007, CGD 89–007a, 58 FR 60266, Nov. 15, 1993; 58 FR 65131, Dec. 13, 1993, as amended by CGD 95–014, 60 FR 31605, June 15, 1995]

§ 67.321 Requirement to report change of address of managing owner.

Upon the change of address of the managing owner of a documented vessel, the managing owner shall report the change of address to the National Vessel Documentation Center within 10 days of its occurrence.

[CGD 94–008, 59 FR 49847, Sept. 30, 1994, as amended by CGD 95–014, 60 FR 31605, June 15, 1995]

§ 67.323 Operation without documentation.

No vessel which is required by § 67.7 to be documented may engage in unlimited coastwise trade or the fisheries without being documented in accordance with the requirements of this part.

[CGD 89–007, CGD 89–007a, 58 FR 60266, Nov. 15, 1993, as amended by USCG–2009–0702, 74 FR 49230, Sept. 25, 2009]

§ 67.325 Violation of endorsement.

A vessel may not be employed in any trade other than a trade endorsed upon the Certificate of Documentation issued for that vessel. A vessel documented exclusively for recreation may not be used for purposes other than pleasure.

§ 67.327 Operation under Certificate of Documentation with invalid endorsement.

Except for vessels identified in § 67.9, no vessel may be operated under a Certificate of Documentation with endorsements which have become invalid under subpart L of this part.

§ 67.329 Unauthorized name change.

The owner of a documented vessel may not change or allow the change of the name of that vessel without exchanging the vessel's Certificate of Documentation in accordance with subpart K of this part. The new name of the vessel must be marked on the vessel upon receipt of the new Certificate of Documentation.

§ 67.331 Improper markings.

The owner of a documented vessel shall not permit the operation of that vessel unless it is marked in accordance with subpart I of this part.

Subpart V—Exception From Fishery Endorsement Requirements Due to Conflict With International Agreements

SOURCE: USCG–1999–6095, 65 FR 76576, Dec. 7, 2000, unless otherwise noted.

§ 67.350 Conflicts with international agreements.

(a) If you are an owner or mortgagee of a fishing vessel less than 100 feet in length and believe that there is a conflict between 46 CFR part 67 and any international treaty or agreement to which the United States is a party on October 1, 2001, and to which the United States is currently a party, you may petition the National Vessel Documentation Center (NVDC) for a ruling that all or sections of part 67 do not apply to you with respect to a particular vessel, provided that you had an ownership interest in the vessel or a mortgage on the vessel on October 1, 2001. You may file your petition with the NVDC before October 1, 2001, with respect to international treaties or agreements in effect at the time of your petition which are not scheduled to expire before October 1, 2001.

§ 67.352

(b) If you are filing a petition for exemption with the NVDC for reasons stated in paragraph (a) of this section, your petition must include:

(1) Evidence of the ownership structure of the vessel petitioning for an exemption as of October 1, 2001, and any subsequent changes to the ownership structure of the vessel;

(i) If you are filing your petition before October 1, 2001, you may substitute evidence of the ownership structure as it exists on the date you file your petition;

(2) A copy of the provisions of the international agreement or treaty that you believe is in conflict with this part;

(3) A detailed description of how the provisions of the international agreement or treaty conflict with this part;

(4) For all petitions filed before October 1, 2001, a certification that the owner intends to transfer no ownership interest in the vessel to a non-U.S. citizen for the following year.

(5) For all petitions filed after October 1, 2001, a certification that no ownership interest was transferred to a non-U.S. citizen after September 30, 2001.

(c) You must file a separate petition for each vessel requiring an exemption unless the NVDC authorizes consolidated filing. Petitions should include two copies of all required materials and should be sent to the following address: National Vessel Documentation Center, 792 TJ Jackson Drive, Falling Water, West Virginia, 25419.

(d) Upon receipt of a complete petition, the NVDC will review the petition to determine whether the effective international treaty or agreement and the requirements of this part are in conflict. If the NVDC determines that this part conflicts with the effective international treaty or agreement, then the NVDC will inform you of the guidelines and requirements you must meet and maintain to qualify for a fisheries endorsement.

(e) If the vessel is determined through the petition process to be exempt from all or sections of the requirements of this part, then you must annually, from the date of exemption, submit the following evidence of its ownership structure to the NVDC:

(1) The vessel's current ownership structure;

(2) The identity of all non-citizen owners and the percentages of their ownership interest in the vessel;

(3) Any changes in the ownership structure that have occurred since you last submitted evidence of the vessel's ownership structure to the NVDC; and

(4) A statement ensuring that no interest in the vessel was transferred to a non-citizen during the previous year.

§ 67.352 Applicability.

The exemption in this subpart shall not be available to:

(a) Owners and mortgagees of a fishing vessel less than 100 feet in length who acquired an interest in the vessel after October 1, 2001; or

(b) Owners of a fishing vessel less than 100 feet in length, if any ownership interest in that vessel is transferred to or otherwise acquired by a non-U.S. citizen after October 1, 2001.

Subparts W-X [Reserved]

Subpart Y—Fees

§ 67.500 Applicability.

(a) This subpart specifies documentation services provided for vessels for which fees are applicable. No documentation service for which a fee is applicable will be performed until the appropriate fee has been paid. Fees are contained in Table 67.550.

(b) There is no fee for the annual renewal of endorsements upon the Certificate of Documentation, unless renewal is late.

(c) There is no fee for replacement of a Certificate of Documentation due to a wrongful withholding.

(d) The Director, National Vessel Documentation Center may waive collection of fees applicable under this subpart for a service provided to a Federal agency when the fee would be directly paid with federally-appropriated funds by a Federal agency acting in its own behalf.

Coast Guard, Dept. of Homeland Security §67.517

(e) Application fees under this subpart are not refundable.

[CGD 89–007, CGD 89–007a, 58 FR 60266, Nov. 15, 1993; 58 FR 65131, Dec. 13, 1993, as amended by CGD 95–014, 60 FR 31605, June 15, 1995; CGD 95–070, 60 FR 40241, Aug. 7, 1995; USCG–1998–4442, 63 FR 52191, Sept. 30, 1998]

§67.501 Application for Certificate of Documentation.

An application fee is charged for an initial Certificate of Documentation in accordance with subpart K of this part. If application is made for any trade endorsement, the applicable fee under §67.511 will be charged in addition to the application fee for the Certificate. The application fee does not include the fee under §67.527 for filing and recording any required bills of sale or instruments in the nature of a bill of sale, or the application fee under §67.519 for waivers in accordance with §§67.89 or 67.101.

§67.503 Application for exchange or replacement of a Certificate of Documentation.

(a) An application fee is charged for exchange or the simultaneous exchange and replacement of a Certificate of Documentation in accordance with subpart K of this part. Only a single application fee will be assessed when two or more reasons for exchange occur simultaneously. If application is made for any trade endorsement, the applicable fee under §67.511 will be charged in addition to the application fee for the exchange or replacement.

(b) The application fee for exchange or replacement does not apply to:

(1) Endorsement of a change in the owner's address;

(2) Exchange or replacement solely by reason of clerical error on the part of a documentation officer; or

(3) Deletion of a vessel from documentation.

§67.505 Application for return of vessel to documentation.

An application fee is charged for a return of a vessel to documentation after deletion in accordance with subpart K of this part. If application is made for any trade endorsement, the applicable fee under §67.511 will be charged in addition to the application fee for return to documentation.

§67.507 Application for replacement of lost or mutilated Certificate of Documentation.

An application fee is charged for replacement of a lost or mutilated Certificate of Documentation in accordance with subpart K of this part.

§67.509 Application for approval of exchange of Certificate of Documentation requiring mortgagee consent.

An application fee is charged for approval of exchange of a Certificate of Documentation requiring mortgagee consent in accordance with subpart K of this part.

§67.511 Application for trade endorsement(s).

(a) *Coastwise endorsement.* An application fee is charged for a coastwise endorsement, in accordance with subpart B of this part.

(b) *Coastwise Bowaters endorsement.* An application fee is charged for a coastwise Bowaters endorsement in accordance with 46 CFR part 68.

(c) *Fishery endorsement.* An application fee is charged for a fishery endorsement in accordance with subpart B of this part.

(d) *Registry or recreational endorsement.* There is no application fee for a registry or recreational endorsement, or both.

(e) When multiple trade endorsements are requested on the same application, only the single highest applicable endorsement fee will be charged.

[CGD 89–007, CGD 89–007a, 58 FR 60266, Nov. 15, 1993, as amended by USCG–2009–0702, 74 FR 49230, Sept. 25, 2009]

§67.513 Application for evidence of deletion from documentation.

An application fee is charged for evidence of deletion from documentation in accordance with subpart L of this part.

§67.515 [Reserved]

§67.517 Application for late renewal.

An application fee is charged for a late renewal in accordance with subpart L of this part.

§ 67.519 Application for waivers.

An application fee is charged for waiver of original build evidence in accordance with subpart F of this part, or for waiver of bill of sale eligible for filing and recording in accordance with subpart E of this part. In cases where more than one waiver is required, each waiver application is subject to this fee.

[CGD 89–007, CGD 89–007a, 58 FR 60266, Nov. 15, 1993, as amended by USCG–1998–4442, 63 FR 52191, Sept. 30, 1998]

§ 67.521 Application for new vessel determination.

An application fee is charged for a new vessel determination in accordance with subpart M of this part.

§ 67.523 Application for wrecked vessel determination.

An application fee is charged for a determination of whether a vessel is entitled to coastwise and fisheries privileges as a result of having been wrecked in waters adjacent to the United States and repaired in accordance with subpart J of this part. This fee is in addition to the cost associated with the vessel appraisals.

[CGD 89–007, CGD 89–007a, 58 FR 60266, Nov. 15, 1993, as amended by USCG–2009–0702, 74 FR 49230, Sept. 25, 2009]

§ 67.525 Application for determination of rebuild.

An application fee is charged for a determination of whether a vessel has been rebuilt in accordance with subpart M of this part. This fee will be assessed for each request for either a preliminary or final determination submitted in writing by the vessel owner or the vessel owner's representative.

§ 67.527 Application for filing and recording bills of sale and instruments in the nature of a bill of sale.

An application fee is charged for filing and recording bills of sale and instruments in the nature of a bill of sale in accordance with subpart P of this part.

§ 67.529 Application for filing and recording mortgages and related instruments.

An application fee is charged for filing and recording mortgages and related instruments in accordance with subpart Q of this part.

§ 67.531 Application for filing and recording notices of claim of lien.

An application fee is charged for filing and recording notices of claim of lien in accordance with subpart R of this part.

§ 67.533 Application for Certificate of Compliance.

An application fee is charged for a Certificate of Compliance to be issued in accordance with regulations set forth in 46 CFR part 68.

§ 67.535 Issuance of Abstract of Title.

An issuance fee is charged for a General Index or Abstract of Title in accordance with subpart T of this part.

§ 67.537 Issuance of Certificate of Ownership.

An issuance fee is charged for a Certificate of Ownership in accordance with subpart T of this part. A supplemental issuance fee is charged for a Certificate of Ownership attachment for each additional vessel with the same ownership and encumbrance information.

§ 67.539 Copies of instruments and documents.

The fee charged for furnishing a copy of any instrument or document is calculated in the same manner as described in 49 CFR 7.95.

[CGD 94–008, 59 FR 49847, Sept. 30, 1994]

§ 67.550 Fee table.

The fees charged under subpart Y are as set forth in Table 67.550.

Table 67.550—Fees

Activity	Reference	Fee
Applications:		
Initial certificate of documentation	Subpart K	$133.00
Exchange of certificate of documentation	do	84.00
Return of vessel to documentation	do	84.00
Replacement of lost or mutilated certificate of documentation	do	50.00
Approval of exchange of certificate of documentation requiring mortgagee consent.	do	24.00
Trade endorsement(s):		
Coastwise endorsement	Subpart B	29.00
Coastwise Bowaters endorsement	46 CFR part 68	29.00
Fishery endorsement	do	12.00
Registry endorsement	do	none
Recreational endorsement	do	none
Note: When multiple trade endorsements are requested on the same application, only the single highest applicable endorsement fee will be charged, resulting in a maximum endorsement fee of $29.00		
Evidence of deletion from documentation	Subpart L	15.00
Late renewal fee	do	5.00
Waivers:		
Original build evidence	Subpart F	15.00
Bill of sale eligible for filing and recording	Subpart E	15.00
Miscellaneous applications:		
Wrecked vessel determination	Subpart J	555.00
New vessel determination	Subpart M	166.00
Rebuild determination—preliminary or final	do	450.00
Filing and recording:		
Bills of sale and instruments in nature of bills of sale	Subpart P	8.00([1])
Mortgages and related instruments	Subpart Q	4.00([1])
Notice of claim of lien and related instruments	Subpart R	8.00([1])
Certificate of compliance:		
Certificate of compliance	46 CFR part 68	55.00
Miscellaneous:		
Abstract of Title	Subpart T	25.00
Certificate of ownership	do	125.00
Attachment for each additional vessel with same ownership and encumbrance data.	do	10.00
Copy of instrument or document	([2])	([2])

[1] Per page.
[2] Fees will be calculated in accordance with 49 CFR 7.95.

[CGD 89–007, CGD 89–007a, 58 FR 60266, Nov. 15, 1993; 58 FR 65243, Dec. 13, 1993, as amended by CGD 95–014, 60 FR 31605, June 15, 1995; CGD 95–070, 60 FR 40242, Aug. 7, 1995; USCG–2007–28098, 72 FR 42313, Aug. 2, 2007; USCG–2009–0702, 74 FR 49230, Sept. 25, 2009]

PART 68—DOCUMENTATION OF VESSELS: EXCEPTIONS TO COASTWISE QUALIFICATION

Subpart A—Regulations for Engaging in Limited Coastwise Trade

Sec.
68.1 Purpose of subpart.
68.3 Definitions for the purposes of this subpart.
68.5 Requirements for citizenship under 46 U.S.C. App. 833–1.
68.7 Qualification as an 883–1 corporation.
68.9 Qualification as a parent or subsidiary.
68.11 Cessation of qualifications.
68.13 Privileges conferred—documentation of vessels.
68.15 Privileges conferred—operation of vessels.
68.17 Restrictions.
68.19 Application by an 883–1 corporation to document a vessel.

APPENDIX A TO SUBPART A OF PART 68—OATH FOR THE QUALIFICATION OF CORPORATION AS A CITIZEN OF THE UNITED STATES UNDER THE ACT OF SEPT. 2, 1958 (46 U.S.C. APP. 883–1)

APPENDIX B TO SUBPART A OF PART 68—OATH OF PARENT OR SUBSIDIARY CORPORATION ACT OF SEPTEMBER 2, 1958 (46 U.S.C. APP. 883–1)

Subpart B—Documentation of Certain Vessels for Oil Spill Cleanup

68.25 Purpose and scope.
68.27 Definitions for purpose of this subpart.
68.29 Citizenship requirements for limited coastwise endorsement.
68.31 Vessel eligibility requirements for limited coastwise endorsement.

§ 68.1

68.33 Privileges of a limited coastwise endorsement.
68.35 Application to document a vessel under this subpart.
68.37 Cessation of qualifications.
APPENDIX A TO SUBPART B OF PART 68—OATH FOR QUALIFICATION OF A NOT-FOR-PROFIT OIL SPILL RESPONSE COOPERATIVE
APPENDIX B TO SUBPART B OF PART 68—OATH FOR DOCUMENTATION OF VESSELS FOR USE BY A NOT-FOR-PROFIT OIL SPILL RESPONSE COOPERATIVE

Subpart C—Vessels With a Coastwise Endorsement Issued on or After August 9, 2004, That Are Demised Chartered to Coastwise Qualified Citizens

68.50 Purpose and applicability.
68.55 Definitions.
68.60 Eligibility of a vessel for a coastwise endorsement under this subpart.
68.65 Annual ownership certification.
68.70 Application procedure for vessels other than barges to be operated in coastwise trade without being documented.
68.75 Application procedure for barges to be operated in coastwise trade without being documented.
68.80 Invalidation of a coastwise endorsement.

Subpart D—Vessels With a Coastwise Endorsement Issued Before August 9, 2004, and Their Replacements That Are Demise Chartered to Coastwise-Qualified Citizens

68.100 Purpose and applicability.
68.103 Definitions.
68.105 Eligibility of a vessel for a coastwise endorsement under this subpart.
68.107 Application procedure for vessels other than barges to be operated in coastwise trade without being documented.
68.109 Application procedure for barges to be operated in coastwise trade without being documented.
68.111 Invalidation of a coastwise endorsement.

AUTHORITY: 14 U.S.C. 664; 31 U.S.C. 9701; 42 U.S.C. 9118; 46 U.S.C. 2103, 2110; 46 U.S.C. app. 876; Department of Homeland Security Delegation No. 0170.1.

SOURCE: CGD 80–107, 47 FR 27511, June 24, 1982, unless otherwise noted.

Subpart A—Regulations for Engaging in Limited Coastwise Trade

SOURCE: CGD 80–107, 47 FR 27511, June 24, 1982. Redesignated and amended by USCG–2005–20258, 71 FR 61418, 61419, Oct. 18, 2006]

§ 68.1 Purpose of subpart.

This subpart contains citizen ownership requirements and procedures to allow documentation of vessels that do not meet the requirements of part 67 of this chapter. The requirements are for corporations engaged in a manufacturing or mineral industry in the United States.

[USCG–2005–20258, 71 FR 61419, Oct. 18, 2006]

§ 68.3 Definitions for the purposes of this subpart.

Act means the Act of September 2, 1958 (46 U.S.C. App. 883–1).

883–1 citizen or *883–1 corporation* means a corporation which qualifies for the special citizenship status created by the Act of September 2, 1958 (46 U.S.C. App. 883–1).

Parent corporation means one incorporated under the laws of the United States, or any state, territory, or district of the United States, which controls (directly or indirectly) at least 50 percent of the voting stock of another corporation.

Subsidiary corporation means one incorporated under the laws of the United States, or any state, territory, or district of the United States, which has not less than 50 percent of its voting stock controlled (directly or indirectly) by another corporation.

[CGD 80–107, 47 FR 27511, June 24, 1982, as amended by CGD 95–028, 62 FR 51203, Sept. 30, 1997. Redesignated by USCG–2005–20258, 71 FR 61418, Oct. 18, 2006]

§ 68.5 Requirements for citizenship under 46 U.S.C. App. 883–1.

A corporation seeking to establish its citizenship under the Act of September 2, 1958 (46 U.S.C. App. 883–1) must meet the following criteria as specified in the Act:

(a) It must be incorporated under the laws of the United States, or any state, territory, district, or possession of the United States;

(b) A majority of the officers and directors of the corporation must be citizens of the United States;

(c) Not less than 90 percent of the employees of the corporation must be residents of the United States;

(d) Such corporation must be engaged primarily in a manufacturing or mineral industry in the United States or any territory, district, or possession of the United States;

(e) The aggregate book value of the vessels owned by the corporation must not exceed 10 percent of the aggregate book value of the assets of the corporation; and

(f) The corporation must purchase or produce in the United States, its territories or possessions, not less than 75 percent of the raw materials used or sold in its operations.

NOTE: A corporation which qualifies as an 883–1 citizen by meeting the criteria in paragraph (a) of this section is not thereby precluded from qualifying as a citizen under any definition in part 67 upon compliance with all applicable requirements.

[CGD 80–107, 47 FR 27494, June 24, 1982, as amended at 47 FR 35488, Aug. 16, 1982; CGD 95–028, 62 FR 51203, Sept. 30, 1997. Redesignated by USCG–2005–20258, 71 FR 61418, Oct. 18, 2006]

§ 68.7 Qualification as an 883–1 corporation.

(a) To be formally qualified as an 883–1 corporation for all purposes under the Act, a corporation which meets the requirements of § 68.5 must file with the Director, National Vessel Documentation Center a certificate under oath as described in appendix A.

(b) Upon the filing of the certificate required under paragraph (a) of this section, the Director, National Vessel Documentation Center will furnish the corporation a Certificate of Compliance which is valid for a period of 3 years from the date of its issuance, unless there is a change in corporate status requiring a report under § 68.11(a). On or before the date of expiration of the Certificate of Compliance, a new certificate under oath as described in appendix A of this subpart must be filed with the Director, National Vessel Documentation Center.

(Approved by the Office of Management and Budget under control number 1625–0027)

[GCD 89–007; GCD 89–007a, 58 FR 60266, Nov. 15, 1993, 58 FR 65131, Dec. 13, 1993, as amended by CGD 95–014, 60 FR 31605, June 15, 1995; USCG–1999–6216, 64 FR 53225, Oct. 1, 1999; USCG–2002–13058, 67 FR 61279, Sept. 30, 2002; USCG–2006–25697, 71 FR 55746, Sept. 25, 2006. Redesignated and amended by USCG–2005–20258, 71 FR 61418, 61419, Oct. 18, 2006]

§ 68.9 Qualification as a parent or subsidiary.

(a) To be formally qualified as a parent corporation, as defined in § 68.3, a corporation must file with the Director, National Vessel Documentation Center a certificate under oath as described in appendix B of this subpart.

(b) To be formally qualified as subsidiary corporation as defined in § 68.3, a corporation must file with the Director, National Vessel Documentation Center a certificate under oath as described in appendix B of this subpart.

(c) Upon the filing of the certificate required under paragraph (a) or (b) of this section, the Director, National Vessel Documentation Center will furnish the corporation a certificate of parent or subsidiary status which is valid for a period of 3 years from the date of its issuance unless there is a change in corporate status requiring a report under § 68.11(a). On or before the date of expiration of the certificate of parent or subsidiary status, a new certificate under oath as described in appendix B of this subpart must be filed with the Director, National Vessel Documentation Center.

[CGD 89–007, CGD 89–007a, 58 FR 60266, Nov. 15, 1993; 58 FR 65131, Dec. 13, 1993, as amended by CGD 95–014, 60 FR 31605, June 15, 1995; USCG–1999–6216, 64 FR 53225, Oct. 1, 1999; USCG–2002–13058, 67 FR 61279, Sept. 30, 2002. Redesignated and amended by USCG–2005–20258, 71 FR 61418, 61419, Oct. 18, 2006]

§ 68.11 Cessation of qualification.

(a) If after filing the certificate required by § 68.7, a change occurs whereby an 883–1 corporation no longer meets the criteria in § 68.5(a), that corporation's qualification for the privileges enumerated in §§ 68.13 and 68.15 is terminated effective as of the date and

§ 68.13

time of the change. The corporation must report the change in writing to the Director, National Vessel Documentation Center.

(b) If, after filing the certificate required by § 68.9, a change occurs whereby the corporation is no longer entitled to be deemed a parent or subsidiary corporation, that corporation's qualification for the privileges in §§ 68.13 and 68.15 is terminated effective as of the date and time of the change. The corporation must report such change in writing to the Director, National Vessel Documentation Center.

[CGD 89–007, CGD 89–007a, 58 FR 60266, Nov. 15, 1993; 58 FR 65131, Dec. 13, 1993, as amended by CGD 95–014, 60 FR 31605, June 15, 1995; USCG–1999–6216, 64 FR 53225, Oct. 1, 1999. Redesignated and amended by USCG–2005–20258, 71 FR 61418, 61419, Oct. 18, 2006]

§ 68.13 Privileges conferred—documentation of vessel.

The special citizenship status created by the Act entitles the 883–1 corporation to document certain vessels for certain limited purposes:

(a) An 883–1 corporation may document under the Act only vessels which are qualified for employment in the coastwise trade and which are either non-self propelled or, if self-propelled, are of less than 500 gross tons.

(b) A vessel owned by an 883–1 corporation and meeting the criteria in paragraph (a) of this section may be documented only for use in the coastwise trade subject to the restrictions in § 68.17.

(c) Section 68.19 contains details concerning the documentation of vessels by an 883–1 corporation.

[CGD 80–107, 47 FR 27511, June 24, 1982. Redesignated and amended by USCG–2005–20258, 71 FR 61418, Oct. 18, 2006]

§ 68.15 Privileges conferred—operation of vessels.

(a) The special citizenship status created by the Act entitles the 883–1 corporation to operate, subject to the restrictions in § 68.17, vessels which are qualified to engage in the coastwise trade and are exempt from documentation. (See § 67.9 for classes of exempt vessels.)

(b) Vessels, documented or exempt from documentation, employed subject to the Act may carry passengers and merchandise of the 883–1 corporation owning such vessels only between points in the United States, including territories, districts, and possessions thereof embraced in the coastwise laws.

(c) The special citizenship status created by the Act entitles an 883–1 corporation owning vessels as described in paragraphs (a) and (b) of this section to transport merchandise or passengers for hire in the coastwise trade as a service for a duly qualified parent or subsidiary corporation as defined in § 68.3.

(d) The special citizenship status created by the Act entitles an 883–1 corporation owning vessels as described in paragraphs (a) and (b) of this section to demise or bareboat charter such vessels to common or contract carriers subject to the restrictions in § 68.17(c).

[CGD 80–107, 47 FR 27511, June 24, 1982, as amended by USCG–2002–13058, 67 FR 61279, Sept. 30, 2002. Redesignated and amended by USCG–2005–20258, 71 FR 61418, Oct. 18, 2006]

§ 68.17 Restrictions.

(a) Vessels employed subject to the Act are entitled to operation only in the coastwise trade and only to the extent described in paragraphs (b) and/or (c) of this section.

(b) A vessel owned by an 883–1 corporation may engage in coastwise transportation for hire as a service to a parent or subsidiary corporation as defined in § 68.3. Such transportation for hire must be between points of the United States, including territories, districts, and possessions thereof embraced in the coastwise laws.

(c) A vessel owned by an 883–1 corporation may be operated under demise or bareboat charter to a common or a contract carrier subject to 49 U.S.C. chapter 101 if the corporation is a U.S. citizen as defined in 46 U.S.C. App. 802.

(1) Such common or contract carrier may not be connected either directly or indirectly by ownership or control with the 883–1 corporation.

(2) The demise or bareboat charter must be at prevailing rates.

Coast Guard, Dept. of Homeland Security **Pt. 68, Subpt. A, App. B**

(3) The vessels under a demise or bareboat charter may not be used in non-contiguous trade.

[CGD 80–107, 47 FR 27511, June 24, 1982, as amended by CGD 95–028, 62 FR 51203, Sept. 30, 1997. Redesignated and amended by USCG–2005–20258, 71 FR 61418, Oct. 18, 2006]

§ 68.19 Application by an 883–1 corporation to document a vessel.

(a) An application by an 883–1 corporation to document a vessel must comply with the applicable requirements in subparts A, D, E, F, G, H, I, K, and L of part 67 of this chapter.

(b) An application by an 883–1 corporation to document a vessel must include a copy of the Certificate of Compliance issued under § 68.7.

[CGD 95–014, 60 FR 31606, June 15, 1995. Redesignated and amended by USCG–2005–20258, 71 FR 61418, Oct. 18, 2006]

APPENDIX A TO SUBPART A OF PART 68—OATH FOR QUALIFICATION OF CORPORATION AS A CITIZEN OF THE UNITED STATES UNDER THE ACT OF SEPTEMBER 2, 1958 (46 U.S.C. APP. 883–1)

Department of Homeland Security, U.S. Coast Guard

Oath for Qualification of Corporation as a Citizen of the United States Under the Act of September 2, 1958 (46 U.S.C. app. 883–1)

Corporation:
 Name _____
 Address [1] _____
 State where incorporated _____
Affiant:
 Name _____
 Address _____
 Company _____
 Title or capacity _____

I, the affiant named above, swear that I am legally authorized to make this oath on behalf of the corporation, that a majority of the officers and directors of the above-named corporation are citizens of the United States, as shown by the attached listing incorporated in and made a part of this oath which truly and correctly names all such officers and directors, giving the home address and citizenship of each; that not less than 90 percent of the employees of the corporation are residents of the United States; that the corporation is engaged primarily in a manufacturing or mineral industry in the United States or in a territory, district or possession thereof; that the aggregate book value of the vessels owned by the corporation does not exceed 10 percent of the aggregate book value of the assets of the corporation; and that the corporation purchases or produces in the United States, its territories or possessions not less than 75 percent of the raw materials used or sold in its operation. [2]

The above named corporation fails to qualify as a citizen within the meaning of § 67.39(c) of this chapter by reason of: [3]
 ____ Non-citizen President
 ____ Non-citizen Chairman of Board
 ____ Failure to meet quorum requirements
 ____ Failure to meet stock ownership requirements
Signature _____
Subscribed and sworn to before me on the day and year shown

_____
(Notary Public)
Date _____

[CGD 80–107, 47 FR 27511, June 24, 1982, as amended by USCG–2002–13058, 67 FR 61279, Sept. 30, 2002; USCG–2003–14505, 68 FR 9535, Feb. 28, 2003. Redesignated and amended by USCG–2007–28098, 71 FR 61418, 61419, Oct. 18, 2006]

APPENDIX B TO SUBPART A OF PART 68—OATH OF PARENT OR SUBSIDIARY CORPORATION ACT OF SEPTEMBER 2, 1958 (46 U.S.C. APP. 883–1)

Department of Homeland Security, U.S. Coast Guard

Oath of Parent or Subsidiary Corporation, Act of September 2, 1958 (46 U.S.C. app. 883–1)

Corporation:
 Name _____
 Address _____
 State of incorporation _____
 Status (Parent) [1] _____ (Subsidiary) [2] _____

---

[2] Attach the required list of the names of all officers and directors of the corporation, giving the home address and citizenship of each.

[3] Check appropriate line or lines.

[1] A "parent corporation" for the purposes of this oath is one incorporated under the laws of the United States, or any State, territory, or district of the United States, which controls (directly or indirectly) at least 50 percent of the voting stock of another corporation. Strike out the inapplicable term.

[2] A "subsidiary corporation" for the purposes of this oath is one incorporated under the laws of the United States, or any State,

Continued

---

[1] Show principal place of business of corporation.

§ 68.25

Name of associated corporation _____
Address _____
State where incorporated _____
Affiant:
Name _____
Address _____
Company _____
Title or capacity _____

I, the affiant named above, swear that the corporation first named herein is the (parent)[1] (subsidiary)[2] of the associated corporation named, that I am the duly authorized officer or agent of the corporation first named, and that the associated corporation has previously established that it is a citizen within the meaning of the Act of September 2, 1958 (46 U.S.C. app. 883–1).

Signature _____
Subscribed and sworn to before me on the day and year shown

_____
(Notary Public)

[CGD 80–107,47 FR 27511, June 24, 1982, as amended by USCG–2003–14505, 68 FR 9535, Feb. 28, 2003. Redesignated and amended by USCG–2007–28098, 71 FR 61418, 61419, Oct. 18, 2006]

Subpart B—Documentation of Certain Vessels for Oil Spill Cleanup

SOURCE: CGD 90–055, 57 FR 7642, Mar. 3, 1992. Redesignated by USCG–2005–20258, 71 FR 61418, Oct. 18, 2006]

§ 68.25 Purpose and scope.

This subpart contains citizen ownership requirements and procedures to allow documentation of vessels which do not meet the requirements of part 67 of this chapter. The requirements are for the limited purposes of training for, implementing, and supporting oil spill cleanup operations.

[CGD 90–055, 57 FR 7642, Mar. 3, 1992. Redesignated by USCG–2005–20258, 71 FR 61418, Oct. 18, 2006]

§ 68.27 Definitions for purposes of this subpart.

Certificate of Documentation means form CG–1270.

Citizen means a citizen as described in part 67 of this chapter.

_____
territory, or district of the United States, which has not less than 50 percent of its voting stock controlled (directly or indirectly) by another corporation. Strike out the inapplicable term.

Exclusive Economic Zone or *EEZ* means the exclusive economic zone established by Presidential Proclamation Numbered 5030, dated March 10, 1983, including the ocean waters of the areas referred to as "eastern special areas" in Article 3(1) of the Agreement between the United States of America and the Union of Soviet Socialist Republics on the Maritime Boundary, signed June 1, 1990.

Not-for-profit oil spill response cooperative means a corporation, partnership, association, trust, joint venture, or other entity established under the laws of the United States, or of a State, with a not-for-profit status and for the limited purposes of training for, carrying out, and supporting oil spill cleanup operations or related research activities.

[CGD 90–055, 57 FR 7642, Mar. 3, 1992. Redesignated by USCG–2005–20258, Oct. 18, 2006]

§ 68.29 Citizenship requirements for limited coastwise endorsement.

(a) Notwithstanding the citizenship requirements set out in part 67 of this chapter, a Certificate of Documentation with a coastwise endorsement for the limited purposes provided in § 68.33 may be issued to a vessel owned by—

(1) A not-for-profit oil spill response cooperative if the vessel meets the requirements of paragraph (b) of this section; or

(2) A member or members of a not-for-profit oil spill response cooperative if the vessel meets the requirements of paragraphs (b) and (c) of this section.

(b) The vessel must be at least 50 percent owned by one or more of the following entities:

(1) An individual who is a native-born, naturalized or derivative citizen of the United States or otherwise qualifies as a United States citizen.

(2) A corporation incorporated under the laws of the United States or of a State where—

(i) The president and, if the president is not the chief executive officer, the chief executive officer, by whatever title, is a citizen;

(ii) The chairman of the board of directors is a citizen; and

Coast Guard, Dept. of Homeland Security § 68.35

(iii) No more of the directors are noncitizens than a minority of the number necessary to constitute a quorum.

(3) A partnership where all the general partners are citizens and at least 50 percent of the equity interest is owned by citizens.

(4) An association or joint venture where all the members are citizens.

(5) A trust where all the trustees and all the beneficiaries with an enforceable interest in the trust are citizens.

(c) The vessel must be owned by a member or members of a not-for-profit oil spill response cooperative who dedicate the vessel to the use of a not-for-profit oil spill response cooperative.

(d) A vessel which meets the criteria of this section is considered to be owned exclusively by citizens of the United States for the purposes of subsequent transfer and documentation under part 67 of this chapter.

[CGD 90–055, 57 FR 7642, Mar. 3, 1992. Redesignated and amended by USCG–2005–20258, 71 FR 61418, Oct. 18, 2006]

§ 68.31 Vessel eligibility requirements for limited coastwise endorsement.

(a) A vessel must comply with all the requirements of part 67 of this chapter, other than citizenship requirements, in order to be eligible for documentation under this subpart.

(b) Notwithstanding 46 U.S.C. App. 883, a vessel remains eligible for documentation under this subpart even if the vessel was formerly owned by a not-for-profit oil spill response cooperative or by one or more members of a not-for-profit oil spill response cooperative and the vessel meets the criteria of § 68.29.

[CGD 90–055, 57 FR 7642, Mar. 3, 1992. Redesignated and amended by USCG–2005–20258, 71 FR 61418, Oct. 18, 2006]

§ 68.33 Privileges of a limited coastwise endorsement.

(a) A vessel which is documented and issued a limited coastwise endorsement under this subpart may operate on the navigable waters of the United States or in the EEZ in coastwise trade only for the following purposes:

(1) To recover oil discharged into the water.

(2) To transport oil discharged into the water.

(3) To transport and deploy equipment, supplies, and personnel for recovering and transporting oil discharged into the water.

(4) To conduct training exercises to prepare for performing the functions in paragraphs (a)(1) through (a)(3) of this section.

(b) This limited coastwise endorsement also entitles the vessel to any other employment for which a registry or fishery license is not required.

(c) A vessel which is documented and issued a limited coastwise endorsement under this subpart may qualify to operate for other purposes by meeting the applicable requirements of part 67 of this chapter.

[CGD 90–055, 57 FR 7642, Mar. 3, 1992. Redesignated by USCG–2005–20258, 71 FR 61418, Oct. 18, 2006; USCG–2009–0702, 74 FR 49230, Sept. 25, 2009]

§ 68.35 Application to document a vessel under this subpart.

(a) To qualify to document a vessel or to accept the dedication of a vessel by a member or members under this subpart, a not-for-profit oil spill response cooperative shall file with the Director, National Vessel Documentation Center the certificate under oath as set forth in appendix A to this subpart.

(b) Upon the filing of the certificate under paragraph (a) of this section, the Director, National Vessel Documentation Center will furnish the not-for-profit oil spill response cooperative with a letter of qualification. The letter of qualification is valid for a period of three years from the date of its issuance, unless there is a change in membership or structure of the not-for-profit oil spill response cooperative or a change in the citizenship status of any of its members requiring a report under § 68.37. In order to renew the letter of qualification, a new certificate under oath must be filed with the Commandant at least 30 days before the date of expiration of the letter of qualification.

(c) A not-for-profit oil spill response cooperative seeking to document a vessel for a limited coastwise endorsement under this subpart, in addition to complying with the requirements of § 68.31(a), shall supply to the National

§ 68.37

Vessel Documentation Center, a copy of the letter of qualification issued under paragraph (b) of this section.

(d) A member or members of a not-for-profit oil spill response cooperative seeking to document a vessel under this subpart shall supply to the National Vessel Documentation Center, a copy of the letter of qualification issued under paragraph (b) of this section to the not-for-profit oil spill response cooperative to which the vessel is dedicated. In addition, the not-for-profit oil spill response cooperative and the vessel owners shall all certify under oath that the vessel for which application is made is dedicated to use by the not-for-profit oil spill response cooperative. This certification must use the format and content described in appendix B to this subpart. If there is a change in the dedicated status of the vessel or its ownership, a report under § 68.37 must be filed.

[GCD 89–007; GCD 89–007a, 58 FR 60266, Nov. 15, 1993, 58 FR 65131, Dec. 13, 1993, as amended by CGD 95–014, 60 FR 31606, June 15, 1995; USCG–1999–6216, 64 FR 53225, Oct. 1, 1999. Redesignated and amended by USCG–2005–20258, 71 FR 61418, Oct. 18, 2006]

§ 68.37 Cessation of qualifications.

(a) If the vessel is owned by a not-for-profit oil spill response cooperative and a change occurs which affects the validity of the certificate required by § 68.35(a), or the ownership of the vessel changes so that it no longer meets the criteria of § 68.29, the qualification for the privileges enumerated in § 68.33 is terminated effective as of the date and time of the change. The not-for-profit oil spill response cooperative shall report the change in writing to the Director, National Vessel Documentation Center.

(b) If the vessel is owned by a member or members of a not-for-profit oil spill response cooperative and a change occurs which affects the validity of the certificate required by § 68.35(a), or the ownership of the vessel changes so that it no longer meets the criteria of § 68.29, the qualification of the member or members for the privileges enumerated in § 68.33 is terminated effective as of the date and time of the change. The member or members shall report the change in writing to the Director, National Vessel Documentation Center.

(c) When qualifications are terminated under this section, the certificate of documentation issued under this subpart must be surrendered or exchanged in accordance with part 67 of this chapter.

[GCD 89–007; GCD 89–007a, 58 FR 60266, Nov. 15, 1993, 58 FR 65131, Dec. 13, 1993, as amended by CGD 95–014, 60 FR 31606, June 15, 1995; USCG–1999–6216, 64 FR 53225, Oct. 1, 1999. Redesignated and amended by USCG–2005–20258, 71 FR 61418, Oct. 18, 2006]

APPENDIX A TO SUBPART B OF PART 68—OATH FOR QUALIFICATION OF A NOT-FOR-PROFIT OIL SPILL RESPONSE COOPERATIVE

Department of Homeland Security, U.S. Coast Guard

Oath for Qualification of a Not-For-Profit Oil Spill Response Cooperative [46 U.S.C. 12106(d)]

Cooperative:

Name _____

Address _____

Jurisdiction where incorporated or organized _____

Affiant:

Name _____

Address _____

Cooperative _____

Title or Capacity _____

I, the affiant, swear that I am legally authorized to make this oath and hold the capacity so bestowed upon me as _____, on behalf of the _____ cooperative and its members, that it is a not-for-profit cooperative, and that it is engaged in training for, carrying out, or supporting oil spill cleanup operations or related research activities.

That all members of the cooperative who may use the letter of qualification issued to this cooperative are truly and correctly named, including home address and citizenship of each on the attached listing incorporated in and made a part of this oath.

Signature _____

Subscribed and sworn to before me on the day and year shown.

_____
(Notary Public)

Date _____

[CGD 90–055, 57 FR 7642, Mar. 3, 1992, as amended by USCG–2003–14505, 68 FR 9535, Feb. 28, 2003. Redesignated by USCG–2007–28098, 71 FR 61418, Oct. 18, 2006]

APPENDIX B TO SUBPART B OF PART 68—OATH FOR DOCUMENTATION OF VESSELS FOR USE BY A NOT-FOR-PROFIT OIL SPILL RESPONSE COOPERATIVE

Department of Homeland Security, U.S. Coast Guard

Oath for Documentation of Vessels For Use by a Not-For-Profit Oil Spill Response Cooperative [46 U.S.C. 12106(d)]

Cooperative:
Name _____
Address _____
Jurisdiction where incorporated or organized _____

I, the undersigned officer of _____, a not-for-profit oil spill response cooperative, swear that I am legally authorized to make this oath on behalf of the cooperative, and its members and that the cooperative has accepted the vessel _____.

I/we _____, am/are the owner(s) of the vessel. I/we further swear that the vessel has been dedicated to the exclusive use of the cooperative for the purpose of training for, carrying out, or supporting oil spill cleanup operations or related research activities for discharges of oil into the navigable waters of the United States and the Exclusive Economic Zone and that the cooperative has accepted the vessel.

For the Cooperative:
Name _____
Address _____
Cooperative _____
Title or Capacity _____
For Each Vessel Owner:
Name _____
Cooperative _____
Title or Capacity _____

Subscribed and sworn to before me on the day and year shown.

(Notary Public)
Date _____

[CGD 90–055, 57 FR 7642, Mar. 3, 1992, as amended by USCG–2003–14505, 68 FR 9535, Feb. 28, 2003. Redesignated by USCG–2007–28098, 71 FR 61418, Oct. 18, 2006]

Subpart C—Vessels With a Coastwise Endorsement Issued on or After August 9, 2004, That Are Demised Chartered to Coastwise Qualified Citizens

SOURCE: USCG–2005–20258, 71 FR 61419, Oct. 18, 2006, unless otherwise noted.

§ 68.50 Purpose and applicability.

(a) This subpart contains requirements, in addition to those in part 67 of this chapter, for obtaining a coastwise endorsement for a U.S.-built vessel—

(1) That is owned by a person that qualifies as a citizen under § 67.35(a), § 67.36(a), § 67.37, or § 67.39(a) of this chapter; and

(2) That is demise chartered to a coastwise qualified citizen under § 67.33, § 67.35(c), § 67.36(c), § 67.37, § 67.39(c), or § 67.41 of this chapter.

(b) This subpart applies to a vessel with a coastwise endorsement issued on or after August 9, 2004. It does not apply to a vessel under subpart D of this part.

§ 68.55 Definitions.

In addition to the terms defined in § 67.3 of this chapter, as used in this subpart—

Affiliate means, with respect to any person, any other person that is—

(1) Directly or indirectly controlled by, under common control with, or controlling that person; or

(2) Named as being part of the same consolidated group in any report or other document submitted to the United States Securities and Exchange Commission or the Internal Revenue Service.

Cargo does not include cargo to which title is held for non-commercial reasons and primarily for the purpose of evading the requirements of § 68.65(a)(2).

Oil has the meaning given that term in 46 U.S.C. 2101(20).

Operation or management, for vessels, means all activities related to the use of vessels to provide services. These activities include, but are not limited to, ship agency; ship brokerage; activities performed by a vessel operator or demise charterer in exercising direction

§ 68.60

and control of a vessel, such as crewing, victualing, storing, and maintaining the vessel and ensuring its safe navigation; and activities associated with controlling the use and employment of the vessel under a time charter or other use agreement. It does not include activities directly associated with making financial investments in vessels or the receipt of earnings derived from these investments.

Passive investment means an investment in which neither the investor nor any affiliate of the investor is involved in, or has the power to be involved in, the formulation, determination, or direction of any activity or function concerning the use, operation, or management of the asset that is the subject of the investment.

Qualified proprietary cargo means—

(1) Oil, petroleum products, petrochemicals, or liquefied natural gas cargo that is beneficially owned by the person who submits to the Director, National Vessel Documentation Center, an application or annual certification under § 68.65(a)(2), or by an affiliate of that person, immediately before, during, or immediately after the cargo is carried in coastwise trade on a vessel owned by that person;

(2) Oil, petroleum products, petrochemicals, or liquefied natural gas cargo not beneficially owned by the person who submits to the Director, National Vessel Documentation Center, an application or an annual certification under § 68.65(a)(2), or by an affiliate of that person, but that is carried in coastwise trade by a vessel owned by that person and which is part of an arrangement in which vessels owned by that person and at least one other person are operated collectively as one fleet, to the extent that an equal amount of oil, petroleum products, petrochemicals, or liquefied natural gas cargo beneficially owned by that person, or an affiliate of that person, is carried in coastwise trade on one or more other vessels, not owned by that person, or an affiliate of that person, if the other vessel or vessels are also part of the same arrangement;

(3) In the case of a towing vessel associated with a non-self-propelled tank vessel where the two vessels function as a single self-propelled vessel, oil, petroleum products, petrochemicals, or liquefied natural gas cargo that is beneficially owned by the person who owns both the towing vessel and the non-self-propelled tank vessel, or any United States affiliate of that person, immediately before, during, or immediately after the cargo is carried in coastwise trade on either of the two vessels; or

(4) Any oil, petroleum products, petrochemicals, or liquefied natural gas cargo carried on any vessel that is either a self-propelled tank vessel having a length of at least 210 meters (about 689 feet) or a tank vessel that is a liquefied natural gas carrier that—

(i) Was delivered by the builder of the vessel to the owner of the vessel after December 31, 1999; and

(ii) Was purchased by a person for the purpose, and with the reasonable expectation, of transporting on the vessel liquefied natural gas or unrefined petroleum beneficially owned by the owner of the vessel, or an affiliate of the owner, from Alaska to the continental United States.

Sub-charter means all types of charters or other contracts for the use of a vessel that are subordinate to a charter. The term includes, but is not limited to, a demise charter, a time charter, a voyage charter, a space charter, and a contract of affreightment.

United States affiliate means, with respect to any person, an affiliate the principal place of business of which is located in the United States.

§ 68.60 Eligibility of a vessel for a coastwise endorsement under this subpart.

(a) To be eligible for a coastwise endorsement under 46 U.S.C. 12106(e) and to operate in coastwise trade under 46 U.S.C. 12106(e) and 12110(b), a vessel must meet the following:

(1) The vessel is eligible for documentation under 46 U.S.C. 12102.

(2) The vessel is eligible for a coastwise endorsement under § 67.19(c) of this chapter and has not lost coastwise eligibility under § 67.19(d) of this chapter.

(3) The person that owns the vessel (or, if the vessel is owned by a trust or similar arrangement, the beneficiary of

the trust or similar arrangement) makes the certification in § 68.65.

(4) The person that owns the vessel has transferred to a qualified U.S. citizen under 46 U.S.C. app. 802 full possession, control, and command of the vessel through a demise charter in which the demise charterer is considered the owner *pro hac vice* during the term of the charter.

(5) The charterer must certify to the Director, National Vessel Documentation Center, that the charterer is a citizen of the United States for engaging in the coastwise trade under 46 U.S.C. app. 802.

(6) The demise charter is for a period of at least 3 years, unless a shorter period is authorized by the Director, National Vessel Documentation Center, under circumstances such as—

(i) When the vessel's remaining life would not support a charter of 3 years; or

(ii) To preserve the use or possession of the vessel.

(b) To apply for a coastwise endorsement for a vessel under a demise charter, see § 68.70 and, for a barge, see § 68.75.

NOTE TO § 68.60: Section 608(b) of Public Law 108–293 provides special requirements for certain vessels in the Alaska trade.

§ 68.65 Annual ownership certification.

(a) At the time of initial application for documentation and at the time for annual renewal of the endorsement as required by § 67.163 of this chapter, the person that owns a vessel with a coastwise endorsement under § 68.60 must certify in writing to the Director, National Vessel Documentation Center—

(1) That the person who owns a vessel with a coastwise endorsement under § 68.60—

(i) Is a leasing company, bank, or financial institution;

(ii) Owns, or holds the beneficial interest in, the vessel solely as a passive investment;

(iii) Does not operate any vessel for hire and is not an affiliate of any person who operates any vessel for hire; and

(iv) Is independent from, and not an affiliate of, any charterer of the vessel or any other person who has the right, directly or indirectly, to control or direct the movement or use of the vessel.

(2) For vessels under paragraph (b) of this section, that—

(i) The aggregate book value of the vessels owned by that person and United States affiliates of that person does not exceed 10 percent of the aggregate book value of all assets owned by that person and its United States affiliates;

(ii) Not more than 10 percent of the aggregate revenues of that person and its United States affiliates is derived from the ownership, operation, or management of vessels;

(iii) At least 70 percent of the aggregate tonnage of all cargo carried by all vessels owned by that person and its United States affiliates and documented under 46 U.S.C. 12106 is qualified proprietary cargo;

(iv) Any cargo other than qualified proprietary cargo carried by all vessels owned by that person and its United States affiliates and documented under 46 U.S.C. 12106 consists of oil, petroleum products, petrochemicals, or liquified natural gas;

(v) No vessel owned by that person or any of its United States affiliates and documented under 46 U.S.C. 12106 carries molten sulphur; and

(vi) That person owned one or more vessels documented as of August 9, 2004, under § 67.20, as that section was in effect on that date.

(b) Paragraph (a)(2) of this section applies only to—

(1) A tank vessel having a tonnage of not less than 6,000 gross tons, as measured under 46 U.S.C. 14502 (or an alternative tonnage measured under 46 U.S.C. 14302 as prescribed under 46 U.S.C. 14104); or

(2) A towing vessel associated with a non-self-propelled tank vessel that meets the requirements of paragraph (b)(1) of this section, where the two vessels function as a single self-propelled vessel.

NOTE TO § 68.65: The Secretary of Transportation may waive or reduce the qualified proprietary cargo requirement of § 68.65(a)(2)(iii) for a vessel if the person that owns the vessel (or, if the vessel is owned by a trust or similar arrangement, the beneficiary of the trust or similar arrangement) notifies the Secretary that circumstances beyond the direct control of the person that owns the vessel or

§ 68.70

its affiliates prevent, or reasonably threaten to prevent, the person that owns the vessel from satisfying this requirement, and the Secretary does not, with good cause, determine otherwise. The waiver or reduction applies during the period of time that the circumstances exist.

§ 68.70 Application procedure for vessels other than barges to be operated in coastwise trade without being documented.

(a) The person that owns the vessel (other than a barge under § 68.75) and that seeks a coastwise endorsement under § 68.60 must submit the following to the National Vessel Documentation Center:

(1) Application for Initial Issue, Exchange, or Replacement of Certificate of Documentation; or Redocumentation (form CG-1258);

(2) Title evidence, if applicable;

(3) Mortgagee consent on form CG-4593, if applicable;

(4) If the application is for replacement of a mutilated document or for exchange of documentation, the outstanding Certificate of Documentation;

(5) The certification required by § 68.65(a)(1) or, if a vessel under § 68.65(b), the certification required by § 68.65(a)(2);

(6) A certification in the form of an affidavit and, if requested by the Director, National Vessel Documentation Center, supporting documentation establishing the following facts with respect to the transaction from an individual who is authorized to provide certification on behalf of the person that owns the vessel and who is an officer in a corporation, a partner in a partnership, a member of the board of managers in a limited liability company, or their equivalent. The certificate must certify that the person that owns the vessel has transferred to a qualified United States citizen under 46 U.S.C. app. 802 full possession, control, and command of the U.S.-built vessel through a demise charter in which the demise charterer is considered the owner *pro hac vice* during the term of the charter.

(7) A copy of the charter, which must provide that the charterer is deemed to be the owner *pro hac vice* for the term of the charter.

(b) The charterer must submit the following to the National Vessel Documentation Center:

(1) A certificate certifying that the charterer is a citizen of the United States for the purpose of engaging in the coastwise trade under 46 U.S.C. app. 802.

(2) Detailed citizenship information in the format of form CG-1258, Application for Documentation, section G, citizenship. The citizenship information may be attached to the form CG-1258 that is submitted under paragraph (a)(1) of this section and must be signed by, or on behalf of, the charterer.

(c) Whenever a charter submitted under paragraph (a)(7) of this section is amended, the vessel owner must file a copy of the amendment with the Director, National Vessel Documentation Center, within 10 days after the effective date of the amendment.

(d) Whenever the charterer of a vessel under paragraph (a) of this section enters into a sub-charter that is a demise charter with another person for the use of the vessel, the charterer must file a copy of the sub-charter and amendments to the sub-charter with the Director, National Vessel Documentation Center, within 10 days after the effective date of the sub-charter and the sub-charterer must provide detailed citizenship information in the format of form CG-1258, Application for Documentation, section G, citizenship.

(e) Whenever the charterer of a vessel under paragraph (a) of this section enters into a sub-charter other than a demise charter with another person for the use of the vessel, the charterer must file a copy of the sub-charter and amendments to the sub-charter with the Director, National Vessel Documentation Center, within 10 days after a request by the Director to do so.

(f) A person that submits a false certification under this section is subject to penalty under 46 U.S.C. 12122 and 18 U.S.C. 1001.

§ 68.75 Application procedure for barges to be operated in coastwise trade without being documented.

(a) The person that owns a barge qualified to engage in coastwise trade must submit the following to the National Vessel Documentation Center:

Coast Guard, Dept. of Homeland Security § 68.80

(1) The certification required by § 68.65(a)(1) or (a)(2).

(2) A certification in the form of an affidavit and, if requested by the Director, National Vessel Documentation Center, supporting documentation establishing the following facts with respect to the transaction from an individual who is authorized to provide certification on behalf of the person that owns the barge and who is an officer in a corporation, a partner in a partnership, a member of the board of managers in a limited liability company, or their equivalent. The certificate must certify the following:

(i) That the person that owns the barge is organized under the laws of the United States or a State.

(ii) That the person that owns the barge has transferred to a qualified United States citizen under 46 U.S.C. app. 802 full possession, control, and command of the U.S.-built barge through a demise charter in which the demise charterer is considered the owner *pro hac vice* during the term of the charter.

(iii) That the barge is qualified to engage in the coastwise trade and that it is owned by a person eligible to own vessels documented under 46 U.S.C. 12102(e).

(3) A copy of the charter, which must provide that the charterer is deemed to be the owner *pro hac vice* for the term of the charter.

(b) The charterer must submit the following to the National Vessel Documentation Center:

(1) A certificate certifying that the charterer is a citizen of the United States for engaging in the coastwise trade under 46 U.S.C. app. 802.

(2) Detailed citizenship information in the format of form CG-1258, Application for Documentation, section G, citizenship. The citizenship information must be signed by, or on behalf of, the charterer.

(c) Whenever a charter under paragraph (a) of this section is amended, the barge owner must file a copy of the amendment with the Director, National Vessel Documentation Center, within 10 days after the effective date of the amendment.

(d) Whenever the charterer of a barge under paragraph (a) of this section enters into a sub-charter that is a demise charter with another person for the use of the barge, the charterer must file a copy of the sub-charter and amendments to the sub-charter with the Director, National Vessel Documentation Center, within 10 days after the effective date of the sub-charter and the sub-charterer must provide detailed citizenship information in the format of form CG-1258, Application for Documentation, section G, citizenship.

(e) Whenever the charterer of a barge under paragraph (a) of this section enters into a sub-charter other than a demise charter with another person for the use of the barge, the charterer must file a copy of the sub-charter and amendments to the sub-charter with the Director, National Vessel Documentation Center, within 10 days after a request by the Director to do so.

(f) A person that submits a false certification under this section is subject to penalty under 46 U.S.C. 12122 and 18 U.S.C. 1001.

§ 68.80 Invalidation of a coastwise endorsement.

In addition to the events in § 67.167(c)(1) through (c)(9) of this chapter, a Certificate of Documentation together with a coastwise endorsement under this subpart becomes invalid when—

(a) The owner fails to make the certification required by § 68.65 or ceases to meet the requirements of the certification on file;

(b) The demise charter expires or is transferred to another charterer; or

(c) The citizenship of the charterer or sub-charterer changes to the extent that they are no longer qualified for a coastwise endorsement.

Subpart D—Vessels With a Coastwise Endorsement Issued Before August 9, 2004, and Their Replacements That Are Demised Chartered to Coastwise-Qualified Citizens

SOURCE: USCG-2005-20258, 71 FR 61421, Oct. 18, 2006, unless otherwise noted.

§ 68.100 Purpose and applicability.

(a) This subpart contains requirements for the documentation of U.S.-built vessels in the coastwise trade that were granted special rights under the Coast Guard and Maritime Transportation Action of 2004 (Pub. L. 108-293).

(b) This subpart applies to—

(1) A vessel under a demise charter that was eligible for, and received, a document with a coastwise endorsement under § 67.19 of this chapter and 46 U.S.C. 12106(e) before August 9, 2004;

(2) A barge deemed eligible under 46 U.S.C. 12106(e) and 12110(b) to operate in coastwise trade without being documented before August 9, 2004; and

(3) A replacement vessel of a similar size and function for any vessel under paragraphs (b)(1) through (b)(3) of this section.

(c) Except for vessels under paragraph (d) of this section, this subpart applies to a certificate of documentation, or renewal of one, endorsed with a coastwise endorsement for a vessel under 46 U.S.C. 12106(e) or a replacement vessel of a similar size and function that was issued before August 9, 2004, as long as the vessel is owned by the person named in the certificate, or by a subsidiary or affiliate of that person, and the controlling interest in the owner has not been transferred to a person that was not an affiliate of the owner as of August 9, 2004.

(d) With respect to offshore supply vessels with a certificate of documentation endorsed with a coastwise endorsement as of August 9, 2004, this subpart applies until August 9, 2007. On and after August 9, 2007, subpart C of this part applies to these vessels.

§ 68.103 Definitions.

In addition to the terms defined in § 67.3 of this chapter, as used in this subpart—

Affiliate means a person that is less than 50 percent owned or controlled by another person.

Group means the person that owns a vessel, the parent of that person, and all subsidiaries and affiliates of the parent of that person.

Offshore supply vessel means a motor vessel of more than 15 gross tons but less than 500 gross tons as measured under 46 U.S.C. 14502, or an alternate tonnage measured under 46 U.S.C. 14302 as prescribed under 46 U.S.C. 14104, that regularly carries goods, supplies, individuals in addition to the crew, or equipment in support of exploration, exploitation, or production of offshore mineral or energy resources.

Operation or management of vessels means all activities related to the use of vessels to provide services. These activities include ship agency; ship brokerage; activities performed by a vessel operator or demise charterer in exercising direction and control of a vessel, such as crewing, victualing, storing, and maintaining the vessel and ensuring its safe navigation; and activities associated with controlling the use and employment of the vessel under a time charter or other use agreement. It does not include activities directly associated with making financial investments in vessels or the receipt of earnings derived from these investments.

Parent means any person that directly or indirectly owns or controls at least 50 percent of another person. If an owner's parent is directly or indirectly controlled at least 50 percent by another person, that person is also a parent of the owner. Therefore, an owner may have multiple parents.

Person means an individual; corporation; partnership; limited liability partnership; limited liability company; association; joint venture; trust arrangement; and the government of the United States, a State, or a political subdivision of the United States or a State; and includes a trustee, beneficiary, receiver, or similar representative of any of them.

Primarily engaged in leasing or other financing transactions means lease financing, in which more than 50 percent of the aggregate revenue of a person is derived from banking, investing, lease financing, or other similar transactions.

Replacement vessel means—

(1) A temporary replacement vessel for a period not to exceed 180 days if the vessel described in § 68.50 is unavailable due to an act of God or a marine casualty; or

(2) A permanent replacement vessel if—

Coast Guard, Dept. of Homeland Security § 68.105

(i) The vessel described in § 68.50 is unavailable for more than 180 days due to an act of God or a marine casualty; or

(ii) A contract to purchase or construct a replacement vessel is executed not later than December 31, 2004.

Sub-charter means all types of charters or other contracts for the use of a vessel that are subordinate to a charter. The term includes, but is not limited to, a demise charter, a time charter, a voyage charter, a space charter, and a contract of affreightment.

Subsidiary means a person at least 50 percent of which is directly or indirectly owned or controlled by another person.

§ 68.105 Eligibility of a vessel for a coastwise endorsement under this subpart.

(a) Except as under paragraphs (b) through (e) of this section, to be eligible for a coastwise endorsement under 46 U.S.C. 12106(e) and to operate in coastwise trade under 46 U.S.C. 12106(e) and 12110(b), a vessel under a demise charter must meet the following:

(1) The vessel is eligible for documentation under 46 U.S.C. 12102.

(2) The vessel is eligible for a coastwise endorsement under § 67.19(c) of this chapter, has not lost coastwise eligibility under § 67.19(d) of this chapter, and was financed with lease financing.

(3) The person that owns the vessel, the parent of that person, or a subsidiary of the parent of that person is primarily engaged in leasing or other financing transactions.

(4) The person that owns the vessel is organized under the laws of the United States or of a State.

(5) None of the following is primarily engaged in the direct operation or management of vessels:
(i) The person that owns the vessel.
(ii) The parent of the person that owns the vessel.
(iii) The group of which the person that owns the vessel is a member.

(6) The ownership of the vessel is primarily a financial investment without the ability and intent to directly or indirectly control the vessel's operations by a person not primarily engaged in the direct operation or management of vessels.

(7) The majority of the aggregate revenues of each of the following is not derived from the operation or management of vessels:
(i) The person that owns the vessel.
(ii) The parent of the person that owns the vessel.
(iii) The group of which the person that owns the vessel is a member.

(8) None of the following is primarily engaged in the operation or management of commercial, foreign-flag vessels used for the carriage of cargo for parties unrelated to the vessel's owner or charterer:
(i) The person that owns the vessel.
(ii) The parent of the person that owns the vessel.
(iii) The group of which the person that owns the vessel is a member.

(9) The person that owns the vessel has transferred to a qualified U.S. citizen under 46 U.S.C. app. 802 full possession, control, and command of the U.S.-built vessel through a demise charter in which the demise charterer is considered the owner *pro hac vice* during the term of the charter.

(10) The charterer must certify to the Director, National Vessel Documentation Center, that the charterer is a citizen of the United States for engaging in the coastwise trade under 46 U.S.C. app. 802.

(11) The demise charter is for a period of at least 3 years, unless a shorter period is authorized by the Director, National Vessel Documentation Center, under circumstances such as—
(i) When the vessel's remaining life would not support a charter of 3 years; or
(ii) To preserve the use or possession of the vessel.

(b) A vessel under a demise charter that was eligible for, and received, a document with a coastwise endorsement under § 67.19 of this chapter and 46 U.S.C. 12106(e) before August 9, 2004, may continue to operate under that endorsement on and after that date and may renew the document and endorsement if the certificate of documentation is not subject to—

(1) Exchange under § 67.167(b)(1) through (b)(3) of this chapter;
(2) Deletion under § 67.171(a)(1) through (a)(6) of this chapter; or

§ 68.107

(3) Cancellation under § 67.173 of this chapter.

(c) A vessel under a demise charter that was constructed under a building contract that was entered into before February 4, 2004, in reliance on a letter ruling from the Coast Guard issued before February 4, 2004, is eligible for documentation with a coastwise endorsement under § 67.19 of this chapter and 46 U.S.C. 12106(e). The vessel may continue to operate under that endorsement and may renew the document and endorsement if the certificate of documentation is not subject to—

(1) Exchange under § 67.167(b)(1) through (b)(3) of this chapter;

(2) Deletion under § 67.171(a)(1) through (a)(6) of this chapter; or

(3) Cancellation under § 67.173 of this chapter.

(d) A barge deemed eligible under 46 U.S.C. 12106(e) and 12110(b) to operate in coastwise trade before August 9, 2004, may continue to operate in that trade after that date unless—

(1) The ownership of the barge changes in whole or in part;

(2) The general partners of a partnership owning the barge change by addition, deletion, or substitution;

(3) The State of incorporation of any corporate owner of the barge changes;

(4) The barge is placed under foreign flag;

(5) Any owner of the barge ceases to be a citizen within the meaning of part 67, subpart C, of this chapter; or

(6) The barge ceases to be capable of transportation by water.

(e) A barge under a demise charter that was constructed under a building contract that was entered into before February 4, 2004, in reliance on a letter ruling from the Coast Guard issued before February 4, 2004, is eligible to operate in coastwise trade under 46 U.S.C. 12106(e) and 12110(b). The barge may continue to operate in coastwise trade unless—

(1) The ownership of the barge changes in whole or in part;

(2) The general partners of a partnership owning the barge change by addition, deletion, or substitution;

(3) The State of incorporation of any corporate owner of the barge changes;

(4) The barge is placed under foreign flag;

(5) Any owner of the barge ceases to be a citizen within the meaning of subpart C of this part; or

(6) The barge ceases to be capable of transportation by water.

§ 68.107 Application procedure for vessels other than barges to be operated in coastwise trade without being documented.

(a) In addition to the items under § 67.141 of this chapter, the person that owns the vessel (other than a barge under § 68.109) and that seeks a coastwise endorsement under this subpart must submit the following to the National Vessel Documentation Center:

(1) A certification in the form of an affidavit and, if requested by the Director, National Vessel Documentation Center, supporting documentation establishing the following facts with respect to the transaction from an individual who is authorized to provide certification on behalf of the person that owns the vessel and who is an officer in a corporation, a partner in a partnership, a member of the board of managers in a limited liability company, or their equivalent. The certificate must certify the following:

(i) That the person that owns the vessel, the parent of that person, or a subsidiary of a parent of that person is primarily engaged in leasing or other financing transactions.

(ii) That the person that owns the vessel is organized under the laws of the United States or a State.

(iii) That none of the following is primarily engaged in the direct operation or management of vessels:

(A) The person that owns the vessel.

(B) The parent of the person that owns the vessel.

(C) The group of which the person that owns the vessel is a member.

(iv) That ownership of the vessel is primarily a financial investment without the ability and intent to directly or indirectly control the vessel's operations by a person not primarily engaged in the direct operation or management of vessels.

(v) That the majority of the aggregate revenues of each of the following is not derived from the operation or management of vessels:

(A) The person that owns the vessel.

Coast Guard, Dept. of Homeland Security § 68.109

(B) The parent of the person that owns the vessel.

(C) The group of which the person that owns the vessel is a member.

(vi) That none of the following is primarily engaged in the operation or management of commercial, foreign-flag vessels used for the carriage of cargo for parties unrelated to the vessel's owner or charterer:

(A) The person that owns the vessel.

(B) The parent of the person that owns the vessel.

(C) The group of which the person that owns the vessel is a member.

(vii) That the person that owns the vessel has transferred to a qualified United States citizen under 46 U.S.C. app. 802 full possession, control, and command of the U.S.-built vessel through a demise charter in which the demise charterer is considered the owner *pro hac vice* during the term of the charter.

(viii) That the vessel is financed with lease financing.

(2) A copy of the charter, which must provide that the charterer is deemed to be the owner *pro hac vice* for the term of the charter.

(b) The charterer must submit the following to the National Vessel Documentation Center:

(1) A certificate certifying that the charterer is a citizen of the United States for the purpose of engaging in the coastwise trade under 46 U.S.C. app. 802.

(2) Detailed citizenship information in the format of form CG–1258, Application for Documentation, section G, citizenship. The citizenship information may be attached to the form CG–1258 that is submitted under § 67.141 of this chapter and must be signed by, or on behalf of, the charterer.

(c) Whenever a charter under paragraph (a) of this section is amended, the vessel owner must file a copy of the amendment with the Director, National Vessel Documentation Center, within 10 days after the effective date of the amendment.

(d) Whenever the charterer of a vessel under paragraph (a) of this section enters into a sub-charter that is a demise charter with another person for the use of the vessel, the charterer must file a copy of the sub-charter and amendments to the sub-charter with the Director, National Vessel Documentation Center, within 10 days after the effective date of the sub-charter and the sub-charterer must provide detailed citizenship information in the format of form CG–1258, Application for Documentation, section G, citizenship.

(e) Whenever the charterer of a vessel under paragraph (a) of this section enters into a sub-charter other than a demise charter with another person for the use of the vessel, the charterer must file a copy of the sub-charter and amendments to the sub-charter with the Director, National Vessel Documentation Center, within 10 days after a request by the Director to do so.

(f) A person that submits a false certification under this section is subject to penalty under 46 U.S.C. 12122 and 18 U.S.C. 1001.

§ 68.109 Application procedure for barges to be operated in coastwise trade without being documented.

(a) The person that owns a barge qualified to engage in coastwise trade under the lease-financing provisions of 46 U.S.C. 12106(e) must submit the following to the National Vessel Documentation Center:

(1) A certification in the form of an affidavit and, if requested by the Director, National Vessel Documentation Center, supporting documentation establishing the following facts with respect to the transaction from an individual who is authorized to provide certification on behalf of the person that owns the barge and who is an officer in a corporation, a partner in a partnership, a member of the board of managers in a limited liability company, or their equivalent. The certificate must certify the following:

(i) That the person that owns the barge, the parent of that person, or a subsidiary of the parent of that person is primarily engaged in leasing or other financing transactions.

(ii) That the person that owns the barge is organized under the laws of the United States or a State.

(iii) That none of the following is primarily engaged in the direct operation or management of vessels:

(A) The person that owns the barge.

(B) The parent of the person that owns the barge.

(C) The group of which the person that owns the barge is a member.

(iv) That ownership of the barge is primarily a financial investment without the ability and intent to directly or indirectly control the barge's operations by a person not primarily engaged in the direct operation or management of the barge.

(v) That the majority of the aggregate revenues of each of the following is not derived from the operation or management of vessels:

(A) The person that owns the barge.

(B) The parent of the person that owns the barge.

(C) The group of which the person that owns the barge is a member.

(vi) That none of the following is primarily engaged in the operation or management of commercial, foreign-flag vessels used for the carriage of cargo for parties unrelated to the vessel's owner or charterer:

(A) The person that owns the barge.

(B) The parent of the person that owns the barge.

(C) The group of which the person that owns the barge is a member.

(vii) That the person that owns the barge has transferred to a qualified United States citizen under 46 U.S.C. app. 802 full possession, control, and command of the U.S.-built barge through a demise charter in which the demise charterer is considered the owner *pro hac vice* for the term of the charter.

(viii) That the barge is qualified to engage in the coastwise trade and that it is owned by a person eligible to own vessels documented under 46 U.S.C. 12102(e).

(ix) That the barge is financed with lease financing.

(2) A copy of the charter, which must provide that the charterer is deemed to be the owner *pro hac vice* for the term of the charter.

(b) The charterer must submit the following to the National Vessel Documentation Center:

(1) A certificate certifying that the charterer is a citizen of the United States for engaging in the coastwise trade under 46 U.S.C. app. 802.

(2) Detailed citizenship information in the format of form CG-1258, Application for Documentation, section G, citizenship. The citizenship information must be signed by, or on behalf of, the charterer.

(c) Whenever a charter under paragraph (a) of this section is amended, the barge owner must file a copy of the amendment with the Director, National Vessel Documentation Center, within 10 days after the effective date of the amendment.

(d) Whenever the charterer of a barge under paragraph (a) of this section enters into a sub-charter that is a demise charter with another person for the use of the barge, the charterer must file a copy of the sub-charter and amendments to the sub-charter with the Director, National Vessel Documentation Center, within 10 days after the effective date of the sub-charter and the sub-charterer must provide detailed citizenship information in the format of form CG-1258, Application for Documentation, section G, citizenship.

(e) Whenever the charterer of a barge under paragraph (a) of this section enters into a sub-charter other than a demise charter with another person for the use of the barge, the charterer must file a copy of the sub-charter and amendments to the sub-charter with the Director, National Vessel Documentation Center, within 10 days after a request by the Director to do so.

(f) A person that submits a false certification under this section is subject to penalty under 46 U.S.C. 12122 and 18 U.S.C. 1001.

§ 68.111 Invalidation of a coastwise endorsement.

(a) In addition to the events in § 67.167(c)(1) through (c)(9) of this chapter, a Certificate of Documentation together with a coastwise endorsement in effect before February 4, 2004, becomes invalid when—

(1) The demise charter expires or is transferred to another charterer;

(2) The citizenship of the charterer or sub-charterer changes to the extent that they are no longer qualified for a coastwise endorsement; or

(3) Neither the person that owns the vessel, nor the parent of that person, nor a subsidiary of the parent of that

Coast Guard, Dept. of Homeland Security

Pt. 69

person is primarily engaged in leasing or other financing transactions.

(b) In addition to the events in §67.167(c)(1) through (c)(9) of this chapter, a Certificate of Documentation together with a coastwise endorsement in effect on or after February 4, 2004, and before August 9, 2004, becomes invalid when—

(1) The demise charter expires or is transferred to another charterer;

(2) The citizenship of the charterer or sub-charterer changes to the extent that they are no longer qualified for a coastwise endorsement;

(3) Neither the person that owns the vessel, nor the parent of that person, nor any subsidiary of the parent of that person is primarily engaged in leasing or other financing transactions;

(4) The majority of the aggregate revenues of at least one of the following is derived from the operation or management of vessels:

(i) The person that owns the vessel.

(ii) The parent of the person that owns the vessel.

(iii) The group of which the person that owns the vessel is a member; or

(5) At least one of the following is primarily engaged in the operation or management of commercial, foreign-flag vessels used for the carriage of cargo for parties unrelated to the vessel's owner or charterer:

(i) The person that owns the vessel.

(ii) The parent of the person that owns the vessel.

(iii) The group of which the person that owns the vessel is a member.

(c) When the coastwise endorsement for a vessel to which this subpart applies becomes invalid under paragraph (a)(1) or (b)(1) of this section, the vessel remains eligible for documentation under this subpart provided it is a vessel to which §68.100(b) or (c) applies.

PART 69—MEASUREMENT OF VESSELS

Subpart A—General

Sec.
69.1 Purpose.
69.3 Applicability.
69.5 Vessels required or eligible to be measured.
69.7 Vessels transiting the Panama and Suez Canals.
69.9 Definitions.
69.11 Determining the measurement system or systems for a particular vessel.
69.13 Deviating from the provisions of a measurement system.
69.15 Authorized measurement organizations.
69.17 Application for measurement services.
69.19 Remeasurement and adjustment of tonnage.
69.21 Right of appeal.
69.23 Fees.
69.25 Penalties.
69.27 Delegation of authority to measure vessels.
69.29 OMB control numbers assigned under the Paperwork Reduction Act.

Subpart B—Convention Measurement System

69.51 Purpose.
69.53 Definitions.
69.55 Application for measurement services.
69.57 Gross tonnage.
69.59 Enclosed spaces.
69.61 Excluded spaces.
69.63 Net tonnage.
69.65 Calculation of volumes.
69.67 Marking of cargo spaces.
69.69 Issuance of an International Tonnage Certificate (1969).
69.71 Change of net tonnage.
69.73 Variance from the prescribed method of measurement.
69.75 Figures.

Subpart C—Standard Measurement System

69.101 Purpose.
69.103 Definitions.
69.105 Application for measurement services.
69.107 Gross and net tonnages.
69.109 Under-deck tonnage.
69.111 Between-deck tonnage.
69.113 Superstructure tonnage.
69.115 Excess hatchway tonnage.
69.117 Spaces exempt from inclusion in gross tonnage.
69.119 Spaces deducted from gross tonnage.
69.121 Engine room deduction.
69.123 Figures.

Subpart D—Dual Measurement System

69.151 Purpose.
69.153 Application of other laws.
69.155 Measurement requirements.
69.157 Definitions.
69.159 Application for measurement services.
69.161 Gross and net tonnages.
69.163 Under-deck tonnage.
69.165 Between-deck tonnage.
69.167 Superstructure tonnage.
69.169 Spaces exempt from inclusion in gross tonnage.

§ 69.1

69.171 When the tonnage mark is considered submerged.
69.173 Tonnage assignments for vessels with only one deck.
69.175 Tonnage assignments for vessels with a second deck.
69.177 Markings.
69.179 Certification of markings.
69.181 Locating the line of the second deck.
69.183 Figures.

Subpart E—Simplified Measurement System

69.201 Purpose.
69.203 Definitions.
69.205 Application for measurement services.
69.207 Measurements.
69.209 Calculation of tonnages.

AUTHORITY: 46 U.S.C. 2301, 14103; Department of Homeland Security Delegation No. 0170.1.

SOURCE: CGD 87–015b, 54 FR 37657, Sept. 12, 1989, unless otherwise noted.

Subpart A—General

§ 69.1 Purpose.

This part implements legislation concerning the measurement of vessels to determine their tonnage (part J of 46 U.S.C. subtitle II). Tonnages are required before a vessel may be documented as a vessel of the United States. Also, tonnages are used to apply commercial vessel safety regulations based on tonnage, to meet the requirements of the International Convention on Tonnage Measurement of Ships, 1969, and to determine Federal and State regulatory fees and private operational charges based on tonnage. Tonnages are determined by the physical measurement of a vessel (Convention, Standard, and Dual Measurement Systems) or by application of a formula based on the vessel's dimensions provided by the owner (Simplified Measurement System). This part indicates the particular measurement system or systems under which the vessel is required or eligible to be measured, describes the application and measurement procedures for each system, identifies the organizations authorized to measure vessels under this part, and provides for the appeal of measurement organizations' decisions.

§ 69.3 Applicability.

This part applies to vessels of the United States over five net tons (as that tonnage is determined under this part) which are required or eligible to be measured under this part, a Federal law, or an international agreement or which are subject to a Federal law or international agreement based on the vessel's tonnage.

§ 69.5 Vessels required or eligible to be measured.

(a) The following vessels (including public vessels) are required to be measured under this part:

(1) Vessels that are to be documented as a vessel of the United States.

(2) Vessels of 79 feet or more in overall length that engage on a foreign voyage.

(3) Vessels subject to a Federal law or regulation based on vessel tonnage.

(4) Vessels determined by the Commandant to require measurement under this part.

(b) The following vessels are not required to be measured under this part but are eligible to be measured, if the owner requests:

(1) Public vessels that are not to be documented and will not engage on a foreign voyage.

(2) Vessels of war.

[CGD 87–015b, 54 FR 37657, Sept. 12, 1989, as amended by CGD 92–058, 57 FR 59938, Dec. 17, 1992]

§ 69.7 Vessels transiting the Panama and Suez Canals.

(a) All vessels intending to transit the Panama Canal, other than vessels of war, must be measured and certificated under the system prescribed in 35 CFR part 135.

(b) All vessels intending to transit the Suez Canal must be measured and certificated under the Arab Republic of Egypt Suez Canal Authority Rules of Navigation, part IV.

(c) Panama Canal and Suez Canal tonnage certificates are in addition to tonnage certificates issued under this part.

(d) Tonnage measurement services for Panama Canal and Suez Canal certificates are provided by measurement organizations authorized by the respective canal authority.

Coast Guard, Dept. of Homeland Security § 69.11

§ 69.9 Definitions.

As used in this part—

Commandant means Commandant of the Coast Guard at the following addresses: Commanding Officer, Marine Safety Center, U.S. Coast Guard, 4200 Wilson Boulevard Suite 400, Arlington, VA 22203 for visitors. Send all mail to Commanding Officer (MSC), Attn: Marine Safety Center, U.S. Coast Guard Stop 7410, 4200 Wilson Boulevard Suite 400, Arlington, VA 20598–7410, in a written or electronic format. Information for submitting the VSP electronically can be found at *http://www.uscg.mil/HQ/MSC*.

Convention means the International Convention on Tonnage Measurement of Ships, 1969.

Convention Measurement System means the system under subpart B of this part.

Dual Measurement System means the system under subpart D of this part.

Great Lakes means the Great Lakes of North America and the St. Lawrence River west of a rhumb line drawn from Cap des Rosiers to West Point, Anticosti Island, and, on the north side of Anticosti Island, the meridian of longitude 63 degrees west.

Gross tonnage means a vessel's approximate volume. Under the Convention Measurement System, it means the total volume of all enclosed spaces modified by a coefficient. Under the Standard and Dual Measurement Systems, it means the total volume of all enclosed spaces less certain exempt spaces. Under the Simplified Measurement Systems, it means the product of a vessel's length, depth, and breadth modified by a coefficient.

National Vessel Documentation Center means the organizational unit designated by the Commandant to process vessel documentation transactions and maintain vessel documentation records. The address can be found in § 67.3 of this subchapter.

Net tonnage means a measure of a vessel's earning capacity. Under the Convention Measurement System, it means the volume of the actual cargo and passenger spaces modified by a formula based on the vessel's volume. Under the Standard and Dual Measurement Systems, it means the gross tonnage less certain deducted spaces. Under the Simplified Measurement System, it means the gross tonnage modified by a coefficient.

Overall length means the horizontal distance between the foremost part of a vessel's stem to the aftermost part of its stern, excluding fittings and attachments.

Simplified Measurement System means the system under subpart E of this part.

Standard Measurement System means the system under subpart C of this part.

Tonnage means the volume of a vessel's enclosed spaces as calculated under a measurement system in this part. Tonnage calculated under the Standard, Dual, or Simplified Measurement System is based on tons of 100 cubic feet each. Tonnage calculated under the Convention Measurement System is based on tons of 100 cubic feet modified by a logarithmic function.

Vessel engaged on a foreign voyage means a vessel—

(a) Arriving at a place under the jurisdiction of the United States from a place in a foreign country;

(b) Making a voyage between places outside of the United States;

(c) Departing from a place under the jurisdiction of the United States for a place in a foreign country; or

(d) Making a voyage between a place within a territory or possession of the United States and another place under the jurisdiction of the United States not within that territory or possession.

Vessel of war means "vessel of war" as defined in 46 U.S.C. 2101.

[GCD 89–007; GCD 89–007a, 58 FR 60266, Nov. 15, 1993, 58 FR 65131, Dec. 13, 1993, as amended by CGD 95–014, 60 FR 31606, June 15, 1995; CGD 95–072, 60 FR 50463, Sept. 29, 1995; 60 FR 54106, Oct. 19, 1995; CGD 96–041, 61 FR 50728, Sept. 27, 1996; USCG–2007–29018, 72 FR 53965, Sept. 21, 2007; USCG–2009–0702, 74 FR 49230, Sept. 25, 2009; USCG 2013–0671, 78 FR 60149, Sept. 30, 2013]

§ 69.11 Determining the measurement system or systems for a particular vessel.

(a) *Convention Measurement System (subpart B)*. (1) Except as otherwise provided in this section, this system applies to a vessel documented or to be documented under part 67 of this chapter and to a vessel engaged on a foreign voyage.

(2) This system does not apply to the following vessels:

(i) A vessel of less than 79 feet in overall length.

(ii) A vessel operating only on the Great Lakes, unless the owner requests measurement under this system.

(iii) A vessel that is not engaged on a foreign voyage and that had its keel laid or was at a similar stage of construction before January 1, 1986, unless the owner requests measurement under the Convention Measurement System or unless, on or after January 1, 1986, the vessel undergoes a change that the Commandant finds substantially affects the vessel's gross tonnage.

(iv) A vessel of war.

(v) A non-self-propelled vessel not engaged on a foreign voyage, unless the owner requests measurement under this system.

(3) A vessel made subject to this system at the request of the owner may be remeasured only under this system.

(4) For the purpose of vessel documentation, a vessel measured under this system is not required to be measured under another system.

(5) A vessel the keel of which was laid or that was at a similar stage of construction before July 18, 1982, (except a vessel measured under this system at the request of the owner or because of a change that substantially affects the vessel's gross tonnage) may retain its tonnage in effect on July 18, 1994, for the application of relevant requirements under an international agreement (except the Convention) or other laws of the United States. However, if the vessel undergoes a change after July 18, 1994, that the Commandant finds substantially affects the vessel's gross tonnage, the vessel must be remeasured only under this system.

(6) A tonnage assignment under this system does not affect the applicability to the vessel of international agreements to which the United States Government is a party that are not in conflict with the Convention or with the application of International Maritime Organization (IMO) Resolutions A.494(XII) of November 19, 1981, A.540(XIII) of November 17, 1983, and A.541(XIII) of November 17, 1983. When applicable to the vessel, these Resolutions provide interim schemes for using the vessel's existing gross tonnage, instead of the gross tonnage under the Convention Measurement System, for applying the International Convention for the Safety of Life at Sea (SOLAS), the International Convention on Standards of Training, Certification, and Watchkeeping for Seafarers, 1978, (STCW), and the International Convention for the Prevention of Pollution from Ships, 1973, (MARPOL), respectively.

(b) *Standard Measurement System (subpart C)*. This system applies to a vessel not required to be measured under the Convention Measurement System if the vessel is to be documented or if the application of a law of the United States to the vessel depends on the vessel's tonnage. Upon request of the owner, this system also applies to a documented vessel measured under the Convention Measurement System when Standard Measurement System tonnages are to be used in applying the provisions of a law under 46 U.S.C. 14305.

(c) *Dual Measurement System (subpart D)*. This system may be applied, at the owner's option, instead of the Standard Measurement System, to a vessel eligible or required to be measured under the Standard Measurement System.

(d) *Simplified Measurement System (subpart E)*. This system may be applied, at the owner's option, instead of the Standard Measurement System to the following vessels:

(1) A vessel that is under 79 feet in overall length.

(2) A vessel of any length that is non-self-propelled and not engaged on a foreign voyage.

(3) A vessel of any length that is operated only for pleasure and operated only on the Great Lakes.

[CGD 87–015b, 54 FR 37657, Sept. 12, 1989, as amended by CGD 92–058, 57 FR 59938, Dec. 17, 1992; CGD 95–028, 62 FR 51203, Sept. 30, 1997]

§ 69.13 **Deviating from the provisions of a measurement system.**

(a) In measuring a vessel under a measurement system in this part, all provisions of that system applicable to the vessel must be observed.

Coast Guard, Dept. of Homeland Security § 69.21

(b) The provisions of more than one measurement system may not be applied interchangeably or combined.

§ 69.15 Authorized measurement organizations.

(a) Except as provided under paragraphs (c) and (d) of this section, all U.S. vessels to be measured or remeasured under the Convention, Standard, or Dual Measurement Systems must be measured by an authorized measurement organization meeting the requirements of § 69.27 of this subpart. A current listing of authorized measurement organizations can be obtained by visitors from the Commanding Officer, Marine Safety Center, U.S. Coast Guard, 4200 Wilson Boulevard Suite 400, Arlington, VA 22203 or by writing to Commanding Officer (MSC), Attn: Marine Safety Center, U.S. Coast Guard Stop 7410, 4200 Wilson Boulevard Suite 400, Arlington, VA 20598–7410.

(b) All vessels to be measured or remeasured under the Simplified Measurement System must be measured by the Coast Guard. Applications for measurement under the Simplified Measurement System are obtainable from the National Vessel Documentation Center.

(c) All U.S. Coast Guard vessels and all U.S. Navy vessels of war to be measured or remeasured under any measurement system must be measured by the Coast Guard.

(d) At the option of the Commandant, the Coast Guard may measure any vessel to determine its tonnage.

(e) The appropriate certificate of measurement is issued by the measuring organization as evidence of the vessel's measurement under this part.

[CGD 87–015b, 54 FR 37657, Sept. 12, 1989, as amended by CGD 92–058, 57 FR 59938, Dec. 17, 1992; CGD 92–053, 59 FR 50508, Oct. 4, 1994; CGD 95–014, 60 FR 31606, June 15, 1995; CGD 97–057, 62 FR 51045, Sept. 30, 1997; USCG–2007–29018, 72 FR 53965, Sept. 21, 2007; USCG–2009–0702, 74 FR 49230, Sept. 25, 2009; USCG 2013–0671, 78 FR 60149, Sept. 30, 2013]

§ 69.17 Application for measurement services.

(a) Applications for measurement are available from and, once completed, are submitted to the authorized measurement organization that will perform the services. The contents of the application are described in this part under the requirement for each system.

(b) Applications for measurement under more than one system may be combined.

(c) For vessels under construction, the application must be submitted before the vessel is advanced in construction. Usually, this means as soon as the decks are laid, holds cleared of encumbrances, engine and boilers installed, and accommodations partitioned.

[CGD 87–015b, 54 FR 37657, Sept. 12, 1989, as amended by CGD 97–057, 62 FR 51045, Sept. 30, 1997]

§ 69.19 Remeasurement and adjustment of tonnage.

(a) If a vessel that is already measured is to undergo a structural alteration or if the use of a space within that vessel is to be changed, a remeasurement may be required. Vessel owners shall report immediately to an authorized measurement organization any intent to structurally alter the vessel or to change the use of a space within the vessel. The organization advises the owner if remeasurement is necessary. Spaces not affected by the alteration or change need not be remeasured.

(b) When there is a perceived error in the application of a regulation or in the tonnage calculations, the vessel owner should contact the responsible measurement organization. If the error is verified, the tonnage is adjusted as necessary.

(c) If a remeasurement or adjustment of tonnage is required, the organization will issue a new tonnage certificate. If the vessel is documented, the vessel's owner must surrender the Certificate of Documentation as required under part 67, subpart 67.25, of this chapter.

(d) A vessel of less than 79 feet in overall length measured under the Standard or Dual Measurement Systems may be remeasured at the owner's request under the Simplified Measurement System.

[CGD 87–015b, 54 FR 37657, Sept. 12, 1989, as amended by CGD 97–057, 62 FR 51045, Sept. 30, 1997]

§ 69.21 Right of appeal.

Any person directly affected by a decision or action taken under this part,

§ 69.23

by or on behalf of the Coast Guard, may appeal therefrom in accordance with subpart 1.03 of this chapter.

[CGD 88–033, 54 FR 50380, Dec. 6, 1989]

§ 69.23 Fees.

Measurement organizations are authorized to charge a fee for measurement services. Information on fees is available directly from the organizations.

[CGD 97–057, 62 FR 51045, Sept. 30, 1997]

§ 69.25 Penalties.

(a) *General violation.* The owner, charterer, managing operator, agent, master, and individual in charge of a vessel in violation of a regulation in this part are each liable to the United States Government for a civil penalty of not more than $20,000. Each day of a continuing violation is a separate violation. The vessel also is liable in rem for the penalty.

(b) *False Statements.* A person knowingly making a false statement or representation in a matter in which a statement or representation is required by this part is liable to the United States Government for a civil penalty of not more than $20,000 for each false statement or representation. The vessel also is liable in rem for the penalty.

§ 69.27 Delegation of authority to measure vessels.

(a) Under 46 U.S.C. 14103 and 49 CFR 1.46, the Coast Guard is authorized to delegate to a "qualified person" the authority to measure vessels and to issue appropriate certificates of measurement for U.S. vessels that are required or eligible to be measured as vessels of the United States.

(b) Authority to measure and certify U.S. vessels under the Convention, Standard, and Dual Measurement Systems may be delegated to an organization that—

(1) Is a full member of the International Association of Classification Societies (IACS);

(2) Is incorporated under the laws of the United States, a State of the United States, or the District of Columbia;

(3) In lieu of the requirements in paragraphs (b)(1) and (2) of this section, is a recognized classification society under the requirements of 46 CFR part 8.

(4) Is capable of providing all measurement services under the Convention, Standard, and Dual Measurement Systems for vessels domestically and internationally;

(5) Maintains a tonnage measurement staff that has practical experience in measuring U.S. vessels under the Convention, Standard, and Dual Measurement Systems; and

(6) Enters into a written agreement, as described in paragraph (d) of this section.

(c) Applications for delegation of authority under this section must be forwarded to the Commandant and include the following information on the organization:

(1) Its name and address.

(2) Its organizational rules and structure.

(3) The location of its offices that are available to provide measurement services under the Convention, Standard, and Dual Measurement Systems.

(4) The name, qualifications, experience, and job title of each full-time or part-time employee or independent contractor specifically designated by the organization to provide measurement services under the Convention, Standard, or Dual Measurement Systems.

(5) Its tonnage measurement training procedures.

(d) If, after reviewing the application, the Coast Guard determines that the organization is qualified to measure and certify U.S. vessels on behalf of the Coast Guard, the organization must enter into a written agreement with the Coast Guard which—

(1) Defines the procedures for administering and implementing the tonnage measurement and certification processes, including the roles and responsibilities of each party;

(2) Outlines the Coast Guard's oversight role;

(3) Prohibits the organization from using an employee or contractor of the organization to measure and certify the tonnage of a vessel if that employee or contractor is acting or has acted as a tonnage consultant for that same vessel; and

(4) Requires the organization to—
(i) Accept all requests to perform delegated services without discrimination and without regard to the vessel's location, unless prohibited from doing so under the laws of the United States or under the laws of the jurisdiction in which the vessel is located;
(ii) Physically inspect each vessel before issuing a tonnage certificate;
(iii) Provide the Coast Guard with current schedules of measurement fees and related charges;
(iv) Maintain a tonnage measurement file for each U.S. vessel that the organization measures and permit access to the file by any person authorized by the Commandant;
(v) Permit observer status representation by the Coast Guard at all formal discussions that may take place between the organization and other vessel tonnage measurement organizations pertaining to tonnage measurement of U.S. vessels or to the systems under which U.S. vessels are measured;
(vi) Comply with and apply all laws and regulations relating to tonnage measurement of U.S. vessels within the scope of authority delegated; and
(vii) Comply with all other provisions, if any, of the written agreement.

[CGD 87–015b, 54 FR 37657, Sept. 12, 1989, as amended by CGD 97–057, 62 FR 51045, Sept. 30, 1997; CGD 95–010, 62 FR 67536, Dec. 24, 1997]

§ 69.29 OMB control numbers assigned under the Paperwork Reduction Act.

(a) *Purpose.* This section collects and displays the control numbers assigned to information collection and record keeping requirements in this part by the Office of Management and Budget (OMB) pursuant to the Paperwork Reduction Act of 1980 (44 U.S.C. 3501 *et seq.*). The Coast Guard intends that this part comply with 44 U.S.C. 3507(f), which requires that agencies display the current control number assigned by the Director of OMB for each approved agency information collection requirement.

(b) *Display*—

Section of 46 CFR part 69	Currently assigned OMB control No.
69.17	1625–0022

Section of 46 CFR part 69	Currently assigned OMB control No.
69.19	1625–0022
69.21	1625–0022
69.27	1625–0022
69.55	1625–0022
69.105	1625–0022
69.121(d)	1625–0022
69.159	1625–0022
69.179	1625–0022
69.205	1625–0022

[CGD 87–015b, 54 FR 37657, Sept. 12, 1989, as amended by USCG–2004–18884, 69 FR 58346, Sept. 30, 2004]

Subpart B—Convention Measurement System

§ 69.51 Purpose.

This subpart prescribes the requirements for measuring a vessel in order to comply with the International Convention on Tonnage Measurement of Ships, 1969 (Convention), and 46 U.S.C. chapter 143.

§ 69.53 Definitions.

As used in this subpart—

Amidships means the midpoint of the registered length, as "registered length" is defined in this section.

Cargo space means an enclosed space appropriated for the transport of cargo which is to be discharged from the vessel. The term does not include a space which qualifies as an excluded space under § 69.61.

Enclosed space is defined in § 69.59.

Excluded space is defined in § 69.61.

Gross tonnage or *GT* means the tonnage determined under § 69.57.

Line of the upper deck means a longitudinal line at the underside of the upper deck or, if that deck is stepped, the longitudinal line of the underside of the lowest portion of that deck parallel with the upper portions of that deck.

Molded depth means the vertical distance amidships between the following points:

(a) From the line of the upper deck at the vessel's side or, if the vessel has rounded gunwales, from the intersection of the line of the upper deck extended to the molded line of the shell plating as though the gunwales were of angular design.

§ 69.55

(b) To the top of the flat keel, to the lower edge of the keel rabbet if the vessel is of wood or composite structure, or to the point where the line of the flat of the bottom extended inward cuts the side of the keel if the vessel's lower part is hollow or has thick garboards.

Molded draft means—

(a) For vessels assigned a load line under parts 42, 44, 45, or 47 of this chapter, the draft corresponding to the Summer Load Line (other than a timber load line);

(b) For passenger vessels assigned a load line under part 46 of this chapter, the draft corresponding to the deepest subdivision load line assigned;

(c) For vessels to which parts 42, 44, 45, 46, or 47 of this chapter do not apply but which otherwise have been assigned a load line, the draft corresponding to the Summer Load Line so assigned;

(d) For vessels to which no load line has been assigned but the draft of which is restricted under any Coast Guard requirement, the maximum draft permitted under the restriction; and

(e) For other vessels, 75 per cent of the molded depth.

Net tonnage or *NT* means tonnage determined under § 69.63.

Passenger means a person on board a vessel other than—

(a) The master, a member of the crew, or other person employed or engaged in any capacity in the business of the vessel; and

(b) A child under one year of age.

Registered breadth means the maximum breadth of a vessel measured amidships to the molded line of the frame in a vessel with a metal shell and to the outer surface of the hull in all other vessels.

Registered length means either 96 percent of the length on a waterline at 85 percent of the least molded depth measured from the top of the flat keel or the length from the fore side of the stem to the axis of the rudder stock on that waterline, whichever is greater. In vessels designed with a rake of keel, this length is measured on a waterline parallel to the design waterline.

Upper deck means the uppermost complete deck exposed to weather and sea, which has permanent means of weathertight closing of all openings in the weather part of the deck, and below which all openings in the sides of the vessel are fitted with permanent means of watertight closing.

Weathertight means secure against penetration of water into the vessel in any sea condition.

§ 69.55 **Application for measurement services.**

Applications for measurement under this subpart must include the following information and plans:

(a) Type of vessel.

(b) Vessel's name and official number (if assigned).

(c) Builder's name and the vessel hull number assigned by builder.

(d) Place and year built.

(e) Date keel was laid.

(f) Overall length, breadth, and depth of vessel.

(g) Lines plan.

(h) Booklet of offsets at stations.

(i) Capacity plans for tanks and cargo compartments.

(j) Hydrostatic curves.

(k) Construction plans showing measurements and scantlings of deck structures, hatches, appendages, recesses, and other enclosed spaces.

(l) Arrangement plans.

[GCD 89–007; GCD 89–007a, 58 FR 60266, Nov. 15, 1993, 58 FR 65131, Dec. 13, 1993, as amended by CGD 95–014, 60 FR 31606, June 15, 1995]

§ 69.57 **Gross tonnage.**

Gross tonnage (GT) is determined by the following formula $GT = K_1 V$, in which V=total volume of all enclosed spaces in cubic meters and $K_1 = 0.2 + 0.02 \log_{10} V$.

§ 69.59 **Enclosed spaces.**

Enclosed space means a space which is bounded by the vessel's hull, by fixed or portable partitions or bulkheads, or by decks or coverings other than permanent or movable awnings. No break in a deck, nor any opening in the vessel's hull, in a deck or in a covering of a space, or in the partitions or bulkheads of a space, nor the absence of a partition or bulkhead precludes the space from being included in the enclosed space.

§ 69.61 Excluded spaces.

(a) *Excluded space* means an enclosed space which is excluded from volume (V) in calculating gross tonnage. Except as under paragraph (g) of this section, this section lists the excluded spaces.

(b) A space that is within a structure and that is opposite an end opening extending from deck to deck (except for a curtain plate of a height not exceeding by more than one inch the depth of the adjoining deck beams) and having a breadth equal to or greater than 90 percent of the breadth of the deck at the line of the opening is an excluded space, subject to the following:

(1) Only the space between the actual end opening and a line drawn parallel to the line or face of the opening at a distance from the opening equal to one-half of the breadth of the deck at the line of the opening is excluded. (See § 69.75, figure 1.)

(2) If, because of any arrangement (except convergence of the outside plating as shown in § 69.75, figure 3), the breadth of the space is less than 90 percent of the breadth of the deck, only the space between the line of the opening and a parallel line drawn through the point where the athwartship breadth of the space is equal to 90 percent or less of the breadth of the deck is excluded. (See § 69.75, figures 2 and 4.)

(3) When any two spaces, either of which is excluded under paragraphs (b)(1) or (b)(2) of this section, are separated by an area that is completely open except for bulwarks or open rails, these two spaces must not be excluded if the separation between the two spaces is less than the least half breadth of the deck in way of the separation. (See § 69.75, figures 5 and 6.)

(4) When the deck at the line of an opening has rounded gunwales, the breadth of the deck is the distance between the tangent points indicated in § 69.75, figure 11.

(c) A space that is open to the weather and that is under an overhead deck covering with no connection on the space's exposed sides between the covering and the deck other than the stanchions necessary for the covering's support is an excluded space. An open rail or bulwark fitted at the vessel's side does not disqualify the space from being an excluded space if the height between the top of the rail or bulwark and the overhead structure or curtain plate (if fitted) is not less than 2.5 feet or one-third of the height of the space, whichever is greater. (See § 69.75, figure 7.)

(d) A space in a side-to-side structure directly in way of opposite side openings not less than 2.5 feet in height or one-third of the height of the structure, whichever is greater, is an excluded space. If the opening is only on one side of the structure, the space to be excluded is limited inboard from the opening to a maximum of one-half of the breadth of the deck in way of the opening. (See § 69.75, figure 8.)

(e) A space in a structure immediately below an uncovered opening in the deck overhead is an excluded space, if the opening is exposed to the weather and the space to be excluded is limited to the area of the opening. (See § 69.75, figure 9.)

(f) A recess in the boundary bulkhead of a structure which is exposed to the weather and which has an opening that extends from deck to deck without a means of closing is an excluded space, if the interior width of the space is not greater than the width of the opening and extension of the space into the structure is not greater than twice the width of the opening. (See § 69.75, figure 10.)

(g) Any space described in paragraphs (b) through (f) of this section which fulfills at least one of the following conditions is not an excluded space:

(1) The space is fitted with shelves or other means designed for securing cargo or stores.

(2) The opening that would otherwise permit the space to be excluded space is fitted with a means of closure.

(3) Other features of the space make it possible for the space to be closed.

§ 69.63 Net tonnage.

Net tonnage (NT) is determined by the formula:

$$NT = K_2 V_C \left(\frac{4d}{3D}\right)^2 + K_3 \left(N_1 + \frac{N_2}{10}\right),$$

in which:

V_c = total volume of cargo spaces in cubic meters.

§ 69.65

$K_2 = 0.2 + 0.02 \log_{10} V_c$.

$$K3 = 1.25\left(\frac{GT + 10{,}000}{10{,}000}\right)$$

D = molded depth amidships in meters, as "molded depth" is defined in § 69.53.
d = molded draft amidships in meters, as "molded draft" is defined in § 69.53.
N_1 = number of passengers in cabins with not more than eight berths, as "passenger" is defined in § 69.53.
N_2 = number of other passengers, as "passenger" is defined in § 69.53.
GT = gross tonnage as determined under § 69.57.
N_1 plus N_2 must equal the total number of passengers the vessel is permitted to carry as indicated on the ship's Passenger Certificate. If N_1 plus N_2 is less than 13, both N_1 and N_2 are zero.

$\left(\dfrac{4d}{3D}\right)^2$ must not be greater than unity.

$K_2 V_c \left(\dfrac{4d}{3D}\right)^2$ must not be less than 0.25 GT.

NT must not be less than 0.30 GT.

[CGD 97–057, 62 FR 51045, Sept. 30, 1997]

§ 69.65 Calculation of volumes.

(a) Volumes V and V_c used in calculating gross and net tonnages, respectively, must be measured and calculated according to accepted naval architectural practices for the spaces concerned.

(b) The volume of the hull below the upper deck is determined as follows:

(1) If the number and location of sections originally used in making other calculations which relate to the form of the vessel (such as displacement volumes and center of buoyancy) are reasonably available, Simpson's first rule may be applied using those sections.

(2) If the number and location of stations originally used are not reasonably available or do not exist and the hull is of conventional design with faired lines, Simpson's first rule may be applied using a number and location of stations not less than those indicated in § 69.109(g)(1).

(3) If the hull is of standard geometric shape, a simple geometric formula that yields a more accurate volume may be used.

(4) If the lines of the hull are not fair, the volume may be measured by using a combination of methods under this section.

(c) The volume of structures above the upper deck may be measured by applying the superstructure provisions in § 69.113 or by any accepted method or combinations of methods.

(d) Measurements must be taken, regardless of the fitting of insulation or the like—

(1) To the inner side of the shell or structural boundary plating, in vessels constructed of metal; and

(2) To the outer surface of the shell or to the inner side of structural boundary surfaces, in all other vessels.

(e) When determining the volume of a cargo space, measurements must be taken without consideration for insulation, sparring, or ceiling fitted within the space.

(f) Measurements must be to the nearest one-twentieth of a foot.

(g) Calculations must be made on a worksheet and must be sufficiently detailed to permit easy review. The measurement procedures used must be identified on the worksheet.

§ 69.67 Marking of cargo spaces.

Cargo spaces used in determining volume (Vc) for calculating net tonnage must be permanently marked with the letters "CC" (cargo compartment) which are at least four inches in height and positioned so as to be visible at all times.

§ 69.69 Issuance of an International Tonnage Certificate (1969).

On request of the vessel owner, an International Tonnage Certificate (1969) is issued for a vessel measured under this subpart that is 79 feet or more in registered length and that will engage on a foreign voyage. The Certificate is issued to the vessel owner or master and must be maintained on board the vessel when it is engaged on a foreign voyage.

§ 69.71 Change of net tonnage.

(a) When a vessel is altered so that the net tonnage is increased, the new net tonnage must be applied immediately.

Coast Guard, Dept. of Homeland Security § 69.75

(b) A vessel concurrently assigned load lines under both the International Convention on Load Lines and either the International Convention for the Safety of Life at Sea (SOLAS) or other international agreement must be assigned only one net tonnage. The net tonnage assigned must be the net tonnage applicable to the load line assigned under the International Convention on Load Lines, SOLAS or other international agreement for the trade in which the vessel in engaged.

(c) When a vessel is altered so that the net tonnage is decreased or the vessel's trade is changed so that the load line assigned for that trade under paragraph (b) of this section is no longer appropriate and results in a decrease in its net tonnage, a new International Tonnage Certificate (1969) incorporating that net tonnage may not be issued until twelve months after the date on which the current Certificate was issued. However, if one of the following apply, a new Certificate may be issued immediately:

(1) The vessel is transferred to the flag of another nation.

(2) The vessel undergoes alterations or modifications which the Coast Guard deems to be of a major character, such as the removal of a superstructure which requires an alteration of the assigned load line.

[CGD 87–015b, 54 FR 37657, Sept. 12, 1989, as amended by USCG–1999–6216, 64 FR 53225, Oct. 1, 1999]

§ 69.73 Variance from the prescribed method of measurement.

(a) When application of this subpart to a novel type vessel produces unreasonable or impractical results, the Commandant may determine a more suitable method of measurement.

(b) Requests for a determination must be submitted to the Commandant, explaining the problem, and including plans and sketches of the spaces in question.

[CGD 87–015b, 54 FR 37657, Sept. 12, 1989, as amended by CGD 97–057, 62 FR 51045, Sept. 30, 1997; USCG–1999–6216, 64 FR 53225, Oct. 1, 1999]

§ 69.75 Figures.

0=excluded space.
C=enclosed space.
I=space to be considered as an enclosed space.
B=breadth of deck in way of the opening.

§ 69.75

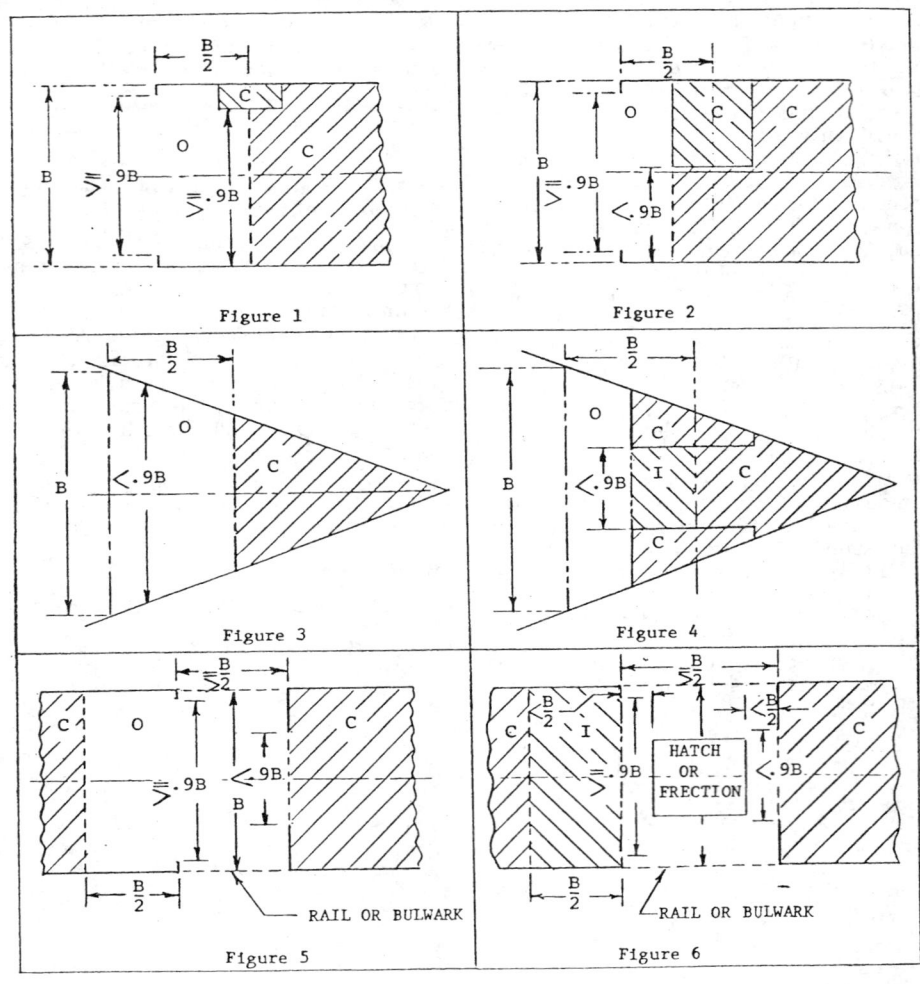

Coast Guard, Dept. of Homeland Security § 69.103

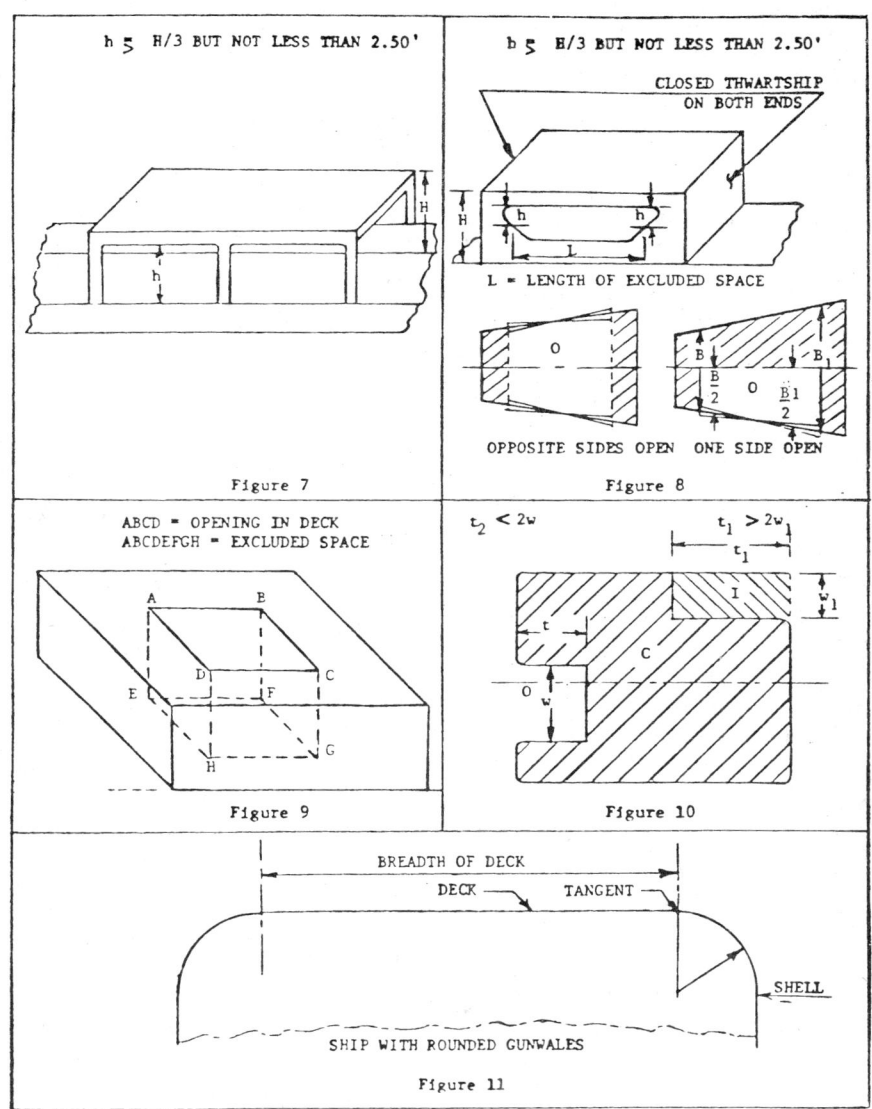

Subpart C—Standard Measurement System

§ 69.101 Purpose.

This subpart prescribes the procedures for measuring a vessel under the Standard Measurement System described in 46 U.S.C. 14512.

§ 69.103 Definitions.

As used in this subpart—

§ 69.105

Between-deck means the space above the line of the tonnage deck and below the line of the deck next above.

Break means the space between the line of a deck and the upper portion of that deck, in cases where that deck is stepped and continued at a higher elevation.

Camber means the perpendicular rise or crown of a deck at the centerline of the vessel measured above the skin of the vessel at the vessel's sides.

Ceiling means the permanent planking or plating fitted directly on the inboard side of frames, floors, or double bottom and includes cargo battens and refrigeration insulation but does not include false ceiling which stands off from the framing.

Coaming means both the vertical plating around a hatch or skylight and the sill below an opening in a bulkhead.

Deckhouse means a structure that is on or above the uppermost complete deck and that does not extend from side to side of the vessel. The term includes cabin trunks and closed-in spaces over the holds of vessels.

Depth of frame means the perpendicular depth of a bottom frame and the athwart distance between the inboard and outboard faces of a side frame.

Double bottom means a space at the bottom of a vessel between the inner and outer bottom plating and used solely for water ballast.

Floor means a vertical plate or timber extending from bilge to bilge in the bottom of a vessel. In a wooden vessel, "floor" means the lowermost timber connecting the main frames at the keel when that timber extends the full depth of the frames to which it is fastened. In a double bottom, floors usually extend from the outer to the inner bottom.

Gross tonnage is defined in § 69.107(a).

Hatch means an opening in a deck through which cargo is laden or discharged.

Line of tonnage deck means the line determined under § 69.109(e).

Line of uppermost complete deck means the line determined under § 69.111(b).

Net tonnage is defined in § 69.107(b).

Registered breadth is defined in § 69.53.

Registered depth means "molded depth" as defined in § 69.53.

Registered length is defined in § 69.53.

Shelter deck means the uppermost deck that would have qualified as the uppermost complete deck had it not been fitted with a middle line opening.

Step means a cutoff in a deck or in the bottom, top, or sides of a space resulting in varying heights of a deck or varying heights or widths of a space.

Superstructure means all permanent structures (such as forecastle, bridge, poop, deckhouse, and break) on or above the line of the uppermost complete deck or, if the vessel has a shelter deck, on or above the line of the shelter deck.

Tonnage deck is defined in § 69.109(c).

Tonnage length is defined in § 69.109(f).

Uppermost complete deck means the uppermost deck—

(a) Which extends from stem to stern and from side to side at all points of its length;

(b) The space below which is enclosed by the sides of the vessel;

(c) Through which there is no opening that would exempt the space below from being included in gross tonnage; and

(d) Below which there is no opening through the hull that would exempt the space below from being included in gross tonnage.

§ 69.105 Application for measurement services.

Applications for measurement services under this subpart must include the following information and plans:

(a) Type of vessel.
(b) Vessel's name and official number (if assigned).
(c) Builder's name and the vessel hull number assigned by the builder.
(d) Place and year built.
(e) Date keel was laid.
(f) Overall length, breadth, and depth of vessel.
(g) Lines plan.
(h) Booklet of offsets.
(i) Capacity plans for tanks
(j) Construction plans showing measurements and scantlings of hull and superstructure.
(k) Tonnage drawing showing tonnage length in profile and tonnage sections.

(1) Arrangement plans.

[CGD 87–015b, 54 FR 37657, Sept. 12, 1989, as amended by CGD 95–014, 60 FR 31606, June 15, 1995]

§ 69.107 Gross and net tonnages.

(a) Gross tonnage is the sum of the following tonnages, less certain spaces exempt under § 69.117:

(1) Under-deck tonnage (§ 69.109).
(2) Between-deck tonnage (§ 69.111).
(3) Superstructure tonnage (§ 69.113).
(4) Excess hatchway tonnage (§ 69.115(c)).
(5) Tonnage of framed-in propelling machinery spaces included in calculating gross tonnage (§ 69.121(d)(1)).

(b) Net tonnage is gross tonnage less deductions under §§ 69.119 and 69.121.

§ 69.109 Under-deck tonnage.

(a) *Defined.* "Under-deck tonnage" means the tonnage of the space below the line of the tonnage deck, as that volume is calculated under this section.

(b) *Method of calculating tonnage.* Under-deck tonnage is calculated by applying Simpson's first rule using the tonnage length and the areas of the transverse sections prescribed by this section.

(c) *Identifying the tonnage deck.* In vessels with two or less decks, the tonnage deck is the uppermost complete deck. In vessels with more than two decks, the tonnage deck is the second deck from the keel as determined in paragraph (d) of this section.

(d) *Enumerating the decks to identify the second deck from the keel.* Only decks without openings that permit space below to be exempt from inclusion in under-deck tonnage are enumerated. Partial decks are not considered decks for the purpose of enumerating decks. However, the presence of engine and boiler casings, peak tanks, or cofferdams that penetrate a deck do not disqualify the deck from being enumerated.

(e) *Identifying the line of the tonnage deck.* (1) If the tonnage deck runs in a continuous line from stem to stern, the line of the tonnage deck is the longitudinal line at the underside of the tonnage deck.

(2) If the tonnage deck runs at different levels from stem to stern, the line of the tonnage deck is the longitudinal line of the underside of the lowest portion of that deck parallel with the upper portions of that deck. (See § 69.123, figures 1 and 2.) Spaces between the line of the tonnage deck and the higher portions of that deck are not included in under-deck tonnage.

(f) *Tonnage length.* (1) "Tonnage length" means the length of a horizontal straight line measured at the centerline of the vessel from the point forward where the line of the tonnage deck intersects the line of the inboard faces of the ordinary side frames to the point aft where the line of the tonnage deck intersects the inboard face of the transom frames or cant frames. (See § 69.123, figure 3.)

(2) For a vessel having a headblock or square end with framing which extends from the tonnage deck to the bottom of the vessel, the tonnage length terminates on the inboard face of the head block or end framing. When a headblock extends inboard past the face of the end side frames or when the headblock plates are excessive in length, the tonnage length terminates at the extreme end of the vessel less a distance equal to the thickness of an ordinary side frame and shell plating. (See § 69.123, figure 4.)

(3) For a vessel having a square bow or stern and tonnage deck with camber, the effect of the camber on the tonnage length must be considered. The tonnage length must be measured below the tonnage deck at a distance equal to one-third of round camber and one-half of straight pitch camber.

(g) *Division of vessel into transverse sections.* (1) Except as under paragraph (m)(1)(iii) of this section, the tonnage length is divided into an even number of equal parts as indicated in the following table:

Class	Tonnage length	Divisions
1	50 ft. or less	6
2	Over 50 ft. but not exceeding 100 ft	8
3	Over 100 ft. but not exceeding 150 ft.	10
4	Over 150 ft. but not exceeding 200 ft.	12
5	Over 200 ft. but not exceeding 250 ft.	14
6	Over 250 ft.	16

(2) Transverse sections are cut at each end of the tonnage length and at each point of division of the tonnage length. Intervals and one-third intervals between the points of division are measured to the nearest thousandth of a foot. (See § 69.123 figures 5 and 6.)

(h) *Depths of transverse sections.* (1) Transverse section depths are measured at each point of division of the tonnage length at the centerline of the vessel from a point below the line of the tonnage deck equal to one-third of the camber or to one-half of the pitch of the beam down to the upper side of the ordinary frames, floors, longitudinals, or tank top of a cellular double bottom, as the case may be.

(2) When a depth falls at a point where the tank top of a double bottom has a straight fall from centerline to the wings, the depth terminates at one-half of the height of fall. (See § 69.123 figure 8.)

(3) When a depth falls at a point where the tank top of a double bottom rises from the centerline to the wings, the depth terminates at one-half the dead rise. (See § 69.123, figure 9.)

(4) The depth at the midpoint of the tonnage length or, when a vessel is measured in parts, the depth at the midpoint of each part determines the number of equal parts into which each depth is divided, as follows:

(i) If the midpoint depth is 16 feet or less, each depth is divided into four equal parts. If the midpoint depth exceeds 16 feet, each depth is divided into six equal parts. (See § 69.123, figure 7.)

(ii) The interval between the points of division of a depth and one-third intervals are carried to the nearest hundredth of a foot.

(i) *Breadths of transverse sections.* (1) Transverse section breadths are measured horizontally at each point of division of each depth and also at the upper and lower points of each depth. Breadths are measured to the inboard face of the ordinary frames or to the line of the ordinary frames. Breadths are measured parallel to each other and at right angle to the vessel's centerline. (See § 69.123, figure 7.)

(2) Upper breadths are not reduced by measuring to deck-beam brackets. In cases of camber when an upper breadth passes through the deck (see § 69.123, figure 7), the breadth is measured to the line of the side frames at the under side of the deck projected vertically up to the height of the upper breadth.

(3) Bottom breadths are measured only as far as the flat of the floor extends. (See § 69.123, figures 7 and 10.) When bottom frames rise immediately from the flat keel, bottom breadths are equal to the breadth of the flat keel. Where there is no double bottom and where there is dead rise of the bottom out to the sides of the vessel, bottom breadths are equal to the part of the bottom plating not affected by dead rise.

(4) Bottom breadths falling in way of a double bottom, the top of which rises or falls from certerline to the wings, are measured between the inboard faces of the frame brackets which connect the double bottom with the frames. (See § 69.123, figures 8 and 9.)

(j) *Measuring spaces having ceiling.* The maximum allowance for terminating measurements on ceiling is three inches on the bottom frames or tank top and three inches on each side frame. When ceiling is less than three inches thick, only the actual thickness is allowed. When ceiling is fitted on a platform directly above the bottom frames, depths are measured down through the platform to the upper side of the frames and the allowable ceiling on the platform is then deducted.

(k) *Area of transverse sections.* (1) A transverse section at an end of the tonnage length may not yield area, except in vessels (such as barges) with an upright bow or stern.

(2) The breadths of each transverse section are numbered from above, the upper being "1", the second down being "2", and so on to the lowest.

(3) Multiply the even numbered breadths by four and the odd numbered breadths by two, except for the first and last breadths, which are multiplied by one.

(4) Add together the products from paragraph (k)(3) of this section.

(5) Multiply the sum from paragraph (k)(4) of this section by one-third of the interval between the breadths. The product is the area of the transverse section.

Coast Guard, Dept. of Homeland Security § 69.111

(1) *Tonnage.* (1) Number the transverse sections successively "1", "2", and so forth, beginning at the bow.

(2) Multiply the area of the even numbered sections by four and the area of the odd numbered sections by two, except the first and last sections, which are multiplied by one.

(3) Add together the products from paragraph (l)(2) of this section and multiply the sum by one-third of the interval between the sections. The product is the volume under-deck.

(4) The volume under-deck is divided by 100 and is, subject to exemptions, the under-deck tonnage.

(m) *Steps in double bottom.* (1) The tonnage length of a vessel having a step exceeding six inches in height in its double bottom is divided into longitudinal parts at the step. Each part is subdivided as follows to determine the number of transverse sections:

(i) Parts 20 feet or under in length are divided into two equal parts.

(ii) Parts over 20 feet and under 40 feet in length are divided into four equal parts.

(iii) Parts 40 feet or over are divided as provided in paragraph (g)(1) of this section.

(2) The tonnage of each part is calculated separately. The sum of the tonnages of the parts is the under-deck tonnage.

(n) *Outside shaft tunnel exclusion.* Any portion of an outside shaft tunnel included in tonnage through the process of measurement is subtracted from the under-deck tonnage.

(o) *Open vessels.* (1) An open vessel is one of any length without a deck or with one or more partial decks, the total length of which is less than one-half the tonnage length.

(2) The line of the tonnage deck for an open vessel is the upper edge of the upper strake. Depths of transverse sections are taken from this line.

(3) Any vessel, other than one having a mechanically refrigerated hold, that is not an open vessel and that has a tonnage length of less than 50 feet is measured as an open vessel, if the distance between the line of its tonnage deck and the upper edge of the upper strake is more than one-sixth of the midship depth. "Midship depth" means the depth measured from the line of the upper edge of the upper strake to the point in the bottom used for measuring tonnage depths.

[CGD 87–015b, 54 FR 37657, Sept. 12, 1989; 54 FR 40240, Sept. 29, 1989]

§ 69.111 Between-deck tonnage.

(a) *Defined.* "Between-deck tonnage" means the tonnage of the space above the line of the tonnage deck and below the line of the uppermost complete deck.

(b) *Identifying the line of the uppermost complete deck.* (1) If the uppermost complete deck runs in a continuous line from stem to stern, the line of the uppermost complete deck is the longitudinal line of the underside of the uppermost complete deck.

(2) If the uppermost complete deck runs at different levels from stem to stern, the line of the uppermost complete deck is the longitudinal line of the underside of the lowest portion of that deck parallel with the upper portions of that deck. Spaces between the line of the uppermost complete deck and the higher portions of the deck are included in superstructure tonnage.

(c) *Method for calculating tonnage.* The tonnage of each level of the between-deck space is calculated separately, as follows:

(1) The length of each level is measured at the mid-height between the line of the deck above and the line of the deck below. Measure from the point forward where the continuation of the line of the inboard face of the normal side frames intersects the center line of the vessel aft to the forward face of the normal transom framing.

(2) Divide the length under paragraph (c)(1) of this section into the same number of equal parts into which the tonnage length is divided under § 69.109(g)(1).

(3) Measure at mid-height between the faces of the normal side frames the inside breadth of the space at each end and at each point of division of the length. Number the breadths successively "1", "2", and so forth beginning at the bow.

(4) Multiply the even numbered breadths by four and the odd numbered breadths by two, except the first and last, which are multiplied by one.

401

(5) Add together the products under paragraph (c)(4) of this section and multiply the sum by one-third of the interval between the points at which the breadths are taken. The product is the square foot area of the space at mid-height.

(6) Multiply the area of the space at mid-height by the average of the heights taken each point of division of the space. The product divided by 100 is the tonnage of that space.

(7) The between-deck tonnage is the sum of the tonnage of each level within the between-deck space.

[CGD 87-015b, 54 FR 37657, Sept. 12, 1989, as amended by CGD 97-057, 62 FR 51045, Sept. 30, 1997]

§ 69.113 Superstructure tonnage.

(a) *Defined.* "Superstructure tonnage" means the tonnage of all permanent structures, such as forecastle, bridge, poop, deckhouse, and break, on or above the line of the uppermost complete deck (or line of shelter deck, if applicable).

(b) *Method of calculating tonnage.* The tonnage of all structures on each level on or above the uppermost complete deck (or shelter deck, if applicable) is calculated separately as follows:

(1) The length of each structure is measured along its centerline at mid-height between the line of the inboard face of the framing on one end to the line of the inboard face of the framing on the other end. (See § 69.123, figure 11.)

(2) Divide the length under paragraph (b)(1) of this section into an even number of equal parts most nearly equal to those into which the tonnage length is divided under § 69.109.

(3) Measure at mid-height the inside breadth at each end and at each point of division of the length. Number the breadths successively "1", "2", and so forth, beginning at the extreme forward end of the structure. If an end of the structure is in the form of a continuous arc or curve, the breadth at that end is one-half the nearest breadth. If an end is in the form of an arc or curve having a decided flat, the breadth at the end is two-thirds of the nearest breadth.

(4) Multiply the even numbered breadths by four and the odd numbered by two, except the first and last breadth, which are multiplied by one.

(5) Add together the products under paragraph (b)(4) of this section and multiply the sum by one-third of the interval between the points at which the breadths are taken. The product is the square foot area of the structure at mid-height.

(6) Multiply this area by the average of the heights taken at each point of division of the structure between its decks or the line of its decks. The product divided by 100 is the tonnage of that structure.

(c) A structure having steps in its deck or side must be measured in parts.

(d) The superstructure tonnage is the sum of tonnages of each level above the line of the uppermost complete deck (or shelter deck, if applicable).

(e) When a structure is located over a cut-away portion of the tonnage deck, the structure's height is measured from the under side of its overhead deck to the line of the tonnage deck. If the tonnage deck has no camber, allow for camber in the overhead deck.

(f) For structures of a standard geometric shape, a simple geometric formula that yields an accurate volume may be used.

§ 69.115 Excess hatchway tonnage.

(a) Hatchways that are above the tonnage deck and are either open to the weather or within open structures are measured to determine excess hatchway tonnage. Hatchways that are in between-deck spaces, on decks within closed-in structures, or on open structures are not measured.

(b) The tonnage of a hatchway is its length times breadth times mean depth divided by 100. Mean depth is measured from the under side of the hatch cover to the top of the deck beam.

(c) From the sum of the tonnage of the hatchways under this section, subtract one-half of one percent of the vessel's gross tonnage exclusive of the hatchway tonnage. The remainder is added as excess hatchway tonnage in calculating gross tonnage.

§ 69.117 Spaces exempt from inclusion in gross tonnage.

(a) *Purpose.* This section lists spaces which are exempt from inclusion in gross tonnage.

(b) *Spaces on or above the line of the uppermost complete deck.* The following spaces or portions of spaces on or above the line of the uppermost complete deck are exempt if the spaces or portions are reasonable in extent and adapted and used exclusively for the purpose indicated:

(1) Spaces for anchor gear, including capstan, windlass, and chain locker, are exempt.

(2) Companions and booby-hatches protecting stairways or ladderways leading to spaces below are exempt, whether or not the spaces below are exempt.

(3) Galley or other spaces fitted with a range or oven for cooking food to be consumed on board the vessel are exempt.

(4) Spaces designed to provide light or air to propelling machinery are exempt, as follows:

(i) When propelling machinery is located entirely on or above the line of the uppermost complete deck, the entire propelling machinery space and all fuel bunker spaces that are also located above that line are exempt as light or air spaces. (See exception in § 69.121(d)(1) for framed-in spaces.)

(ii) When part of the propelling machinery projects above the line of the uppermost complete deck into a space used exclusively to provide light or air to the propelling machinery, the entire space is exempt as light or air space. When any portion of this space is used for purposes other than providing light or air, only the portion of the space used for light or air, the space occupied by the propelling machinery itself, and a propelling machinery working space allowance under § 69.121 limited to two feet, if available, on each side of the propelling machinery are exempt.

(iii) Any part of an escape shaft, or a companion sheltering an escape shaft, above the line of the uppermost complete deck is exempt as light or air space.

(iv) Space that would otherwise be exempt as a light or air space is not exempt when propelling machinery is boxed-in and does not extend above the line of the uppermost complete deck. Any portion of the boxed-in space above the line of the uppermost complete deck is exempt.

(5) Skylights affording light or air to a space below, other than to propelling machinery spaces. Space immediately below the line of the deck on which a skylight is located is exempt only when there is an opening in the next lower deck directly below the skylight to permit light or air to an even lower deck.

(6) Machinery spaces, other than for propelling machinery under § 169.121.

(7) Spaces for steering gear.

(8) Water closet spaces that are fitted with at least a toilet and are intended for use by more than one person.

(9) The space in a wheelhouse necessary for controlling the vessel.

(c) *Passenger spaces.* (1) As used in this section, the term "passenger" includes officers and enlisted men on military vessels who are not assigned ship's duties and not entered on the ship's articles.

(2) As used in this section, "passenger space" means a space reserved exclusively for the use of passengers and includes, but is not limited to, berthing areas, staterooms, bathrooms, toilets, libraries, writing rooms, lounges, dining rooms, saloons, smoking rooms, and recreational rooms. The space need not be part of or adjacent to a berthing area to be considered a passenger space.

(3) A passenger space located on or above the first deck above the uppermost complete deck is exempt from gross tonnage.

(4) A passenger space located on the uppermost complete deck is exempt from gross tonnage only when it has no berthing accommodations and is an open structure under paragraph (d) of this section.

(d) *Open structures.* (1) Structures that are located on or above the line of the uppermost complete deck that are under cover (sheltered) but open to the weather are exempt from gross tonnage.

(2) A structure is considered "open to the weather" under paragraph (d)(1) of

§ 69.117

this section when an exterior end bulkhead of the structure is open and, except as provided in paragraphs (d)(4), (d)(5), and (d)(6) of this section, is not fitted with any means of closing. To be considered "open to the weather", the end bulkhead must not have a coaming height of more than two feet in way of any required opening and have one of the following:

(i) Two openings, each at least three feet wide and at least four feet high in the clear, one on each side of the centerline of the structure.

(ii) One opening at least four feet wide and at least five feet high in the clear.

(iii) One opening at least 20 square feet in the clear with a breadth in excess of four feet and a height of not less than three feet.

(3) A compartment within an open structure is considered open to the weather only when an interior bulkhead of that compartment has an opening or openings that meet the requirements for end bulkheads under paragraphs (d)(2)(i) through (d)(2)(iii) of this section. Other compartments within the structure are not considered open to the weather.

(4) An interior or exterior opening that is temporarily closed by shifting boards dropped into channel sections at the sides of the opening is considered open to the weather if battening, caulking, or gaskets of any material are not used.

(5) An interior or exterior opening that is temporarily closed by cover plates or boards held in place only by hook bolts (see § 69.123, Figure 12) is considered open to the weather—

(i) If hook bolts used to secure cover plates or boards are spaced at least one foot apart and hook over a stiffener installed around the perimeter of the opening;

(ii) If the cover plates or boards fit tightly against the bulkhead; and

(iii) If battening, caulking, or gaskets of any material are not used.

(6) An interior or exterior opening that is temporarily closed by cover plates or boards held in place only by bolts and crosspieces is considered open to the weather—

(i) If the bolts are not installed through the bulkhead;

(ii) If the bolts and crosspieces are not held in place by cleats or other attachments to or through the bulkhead;

(iii) If the cover plates or boards fit tightly against the bulkhead; and

(iv) If battening, caulking, or gaskets of any material are not used.

(7) A structure with its aft end entirely open from the under side of its overhead stiffeners down to the deck, to the line of the deck, or to a coaming not exceeding three inches in height and open athwartship between the inboard faces of the side stiffeners is considered open to the weather. The opening may be covered by a wire mesh screen or temporarily closed by canvas secured at the top and lashed or buttoned in place.

(e) *Open space between the shelter deck and the next lower deck.* (1) Space that is between the shelter deck and the next lower deck and that is under cover (sheltered) but open to the weather is exempt from gross tonnage when all openings in the uppermost complete deck are provided with a watertight means of closing.

(2) A space is considered "open to the weather" under paragraph (e)(1) of this section when the shelter deck above the space has a middle line opening which conforms to the following:

(i) The middle line opening must be at least four feet long in the clear and at least as wide as the after cargo hatch on the shelter deck, but not less than one-half the width of the vessel at the midpoint of the length of the opening. The opening may have rounded corners not exceeding a nine inch radius. When a greater radius is required by the Coast Guard or a Coast Guard recognized classification society under § 42.05-60 of this chapter, notification of that requirement must be submitted to the Commandant.

(ii) The middle line opening must be located so that the distance between the aft edge of the middle line opening and the vessel's stern is not less than one-twentieth of the tonnage length of the vessel and the distance between the fore edge of the opening and the vessel's stem is not less than one-fifth of the tonnage length of the vessel.

(iii) The middle line opening must not be within a structure of any type.

Coast Guard, Dept. of Homeland Security §69.117

(iv) If the middle line opening is guarded by rails or stanchions, the rails and stanchions must not be used to secure or assist in securing a cover over the opening.

(v) The coaming of the middle line opening must not exceed one foot mean height above the shelter deck. Bolts must not pass through the stiffeners or flanges on the coaming, nor may there be any other attachments on the coaming for fastening a cover. Portable wood covers may be fitted over the middle line opening if held in place only by lashings fitted to the under side of the covers. Metal covers may be fitted in place only by hook bolts spaced not less than 18 inches apart that pass through the cover and hook over angle stiffeners or flanges fitted to the outside of the coaming.

(vi) The space below the middle line opening must have a minimum length of four feet throughout its entire breadth and height and be in the clear at all times.

(vii) A scupper having a five inch minimum inside diameter and fitted with a screw down non-return valve geared to and operated from the shelter deck must be fitted on each side of the upper deck in way of the middle line opening.

(3) When the shelter deck space forward or aft of the middle line opening is divided by interior bulkheads, only those compartments with at least two openings that progress to the middle line opening are considered "open to the weather" under paragraph (e)(1) of this section. Each required opening must be at least three feet wide and at least four feet high in the clear, must not have a coaming height of more than two feet, and must not be fitted (except as provided in paragraphs (d)(4), (d)(5), and (d)(6) of this section) with any means of closing. Other compartments within the shelter deck space are not considered "open to the weather" under paragraph (e)(1) of this section.

(f) *Water ballast spaces.* A space, regardless of location, adapted only for water ballast and not available for stores, supplies, fuel, or cargo (other than water to be used for underwater drilling, mining, and related purposes, including production), upon request, may be exempt from gross tonnage if the following are met:

(1) The space must be available at all times only for water ballast that is piped through a system independent of other systems (except fire fighting and bilge suction systems). Pumps, pipes, and other equipment for loading and unloading water ballast must be of a size suitable for the efficient handling of the water ballast within a reasonable time frame. All manholes providing access to a water ballast space must be oval or circular and not greater than 34 inches in diameter. Except for those on a deck exposed to the weather, the manholes may have a coaming not exceeding six inches in height. Existing hatches over spaces being converted to water ballast spaces must have a watertight cover plate welded to the hatch and a manhole, as described in this paragraph, fitted in the plating.

(2) The primary purpose of the water ballast must be to afford a means of maintaining the vessel's stability, immersion, trim, pre-loading conditions, or seakeeping capabilities.

(3) If the space is in a vessel that is subject to inspection under 46 U.S.C. 3301, the space must be considered when determining the adequacy of the vessel's stability under 46 CFR chapter I.

(4) If the total of all water ballast spaces to be exempted from gross tonnage exceeds 30 percent of the vessel's gross tonnage (as calculated under this subpart without any allowance for water ballast), a justification of the operating conditions that require water ballast must be submitted to the measuring organization for approval. Although a single condition may justify all water ballast spaces, several conditions may be necessary in other cases. However, a particular tank is not justified by a condition if another tank already justified by another condition could be used as effectively. The justification must—

(i) Designate the vessel's service;

(ii) Explain for what purpose under paragraph (f)(2) of this section the water ballast is being used;

(iii) Provide the calculations required in paragraphs (f)(4)(vi) through (f)(4)(ix) of this section for those uses

§ 69.119

on a form similar to Coast Guard Stability Test Form CG-993-9;

(iv) Include the capacity, tank arrangement, and piping plans for the vessel;

(v) Include a statement certifying that the space will be used exclusively for water ballast as prescribed by this section;

(vi) If water ballast is used for stability, describe each loading condition and the resultant metacentric height (GM) and include calculations;

(vii) If water ballast is used for immersion or trim, describe those conditions and include loading and trim calculations;

(viii) If water ballast is used for preloading, describe how it is used and include strength and weight calculations; and

(ix) If water ballast is used for seakeeping, describe each loading condition, GM, period of roll, and, if speed is involved, speed versus trim and draft and include calculations.

(5) If the water ballast space or its use, purpose, or piping are changed, the vessel owner or operator must report the change promptly to a measurement organization listed in § 69.15 for a determination as to whether a tonnage remeasurement is required.

(g) *Methods for measuring exempt spaces.* (1) If the exempt space is located within the superstructure, the exempt space is measured using the same procedures used to measure superstructure tonnage under § 69.113.

(2) If the exempt space is located between-deck, the space is measured using the same procedures used for between-deck tonnage under § 69.111(c), except that the length of the exempt space is divided into the even number of spaces most equal to the number of spaces into which the between-deck was divided.

(3) If the exempt space is located under-deck, the space is measured using the same procedures used for under-deck tonnage under § 69.109, except that the length of the exempt space is divided into the even number of spaces most equal to the number of spaces into which the under-deck was divided.

[CGD 87–015b, 54 FR 37657, Sept. 12, 1989; 54 FR 40240, Sept. 29, 1989; CGD 97–057, 62 FR 51045, Sept. 30, 1997; CGD 95–028, 62 FR 51203, Sept. 30, 1997; USCG–1999–5118, 64 FR 47404, Aug. 31, 1999]

§ 69.119 Spaces deducted from gross tonnage.

(a) *Purpose.* This section lists the requirements for spaces (other than propelling machinery spaces under § 69.121) which, though included in calculating gross tonnage (i.e., are not exempt under § 69.117), are deducted from gross tonnage in deriving net tonnage.

(b) *General.* (1) A deductible space must be used exclusively for, and be reasonable in size for, its intended purpose.

(2) When a space is larger than necessary for the safe and efficient operation of deductible equipment, only the space occupied by the equipment plus a two foot maximum working space on each side of the equipment, if available, is deductible.

(3) Space specified in this section may be located anywhere within the vessel, unless otherwise specified.

(c) *Anchor gear.* A space below the line of the uppermost complete deck occupied by the anchor gear, capstan, windlass, and chain locker is deductible. A fore peak used exclusively as chain locker is measured by the method prescribed under § 69.117(g)(3).

(d) *Boatswain's stores.* A space containing oils, blocks, hawsers, rigging, deck gear, or other boatswain's stores for daily use is deductible. The maximum deduction allowed for vessels less than 100 gross tons is one ton and, for vessels 100 gross tons or over, is one percent of the gross tonnage, not to exceed 100 tons.

(e) *Chart room.* A space for keeping charts and nautical instruments and for plotting the vessel's course is deductible. For a combined wheelhouse and chart room, that part not exempted as wheelhouse under § 69.117(b)(9) is deductible. For small vessels in which the only space for a chart room is in a cabin or saloon, one half the space not to exceed 1.5 tons is deductible as chart room.

Coast Guard, Dept. of Homeland Security § 69.119

(f) *Donkey engine and boiler.* Donkey engine and boiler space is deductible when connected with the main (non-cargo) pumps of the vessel, except as follows:

(1) If the space is within the engine room or within the casing above the engine room and if the donkey engine is an auxiliary to the main propelling machinery, the space is an engine room deduction under § 69.121(b).

(2) If the space is above the line of the uppermost complete deck and if the donkey engine is not an auxiliary to the main propelling machinery, the space is exempt under § 69.117(b).

(g) *Spaces for the exclusive use of officers or crew.* (1) The following spaces, regardless of their location (unless otherwise noted), are deductible if not used by passengers:

(i) Sleeping rooms.

(ii) Bathrooms with a bath tub or shower but without a water closet.

(iii) Water closets below the line of the uppermost complete deck serving more than one person, with or without a bath tub or shower. Water closets, regardless of location, that serve only one person or that are accessible only through a stateroom or bedroom serving one person are considered as part of the space they serve and are deductible only if that space is deductible.

(iv) Clothes drying rooms.

(v) Drinking water filtration or distilling plant below the line of the uppermost complete deck.

(vi) Hospitals.

(vii) Mess rooms.

(viii) Office of the chief engineer.

(ix) Oil skin lockers.

(x) Pantries.

(xi) Recreation rooms.

(xii) Smoking rooms.

(xiii) Galleys below the line of the uppermost complete deck.

(2) Shops for engineers, carpenters, plumbers, or butchers and offices for clerks, pursers, or postmasters are not deductible, wherever located.

(h) *Master's cabin.* The master's sleeping room, dressing room, bathroom, observation room, reception room, sitting room, water closet, and office are deductible.

(i) *Radio room.* Spaces in which radio apparatus is installed and messages are sent and received and which may provide off-duty operator accommodations are deductible.

(j) *Steering gear.* Spaces for steering gear below the line of the uppermost complete deck are deductible.

(k) *Generators.* Spaces for generators below the line of the uppermost complete deck are deductible regardless of what space the generators serve. These spaces may include other equipment necessary for the generator's operation.

(l) *Pump room.* Spaces below the line of the uppermost complete deck containing pumps that are not capable of handling cargo and that are not fuel oil transfer pumps considered part of the propelling machinery under § 69.121(b)(2)(v) are deductible.

(m) *Sail stowage.* A space for stowing sails on a vessel propelled only by sails is deductible up to two and one-half percent of the vessel's gross tonnage.

(n) *Waste material space.* (1) A tank or collection space, regardless of location, used for the carriage or collection of sewage, garbage, galley waste, trash, slop-oil mixture, tank cleaning residue, bilge residue, or other waste material generated aboard the vessel is deductible.

(2) Space below the line of the uppermost complete deck used exclusively to separate, clarify, purify, or otherwise process waste material generated aboard the vessel is deductible.

(o) *Passageways.* A passageway or companionway is deductible—

(1) If it serves deductible spaces only; or

(2) If it serves deductible spaces and is also the sole means of access to one of the following non-deductible spaces:

(i) Lockers of less than two tons each, containing medicine, linen, mops, or other items for the free use of the crew.

(ii) A ship's office.

(iii) Spare rooms (not exceeding two) used by a pilot, customs officer, reserve engineer, or employee or agent of the vessel's owner or operator.

(p) *Markings for deductible spaces.* (1) Each space deducted under this section

§ 69.121

must be marked with the words "Certified ____" (inserting the space designation, such as "Seaman", "Generator", Office of Chief Engineer", "Hospital", or "Anchor Gear"). If a deductible space berths more than one crew member, the marking must indicate the number of crew members berthed, such as "Certified ____ Seamen" (inserting the number of crew).

(2) The abbreviations "Cert." for "certified" and "W.C." for "water closet" may be used.

(3) The markings must be in Roman letters and Arabic numerals at least ½ inch in height, must be painted in a light color on a dark background, must be embossed, center-punched, carved, or permanently cut in a bulkhead or metal plate, and must be placed in a legible location over a doorway on the inside of the space. A metal plate, if used, must be permanently fastened in place by welding, riveting, lock screws, or a Coast Guard-approved bonding agent.

(q) *Method for measuring deductible spaces.* (1) A rectangular space must be measured by taking the product of its length, breadth, and height.

(2) A space with curved sides on or above the tonnage deck is measured according to § 69.109.

(3) Space less than 15 feet in length may be measured by any practical method.

(4) Spaces below the tonnage deck exceeding 15 feet in length and bounded by a curved surface conforming to the side of the vessel must be measured by the formula used for measuring the superstructure under § 69.113.

(5) The height of a space located on a platform in the hull must be measured from the top of the bottom hull frames, if the platform is used only to form a flat surface at the bottom of the space, if the platform is not more than one foot above the top of the bottom frames, and if the space below the platform is not usable.

(6) The height of a space is measured through any ceiling, paneling, false overhead, or other covering, to the space's structural boundary, unless the space enclosed by the covering is available for a non-deductible use.

[CGD 87–015b, 54 FR 37657, Sept. 12, 1989; 54 FR 40240, Sept. 29, 1989; CGD 92–058, 57 FR 59938, Dec. 17, 1992]

§ 69.121 Engine room deduction.

(a) *General.* The engine room deduction is either a percentage of the vessel's total propelling machinery spaces or a percentage of the vessel's gross tonnage.

(b) *Propelling machinery spaces.* (1) Propelling machinery spaces are the spaces occupied by the main propelling machinery and auxiliary machinery and spaces reasonably necessary for the operation and maintenance of the machinery. Propelling machinery spaces do not include spaces for fuel tanks, spaces exempt from gross tonnage under § 69.117, and spaces not used or not available for use in connection with the propelling machinery.

(2) Propelling machinery spaces are—

(i) Space below the crown. The crown is the top of the main space of the engine room to which the heights of the main space are taken. The crown is either the underside of a deck or, if the side bulkheads are sloping, the uppermost point at which the slope terminates. (See § 69.123, figures 13 and 14.)

(ii) Framed-in space located between the crown and the uppermost complete deck and used for propelling machinery or for the admission of light or air to propelling machinery spaces. (See § 69.123, figures 13 and 14.)

(iii) Shaft tunnel space and thrust block recess space.

(iv) Space below the uppermost complete deck used for escape shafts or trunked ladderways leading from the aft end of the shaft tunnel to the deck above.

(v) Space containing a fuel oil transfer pump located in a separate space and not used for bunkering the vessel. When the pump serves both ballast and fuel oil, only one-half of the pump's space is considered a propelling machinery space.

(vi) Spaces containing fuel oil settling tanks used solely for the main boilers. The space must not exceed one percent of the vessel's gross tonnage.

Coast Guard, Dept. of Homeland Security §69.121

(vii) Spaces for engineers' stores and workshops located below the uppermost complete deck and either open to a propelling machinery space or separated from a propelling machinery space only by a screen bulkhead. The space must not exceed three-quarters of one percent of the vessel's gross tonnage.

(viii) Framed-in space located above the line of the uppermost complete deck and used for propelling machinery or for the admission of light or air to a propelling machinery space, when requested under paragraph (d) of this section.

(ix) If the propelling machinery is boxed-in below the tonnage deck, the boxed-in space plus the spaces outside of the boxing for the shaft, auxiliary engines, and related propelling machinery. If a portion of the boxed-in space extends above a platform or partial deck that is below the uppermost complete deck, that portion is also considered part of the propelling machinery space.

(c) *Methods for measuring propelling machinery spaces.* (1) If the propelling machinery space is bulkheaded off or is not larger than necessary for the safe operation and maintenance of the propelling machinery, the entire space, or, if bulkheaded off, the portion bulkheaded off, is measured for the engine room deduction.

(2) If the propelling machinery space is not bulkheaded off or is larger than necessary for the safe operation and maintenance of the propelling machinery, only the space occupied by the propelling machinery itself plus a working space of two feet, if available, on each side of the propelling machinery is measured for the engine room deduction. If the working space overlaps another working space not related to the propelling machinery, only one-half of the overlapping working space is included in the propelling machinery space. The height of the working space is measured as provided in paragraph (c) of this section.

(3) If the propelling machinery is located in more than one space, each space must be measured separately.

(4) If the propelling machinery is located in a space with a step in the bottom or side lines, each stepped portion of the space must be measured separately.

(5) The length of a space under paragraph (c)(1) of this section is measured from the bulkhead just forward of the propelling machinery to the bulkhead just aft of the propelling machinery. The length of a space under paragraph (c)(2) of this section is measured from the forward edge of the working space to the aft edge of the working space.

(6) If the boundaries of the propelling machinery space form a rectangle, the product of the length, breadth, and height, divided by 100, is the tonnage of the space.

(7) If the boundaries of the propelling machinery space are continuous fair lines, heights are measured at the fore and aft ends and at the center of the space from the bottom frames, floors, or tank top of a double bottom up to the line of the crown. A breadth is measured at half-height of each height. The product of the length, mean breadth, and mean height, divided by 100, is the tonnage of the space.

(8) If the propelling machinery space is in the aft end of the hull, extends from side to side of the hull, and has a continuous bottom line, the length of the space is divided into the even number of equal parts most nearly equal to the number of parts that the tonnage length under §69.109(g) was divided. The tonnage is then calculated by the same method used for calculating the under-deck tonnage in §69.109(1).

(9) The tonnage of a framed-in space located between the crown and the uppermost complete deck and used for propelling machinery or for the admission of light or air to the propelling machinery space, is the product of its length, breadth, and height, divided by 100.

(10) The tonnage of a shaft tunnel, or a thrust block recess, having a flat top is the product of its length, breadth, and height, divided by 100. If the shaft tunnel or thrust block recess top is not flat, the space above must be calculated by using the appropriate geometrical formula. If the space aft of the shaft tunnel extends from side to side of the vessel, the tonnage of the space is found by the formula for measuring peak tanks in §69.109(1).

(11) The length and breadth of the space for a shaft tunnel, or a thrust block recess, when not cased is that which is necessary for maintenance of the shaft. The height allowed for thrust block recess space must not exceed seven feet. The mean height allowed for the shaft tunnel space must not exceed six feet. In a multi-screw vessel where the shaft tunnel or thrust block recess space is open from side to side, measure only the space used for purposes of propelling the vessel.

(12) When the propelling machinery is on a bed at the vessel's bottom, the height of the propelling machinery space is measured from the top of the bottom frames or floors.

(d) *Request to treat certain framed-in engine room spaces as part of a propelling machinery space.* (1) Under §69.117(b)(4), framed-in spaces located above the line of the uppermost complete deck and used for propelling machinery or for admitting light or air to a propelling machinery space are exempt from inclusion in gross tonnage. However, upon written request to a measurement organization listed in §69.15, the vessel owner may elect to have these spaces included in calculating gross tonnage, then deducted from gross tonnage as propelling machinery spaces under paragraph (b)(2)(viii) of this section.

(2) The framed-in space must be safe, seaworthy, and used only for propelling machinery or for the admission of light or air to the propelling machinery space. The length of the space must not exceed the length of the propelling machinery space and the breadth must not exceed one-half of the extreme inside midship breadth of the vessel. Portions of the framed-in space that are plated over are not included in the propelling machinery space.

(3) To exercise the option in paragraph (d)(1) of this section, all of the framed-in space need not be treated as propelling machinery space, but only that portion required to entitle the vessel to have 32 percent of its gross tonnage deducted as an engine room deduction under paragraph (e) of this section.

(e) *Calculating the engine room deduction.* (1) The engine room deduction is based on a percentage of the vessel's gross tonnage or a percentage of the total propelling machinery space.

(2) For vessels propelled in whole or in part by screw—

(i) If the total propelling machinery space is 13 percent or less of the vessel's gross tonnage, deduct $32/13$ times the total propelling machinery space;

(ii) If the total propelling machinery space is more than 13 but less than 20 percent of the vessel's gross tonnage, deduct 32 percent of the vessel's gross tonnage; or

(iii) If the total propelling machinery space is 20 percent or more of the vessel's gross tonnage, deduct either 32 percent of the vessel's gross tonnage or 1.75 times the total propelling machinery space, whichever the vessel's owner elects.

(3) For vessels propelled in whole or in part by paddle-wheel—

(i) If the total propelling machinery space is 20 percent or less of the vessel's gross tonnage, deduct $37/20$ times the total propelling machinery space;

(ii) If the total propelling machinery space is more than 20 but less than 30 percent of the vessel's gross tonnage, deduct 37 percent of the vessel's gross tonnage; or

(iii) If the total propelling machinery space is 30 percent or more of the vessel's gross tonnage, deduct either 37 percent of the vessel's gross tonnage or 1.5 times the total propelling machinery space, whichever the vessel's owner elects.

[CGD 87–015b, 54 FR 37657, Sept. 12, 1989; 54 FR 40240, Sept. 29, 1989]

§ **69.123 Figures.**

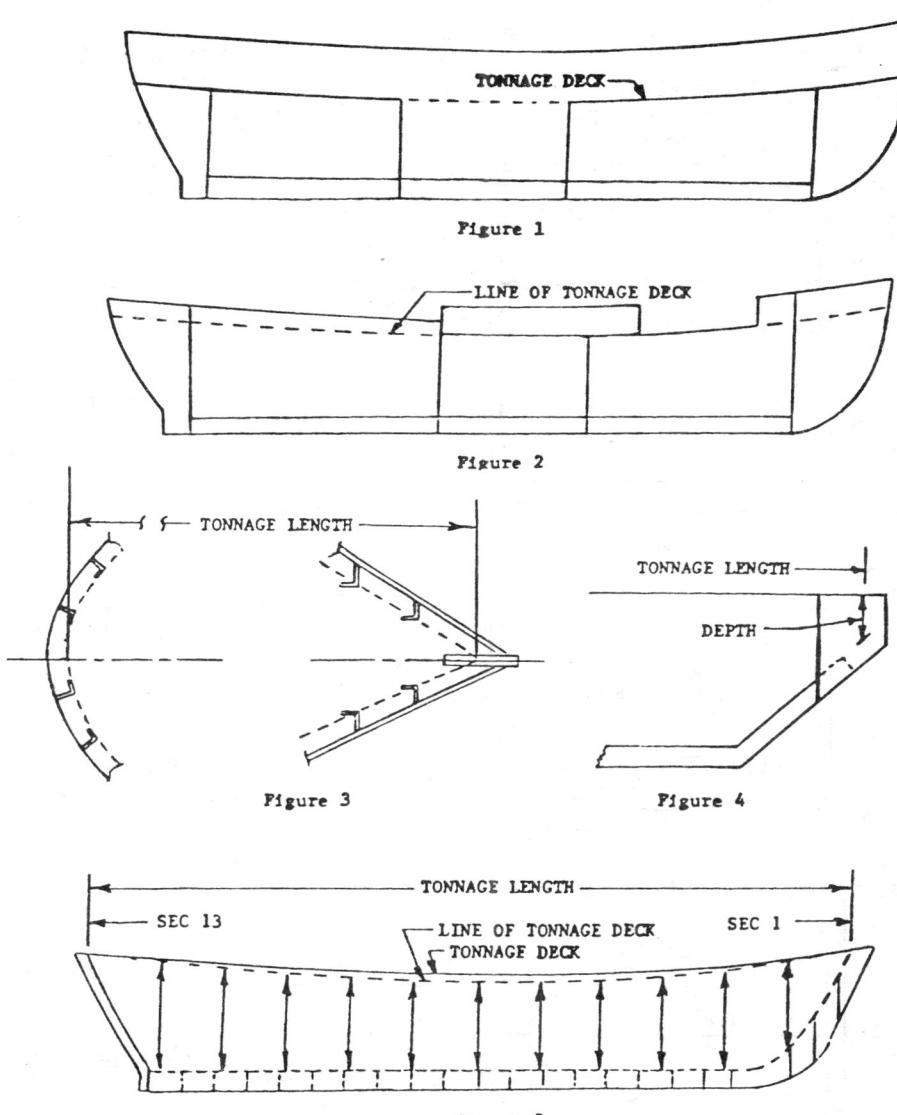

Figure 1

Figure 2

Figure 3

Figure 4

Figure 5

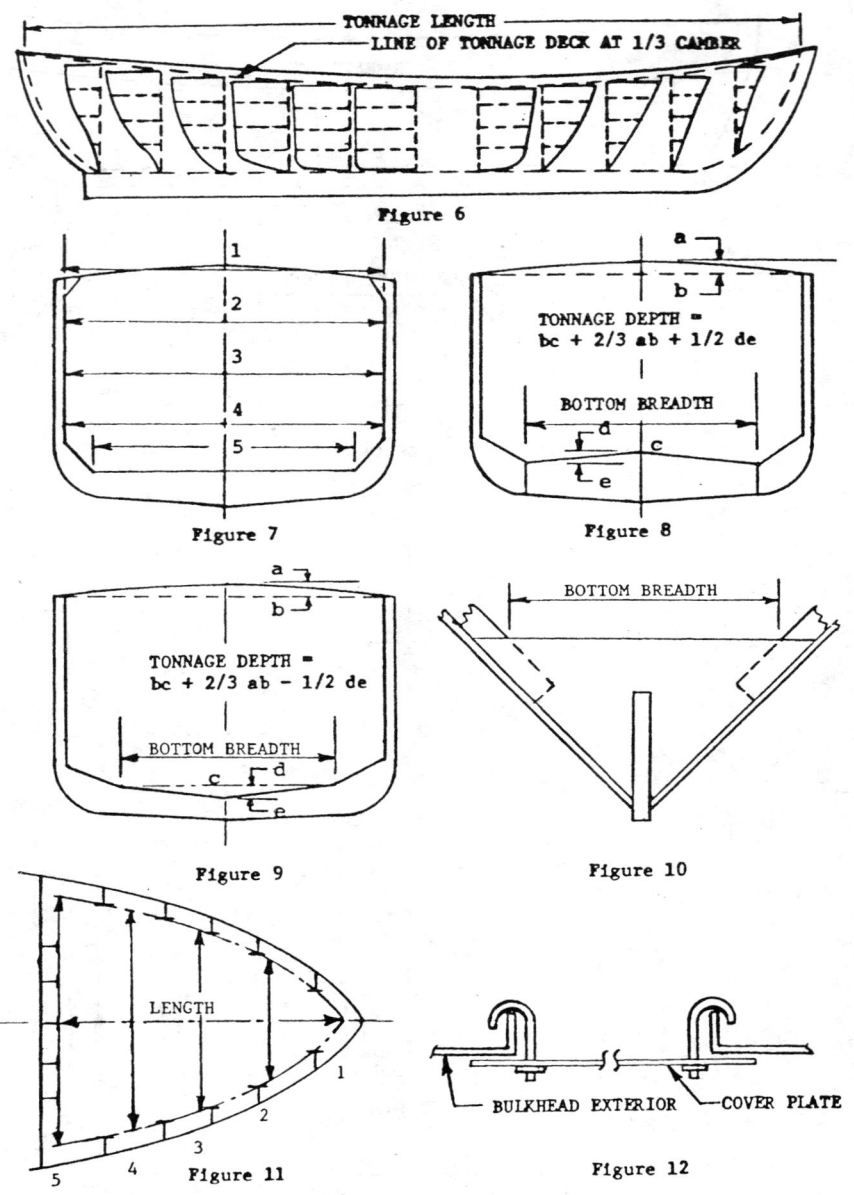

Coast Guard, Dept. of Homeland Security § 69.123

H = Height of main space.
H' = Height between crown and upper deck.
L/A = Light or air space above the upper deck.

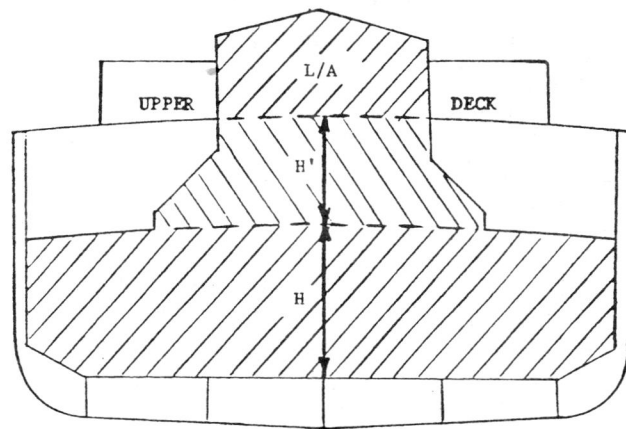

Figure 13

H = Height of main space.
H' = Height between crown and upper deck.
L/A = Light or air space above the upper deck.

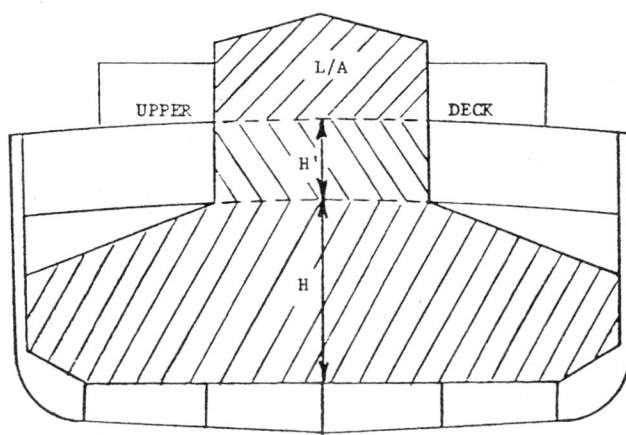

Figure 14

Subpart D—Dual Measurement System

§ 69.151 Purpose.

This subpart prescribes measurement requirements for the assignment of either one gross and one net tonnage or two gross and two net tonnages to vessels under the Dual Measurement System.

§ 69.153 Application of other laws.

(a) If a vessel is assigned two gross tonnages under § 69.175(b), the higher gross tonnage is the tonnage used when applying inspection, manning, and load line laws and regulations to the vessel.

(b) Tonnage marks are not to be construed as additional load line marks. Whether or not a tonnage mark is submerged under § 69.171 has no effect on the applicability of load line laws and regulations.

§ 69.155 Measurement requirements.

Except as otherwise required by this subpart, the measurement requirements under the Standard Measurement System in subpart C of this part apply to the measurement of vessels under the Dual Measurement System.

§ 69.157 Definitions.

Terms used in this subpart that are defined in § 69.103 have the same meaning as in § 69.103, except the terms listed below. As used in this subpart,—

Gross tonnage is defined in § 69.161(a).

Line for fresh and tropical waters means the line described in § 69.177(b)(2).

Line of the second deck means the line described in § 69.181.

Line of the uppermost complete deck means a longitudinal line at the underside of the uppermost complete deck or, if that deck is stepped, the longitudinal line of the underside of the lowest portion of that deck parallel with the upper portions of that deck.

Net tonnage is defined in § 69.161(b).

Second deck means the next deck below the uppermost complete deck that meets the following:

(a) Is continuous athwartships and in a fore-and-aft direction at least between peak bulkheads, even though the deck may have interruptions or openings due to propelling machinery spaces, to hatch and ventilation trunks not extending longitudinally completely between main transverse bulkheads, to ladder and stairway openings, to chain lockers, or to cofferdams.

(b) Is fitted as an integral and permanent part of the vessel.

(c) Has proper covers to all main hatchways.

(d) Does not have steps the total of which exceed 48 inches in height.

Tonnage deck means, for a vessel with only one deck, the uppermost complete deck and, for a vessel with a second deck, the second deck.

Tonnage mark means the line described in § 69.177(a)(2).

§ 69.159 Application for measurement services.

Applications for measurement services under this subpart must include the application information and plans required for the Standard Measurement System under § 69.105. The application must indicate whether a line for fresh and tropical waters is requested under § 69.177(b) and, for vessels with more than one deck, indicate whether one or two sets of tonnages are desired under § 69.175.

§ 69.161 Gross and net tonnages.

(a) *Gross tonnage* means the tonnage of a vessel, less certain spaces exempt under § 69.169, and is the sum of the following:

(1) Under-deck tonnage (§ 69.163).

(2) Between-deck tonnage (§ 69.165).

(3) Superstructure tonnage (§ 69.167).

(4) Excess hatchway tonnage (§ 69.115).

(5) Tonnage of framed-in propelling machinery spaces included in calculating gross tonnage (§ 69.121(d)(1)).

(b) *Net tonnage* means gross tonnage less deductions under § 69.119 and § 69.121.

§ 69.163 Under-deck tonnage.

The under-deck tonnage provisions in § 69.109 apply; except that, under the Dual Measurement System, spaces between the line of the tonnage deck and the tonnage deck itself due to a stepped tonnage deck are included in under-deck tonnage.

§ 69.165 Between-deck tonnage.

The between-deck tonnage provisions in § 69.111 apply, except that, under the Dual Measurement System, between-deck space extends from the tonnage deck to the uppermost complete deck, rather than from the line of the tonnage deck to the line of the uppermost complete deck.

§ 69.167 Superstructure tonnage.

The superstructure tonnage provisions in § 69.113 apply; except that, under the Dual Measurement System, spaces between the line of the uppermost complete deck and the uppermost complete deck itself due to a stepped uppermost complete deck are not included in the superstructure tonnage.

§ 69.169 Spaces exempt from inclusion in gross tonnage.

The tonnage of the following spaces is exempt from inclusion in gross tonnage:

(a) Spaces listed in § 69.117(b) when located within the superstructure.

(b) Spaces listed in § 69.117(c)(1) through (c)(3) when located above, but not on, the uppermost complete deck.

(c) Spaces listed in § 69.117(f), regardless of location.

(d) Spaces available for carrying dry cargo and stores when located on or above the uppermost complete deck.

(e) When a vessel is assigned a tonnage mark and the tonnage mark is not submerged,—

(1) Spaces listed in § 69.117(b) when located between the uppermost complete deck and the second deck;

(2) Spaces listed in § 69.117(c)(1) through (c)(3) when located on the uppermost complete deck; and

(3) Spaces available for carrying dry cargo and stores when located between the uppermost complete deck and the second deck.

[CGD 87–015b, 54 FR 37657, Sept. 12, 1989, as amended by CGD 92–058, 57 FR 59938, Dec. 17, 1992]

§ 69.171 When the tonnage mark is considered submerged.

For the purpose of this subpart, a tonnage mark is considered submerged when—

(a) In salt or brackish water, the upper edge of the tonnage mark is submerged; and

(b) In fresh or tropical water, the upper edge of the line for fresh and tropical waters is submerged.

§ 69.173 Tonnage assignments for vessels with only one deck.

A vessel without a second deck is assigned only one gross and one net tonnage. In calculating the gross tonnage, only the exemptions in § 69.169 (a) through (d) are allowed. Markings under § 69.177 are not permitted on these vessels.

§ 69.175 Tonnage assignments for vessels with a second deck.

(a) At the option of the vessel owner, a vessel having a second deck is assigned either two gross and two net tonnages or one gross and one net tonnage.

(b) If two gross and two net tonnages are assigned, the higher tonnages (i.e. those based only on exemptions under § 69.169 (a) through (d)) are applicable when the upper edge of the tonnage mark is submerged and the lower tonnages (i.e. those based only on all exemptions under § 69.169) are applicable when the upper edge of the tonnage mark is not submerged.

(c) If only the low gross and low net tonnages, as calculated under paragraph (b) of this section, are assigned, these tonnages are applicable at all times. On these vessels, the tonnage mark must be located in accordance with § 69.177(a)(6) at the level of the uppermost part of the load line grid.

§ 69.177 Markings.

(a) *Tonnage mark.* (1) All vessels with a second deck that are measured under the Dual Measurement System must have, on each side of the vessel, a tonnage mark, and an inverted triangle identifying the tonnage mark, as described and located under this section. (See the figure in § 69.183(a).) Vessels with only one deck are not assigned markings under this section.

(2) The tonnage mark is a horizontal line 15 inches long and one inch wide. The tonnage mark must be designated by a welded bead or other permanent

§ 69.177

mark 15 inches long placed along the top edge of the tonnage mark.

(3) Above the tonnage mark is placed an inverted equilateral triangle, each side of which is 12 inches long and one inch wide, with its apex touching the upper edge of the center of the tonnage mark.

(4) If the vessel has a load line mark, the longitudinal location of the center of the tonnage mark must be between 21 inches and six feet six inches aft of the vertical centerline of the load line ring. (See the figures in § 69.183 (b) and (c).) If the vessel does not have a load line mark, the center of the tonnage mark must be located amidships.

(5) Except as under paragraph (a)(6) of this section, the upper edge of the tonnage mark must be located below the line of the second deck at the distance indicated in Table 69.177(a)(5). (See the figure in § 69.183(b).)

TABLE 69.177(a)(5)—MINIMUM DISTANCE IN INCHES BETWEEN THE TONNAGE MARK AND THE LINE OF THE SECOND DECK

L (in feet)	L divided by D								
	12	13	14	15	16	17	18	19	20
220 and under	2.0	2.0	2.0	2.0	2.0	2.0	2.0	2.0	2.0
230	3.2	2.0	2.0	2.0	2.0	2.0	2.0	2.0	2.0
240	4.7	2.0	2.0	2.0	2.0	2.0	2.0	2.0	2.0
250	6.3	3.3	2.0	2.0	2.0	2.0	2.0	2.0	2.0
260	8.0	4.8	2.1	2.0	2.0	2.0	2.0	2.0	2.0
270	9.9	6.4	3.5	2.0	2.0	2.0	2.0	2.0	2.0
280	11.8	8.1	4.9	2.1	2.0	2.0	2.0	2.0	2.0
290	13.9	9.9	6.5	3.5	2.0	2.0	2.0	2.0	2.0
300	16.0	11.7	8.1	4.9	2.1	2.0	2.0	2.0	2.0
310	18.3	13.7	9.8	6.4	3.5	2.0	2.0	2.0	2.0
320	20.7	15.8	11.7	8.1	4.9	2.1	2.0	2.0	2.0
330	23.2	18.0	13.6	9.8	6.4	3.5	2.0	2.0	2.0
340	25.9	20.4	15.7	11.6	8.1	4.9	2.1	2.0	2.0
350	28.7	22.9	17.9	13.6	9.8	6.5	3.6	2.0	2.0
360	31.7	25.5	20.2	15.7	11.7	8.2	5.0	2.2	2.0
370	34.7	28.3	22.7	17.9	13.6	9.9	6.6	3.7	2.0
380	38.0	31.1	25.3	20.2	15.7	11.8	8.3	5.2	2.4
390	41.3	34.1	27.9	22.6	17.9	13.8	10.1	6.8	3.8
400	44.8	37.2	30.7	25.0	20.1	15.8	11.9	8.4	5.3
410	48.2	40.3	33.5	27.7	22.6	18.1	14.0	10.4	7.2
420	51.5	43.4	36.4	30.4	25.2	20.6	16.4	12.7	9.7
430	54.8	46.5	39.4	33.3	27.9	23.2	19.0	15.2	11.8
440	58.4	49.9	42.6	36.4	30.9	26.0	21.7	17.8	14.4
450	62.1	53.4	46.0	39.6	33.9	29.0	24.6	20.6	17.1
460	65.9	57.0	49.5	42.9	37.1	32.1	27.6	23.5	19.9
470	69.8	60.7	53.0	46.3	40.4	35.2	30.6	26.5	22.8
480	73.7	64.4	56.5	49.7	43.7	38.4	33.7	29.5	25.7
490	77.5	68.1	60.0	53.0	46.9	41.5	36.7	32.4	28.5
500	81.2	71.6	63.4	56.2	50.0	44.5	39.6	35.2	31.2
510	84.9	75.1	66.7	59.4	53.0	47.4	42.4	37.9	33.9
520	88.4	78.4	69.9	62.4	55.9	50.2	45.1	40.5	36.4
530	91.8	81.6	72.9	65.3	58.7	52.9	47.7	43.0	38.8
540	95.2	84.8	75.9	68.1	61.4	55.5	50.2	45.4	41.2
550	98.4	87.8	78.8	70.9	64.0	58.0	52.6	47.8	43.4
560	101.6	90.8	81.6	73.6	66.6	60.5	55.0	50.1	45.6
570	104.8	93.8	84.4	76.3	69.2	62.9	57.3	52.3	47.8
580	107.9	96.8	87.2	78.9	71.7	65.3	59.6	54.5	49.9
590	111.0	99.7	90.0	81.5	74.2	67.7	61.9	56.7	52.0
600	114.0	102.5	92.6	84.0	76.5	69.9	64.0	58.8	54.0
610	117.0	105.3	95.2	86.5	78.9	72.1	66.2	60.8	56.0
620	120.0	108.0	97.8	88.9	81.2	74.4	68.3	62.8	58.0
630	122.9	110.7	100.4	91.3	83.5	76.6	70.4	64.8	59.9
640	125.7	113.4	102.9	93.7	85.8	78.7	72.4	66.8	61.7
650	128.6	116.1	105.4	96.1	88.0	80.8	74.4	68.7	63.6
660	131.4	118.7	107.8	98.3	90.1	82.8	76.3	70.6	65.3
670	134.2	121.2	110.2	100.6	92.2	84.8	78.3	72.4	67.1
680	136.9	123.8	112.8	102.9	94.3	86.8	80.2	74.2	68.9
690	139.6	126.3	115.0	105.1	96.4	88.8	82.1	76.0	70.6
700	142.3	128.8	117.3	107.3	98.5	90.8	83.9	77.8	72.3
710	144.9	131.3	119.6	109.4	100.5	92.7	85.7	79.5	73.9
720	147.5	133.7	121.8	111.5	102.5	94.6	87.5	81.2	75.5
730	150.1	136.1	124.0	113.6	104.5	96.5	89.3	82.9	77.1
740	152.7	138.5	126.2	115.7	106.5	98.3	91.5	84.5	78.7

Coast Guard, Dept. of Homeland Security §69.181

TABLE 69.177(a)(5)—MINIMUM DISTANCE IN INCHES BETWEEN THE TONNAGE MARK AND THE LINE OF THE SECOND DECK—Continued

L (in feet)	L divided by D								
	12	13	14	15	16	17	18	19	20
750	155.3	140.8	128.5	117.8	108.4	100.1	92.8	86.1	80.3
760	157.8	143.1	130.6	119.7	110.3	101.9	94.4	87.8	81.7
770	160.2	145.4	132.7	121.7	112.1	103.6	96.0	89.3	83.2
780	162.6	147.6	134.8	123.7	113.9	105.3	97.6	90.8	84.7
790	165.1	149.9	136.9	125.6	115.7	107.0	99.2	92.3	86.1
800	167.5	152.1	138.9	127.4	117.4	108.6	100.8	93.8	87.4

L=the length in feet of the line of the second deck at the centerline of the vessel from the inner surface of the frames at the vessel's stem to the inner surface of the frames at the vessel's stern.
D=The vertical distance in feet from the top of the flat keel of the vessel to the line of the second deck.
EXAMPLE (1) For a vessel in which L=450 feet and L/D=15 feet, read down from the L/D column "15" and to the right on the column "450" to where the two columns intersect at 39.6. The tonnage mark must be located 39.6 inches below the line of the second deck.
EXAMPLE (2) If L or L/D is an intermediate number, the distance "a" between the tonnage mark and the line of the second deck must be obtained by linear interpolation. For a vessel in which L=424.80 feet and L/D=15.17:

L	Table L/D=15	Actual L/D=15.17	Table L/D=16
Table 420	30.4		25.2
Actual 424.80	r	a	s
Table 430	33.3		27.9

Interpolation:
r=30.4+0.48 (33.3−30.4)=31.79
s=25.2+0.48 (27.9−25.2)=26.50
a=r−0.17 (r−s)=31.79−0.17 (31.79−26.50)=30.89 inches

(6) For the following vessels with a load line mark, the upper edge of the tonnage mark must be located at the level of the uppermost part of the load line grid:

(i) Vessels assigned only one gross and one net tonnage under §69.175(c).

(ii) Vessels for which a load line assigning authority certifies that the vessel's load line mark was located as though the second deck were the freeboard deck.

(b) *Line for fresh and tropical waters.* (1) Except as under paragraph (b)(4) of this section, a horizontal line for fresh and tropical waters may be assigned at the vessel owner's request.

(2) The line must be nine inches long and one inch wide and located above and to the left of the tonnage mark at a distance equal to one forty-eighth of the distance from the top of the flat keel to the tonnage mark. The tonnage mark and the line for fresh and tropical waters must be connected by a vertical line one inch wide. (See the figure in §69.183(a).)

(3) The line for fresh and tropical waters must be designated by a welded bead or other permanent mark nine inches long placed along the upper edge of the line.

(4) For vessels with a load line mark, if the load line assigning authority certifies that the load line mark was located as though the second deck were the freeboard deck, a line for fresh and tropical waters must not be placed on the vessel.

(c) *Freeboard deck mark.* A vessel assigned two gross and two net tonnages which has more than one deck and no load line mark assigned must have a mark on each side of the vessel with the same dimensions and location as the freeboard deck line mark under §42.13–20 of this chapter, except that the mark must be located directly above the tonnage mark.

(d) *The line of the second deck.* The line of the second deck must not be marked on the side of the vessel.

(e) *Color of markings.* All markings under this section must be maintained in either a light color on a dark background or a dark color on a light background.

§69.179 Certification of markings.

(a) Before a certificate of measurement is issued for a vessel requiring a tonnage mark, a certification by a measurement organization under §69.15 that all markings meet the requirements of this subpart is required.

(b) The Coast Guard, at any time, may verify markings under this subpart.

§69.181 Locating the line of the second deck.

(a) If the second deck is not stepped, the line of the second deck is the longitudinal line of the underside of the second deck at the side of the hull.

(b) If the second deck is stepped (as in the examples following this paragraph), the line of the second deck is a longitudinal line extended parallel to each portion of the second deck and located at the height of the underside of the amidships portion of the second deck at the side of the hull—

(1) Plus, for each stepped portion of the second deck higher than the second deck at amidships, a distance equal to the length of the stepped portion divided by the total length of the second deck times the height that the step is above the height of the amidship portion of the second deck; and

(2) Minus, for each stepped portion of the second deck lower than the second deck at amidships, a distance equal to the length of the stepped portion divided by the total length of the second deck times the height that the amidship portion of the second deck is above the height of the step.

EXAMPLE: (1)

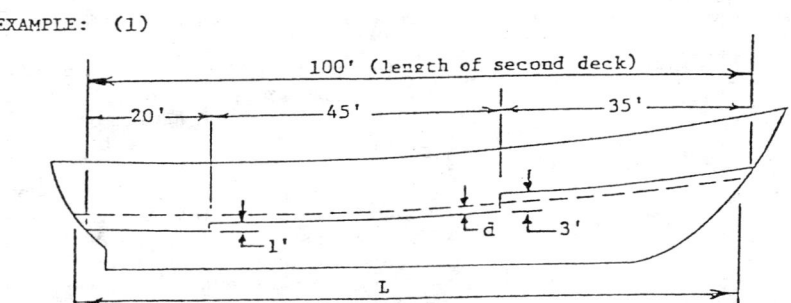

L = Length of the line of the second deck.
d = Distance from amidship portion of second deck to line of second deck.
$d = \dfrac{35 \times 3}{100} - \dfrac{20 \times 1}{100} = +0.85$ feet.

EXAMPLE: (2)

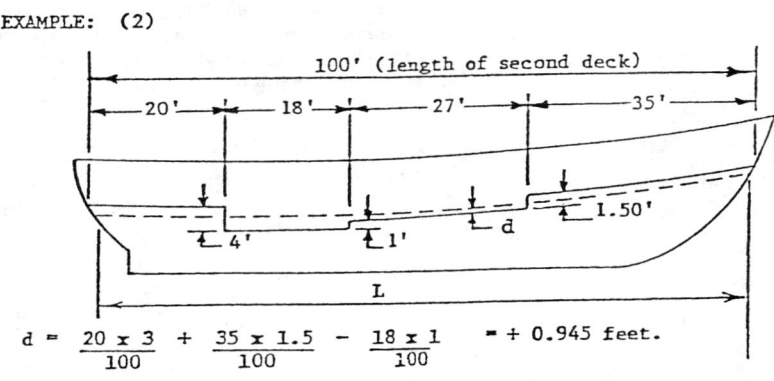

$d = \dfrac{20 \times 3}{100} + \dfrac{35 \times 1.5}{100} - \dfrac{18 \times 1}{100} = +0.945$ feet.

§ 69.183 Figures.

(a) *Tonnage mark with an equilateral triangle and a line for fresh and tropical waters.*

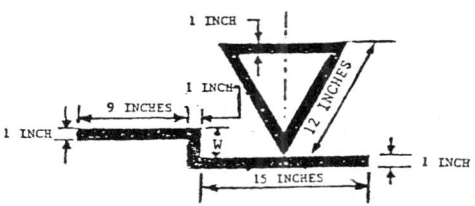

W=1/48 of the distance from the top of the flat keel to the tonnage mark. (See § 69.177(b)(2).)

(b) *Tonnage mark location if the load line mark is not placed as though the second deck were the freeboard deck.*

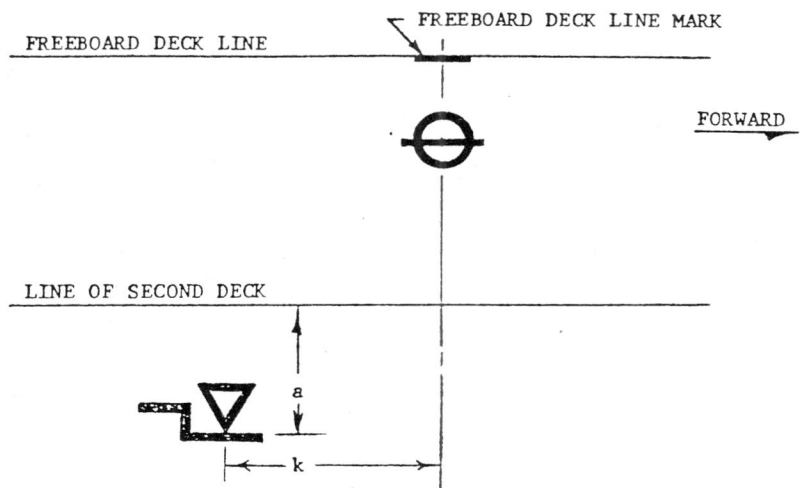

k=a distance between 21 inches and six feet six inches.
a=distance derived from Table 69.177(a)(5).

(c)—*Tonnage mark location if the load line mark is placed as though the second deck were the freeboard deck.*

§ 69.201

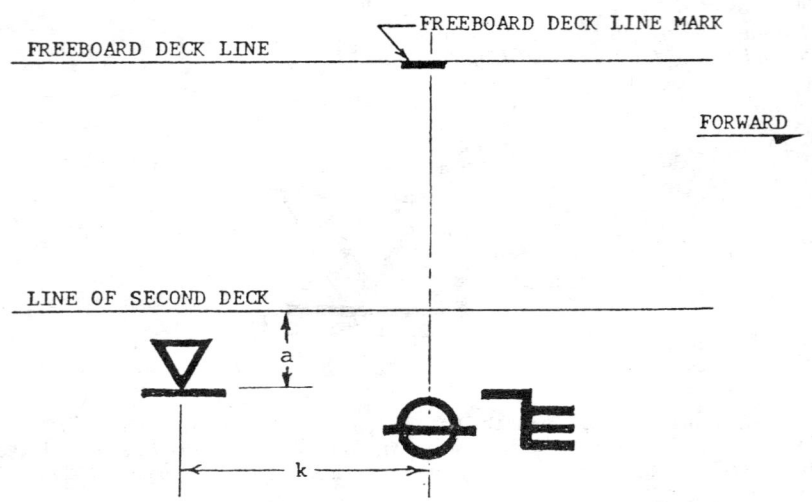

k=a distance between 21 inches and six feet six inches.
a=the distance between the line of the second deck and the uppermost part of the load line grid.

Subpart E—Simplified Measurement System

§ 69.201 Purpose.

This subpart prescribes the procedures for measuring a vessel under the Simplified Measurement System described in 46 U.S.C. chapter 145, subchapter III.

§ 69.203 Definitions.

As used in this subpart and in Coast Guard Form CG–5397 under § 69.205—

Overall breadth means the horizontal distance taken at the widest part of the hull, excluding rub rails, from the outboard side of the skin (outside planking or plating) on one side of the hull to the outboard side of the skin on the other side of the hull.

Overall depth means the vertical distance taken at or near midships from a line drawn horizontally through the uppermost edges of the skin (outside planking or plating) at the sides of the hull (excluding the cap rail, trunks, cabins, and deckhouses) to the outboard face of the bottom skin of the hull, excluding the keel. For a vessel that is designed for sailing and has a keel faired to the hull, the keel is included in "overall depth" if the distance to the bottom skin of the hull cannot be determined reasonably.

Overall length means the horizontal distance between the outboard side of the foremost part of the stem and the outboard side of the aftermost part of the stern, excluding rudders, outboard motor brackets, and other similar fittings and attachments.

Registered breadth means—

(a) For a single-hull vessel, the vessel's overall breadth; and

(b) For a multi-hull vessel, the horizontal distance taken at the widest part of the complete vessel between the outboard side of the skin (outside planking or plating) on the outboardmost side of one of the outboardmost hulls to the outboard side of the skin on the outboardmost side of the other outboardmost hull, excluding rubrails.

Registered depth means—

(a) For a single-hull vessel, the vessel's overall depth; and

(b) For a multi-hull vessel, the overall depth of the deepest hull.

Registered length means—

(a) For a single-hull vessel, the vessel's overall length; and

420

Coast Guard, Dept. of Homeland Security §69.209

(b) For a multi-hull vessel, the horizontal distance between the outboard side of the foremost part of the stem of the foremost hull and the outboard side of the aftermost part of the stern of the aftermost hull, excluding fittings or attachments.

Vessel designed for sailing means a vessel which has the fine lines of a sailing craft and is capable of being propelled by sail, whether or not the vessel is equipped with an auxiliary motor, a decorative sail, or a sail designed only to steady the vessel.

[CGD 87–015b, 54 FR 37657, Sept. 12, 1989; 54 FR 40240, Sept. 29, 1989; USCG–1999–6216, 64 FR 53225, Oct. 1, 1999]

§69.205 Application for measurement services.

To apply for measurement under the Simplified Measurement System, the owner of the vessel must complete either an Application for Simplified Measurement (form CG–5397), or a Builder's Certification and First Transfer of Title (form CG–1261) which has the information in Part III "Dimensions" completed, and submit it to the National Vessel Documentation Center.

[CGD 95–014, 60 FR 31606, June 15, 1995]

§69.207 Measurements.

(a) All lengths and depths must be measured in a vertical plane at centerline and breadths must be measured in a line at right angles to that plane. All dimensions must be expressed in feet and inches to the nearest half inch or in feet and tenths of a foot to the nearest .05 of a foot.

(b) For a multi-hull vessel, each hull must be measured separately for overall length, breadth, and depth and the vessel as a whole must be measured for registered length, breadth, and depth.

(c) The Coast Guard may verify dimensions of vessels measured under this subpart.

§69.209 Calculation of tonnages.

(a) *Gross tonnage.* (1) Except as in paragraphs (a)(2) through (a)(5) of this section, the gross tonnage of a vessel designed for sailing is one-half of the product of its overall length, overall breadth, and overall depth (LBD) divided by one hundred (i.e., 0.50 LBD/100), and the gross tonnage of a vessel not designed for sailing is 0.67 LBD/100.

(2) The gross tonnage of a vessel with a hull that approximates in shape a rectangular geometric solid (barge-shape) is 0.84 LBD/100.

(3) The gross tonnage of a multi-hull vessel is the sum of all the hulls as calculated under this section.

(4) If the volume of the principal deck structure of a vessel is as large as, or larger than, the volume of the vessel's hull, the volume of the principal deck structure in tons of 100 cubic feet is added to the tonnage of the hull to establish the vessel's gross tonnage. The volume of the principal deck structure of a vessel is determined by the product of its average dimensions.

(5) If the overall depth of a vessel designed for sailing includes the keel, only 75 percent of that depth is used for gross tonnage calculations.

(b) *Net tonnage.* (1) For a vessel having propelling machinery in its hull—

(i) The net tonnage is 90 percent of its gross tonnage, if it is a vessel designed for sailing; or

(ii) The net tonnage is 80 percent of its gross tonnage, if it is not a vessel designed for sailing.

(2) For a vessel having no propelling machinery in its hull, the net tonnage is the same as its gross tonnage.

[CGD 87–015b, 54 FR 37657, Sept. 12, 1989, as amended by CGD 97–057, 62 FR 51045, Sept. 30, 1997]

FINDING AIDS

A list of CFR titles, subtitles, chapters, subchapters and parts, and an alphabetical listing of agencies publishing in the CFR are included in the CFR Index and Finding Aids volume to the Code of Federal Regulations which is published separately and revised annually.

Table of CFR Titles and Chapters
Alphabetical List of Agencies Appearing in the CFR
List of CFR Sections Affected

Table of CFR Titles and Chapters
(Revised as of October 1, 2013)

Title 1—General Provisions

I	Administrative Committee of the Federal Register (Parts 1—49)
II	Office of the Federal Register (Parts 50—299)
III	Administrative Conference of the United States (Parts 300—399)
IV	Miscellaneous Agencies (Parts 400—500)

Title 2—Grants and Agreements

SUBTITLE A—OFFICE OF MANAGEMENT AND BUDGET GUIDANCE FOR GRANTS AND AGREEMENTS

I	Office of Management and Budget Governmentwide Guidance for Grants and Agreements (Parts 2—199)
II	Office of Management and Budget Circulars and Guidance (200—299)

SUBTITLE B—FEDERAL AGENCY REGULATIONS FOR GRANTS AND AGREEMENTS

III	Department of Health and Human Services (Parts 300— 399)
IV	Department of Agriculture (Parts 400—499)
VI	Department of State (Parts 600—699)
VII	Agency for International Development (Parts 700—799)
VIII	Department of Veterans Affairs (Parts 800—899)
IX	Department of Energy (Parts 900—999)
XI	Department of Defense (Parts 1100—1199)
XII	Department of Transportation (Parts 1200—1299)
XIII	Department of Commerce (Parts 1300—1399)
XIV	Department of the Interior (Parts 1400—1499)
XV	Environmental Protection Agency (Parts 1500—1599)
XVIII	National Aeronautics and Space Administration (Parts 1800—1899)
XX	United States Nuclear Regulatory Commission (Parts 2000—2099)
XXII	Corporation for National and Community Service (Parts 2200—2299)
XXIII	Social Security Administration (Parts 2300—2399)
XXIV	Housing and Urban Development (Parts 2400—2499)
XXV	National Science Foundation (Parts 2500—2599)
XXVI	National Archives and Records Administration (Parts 2600—2699)
XXVII	Small Business Administration (Parts 2700—2799)
XXVIII	Department of Justice (Parts 2800—2899)

Title 2—Grants and Agreements—Continued

Chap.	
XXX	Department of Homeland Security (Parts 3000—3099)
XXXI	Institute of Museum and Library Services (Parts 3100—3199)
XXXII	National Endowment for the Arts (Parts 3200—3299)
XXXIII	National Endowment for the Humanities (Parts 3300—3399)
XXXIV	Department of Education (Parts 3400—3499)
XXXV	Export-Import Bank of the United States (Parts 3500—3599)
XXXVII	Peace Corps (Parts 3700—3799)
LVIII	Election Assistance Commission (Parts 5800—5899)

Title 3—The President

I	Executive Office of the President (Parts 100—199)

Title 4—Accounts

I	Government Accountability Office (Parts 1—199)
II	Recovery Accountability and Transparency Board (Parts 200—299)

Title 5—Administrative Personnel

I	Office of Personnel Management (Parts 1—1199)
II	Merit Systems Protection Board (Parts 1200—1299)
III	Office of Management and Budget (Parts 1300—1399)
V	The International Organizations Employees Loyalty Board (Parts 1500—1599)
VI	Federal Retirement Thrift Investment Board (Parts 1600—1699)
VIII	Office of Special Counsel (Parts 1800—1899)
IX	Appalachian Regional Commission (Parts 1900—1999)
XI	Armed Forces Retirement Home (Parts 2100—2199)
XIV	Federal Labor Relations Authority, General Counsel of the Federal Labor Relations Authority and Federal Service Impasses Panel (Parts 2400—2499)
XV	Office of Administration, Executive Office of the President (Parts 2500—2599)
XVI	Office of Government Ethics (Parts 2600—2699)
XXI	Department of the Treasury (Parts 3100—3199)
XXII	Federal Deposit Insurance Corporation (Parts 3200—3299)
XXIII	Department of Energy (Parts 3300—3399)
XXIV	Federal Energy Regulatory Commission (Parts 3400—3499)
XXV	Department of the Interior (Parts 3500—3599)
XXVI	Department of Defense (Parts 3600— 3699)
XXVIII	Department of Justice (Parts 3800—3899)
XXIX	Federal Communications Commission (Parts 3900—3999)
XXX	Farm Credit System Insurance Corporation (Parts 4000—4099)
XXXI	Farm Credit Administration (Parts 4100—4199)

Title 5—Administrative Personnel—Continued

Chap.	
XXXIII	Overseas Private Investment Corporation (Parts 4300—4399)
XXXIV	Securities and Exchange Commission (Parts 4400—4499)
XXXV	Office of Personnel Management (Parts 4500—4599)
XXXVII	Federal Election Commission (Parts 4700—4799)
XL	Interstate Commerce Commission (Parts 5000—5099)
XLI	Commodity Futures Trading Commission (Parts 5100—5199)
XLII	Department of Labor (Parts 5200—5299)
XLIII	National Science Foundation (Parts 5300—5399)
XLV	Department of Health and Human Services (Parts 5500—5599)
XLVI	Postal Rate Commission (Parts 5600—5699)
XLVII	Federal Trade Commission (Parts 5700—5799)
XLVIII	Nuclear Regulatory Commission (Parts 5800—5899)
XLIX	Federal Labor Relations Authority (Parts 5900—5999)
L	Department of Transportation (Parts 6000—6099)
LII	Export-Import Bank of the United States (Parts 6200—6299)
LIII	Department of Education (Parts 6300—6399)
LIV	Environmental Protection Agency (Parts 6400—6499)
LV	National Endowment for the Arts (Parts 6500—6599)
LVI	National Endowment for the Humanities (Parts 6600—6699)
LVII	General Services Administration (Parts 6700—6799)
LVIII	Board of Governors of the Federal Reserve System (Parts 6800—6899)
LIX	National Aeronautics and Space Administration (Parts 6900—6999)
LX	United States Postal Service (Parts 7000—7099)
LXI	National Labor Relations Board (Parts 7100—7199)
LXII	Equal Employment Opportunity Commission (Parts 7200—7299)
LXIII	Inter-American Foundation (Parts 7300—7399)
LXIV	Merit Systems Protection Board (Parts 7400—7499)
LXV	Department of Housing and Urban Development (Parts 7500—7599)
LXVI	National Archives and Records Administration (Parts 7600—7699)
LXVII	Institute of Museum and Library Services (Parts 7700—7799)
LXVIII	Commission on Civil Rights (Parts 7800—7899)
LXIX	Tennessee Valley Authority (Parts 7900—7999)
LXX	Court Services and Offender Supervision Agency for the District of Columbia (Parts 8000—8099)
LXXI	Consumer Product Safety Commission (Parts 8100—8199)
LXXIII	Department of Agriculture (Parts 8300—8399)
LXXIV	Federal Mine Safety and Health Review Commission (Parts 8400—8499)
LXXVI	Federal Retirement Thrift Investment Board (Parts 8600—8699)
LXXVII	Office of Management and Budget (Parts 8700—8799)
LXXX	Federal Housing Finance Agency (Parts 9000—9099)
LXXXII	Special Inspector General for Iraq Reconstruction (Parts 9200—9299)

Title 5—Administrative Personnel—Continued

Chap.

LXXXIII Special Inspector General for Afghanistan Reconstruction (Parts 9300—9399)
LXXXIV Bureau of Consumer Financial Protection (Parts 9400—9499)
LXXXVI National Credit Union Administration (9600—9699)
XCVII Department of Homeland Security Human Resources Management System (Department of Homeland Security—Office of Personnel Management) (Parts 9700—9799)
XCVII Council of the Inspectors General on Integrity and Efficiency (Parts 9800—9899)

Title 6—Domestic Security

I Department of Homeland Security, Office of the Secretary (Parts 1—99)
X Privacy and Civil Liberties Oversight Board (Parts 1000—1099)

Title 7—Agriculture

SUBTITLE A—OFFICE OF THE SECRETARY OF AGRICULTURE (PARTS 0—26)

SUBTITLE B—REGULATIONS OF THE DEPARTMENT OF AGRICULTURE

I Agricultural Marketing Service (Standards, Inspections, Marketing Practices), Department of Agriculture (Parts 27—209)
II Food and Nutrition Service, Department of Agriculture (Parts 210—299)
III Animal and Plant Health Inspection Service, Department of Agriculture (Parts 300—399)
IV Federal Crop Insurance Corporation, Department of Agriculture (Parts 400—499)
V Agricultural Research Service, Department of Agriculture (Parts 500—599)
VI Natural Resources Conservation Service, Department of Agriculture (Parts 600—699)
VII Farm Service Agency, Department of Agriculture (Parts 700—799)
VIII Grain Inspection, Packers and Stockyards Administration (Federal Grain Inspection Service), Department of Agriculture (Parts 800—899)
IX Agricultural Marketing Service (Marketing Agreements and Orders; Fruits, Vegetables, Nuts), Department of Agriculture (Parts 900—999)
X Agricultural Marketing Service (Marketing Agreements and Orders; Milk), Department of Agriculture (Parts 1000—1199)
XI Agricultural Marketing Service (Marketing Agreements and Orders; Miscellaneous Commodities), Department of Agriculture (Parts 1200—1299)
XIV Commodity Credit Corporation, Department of Agriculture (Parts 1400—1499)
XV Foreign Agricultural Service, Department of Agriculture (Parts 1500—1599)

Title 7—Agriculture—Continued

Chap.
XVI Rural Telephone Bank, Department of Agriculture (Parts 1600—1699)
XVII Rural Utilities Service, Department of Agriculture (Parts 1700—1799)
XVIII Rural Housing Service, Rural Business-Cooperative Service, Rural Utilities Service, and Farm Service Agency, Department of Agriculture (Parts 1800—2099)
XX Local Television Loan Guarantee Board (Parts 2200—2299)
XXV Office of Advocacy and Outreach, Department of Agriculture (Parts 2500—2599)
XXVI Office of Inspector General, Department of Agriculture (Parts 2600—2699)
XXVII Office of Information Resources Management, Department of Agriculture (Parts 2700—2799)
XXVIII Office of Operations, Department of Agriculture (Parts 2800—2899)
XXIX Office of Energy Policy and New Uses, Department of Agriculture (Parts 2900—2999)
XXX Office of the Chief Financial Officer, Department of Agriculture (Parts 3000—3099)
XXXI Office of Environmental Quality, Department of Agriculture (Parts 3100—3199)
XXXII Office of Procurement and Property Management, Department of Agriculture (Parts 3200—3299)
XXXIII Office of Transportation, Department of Agriculture (Parts 3300—3399)
XXXIV National Institute of Food and Agriculture (Parts 3400—3499)
XXXV Rural Housing Service, Department of Agriculture (Parts 3500—3599)
XXXVI National Agricultural Statistics Service, Department of Agriculture (Parts 3600—3699)
XXXVII Economic Research Service, Department of Agriculture (Parts 3700—3799)
XXXVIII World Agricultural Outlook Board, Department of Agriculture (Parts 3800—3899)
XLI [Reserved]
XLII Rural Business-Cooperative Service and Rural Utilities Service, Department of Agriculture (Parts 4200—4299)

Title 8—Aliens and Nationality

I Department of Homeland Security (Immigration and Naturalization) (Parts 1—499)
V Executive Office for Immigration Review, Department of Justice (Parts 1000—1399)

Title 9—Animals and Animal Products

I Animal and Plant Health Inspection Service, Department of Agriculture (Parts 1—199)

Title 9—Animals and Animal Products—Continued

Chap.

II	Grain Inspection, Packers and Stockyards Administration (Packers and Stockyards Programs), Department of Agriculture (Parts 200—299)
III	Food Safety and Inspection Service, Department of Agriculture (Parts 300—599)

Title 10—Energy

I	Nuclear Regulatory Commission (Parts 0—199)
II	Department of Energy (Parts 200—699)
III	Department of Energy (Parts 700—999)
X	Department of Energy (General Provisions) (Parts 1000—1099)
XIII	Nuclear Waste Technical Review Board (Parts 1300—1399)
XVII	Defense Nuclear Facilities Safety Board (Parts 1700—1799)
XVIII	Northeast Interstate Low-Level Radioactive Waste Commission (Parts 1800—1899)

Title 11—Federal Elections

I	Federal Election Commission (Parts 1—9099)
II	Election Assistance Commission (Parts 9400—9499)

Title 12—Banks and Banking

I	Comptroller of the Currency, Department of the Treasury (Parts 1—199)
II	Federal Reserve System (Parts 200—299)
III	Federal Deposit Insurance Corporation (Parts 300—399)
IV	Export-Import Bank of the United States (Parts 400—499)
V	Office of Thrift Supervision, Department of the Treasury (Parts 500—599)
VI	Farm Credit Administration (Parts 600—699)
VII	National Credit Union Administration (Parts 700—799)
VIII	Federal Financing Bank (Parts 800—899)
IX	Federal Housing Finance Board (Parts 900—999)
X	Bureau of Consumer Financial Protection (Parts 1000—1099)
XI	Federal Financial Institutions Examination Council (Parts 1100—1199)
XII	Federal Housing Finance Agency (Parts 1200—1299)
XIII	Financial Stability Oversight Council (Parts 1300—1399)
XIV	Farm Credit System Insurance Corporation (Parts 1400—1499)
XV	Department of the Treasury (Parts 1500—1599)
XVI	Office of Financial Research (Parts 1600—1699)
XVII	Office of Federal Housing Enterprise Oversight, Department of Housing and Urban Development (Parts 1700—1799)
XVIII	Community Development Financial Institutions Fund, Department of the Treasury (Parts 1800—1899)

Chap.	Title 13—Business Credit and Assistance
I	Small Business Administration (Parts 1—199)
III	Economic Development Administration, Department of Commerce (Parts 300—399)
IV	Emergency Steel Guarantee Loan Board (Parts 400—499)
V	Emergency Oil and Gas Guaranteed Loan Board (Parts 500—599)

Title 14—Aeronautics and Space

I	Federal Aviation Administration, Department of Transportation (Parts 1—199)
II	Office of the Secretary, Department of Transportation (Aviation Proceedings) (Parts 200—399)
III	Commercial Space Transportation, Federal Aviation Administration, Department of Transportation (Parts 400—1199)
V	National Aeronautics and Space Administration (Parts 1200—1299)
VI	Air Transportation System Stabilization (Parts 1300—1399)

Title 15—Commerce and Foreign Trade

SUBTITLE A—OFFICE OF THE SECRETARY OF COMMERCE (PARTS 0—29)

SUBTITLE B—REGULATIONS RELATING TO COMMERCE AND FOREIGN TRADE

I	Bureau of the Census, Department of Commerce (Parts 30—199)
II	National Institute of Standards and Technology, Department of Commerce (Parts 200—299)
III	International Trade Administration, Department of Commerce (Parts 300—399)
IV	Foreign-Trade Zones Board, Department of Commerce (Parts 400—499)
VII	Bureau of Industry and Security, Department of Commerce (Parts 700—799)
VIII	Bureau of Economic Analysis, Department of Commerce (Parts 800—899)
IX	National Oceanic and Atmospheric Administration, Department of Commerce (Parts 900—999)
XI	Technology Administration, Department of Commerce (Parts 1100—1199)
XIII	East-West Foreign Trade Board (Parts 1300—1399)
XIV	Minority Business Development Agency (Parts 1400—1499)

SUBTITLE C—REGULATIONS RELATING TO FOREIGN TRADE AGREEMENTS

XX	Office of the United States Trade Representative (Parts 2000—2099)

SUBTITLE D—REGULATIONS RELATING TO TELECOMMUNICATIONS AND INFORMATION

XXIII	National Telecommunications and Information Administration, Department of Commerce (Parts 2300—2399)

Chap.

Title 16—Commercial Practices

- I Federal Trade Commission (Parts 0—999)
- II Consumer Product Safety Commission (Parts 1000—1799)

Title 17—Commodity and Securities Exchanges

- I Commodity Futures Trading Commission (Parts 1—199)
- II Securities and Exchange Commission (Parts 200—399)
- IV Department of the Treasury (Parts 400—499)

Title 18—Conservation of Power and Water Resources

- I Federal Energy Regulatory Commission, Department of Energy (Parts 1—399)
- III Delaware River Basin Commission (Parts 400—499)
- VI Water Resources Council (Parts 700—799)
- VIII Susquehanna River Basin Commission (Parts 800—899)
- XIII Tennessee Valley Authority (Parts 1300—1399)

Title 19—Customs Duties

- I U.S. Customs and Border Protection, Department of Homeland Security; Department of the Treasury (Parts 0—199)
- II United States International Trade Commission (Parts 200—299)
- III International Trade Administration, Department of Commerce (Parts 300—399)
- IV U.S. Immigration and Customs Enforcement, Department of Homeland Security (Parts 400—599)

Title 20—Employees' Benefits

- I Office of Workers' Compensation Programs, Department of Labor (Parts 1—199)
- II Railroad Retirement Board (Parts 200—399)
- III Social Security Administration (Parts 400—499)
- IV Employees' Compensation Appeals Board, Department of Labor (Parts 500—599)
- V Employment and Training Administration, Department of Labor (Parts 600—699)
- VI Office of Workers' Compensation Programs, Department of Labor (Parts 700—799)
- VII Benefits Review Board, Department of Labor (Parts 800—899)
- VIII Joint Board for the Enrollment of Actuaries (Parts 900—999)
- IX Office of the Assistant Secretary for Veterans' Employment and Training Service, Department of Labor (Parts 1000—1099)

Chap.

Title 21—Food and Drugs

I Food and Drug Administration, Department of Health and Human Services (Parts 1—1299)
II Drug Enforcement Administration, Department of Justice (Parts 1300—1399)
III Office of National Drug Control Policy (Parts 1400—1499)

Title 22—Foreign Relations

I Department of State (Parts 1—199)
II Agency for International Development (Parts 200—299)
III Peace Corps (Parts 300—399)
IV International Joint Commission, United States and Canada (Parts 400—499)
V Broadcasting Board of Governors (Parts 500—599)
VII Overseas Private Investment Corporation (Parts 700—799)
IX Foreign Service Grievance Board (Parts 900—999)
X Inter-American Foundation (Parts 1000—1099)
XI International Boundary and Water Commission, United States and Mexico, United States Section (Parts 1100—1199)
XII United States International Development Cooperation Agency (Parts 1200—1299)
XIII Millennium Challenge Corporation (Parts 1300—1399)
XIV Foreign Service Labor Relations Board; Federal Labor Relations Authority; General Counsel of the Federal Labor Relations Authority; and the Foreign Service Impasse Disputes Panel (Parts 1400—1499)
XV African Development Foundation (Parts 1500—1599)
XVI Japan-United States Friendship Commission (Parts 1600—1699)
XVII United States Institute of Peace (Parts 1700—1799)

Title 23—Highways

I Federal Highway Administration, Department of Transportation (Parts 1—999)
II National Highway Traffic Safety Administration and Federal Highway Administration, Department of Transportation (Parts 1200—1299)
III National Highway Traffic Safety Administration, Department of Transportation (Parts 1300—1399)

Title 24—Housing and Urban Development

SUBTITLE A—OFFICE OF THE SECRETARY, DEPARTMENT OF HOUSING AND URBAN DEVELOPMENT (PARTS 0—99)

SUBTITLE B—REGULATIONS RELATING TO HOUSING AND URBAN DEVELOPMENT

I Office of Assistant Secretary for Equal Opportunity, Department of Housing and Urban Development (Parts 100—199)

Title 24—Housing and Urban Development—Continued

Chap.	
II	Office of Assistant Secretary for Housing-Federal Housing Commissioner, Department of Housing and Urban Development (Parts 200—299)
III	Government National Mortgage Association, Department of Housing and Urban Development (Parts 300—399)
IV	Office of Housing and Office of Multifamily Housing Assistance Restructuring, Department of Housing and Urban Development (Parts 400—499)
V	Office of Assistant Secretary for Community Planning and Development, Department of Housing and Urban Development (Parts 500—599)
VI	Office of Assistant Secretary for Community Planning and Development, Department of Housing and Urban Development (Parts 600—699) [Reserved]
VII	Office of the Secretary, Department of Housing and Urban Development (Housing Assistance Programs and Public and Indian Housing Programs) (Parts 700—799)
VIII	Office of the Assistant Secretary for Housing—Federal Housing Commissioner, Department of Housing and Urban Development (Section 8 Housing Assistance Programs, Section 202 Direct Loan Program, Section 202 Supportive Housing for the Elderly Program and Section 811 Supportive Housing for Persons With Disabilities Program) (Parts 800—899)
IX	Office of Assistant Secretary for Public and Indian Housing, Department of Housing and Urban Development (Parts 900—1699)
X	Office of Assistant Secretary for Housing—Federal Housing Commissioner, Department of Housing and Urban Development (Interstate Land Sales Registration Program) (Parts 1700—1799)
XII	Office of Inspector General, Department of Housing and Urban Development (Parts 2000—2099)
XV	Emergency Mortgage Insurance and Loan Programs, Department of Housing and Urban Development (Parts 2700—2799)
XX	Office of Assistant Secretary for Housing—Federal Housing Commissioner, Department of Housing and Urban Development (Parts 3200—3899)
XXIV	Board of Directors of the HOPE for Homeowners Program (Parts 4000—4099)
XXV	Neighborhood Reinvestment Corporation (Parts 4100—4199)

Title 25—Indians

I	Bureau of Indian Affairs, Department of the Interior (Parts 1—299)
II	Indian Arts and Crafts Board, Department of the Interior (Parts 300—399)
III	National Indian Gaming Commission, Department of the Interior (Parts 500—599)
IV	Office of Navajo and Hopi Indian Relocation (Parts 700—799)
V	Bureau of Indian Affairs, Department of the Interior, and Indian Health Service, Department of Health and Human Services (Part 900)

Chap.

Title 25—Indians—Continued

VI	Office of the Assistant Secretary-Indian Affairs, Department of the Interior (Parts 1000—1199)
VII	Office of the Special Trustee for American Indians, Department of the Interior (Parts 1200—1299)

Title 26—Internal Revenue

I	Internal Revenue Service, Department of the Treasury (Parts 1—End)

Title 27—Alcohol, Tobacco Products and Firearms

I	Alcohol and Tobacco Tax and Trade Bureau, Department of the Treasury (Parts 1—399)
II	Bureau of Alcohol, Tobacco, Firearms, and Explosives, Department of Justice (Parts 400—699)

Title 28—Judicial Administration

I	Department of Justice (Parts 0—299)
III	Federal Prison Industries, Inc., Department of Justice (Parts 300—399)
V	Bureau of Prisons, Department of Justice (Parts 500—599)
VI	Offices of Independent Counsel, Department of Justice (Parts 600—699)
VII	Office of Independent Counsel (Parts 700—799)
VIII	Court Services and Offender Supervision Agency for the District of Columbia (Parts 800—899)
IX	National Crime Prevention and Privacy Compact Council (Parts 900—999)
XI	Department of Justice and Department of State (Parts 1100—1199)

Title 29—Labor

SUBTITLE A—OFFICE OF THE SECRETARY OF LABOR (PARTS 0—99)
SUBTITLE B—REGULATIONS RELATING TO LABOR

I	National Labor Relations Board (Parts 100—199)
II	Office of Labor-Management Standards, Department of Labor (Parts 200—299)
III	National Railroad Adjustment Board (Parts 300—399)
IV	Office of Labor-Management Standards, Department of Labor (Parts 400—499)
V	Wage and Hour Division, Department of Labor (Parts 500—899)
IX	Construction Industry Collective Bargaining Commission (Parts 900—999)
X	National Mediation Board (Parts 1200—1299)
XII	Federal Mediation and Conciliation Service (Parts 1400—1499)
XIV	Equal Employment Opportunity Commission (Parts 1600—1699)

Title 29—Labor—Continued

Chap.

XVII Occupational Safety and Health Administration, Department of Labor (Parts 1900—1999)

XX Occupational Safety and Health Review Commission (Parts 2200—2499)

XXV Employee Benefits Security Administration, Department of Labor (Parts 2500—2599)

XXVII Federal Mine Safety and Health Review Commission (Parts 2700—2799)

XL Pension Benefit Guaranty Corporation (Parts 4000—4999)

Title 30—Mineral Resources

I Mine Safety and Health Administration, Department of Labor (Parts 1—199)

II Bureau of Safety and Environmental Enforcement, Department of the Interior (Parts 200—299)

IV Geological Survey, Department of the Interior (Parts 400—499)

V Bureau of Ocean Energy Management, Department of the Interior (Parts 500—599)

VII Office of Surface Mining Reclamation and Enforcement, Department of the Interior (Parts 700—999)

XII Office of Natural Resources Revenue, Department of the Interior (Parts 1200—1299)

Title 31—Money and Finance: Treasury

SUBTITLE A—OFFICE OF THE SECRETARY OF THE TREASURY (PARTS 0—50)

SUBTITLE B—REGULATIONS RELATING TO MONEY AND FINANCE

I Monetary Offices, Department of the Treasury (Parts 51—199)

II Fiscal Service, Department of the Treasury (Parts 200—399)

IV Secret Service, Department of the Treasury (Parts 400—499)

V Office of Foreign Assets Control, Department of the Treasury (Parts 500—599)

VI Bureau of Engraving and Printing, Department of the Treasury (Parts 600—699)

VII Federal Law Enforcement Training Center, Department of the Treasury (Parts 700—799)

VIII Office of International Investment, Department of the Treasury (Parts 800—899)

IX Federal Claims Collection Standards (Department of the Treasury—Department of Justice) (Parts 900—999)

X Financial Crimes Enforcement Network, Department of the Treasury (Parts 1000—1099)

Title 32—National Defense

SUBTITLE A—DEPARTMENT OF DEFENSE

I Office of the Secretary of Defense (Parts 1—399)

Title 32—National Defense—Continued

Chap.

V	Department of the Army (Parts 400—699)
VI	Department of the Navy (Parts 700—799)
VII	Department of the Air Force (Parts 800—1099)

SUBTITLE B—OTHER REGULATIONS RELATING TO NATIONAL DEFENSE

XII	Defense Logistics Agency (Parts 1200—1299)
XVI	Selective Service System (Parts 1600—1699)
XVII	Office of the Director of National Intelligence (Parts 1700—1799)
XVIII	National Counterintelligence Center (Parts 1800—1899)
XIX	Central Intelligence Agency (Parts 1900—1999)
XX	Information Security Oversight Office, National Archives and Records Administration (Parts 2000—2099)
XXI	National Security Council (Parts 2100—2199)
XXIV	Office of Science and Technology Policy (Parts 2400—2499)
XXVII	Office for Micronesian Status Negotiations (Parts 2700—2799)
XXVIII	Office of the Vice President of the United States (Parts 2800—2899)

Title 33—Navigation and Navigable Waters

I	Coast Guard, Department of Homeland Security (Parts 1—199)
II	Corps of Engineers, Department of the Army (Parts 200—399)
IV	Saint Lawrence Seaway Development Corporation, Department of Transportation (Parts 400—499)

Title 34—Education

SUBTITLE A—OFFICE OF THE SECRETARY, DEPARTMENT OF EDUCATION (PARTS 1—99)

SUBTITLE B—REGULATIONS OF THE OFFICES OF THE DEPARTMENT OF EDUCATION

I	Office for Civil Rights, Department of Education (Parts 100—199)
II	Office of Elementary and Secondary Education, Department of Education (Parts 200—299)
III	Office of Special Education and Rehabilitative Services, Department of Education (Parts 300—399)
IV	Office of Vocational and Adult Education, Department of Education (Parts 400—499)
V	Office of Bilingual Education and Minority Languages Affairs, Department of Education (Parts 500—599)
VI	Office of Postsecondary Education, Department of Education (Parts 600—699)
VII	Office of Educational Research and Improvement, Department of Education (Parts 700—799) [Reserved]

SUBTITLE C—REGULATIONS RELATING TO EDUCATION

XI	National Institute for Literacy (Parts 1100—1199)
XII	National Council on Disability (Parts 1200—1299)

Title 35 [Reserved]

Title 36—Parks, Forests, and Public Property

Chap.
I	National Park Service, Department of the Interior (Parts 1—199)
II	Forest Service, Department of Agriculture (Parts 200—299)
III	Corps of Engineers, Department of the Army (Parts 300—399)
IV	American Battle Monuments Commission (Parts 400—499)
V	Smithsonian Institution (Parts 500—599)
VI	[Reserved]
VII	Library of Congress (Parts 700—799)
VIII	Advisory Council on Historic Preservation (Parts 800—899)
IX	Pennsylvania Avenue Development Corporation (Parts 900—999)
X	Presidio Trust (Parts 1000—1099)
XI	Architectural and Transportation Barriers Compliance Board (Parts 1100—1199)
XII	National Archives and Records Administration (Parts 1200—1299)
XV	Oklahoma City National Memorial Trust (Parts 1500—1599)
XVI	Morris K. Udall Scholarship and Excellence in National Environmental Policy Foundation (Parts 1600—1699)

Title 37—Patents, Trademarks, and Copyrights

I	United States Patent and Trademark Office, Department of Commerce (Parts 1—199)
II	U.S. Copyright Office, Library of Congress (Parts 200—299)
III	Copyright Royalty Board, Library of Congress (Parts 300—399)
IV	Assistant Secretary for Technology Policy, Department of Commerce (Parts 400—599)

Title 38—Pensions, Bonuses, and Veterans' Relief

I	Department of Veterans Affairs (Parts 0—199)
II	Armed Forces Retirement Home (Parts 200—299)

Title 39—Postal Service

I	United States Postal Service (Parts 1—999)
III	Postal Regulatory Commission (Parts 3000—3099)

Title 40—Protection of Environment

I	Environmental Protection Agency (Parts 1—1099)
IV	Environmental Protection Agency and Department of Justice (Parts 1400—1499)
V	Council on Environmental Quality (Parts 1500—1599)
VI	Chemical Safety and Hazard Investigation Board (Parts 1600—1699)

Title 40—Protection of Environment—Continued

Chap.

VII Environmental Protection Agency and Department of Defense; Uniform National Discharge Standards for Vessels of the Armed Forces (Parts 1700—1799)

Title 41—Public Contracts and Property Management

SUBTITLE A—FEDERAL PROCUREMENT REGULATIONS SYSTEM [NOTE]

SUBTITLE B—OTHER PROVISIONS RELATING TO PUBLIC CONTRACTS

50 Public Contracts, Department of Labor (Parts 50–1—50–999)
51 Committee for Purchase From People Who Are Blind or Severely Disabled (Parts 51–1—51–99)
60 Office of Federal Contract Compliance Programs, Equal Employment Opportunity, Department of Labor (Parts 60–1—60–999)
61 Office of the Assistant Secretary for Veterans' Employment and Training Service, Department of Labor (Parts 61–1—61–999)
62—100 [Reserved]

SUBTITLE C—FEDERAL PROPERTY MANAGEMENT REGULATIONS SYSTEM

101 Federal Property Management Regulations (Parts 101–1—101–99)
102 Federal Management Regulation (Parts 102–1—102–299)
103—104 [Reserved]
105 General Services Administration (Parts 105–1—105–999)
109 Department of Energy Property Management Regulations (Parts 109–1—109–99)
114 Department of the Interior (Parts 114–1—114–99)
115 Environmental Protection Agency (Parts 115–1—115–99)
128 Department of Justice (Parts 128–1—128–99)
129—200 [Reserved]

SUBTITLE D—OTHER PROVISIONS RELATING TO PROPERTY MANAGEMENT [RESERVED]

SUBTITLE E—FEDERAL INFORMATION RESOURCES MANAGEMENT REGULATIONS SYSTEM [RESERVED]

SUBTITLE F—FEDERAL TRAVEL REGULATION SYSTEM

300 General (Parts 300–1—300–99)
301 Temporary Duty (TDY) Travel Allowances (Parts 301–1—301–99)
302 Relocation Allowances (Parts 302–1—302–99)
303 Payment of Expenses Connected with the Death of Certain Employees (Part 303–1—303–99)
304 Payment of Travel Expenses from a Non-Federal Source (Parts 304–1—304–99)

Title 42—Public Health

I Public Health Service, Department of Health and Human Services (Parts 1—199)
IV Centers for Medicare & Medicaid Services, Department of Health and Human Services (Parts 400—599)

Chap.

Title 42—Public Health—Continued

V   Office of Inspector General-Health Care, Department of Health and Human Services (Parts 1000—1999)

Title 43—Public Lands: Interior

SUBTITLE A—OFFICE OF THE SECRETARY OF THE INTERIOR (PARTS 1—199)

SUBTITLE B—REGULATIONS RELATING TO PUBLIC LANDS

I   Bureau of Reclamation, Department of the Interior (Parts 400—999)

II Bureau of Land Management, Department of the Interior (Parts 1000—9999)

III Utah Reclamation Mitigation and Conservation Commission (Parts 10000—10099)

Title 44—Emergency Management and Assistance

I   Federal Emergency Management Agency, Department of Homeland Security (Parts 0—399)

IV Department of Commerce and Department of Transportation (Parts 400—499)

Title 45—Public Welfare

SUBTITLE A—DEPARTMENT OF HEALTH AND HUMAN SERVICES (PARTS 1—199)

SUBTITLE B—REGULATIONS RELATING TO PUBLIC WELFARE

II Office of Family Assistance (Assistance Programs), Administration for Children and Families, Department of Health and Human Services (Parts 200—299)

III Office of Child Support Enforcement (Child Support Enforcement Program), Administration for Children and Families, Department of Health and Human Services (Parts 300—399)

IV Office of Refugee Resettlement, Administration for Children and Families, Department of Health and Human Services (Parts 400—499)

V   Foreign Claims Settlement Commission of the United States, Department of Justice (Parts 500—599)

VI National Science Foundation (Parts 600—699)

VII Commission on Civil Rights (Parts 700—799)

VIII Office of Personnel Management (Parts 800—899)

X   Office of Community Services, Administration for Children and Families, Department of Health and Human Services (Parts 1000—1099)

XI National Foundation on the Arts and the Humanities (Parts 1100—1199)

XII Corporation for National and Community Service (Parts 1200—1299)

XIII Office of Human Development Services, Department of Health and Human Services (Parts 1300—1399)

Title 45—Public Welfare—Continued

Chap.

XVI Legal Services Corporation (Parts 1600—1699)
XVII National Commission on Libraries and Information Science (Parts 1700—1799)
XVIII Harry S. Truman Scholarship Foundation (Parts 1800—1899)
XXI Commission on Fine Arts (Parts 2100—2199)
XXIII Arctic Research Commission (Part 2301)
XXIV James Madison Memorial Fellowship Foundation (Parts 2400—2499)
XXV Corporation for National and Community Service (Parts 2500—2599)

Title 46—Shipping

I Coast Guard, Department of Homeland Security (Parts 1—199)
II Maritime Administration, Department of Transportation (Parts 200—399)
III Coast Guard (Great Lakes Pilotage), Department of Homeland Security (Parts 400—499)
IV Federal Maritime Commission (Parts 500—599)

Title 47—Telecommunication

I Federal Communications Commission (Parts 0—199)
II Office of Science and Technology Policy and National Security Council (Parts 200—299)
III National Telecommunications and Information Administration, Department of Commerce (Parts 300—399)
IV National Telecommunications and Information Administration, Department of Commerce, and National Highway Traffic Safety Administration, Department of Transportation (Parts 400—499)

Title 48—Federal Acquisition Regulations System

1 Federal Acquisition Regulation (Parts 1—99)
2 Defense Acquisition Regulations System, Department of Defense (Parts 200—299)
3 Health and Human Services (Parts 300—399)
4 Department of Agriculture (Parts 400—499)
5 General Services Administration (Parts 500—599)
6 Department of State (Parts 600—699)
7 Agency for International Development (Parts 700—799)
8 Department of Veterans Affairs (Parts 800—899)
9 Department of Energy (Parts 900—999)
10 Department of the Treasury (Parts 1000—1099)
12 Department of Transportation (Parts 1200—1299)
13 Department of Commerce (Parts 1300—1399)
14 Department of the Interior (Parts 1400—1499)

Title 48—Federal Acquisition Regulations System—Continued

Chap.
- 15 Environmental Protection Agency (Parts 1500—1599)
- 16 Office of Personnel Management, Federal Employees Health Benefits Acquisition Regulation (Parts 1600—1699)
- 17 Office of Personnel Management (Parts 1700—1799)
- 18 National Aeronautics and Space Administration (Parts 1800—1899)
- 19 Broadcasting Board of Governors (Parts 1900—1999)
- 20 Nuclear Regulatory Commission (Parts 2000—2099)
- 21 Office of Personnel Management, Federal Employees Group Life Insurance Federal Acquisition Regulation (Parts 2100—2199)
- 23 Social Security Administration (Parts 2300—2399)
- 24 Department of Housing and Urban Development (Parts 2400—2499)
- 25 National Science Foundation (Parts 2500—2599)
- 28 Department of Justice (Parts 2800—2899)
- 29 Department of Labor (Parts 2900—2999)
- 30 Department of Homeland Security, Homeland Security Acquisition Regulation (HSAR) (Parts 3000—3099)
- 34 Department of Education Acquisition Regulation (Parts 3400—3499)
- 51 Department of the Army Acquisition Regulations (Parts 5100—5199)
- 52 Department of the Navy Acquisition Regulations (Parts 5200—5299)
- 53 Department of the Air Force Federal Acquisition Regulation Supplement (Parts 5300—5399)[Reserved]
- 54 Defense Logistics Agency, Department of Defense (Parts 5400—5499)
- 57 African Development Foundation (Parts 5700—5799)
- 61 Civilian Board of Contract Appeals, General Services Administration (Parts 6100—6199)
- 63 Department of Transportation Board of Contract Appeals (Parts 6300—6399)
- 99 Cost Accounting Standards Board, Office of Federal Procurement Policy, Office of Management and Budget (Parts 9900—9999)

Title 49—Transportation

SUBTITLE A—OFFICE OF THE SECRETARY OF TRANSPORTATION (PARTS 1—99)

SUBTITLE B—OTHER REGULATIONS RELATING TO TRANSPORTATION

- I Pipeline and Hazardous Materials Safety Administration, Department of Transportation (Parts 100—199)
- II Federal Railroad Administration, Department of Transportation (Parts 200—299)
- III Federal Motor Carrier Safety Administration, Department of Transportation (Parts 300—399)
- IV Coast Guard, Department of Homeland Security (Parts 400—499)

Title 49—Transportation—Continued

Chap.
V National Highway Traffic Safety Administration, Department of Transportation (Parts 500—599)
VI Federal Transit Administration, Department of Transportation (Parts 600—699)
VII National Railroad Passenger Corporation (AMTRAK) (Parts 700—799)
VIII National Transportation Safety Board (Parts 800—999)
X Surface Transportation Board, Department of Transportation (Parts 1000—1399)
XI Research and Innovative Technology Administration, Department of Transportation (Parts 1400—1499)[Reserved]
XII Transportation Security Administration, Department of Homeland Security (Parts 1500—1699)

Title 50—Wildlife and Fisheries

I United States Fish and Wildlife Service, Department of the Interior (Parts 1—199)
II National Marine Fisheries Service, National Oceanic and Atmospheric Administration, Department of Commerce (Parts 200—299)
III International Fishing and Related Activities (Parts 300—399)
IV Joint Regulations (United States Fish and Wildlife Service, Department of the Interior and National Marine Fisheries Service, National Oceanic and Atmospheric Administration, Department of Commerce); Endangered Species Committee Regulations (Parts 400—499)
V Marine Mammal Commission (Parts 500—599)
VI Fishery Conservation and Management, National Oceanic and Atmospheric Administration, Department of Commerce (Parts 600—699)

CFR Index and Finding Aids

Subject/Agency Index
List of Agency Prepared Indexes
Parallel Tables of Statutory Authorities and Rules
List of CFR Titles, Chapters, Subchapters, and Parts
Alphabetical List of Agencies Appearing in the CFR

Alphabetical List of Agencies Appearing in the CFR
(Revised as of October 1, 2013)

Agency	CFR Title, Subtitle or Chapter
Administrative Committee of the Federal Register	1, I
Administrative Conference of the United States	1, III
Advisory Council on Historic Preservation	36, VIII
Advocacy and Outreach, Office of	7, XXV
Afghanistan Reconstruction, Special Inspector General for	22, LXXXIII
African Development Foundation	22, XV
Federal Acquisition Regulation	48, 57
Agency for International Development	2, VII; 22, II
Federal Acquisition Regulation	48, 7
Agricultural Marketing Service	7, I, IX, X, XI
Agricultural Research Service	7, V
Agriculture Department	2, IV; 5, LXXIII
Advocacy and Outreach, Office of	7, XXV
Agricultural Marketing Service	7, I, IX, X, XI
Agricultural Research Service	7, V
Animal and Plant Health Inspection Service	7, III; 9, I
Chief Financial Officer, Office of	7, XXX
Commodity Credit Corporation	7, XIV
Economic Research Service	7, XXXVII
Energy Policy and New Uses, Office of	2, IX; 7, XXIX
Environmental Quality, Office of	7, XXXI
Farm Service Agency	7, VII, XVIII
Federal Acquisition Regulation	48, 4
Federal Crop Insurance Corporation	7, IV
Food and Nutrition Service	7, II
Food Safety and Inspection Service	9, III
Foreign Agricultural Service	7, XV
Forest Service	36, II
Grain Inspection, Packers and Stockyards Administration	7, VIII; 9, II
Information Resources Management, Office of	7, XXVII
Inspector General, Office of	7, XXVI
National Agricultural Library	7, XLI
National Agricultural Statistics Service	7, XXXVI
National Institute of Food and Agriculture	7, XXXIV
Natural Resources Conservation Service	7, VI
Operations, Office of	7, XXVIII
Procurement and Property Management, Office of	7, XXXII
Rural Business-Cooperative Service	7, XVIII, XLII, L
Rural Development Administration	7, XLII
Rural Housing Service	7, XVIII, XXXV, L
Rural Telephone Bank	7, XVI
Rural Utilities Service	7, XVII, XVIII, XLII, L
Secretary of Agriculture, Office of	7, Subtitle A
Transportation, Office of	7, XXXIII
World Agricultural Outlook Board	7, XXXVIII
Air Force Department	32, VII
Federal Acquisition Regulation Supplement	48, 53
Air Transportation Stabilization Board	14, VI
Alcohol and Tobacco Tax and Trade Bureau	27, I
Alcohol, Tobacco, Firearms, and Explosives, Bureau of	27, II
AMTRAK	49, VII
American Battle Monuments Commission	36, IV
American Indians, Office of the Special Trustee	25, VII

Agency	CFR Title, Subtitle or Chapter
Animal and Plant Health Inspection Service	7, III; 9, I
Appalachian Regional Commission	5, IX
Architectural and Transportation Barriers Compliance Board	36, XI
Arctic Research Commission	45, XXIII
Armed Forces Retirement Home	5, XI
Army Department	32, V
Engineers, Corps of	33, II; 36, III
Federal Acquisition Regulation	48, 51
Bilingual Education and Minority Languages Affairs, Office of	34, V
Blind or Severely Disabled, Committee for Purchase from People Who Are	41, 51
Broadcasting Board of Governors	22, V
Federal Acquisition Regulation	48, 19
Bureau of Ocean Energy Management, Regulation, and Enforcement	30, II
Census Bureau	15, I
Centers for Medicare & Medicaid Services	42, IV
Central Intelligence Agency	32, XIX
Chemical Safety and Hazardous Investigation Board	40, VI
Chief Financial Officer, Office of	7, XXX
Child Support Enforcement, Office of	45, III
Children and Families, Administration for	45, II, III, IV, X
Civil Rights, Commission on	5, LXVIII; 45, VII
Civil Rights, Office for	34, I
Council of the Inspectors General on Integrity and Efficiency	5, XCVIII
Court Services and Offender Supervision Agency for the District of Columbia	5, LXX
Coast Guard	33, I; 46, I; 49, IV
Coast Guard (Great Lakes Pilotage)	46, III
Commerce Department	2, XIII; 44, IV; 50, VI
Census Bureau	15, I
Economic Analysis, Bureau of	15, VIII
Economic Development Administration	13, III
Emergency Management and Assistance	44, IV
Federal Acquisition Regulation	48, 13
Foreign-Trade Zones Board	15, IV
Industry and Security, Bureau of	15, VII
International Trade Administration	15, III; 19, III
National Institute of Standards and Technology	15, II
National Marine Fisheries Service	50, II, IV
National Oceanic and Atmospheric Administration	15, IX; 50, II, III, IV, VI
National Telecommunications and Information Administration	15, XXIII; 47, III, IV
National Weather Service	15, IX
Patent and Trademark Office, United States	37, I
Productivity, Technology and Innovation, Assistant Secretary for	37, IV
Secretary of Commerce, Office of	15, Subtitle A
Technology Administration	15, XI
Technology Policy, Assistant Secretary for	37, IV
Commercial Space Transportation	14, III
Commodity Credit Corporation	7, XIV
Commodity Futures Trading Commission	5, XLI; 17, I
Community Planning and Development, Office of Assistant Secretary for	24, V, VI
Community Services, Office of	45, X
Comptroller of the Currency	12, I
Construction Industry Collective Bargaining Commission	29, IX
Consumer Financial Protection Bureau	5, LXXXIV; 12, X
Consumer Product Safety Commission	5, LXXI; 16, II
Copyright Royalty Board	37, III
Corporation for National and Community Service	2, XXII; 45, XII, XXV
Cost Accounting Standards Board	48, 99
Council on Environmental Quality	40, V
Court Services and Offender Supervision Agency for the District of Columbia	5, LXX; 28, VIII
Customs and Border Protection	19, I

446

Agency	CFR Title, Subtitle or Chapter
Defense Contract Audit Agency	32, I
Defense Department	2, XI; 5, XXVI; 32, Subtitle A; 40, VII
Advanced Research Projects Agency	32, I
Air Force Department	32, VII
Army Department	32, V; 33, II; 36, III; 48, 51
Defense Acquisition Regulations System	48, 2
Defense Intelligence Agency	32, I
Defense Logistics Agency	32, I, XII; 48, 54
Engineers, Corps of	33, II; 36, III
National Imagery and Mapping Agency	32, I
Navy Department	32, VI; 48, 52
Secretary of Defense, Office of	2, XI; 32, I
Defense Contract Audit Agency	32, I
Defense Intelligence Agency	32, I
Defense Logistics Agency	32 XII; 48, 54
Defense Nuclear Facilities Safety Board	10, XVII
Delaware River Basin Commission	18, III
District of Columbia, Court Services and Offender Supervision Agency for the	5, LXX; 28, VIII
Drug Enforcement Administration	21, II
East-West Foreign Trade Board	15, XIII
Economic Analysis, Bureau of	15, VIII
Economic Development Administration	13, III
Economic Research Service	7. XXXVII
Education, Department of	2 XXXIV; 5, LIII
Bilingual Education and Minority Languages Affairs, Office of	34, V
Civil Rights, Office for	34, I
Educational Research and Improvement, Office of	34, VII
Elementary and Secondary Education, Office of	34, II
Federal Acquisition Regulation	48, 34
Postsecondary Education, Office of	34, VI
Secretary of Education, Office of	34, Subtitle A
Special Education and Rehabilitative Services, Office of	34, III
Vocational and Adult Education, Office of	34, IV
Educational Research and Improvement, Office of	34, VII
Election Assistance Commission	2, LVIII; 11, II
Elementary and Secondary Education, Office of	34, II
Emergency Oil and Gas Guaranteed Loan Board	13, V
Emergency Steel Guarantee Loan Board	13, IV
Employee Benefits Security Administration	29, XXV
Employees' Compensation Appeals Board	20, IV
Employees Loyalty Board	5, V
Employment and Training Administration	20, V
Employment Standards Administration	20, VI
Endangered Species Committee	50, IV
Energy, Department of	2, IX; 5, XXIII; 10, II, III, X
Federal Acquisition Regulation	48, 9
Federal Energy Regulatory Commission	5, XXIV; 18, I
Property Management Regulations	41, 109
Energy, Office of	7, XXIX
Engineers, Corps of	33, II; 36, III
Engraving and Printing, Bureau of	31, VI
Environmental Protection Agency	2, XV; 5, LIV; 40, I, IV, VII
Federal Acquisition Regulation	48, 15
Property Management Regulations	41, 115
Environmental Quality, Office of	7, XXXI
Equal Employment Opportunity Commission	5, LXII; 29, XIV
Equal Opportunity, Office of Assistant Secretary for	24, I
Executive Office of the President	3, I
Administration, Office of	5, XV
Environmental Quality, Council on	40, V
Management and Budget, Office of	2, Subtitle A; 5, III, LXXVII; 14, VI; 48, 99

Agency	CFR Title, Subtitle or Chapter
National Drug Control Policy, Office of	21, III
National Security Council	32, XXI; 47, 2
Presidential Documents	3
Science and Technology Policy, Office of	32, XXIV; 47, II
Trade Representative, Office of the United States	15, XX
Export-Import Bank of the United States	2, XXXV; 5, LII; 12, IV
Family Assistance, Office of	45, II
Farm Credit Administration	5, XXXI; 12, VI
Farm Credit System Insurance Corporation	5, XXX; 12, XIV
Farm Service Agency	7, VII, XVIII
Federal Acquisition Regulation	48, 1
Federal Aviation Administration	14, I
Commercial Space Transportation	14, III
Federal Claims Collection Standards	31, IX
Federal Communications Commission	5, XXIX; 47, I
Federal Contract Compliance Programs, Office of	41, 60
Federal Crop Insurance Corporation	7, IV
Federal Deposit Insurance Corporation	5, XXII; 12, III
Federal Election Commission	5, XXXVII; 11, I
Federal Emergency Management Agency	44, I
Federal Employees Group Life Insurance Federal Acquisition Regulation	48, 21
Federal Employees Health Benefits Acquisition Regulation	48, 16
Federal Energy Regulatory Commission	5, XXIV; 18, I
Federal Financial Institutions Examination Council	12, XI
Federal Financing Bank	12, VIII
Federal Highway Administration	23, I, II
Federal Home Loan Mortgage Corporation	1, IV
Federal Housing Enterprise Oversight Office	12, XVII
Federal Housing Finance Agency	5, LXXX; 12, XII
Federal Housing Finance Board	12, IX
Federal Labor Relations Authority	5, XIV, XLIX; 22, XIV
Federal Law Enforcement Training Center	31, VII
Federal Management Regulation	41, 102
Federal Maritime Commission	46, IV
Federal Mediation and Conciliation Service	29, XII
Federal Mine Safety and Health Review Commission	5, LXXIV; 29, XXVII
Federal Motor Carrier Safety Administration	49, III
Federal Prison Industries, Inc.	28, III
Federal Procurement Policy Office	48, 99
Federal Property Management Regulations	41, 101
Federal Railroad Administration	49, II
Federal Register, Administrative Committee of	1, I
Federal Register, Office of	1, II
Federal Reserve System	12, II
Board of Governors	5, LVIII
Federal Retirement Thrift Investment Board	5, VI, LXXVI
Federal Service Impasses Panel	5, XIV
Federal Trade Commission	5, XLVII; 16, I
Federal Transit Administration	49, VI
Federal Travel Regulation System	41, Subtitle F
Financial Crimes Enforcement Network	31, X
Financial Research Office	12, XVI
Financial Stability Oversight Council	12, XIII
Fine Arts, Commission on	45, XXI
Fiscal Service	31, II
Fish and Wildlife Service, United States	50, I, IV
Food and Drug Administration	21, I
Food and Nutrition Service	7, II
Food Safety and Inspection Service	9, III
Foreign Agricultural Service	7, XV
Foreign Assets Control, Office of	31, V
Foreign Claims Settlement Commission of the United States	45, V
Foreign Service Grievance Board	22, IX
Foreign Service Impasse Disputes Panel	22, XIV
Foreign Service Labor Relations Board	22, XIV
Foreign-Trade Zones Board	15, IV

Agency	CFR Title, Subtitle or Chapter
Forest Service	36, II
General Services Administration	5, LVII; 41, 105
Contract Appeals, Board of	48, 61
Federal Acquisition Regulation	48, 5
Federal Management Regulation	41, 102
Federal Property Management Regulations	41, 101
Federal Travel Regulation System	41, Subtitle F
General	41, 300
Payment From a Non-Federal Source for Travel Expenses	41, 304
Payment of Expenses Connected With the Death of Certain Employees	41, 303
Relocation Allowances	41, 302
Temporary Duty (TDY) Travel Allowances	41, 301
Geological Survey	30, IV
Government Accountability Office	4, I
Government Ethics, Office of	5, XVI
Government National Mortgage Association	24, III
Grain Inspection, Packers and Stockyards Administration	7, VIII; 9, II
Harry S. Truman Scholarship Foundation	45, XVIII
Health and Human Services, Department of	2, III; 5, XLV; 45, Subtitle A,
Centers for Medicare & Medicaid Services	42, IV
Child Support Enforcement, Office of	45, III
Children and Families, Administration for	45, II, III, IV, X
Community Services, Office of	45, X
Family Assistance, Office of	45, II
Federal Acquisition Regulation	48, 3
Food and Drug Administration	21, I
Human Development Services, Office of	45, XIII
Indian Health Service	25, V
Inspector General (Health Care), Office of	42, V
Public Health Service	42, I
Refugee Resettlement, Office of	45, IV
Homeland Security, Department of	2, XXX; 6, I; 8, I
Coast Guard	33, I; 46, I; 49, IV
Coast Guard (Great Lakes Pilotage)	46, III
Customs and Border Protection	19, I
Federal Emergency Management Agency	44, I
Human Resources Management and Labor Relations Systems	5, XCVII
Immigration and Customs Enforcement Bureau	19, IV
Transportation Security Administration	49, XII
HOPE for Homeowners Program, Board of Directors of	24, XXIV
Housing and Urban Development, Department of	2, XXIV; 5, LXV; 24, Subtitle B
Community Planning and Development, Office of Assistant Secretary for	24, V, VI
Equal Opportunity, Office of Assistant Secretary for	24, I
Federal Acquisition Regulation	48, 24
Federal Housing Enterprise Oversight, Office of	12, XVII
Government National Mortgage Association	24, III
Housing—Federal Housing Commissioner, Office of Assistant Secretary for	24, II, VIII, X, XX
Housing, Office of, and Multifamily Housing Assistance Restructuring, Office of	24, IV
Inspector General, Office of	24, XII
Public and Indian Housing, Office of Assistant Secretary for	24, IX
Secretary, Office of	24, Subtitle A, VII
Housing—Federal Housing Commissioner, Office of Assistant Secretary for	24, II, VIII, X, XX
Housing, Office of, and Multifamily Housing Assistance Restructuring, Office of	24, IV
Human Development Services, Office of	45, XIII
Immigration and Customs Enforcement Bureau	19, IV
Immigration Review, Executive Office for	8, V
Independent Counsel, Office of	28, VII
Indian Affairs, Bureau of	25, I, V

Agency	CFR Title, Subtitle or Chapter
Indian Affairs, Office of the Assistant Secretary	25, VI
Indian Arts and Crafts Board	25, II
Indian Health Service	25, V
Industry and Security, Bureau of	15, VII
Information Resources Management, Office of	7, XXVII
Information Security Oversight Office, National Archives and Records Administration	32, XX
Inspector General	
Agriculture Department	7, XXVI
Health and Human Services Department	42, V
Housing and Urban Development Department	24, XII, XV
Institute of Peace, United States	22, XVII
Inter-American Foundation	5, LXIII; 22, X
Interior Department	2, XIV
American Indians, Office of the Special Trustee	25, VII
Bureau of Ocean Energy Management, Regulation, and Enforcement	30, II
Endangered Species Committee	50, IV
Federal Acquisition Regulation	48, 14
Federal Property Management Regulations System	41, 114
Fish and Wildlife Service, United States	50, I, IV
Geological Survey	30, IV
Indian Affairs, Bureau of	25, I, V
Indian Affairs, Office of the Assistant Secretary	25, VI
Indian Arts and Crafts Board	25, II
Land Management, Bureau of	43, II
National Indian Gaming Commission	25, III
National Park Service	36, I
Natural Resource Revenue, Office of	30, XII
Ocean Energy Management, Bureau of	30, V
Reclamation, Bureau of	43, I
Secretary of the Interior, Office of	2, XIV; 43, Subtitle A
Surface Mining Reclamation and Enforcement, Office of	30, VII
Internal Revenue Service	26, I
International Boundary and Water Commission, United States and Mexico, United States Section	22, XI
International Development, United States Agency for	22, II
Federal Acquisition Regulation	48, 7
International Development Cooperation Agency, United States	22, XII
International Joint Commission, United States and Canada	22, IV
International Organizations Employees Loyalty Board	5, V
International Trade Administration	15, III; 19, III
International Trade Commission, United States	19, II
Interstate Commerce Commission	5, XL
Investment Security, Office of	31, VIII
Iraq Reconstruction, Special Inspector General for	5, LXXXVII
James Madison Memorial Fellowship Foundation	45, XXIV
Japan–United States Friendship Commission	22, XVI
Joint Board for the Enrollment of Actuaries	20, VIII
Justice Department	2, XXVIII; 5, XXVIII; 28, I, XI; 40, IV
Alcohol, Tobacco, Firearms, and Explosives, Bureau of	27, II
Drug Enforcement Administration	21, II
Federal Acquisition Regulation	48, 28
Federal Claims Collection Standards	31, IX
Federal Prison Industries, Inc.	28, III
Foreign Claims Settlement Commission of the United States	45, V
Immigration Review, Executive Office for	8, V
Offices of Independent Counsel	28, VI
Prisons, Bureau of	28, V
Property Management Regulations	41, 128
Labor Department	5, XLII
Employee Benefits Security Administration	29, XXV
Employees' Compensation Appeals Board	20, IV
Employment and Training Administration	20, V

Agency	CFR Title, Subtitle or Chapter
Employment Standards Administration	20, VI
Federal Acquisition Regulation	48, 29
Federal Contract Compliance Programs, Office of	41, 60
Federal Procurement Regulations System	41, 50
Labor-Management Standards, Office of	29, II, IV
Mine Safety and Health Administration	30, I
Occupational Safety and Health Administration	29, XVII
Office of Workers' Compensation Programs	20, VII
Public Contracts	41, 50
Secretary of Labor, Office of	29, Subtitle A
Veterans' Employment and Training Service, Office of the Assistant Secretary for	41, 61; 20, IX
Wage and Hour Division	29, V
Workers' Compensation Programs, Office of	20, I
Labor-Management Standards, Office of	29, II, IV
Land Management, Bureau of	43, II
Legal Services Corporation	45, XVI
Library of Congress	36, VII
Copyright Royalty Board	37, III
U.S. Copyright Office	37, II
Local Television Loan Guarantee Board	7, XX
Management and Budget, Office of	5, III, LXXVII; 14, VI; 48, 99
Marine Mammal Commission	50, V
Maritime Administration	46, II
Merit Systems Protection Board	5, II, LXIV
Micronesian Status Negotiations, Office for	32, XXVII
Millennium Challenge Corporation	22, XIII
Mine Safety and Health Administration	30, I
Minority Business Development Agency	15, XIV
Miscellaneous Agencies	1, IV
Monetary Offices	31, I
Morris K. Udall Scholarship and Excellence in National Environmental Policy Foundation	36, XVI
Museum and Library Services, Institute of	2, XXXI
National Aeronautics and Space Administration	2, XVIII; 5, LIX; 14, V
Federal Acquisition Regulation	48, 18
National Agricultural Library	7, XLI
National Agricultural Statistics Service	7, XXXVI
National and Community Service, Corporation for	2, XXII; 45, XII, XXV
National Archives and Records Administration	2, XXVI; 5, LXVI; 36, XII
Information Security Oversight Office	32, XX
National Capital Planning Commission	1, IV
National Commission for Employment Policy	1, IV
National Commission on Libraries and Information Science	45, XVII
National Council on Disability	34, XII
National Counterintelligence Center	32, XVIII
National Credit Union Administration	5, LXXXVI; 12, VII
National Crime Prevention and Privacy Compact Council	28, IX
National Drug Control Policy, Office of	21, III
National Endowment for the Arts	2, XXXII
National Endowment for the Humanities	2, XXXIII
National Foundation on the Arts and the Humanities	45, XI
National Highway Traffic Safety Administration	23, II, III; 47, VI; 49, V
National Imagery and Mapping Agency	32, I
National Indian Gaming Commission	25, III
National Institute for Literacy	34, XI
National Institute of Food and Agriculture	7, XXXIV
National Institute of Standards and Technology	15, II
National Intelligence, Office of Director of	32, XVII
National Labor Relations Board	5, LXI; 29, I
National Marine Fisheries Service	50, II, IV
National Mediation Board	29, X
National Oceanic and Atmospheric Administration	15, IX; 50, II, III, IV, VI
National Park Service	36, I
National Railroad Adjustment Board	29, III

Agency	CFR Title, Subtitle or Chapter
National Railroad Passenger Corporation (AMTRAK)	49, VII
National Science Foundation	2, XXV; 5, XLIII; 45, VI
Federal Acquisition Regulation	48, 25
National Security Council	32, XXI
National Security Council and Office of Science and Technology Policy	47, II
National Telecommunications and Information Administration	15, XXIII; 47, III, IV
National Transportation Safety Board	49, VIII
Natural Resources Conservation Service	7, VI
Natural Resource Revenue, Office of	30, XII
Navajo and Hopi Indian Relocation, Office of	25, IV
Navy Department	32, VI
Federal Acquisition Regulation	48, 52
Neighborhood Reinvestment Corporation	24, XXV
Northeast Interstate Low-Level Radioactive Waste Commission	10, XVIII
Nuclear Regulatory Commission	2, XX; 5, XLVIII; 10, I
Federal Acquisition Regulation	48, 20
Occupational Safety and Health Administration	29, XVII
Occupational Safety and Health Review Commission	29, XX
Ocean Energy Management, Bureau of	30, V
Offices of Independent Counsel	28, VI
Office of Workers' Compensation Programs	20, VII
Oklahoma City National Memorial Trust	36, XV
Operations Office	7, XXVIII
Overseas Private Investment Corporation	5, XXXIII; 22, VII
Patent and Trademark Office, United States	37, I
Payment From a Non-Federal Source for Travel Expenses	41, 304
Payment of Expenses Connected With the Death of Certain Employees	41, 303
Peace Corps	2, XXXVII; 22, III
Pennsylvania Avenue Development Corporation	36, IX
Pension Benefit Guaranty Corporation	29, XL
Personnel Management, Office of	5, I, XXXV; 45, VIII
Human Resources Management and Labor Relations Systems, Department of Homeland Security	5, XCVII
Federal Acquisition Regulation	48, 17
Federal Employees Group Life Insurance Federal Acquisition Regulation	48, 21
Federal Employees Health Benefits Acquisition Regulation	48, 16
Pipeline and Hazardous Materials Safety Administration	49, I
Postal Regulatory Commission	5, XLVI; 39, III
Postal Service, United States	5, LX; 39, I
Postsecondary Education, Office of	34, VI
President's Commission on White House Fellowships	1, IV
Presidential Documents	3
Presidio Trust	36, X
Prisons, Bureau of	28, V
Private and Civil Liberties Oversight Board	6, X
Procurement and Property Management, Office of	7, XXXII
Productivity, Technology and Innovation, Assistant Secretary	37, IV
Public Contracts, Department of Labor	41, 50
Public and Indian Housing, Office of Assistant Secretary for	24, IX
Public Health Service	42, I
Railroad Retirement Board	20, II
Reclamation, Bureau of	43, I
Recovery Accountability and Transparency Board	4, II
Refugee Resettlement, Office of	45, IV
Relocation Allowances	41, 302
Research and Innovative Technology Administration	49, XI
Rural Business-Cooperative Service	7, XVIII, XLII, L
Rural Development Administration	7, XLII
Rural Housing Service	7, XVIII, XXXV, L
Rural Telephone Bank	7, XVI
Rural Utilities Service	7, XVII, XVIII, XLII, L

Agency	CFR Title, Subtitle or Chapter
Saint Lawrence Seaway Development Corporation	33, IV
Science and Technology Policy, Office of	32, XXIV
Science and Technology Policy, Office of, and National Security Council	47, II
Secret Service	31, IV
Securities and Exchange Commission	5, XXXIV; 17, II
Selective Service System	32, XVI
Small Business Administration	2, XXVII; 13, I
Smithsonian Institution	36, V
Social Security Administration	2, XXIII; 20, III; 48, 23
Soldiers' and Airmen's Home, United States	5, XI
Special Counsel, Office of	5, VIII
Special Education and Rehabilitative Services, Office of	34, III
State Department	2, VI; 22, I; 28, XI
Federal Acquisition Regulation	48, 6
Surface Mining Reclamation and Enforcement, Office of	30, VII
Surface Transportation Board	49, X
Susquehanna River Basin Commission	18, VIII
Technology Administration	15, XI
Technology Policy, Assistant Secretary for	37, IV
Tennessee Valley Authority	5, LXIX; 18, XIII
Thrift Supervision Office, Department of the Treasury	12, V
Trade Representative, United States, Office of	15, XX
Transportation, Department of	2, XII; 5, L
Commercial Space Transportation	14, III
Contract Appeals, Board of	48, 63
Emergency Management and Assistance	44, IV
Federal Acquisition Regulation	48, 12
Federal Aviation Administration	14, I
Federal Highway Administration	23, I, II
Federal Motor Carrier Safety Administration	49, III
Federal Railroad Administration	49, II
Federal Transit Administration	49, VI
Maritime Administration	46, II
National Highway Traffic Safety Administration	23, II, III; 47, IV; 49, V
Pipeline and Hazardous Materials Safety Administration	49, I
Saint Lawrence Seaway Development Corporation	33, IV
Secretary of Transportation, Office of	14, II; 49, Subtitle A
Surface Transportation Board	49, X
Transportation Statistics Bureau	49, XI
Transportation, Office of	7, XXXIII
Transportation Security Administration	49, XII
Transportation Statistics Bureau	49, XI
Travel Allowances, Temporary Duty (TDY)	41, 301
Treasury Department	5, XXI; 12, XV; 17, IV; 31, IX
Alcohol and Tobacco Tax and Trade Bureau	27, I
Community Development Financial Institutions Fund	12, XVIII
Comptroller of the Currency	12, I
Customs and Border Protection	19, I
Engraving and Printing, Bureau of	31, VI
Federal Acquisition Regulation	48, 10
Federal Claims Collection Standards	31, IX
Federal Law Enforcement Training Center	31, VII
Financial Crimes Enforcement Network	31, X
Fiscal Service	31, II
Foreign Assets Control, Office of	31, V
Internal Revenue Service	26, I
Investment Security, Office of	31, VIII
Monetary Offices	31, I
Secret Service	31, IV
Secretary of the Treasury, Office of	31, Subtitle A
Thrift Supervision, Office of	12, V
Truman, Harry S. Scholarship Foundation	45, XVIII
United States and Canada, International Joint Commission	22, IV
United States and Mexico, International Boundary and Water Commission, United States Section	22, XI

Agency	CFR Title, Subtitle or Chapter
U.S. Copyright Office	37, II
Utah Reclamation Mitigation and Conservation Commission	43, III
Veterans Affairs Department	2, VIII; 38, I
Federal Acquisition Regulation	48, 8
Veterans' Employment and Training Service, Office of the Assistant Secretary for	41, 61; 20, IX
Vice President of the United States, Office of	32, XXVIII
Vocational and Adult Education, Office of	34, IV
Wage and Hour Division	29, V
Water Resources Council	18, VI
Workers' Compensation Programs, Office of	20, I
World Agricultural Outlook Board	7, XXXVIII

List of CFR Sections Affected

All changes in this volume of the Code of Federal Regulations (CFR) that were made by documents published in the FEDERAL REGISTER since January 1, 2008 are enumerated in the following list. Entries indicate the nature of the changes effected. Page numbers refer to FEDERAL REGISTER pages. The user should consult the entries for chapters, parts and subparts as well as sections for revisions.

For changes to this volume of the CFR prior to this listing, consult the annual edition of the monthly List of CFR Sections Affected (LSA). The LSA is available at *www.fdsys.gov*. For changes to this volume of the CFR prior to 2001, see the "List of CFR Sections Affected, 1949–1963, 1964–1972, 1973–1985, and 1986–2000" published in 11 separate volumes. The "List of CFR Sections Affected 1986–2000" is available at *www.fdsys.gov*.

2008

46 CFR

73 FR Page

Chapter I
- 50.20-33 Removed 65160
- 50.25-1 (e) amended 65160
- 52.01-1 Revised 65160
- 52.01-2 (a) revised 65160
- 52.01-5 (a) revised 65160
- 52.01-50 (a) revised 65160
- 52.01-90 Revised 65161
- 52.01-95 (a) and (f) revised 65161
- 52.01-100 (a) and (b) revised 65161
- 52.01-105 (a) and (b) revised 65161
- 52.01-110 (a) and (c) revised 65161
- 52.01-115 Revised 65161
- 52.01-120 (a)(1), (2)(i), (4), (6), (b)(1), (c)(1), (3), (d)(1) and (2) amended 65161
- 52.01-135 (a), (b) and (c) amended 65162
- 52.01-140 (a), (b)(3), (c) and (d) amended 65162
- 52.01-145 Amended 65162
- 52.05-1 (a) amended 65162
- 52.05-15 (a) amended 65162
- 52.05-20 Revised 65162
- 52.05-30 (a), (b) and (c) amended 65162
- 52.05-45 (a), (b) and (c) amended 65162
- 52.15-1 Amended 65162
- 52.15-5 (a) and (b) amended 65162
- 52.20-1 Revised 65162
- 52.20-25 (a) amended 65162
- 52.25-3 Amended 65162

46 CFR—Continued

73 FR Page

Chapter I—Continued
- 52.25-5 Amended 65162
- 52.25-7 Amended 65162
- 52.25-10 (a) amended 65162
- 53.01-1 Revised 65163
- 53.01-3 (a), (b) and (c) introductory text revised 65163
- 53.01-5 Revised 65163
- 53.01-10 (a), (c)(1), (e) introductory text and (1) revised 65163
- 53.05-1 (a) revised 65163
- 53.05-2 (a) revised 65164
- 53.05-3 Revised 65164
- 53.05-5 Revised 65164
- 53.10-1 Revised 65164
- 53.10-3 (a) revised 65164
- 53.10-10 Revised 65164
- 53.10-15 Revised 65164
- 53.12-1 (Subpart 53.12) Heading revised 65164
- 53.12-1 (a) revised 65164
- 54.01-1 Revised 65164
- 54.01-2 Heading, (a), (b) and (c) introductory text revised 65165
- 54.01-5 (b) Table revised; (c)(3) and (e) amended 65165
- 54.01-10 Heading revised 65166
- 54.01-15 Heading, (a)(1), (2)(i) through (iv), (3)(i) and (4) revised 65166
- 54.01-18 (b)(5) amended 65167
- 54.01-25 (a) and (b) amended 65167
- 54.01-30 (a) and (b) introductory text amended 65167

46 CFR—Continued

73 FR Page

Chapter I—Continued
54.01–35 (a), (b)(4) and (d)(2) note amended 65167
54.03–1 Amended 65167
54.05–1 Amended 65167
54.10–1 Amended 65167
54.10–3 (b) amended 65167
54.10–5 Revised 65167
54.10–10 (b) and (e) amended 65170
54.10–15 (c) revised 65170
54.10–20 (a)(6) revised 65170
54.15–1 Heading and (a) revised 65170
54.15–3 Heading revised 65170
54.15–5 (a) amended 65170
54.15–10 (e), (h)(1), (2) and (3) amended 65170
54.15–13 (a) amended 65170
54.20–1 (a) amended 65170
54.20–3 (b), (c) and (d) amended 65170
54.25–1 Amended 65170
54.25–3 Revised 65170
54.25–5 Revised 65170
54.25–8 (b) amended 65170
54.25–10 (b) introductory text and (c) amended 65170
54.25–15 (a), (b) and (c) amended 65171
54.25–20 (b) introductory text, (c) and (e) revised 65171
54.25–25 (a) revised 65171
54.30–3 (c) revised 65171
54.30–5 (a)(1), (4) and (6) amended 65171
54.30–10 (a)(1) amended 65171
56.01–1—56.01–10 (Subpart 56.01) Note removed 65171
56.01–2 Revised 65171
56.01–3 Heading and (b) revised 65174
56.01–5 Revised 65175
56.07–5 (a) introductory text, (c) and (f) revised 65175
56.07–10 (a) heading, (1), (b) heading, (d) heading, introductory text, (1), (e) heading, (1), (f) heading and introductory text revised 65175
56.10–1 (b) revised 65175
56.10–5 (c)(2–a), (3), (4) and (5) redesignated as (c)(3) through (6) 65175
56.15–1 (c)(2)(i), (ii), (4)(ii)(B) and (e) amended 65176
56.15–5 (c)(2)(ii)(A) and (B) amended 65176
56.20–1 (c)(2)(i), (ii) and (d) amended 65176
56.20–5 Revised 65176

46 CFR—Continued

73 FR Page

Chapter I—Continued
56.20–9 (a) revised 65176
56.20–15 (c) revised 65176
56.20–20 (a) revised 65176
56.25–5 Amended 65176
56.25–7 Revised 65176
56.25–10 (a) revised 65176
56.25–15 Heading revised; (b) and (c) redesignated as (c) and (d); new (b) added 65176
56.25–20 (a)(1), (b), (d) and (e) revised 65176
56.30–1 Revised 65177
56.30–5 (b)(3), (c)(1), (3) and (d) revised 65177
56.30–10 (b) introductory text, (1), (3), (4) and (5) revised; Figure 56.30–10(b) note removed 65177
(b) correctly revised 76247
56.30–20 (b) and (d) revised 65178
56.30–30 (b)(1) amended 65178
56.35–1 (b) revised 65178
56.50–1 Heading and introductory text revised 65178
56.50–10 Heading and (a) revised 65178
56.50–15 (b) amended; (f) revised 65178
56.50–30 (b)(1) revised 65178
56.50–40 Heading and (a)(1) revised 65178
56.50–60 (d)(1) introductory text and (2) amended 65178
56.50–65 (a) amended 65178
56.50–70 (a)(2) and (b)(2) revised 65178
56.50–97 Heading and (a) introductory text revised 65178
56.50–105 Table note added 65178
56.60–1 Revised 65179
56.60–2 (c)(1)(ii) and table 56.60–2(a) revised 65182
56.60–3 (b) revised 65183
56.60–5 (a) and (b) revised 65183
56.60–10 (a) revised 65183
56.60–15 (a) and (b)(2) revised 65183
56.60–25 (a) introductory text, (b)(1), (2), (3) and (5) revised; (b)(6) added 65183
56.65–1 Revised 65184
56.70–5 (a) revised 65184
56.70–10 (a) heading, (1)(ii) and (b) revised; (a)(3) amended 65184

List of CFR Sections Affected

46 CFR—Continued

73 FR Page

Chapter I—Continued
56.70–15 (b)(1), (5) introductory text, (6), (f) introductory text heading, (g) introductory text heading and (4) revised; (b)(8)(ii), (c), (d)(1) and (g)(1) through (7) amended 65184
56.70–20 (a) revised 65184
56.75–5 (c) revised 65184
56.75–10 Heading revised 65184
56.75–15 Heading revised 65184
56.75–20 (a) revised 65184
56.75–25 (b) revised 65184
56.80–5 Amended 65185
56.80–15 (a), (c), (d), (e) and (g) revised 65185
56.85–5 Revised 65185
56.85–10 (b) and (c) revised 65185
56.85–15 (d), (e) and (i) revised 65185
56.90–5 (b) and (d) revised 65185
56.90–10 Heading revised 65185
56.95–1 (a) and (b) amended 65185
56.95–10 (a) introductory text, (c)(1)(i), (ii), (4) introductory text and (c)(5) amended 65185
56.97–1 (a) amended 65185
56.97–25 Heading revised 65185
56.97–30 Heading revised 65185
58.01–5 Amended 65185
58.01–10 (a)(3) revised 65186
58.01–50 (a) revised 65186
58.03–1 Revised 65186
58.05–1 Revised 65186
58.10–5 (b)(3)(i) and (d)(1) introductory text revised 65187
58.10–15 (a) amended 65187
58.16–10 (b)(1) and (c) revised 65187
58.20–5 (a) revised 65187
58.20–20 (b) amended 65187
58.25–5 (d) amended 65187
58.25–60 Revised 65187
58.30–10 (e) amended 65187
58.30–15 (b) and (c) revised 65187
58.50–5 (a) table revised 65187
58.50–10 (a) table revised 65188
58.50–15 Revised 65188
58.60–7 Revised 65188
58.60–9 Revised 65188
59.01–2 Revised 65188
59.01–3 Removed 65189
59.01–5 (e) revised 65189
59.10–5 (i), (j) and (k) amended 65189
59.10–10 (f) amended 65189
61.15–10 Heading and (b) revised... 65189
62.05–1 Revised 65189
62.25–1 (c) revised 65189

46 CFR—Continued

73 FR Page

Chapter I—Continued
62.25–5 (a) revised 65189
62.25–30 (a)(1), (2), (3) and (5) revised.. 65189
62.35–5 Heading and (d) revised 65189
62.35–35 Revised 65189
62.35–40 (c) revised 65190
62.35–50 Table footnotes 1, 2, 8 and 9 and notes 1 and 9 revised 65190
62.50–30 (c) and (k) introductory text revised 65190
63.05–1 Revised 65190
63.10–1 Introductory text, (a), (b) introductory text and (1) revised.. 65190
63.15–1 (b) revised 65191
63.15–3 (e) revised 65191
63.15–5 (c) revised 65191
63.20–1 Introductory text revised.. 65191
63.25–1 Introductory text revised.. 65191
63.25–3 (a) and (j) revised 65191
63.25–9 Revised 65191

2009

46 CFR

74 FR Page

Chapter I
42.05–27 Added 11265
42.07–50 (b)(5) amended 11265
44.320 (a) amended 49228
46.10–10 (d) amended 49228
50.10–23 Amended 49228
52.01–1 (a) amended 49228
53.01–1 (a) amended 49228
54.01–1 (a) amended 49228
54.05–30 (b) and (c) amended 49228
54.15–25 (c) and (c–1) amended 49228
56.01–2 (a) amended 49229
56.50–105 Table amended 49229
57.02–1 (a) amended 49229
58.03–1 (a) amended 49229
58.16–19 (b) amended 11265
59.01–2 (a) amended 49229
61.03–1 (a) amended 49229
61.15–10 (a) amended 11265
61.20–17 (f)(2) amended 49229
61.20–21 Amended 49229
61.40–10 (b) amended 49229
62.05–1 (a) amended 49229
62.35–40 (b) amended 49229
63.05–1 (a) amended 49230
63.10–1 Amended 49230
63.25–9 (a) amended 49230
67.7 Amended 49230
67.15 (b) amended 49230

46 CFR—Continued

Chapter I—Continued

74 FR Page

67.17 (a) amended	49230
67.19 (b) removed; (c) through (f) redesignated as new (b) through (e); heading, (a) and new (b) through (e) amended	49230
67.21 (a) amended	49230
67.35 (c) amended	49230
67.36 (c) amended	49230
67.39 (c) amended	49230
67.50 (a) amended	49230
67.57 (a)(1) and (b)(1) amended	49230
67.59 (c) amended	49230
67.61 Note amended	49230
67.63 (a) and (b)(1) amended	49230
67.95 Amended	49230
67.132 (a) amended	49230
67.177 (e) and (f) amended	49230
67.211 Note amended	49230
67.323 Amended	49230
67.511 (a) amended	49230
67.523 Amended	49230
67.550 Amended	49230
68.33 (b) amended	49230
69.9 Amended	49231
69.15 (a) amended	49231

2010

46 CFR

75 FR Page

Chapter I

45.171 (c) table revised; (d) added	70601
Regulation at 75 FR 70601 eff. date delayed in part; comment period reopened	78928
45.173 (c) and (d) revised; (e) added	70603
45.175 Revised	70604
45.181 (a) and (b)(1) revised	70604
45.183 (a)(2) and (b)(2)(vi) amended	70604
45.185 (b) and (c) revised	70604
45.187 Revised	70604
Regulation at 75 FR 70604 eff. date delayed; comment period reopened	78928
45.191 (a) and (b)(5) revised	70604
Regulation at 75 FR 70604 eff. date delayed in part; comment period reopened	78928
45.193 (a) amended	70604
45.197 Introductory text amended	70604
54.01–15 (a)(4) and (5) revised	60002

2011

46 CFR

76 FR Page

Chapter I

45.171 (c) table revised	32326
45.187 Revised	32327
45.191 (a) revised	32327
62.35–5 (c)(3) amended	60754

2012

46 CFR

77 FR Page

Chapter I

42.07-60 (a), (b) and (c) amended	59777
46.10-60 Revised	59777
50.25-1 (e) amended	59777
52.01-1 (a) amended	59777
53.01-1 (a) amended	59777
54.01-1 (a) amended	59777
54.05-30 (b) and (c) amended	59777
54.15-25 (c-1) amended	59777
56.01-2 (a) amended	59777
56.50-105 Table Note 3 amended	59777
57.02-1 (a) amended	59778
58.03-1 (a) amended	59778
58.50-15 (a) amended	59778
59.01-2 (a) amended	59778
61.03-1 (a) amended	59778
61.20-17 (f)(2) amended	59778
61.20-21 Amended	59778
61.40-10 (b) amended	59778
62.01–1 Heading revised; amended	33874
62.05-1 (a) amended	59778
62.25–20 (d)(1)(ii) revised	33874
63.05-1 (a) amended	59778
64.2 (a) amended	59778
67.3 Amended	59778
67.177 Actions on petitions	16172

2013

(Regulations published from January 1, 2013 through October 1, 2013)

46 CFR

78 FR Page

Chapter I

42.05-20 Amended	60147
44.320 (a) revised	60147
46.10-20 Amended	60147
50.10-20 Amended	60147
50.10-23 Amended	60147
52.01-1 (a) amended	60148
53.01-1 (a) amended	60148
54.01-1 (c) introductory text and (2) revised	13249

List of CFR Sections Affected

46 CFR—Continued

78 FR Page

Chapter I—Continued
(a) amended 60148
54.05-30 (b) amended......................60148
56.01-2 (a) amended 60148
 (e)(9) through (82) redesignated as (e)(10) through (83); second paragraph of (e)(8) redesignated as new (e)(9); (e) introductory text, (6) and new (10), (17), (40), (41), (42), (69) through (76), (78), (79) and (80) revised 13250
57.02-1 (a) amended 60148

46 CFR—Continued

78 FR Page

Chapter I—Continued
58.03-1 (a) amended 60148
59.01-2 (a) amended 60148
61.03-1 (a) amended 60149
62.05-1 (a) amended 60149
63.05-1 (a) amended 60149
63.10-1 Introductory text revised..60149
63.25-9 (a) amended 60149
64.2 (a) amended...........................60149
69.9 Amended................................60149
69.15 (a) amended 60149